The Wine Roads of Italy

By the same authors

The Wine Roads of France
The Wine and Food of Europe
The Wine Roads of Europe
The Taste of Britain
Flavours of Korea

The Wine Roads
— of —
ITALY

MARC AND KIM MILLON

Photographs by Kim Millon

HarperCollins*Publishers*

HarperCollins*Publishers*
77–85 Fulham Palace Road,
Hammersmith, London W6 8JB

Published by HarperCollins*Publishers* 1991

10 9 8 7 6 5 4 3 2 1

British Library Cataloguing in Publication Data

Millon, Marc
   The wine roads of Italy.
   1. Italy. Wine-growing regions – visitors' guides
   I. Title   II. Millon, Kim
   914.504929

ISBN 0-246-13736-3

Phototypeset by
Computape (Pickering) Ltd, North Yorkshire
Printed in Great Britain by
Butler & Tanner Ltd, Frome, Somerset

To my mother, Lori

CONTENTS

Introduction   1

The North-west   15

Piedmont and the Valle d'Aosta   17

Liguria   85

Lombardy   96

The North-east   117

Veneto   119

Trentino-Alto Adige   179

Friuli-Venezia Giulia   208

The Centre   229

Tuscany   231

Umbria   329

Emilia-Romagna   356

The Marches   372

The Mezzogiorno   385

Latium   387

Abruzzi and Molise   405

Campania   414

Apulia   431

Basilicata   457

Calabria   468

The Islands	483
Sicily	485
Sardinia	504
Select Bibliography	513
Glossary	515
Acknowledgements	517
Index	519

INTRODUCTION

The wine roads of Italy.

In Italy, all roads lead eventually to the wine country. In every one of her 20 regions, wine is produced. From the snow-covered peaks of the Südtirol, the Valle d'Aosta and the Julian Alps, down across the wide fertile belly of the Po valley along the Via Emilia that leads to the Adriatic coast; from the great northern vineyards of Piedmont and Veneto, down south past the tortuous terraces of Liguria to the classic vine and olive landscapes of Tuscany and Umbria; around Rome, of course, and beyond, to Campania; Apulia; Basilicata; even way down to Calabria, the poor, bruised forgotten toe of Italy. Indeed, the prolific vine extends beyond the mainland, off-shore to islands such as Sicily and Sardinia, as well as to Pantelleria, Lipari, Elba, Capri, Ischia, and scores of others.

The ancient Greeks called Italy Enotria because of the country's suitability to the cultivation of the vine. But even before those ancient seafarers introduced *Vitis vinifera* to the lands that they colonized, grapes were grown and wine was made on the Italian peninsula. The Etruscans, that mysterious but advanced civilization, were particular acolytes of the art of wine and wine making. Later, under the Romans, the vine did indeed come, see, and conquer all. At the height of the Roman Empire there were already at least 60 named regional wines, that is, wines that were fine enough and in sufficient demand to be traded under the *denominazioni* of their region or locality of production, in addition to the many hundreds or thousands of anonymous wines consumed young or locally only. The Romans, furthermore, took the vine with them to the lands they colonized, notably planting the vineyards of France and the Rhineland along the way to quench the legendary thirst of the conquering legions.

Vino da Pasto: Wine as Food

Today, Italy remains the greatest wine producing and wine drinking country in the world; in terms of sheer volume alone, she ranks first overall, and Italians still drink more wine per capita than virtually anyone else in the world. So basic is wine in the scheme of Italian life that even criminals in State prisons are given a daily ration, for, indeed, to deprive a man of wine with his daily meal would be considered too cruel and unusual a punishment.

Sheer quantity alone, of course, should not be considered a measure of achievement in itself. Undoubtedly, here, as in other wine producing nations (France included), the everyday beverage that the man in the street drinks to accompany his *pasta asciutta* may not be anything to write home or books about: at best, it should be bracing, honest, and inexpensive. Such wine (usually red) may display little character or elegance, but it strives for none.

Many Italians still purchase their wine weekly or monthly in bulk, in wicker- or plastic-covered *damigiane* – 54- or 25-litre demi-johns – from the local grower. This is then carted back home and siphoned into unlabelled bottles for everyday consumption. Such wine, frankly, is a food, and a basic and essential one, to be consumed daily, quite without fuss or pretension: as such, it quenches an enormous national thirst.

Damigiane.

Italy, the Home of Great Wines

However, if *vino da pasto* – ordinary table wine – remains the staple beverage, this is a country none the less which appreciates its bounty, and it would be a poor household (in spirit, not money) that did not on special occasions or at weekends enjoy the superior fruits of its particular corner of the land. Moreover, in common with trends throughout the world, in recent years wine consumption per capita has fallen, but discerning drinkers are enjoying better wines.

In respect of quality, Italy can claim her rightful place among the greatest wine nations on earth. This is the home, after all, of classic and historic wines that can compare and compete on equal terms with the very greatest from anywhere: I am thinking of single *bricco* wines from Barolo and Barbaresco; classics from Tuscany, such as Brunello di Montalcino, Carmignano, and certain estate-bottled Chianti *riserve*; super-*vini da tavola*, wines such as Tignanello, Sassicaia, Querciagrande, Canetto, and Ghaie delle Furbe, made outside the stringent and constricting limitations of *denominazione di origine controllata* but with such care and selection that they are rightly regarded as the nation's finest; and age-old classics such as Recioto and Recioto Amarone di Valpolicella, made by unique methods carried out nowhere else, methods that have changed not one iota since Roman days.

An Italian 'Wine Renaissance'

In the cinquecento the Florentines turned their backs on centuries of Dark Ages to rediscover the classical heritage of ancient Rome. Today in Italy, after decades or even centuries of neglect, the wine makers of the country have also reclaimed their rightful patrimony. For example, in Verona's Valpolicella, the estate of Serègo Alighieri was founded by the poet Dante's son in 1353, and today is still owned and worked by his direct descendants. It must rank among the oldest private wine estates in the world in continuous ownership. Yet even only a decade ago this historic estate made and sold all its wine in bulk, to be sent to merchants for blending. Today, working in conjunction with the firm of Masi, it produces wines like Serègo Alighieri Valpolicella Classico and the *cru* Vajo Armaron which are rightly regarded as among Italy's finest.

Elsewhere, in Campania for example, Antonio Mastroberardino has safeguarded a vinous heritage that extends back even before the Romans. Today this archaeologist of the vine cultivates only the unique historical grape varieties of his zone – Fiano, indigenous to the hills of Avellino, and Aglianico and Greco, both introduced into Italy by the ancient Greeks. Yet if the grapes themselves come from an antique lineage, there is nothing behind the times in Mastroberardino's ultra-modern winery, and the wines produced are among the classics of the wine world.

In Tuscany, Chianti, which suffered decades of neglect while it was downed without serious consideration from millions of wicker flasks not only in the zone but in *trattorie* in Soho or Greenwich Village alike, has reassessed itself. Now, under stricter DOCG guidelines, serious estate-bottled wines are being produced in the Classico, Rufina, and elsewhere that are truly worthy of the heritage that extends back long before the Middle Ages. And less well-known wines such as Carmignano and Pomino have reclaimed a patrimony that was appreciated by the Medici Grand Dukes in a 17th-century decree, probably Italy's and the world's first example of *denominazione di origine controllata*.

Even way down in sun-baked Apulia, the vinous potential of a rich and fertile land is now being realized. After decades of supplying France, Germany, and northern Italy with robust wines for blending, Apulia is now turning her hand to the production of fine estate wines; utilizing both native and foreign grape varieties, they are made with the most modern technologies and thus are something of a revelation to those who believe that only coarse, baked wines come from the Mezzogiorno.

As Italy rediscovers her historic vinous splendour, this renaissance in wine forges ahead, moreover, with advances in the vineyard and cantina; indeed, creative and forward-thinking innovations and experiments positively look to the future and the next millennia. The plantation of classic French varieties alongside traditional, the experimentation with clonal grape selection and new vinification techniques, the not always successful profusion of 'designer' wines and super-*vini da tavola* made outside the limiting disciplines of DOC, the passion (of the most dedicated) ever to create something new and wondrous and exciting: certainly this is evidence of artistic creativity at the highest level.

Wine Tourism

Italy remains a nation of individual provinces, regions that correspond broadly to former independent city-states which historically deemed themselves to have little in common with their neighbours. Even today, an intensely insular and chauvinistic attitude remains. Thus, every Italian is first and foremost a citizen of his region, and only second (sometimes a very distant second) a citizen of his nation. As applied to wine drinking, this means that except in cities where there may be exceptional private *enoteche* (specialist wine shops), it may well be impossible to find interesting wines from outside the immediate locality. Intelligent wine drinkers from, say, Florence, may well know the best *aziende agricole* in the Chianti Classico region, but it is probable that they rarely drink wines from even as famous a wine region as Piedmont. Perhaps they have tasted a Barolo, yes, or a Barbaresco or a Barbera d'Asti or d'Alba: but mention Grignolino, Dolcetto, or Carema, and they will probably raise not even a flicker of recognition. Ask a Florentine if he has tasted a Kalterersee Auslese, Vin Blanc de Morgex,

Stop to taste; stop to buy.

Sagrantino di Montefalco *passito*, Aglianico del Vulture, or Primitivo di Manduria and he may be even more baffled. Indeed, even within small areas, old traditions and loyalties die hard: those who live within the area of Alba hardly ever consider drinking wine from nearby Asti, and vice versa.

National prejudices may be even more marked. Northerners may well honestly (if a little maliciously) believe that the Mezzogiorno begins at Rome or even further north ('Asti', says our charming but incorrigible friend from Turin); certainly they do not believe that the south is capable of producing wines of note, but is suited only to the production of bulk, hot country wines high in alcohol and merely useful for blending. Southerners, too, may hold similar prejudices. I have a friend from Apulia who will drink wine from no other region, even though he lives in Piedmont. These northern wines, they have no guts, he states simply. Barolo, no guts? But there is no shaking him from his firm conviction.

The thirsty wine traveller need bring along with him no prejudices, and thus he or she is in the fortunate position of being able to sample and enjoy all that this rich and varied country has to offer.

Visiting Wineries

Wine tourism in an organized sense is not yet as developed in Italy as it is, say, in France (apart from Piedmont with its wine roads and regional *enoteche*, and Tuscany's Chianti Classico, where many wine estates encour-

INTRODUCTION

age tastings and direct sales). There are signposted wine roads – *strade dei vini* – in many areas, but on the whole, Italy's wine roads remain uncharted, since to do so would require virtually a map of entire regions and areas, so prolific and prevalent is the vine. Also, wine – and the vineyards and grapes that it is made from – is considered such a basic everyday commodity that it may not always be perceived as of specific touristic interest, either to Italians or to those of us from outside who consider this annual transubstantiation nothing short of a minor miracle.

Few *aziende agricole* (private wine estates) keep open house for visitors as is often the case in France, and when asked, most state that they would like an appointment made in advance for visits, that is, at least a telephone call the morning that you intend to come if only to ensure that someone is on hand to receive you. On the other hand, there is a long-standing tradition in Italy of purchasing wine direct from the farm (in bottle, or in bulk as *vino sfuso*) and visits for direct sales are expected and indeed welcomed by almost all, including the most famous.

So be in no doubt: provided you don't arrive at an inconvenient time (such as lunchtime), it has certainly been our experience that most wine estates will make you very welcome indeed. For your visit is important, and not just for any direct sales that may result. Visits from foreigners in many cases may still be something of a novelty, and a warm, inborn tradition of hospitality to the stranger remains. Moreover, you, the non-professional consumer, the discerning consumer, the international consumer, may be perceived as an important gauge of opinion and taste, or as a means of confirming excellence. For here, in this country of artists, what is often most important – certainly more important than mere economic considerations – is the opportunity to share interests, passions, and enthusiasms with likeminded folk. Wine, after all, is the ultimate cup of *amicizia*: one glass leads to another, and a visit to a wine estate may truly be the start of lasting friendships.

We have visited, talked on the telephone, or corresponded with all the producers included in the book, and they have supplied their own factual visiting details. Our selection, of course, is a highly personal one, and makes no claim at comprehensiveness. Well-known producers may be missing simply because they did not answer our letters, or because we are not familiar with their wines, or because space did not permit. Similarly, it has not been possible – probably it would not even have been desirable – to cover all the hundreds of wine zones of Italy with equal emphasis. Our aim throughout has been to explore as thoroughly as possible not only the most important wine regions, but also those zones of less importance viticulturally, but which are well-visited and popular with tourists.

Enoteche: National, Regional, and Private 'Wine Libraries'

For the wine lover and wine tourist, Italian *enoteche* are among the nation's greatest assets, for they provide unique and unrivalled opportunities for tasting and purchasing. Visitors to central Italy, for example, will not want to miss visiting Siena's *Enoteca Permanente*, a virtual national monument to the nation's wines in all their regional variety, with samples from each of Italy's 20 regions that can all be tasted (by the glass or bottle) and purchased. In Piedmont, there are 8 *Enoteche Regionali*; these important institutions, housed in castles, deconsecrated churches, or ancient restored *palazzi*, are crucial links between the wine producer and the consumer. Wines from leading producers within each locality are displayed and can be tasted and purchased and the *enoteche* furthermore often sponsor wine-related exhibitions, tutored tastings, and professional conferences. Some also have within their premises excellent restaurants serving regional foods accompanied by the same local wines. Elsewhere, private *enoteche* may seem no more than good wine shops. Yet, none the less, they are usually the source of the best wines of their locality, and can serve as points of reference, advising on the best local properties, and in many cases helping to arrange visits to them.

Ristoranti: Wine Producers' and Our Own Recommendations

Wine and food, in Italy, are virtually inseparable. Italian wine (with few exceptions) is made foremost to be drunk with meals, and indeed best displays its character at the table. Moreover, if wine is one of Italy's greatest pleasures, so undoubtedly is eating. Nowhere else in Europe can you eat so well, of unpretentious and genuine regional or local foods, accompanied by the true wines of the land.

In the course of researching this, and previous books, we have found that the wine producers themselves are invariably the best guides to their local restaurants, and thus we naturally always seek their opinions. Such recommended restaurants, together with many others that we have enjoyed on

INTRODUCTION

both recent research trips and over the course of years, form the core of the restaurant sections for each chapter. They range from the most elegant and refined, to humble (but delicious) *trattorie* or *osterie* serving simple home cooking – *cucina casalinga*.

This book is not a hotel guide, but we have indicated restaurants with rooms available, as well as some hotel-restaurants particularly in out-of-the-way wine zones. Don't overlook the *agriturismo* sections, either, for both eating and sleeping opportunities.

Prices

Since prices always rise, we have used the following simple rating system for a full 3- or 4-course meal and local wine based on Italian restaurant prices current in 1990 (at the time of writing, the pound is equivalent to about 2100 Italian *lire*; the US dollar is worth about 1200 *lire*):

Very Inexpensive	Less than 15,000 *lire*
Inexpensive	15,000–30,000 *lire*
Moderate	30,000–50,000 *lire*
Expensive	50,000–75,000 *lire*
Very Expensive	Over 75,000 *lire*

La Civiltà del Bere: Wine as Civilization

Our primary interest in exploring the wine lands of the world – and in this instance, those of Italy – remains as always not simply that of studying this or that liquid in isolation. For us, it is not possible to separate a wine from the land and the people that produce it. Obviously, wine is a beverage to be enjoyed wholeheartedly in its own right: but more than that, it can serve most pleasantly to lubricate a journey that takes us not only into the wine *cantina* or vineyard but to the essential heart of a region itself.

We therefore make no apologies if, over these pages, we wander from time to time out of the vineyard and into this church, or that museum or olive oil mill, for such experiences – apart from simply being enjoyable in themselves – are what we consider essential elements of the land.

For in Italy, more so than anywhere else, wine is inseparable from the totality of its civilization. The great legacy that this country has given the world, from the Romans through the Renaissance even to today, is in essence one foremost that uplifts the soul, lightens the human condition,

AGRITURISMO: HOME COOKING AND FARMHOUSE ACCOMMODATION

One of the most exciting concepts that we encountered throughout Italy is that of *agriturismo* – organized farmhouse tourism, which takes many different manifestations in various regions. In the German-speaking Südtirol, for example, there is a long-standing tradition of offering farmhouse hospitality to visitors, usually on a bed and breakfast basis, often with evening meals taken with the family. In the Veneto, we encountered wonderfully simple but delicious *'punti di ristoro agrituristico'* – farmhouse restaurants serving simple outdoor meals – homemade *salame*, fresh pasta or soups, grilled meats, together with vegetables or salad from the garden, and of course own-produced wines. Tuscany's *agriturismo* is more sophisticated; here, former sharecroppers' cottages have been restored into lovely farmhouses for rent, sometimes with added luxuries like swimming pools. And farmhouse restaurants attached to wine estates serve foods that are as delicious – and sometimes as expensive – as those found in good restaurants. In Umbria and Latium there are opportunities to stay on wine farms, eating evening meals with the families around communal trestles. Way down south in Apulia, meanwhile, it is even possible to rent a *trullo*, the weird, whitewashed beehive hut that is the ancient form of habitation amidst the vineyards.

Agriturismo is an important concept for us. For in such rural settings one is best able to experience the real flavours of the land, as well as, more significantly, to make lasting and worthwhile human contacts. Staying on a wine farm, for only a few days, or for a fortnight or longer, moreover, provides one of the best opportunities for learning about wine and how it is made.

We have included the addresses of all major *agriturismo* offices in each region, as well as a brief selection of places that we found *simpatico*. But this is an area where the intrepid and open visitor will find endless scope for further exploration. Do bear in mind, however, that, given the informal nature of farmhouse tourism, you may find, for example, that rural *trattorie* are open by reservation only, or else just at weekends. So it is important always to telephone in advance.

INTRODUCTION

Bacchus.

and sees joy in the cypress trees punctuating the hills, in the timeless beauty of the human form, and in a glass of wine. Wine – Italian wine – certainly has the capacity to uplift our daily lives. For those of us who believe in that legacy, the wine roads of Italy take us directly to the heart and soul of the country.

Marc and Kim Millon
Topsham, Devon, England

LA VENDEMMIA: THE HARVEST

Autumn is undoubtedly the best time to visit the wine lands of Italy. To those of us from northern Europe or North America, the grape harvest beckons as a timeless, bucolic event tinted in poetic autumnal colours. Up and down the country, from mid-September to early November, men and women are at work in the fields, and tractors pulling laden trailers chug up and down country lanes and roads, delivering the grapes to the *cantina* where they are destalked, crushed, and pumped into wooden, concrete, or stainless steel fermentation tanks. Then, as the *mosto* – sugar-rich grape juice – begins to work, there is that distinctive, slightly sour, yeasty alcoholic aroma that drifts beyond the *cantina*, and spreads out to permeate the very countryside itself.

On a large estate, the *vendemmia* can last for up to a month, maybe even longer. When the last tractor-load of grapes has been delivered to the *cantina*, and the vines, already turning shades of yellow, red and orange, stand stripped of their fruit, there is inevitably a sense of relief all around. The work in the *cantina* may just be beginning, but in the vineyards another annual cycle is completed. The wine festivals – *feste* and *sagre* – that take place up and down the country celebrate this fact, while the workers usually enjoy a raucous harvest meal at the *padrone*'s expense.

KEY TO MAPS

Wine producer

Restaurant

Agriturismo

Enoteca

Museum

DENOMINAZIONE DI ORIGINE CONTROLLATA: A GUARANTEE OF EXCELLENCE?

Denominazione di origine controllata, or DOC for short, is Italy's equivalent of the French system of *appellation d'origine contrôlée* (AOC). DOC attempts to guarantee the provenance and authenticity of a wine by laying down specific strictures concerning its delimited zone of production, permitted grape varieties, maximum yield (expressed as *quintali* (100 kg) of grapes per hectare), minimum alcohol levels, and on ageing and methods of production. *Denominazione di origine controllata e garantita*, or DOCG, attempts to go a step further. In theory, DOCG applies only to Italy's greatest wines (Barolo, Barbaresco, Brunello di Montalcino among others); disciplines are usually even stricter and more rigorously applied and the wines must furthermore undergo a mandatory tasting before approval and the granting of a government seal.

There are at present well over 220 separate categories of DOC and DOCG and the list seems to grow each year. There is thus a tendency to dismiss DOC as of little consequence. Undoubtedly there are a number of anomalies in the system, disciplines that are too lax and which allow, for example, overproduction at the expense of quality, or wines that are so limited and obscure that they are rarely encountered outside their locality. Many quality producers, moreover, have chosen to produce wines outside the limitations imposed by DOC regulations, and we have now reached the position where some of Italy's greatest wines are simply labelled as *vino da tavola* – humble table wine (though there is nothing humble about their heavy bottles, designer labels, and hefty price tags).

Be that as it may, DOC still provides us with the best map through the dense jungle of Italian wines, providing an order (of sorts) out of the intertwined chaos of thousands of wines produced throughout this lengthy peninsula. But DOC alone, or even DOCG, is no more a guarantee of quality than is the French system of AOC: for within each category, there will undoubtedly exist average wines, good or even great wines, and (hopefully not too many) downright bad ones. As always, the best guarantee is the reputation and name of the wine producer himself or herself.

VIDE is a voluntary association founded in 1978 by a grouping of some of Italy's leading wine estates in an effort to affirm and further the reputation of Italian quality wines at the highest level. Today there are about 30 member estates, all *vinificatori-viticoltori* who vinify only grapes grown in their own vineyards. Member estates do not automatically qualify to utilize the VIDE neckband for all of their wines: rather this is awarded only to wines that have been submitted each year for independent analysis and approval undertaken by a commission at the laboratory of the Istituto Agrario Provinciale di San Michele all'Adige, one of Italy's leading and most respected wine institutions. The VIDE seal thus serves to identify serious wine estates with aspirations above all to quality (there are of course many other such estates who are not members of this select voluntary organization), and furthermore can be relied upon as a guarantee of quality for the wines to which it has been granted.

INTRODUCTION

THE NORTH-WEST

Piedmont and the Valle d'Aosta
Liguria
Lombardy

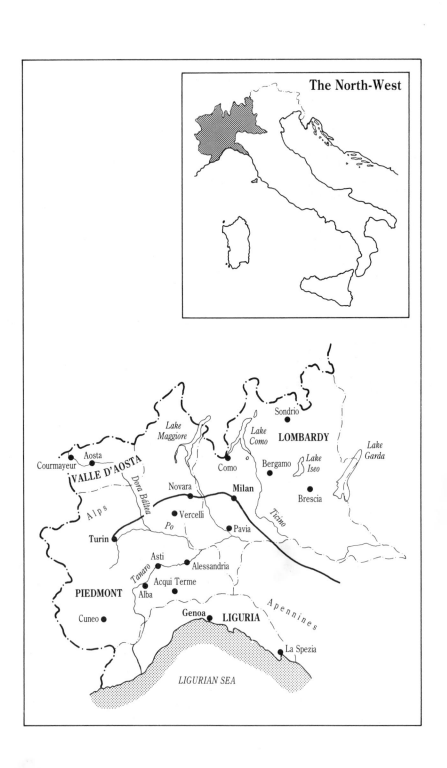

The North-West

PIEDMONT AND THE VALLE D'AOSTA

I Vini: THE WINES OF PIEDMONT
AND THE VALLE D'AOSTA   19

La Gastronomia   24

Le Strade dei Vini: THE WINE ROADS OF
PIEDMONT AND THE VALLE D'AOSTA

The *Route des Vins* of the Valle d'Aosta   27

The Wine Roads of Piedmont   34

The Langhe   37

   La Terra del Barolo   37

   Barbaresco   50

   The Roero   56

Asti and the Monferrato   59

   Asti to Acqui Terme   61

   Asti to Vignale Monferrato   71

Gavi: An Exceptional Wine Island   75

Northern Piedmont   78

Le Sagre: WINE AND OTHER RELATED FESTIVALS   84

Additional Information   84

Serralunga d'Alba

Piedmont means 'foot of the mountain', for indeed this vast north-western corner of the country (including the autonomous region of Valle d'Aosta) is framed by a dramatic corona of peaks forming its northern border with Switzerland as well as its northern and western frontiers with France. To the south, the spiny range of the Apennines separates Piedmont from Liguria.

South of Turin, the elegant capital of the region which is situated at the base of the mountains on the plain that marks the beginning of the broad Po valley, lie the prestigious vineyards of the Langhe, Asti, and Monferrato. These are the source not only of some of Italy's very greatest wines – notably Barolo and Barbaresco – but also of an astonishing range that includes such international superstars as sparkling Asti Spumante; everyday red work-horses such as Barbera and Dolcetto, wines which, in the hands of the best wine makers, can rise well above their humble station; prestigious but virtually unknown dry white wines such as Arneis and Favorita; and relatively obscure, local wines that are wonderful when drunk *in situ*, such as the frothy red Brachetto d'Acqui and Freisa, or the delicious, yet rare Grignolino.

THE NORTH-WEST

If Piedmont produces both aristocratic vintages and plentiful everyday wines, its essential character is also a mixture of the noble and the down-to-earth. Simple, humble stone dwellings stand proudly alongside palaces and fortresses. And the distinctive *cucina piemontese* is based on a similar duality, between simple peasant fare and the elegant sophistication that emanated from the royal kitchens of the House of Savoy.

The wine country itself remains rustic and unspoiled to a degree that is almost unbelievable. Famous producers are more than willing to open their *cantine* and wines to interested visitors, not for the direct sales that might result, but simply out of the passion of sharing mutual enthusiasms with true amateurs. And, of course, the *Enoteche Regionali*, located in old castles, palaces and the like, provide the interested wine traveller with probably the best opportunities for serious wine sampling that will be encountered any-where in the country (only Siena's *Enoteca Permanente* can rival them).

The Valle d'Aosta is best-known as an alpine resort for winter sports at such notable venues as Courmayeur and Breuil-Cervinia. Others may find that it serves as the point of entry to Italy via the Monte Bianco tunnel. The majority will pass through, en route to more famous stopping points in the Veneto, Tuscany, Lombardy and elsewhere. But this north-west corner of the country is an area that deserves an extended stay. Whether for dedicated wine touring, for relaxation in quiet rural areas far from the madness of the cities, or for combining walking in hills and mountains with serious explor-ation of regional wines and unsurpassed *cucina*, this is a region that cannot fail to satisfy.

ORIENTATION

Piedmont is Italy's largest mainland region and comprises the provinces of Alessandria, Asti, Cuneo, Novara, Vercelli, and Turin. The Valle d'Aosta is an autonomous, bilingual (French–Italian) region whose capital is the former Roman town of Aosta. Located in the far north-western corner of the country, Piedmont and the Valle d'Aosta are well-served by an extensive road network, with no fewer than 6 major *auto-strade* extending throughout the regions. Turin's Caselle International Airport is located about 10 miles from the capital's centre. Rail connec-tions with both international and domestic destinations are good, while local trains link Turin with Asti, Alessandria, and Acqui Terme. But to explore the wine country in full, the use of a car is essential.

Map Touring Club Italiano 1:200 000 Piemonte e Valle d'Aosta.

THE HOUSE OF SAVOY AND THE *RISORGIMENTO*

It is easy today to overlook the fact that for centuries Italy was not a unified nation but a disparate collection of city-states, duchies, republics, and kingdoms, ruled variously by warrior-statesmen, popes, foreign kings, and emperors. The House of Savoy, for example, ruled over not only the area now known as Piedmont but also the French Savoie for some 9 centuries. After the Congress of Vienna in 1815, the Italian peninsula was parcelled out like spoils to the victors, with the Austrians maintaining their dominant role, though the Duchy of Savoy survived intact. However, the *Risorgimento* – the 'awakening' of a national consciousness and the formation of a movement for unification – took root in Piedmont, where, under the patronage of the House of Savoy, such national heroes as Cavour, Mazzini, and Garibaldi planned for and dreamed of a united Italy. That they were ultimately successful is part of European history: in 1861 the Duchy of Savoy's Vittorio Emanuele II was declared the first King of Italy, and Turin (until the later incorporation of Rome) served as the first capital of the fledgling nation.

I VINI: GLOSSARY TO THE WINES OF PIEDMONT AND VALLE D'AOSTA

Wines of *Denominazione di Origine Controllata* (DOC) and Wines of *Denominazione di Origine Controllata e Garantita* (DOCG)

Asti Spumante; Moscato d'Asti Spumante DOC Famous sparkling wine produced from Moscato Bianco grapes grown widely throughout the provinces of Asti and parts of Alessandria. Usually produced by the Charmat method of secondary fermentation in the tank, the wine is invariably sweet with the delicate grapey perfume of the Moscato. Minimum alcohol 11.5 degrees.

Barbaresco DOCG Prestigious red wine produced from the Nebbiolo grape in the communes of

Barbaresco, Neive, Treiso, and part of San Rocco Senodelvio d'Alba. Minimum alcohol 12.5 degrees; minimum ageing in oak or chestnut casks at least 2 years. If aged for at least 3 years in wood the wine may be labelled Riserva; 4 years minimum for Riserva Speciale.

Barbera; Barbera d'Alba DOC; Barbera d'Asti DOC; Barbera del Monferrato DOC The Barbera grape is Piedmont's most prolific variety, and is utilized to produce a range of sound red wines from a vast area covering the vineyards of Alba, Asti, and the Monferrato. Minimum alcohol content is between 11.5 and 12.5 degrees, and the styles of wine vary considerably, from light, everyday table wines to serious *barrique*-aged reds.

Barolo DOCG Possibly Italy's greatest red wine, produced from Nebbiolo grapes grown in hills south-east of Alba centred on the hill town of Barolo, and other communities such as Serralunga d'Alba, Monforte d'Alba, Castiglione Falletto, La Morra and Grinzane Cavour. Minimum alcohol 13 degrees; minimum ageing at least 3 years, 2 of which must be in oak or chestnut casks; wines aged for at least 4 years may be labelled Riserva; 5 years minimum for Riserva Speciale.

Boca DOC Undervalued red wine from northern Piedmont vineyards of Boca and surrounding communes. Produced from Nebbiolo 45–70%, together with Vespolina and Bonarda Novarese. Minimum alcohol 12 degrees; minimum ageing of 3 years, 2 of which must be in oak or chestnut cask.

Brachetto d'Acqui DOC Unusual local red wine that is usually sweet and either slightly *frizzante* or fully sparkling, produced from the Brachetto grape grown in the provinces of Alessandria and Asti mainly around the spa town of Acqui Terme. Minimum alcohol 11.5 degrees.

Bramaterra DOC Red wine from northern Piedmont vineyards around Brusnengo, west of Gattinara. Grapes include Nebbiolo (50–70%) together with Croatina, Bonarda Novarese, and Vespolina. Minimum alcohol 12 degrees; minimum ageing 2 years, 18 months of which must be in wood barrels. Wines aged for at least 3 years may be labelled Riserva.

Carema DOC Tiny but prestigious Nebbiolo vineyard situated at Piedmont's border with the Valle d'Aosta, producing red wines capable of great scent and elegance. Minimum alcohol 12 degrees; minimum ageing 4 years, at least 2 of which must be in oak or chestnut cask.

Colli Tortonesi DOC Zonal *denominazione* for vineyards around town of Tortona (in south-east of region near Novi Ligure) for both mainly red wines produced from Barbera with the addition of some Freisa, Bonarda, and Dolcetto (minimum alcohol 12 degrees), and white wines produced from Cortese (minimum alcohol 10.5 degrees).

Cortese dell'Alto Monferrato DOC Fairly undistinguished white wine from Cortese grapes grown in the hills of the Alto Monferrato. Minimum alcohol 10 degrees.

Dolcetto delle Langhe Monregalesi DOC; Dolcetto d'Acqui DOC; Dolcetto di Asti DOC; Dolcetto d'Alba DOC; Dolcetto di Diano d'Alba DOC; Dolcetto di Dogliani DOC; Dolcetto di Ovada DOC
7 separate zonal *denominazioni* covering a vast area for the production of red wines from the Dolcetto grape, a local variety with great character and potential for producing both grapey wines for immediate consumption, as well as sturdier, more profound examples capable of improving with age. Minimum alcohol is between 11 and 12 degrees; wines with at least 12.5 degrees may be labelled Superiore.

Erbaluce di Caluso DOC; Caluso Passito DOC; Caluso Passito Liquoroso Dry white, sweet, and sweet fortified wines produced from the distinctive Erbaluce grape grown on vineyards mainly south of Ivrea. Dry white Erbaluce di Caluso must reach at least 11 degrees of alcohol; 13.5 degrees for Caluso Passito; 16 degrees for Liquoroso.

Fara DOC Fine red wine produced from Nebbiolo, Vespolina, and Bonarda Novarese grapes grown in northern Piedmont vineyards around town of Fara, north of Novara. Minimum alcohol 12 degrees; minimum ageing 3 years, 2 of which must be in oak or chestnut cask.

Favorita Distinctive, fashionable light dry white wine from Favorita grapes grown in the Roeri hills north of Alba. Probable candidate for Piedmont's next DOC.

Freisa di Asti DOC; Freisa di Chieri DOC Dry red wines of character, sometimes *frizzante* or even fully sparkling, produced from Freisa grapes grown in vineyards around Asti and in the smaller delimited zone around Chieri. Minimum alcohol 11 degrees.

Gabiano DOC Obscure *denominazione* for red wine produced from Barbera grapes grown around the communities of Gabiano and Moncestino. Minimum alcohol 12 degrees.

Gattinara DOC Distinguished Nebbiolo (90% at least) red wine produced from northern vineyards around the community of Gattinara. Minimum alcohol 12 degrees; minimum ageing 4 years, with at least 2 in oak or chestnut cask.

Gavi DOC; **Cortese di Gavi DOC** Prestigious vineyard around town of Gavi Ligure for the production of fine, classy white wine from Cortese grape. Minimum alcohol 10.5 degrees.

Ghemme DOC Red wine produced from vineyards adjoining Gattinara, from Nebbiolo (60–85%) together with Vespolina and Bonarda Novarese. Minimum alcohol 12 degrees; minimum ageing 4 years, with at least 2 in oak or chestnut cask.

Grignolino del Monferrato Casalese DOC; **Grignolino di Asti DOC** Delicate, increasingly rare red wine produced from this distinctive Piedmont grape variety with the addition of up to 10% Freisa. Minimum alcohol 11 degrees.

Lessona DOC Tiny vineyard north of Vercelli, producing red wines from Nebbiolo (75%) and Vespolina and Bonarda. Minimum alcohol 12 degrees; minimum ageing 2 years.

Malvasia di Casorzo di Asti DOC; Malvasia di Castelnuovo Don Bosco DOC Interesting local sweet, sparkling or *frizzante* red wines produced from Malvasia Nera with the addition of Freisa. Minimum alcohol 10.5 degrees.

Moscato d'Asti DOC Outstanding, fragrant medium dry to sweet table wine produced from Moscato Bianco grapes. Generally low in alcohol (6–8 degrees), and drunk in the zone as an *aperitivo*. **Moscato d'Asti Spumante DOC** (see Asti Spumante above).

Nebbiolo d'Alba DOC Basic *denominazione* for varietal wine produced from Nebbiolo grapes grown throughout the Alba vineyard. Usually lighter and considerably less expensive than more prestigious wines named after principal communities, but none the less capable of some distinction in its own right. Minimum alcohol 12 degrees.

Roero Arneis DOC Outstanding white wine produced from local Arneis grape grown in the Roero hills north of Alba. Minimum alcohol 10.5 degrees.

Roero DOC Historic delimited vineyard north of Alba producing red wine mainly from the Nebbiolo grape (with tiny addition of Arneis). Minimum alcohol 11.5 degrees.

Rubino di Cantavenna DOC Tiny delimited vineyard overlapping that of Gabiano, for the production of red wine from Barbera (mainly) with the addition of Grignolino and Freisa. Minimum alcohol 11.5 degrees.

Ruchè di Castagnole del Monferrato DOC Rare Ruchè grape produces this little-known red wine in vineyards north of Asti around town of Castagnole Monferrato. Minimum alcohol 12 degrees.

Sizzano DOC Red wine from tiny delimited vineyard north of Novara, produced from Nebbiolo (40–60%), together with Vespolina and Bonarda Novarese. Minimum alcohol 12 degrees; minimum ageing 3 years, 2 of which must be in oak or chestnut cask.

VERMOUTH

It is not surprising that Piedmont is the principal source of vermouth, for this mountainous zone has traditionally had a plentiful supply of fragrant mountain herbs, roots, and flavourings at hand. Indeed, the process of infusing wine with such aromatics dates back to Roman times at least, though the name 'vermouth' comes from the German *Wermut*, referring to the shrub wormwood which adds its distinctive flavour, along with cinnamon, nutmeg, orange and lemon peel, quinine and other barks, coriander, and numerous other herbs and ingredients. Indeed, these myriad flavourings are much more important than the wine itself, which should be neutral and strong, and which has traditionally come from Apulia. There are basically 4 styles of vermouth: *bianco* (sweet white); *rosso* (sweet, caramel coloured); *rosato* (medium-sweet, pink); and *secco* (dry white). Though, outside Italy, vermouth is popular as a mixer for various cocktails, in Italy it is most often enjoyed as an unmixed *aperitivo*, for the blend of herbs and bitters encourages the gastric juices to flow in anticipation of the meal which follows.

THE NORTH-WEST

Spanna Local name for Nebbiolo grape in northern Piedmont. Wine labelled as such, though not entitled to DOC, is generally good varietal *vino da tavola*.

Valle d'Aosta DOC The regional *denominazione* is utilized to encompass all of the Valle d'Aosta's varied wines, and applies to some 15 different wines from throughout the zone, including both generic as well as wines from specific communes: Arnad Montjovet; Bianco (Blanc); Blanc de Morgex et de La Salle; Chambave Moscato (Muscat); Chambave Rosso (Rouge); Donnaz (Donnas); Enfer d'Arvier; Gamay; Müller-Thurgau; Nus Malvoisie; Nus Rosso (Vien de Nus); Pinot Nero (Pinot Noir); Rosato (Rosé); Rosso (Rouge); Torrette.

LA GASTRONOMIA: FOODS OF PIEDMONT AND VALLE D'AOSTA

Piedmont is not only Italy's greatest quality vineyard, it can also claim distinction as one of her foremost culinary zones. Indeed, arguably nowhere else can you enjoy such unselfconscious local foods (including rare truffles and *funghi porcini*) in such ample proportions. The proximity to France has undoubtedly influenced the cooks of the region, who display considerably more elegant skills in the preparation of a number of sophisticated dishes; but the proximity of the mountains to both Piedmont and the autonomous Valle d'Aosta has also resulted in a range of robust, hearty, and simple alpine foods that satisfy man-sized appetites after days spent out of doors.

Piedmont has an almost embarrassingly wide choice of excellent restaurants, especially throughout the wine zones, ranging from the simplest serving *cucina casalinga* to those set in more sophisticated and elegant surroundings, catering inevitably to the wealthy businessmen from nearby industrial Turin. However, the zone is so famous for its food and drink that gastronomes converge on centres such as Alba and Asti, especially in autumn to enjoy great truffle feasts. Valle d'Aosta has no shortage of good restaurants serving the principal winter and summer mountain resorts.

PIATTI TIPICI:
REGIONAL SPECIALITIES

Agnolotti Favourite local 'ravioli' stuffed with meat or spinach.

Antipasti piemontesi Virtually a meal in itself: vast trolley or table laden with astonishing array of 'appetizers', such as roasted marinated vegetables; raw meat; trout in aspic; stuffed eggs; *vitello tonnato*; and much else.

Carne cruda Very finely sliced raw *sotto filetto*, arranged on a plate with thin slices of *parmigiano reggiano*, slivers of mushrooms (or truffles in season), and a creamy sauce.

Bagna cauda Pungent hot anchovy, olive oil, and garlic mixture, served with grated truffles in season. This can be spread over vegetables or meat, or else the bubbling pot is brought to the table fondue-style, as a dip for raw vegetables and *grissini*.

Riso al Barbera *Arborio* rice cooked with good homemade stock, Barbera wine, and (usually) *funghi porcini*.

Tajarin; **tagliarin** Very fine, homemade egg noodles, usually served in autumn with butter and grated truffles, and in summer with fresh tomato sauce.

Bollito misto Gargantuan trolley of boiled meats, including beef, chicken, veal, calf's foot, tongue, served with boiled vegetables and *salsa verde* and *salsa rossa*.

Brasato al Barolo Large joint of beef marinated then stewed in Barolo wine.

Costolette alla valdostana Veal chop layered with *prosciutto* and Fontina cheese, then fried.

Finanziera Extremely rich speciality: chicken giblets, calf's sweetbreads, chicken breast, even cock's comb (literally), cooked separately, then mixed with cream and truffles.

Fonduta Melted Fontina cheese, cream, and grated truffles, served at the table fondue-style or else spread on cooked vegetables, toasted bread or potatoes.

Gallo al Barbera Chicken stewed in Barbera wine: a classic rustic dish of the country.

Rane dorate Frogs' legs, dipped

in flour and fried in olive oil – speciality of Vercelli province.

Tartufi bianchi The highly prized white truffles of Piedmont, in season to be eaten raw, shaved into razor-thin slices and sprinkled over virtually everything. A great delicacy not to be missed.

Zabaione; **zabaglione** Favourite dessert invented by cooks for the House of Savoy, made of beaten egg yolks, sugar and Marsala (some local cooks today use Barbera).

Cheeses: *Fontina* Large, smooth, creamy cheese from Valle d'Aosta. *Toma* Small disc of mountain cheese, usually made from sheep's milk. *Raschera* Rind-washed, traditional handmade cheese made from cow's milk. *Robiola di Murazzano* Creamy, fresh sheep's milk cheese from Langhe hills south of Alba. *Robiola di Roccaverano* Similar sheep's milk cheese from steep hills south-west of Acqui Terme. *Brúsa* (*fromage fort*) Robiola cheese packed in pots and aged in *grappa* for upwards of a year: not for the faint-hearted.

IN SEARCH OF FUNGHI

One of the most popular autumn activities in the Piedmont as well as throughout the country is the annual exodus into the woods in search of funghi. This is a regional – indeed national – passion that borders on the obsessive. Around Alba, Asti and the Monferrato hills, professional truffle hunters search for the unbelievably expensive *tartufi bianchi*. But ordinary folk – office workers from Turin, manual workers from the Fiat and Olivetti factories, whole families, *nonni* and *nonne*, everybody – turn out at weekends in search of mushrooms such as the pungent and highly prized *funghi porcini*, delicate *ovuli*, *le crave* (brown birch boletus) and scores of lesser varieties. It should perhaps be pointed out, though, that this activity is not without its risks: it can be extremely difficult to distinguish the delicious from the deadly poisonous. Offices of hygiene exist, therefore, in most areas, where licensed experts can determine whether your efforts are fit to eat or not. If in doubt, resist temptation.

THE *ROUTE DES VINS* OF THE VALLE D'AOSTA

In Brief: For those entering or leaving Italy by the Monte Bianco/Mont Blanc tunnel, the *Route des Vins* of the Valle d'Aosta is the road that is followed, leading through tiny wine hamlets where vineyards hug the precipitous slopes above the raging Dora Báltea valley. Though the *autostrada* begins outside Aosta, forgo this and meander through such wine hamlets as Nus and Chambave, stopping in the latter where there are 2 of the few opportunities to visit producers and (if you are lucky) taste wines.

Excursions through the wine country also provide interesting relief for those who have come to the region for winter sports. Otherwise, simply enjoy the local wines in your hotel or in restaurants, not begrudging their rather steep prices, for they are produced only at the greatest effort at the utmost limits of the vine's feasibility, and it is unlikely that there will ever be opportunities to sample them anywhere else.

Emerging from the long darkness of the Monte Bianco (or Mont Blanc – both names are used in this bilingual region) tunnel from France into Italy, it comes as something of a shock to find yourself in the bright and blinding glare of the mountains once more. The majestic, almost always snow-covered peaks dominate in all directions, and villages such as Courmayeur and Cervinia are a reminder that this alpine land is today principally noted for its world-famous winter sports venues.

Yet here, on steep, stony terraces, below the snow-line and on virtually every patch of suitable soil, vines are trained on low *pergole*, fanned out to expose themselves to every minute of fleeting but fierce alpine sun. These vineyards of the Valle d'Aosta, though necessarily limited and producing only tiny quantities of wine, are Italy's first for the wine traveller coming to the country from northern Europe. Established in this remote valley even before the Roman occupation, they remain today some of the most beautiful and striking that will ever be encountered. Those at La Salle, planted a dizzying 1000 metres above sea level underneath Monte Bianco, are the highest in Europe. For these reasons alone, the Valle d'Aosta is noteworthy as a wine region. The wines produced, though admittedly not classics in any world sense, are varied and interesting; they provide a most enjoyable *apéritif* – or should we say *aperitivo* – for the thirsty, and promise further of

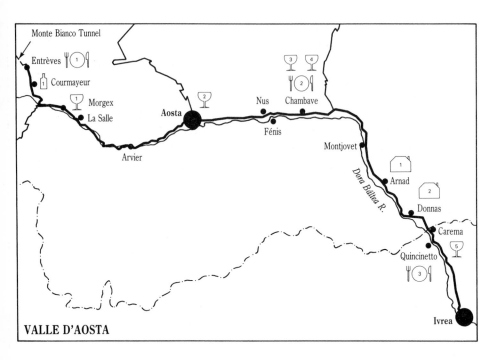

VALLE D'AOSTA

all that lies ahead to the south.

And yet: the traveller heading south – and this valley has been an important international corridor for millennia, via the later-named Great St Bernard and Little St Bernard passes, and now via the Monte Bianco tunnel – through mountain hamlets such as Morgex, La Salle, Arvier, Nus, Chambave, or Donnas might quite feasibly pass by hardly realizing that he or she is in a historic and ancient wine land. Indeed, those who stop at small villages to shop for provisions may not even be able to purchase a bottle of Malvoisie de Nus, Muscat de Chambave, Enfer d'Arvier or Vin Blanc de Morgex. The growers, many of whom tend only tiny patches of vines alongside other fruit orchards or meadows for alpine herds, guard much of the fruits of their efforts jealously for themselves. The rest, produced by small individual growers or in a few large co-operative wine cellars, find a ready market, to be drunk in quantity by the thousands of holidaymakers to the region's many winter resorts. In a case where demand always outstrips meagre supply, and where wine making is carried out in such extreme labour-intensive conditions, at the very limits of feasibility and possibility, the wines produced can never be inexpensive.

The *Route des Vins* broadly follows the valley south and east and as such provides the opportunity to view in wonder – if not to taste, since some of the region's most notable wines are virtually impossible to obtain – the region from where Italy's most northernmost wines hail. The first wine communes of note are Morgex and La Salle. Together, both produce one of the region's most distinctive white wines, Vin Blanc de Morgex et de La Salle, rather low in alcohol, dry, and slightly sharp – not surprising, considering the severe conditions under which the grapes must be cultivated. These wines, though rare and necessarily produced in limited quantities, may be sampled and purchased at the *Cave du Vin Blanc de Morgex et de La Salle*, located in the little hamlet of Les Iles up the valley towards the Little St Bernard Pass. Morgex, incidentally, is also famous for its *boudin* sausage, reputedly delicious with the local white wine.

Further down the valley, the next wine commune of note is little Arvier, where Petit Rouge grapes grow on such sheltered, south-facing, sun-baked slopes that the wine produced is called Enfer d'Arvier. Those who may expect such alpine mountain wines to be light at best, may well be surprised by the body, depth, and indeed rather rough and powerful edge that Enfer can possess, for the microclimate here is exceptional, and the grapes are allowed to ripen fully and thus maintain high levels of tannin and pigmentation.

Aosta, the region's capital, is an elegant town. Its position from time immemorial at the junction of important passes has given it a rather worldly outlook, and a veneer of considerable sophistication. Of course, Aosta was a Roman city of importance (named after the emperor Augustus), and reminders from that imperial age are still impressive: the well-preserved town walls, the triumphal Arch of Augustus, and the remains of a Roman theatre and amphitheatre. The latter dates from the 1st century BC and was capable of holding some 20,000 spectators.

Today Aosta is the home of one of Italy's pre-eminent regional agricultural schools, the Institut Agricol Regional, and indeed this important institution has done much to further viticulture in the region. In addition to considerable experimentation regarding grape varieties, clonal selection, and oenological techniques, the Institut has its own considerable vineyard holdings and itself produces notable wines from Gamay, Pinot Nero, Pinot Grigio, Petit Rouge, Petit Arvine, Merlot, Grenache, and Malvoisie grapes. The Institut can be visited by appointment, and the wines are available for purchase.

Just south of Aosta, the tiny wine hamlet of Nus produces a legendary *passito* wine from semi-dried Malvoisie grapes, a reputedly exceptional dessert wine, though we cannot confirm this: we scoured the village, but were unable to purchase a single bottle, nor could we acquire a bottle of Nus Rouge, a red wine produced from Vien de Nus grapes blended with Petit Rouge, Pinot Noir, and/or Freisa.

The intrepid wine traveller, however, need not despair totally, for refreshment is at hand in the next wine hamlet of Chambave where the local growers have banded together to form a co-operative known as *La Crotta di Vegneron*. Chambave is famous particularly for its *passito* dessert wine, produced from semi-dried Muscat grapes, for its dry Muscat wine, and for its Chambave Rouge, produced mainly from Petit Rouge. These wines may be tasted and purchased at *La Crotta*; upstairs there is an inexpensive restaurant serving local foods and wines. At Fénis, opposite Chambave, there is a fine, well-preserved medieval castle that can be visited.

Below Chambave, the Aosta valley begins to broaden out somewhat, and is dominated by the immense feudal castles that once guarded the road to Aosta. Grape growing continues, here, there, anywhere that it is possible, and the wines produced may be drunk locally by the carafe, or else are bottled and labelled varietally (Pinot Nero, Gamay, Petit Rouge, Riesling, Müller-Thurgau, and others) then sent down to the Piedmont, where they are much enjoyed.

Valle d'Aosta wine hamlet.

Donnas is a fine, lively, rather larger wine town, nestled in a curve of the

Dora Báltea valley, its steep terraced vineyards rising dramatically above it. Donnas is poised virtually on the autonomous region's southern limits, and, indeed, the neighbouring wine community of Carema, though theoretically within the Piedmont region, produces wines that are remarkably similar. Donnas and Carema are both made varietally from the aristocratic Nebbiolo (known in the former commune as Picotendro, in the latter as Spanna). Carema's vineyards, planted by the Romans with the vines supported by corridors of stone pillars, have a pleasing architectural quality about them, and appear almost like hanging gardens. Both wines, as well as the much rarer Arnad Mont-jovet (from the wine community north of Donnas), have a character that is at once elegant and highly perfumed; they are undoubtedly big, serious red wines which are light only in comparison to the Nebbiolo heavyweights of the Langhe to the south.

The wines of the Valle d'Aosta will probably always remain little more than curiosities rarely encountered outside their region of provenance: how can they be otherwise when they are necessarily produced in such minute quantities and with such back-breaking, one might even say soul-destroying, effort? None the less, they are an important and necessary strand in the great Italian *tappeto*, woven from all her varied wine lands.

LA GROLLA

The alpine climate of the Valle d'Aosta sometimes requires a drink more warming even than wine. At such times, the *grolla* is passed. This hand-carved wooden receptacle has half a dozen or so mouthpieces sprouting from its top. The *grolla* is filled with strong black coffee, and to this is usually added a generous dose of locally-distilled *grappa*. It is then passed around the table, each person drinking from his own spout, refilled, and inevitably refilled yet again. It is a wonderful communal pot of hospitality.

Degustazione: Stop to Taste; Stop to Buy

1

CAVE DU VIN BLANC DE MORGEX ET
  DE LA SALLE
SOC. COOP. A.R.L.
LOCALITÀ LES ILES
FRAZIONE LA RULNE
11017 MORGEX AO
TEL: 0165/800331

WINES PRODUCED: Blanc de Morgex et de La Salle still and sparkling (*metodo champenois*).
VISITS: daily by appointment, preferably 15 days in advance.
Charge for *degustazione*.

The vineyards of Morgex and La Salle, sited between 900 and 1300 metres above sea level, are the highest in Europe, and because of this they were not affected by the phylloxera disaster. Come to this *cave cooperative* to taste and purchase these little encountered wines when *en route* to or from the Monte Bianco tunnel.
French spoken.

THE NORTH-WEST

2 INSTITUT AGRICOL REGIONAL
LA ROCHÈRE 1/A
11100 AOSTA
TEL: 0165/553304

WINES PRODUCED: Vin du Conseil
Petite Arvine; Gamay Valle
d'Aosta; Pinot Nero Valle d'Aosta;
Petit Rouge Valle d'Aosta.

VISITS: by appointment.
Founded in 1949, this important
regional agricultural school has
done much to further viticulture in
the region. The well-made wines
may be sampled and purchased by
appointment.

---

3 SOCIETÀ COOPERATIVA 'LA CROTTA
DI VEGNERON'
PIAZZA RONCAS 2
11023 CHAMBAVE AO
TEL: 0166/46670

WINES PRODUCED: Chambave
Rouge; Chambave Muscat;
Chambave Muscat Passito.
VISITS: Mon–Fri 9–12h; 14–17h.
Welcoming co-operative winery
with adjoining restaurant.

---

4 AZIENDA VITIVINICOLA EZIO VOYAT
VIA ARBERAZ 13
11023 CHAMBAVE AO
TEL: 0166/46139

WINES PRODUCED: Rosso Le
Muraglie (Chambave Rouge);
Passito Le Muraglie; La Gazzella
(Moscato Secco di Chambave).
VISITS: daily, by appointment.
Ezio Voyat is probably the most
famous wine producer in the Valle
d'Aosta. He cultivates his steep
vineyards above Chambave
biologically, and his *cru* wines are
named after the *muraglie*,
dry-stone walls that contain the
terraces and the loose scree and

topsoil ('La Gazzella', on the other
hand, is not named after a vineyard
but after Voyat's daughter
Marilena, a national class sprinter
over 100 and 200 metres, known
locally as the 'gazelle of
Chambave').

Voyat's are true artisan-made
wines, rare, distinguished, and in
great demand by all *amatori* of the
grape: they may be available for
purchase, but so scarce are they
that they probably cannot be
tasted. Ezio Voyat's house is located
above the pharmacy in Chambave.
French and a little English spoken.

5 CANTINA DEI PRODUTTORI
'NEBBIOLO DI CAREMA'
VIA NAZIONALE 28
10010 CAREMA TO
TEL: 0125/85256

WINES PRODUCED: Carema, Carema Riserva; 'Turel' *vino rosso da tavola*; *bianco e rosato da tavola*.

VISITS: daily 9–12h30; 14h30–19h30.
The *cantina* of this important co-operative wine cellar is located on the main north–south route, and is therefore an important source of the rare and undervalued Carema wines.
English, French spoken.

Enoteca

1 ENOTECA 'LA CROTTA'
VIA CIRCONVALLAZIONE 102
11013 COURMAYEUR AO
TEL: 0165/841735

OPEN: daily year round 9–12h30; 14–20h.
This *enoteca* in the stylish ski town is run by enthusiast Sergio Migliore and provides one of the best opportunities to purchase the full gamut of often elusive Valle d'Aosta wines from the region's best producers, as well as a selection of fine wines from throughout the country. Located near the entrance to the Monte Bianco tunnel, it may be useful for those wishing to stock up on quality wines before heading north.

Ristoranti

1 MAISON DE FILIPPO
LOC. ENTRÈVES
11013 COURMAYEUR AO
TEL: 0165/89968

Closed Tue.
This old favourite, located just near the entrance to the Monte Bianco tunnel in a typical mountain house, serves ample, warming foods of the region: *antipasti locali*, *tortelloni*, *fonduta*, *polenta* and a good range of both own-produced and other local wines.
Moderate

THE NORTH-WEST

2 RISTORANTE-BAR 'LA CROTTA'
PIAZZA RONCAS 4
11023 CHAMBAVE AO
TEL: 0166/46670

Closed Thurs.
Located above the Cooperativa 'La

Crotta di Vegneron', this simple restaurant serves local foods, including *fonduta* and *agnolotti*, accompanied by the excellent wines of the co-operative.
Inexpensive

---

3 RISTORANTE 'DA GIOVANNI'
PIAZZA CHIESA PARROCCHIALE
10010 QUINCINETTO TO
TEL: 0125/757927

Closed Tue.
Fine local *trattoria* literally minutes off the *autostrada* in the colourful main square of this

Carema wine village north of Ivrea. Good local foods include: *antipasti, funghi porcini sott'olio, risotto ai funghi, costolette alla valdostana, funghi ai ferri, panna cotta,* together with a good selection of local wines.
Moderate

Agriturismo

1 AZIENDA AGRITURISTICA 'LO DZERBY'
LOC. PIED DE VILLE
11010 ARNAD AO
TEL: 0125/966067

Rural *trattoria* near the wine town of Arnad, open May–July and Sept,

weekends only (daily August) or by reservation, serving local foods and own-produced wines and *salami* in a mountain setting 720 metres above sea level.

---

2 'LES VIGNOBLES' TURISMO RURALE
VIA GEAN BREAN 8
11020 DONNAS AO
TEL: 0125/85469

Apartment available for weekly rental year round; attached to wine grower's own house.

THE WINE ROADS OF PIEDMONT

Piedmont takes its position as Italy's greatest single wine region seriously, and wine tourism is more highly developed here than probably anywhere else in the country. Indeed, wine and gastronomy are rightly appreciated as two of the region's major attractions. The vineyard centres of Alba and Asti

ENOTECHE REGIONALI AND *BOTTEGHE DEL VINO*

Located throughout the Piedmont are 8 *Enoteche Regionali*, important wine centres in castles or other historic buildings which serve as a direct link between the producer and the consumer, and which provide unsurpassed tasting and purchasing opportunities. Many also have restaurants serving superlative regional *cucina* together with local wines. Any wine tourist, therefore, should most certainly plan on visiting at least one or two of these unique institutions as part of an itinerary along the wine roads of Piedmont. They are incorporated into the principal wine tours below.

There are furthermore numerous smaller *Botteghe del Vino* which serve as municipal or communal outlets for the display and sale of wines. Most have limited opening times, often only at weekends or holidays, but they too provide excellent opportunities for tasting and purchasing wines. The addresses are included below.

are the best-known and most important, but other localities within this vast region are equally proud of their local products, and eager to promote them to visitors. Thus, a fine and extensive network of *strade dei vini* – wine roads – winds throughout Piedmont. They are identified by signs designed with crenellated corners representing the many castles of Piedmont, a wine glass, a bunch of grapes, and a winding road, all on a yellow background.

These *strade dei vini*, however, are not necessarily roads or routes which one follows from one point to another. No comprehensive or logical map charting all of them seems to exist. Rather, they serve as important and essential points of reference within a total landscape complex of which the grapes are but a part.

There are so many different wines produced in Piedmont, and over such a vast area, that it would hardly be possible to travel over every signposted wine road in the region. We have chosen to concentrate on the principal and most important zones of production, primarily around Asti and Alba, but that still leaves plenty of opportunity for further exploration.

THE NORTH-WEST

MARTINI MUSEUM OF THE HISTORY OF WINE MAKING

The Martini Museum, located at Pessione, south of Turin, is one of the most extensive and important wine museums in Europe. Here, in the vaulted cellars of the 18th-century mansion that remains the headquarters of this world-famous vermouth and sparkling wine firm, some 18 rooms have been given over to tracing the history of wine through the ages. It is above all the collection of wine-related objects from antiquity that is unsurpassed, including well-preserved and restored examples of 7th-century BC Etruscan wine cups made from shiny black *bucchero* (clay mixed with magnesium); finely-decorated 4th-century BC Greek *idrie* and *crateri* (water and wine serving vessels); enormous Roman terracotta fermentation *dolium* (with a model showing how such vessels, in a Roman cellar, would be buried in the earth or sand up to their necks); magnificent drinking cups shaped like rams' heads, as well as the first Roman glass vessels, and much else. This establishment, though private, is by no means a commercial publicity vehicle for Martini, but a serious and fascinating museum which all wine lovers should make the effort to visit.

Martini Museum of the History of Wine Making
Martini & Rossi SpA
10023 Pessione TO
tel: 011/57451 ext 377

Open: daily, including weekends but excluding holidays, 9–12h30; 14h30–17h30. Appointment not essential but advisable by telephoning the above number. English-, French-, and German-speaking guides available. Appointments can also be made to visit the Martini factory, as well as the botanical and herb gardens.

Roman amphora

THE LANGHE

South-east of Turin, below Asti and Monferrato, and above the Ligurian Apennines and Maritime Alps lies a land of rare majesty: the Langhe. This is an ancient and long-established region, divided by the slow Tanaro river into the Langa to the south, a most prestigious vineyard region of high hills cut by deep gorges, and the Roero to the north, also hilly and vine covered, though more irregularly so. Throughout the region, there are dozens of imposing castles and medieval *palazzi*, testimony to a grander past when feudal counts and lords stared across at one another from their lofty hilltop fortresses. Later, King Vittorio Emanuele II had a hunting lodge at Pollenzo, while another king, Carlo Alberto, built a castle at Verduno. Today, the Langhe is a rich, proud, isolated land, the source not only of some of Italy's greatest wines, but also of a regional gastronomy that many consider to be unsurpassed.

Alba, capital of the Langhe, is in every way one of the great wine towns of Italy. Located at the hub of the major viticultural zones of Barbaresco, Barolo, and Roero, the medieval town remains very much the centre of the zone's economic and social activity. Though today prosperity has meant that the town has rather sprawled out into the surrounding countryside, the historic centre, with its 'hundred medieval towers' and houses arranged around a circle, maintains a timeless and most pleasant atmosphere, especially in autumn, traditionally the busiest time of year, when the very air is pungent with the aroma of *tartufi*. Many of the region's most famous wine growers and producers have their headquarters in or just outside Alba, and there is no shortage of really fine restaurants serving the ample and generous foods of the Langhe. Alba is the starting point for our 3 wine tours of the Langhe.

La Terra del Barolo

Barolo is arguably Italy's greatest delimited red wine (only Brunello di Montalcino vies for supremacy). The land from which it comes is equally majestic, a small wine region to the south-west of Alba that spreads over 11 principal communes, mainly hill hamlets that stare across at one another in stony silence over bare, sometimes white hills ringed with concentric circles of vines. Hellishly hot in summer, in autumn the region is often blanketed by a thick layer of fog. Indeed, the Nebbiolo, temperamental but aristocratic grape, and the single variety used to produce Barolo (and neighbouring

THE NORTH-WEST

In Brief: The Barolo wine zone is not large, and the circuit can easily be covered in a day, though further time is necessary to explore fully this fascinating and important vineyard. In addition to visiting wine producers, there are 2 important *Enoteche Regionali*, the first at Grinzane Cavour, the second at Barolo itself. There is no shortage of restaurants, either, serving both elegant and everyday foods of the Langhe. In autumn, the region is at its busiest, so it is wise both to book restaurants in advance, as well as to make appointments to visit wine producers as far in advance as possible.

Barbaresco), takes its name from *nebbia* for it is often harvested in late October or even November, well into the season of mists.

The Nebbiolo produces austere, well-structured wine, nowhere more so than in these mainly calcareous hills of Barolo. Produced by age-old methods, that is, with lengthy maceration of up to 30–40 days, with the *capello* of skins continually submerged below the surface of the fermenting must, the resulting wines may be in need of considerable ageing to soften their harsh robe of tannins, in some cases upwards of 5–10 years in the large Slavonian oak *botte* prior to bottling. Even after such lengthy sojourns in the cask, the wines may still retain too much tannin at the expense of perfume and fruit, argue some. Thus, today, the trend by some wine makers is towards the production of somewhat lighter, less tannic, more elegant and fruity wines. They achieve this through much shorter maceration (10–20 days only) utilizing *rimontaggio* (pumping the must back over the mass of skins 3–4 times a day to extract colour and tannin), followed by the bare legal minimum of 2 years in *botte*. Such wines, argue their proponents, are able to be enjoyed at a far younger age, but remain capable of lengthy conservation none the less.

Though the wine zone is scattered with castles, mansions, ancient *palazzi*, and royal hunting lodges, viticulture here traditionally remains somewhat fragmented, not based on large and intact estates. Families have, over the years, acquired parcels of land here and there, throughout not only the Barolo zone, but extending across into Barbaresco, Roero, and further afield. In this wine zone near the Alps, where the threat of hail is a constant one, it has always made sense to scatter one's resources and lessen the risk of total ruination. Traditionally, though, the grapes would be harvested and pressed together to produce, say, a generic Barolo, albeit (depending on the producer) either an ordinary or a very fine one.

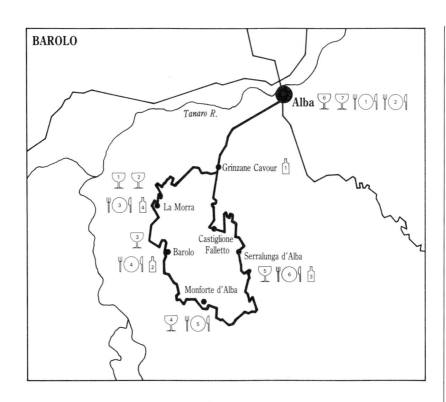

Today, however, there is great interest in the production of single *cru* or *vigneto* wines – a most important development for the consumer, for it adds a further tier of enjoyment and the opportunity to appreciate the subtle nuances of microclimate. This is not an entirely new departure, it should be noted, for wine growers here have long valued certain vineyards over others, and have known them by name since at least the 18th century. The difference is that now estate wines are being produced and sold under the name of such single vineyards (in some cases designated by the term '*bricco*' which means top of the hill), and they can be among the region's most exciting and outstanding. Indeed, the difference between a straight generic supermarket Barolo and a single-*vigneto* wine produced by one of the top growers can be as great as that between a straight generic Burgundy and a classified *Premier* or *Grand Cru*.

On the other hand, it should be pointed out that, as in Burgundy (the comparison between the two regions seems obvious and inevitable), the fact that a wine comes from a single vineyard is not evidence in itself of excellence. Some producers here act in the role of *négociant-éleveur*, pur-

THE NORTH-WEST

chasing either grapes or wines from growers located throughout the zone, then assembling the wines in their *cantine* in Alba or elsewhere. They maintain that by so doing, by assembling wines from the commune of Barolo with, say, wines from Serralunga and Monforte, they are able to produce

THE *PRIME CATEGORIE, GRANDS CRUS* OF BAROLO

There is not, as yet, an official classification of the vineyards of Barolo and until there is, the consumer is apt to remain somewhat confused. For simply because a wine bears the name of a single *vigneto* is no guarantee of excellence in itself unless that *vigneto* is noted and accepted as capable of producing wine that can make a particular statement about its provenance. The late Renato Ratti, wine maker and historian, classified the Barolo vineyard into historic sub-zones of excellence (Monfortino, Zonchetta, Arione, Marcenasco, Fontanafredda are a few of the better-known examples), sub-regions with special or particular characteristics (Bussia Soprana, Rocchette, Monfalletto, Santo Stefano and some 19 others), and finally 10 *Prime Categorie* vineyards of unsurpassed excellence, the *Grands Crus* as it were of the Barolo vineyard. Admittedly, any classification of vineyards is without doubt a tightrope exercise in local politics, and fierce disagreements may continue over the inclusion or exclusion of vineyards from this élite list. However, Ratti was held in wide esteem in the region, and few would disagree that his 10 *Prime Categorie* vineyards are all capable of undoubted excellence.

Vigneto	Commune
Rocche	La Morra
Brunate	La Morra; Barolo
Cerequio	La Morra; Barolo
Cannubi	Barolo
Momprivato	Castiglione Falletto
Villero	Castiglione Falletto
Rocche	Castiglione Falletto
Gubutti-Parafada	Serralunga d'Alba
Lazzarito	Serralunga d'Alba
Marenca-Rivette	Serralunga d'Alba

more balanced, consistent wines that combine elegance with structure and longevity. Such wines may not have the individuality of those from single *vigneti*, but they can be equally outstanding none the less.

To begin a wine tour of the Barolo vineyard, leave Alba on the Alba–Gallo Grinzane road. Grinzane Cavour is located above the one-street town of Gallo d'Alba, itself famous for its sweet *torrone piemontese*. A visit to the important *Enoteca Regionale* of Grinzane Cavour, located in the Castello di Grinzane, should be high on the priorities for any wine tourist. Opened in 1971 as the first *Enoteca Regionale* in Piedmont, it provides a magnificent introduction to the history of viticulture in the region within a majestic 12th-century setting. In addition to an extensive display of wine and *grappa* from throughout the Piedmont vineyard (available for tasting and purchase), there are various museum rooms on different floors of the castle, including examples of 15th- and 17th-century kitchens, a smithy and threshing room, a 16th-century distillery, and a 17th-century wine cellar and cooper's workshop. The adjoining restaurant serves the fine foods of Alba together with wines selected by the *Ordine dei Cavalieri del Tartufo e dei Vini di Alba*. There is also an important school of viticulture located in the Grinzane castle.

After visiting the *enoteca*, return to Gallo, then find the road that leads to the right towards La Morra. By the time the little wine hamlet of Santa Maria is reached, the wine road has begun to climb into the vineyards. Before La Morra is reached, a turning to the left leads to the well-known and important wine commune of La Annunziata, home of some important and notable growers, such as the Antiche Cantine dell' Abbazia dell'Annunziata. To gain a historical perspective of the Barolo vineyard, as well as to learn about modern trends in viticulture, it is certainly worth making an appointment with Massimo Martinelli, nephew of the late Renato Ratti, to visit the important Museo Ratti and the wine *cantina*.

The Barolo region is broadly divided into two valleys, the valley of Barolo which includes the communes of Barolo, La Morra and Annunziata, and the valley of Serralunga which takes in the communes of Serralunga d'Alba, Castiglione Falletto and Monforte. In general the latter, whose vineyards extend over particularly chalky soil, is the source of the richest, fullest, and most long-lived wines. The former, on the other hand, is capable of producing wines that, if somewhat lighter, may possess considerably more perfume and elegance. La Morra itself is the most important single wine commune in the Barolo zone, accounting for some 40% of the whole area of the DOC. La Morra takes its position as a centre of considerable importance

THE NORTH-WEST

seriously, and does much to welcome the wine tourist and wine lover. One of the most imaginative schemes is the system of 5 colour-coded signposted footpaths through the vineyards, known as '*sentieri del vino*', together with suggested restaurant stops along the way. For those who don't want to risk driving, they provide a singular opportunity for gaining a more intimate acquaintance with the *terra del Barolo*. Ask for details or a map at the Cantina Communale di La Morra (address below).

From La Morra, continue on to Barolo itself. Here the wine road passes by or through some of the region's undoubtedly finest vineyards, among them Brunate, Cerequio, and Cannubi, en route to the little town that has given its name to this famous wine. Like other great eponymous wine towns whose names are known throughout the world (Sauternes, Chablis, Piesport come to mind), Barolo remains surprisingly unassuming and modest, almost somnolent, surrounded by its bare prestigious vineyards. Of course, this is quiet, still little visited wine country, far off the beaten track, and all the better for it. Those who wish to study at leisure, taste, or purchase from an

unsurpassed selection of more than a hundred different Barolos must come to the *Enoteca Regionale*, located in the 13th-century communal castle.

From Barolo, the wine road leads first down the steep valley, then around to Monforte d'Alba, another important wine commune, whose wines are primarily noted for their great structure and body. Those modernists who consider that such wines may suffer from excessive tannin at the expense of elegance or fruit should visit a traditionalist in the zone such as Giovanni Conterno. To taste his special *riserva* Monfortino from the cask is to gain an

Man-sized bottles and barrels in Barolo.

understanding of how great wine evolves. The 1988 Monfortino, for example, tasted the summer after the harvest, was intense and enormous, so rich in extract and locked in tannin that it was almost impossible to consider. The 1987 Monfortino, another great year, was almost equally enormous and mouth-numbing. The 1985 Monfortino, though, had already mellowed after 3 ½ years in *botte*, and underneath the layers of immense tannin and extract there was still fruit and charm, as the complex bouquet of tar, violets, and dense vegetal undergrowth began to emerge and knit together. Though destined to age in the Slavonian oak casks for another 3 years at least, it was, perhaps surprisingly, already pleasing to drink, and clearly destined to be a great wine.

I asked Giovanni Conterno how he makes his wines. He smiled gently, spread his hands palms up, and stated simply, '*Come sempre.*' As always, in the traditional manner of the Barolo zone, that is, through lengthy maceration with the *capello* – the dense mass of crushed grape skins – continually submerged to extract maximum tannin, colour, and flavouring elements. Clearly, if there are today two schools of wine making in the Barolo zone, wine lovers should be grateful for the variety in styles and wines that they provide; from each school, outstanding wines are made.

From Monforte, circle around towards Serralunga d'Alba. Between Monforte, Castiglione Falletto, and Serralunga, these stark hills have soil as white as the bare chalk *albariza pagos* of Jerez de la Frontera. This soil gleams through the vines, planted around the hilltops in concentric circles,

ORDINE DEI CAVALIERI DEL TARTUFO E DEI VINI DI ALBA

The Order of the Knights of the Truffle and Wines of Alba was founded in 1967 and has its headquarters at the Castello di Grinzane, where it meets in splendour in the magnificent Hall of Honour. This important organization, with more than 1000 members worldwide, serves to promote the foods and wines of Alba and the Langhe, with the *Enoteca Regionale* as its principal showcase. Each year the best estates bring their wines to be tasted by a commission from the *Ordine*: the finest bottles only are designated part of the 'Great Alba Wine Selection', and are displayed in the *enoteca*. Rather like Burgundy's *Chevaliers du Tastevin*, the *Cavalieri del Tartufo* serve as an important link with history and tradition, and a safeguard for the quality and integrity of the wine zone.

THE NORTH-WEST

giving the hills a bald, imposing look. Indeed, this is a grand, singular land, capable of producing as majestic and uncompromising a wine as any. Serralunga d'Alba is a tiny medieval hill hamlet, topped by its impressive fortified castle. Park in the square below, and walk up the cobbled road to the castle to enjoy the views over this outstanding landscape.

From Serralunga, the wine road descends once more to meet the main road leading back to Alba. Climb up to Castiglione Falletto first, then return towards Alba, passing along the way the famous estate of Fontanafredda.

Degustazione: Stop to Taste; Stop to Buy

THE *ALBEISA* BOTTLE

In a land where history and tradition are so highly valued, it was natural that the wine growers should want to bottle their wines in a traditional container unique to the region. Thus, in 1973, the Unione Produttori Vini Albesi, after careful research of historic bottles dating back to the 17th century, rediscovered the *Albeisa*, a fine, proud-looking bottle whose shoulders slope down towards its base, and which, in today's modern version, has the word *Albeisa* embossed across its shoulders. Today some 140 local wine growers utilize the *Albeisa*: not only a guarantee to the consumer of authenticity, but an important link with the past.

1

AZIENDA AGRICOLA RENATO RATTI
ANTICHE CANTINE DELL'ABBAZIA
  DELL'ANNUNZIATA
FRAZ. ANNUNZIATA 7
12064 LA MORRA CN
TEL: 0173/50185

WINES PRODUCED: Barolo 'Conca dell' Abazzia dell' Annunziata', Barolo 'Marcenasco', Barolo 'Rocche'; Dolcetto d'Alba; Barbera d'Alba; Nebbiolo d'Alba; Dolcetto d'Alba Colombé; Villa Pattono (super-*vino da tavola* from a blend of Barbera, Freisa, Uvalino, and Cabernet Sauvignon aged in *barrique*).

VISITS: Mon–Fri 8h30–12h; 14h30–18 h. Saturday and Sunday by appointment.
The Ratti family have been instrumental in pioneering modern viticultural techniques in Alba, eschewing traditional practices of lengthy maceration and ageing in *botte* in favour of shorter maceration in stainless steel, thus resulting in elegant and refined wines that can be bottled and enjoyed considerably earlier. The late Renato Ratti was a historian of the region, and visitors to the

Abbazia dell'Annunziata may also visit the important *Museo Ratti dei Vini di Alba*, itself actually located in the ancient abbey. French spoken.

---

2 AZIENDA AGRICOLA MONFALLETTO S.S.
CORDERO DI MONTEZEMOLO
CASCINA MONFALLETTO
FRAZ. ANNUNZIATA 67
12064 LA MORRA CN
TEL: 0173/50344

WINES PRODUCED: Barolo; Dolcetto d'Alba.
VISITS: Mon–Fri 8h30–12h; 14h30–18h. It is advisable to telephone or write prior to the visit. The Cordero di Montezemolo family have owned and farmed the lands of Monfalletto since 1340, and today strive to combine ancient and traditional skills with modern technology, producing highly respected estate-bottled wines. A little English spoken.

---

3 CANTINE MARCHESI DI BAROLO SPA
VIA ALBA 12
12060 BAROLO CN
TEL: 0173/56101

WINES PRODUCED: Barolo, Barolo *crus*; Barbaresco; Barbera d'Alba; Dolcetto d'Alba; Nebbiolo d'Alba; Gavi; Freisa d'Asti; Moscato d'Asti Zagara; Verbesco; *grappa di Barolo*.
VISITS: Mon–Fri 8–12h; 14–18h. Sat and Sun mornings only by appointment.
The estate of the Marchesi di Barolo has been credited with the creation and commercialization in the 19th century of the wine that came to be known as Barolo. Today, this historic *cantina* is best-known for its range of Barolo *crus* from selected vineyards, including Cannubi, Valletta, Cannubi-Muscatel, Sarmassa, Brunate, and Coste di Rose. Though the concept of *cru* wines in Barolo is a relatively recent one, the tradition of selection by vineyard on this estate has a lengthy pedigree: for example, two bottles still exist of a wine labelled Cannubi 1752.

English, French spoken.

---

4 AZIENDA VITIVINICOLA CONTERNO GIACOMO
LOC. ORNATI 2
12064 MONFORTE D'ALBA CN
TEL: 0173/78221

WINES PRODUCED: Barolo, Barolo Riserva Monfortino; Dolcetto d'Alba; Barbera d'Alba; Freisa.
VISITS: by appointment.

Giovanni Conterno represents the traditionalist school in Barolo, and is renowned for the production of outstanding immense and long-lived wines that require lengthy ageing in oak *botte* prior to release. Such wines as Conterno's Barolo Riserva and the even more remarkable Monfortino may need considerable time for the tannins to mellow and come around, but great wines are always for people with patience. In the meantime, enjoy his only somewhat lighter Dolcetto, Barbera, and Freisa.
A little English spoken.

---

5 TENIMENTI DI BAROLO E
FONTANAFREDDA
CANTINE FONTANAFREDDA
VIA ALBA 15
12050 SERRALUNGA D'ALBA CN
TEL: 0173/53161

WINES PRODUCED: Barolo, Barolo *crus*; Barbaresco; Barbera d'Alba; Dolcetto d'Alba; Freisa delle Langhe *frizzante*; Nebbiolo Langhe; Gavi; Chardonnay delle Langhe; Moscato d'Asti; Asti Spumante; Contessa Rosa (*metodo champenois*); *grappa*.
VISITS: programmed visits by appointment, April–Nov Sat and Sun only at 9h30; 11h; 15h30; 17h. One of the most historic estates in the Barolo zone, founded over 100 years ago by King Vittorio Emanuele II's son Conte Emanuele and Contessa Rosa di Mirafiori e di Fontanafredda. Today, Fontanafredda is owned by the large financial group Monte dei Paschi di Siena, and continues to produce a large range of highly-respected wines. Most notable are the single-vineyard Barolo *crus* produced in severely limited, numbered bottles: Vigna San Pietro, Vigna Lazzarito, Vigna Gallaretto, Vigna La Villa, Vigna La Delizia, Vigna La Rosa, Vigna Bianca, Vigna Gattinera.

---

6 AZIENDA VITIVINICOLE CERETTO
S.R.L.
'LA BERNARDINA'
LOC. SAN CASSIANO 34
12051 ALBA CN
TEL: 0173/282582

WINES PRODUCED: Barolo Bricco Rocche Brunate, Barolo Bricco Rocche Bricco Rocche, Barolo Bricco Rocche Prapó; Barbaresco Bricco Asili Bricco Asili, Barbaresco Bricco Asili Fasset; Arneis Blangé; Dolcetto d'Alba Rossana; Moscato d'Asti, Asti Spumante; *grappa Nebbiolo*.
VISITS: by appointment.
Bruno Ceretto is a highly regarded producer of traditional single

vineyard wines (known in Piedmont as '*bricchi*', indicating lofty hilltop positions). Though such sites have never been classified as in, say, the Côte d'Or, none the less they are comparable great growths, and have always been in demand by *conoscenti* both throughout Italy and internationally: indeed today they fetch prices comparable with the greatest wines in the world. The Ceretto brothers in recent years continue to expand, and now oversee a vast wine empire from new premises at 'La Bernardina' south of Alba.

English, some French spoken.

---

7 FRANCO-FIORINA S.A.S
VIA LIBERAZIONE 3
12051 ALBA CN
TEL: 0173/42248; 42249

WINES PRODUCED: Barolo; Barbaresco; Dolcetto d'Alba; Nebbiolo d'Alba; Barbera d'Alba; Grignolino Monferrato Casalese.
VISITS: weekdays, 9–12h; 15–18h. Telephone or write prior to visit. Family *négociant* established in 1925 which continues founder Andrea Franco's policy of purchasing grapes by long-standing contract. 'Aware that no single vineyard can produce a wine which is complete in all its characteristics, the Franco-Fiorina company has never acquired its own vineyards. It is company practice to ferment, in the same vat, grapes from identical vines but grown in vineyards on different hills.' As such, the winery acts in a similar role to the Burgundian *négociant-éleveur*, and the wines produced, if lacking the individuality of *crus* from single vineyards, are none the less of a very high overall standard.

English, French spoken.

ENOTECHE REGIONALI AND BOTTEGHE DEL VINO

1 ENOTECA REGIONALE PIEMONTESE
CAVOUR
CASTELLO DI GRINZANE
VIA CASTELLO 5
12060 GRINZANE CAVOUR CN
TEL: 0173/62159

OPEN: daily except Tue: summer 9–12h; 14h30–18h30; winter 9–12h; 14–18h. Closed Jan.

Piedmont's first *Enoteca Regionale* was realized in 1971 and is still probably the region's most important, prestigious, and welcoming. It is thus an essential for every wine lover to the region: the range of wines on display for purchase and tasting is extensive, picked each year by the *Cavalieri*

THE NORTH-WEST

del Tartufo e dei Vini dell'Alba, and the museum, located on various floors of the castle, is important and fascinating. The Ristorante Enoteca (**Moderate to Expensive**) further safeguards the traditional gastronomy of Alba, and serves authentically prepared foods of the region, alongside the wines and *grappe* of the *enoteca*.

2
ENOTECA REGIONALE DI BAROLO
CASTELLO COMMUNALE
PIAZZA FALLETTI
12060 BAROLO CN
TEL: 0172/56277

OPEN: daily except Tue 10–12h30; 15–18h30. Holidays by appointment only.
Barolo, the wine town that has given its name to Italy's greatest and most famous red wine, takes its position seriously: the ancient castle, now owned by the commune, is a fitting home for this important *Enoteca Regionale* dedicated to what many consider to be the 'King of Italian Wines'.

Numerous events are held here to promote the region's wine, gastronomy, and culture. The *enoteca* itself is located in the castle's ancient restored *cantina*, where an extensive range of Barolo and other wines is displayed. Wines are available for tasting and purchase, and special organized tastings for groups can be pre-arranged. The castle also has an ethnographic exhibition of the Barolo region, and is the headquarters for an important professional catering training centre.

3
BOTTEGA COMMUNALE
VIA FOGLIO 1
12050 SERRALUNGA D'ALBA CN
TEL: 0173/53101

OPEN: Sat and holidays only 9–12h30; 15–19h.
Selections of Barolos from the prestigious vineyards of Serralunga d'Alba.

4
CANTINA COMMUNALE DI LA
  MORRA
VIA CARLO ALBERTO 2
12064 LA MORRA CN
TEL: 0173/509204

OPEN: Wed, Thur, Fri 11–12h30; 14h30–17h30. Sat and Sun 10–12h30; 14h30–17h30.
Founded in 1973 in the 17th-century *cantina* of the

palace of the Marchesi di Barolo, this communal *bottega* offers an extensive range of wines from La Morra which can be tasted and purchased.

Ristoranti

1

RISTORANTE LA CAPANNINA
LOC. BORGO MORETTA
STRADA PROFONDA 21
12051 ALBA CN
TEL: 0173/43952

Closed Mon.
The Gallina brothers run this charming old favourite located just outside Alba, serving authentic, faithfully prepared foods of the Langhe, such as *carne cruda, risotto al Barolo, tajarin, fonduta, coniglio al Barbaresco*, accompanied by an outstanding range of local wines. They are enthusiasts and fine ambassadors not only for the gastronomy of the region but for its culture and history.
Inexpensive to Moderate

2

OSTERIA DELL'ARCO
COOPERATIVA 'I TAROCCHI'
VICOLO DELL'ARCO
12051 ALBA CN
TEL: 0173/363974

Closed Sun.
Authentic *osteria* in the historic centre of Alba near the Duomo serving traditional foods and a good selection of wines.
Inexpensive to Moderate

3

RISTORANTE BELVEDERE
PIAZZA CASTELLO 5
12064 LA MORRA CN
TEL: 0173/50190

Closed Sun eve; Mon.
Classic foods of the Piedmont – *antipasti, carne cruda, agnolotti, tajarin, finanziera, brasato al Barolo* – together with a vast choice of local and national wines, in this popular wine growers' favourite. The name is apt, for the restaurant affords splendid views of the majestic surrounding wine country. English, French spoken.
Moderate to Expensive

THE NORTH-WEST

4 ALBERGO RISTORANTE DEL BUON
PADRE
FRAZ. VERGNE 50
12060 BAROLO CN
TEL: 0173/56192; 56329

Closed Wed. Reservations
advisable.

Rustic hotel-restaurant in the
Barolo countryside serving
homemade *salami, bagna cauda,
capretto, brasato al Barolo*, and
local wines.
English, French spoken.
Moderate

---

5 ALBERGO RISTORANTE GIARDINO DA
FELICIN
VIA VALLADA 18
12065 MONFORTE D'ALBA CN
TEL: 0173/78225

Closed Wed.
Fine, highly regarded
hotel-restaurant in the heart of the

wine country serving the classic
foods of the region revised for
modern tastes. All rooms have
private facilities.
English, French, German spoken.
Moderate to Expensive

---

6 ALBERGO RISTORANTE ITALIA
12050 SERRALUNGA D'ALBA CN
TEL: 0173/53124

Very basic but friendly family
hotel-restaurant with commanding
position overlooking the Barolo

hills: simple but delicious home
cooking includes *tajarin, fonduta,
bagna cauda, bollito*, served with
robust house Nebbiolo d'Alba. 8
rooms without bath.
Inexpensive

Barbaresco: *La Strada del Vino*

In Brief: The Barbaresco vineyard extends to the north-east of Alba over
low-lying hills on the south side of the Tanaro valley. It is a small,
compact wine region, but an important one, and it can easily be covered
in a half or full day excursion. Our route leads to two *Enoteche Regionali*,
the first in Barbaresco itself, the second in nearby Mango, where the
Nebbiolo vineyards have given way primarily to Moscato for the production of Moscato d'Asti and Asti Spumante.

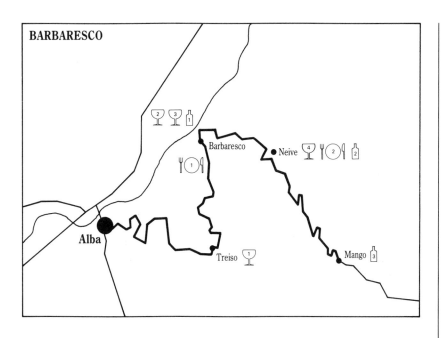

Outside its zone of production, Barbaresco is most often talked about – and drunk – as an afterthought to Barolo. Both wines are produced from the temperamental Nebbiolo, on vineyards that are almost contiguous, though the lower hills and lighter soil of Barbaresco usually results in wines that are slightly less austere, if generally more perfumed and elegant. But make no mistake, Barbaresco is no lightweight feminine cousin to manly Barolo: it is a serious, aristocratic red wine that ranks among the very best wines in Italy, awarded, like Barolo, the exclusive DOCG *denominazione*. However, perhaps because the vineyard region is so much smaller – less than half the size of Barolo, in fact – Barbaresco remains considerably less well-known, abroad at least, than its illustrious neighbour. Quite simply, there is far less of it to go round. Thus, for the serious wine tourist, a tour through the Barbaresco vineyard provides a rare opportunity to encounter, taste, and purchase this prestigious and aristocratic wine at source.

From Alba, leave the town on the road that climbs out in the direction of Treiso-Barbaresco, pausing to look back at the superb view of the red roofs and towers of Alba. At Altavilla, the road descends back down to the Pertinace valley and continues along the valley floor. Turn right at the signpost to visit Treiso, one of the zone's 3 principal communes, noted above all for wines of extreme finesse and elegance. Circle back then to the

Barbaresco road, and pass through the tiny wine hamlet of Tre Stelle where there is a good, unpretentious country inn.

The wine road leads to Barbaresco itself, passing along the way some of the zone's most prestigious single *vigneti*: Pora, Asili, Moccagatta, and Rabajà. Barbaresco is a small, industrious wine town, and the home of world-famous and small growers alike, as well as the important and high-quality co-operative Cantina Produttori del Barbaresco. Barbaresco also boasts a notable shrine for wine lovers, for the ex-San Donato church, located in the main *piazza*, has been given over to the *Enoteca Regionale di Barbaresco*. Within the deconsecrated 18th-century walls of this temple to wine, there are displays illustrating the various phases of wine growing in the region, as well as a selection of wines from the majority of growers and producers. Each week, on a rota basis, the *enoteca* selects 10 different wines for tasting by the glass.

Barbaresco's most famous producer – indeed one of the most famous wine producers in Italy – is Angelo Gaja, whose wines, particularly his single *vigneti* Barbarescos aged in new oak *barriques* such as Costa Russi, Sorì Tildin, and Sorì San Lorenzo rank (if price is a valid indication of stature and quality) alongside the very greatest in the world: Italy's answer to Château Petrus or La Romanée. These clearly are not wines to pick up at the source for a vineyard picnic! But it should be pointed out that almost all the great producers in the Barbaresco and Barolo zones, Gaja and Ceretto not-withstanding, offer in addition to their prestigious – and fabulously expensive – flagship names, an extensive range of more accessible wines that are more immediately enjoyable, produced from local grapes such as Dolcetto and Barbera. Indeed, Dolcetto d'Alba and Barbera d'Alba are both wines capable of excellence in their own right, much enjoyed locally on those occasions when Barbaresco or Barolo would be considered too grand, too momentous, or simply too heavy.

From Barbaresco, the wine tour passes next through the vineyards to Neive, the zone's third principal wine commune, whose wines are noted above all for their exceptional structure and body. From Neive, find the winding road that leads over to Mango, passing by the imposing hilltop Bricco di Neive. These vineyards follow a transition from those planted almost exclusively with the prestigious Nebbiolo to those planted with Dolcetto, Barbera, and, especially around Mango, fragrant Moscato.

Mango is a fine hill town topped by an imposing 15th-century castle that today is the home of the *Enoteca Regionale di Mango*, which specializes in the sweet dessert wines of Piedmont, principally Moscato d'Asti and Asti

Spumante. The well-restored castle not only has an extensive display of such dessert wines available for tasting and purchase, there are also collections of tools, domestic equipment, and agricultural implements, as well as, in keeping with the sweet theme, an exhibition on the production of local confectionery and a professional confectionery school. Such sweets and sweet wines provide a fitting finale to Piedmont meals, and to our tour.

Degustazione: Stop to Taste; Stop to Buy

1

AZIENDA AGRICOLA VITIVINICOLA
  PELISSERO
VIA FERRERE 19
12050 TREISO CN
TEL: 0173/638136

WINES PRODUCED: Dolcetto d'Alba Vigneto Augenta; Dolcetto d'Alba Vigneto Munfri'na; Barbera d'Alba Vigna Ronchi; Barbaresco Vanotu; Freisa delle Langhe; Favorita; Grignolino.

VISITS: daily, telephone call in advance preferred.

Family production of an impressive range of wines of differing styles: Favorita, Freisa, and Grignolino are vinified to maximize fruit, perfume, and freshness while the *cru* Dolcettos, Barbera, and Barbaresco are vinified traditionally with lengthy maceration for maximum extract and structure.

A little English and French spoken.

2

AZIENDA AGRICOLA ANGELO GAJA
VIA TORINO 36/A
12050 BARBARESCO CN
TEL: 0173/635158

WINES PRODUCED: Barbaresco, Barbaresco Costa Russi, Barbaresco Sorì Tildin, Barbaresco Sorì San Lorenzo; Barbera d'Alba Vignarey; Dolcetto d'Alba; Nebbiolo d'Alba; Chardonnay Gaia & Rey, Chardonnay RossJ Bass; Darmagi Cabernet Sauvignon.

VISITS: weekdays and Saturday morning by appointment only.

Angelo Gaja is best known for his superlative estate Barbarescos, which can compare in quality as well as in price with the greatest wines from the Côte d'Or or Médoc. The wines have achieved a sort of cult status and are consequently always in the greatest demand; they are earmarked for customers almost before they are even produced, and thus cannot be purchased direct at the *azienda*.

English, French spoken.

THE NORTH-WEST

3 COOP. PRODUTTORI DEL BARBARESCO
S.R.L.
VIA TORINO 52
12050 BARBARESCO CN
TEL: 0173/635139

WINES PRODUCED: Barbaresco,
Barbaresco Riserva; Langhe
Nebbiolo *vino da tavola*.
VISITS: by appointment. Visits with
tasting take at least 1 hour. Open
working hours for direct sales.
The co-operative cellar of
Barbaresco was founded in 1958,
and there are 66 members from the
area, whose holdings together
comprise 110 hectares. The winery
employs traditional vinification
methods utilizing modern
equipment: initial fermentation in
stainless steel vats, followed by
ageing in oak *botte* and *barrique* for
a minimum of 2 years and in some
cases upwards of 6–8. In the best
years, grapes from individual sites
and localities (Pora, Montefico,
Montestefano, Rio Sordo, Rabajà,
Asili, Moccagatta, Ovello, and
others) may be vinified separately;
such special *cru* wines will receive
particular attention, and when
bottled will bear the name of the
locality, as well as that of the
growers.

---

4 CASA VINICOLA GIACOSA BRUNO
VIA XX SETTEMBRE 52
12057 NEIVE CN
TEL: 0173/67027

WINES PRODUCED: Barbaresco,
Barbaresco *cru* Santo Stefano;
Barolo, Barolo *crus*; Nebbiolo;
Dolcetto d'Alba; Barbera d'Alba;
Grignolino d'Asti; Arneis; Spumante
metodo champenois.
VISITS: Mon–Sat, by appointment.
One of the great wine makers of
Piedmont, producing an extremely
select, virtually handmade range of
wines of the highest quality.
English spoken.

ENOTECHE REGIONALI AND BOTTEGHE DEL VINO

1 ENOTECA REGIONALE DEL
BARBARESCO
VIA TORINO 8/A
12050 BARBARESCO CN
TEL: 0173/635251

OPEN: Wed, Thur, Fri 15–19h;
Sat, Sun 10–12h; 15–19h.
18th-century shrine for wine
lovers in the deconsecrated San
Donato church in the main
square. Most zones are
represented, and each week a
range of wines is available for
tasting by the glass.
A little English spoken.

2 BOTTEGA DEI QUATTRO VINI
PIAZZA ITALIA
12057 NEIVE CN
TEL: 0173/67110

OPEN: weekends and holidays
only, or by appointment.
Communal *bottega* with a selection of wines from about 25
local growers in this commune
that is the intersection for 4
DOCs: Barbaresco, Barbera
d'Alba, Dolcetto d'Alba, and
Moscato d'Asti.

---

3 ENOTECA REGIONALE DI MANGO
CASTELLO DI BUSCA
PIAZZA XX SETTEMBRE
12056 MANGO CN
TEL: 0141/89127

OPEN: Sat, Sun and holidays only
9–12h; 15–19h.
The restored Castello di Busca is
more a *palazzo* than a castle, once
home of the noble Marchesi di
Busca in the 17th and 18th
centuries. Today, it
specializes above all in the sweet white wines of Piedmont which
are so loved throughout the world:
Moscato d'Asti and Asti
Spumante. These are wines to
drink on their own, or with
preserved bottled fruit, pastries,
and confectionery, the production
of which is also highlighted in the
enoteca. The restaurant of the
enoteca serves classic *cucina
langarola*.
Moderate

Ristoranti

1 ALBERGO RISTORANTE 'VECCHIO TRE
STELLE'
VIA RIO SORDO 13
FRAZ. TRE STELLE
12050 BARBARESCO CN
TEL: 0173/638192

Closed Tue.

This small hotel has a good
restaurant serving local foods and
wines. Isolated, with splendid
panoramic views of the Barbaresco
wine country.
English, French, German spoken.
Inexpensive

---

2 LA CONTEA
PIAZZA COCITO 8
12057 NEIVE CN
TEL: 0173/67126

Closed Sun eve, Mon.

Classic foods of the Piedmont and
an exceptional selection of the
region's best wines.
Moderate to Expensive

THE NORTH-WEST

The Roero

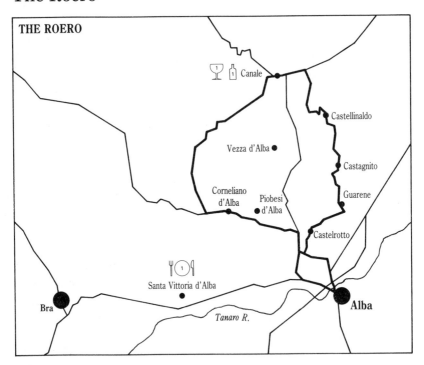

THE ROERO

Canale

Castellinaldo

Vezza d'Alba ●

Castagnito

Corneliano
d'Alba

Piobesi
● d'Alba

Guarene

Castelrotto

Santa Vittoria d'Alba
●

Bra

Alba

Tanaro R.

In Brief: The Roero lies to the north of Alba and the Tanaro river. Primarily a zone for the production of Roero, Arneis, Favorita, and Nebbiolo d'Alba, it is not as well known as either the Barolo or Barbaresco vineyards. It deserves exploration, none the less, not only as an increasingly important source of good reds and outstanding dry white wines, but also for its natural beauty, fine villages rich in art and archaeology, and outstanding castles and *palazzi*. This brief tour begins from Alba and can be completed in half a day, or else en route to Turin.

In such a long-standing wine region as Piedmont, it is perhaps surprising to find that exciting new wines are still coming to the fore. The Roero is an ancient traditional wine growing region, but it has always been over-shadowed by the prestigious vineyards that lie on the hills to the south of the Tanaro river. However, the region has gained in stature especially over the last decade, and is now a wine zone of considerable importance in its own right, the source not only of sound red country wines, but most importantly of outstanding dry white wines, mainly from the local Arneis grape as well as from the rare and little encountered Favorita.

Indeed, the Arneis grape grown in Roero has recently been rewarded with elevation to *denominazione di origine controllata* status, along with Roero, the new DOC for light, vivacious red wine made from Nebbiolo together with smaller amounts of Arneis. In the past the two varieties were planted in the zone somewhat indiscriminately, perhaps 3 rows of Nebbiolo, then a row of Arneis, and so on. The grapes were all harvested and pressed together to result in a delicious and locally enjoyed red wine. When Arneis was vinified alone, it was more often than not made into a sweet wine.

However, through improvements and developments in modern white wine making, it was discovered that Arneis is indeed capable of producing exceptional dry white wine, rich in perfume and extract, well-balanced, with fresh intense bouquet and a crisp lively flavour. Thus, the last 10 years or so have seen a considerable renaissance for this age-old local variety, with new plantations of up to 200 hectares. It is my guess that in years to come Arneis, now little-known, will soon be appreciated as one of the great dry white wines of Italy. The Favorita, another little-known local grape variety, is similarly enjoying a revival, and is also producing white wines that can be exciting and vivid.

For a brief tour through the vineyards of the Roero, leave Alba on the N29 Corso Torino, crossing the Tanaro river. This road leads directly to Canale, but the vineyards lie mainly over hillside slopes to the right and left of the valley corridor. To make a circular tour, therefore, find the road left to Piobesi d'Alba and Corneliano, which has an interesting 12-sided tower. From Corneliano, look for the road right to Canale. This leads over the valley floor, and the *aziende* here practise traditional mixed farming, some viticulture, but also wheat, grain, and fruit orchards. The peaches from Roero are particularly succulent. As the road begins to climb, the vines soon become more dominant. Off to the right is Vezza d'Alba, an important viticultural community where much new planting has taken place recently.

Canale, surrounded by an impressive amphitheatre of vines, is an important agricultural and economic centre for the surrounding country and a fine, pleasant old town. Its late medieval Church of San Vittore has a particularly beautiful bas-relief embellishing the main façade. Canale has a *Bottega del Vino* which is a good source for the little encountered wines of the Roero: Roero, Arneis, Favorita, as well as Nebbiolo d'Alba and Barbera d'Alba.

THE NORTH-WEST

Leave Canale on the main road to Asti, then turn right along a winding road to the steep hill town of Castellinaldo, an important wine centre set amidst some of the zone's finest vineyards. The Azienda Agricola Blangé Ceretto was established here in recent years, a super-modern, computer controlled winery for the production of the outstanding and highly regarded Arneis Blangé. The Ceretto brothers, long known for their exceptional estate Barolos and Barbarescos from select hill-top vineyards, have expanded in recent years and now produce an unrivalled range of quality Piedmont wines from the family-owned estates of Bricco Rocche at Castiglione Falletto, Bricco Asili at Barbaresco, Blangé, and Bernardina outside Alba. The family also has a distillery for the production of estate bottled *grappe*, and is in partnership with I Vignaioli di Santo Stefano for the production of Moscato d'Asti and Asti Spumante.

From Castellinaldo, return to Alba via the hill towns of Castagnito, Guarene, and Castelrotto. The views over the valleys from Guarene, to the right the Roero, to the left the hills of Barbaresco, are outstanding.

One final detour for the interested wine tourist should be made: just off the main road from Alba to Bra lies the little village of Santa Vittoria d'Alba. This is the home of the great vermouth and sparkling wine firm of Cinzano, and today the village of Cinzano d'Alba, inhabited mainly by employees of this enormous and worldwide firm, sprawls into the older hill town where King Carlo Alberto once had a country villa. Santa Vittoria is equally famous for its 'secret', the subject of a feature film based on the true events that occurred during World War II, when the locals outwitted the occupying Germans' attempt to steal their wine by walling up Cinzano's ancient cellars.

Degustazione: Stop to Taste; Stop to Buy

1 AZIENDA AGRICOLA DELTETTO
CARLO
CORSO ALBA 43
12043 CANALE D'ALBA CN
TEL: 0173/9383; 95125

WINES PRODUCED: Roero; Arneis; Favorita; Ruchè; Barbera d'Alba; Dolcetto d'Alba; Gavi; Grignolino d'Asti.

VISITS: weekdays, by appointment. Carlo Deltetto is a highly-regarded producer of premium wines, and offers a full range of the little-encountered and sometimes elusive wines of Roero for tasting and purchase.
English, French spoken.

BOTTEGA DEL VINO

1

BOTTEGA DEL VINO DEL ROERO
CORSO TORINO 11
12043 CANALE D'ALBA CN
TEL: 0173/95057

OPEN: Sat 15–19h, Sun 9–12h;
15–19h. Other times by
appointment.
Good source for a selection of
these undervalued wines: Arneis,
Favorita, Roero, Nebbiolo d'Alba.

Ristorante

1

HOTEL SOGGIORNO
  S. VITTORIA/RISTORANTE AL
  CASTELLO
CASTELLO DI S. VITTORIA
12060 S. VITTORIA D'ALBA CN
TEL: 0172/478198 (HOTEL);
  0172/478147 (RESTAURANT)

Restaurant closed Wed; hotel closed
January.

The restaurant of this traditional
hotel located in the town with the
'secret' serves good *piemontesi*
specialities, including *carne cruda*,
bagna cauda, and in season *funghi*
and *tartufi*. Hotel has 45 rooms.
Moderate

ASTI AND THE MONFERRATO

The province of Asti comprises the hilly district known as the Monferrato, an area of rippling vine-covered hills south of the province of Turin, west of Alessandria, east of the Langhe, and north of the Ligurian coast.

Best-known to the world as the source of one of the gayest and most easily loved wines, Asti Spumante, it in fact produces an extensive and impressive range, more extensive and varied even than its prestigious vineyard neighbour Alba to the west. Barbera is the most widely planted grape in the Piedmont, taking up fully half of the total area under plantation, so, not surprisingly, this prolific and tough variety provides the everyday beverage wines of the region. Barbera d'Asti and Barbera di Monferrato are strong, bright, full-bodied reds that are usually enjoyed while still young and vivid, though the former at least does have the capacity to age.

Dolcetto is also grown extensively in the Asti province; like the Dolcettos from Alba and elsewhere, it is another typical variety that produces deep, gutsy red wine which in spite of its name is not at all sweet but even slightly

THE NORTH-WEST

bitter. Grignolino is an ancient Piedmont grape variety that is much loved locally, though production in recent years has dwindled considerably. Light in colour, dry, with a slightly bitter, even austere finish, it is a very enjoyable wine for those occasions that do not call for the heavier, darker wines of the Piedmont. Grignolino is cultivated in the vineyards of both Asti and Alba, but especially around the wine town of Casale Monferrato. Freisa is another delightful local wine, little encountered outside its region of production. Widely cultivated at the turn of the century, it is now grown mainly in the northern part of the Asti province, especially near the town of Chieri. Made in both dry or *amabile* versions, Freisa usually has a semi-sparkling *frizzante* quality that makes this delicious, foaming raspberry-scented wine so particularly vivid and delightful.

It is interesting to note that it was only within the last 100 years that even such austere and heavyweight wines as Barolo were first produced in dry versions. Prior to this, such wines almost always retained a residual sweetness. At that time, a young French noblewoman married into the family of the Marchesi Falleti, who owned the Castello di Barolo, and, wishing to drink wines in the Bordeaux style that she was accustomed to, brought over a French oenologist to produce the first dry Barolo.

However, the local predilection for such sweet or semi-sweet red wines, often *frizzante* or even fully sparkling, remains. Brachetto d'Acqui is another such soft wine with a delicate, quickly fading bouquet, usually semi-sweet to sweet, and made in still, *frizzante*, or fully sparkling versions: it is an unusual speciality that should be tried when in the region, especially around the spa town of Acqui Terme. The Malvasia Nera, an ancient grape first brought to Italy by the Greeks, also produces fragrant, sweet, often foaming red wines, especially around the areas of Casorzo and Castelnuovo Don Bosco. Such wines may seem at odds with our modern tastes, but they can be delicious, either drunk on their own, or with desserts or fruit.

Asti is the provincial capital, at once a busy industrial town, an important agricultural centre, and an ancient municipality rich in history, art, culture, and folklore. Hasta Pompeia, as Asti was known to the Romans, was one of the most important colonies of ancient Liguria. From that time on, it grew steadily in importance, strategically located as it was on the main north–south axis from Rome to northern Europe, as well as on the east–west route leading from France to Lombardy, Emilia, and the Veneto. By the 13th century, it was one of the richest and most powerful communes in Italy, with strong commercial ties with France, England and the Low Countries. Today, Asti still preserves many of the 120 towers that existed at that time, as well as other notable medieval buildings, Renaissance and baroque palaces and churches.

Asti's illustrious past is recalled each September with the colourful and historic Palio, an event which goes back at least as far as 1275. For this annual horserace, the youth and men of the city dress in period costumes bearing the colours of the various *borghi* (districts) of Asti; there is a colourful procession of horsemen, pages, ladies and girls, and standard-bearers, then the horsemen race across the Campo del Palio, Asti's principal square. The victors are awarded the Palio itself, a crimson cloth in honour of San Secondo, the city's patron saint, which, the next May, is re-offered to the Collegiate Church of San Secondo to mark the start of that year's celebrations.

If the Palio looks back on the illustrious history of Asti, another autumn festival celebrates the present: the Douja d'Or is a wine festival of national importance which takes place each September for 15 days, during which there are serious wine tastings, competitions, and awards, as well as much singing, dancing, drinking, and eating. The following month, the province's other most famous product, the prized *tartufo bianco* – white truffle – is honoured with the *Mostra Mercato del Tartufo* which lasts for over a month, a period of local and village festivities, truffle auctions, and gastronomic events at restaurants throughout the region.

The Asti province is such a prolific wine region that virtually all roads lead quite pleasurably into the vineyards. We suggest two tours below, but in truth the wine tourist to Asti can scarcely make a wrong turn.

Asti to Acqui Terme

In Brief: This wine tour provides an excursion over the southern Monferrato hills, leaving from Asti and ending up in the spa town of Acqui Terme. Along the way there are visits to the *Enoteca Regionale* at Costigliole d'Asti, the town of Nizza Monferrato where the wine firm of Bersano has an important wine museum, Canelli, centre for the production of Moscato sparkling wines, ending at the stylish spa town of Acqui Terme where there is another *Enoteca Regionale*. This tour, with a stop for lunch along the way, will take a full day.

From Asti, leave the town over the Tanaro river in the direction of Alba (N456) then, at Isola d'Asti, climb up into the hills to the important wine

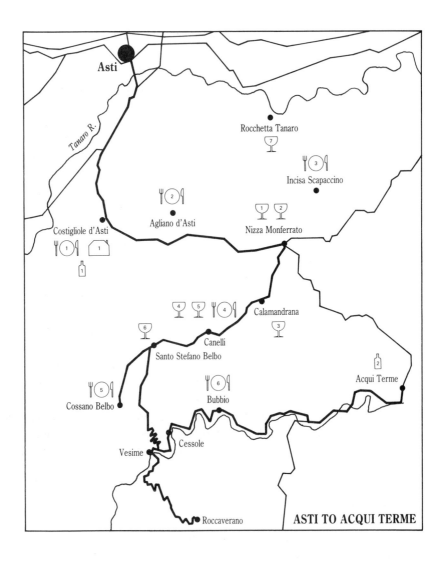

ASTI TO ACQUI TERME

town of Costigliole d'Asti. Costigliole is dominated by its Castello di Costigliole, an imposing 18th-century residence made famous by the Contessa di Costigliole. Today the castle is in the process of being restored and is one of Piedmont's *Enoteche Regionali*. There is a display of wines selected each year at the Douja d'Or, a permanent exhibition of humorous graphics on the theme of wine, and a fine restaurant serving foods of Asti and Monferrato. However, to visit the *Enoteca* itself, it is at present necessary to make arrangements through the restaurant.

From Costigliole, find the road that leads to Nizza Monferrato. This is undoubtedly single-minded country. It is almost everywhere intensively cultivated with the vine, primarily Barbera, Piedmont's most common and one of the few that have transplanted successfully to many other Italian wine regions. Though prolific, able to be cultivated where other more temperamental vines fail, the wines produced are in no way common. True, vast amounts of jug Barbera continue to be made and consumed in prodigious quantities as an everyday beverage of the region. But Barbera shows its versatility by the fact that it can result in such different styles of wine: youthful, dark purple, foaming in the glass with the *frizzante* character that comes from a pleasing malo-lactic secondary fermentation; rich in colour and alcohol but with a rather rasping and bitter finish, due to a natural high acidity that makes it go so well with the rich foods of the region; or altogether more profound, deeper, as in the single *bricco* wines from Giacomo Bologna, wines which, finished in new oak *barriques*, prove that Barbera, like its aristocratic cousin Nebbiolo, does indeed have the capacity and breed to improve with age.

Nizza Monferrato is a fine old market town, and an important agricultural and commercial centre for the surrounding countryside, with a large ample town square and impressive town hall. It is especially famous not only for its wines, but also for its truffles, and for a vegetable, the *cardo*, an edible thistle much enjoyed in autumn. Nizza is the home of important wine growers and is a pleasant base from which to explore the region further. The highly-respected Bersano firm, owned by Seagrams, has its headquarters near the railway station, and has a fine wine and country-life museum that is well worth visiting.

From Nizza, follow the Belbo valley through Calamandrana to Canelli. Calamandrana, today a small but prestigious wine commune, was once an important and strategic village, as its ruined castle and numerous towers attest. Canelli is the capital of Asti Spumante, one of the most famous wines of Piedmont if not all of Italy. Like Valpolicella, Soave, or Lambrusco, Asti Spumante is one of that Italian breed with seemingly universal appeal that has gone out to conquer the world and successfully introduced millions to the pleasures of drinking wine.

Its very popularity – some 80 million bottles are produced and drunk annually – has perhaps caused Asti to suffer the scorn of pseudo-sophisticates and -connoisseurs who turn their noses up at such straightforward pleasure. But make no mistake, Asti Spumante is no lightweight soda-pop (the same cannot be said for much export Lambrusco, especially

THE NORTH-WEST

that which finds its way across the Atlantic). Fizzy, slightly or considerably sweet, and with the delicious fresh fragrance of the Moscato Bianco, Asti Spumante is a truly delightful wine, easy to drink, certainly, easy to enjoy, but where is the harm in that?

Admittedly, if you compare Asti Spumante to Champagne, the wines are totally dissimilar, sharing only the fact that both are sparkling. This denominator, perhaps, has caused Asti unfairly to be viewed as a cheap alternative to the French prototype. But Asti is an altogether different wine. For a start, it gains its sparkle not through the Champagne method of secondary fermentation in the bottle, but by the Charmat transfer method, whereby the clarified grape must undergoes fermentation in sealed pressurized autoclaves. As the specially selected yeasts feed on the natural grape sugars, carbon dioxide is given off as a natural by-product, and, since the vats are sealed, this remains dissolved in the wine, giving its sparkle. The ripe Moscato Bianco grapes, moreover, are extremely rich in sugar, and some of this remains unfermented, providing the natural residual sweetness that is the hallmark of Asti. Afterwards, the wine undergoes sterile filtering (to ensure that the remaining sugar does not begin to 'work' again), and is then transferred under pressure to the bottle.

The transfer method of production of sparkling wines is considerably less expensive to undertake than the costly *metodo champenois*, the process of secondary fermentation in the bottle. However, it is by no means utilized simply as a means of cutting costs, for the transfer method also requires considerable oenological expertise and the most modern technology. By utilizing a lengthy, slow secondary fermentation at low temperatures, the essential fragrance and fresh grapey bouquet of the Moscato is better preserved, even intensified, and the finished wine can be released while still young, fresh, and at its most vivid. Asti Spumante is a wine to drink as an *aperitivo*, with desserts or fruit, or simply whenever you have an excuse for a celebration. It is, quite unashamedly, one of our favourite wines: would that other more prestigious and expensive wines could give such generous pleasure so unstintingly and consistently.

While Asti Spumante is not, nor is it trying to be, a wine in the style of Champagne, it should be pointed out that there are many Italian alternatives to the real French thing, produced in Piedmont, as well as Lombardy, Trento, the Veneto and elsewhere, from a similar *uvaggio* as Champagne (usually Pinot Nero and Chardonnay, with the addition of some Pinot Bianco and Pinot Grigio). Such wines produced by the laborious *metodo champenois* can be excellent, truly fine wines that rightly stand alongside the best sparkling wines in the world. Certainly the best command prices that equal even Champagne: many are produced by the same world-famous Piedmont firms that specialize in Asti, including Gancia, Martini, Cinzano, Fontana-fredda, and others.

Canelli's beautiful castle which dominates the town, incidentally, was purchased and restored by the Gancia family in 1929. But as long ago as 1616, this castle was a storehouse for fine wines, praised by the Marchese di Mortara, who, on taking up command of Spanish forces there, found in its cellars some 'very delicate and lovable Moscatos'.

The wine zone for Asti Spumante and Moscato d'Asti is a vast one, extending over some 52 communes across 3 provinces, Alessandria and Cuneo in addition to Asti. However, it is generally recognized that some of the finest Moscato grapes are grown in the Belbo valley, on the calcium-rich limestone hills that extend from Canelli to San Stefano Belbo and Cossano Belbo. The wine tour thus continues down the valley. San Stefano was the birthplace of Cesare Pavese, and today there is an *enoteca* and museum in the house where the writer was born.

Either continue on to Cossano (and so link up with the vineyards of the Langhe, for here we have entered the province of Cuneo), or else, just out of San Stefano, find the road left that strikes into the majestic hills and leads across the Bormida valley at Vésime. This is a stunning wine road through the steep hill vineyards, with dramatic views back over the surrounding countryside. It is from these steep chalk hills where Moscato grapes are grown up to an altitude of 550 metres above sea level, that the finest wines come, those with the freshest, most intense, and persistent bouquet combined with long, lingering, delicate flavours. Asti Spumante produced from grapes grown on the richer, flatter plains, on the other hand, is generally more richly flavoured, perhaps somewhat coarser. But (and here it does share a common trait with Champagne), most Asti Spumante is not produced from grapes grown in single vineyards, but rather is a blend of wines from various zones to achieve a consistent and harmonious balance, as well as a consistent house style. The finest selected Moscato grapes, on the other hand, may be utilized by artisan-producers for the production of still Moscato d'Asti, a generally low in alcohol, medium-dry to dry table wine of outstanding scent and freshness.

The vineyards finally peter out by the top of the hill, then the road winds up and over to the quiet, little-visited Bormida valley. Upon reaching the main road, either climb up into the hills again to Roccaverano, an ancient hill village and centre for the production of a notable cheese, Robiola (known also as Formaggetta di Roccaverano). Or else follow the road left to Acqui Terme, passing through quiet wine hamlets like Cessole (noted also for its fine herbs, utilized in a popular local *digestivo*) and Bubbio. Bubbio's vineyards produce no less than 6 DOC wines, but the small town is most famous for its annual *Polentone*, a *polenta* festival that takes place each year the Sunday after Easter.

Acqui Terme, whose hot sulphurous mineral springs have been renowned since Roman days at least, is the capital of the Alto Monferrato. The ruined Roman aqueduct that still spans the Bormida valley is most impressive, and there is a considerable collection of ancient artefacts in the civic archaeological museum. The cathedral and Castello dei Paleologhi date originally from the 11th century, though both were rebuilt and restored, notably in the 16th and 18th centuries when the town enjoyed something of a heyday. Today, Acqui remains a stylish and popular spa town, as well as an important commercial and political centre.

The *Enoteca Regionale di Acqui Terme*, located in the vaulted cellars of the 11th-century Palazzo Robellini, is dedicated to the wines of the Alto Monferrato, notably Barbera d'Asti, Barbera del Monferrato, Moscato d'Asti, Asti Spumante, Cortese dell'Alto Monferrato, and above all Dolcetto d'Acqui and Brachetto d'Acqui. The latter is a rare ancient wine, praised by the Roman Pliny the Elder, today produced in small quantity only. Delicate, sweet, usually slightly or fully sparkling, it should definitely be tried when in the region.

Degustazione: Stop to Taste; Stop to Buy

1

BERSANO
ANTICO PODERE CONTI DELLA
 CREMOSINA SPA
PIAZZA DANTE 21
14049 NIZZA MONFERRATO AT
TEL: 0141/721273

WINES PRODUCED: Asti Spumante; Gavi; Grignolino d'Asti; Barbaresco; Barolo; Nebbiolo d'Alba; Barbera d'Alba.
VISITS: daily by appointment.
Museums open weekdays 9–11h.

Bersano is one of the larger producers in the Asti region, with 8 estates which together supply the company with 85% of its grapes for the production of a full range of Piedmont wines, including Asti Spumante, and Pinot Spumante (from Oltrepò Pavese). The *Museo delle Contadinerie* and the *Museo delle Stampe sul Vino* are both well worth visiting.
English spoken.

2 CASA VINICOLA GUASTI CLEMENTE E FIGLI SPA
CORSO IV NOVEMBRE 80
14049 NIZZA MONFERRATO AT
TEL: 0141/721350

WINES PRODUCED: Barbera d'Asti; Grignolino d'Asti; Moscato d'Asti; Asti Spumante; Gavi; Brachetto d'Acqui; Barolo; Barbaresco; Dolcetto d'Alba.
VISITS: daily, telephone before coming.
The Guasti family have been making wine in this region since 1800, but the present family firm was founded in 1946. The speciality is Barbera, and a full range is produced which demonstrates this grape's versatility: Il Mio Vino Barbera Frizzante; Barbera del Monferrato; Barbera d'Asti, Barbera d'Asti Superiore; and Barberas from 3 individual and superior estates: Cascine Fonda, Boschetto, and Baldi.
A little English and French spoken.

---

3 CANTINE DUCA D'ASTI
STRADA NIZZA-CANELLI
14042 CALAMANDRANA AT
TEL: 0141/75231

WINES PRODUCED: Barolo; Barbaresco; Gavi; Barbera d'Asti; Moscato d'Asti; Dolcetto d'Alba; Barilot.
VISITS: daily, working hours by appointment.
Highly-regarded producer of a full range of Piedmont wines.
English, French spoken.

---

4 TENUTE LUIGI IV S.R.L.
BOSCA HOLDING S.R.L.
VIA LUIGI BOSCA 2
14053 CANELLI AT
TEL: 0141/832508

WINES PRODUCED: Barolo; Barbaresco; Chardonnay di Moirano; Nebbiolo d'Alba; Grignolino d'Asti; Ruchè; Barbera d'Asti.
VISITS: daily by appointment.
Charge for *degustazione*.
The firm of Bosca is a large one, with considerable estates extending throughout Asti and Alba, in Canelli, Castagnol Monferrato, Cassinasco, Acqui Terme, Castelrocchero, Trezzo Tinella, Barbaresco, Monforte d'Alba, La Morra, and Neviglie. All the wines are produced entirely from own-grown grapes.
English spoken.

THE NORTH-WEST

5 F.LLI GANCIA & C SPA
CORSO LIBERTÀ 16
14053 CANELLI AT
TEL: 0141/8301

WINES PRODUCED: Gancia Asti
Spumante; Pinot di Pinot; Gancia
dei Gancia; vermouth; table wines.
VISITS: Mon–Fri 9h30–12h;
14h30–17h. Gancia ask, if possible,
to be informed of visits 15 days in
advance.
Canelli is the principal centre for
the production of Asti Spumante,
and the firm of Gancia, founded in
1850, is a well-known and
important one. Gancia produce not
only Asti Spumante from fragrant
Moscato grapes, but also a range of
superlative sparkling wines, such as
Pinot di Pinot by the *metodo
champenois*. Gancia is also a large
producer of vermouth and other
aperitivi.
English, French spoken.

---

6 I VIGNAIOLI DI SANTO STEFANO
FRAZ. MARINI 12
12058 SANTO STEFANO BELBO CN
TEL: 0141/840419

WINES PRODUCED: Moscato d'Asti;
Asti Spumante; Passito di Moscato
VISITS: working hours, appointment
preferable.
This small but prestigious winery
belongs to a consortium of owners,
among them the Ceretto brothers of
Alba, and produces excellent
Moscato sparkling wines, as well as
a rare *passito* wine made from
semi-dried Moscato Bianco grapes.
The wines may be available for
tasting but usually not for purchase.

---

7 BRAIDA DI GIACOMO BOLOGNA
VIA ROMA 94
14030 ROCCHETTA TANARO AT
TEL: 0141/644113; 644584

WINES PRODUCED: Barbera La
Monella, Barbera Bricco Uccellone;
Barbera Bricco Bigotta; Grignolino
d'Asti; Moscato d'Asti; Brachetto
d'Acqui.
VISITS: Mon–Fri, by appointment.
Giacomo Bologna's outstanding
wines are evidence, if any is needed,
that the Barbera, long considered
the everyday workhorse grape of the
Piedmont, is capable of producing
wines of the highest class and
stature.
English, French spoken.

ENOTECHE REGIONALI

1

ENOTECA REGIONALE DI
  COSTIGLIOLE D'ASTI
CASTELLO DI COSTIGLIOLE
14055 COSTIGLIOLE D'ASTI AT
TEL: 0141/966015

OPEN: daily except Mon.
The magnificent Castello di Costigliole dominates this small hill village and is currently in the process of being restored as one of Piedmont's principal showcases. It is best known for its fine restaurant which takes great pride in honouring and safeguarding the country cooking by serving local foods and wines of the *enoteca* at reasonable prices (**Moderate**). At present, visits to the *enoteca* must be made through the Ristorante del Castello.

2

ENOTECA REGIONALE DI ACQUI
  TERME
PALAZZO ROBELLINI
15011 ACQUI TERME AL
TEL: 0144/770274

OPEN: 10–12h; 15–18h30. Closed Mon, Wed, Thurs morning.
The vaulted *cantina* of this splendid *palazzo*, the oldest part of which dates back to the 11th century, serves as an atmospheric setting for this *Enoteca Regionale* dedicated to the wines of the Alto Monferrato. Run by enthusiasts, it provides ample tasting opportunities, as well as the chance to purchase from a full range of wines from throughout the zone. Its specialities, in particular, are Dolcetto d'Acqui, and the now rare but delightful Brachetto d'Acqui.

Ristoranti

1

RISTORANTE COLLAVINI
VIA ASTI-NIZZA 84
14055 COSTIGLIOLE D'ASTI AT
TEL: 0141/966440

Simple family cooking: homemade *tagliarini* and *agnolotti*, *brasato*, *faraona*, *coniglio*, together with local wines.
German, French, a little English spoken.
Inexpensive to Moderate

THE NORTH-WEST

2 HOTEL-RISTORANTE FONS SALUTIS
VIA FONTI 19
14041 AGLIANO D'ASTI AT
TEL: 0141/954018

Closed Mon.
Spa hotel in thermal town with a
pleasant shaded outdoor terrace
where meals are served in summer.
Moderate

---

3 RISTORANTE LA TAVOLACCIA
VIA POGGIO 5
INCISA SCAPACCINO AT
TEL: 0141/74639

Closed Tue.
Creative cuisine with homemade

bread, fresh *pasta*, and dishes
inspired from throughout Italy:
*antipasti assortiti, insalata di
Modena, saltimbocca alla romana.*
English, French spoken.
Moderate

---

4 RISTORANTE SAN MARCO
VIA ALBA 136
14053 CANELLI AT
TEL: 0141/833544

Closed Wed. Open Mon and Tue
midday only.
Specialities include *antipasti caldi,*

*fonduta con tartufi, agnolottini,
coniglio alla Monferrina, finanziera,*
served together with local wines
such as Arneis, Gavi, Moscato
d'Asti, and others.
English, French spoken.
Moderate

---

5 TRATTORIA DELLA POSTA 'DA
   CAMULIN'
CORSO F.LLI NEGRO 3
12054 COSSANO BELBO CN
TEL: 0141/88126

Closed Mon.
In the heart of the Moscato country,
a country *trattoria* serving
homemade *tajarin, fritto misto alla
piemontese, fonduta,* accompanied
by a good selection of local wines.
Moderate

---

6 RISTORANTE-ALBERGO 'DA TERESIO'
VIA ROMA 16
14051 BUBBIO AT
TEL: 0144/8128-8100

Closed Wed; 25 Sept–mid-Oct

(during the *vendemmia*).
Simple, friendly family
hotel-restaurant in this quiet town
most famous for its annual
Polentone, serving well-prepared

cucina casalinga: *minestra di verdura, penne al forno, bollito, polenta* (of course), and *budino di* *panna*, accompanied by own-produced Barbera.
Inexpensive

Agriturismo

1

PODERE LA PIAZZA
FRAZ. S. MARGHERITA
14055 COSTIGLIOLE D'ASTI AT
TEL: 0141/966267

Outstanding rural *trattoria* with rooms for rent together with outdoor activities (horse riding and tennis) on a wine estate in the heart of the Astigiana vineyard. Telephone for reservations for meals or rooms.

Asti to Vignale Monferrato

In Brief: The second wine tour leads north of Asti into the Monferrato hills through small wine towns, ending eventually at the *Enoteca Regionale di Vignale Monferrato*, before circling back to Asti. It provides a brief but most pleasant excursion into the wine country that can comfortably be completed in a half or full day. There are opportunities to taste less well known but fascinating and delicious wines, especially Grignolino and Malvasia.

Leave Asti on the N457 road to Casale Monferrato. Portacomaro is the first wine commune of note, with remains of considerable ancient fortifications. Turn off the main road left to visit the perched village of Castell'Alfero, topped by its impressive 18th-century castle. The nearby hamlet of Callianetto is the home of the popular Piedmont masque-character Gianduja, a satiric, wily peasant of humble country origin who delights in poking fun at the actions of government or local rulers. Gianduja (*duja* is dialect for jug or pitcher) each year opens the Piedmont *Carnevale* as he leads a procession of festive, costumed girls from his native *ciobata* cottage.

Continue through the vineyards and wine towns of Calliano and Penango to Moncalvo, once a fief of the church of Asti and the counts of Monferrato,

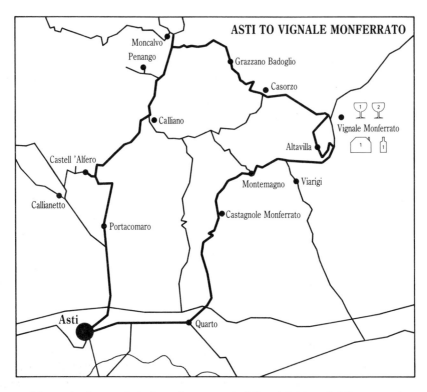

and important enough to have been granted the right to mint its own coins. The ruins of the ancient castle, with its towers, moat, and buttresses, can still be seen, while the Chiesa di San Francesco, built in the Lombard-Gothic style, contains some notable works of art by the painter Guglielmo Caccia. Moncalvo is an important agricultural centre: the large main square at the summit of the hill is the site of a lively cattle and agricultural market, while the town is also a centre not only for wines but also for truffles.

From Moncalvo, strike out into the Monferrato hills to the small wine towns of Grazzano Badóglio and Casorzo. Casorzo is the centre for the production of an unusual but delicious local wine, Malvasia di Casorzo d'Asti, a pale pink wine that is usually sweet and either *frizzante* or fully sparkling. Try a glass in the local bar. This is simply lovely wine country to meander through, characterized by fields of vines interspersed with rambling *aziende* and small cottages made of tufa, the underlying sub-stratum which so nourishes the vines.

The wine road continues next to Vignale Monferrato, an important regional centre since Roman times, though the town enjoyed its heyday

TRUFFLE AUCTIONS

The famous white truffle of Piedmont comes from the hills of both Alba and Asti. It is sought by professional truffle hunters (known in dialect as *trifolau*) who, with the aid of trained mongrels, usually find the rare and mysterious tuber buried under the earth beneath certain oak trees. The brief truffle season lasts only from the end of August until January, but during that time gastronomes from all over Italy converge on the region to pay it homage.

Truffle auctions take place in towns throughout the region such as Alba, Asti, Nizza Monferrato and elsewhere, and they are rare and remarkable events. The truffles on display tranfuse a throbbing, almost overpowering aroma. Bidding is fast and the prices fetched are quite astronomical. Afterwards, the entire town celebrates with a series of feasts to honour (and consume liberally) this magical fungus which many claim has aphrodisiac properties. Our research to verify this belief continues.

between the 15th and 17th centuries and retains much of architectural interest from that period, notably the austere, symmetrical Palazzo Callori. Today the Palazzo serves as the home for the important *Enoteca Regionale di Vignale Monferrato*, enclosed within the castle walls. There, in the vaulted cellars carved out of the soft tufa, wines from more than 100 properties are displayed, the finest kept in the *infernotto*. This is the traditional name for a secret cellar, known also as *crutin* in Piedmontese dialect, generally carved out of tufa or rock as a special place to store the rarest and most precious bottles. Such wine tabernacles not only stored the wine in perfect conditions, they also often served as religious shrines as well as places to receive privileged guests. The *enoteca* has a fine regional restaurant, and in summer the palace is the setting for many cultural and folk events.

From Vignale Monferrato, return to Asti by way of the perched town of Altavilla, Viarigi (the crenellated tower remains from feudal times when it was the residence of the counts of Monferrato and later the House of Savoy), and Montemagno, which also has an imposing castle. Continue back down towards the Tanaro valley by way of Castagnole Monferrato, source of another rarely encountered Piedmont wine curiosity, Ruchè di Castagnole Monferrato, a very particular, aromatic, deep red wine. At Quarto, turn right on the main road to return to Asti.

THE NORTH-WEST

Degustazione: Stop to Taste; Stop to Buy

1 AZIENDA AGRICOLA CASCINA
   ALBERTA
CA' PRANO 14
15049 VIGNALE MONFERRATO AL
TEL: 0142/923313

WINES PRODUCED: Grignolino del
Monferrato Casalese 'Vigneto
Poggio Superiore'; Barbera del
Monferrato; 'Bruga' *vino rosato da
tavola.*
VISIT: daily, working hours.
Grignolino can be a hard wine to
track down; a notoriously difficult
vine to cultivate, it has in recent
years been replaced with more
prolific and easier varieties. But the
Cristoforo family continue to
specialize in its production, and
make a good *cru* example from
their hilltop vineyard. The farm is
located about 2 km off the road
from Vignale to Camagna
Monferrato.
English spoken.

2 AZIENDA AGRICOLA IL MONGETTO
CASCINA MONGETTO
15049 VIGNALE MONFERRATO AL
TEL: 0142/923442; 923469

WINES PRODUCED: Grignolino del
Monferrato Casalese; Barbera
d'Asti.
VISITS: daily, by appointment.
Another source of the rare but
delicious Grignolino, as well as a
range of other home-produced
goodies, including honey, conserves,
and sauces.
A little English and French
spoken.

ENOTECA REGIONALE

1 ENOTECA REGIONALE DEL
   MONFERRATO
PALAZZO CALLORI
15049 VIGNALE MONFERRATO AL
TEL: 0142/923243

OPEN: daily except Tue.
The historic Palazzo Callori is the
splendid setting for this important
Enoteca Regionale. Built and
expanded over the centuries,
particularly from the 15th to the
17th, it is today administered by a
consorzio whose aims are to
promote the viticultural and
cultural traditions of the
Monferrato. Each year the wines
to be displayed in the *cantina* are
selected only after a most rigorous
tasting. The restaurant serves the
typical foods of the Monferrato in
an elegant historic setting.
Moderate.

Agriturismo

1

AZIENDA AGRICOLA CASCINA
   ALBERTA
(address above)

In addition to its role as a producer of serious wines, Cascina Alberta is also an important *azienda agrituristica*: local foods and *piatti tipici* can be enjoyed in the rural *trattoria* by reservation, and there are 3 double rooms for rent by the night or week.

GAVI: AN EXCEPTIONAL WINE ISLAND

In Brief: The wine region of Gavi, like that of Burgundy's Chablis, lies like an island, located in the far south of the province of Alessandria, separated from the main body of prestigious Piedmont vineyards that extend mainly over the provinces of Cuneo and Asti. It is thus easy to overlook it: but Gavi Ligure is a fascinating historic town, and the wine hamlets that encircle it are the source of one of Italy's great dry white wines, Gavi DOC.

The Alto Monferrato produces a vast range of wines, among them Cortese dell'Alto Monferrato, a plentiful if relatively undistinguished wine that is the everyday white of the region. However, in the far south of the Alto Monferrato, on the lime-rich foothills leading up to the Ligurian Apennines, particularly around the town of Gavi Ligure and its surrounding wine communities, the Cortese grape rises above its humble station to produce outstanding dry white wines that are among the finest of the region, if not the country. Gavi, or Gavi di Gavi, as some producers label their wines to indicate an unofficial 'cru' zone, is a modern, exceptionally clean wine that combines scent, structure, and delicacy. Moreover, like all great white wines, it has the further capacity to improve with bottle age.

Such are the dictates of supply and demand in this country which follows fashion sometimes to slavish degrees, that the conspicuous popularity of Gavi (and in particular Gavi dei Gavi produced by the Soldati family at Villa Scolca) has brought the wine not only wide acclaim but at the same time allowed it to carry a not inconsiderable premium that may or may not always be valid. Like the designer labels that Italians are so fond and aware of, Gavi has become one of *the* wines to be seen to be drinking.

THE NORTH-WEST

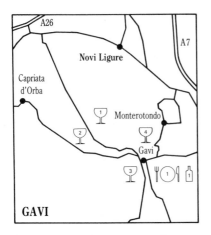

Gavi Ligure itself is a notable town, located in the beautiful Val Lemme along an ancient and important thoroughfare that once connected Liguria with the north. Indeed Gavi came under Genoese rule for some 6 centuries, and as its name suggests the town retains many distinctive Ligurian characteristics. It is dominated above all by its massive Fortezza Genovese that covers virtually the entire brow of the hill that overlooks the town. Construction of this formidable and imposing military structure, one of the largest in Italy, began in the 10th century, but it was further extended over succeeding centuries, particularly the 16th and 17th. While it then allowed the Ligurians to exercise control over transport in or out of the region, in later centuries it served primarily as a penal colony and prison, even until the end of World War II. Today the castle can be visited: it provides one of the best views of the surrounding wine country. Also worth visiting is the 12th-century Lombard-Gothic Parocchia di San Giacomo which is famous for its baroque frescoes.

Gavi today is located administratively in the region of Piedmont, and coming to this somewhat isolated wine island from Asti or further inland, it is perhaps not immediately obvious that it is located only 35 kilometres from the sea. The region's history as part of Liguria, its mild and pleasant climate, and its ease of communications with nearby Genoa, led to the construction of numerous stately *palazzi* and country villas for the nobility and merchants of what was once one of Europe's most important maritime republics. These villas remain today and are a feature in particular of the wine country to the north of Gavi where some of the best and most famous wines are produced.

The intrepid wine tourist in search of good wine and splendid vineyard scenery, therefore, will strike out from Gavi and explore the myriad tiny wine hamlets and villages such as Rovereto di Gavi, Capriata d'Orba, Monterotondo and others, located between Gavi and Novi Ligure, another important historic Genoese outpost.

Degustazione: Stop to Taste; Stop to Buy

1 AZIENDA AGRICOLA 'LA SCOLCA'
VILLA SCOLCA
FRAZ. ROVERETO DI GAVI
15066 GAVI AL
TEL: 0143/682176

WINES PRODUCED: Gavi dei Gavi;
Gavi La Scolca; Gavi Villa Scolca;
Gavi Zunot; Gavi Rugrè; Spumante
Classico.
VISITS: Mon–Fri, by appointment,
for wine professionals and trade

members only.
La Scolca was the first wine estate
in the Gavi zone to create a
national and international
reputation for the wine and remains
the leading firm today. So popular is
Villa Scolca's Gavi dei Gavi that
sales have to be rationed, and visits
are only available to wine
professionals.
English, French spoken.

2 AZIENDA AGRICOLA LA FONTANASSA
FRAZ. ROVERETO DI GAVI 65
15066 GAVI AL
TEL: 0143/682250

WINE PRODUCED: Gavi 'La
Fontanassa'.
VISITS: daily, appointment
preferred.

Another favourite, produced by a
dedicated artisan wine maker in the
heart of this prestigious vineyard.
English spoken 'by appointment'.

3 AZIENDA AGRICOLA LA CHIARA
LOC. VALLEGGE 24/2
15066 GAVI AL
TEL: 0143/642293

WINE PRODUCED: Gavi 'La Chiara'.
VISITS: Mon–Sat, by appointment.
Outstanding white wine made with
modern expertise.

4 TENUTA SAN PIETRO
VIA ROMA 20
15066 GAVI AL
TEL: 0143/642598; 42125

WINE PRODUCED: Gavi 'San Pietro'.
VISITS: Mon–Fri, by appointment.
Fine wine from an important VIDE
estate located in the town centre.

THE NORTH-WEST

Enoteca

1 LE COLLINE DEL GAVI
VIA MAMELI 68R
15066 GAVI AL
TEL: 0143/642398

OPEN: 10–12h30; 16–19h30. Closed
Sun afternoon, Mon.

This small shop near the Parocchia
is the best place to examine and
purchase an intelligent selection of
wines from the finest estates of
Gavi.

Ristorante

1 RISTORANTE 'CANTINE DEL GAVI'
VIA MAMELI 50
15066 GAVI AL
TEL: 0143/642458

Closed Mon.
Located in a traditional house in the
historic centre of Gavi, this
outstanding, elegant restaurant

offers local foods such as *risotto al
Gavi* and *costata di manzo al
Barolo*, together with a vast
selection of the wines of Gavi and
Piedmont.
English, French spoken.
Moderate

NORTHERN PIEDMONT

In Brief: The vineyards of the northern Piedmont, though nowhere near
as well-known as those of the south, are located in areas of extreme
beauty and touristic interest, spread across the provinces of Novara and
Vercelli. Those holidaying near or around Lake Maggiore, or the smaller
Lakes Orta and Viverone, will therefore find plenty of opportunities for
wine tasting and touring, while others, en route to northern Europe by
way of the Monte Bianco or Great San Bernard tunnels, may wish to
break their journey with a brief tour through vineyards and wine towns,
ending at the impressive *Enoteca Regionale della Serra* which overlooks
Lake Viverone.

The vinous riches of Alba, Asti and the Monferrato are so varied, the wines
produced so richly satisfying and prestigious, that it is easy to overlook the
vineyards and wine regions of the northern Piedmont. Yet, across both the
provinces of Novara and Vercelli, the vine is cultivated on foothills that look
up towards the snow-covered Alps to the north.

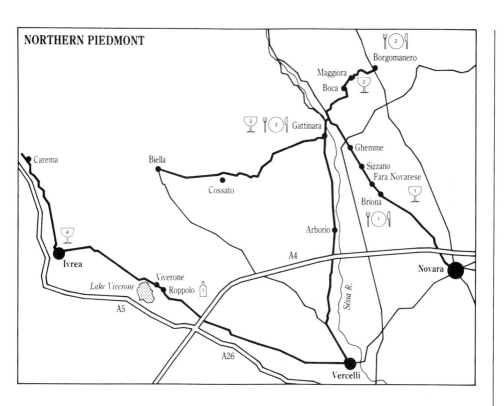

NORTHERN PIEDMONT

The dominant grape in these zones is the Spanna, a local name for the aristocratic Nebbiolo. Much generic wine is produced and bottled under the basic varietal Spanna label, generally robust country wines that can be very satisfying and which on the whole are remarkably good value. The finest, most distinctive wines, on the other hand, are entitled to a clutch of confusing communal *denominazioni*, names that will never be household ones but which none the less provide fascinating comparisons for the intrepid wine tourist as he or she meanders through the vineyards.

A tour through the vineyards of Novara begins in the capital of the province. Novara today is a medium-sized city of 100,000 inhabitants and an important commercial, industrial, and agricultural centre. Probably once an ancient Ligurian settlement in the 5th century BC, it then became a flourishing Roman city known as Novaria, and even today retains the typical layout of a Roman municipality. After a period of decline, Novara then became a free city during the Middle Ages, and the only one in the region entitled to have its own Broletto, or Courts of Justice. Ruled at times by the Visconti, Sforza, and Savoia families, Novara played an important role

THE NORTH-WEST

during the Risorgimento: it was here that King Carlo Alberto, after being defeated by the Austrians at the battle of Bicocca in 1849, abdicated the crown in favour of his son Vittorio Emanuele II, later to be proclaimed first king of unified Italy in 1861.

The vast plains of the Po valley extend over the provinces of both Novara and Vercelli, flooded in spring and summer into vast, mirror-like paddies in which the jagged silhouette of the Alps is reflected. This is the most important rice growing centre in Europe, and the source of the medium-grain variety known as *arborio*, so essential for the *risotti* dishes that are the staple not only of Piedmont, but also of Lombardy and Veneto. The vineyards, on the other hand, extend over the hills, mostly small but sometimes more considerable, that rise up from the flatter plains.

From Novara, a most pleasant excursion can be made through wine towns en route to Borgomanero and the Lakes of Orta and Maggiore. Leave the city not by the direct road to Borgomanero, but by the N299 to Romagnano and Varallo. The principal wine hamlets, each entitled to a DOC for their respective Spanna (primarily) wines, are all spread out along this wine route: first Briona, then Fara, then Sizzano, and finally Ghemme. These are rare wines, little encountered outside the zone of production, but they are excellent all the same, on the whole somewhat lighter, less dense than their complex, tannic cousins from the Langhe, and as such perhaps more immediately appealing and enchanting. But in the best years, make no mistake, such wines can display considerable robust structure in their own right and are capable of improving with age.

Beyond Ghemme, on the opposite bank of the Sésia river lies the wine town of Gattinara, probably the best-known *denominazione* of all the northern Piedmont wines. Gattinara is actually located in the province of Vercelli, its vineyards extending over hills above the lovely alpine Valsesia. The Spanna grape here is capable of producing wines of particularly fine and delicate scent.

From Gattinara, recross the river, and find the small wine road out of Prato that leads to Boca and Maggiora. The vineyards that extend over these lovely hills are also mainly planted with Spanna, and the wines produced are entitled to the Boca DOC. Locally, they are known as 'wines fit for a pope', for in 1903 the Venetian Cardinal Giuseppe Sarto made a pilgrimage to the Sanctuary at Boca together with the Bishop of Novara. When the local parish priest served his illustrious guests lunch together with the local Boca wine, the Bishop of Novara exclaimed, 'Your Eminence, this wine is fit for a Cardinal.' Cardinal Sarto poured himself another glass of Boca, tasted it again, and replied, 'Excellency, this wine is fit for a Pope.' The proclamation was prophetic, for indeed, only a few months later, Cardinal Sarto himself was proclaimed Pope, taking the name of Pius X. From Boca and Maggiora, continue on to Borgomanero, gateway to the lakes.

Vercelli, capital of the province to which it gives its name, is like Novara an ancient city, first established probably by the Ligurians. Its important position along the roads that lead from Rome to the Alpine passes and northern Europe, and its location equidistant between Turin and Milan, allowed it to establish a position of considerable importance by the 12th century, though, in common with so many other cities in the region, it subsequently suffered a succession of virtually continuous wars as different factions, parties, and families struggled for supremacy. Today its strategic position at the junctions of 3 major *autostrade* has led to a highly developed industrial, commercial, and agricultural economy.

Vercelli is virtually an island surrounded by its vast, glass-like rice paddies, but wherever the land rises above the flatter plains, there are likely to be vines planted. The wine tourist may wish to head over the plains north through Arborio (the town that has given its name to Italy's most famous rice) to Gattinara, and then strike west to Cossato and Biella. Or else take the N143 across the rice plains to Lake Viverone, where at Roppolo there is the important *Enoteca Regionale della Serra* located above the town in the splendid, mainly 16th-century castle of Roppolo. The castle tower serves as a repository for a vast selection of wines not only from Vercelli and Novara but from throughout the Piedmont, so it is a fine source for those wishing to stock up before returning home. There is also a restaurant in the *enoteca* serving regional foods.

Beyond Lake Viverone lies Ivrea, a town famous primarily for the single industry that dominates: Olivetti. None the less, around Ivrea and up the Dora Báltea valley leading to the Valle d'Aosta there are significant vineyards. Those around the town of Carema, virtually the last community before the autonomous region is entered, produce particularly fine wines from the Spanna.

THE NORTH-WEST

Degustazione: Stop to Taste; Stop to Buy

1 CANTINA SOCIALE DEI COLLI
    NOVARESI
VIA CESARE BATTISTI 56
28073 FARA NOVARESE NO
TEL: 0321/829234; 829385

WINES PRODUCED: Fara; Ghemme; Caramino.
VISITS: Mon–Fri 8–12h.
Good local co-operative winery producing wines utilizing modern technology, including carbonic maceration.

---

2 ANTONIO VALLANA & FIGLIO S.N.C.
VIA MAZZINI 3
28014 MAGGIORA NO
TEL: 0322/87116

WINES PRODUCED: Gattinara; Boca; Spanna.
VISITS: Mon–Sat 8–12h30; 14–18h.
For visits at weekends or during the month of August, telephone for an appointment.

Giuseppina Vallana and Marina Vallerani produce wines from their own grapes, vinified by the traditional methods of the region. The *azienda* is located near to Lakes Maggiore and Orta, and some self-catering accommodation may be available.
English, French, a little German spoken.

---

3 CANTINA SOCIALE DI GATTINARA
VIA MONTE GRAPPA 6
13045 GATTINARA VC
TEL: 0163/833568

WINES PRODUCED: Gattinara; *vino rosso da tavola*.
VISITS: daily by appointment.
Working hours for purchases.

---

4 AZIENDA AGRICOLA FERRANDO LUIGI
    & FIGLIO S.N.C
CORSO CAVOUR 9
10015 IVREA TO
TEL: 0125/422383

WINES PRODUCED: Carema; Carema Riserva; Erbaluce Caluso; Erbaluce Vendemmia Tardiva; Solativo; Grappa di Carema.
VISITS: open for *vendita diretta* Mon

afternoon – Fri 8h30–12h30; 15–19h.
Carema red wine, from the Spanna grape, as well as rare dry white and late-harvested dessert wines, from the Erbaluce grape, are produced at this highly-regarded family wine estate. Solativo is a white wine produced from Erbaluce aged in *barrique* for one year.

ENOTECA REGIONALE

1 ENOTECA DELLA SERRA
CASTELLO DI ROPPOLO
13040 ROPPOLO VC
TEL: 0161/98501

OPEN: 1 April–30 Sept Wed, Thur, Fri 14–19h; Sat and Sun 9–12h; 14–19h. Oct–March Fri, Sat, and Sun only 9h30–12h; 14h30–18h. Hotel-*ristorante* open all year, but restaurant closed Mon.
The pleasant tasting room and atmospheric *cantine* are located in the castle tower and dungeon. Extensive, nicely displayed selection of wines, not just from the northern Piedmont vineyards but throughout the region, available for purchase and tasting. The hotel-restaurant serves regional foods in a unique and atmospheric setting.
Moderate to Expensive

Ristoranti

1 TRATTORIA DEL PONTE
VIA PER OLEGGIO 1
LOC. PROH
28072 BRIONA NO
TEL: 0321/826282

Closed Mon eve; Tue.

Country *trattoria* serving the rarely encountered wines of northern Piedmont together with *cucina casalinga* and local specialities such as *rane dorate*.
Inexpensive to Moderate

2 RISTORANTE PINOCCHIO
VIA MATTEOTTI 147
28021 BORGOMANERO NO
TEL: 0322/82273; 81906

Closed Mon.
Elegant restaurant serving refined

regional *cucina: bianco di gallina al ginepro in bagna freida; animella con funghi porcini; zabaione con brutti ma buoni.*
English, French spoken.
Expensive

3 ALBERGO RISTORANTE IMPERO
CORSO GARIBALDI 81
13045 GATTINARA VC
TEL: 0163/833232

Closed Fri.
This **Moderate** hotel-restaurant serves classic *cucina piemontese: antipasti, risotti, tagliolini, brasato al Gattinara, fritto misto*

THE NORTH-WEST

piemontese, together with a good selection of Gattinara wines. Visits to the vineyards and wine producers of Gattinara can be arranged.
English, French spoken.

Wine and Other Related *Sagre* and *Feste*

end Jan–early Feb	Fiera dei Vini	Turin
Easter	Festa del Vino	Alba
Sun after Easter	Polentone	Bubbio
end Aug	Festa del Vino Barolo	La Morra
end Aug–early Sept	Festa del Moscato d'Asti	S. Stefano Belbo
mid-Sept	Douja d'Or	Asti
1st Sun Oct	Festa del Tartufo	Alba
mid-Oct–Nov	Grande Feste del Tartufo	Various towns throughout Asti and Alba.

E PER SAPERE DI PIÙ – ADDITIONAL INFORMATION

Ufficio Turistico Regionale
via Magenta 12
10128 Turin
tel: 011/57171

Ufficio Turistico Regionale
Regione Autonoma Valle d'Aosta
Piazza Narbonne 3
11100 Aosta
tel: 0165/303718

Consorzio per la Tutela dell'Asti
  Spumante
Consorzio Barbera d'Asti e
  Barbera dell' Monferrato
Piazza Roma 10
14100 Asti
tel: 0141/54215

Associazione Consorzii del Barolo,
  del Barbaresco e dei Vini d'Alba
Piazza Savona 3
12051 Alba
tel: 0173/43202

Agriturist Comitato Regionale
Corso V. Emanuele 58 (3° piano)
10121 Turin
tel: 011/518167

Assessorato Regionale Agricoltura
Ufficio Agriturismo
Piazza Deffeyes
11100 Aosta
tel: 0165/5533922

LIGURIA

I Vini: THE WINES OF LIGURIA   86

La Gastronomia   87

La Strada del Vino: THE WINE ROAD OF LIGURIA
  The Cinque Terre: By Foot through Terraced
  Vineyards and Fishing Villages   89

Le Sagre: WINE AND OTHER RELATED FESTIVALS   95

Additional Information   95

Stop to taste; stop to buy.

Liguria, the Italian Riviera which curves seductively around Italy's north-west corner to the border with the French Côte d'Azur, is one of the nation's smallest but most beautiful regions. The Apennines, the long spine of mountains that extends virtually the length of the peninsula, begins amazingly near to the rocky, steep Ligurian coastline, so the essential and enduring features of this rugged land are mountains and sea.

ORIENTATION

Liguria consists of 4 provinces: Genoa, Imperia, La Spezia, and Savona. The region's proximity to urban areas such as Turin, Milan, and Florence makes it particularly popular with holidaying Italians, while the twin Rivieras of Ponente (from Genoa to the French border) and Levante (south to La Spezia) have both traditionally attracted well-heeled visitors from northern Europe for their exceptionally mild climates.

Genoa's Cristoforo Colombo international airport serves the region, and connections with Milan, Turin, or Pisa are not difficult. The principal west coast railway extends south from Genoa all the way to Naples, but travel by local train is the best way to explore the region. Indeed, for visits to the Cinque Terre it is virtually the only way, a car being a positive disadvantage. The A10 and A12 *autostrade* follow the coast from the French border south to La Spezia and Tuscany. Indeed, for those heading to Florence by car, the region can be dipped into en route.

Maps Touring Club Italiano 1: 200 000 Liguria. Guida alle Cinque Terre 1: 30 000 (walking map with marked footpaths)

THE NORTH-WEST

Under the aegis of the Maritime Republic of Genoa, Liguria was once one of the most important powers in Europe, but as a wine region, we must admit that it ranks as one of Italy's most minor. The land is simply too rugged, too steep, too schistous for widescale production, so the limited amounts of wines produced are rarely encountered outside the region. That said, the combination of a majestic rocky coastline, charming colourful fishing villages, unique, steeply terraced vineyards, and exceptional local foods to accompany the wines, makes this one of the most enjoyable wine regions to encounter. Wine is produced throughout Liguria. However, we have focused on the wholly exceptional and unique wine land of the Cinque Terre.

BY BOAT ALONG THE LIGURIAN COAST

One of the best ways to gain a more intimate acquaintance with this lovely but at times inaccessible coastline is by boat. A number of companies offer regular services, for example, between Portofino and Lerici, stopping along the way in the Cinque Terre.

For further information contact:

Navigazione
Golfo dei Poeti
19032 Lerici SP
tel: 0187/967676; 900785

I VINI: GLOSSARY TO THE WINES OF LIGURIA

Wines of *Denominazione di Origine Controllata (DOC)*

Cinque Terre DOC Most famous Ligurian wine: dry white, produced from Bosco, Albarola, and Vermentino grapes grown on terraced vineyards along the southern Ligurian coast. Minimum alcohol 11 degrees.

Cinque Terre Sciacchetrà DOC Rare *passito* dessert wine made in the eponymous wine zone from grapes that have been laid on racks to semi-dry. Minimum alcohol 17 degrees.

Riviera di Ponente DOC
Denominazione for vineyards west of Genoa for the production of 4 varietal wines: Pigato and Vermentino (both white) and Rossese and Ormeasco (red).

Rossese di Dolceacqua DOC; **Dolceacqua DOC** Rossese grapes grown on hill vineyards centred on town of Dolceacqua produce Liguria's best red wine: fruity and perfumed. Reputedly Napoleon's favourite tipple. Minimum alcohol 12 degrees.

LA GASTRONOMIA: FOODS OF LIGURIA

Liguria is a poor region of fishermen and hill farmers who from time immemorial have had to scrape a bare living from sea or rocky terrain. The *cucina* of the region may reflect this, but rarely will you encounter such simple foods prepared with such vivacity and colour. Most who come to Liguria will stay on or near the coast, and thus enjoy a profusion of superb shellfish and fish prepared in any number of ways, from imaginative platters of *antipasti* to seafood pastas to simply grilled whole fish.

Ligurian olive oil, produced like the wine from ancient terraced groves in

PESTO

Basil is the perfume of Liguria. In gardens, on windowsills, on every city balcony or rooftop terrace, the terracotta pot of this prized herb takes pride of place, basking in the warm Mediterranean sun. The small, pointed, densely green leaves are gathered daily, torn by hand, then pounded into an emulsion with plenty of garlic, golden Ligurian olive oil, grated *pecorino* cheese, and crushed pine nuts. Around the corner in French Provence, a similar sauce, *pistou*, is equally enjoyed, a reminder that culinary borders do not necessarily correspond with today's political frontiers. Pungent *pesto*, spread thickly on to homemade noodles, or dolloped into a tureen of fresh vegetable soup, encapsulates the taste of Liguria.

proximity to the sea, is lighter, yellower than the dense green Tuscan oil, and therefore it is ideal for the preparation of fish dishes. Indeed, olive oil and pungent, fresh herbs are the hallmarks of the Ligurian *cucina*.

But just a mile or so inland from the coast, there is another, little-visited world of isolated hill communities set amidst rugged mountainous terrain. The local *cucina* reflects this duality, too, with the preparation of surprisingly hearty dishes from locally-hunted boar, hare, pheasant, rabbit and other game.

PIATTI TIPICI: REGIONAL SPECIALITIES

Focaccia Genoese 'pizza' – bread dough dimpled and spread with Ligurian olive oil and coarse sea salt.

Acciughe marinate Fresh anchovies marinated in lemon juice, herbs, and olive oil.

Tartufi di mare Local clams eaten as *antipasto* or with seafood pasta.

Datteri di mare Sea dates, a type of shellfish.

Cozze Mussels.

Minestrone alla genovese Fresh vegetable and bean soup flavoured with pungent *pesto*.

Trenette al pesto Homemade noodles (like thin *tagliatelle*) served with sauce of *pesto*: virtually the hallmark dish of Liguria.

Pansôti Local homemade ravioli, usually served with creamy walnut sauce.

Cappon magro Outrageously sumptuous Genoese fish and vegetable salad arranged in a showcase pyramid shape.

Triglie alla Ligure Red mullet, traditionally baked in olive oil with olives.

Cima di vitello ripieno; cima alla genovese Breast of veal stuffed with vegetables, herbs, hard-boiled eggs, pistachio nuts, to be eaten cold.

Biscotti di Lagaccio Hard biscuits flavoured with fennel seed. Delicious with Sciacchetrà.

Cheese: *Formagette* Small goat's milk cheeses, sometimes flavoured with herbs.

THE CINQUE TERRE: BY FOOT THROUGH TERRACED VINEYARDS AND FISHING VILLAGES

In Brief: The Cinque Terre are 5 fishing villages located on tortuously terraced, vine-covered coastal cliffs between Lévanto and La Spezia. Only Riomaggiore and Monterosso are in theory accessible by car, but in summer even this should be avoided. Better to take the little train that links them all, then strike out on the cliff footpath through the vineyards. There are series of well marked footpaths that extend not only along the coast, but into the steep hinterland as well, thus giving a number of hiking options, from a few hours' ramble to days or more of serious walking. The bonus is that you can always catch the train from the next village.

There is no shortage of fish restaurants and bars where the wines of the Cinque Terre can be sampled; accommodation in the Cinque Terre towns themselves is limited. Lévanto probably makes the best base for exploring this charming wine zone.

Of all of Italy's varied and myriad wine regions, the Cinque Terre is the most dramatic and beautiful. On this brief, hardly accessible stretch of Ligurian coastline the steep cliffs have been carved out of a shifting, inhospitable sedimentary terrain of flint and slate into a wave-like pattern of vine-covered terraces. Held in place only by centuries-old small dry-stone walls, the terraced vineyards extend steeply above the 5 colourful fishing villages of the Cinque Terre, as well as below them, virtually to the water's edge. Some vineyards, say the locals, are accessible only by boat; whether or not this is true, almost all can certainly only be reached by footpath, not by road.

The vineyards of the Cinque Terre are probably among the most labour intensive in the world, so much so that these days more and more are being abandoned. Not only are they virtually inaccessible, they are planted in low *pergole* fashion to protect the grapes from the strong sea winds that blow in the mornings: tending and harvesting the grapes is literally backbreaking. As elsewhere, young people are simply not willing to put in the monumental labour required to keep up the age-old traditions and way of life.

Yet the grapes – mainly Bosco, Albarola, and Vermentino for the production of Cinque Terre DOC – continue to be grown, harvested, and made

THE NORTH-WEST

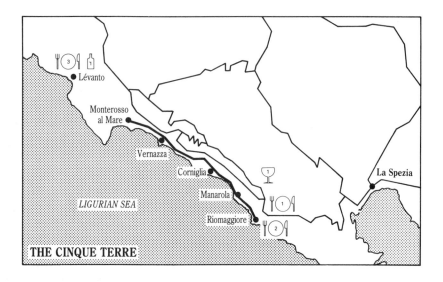

into wine, for home consumption, for sale to local restaurants, and to slake the prodigious thirst of the millions who come each year to visit these charming and timeless villages. Almost all of the grapes, other than those used for home consumption, go to the modern co-operative at Groppo which produces a range of excellent, clean, well-made wines (including 3 selected *cru* bottlings), as well as the rare Sciacchetrà, a *passito* dessert wine rather in the style of Vin Santo and a speciality which must be tried when in the region.

In truth, though, it has to be said that Cinque Terre DOC is not a great wine. It is good; it is particular; it has a character at once rather rasping, flinty, and *salato*, with a sea-fresh bite that goes so well with *antipasti di mare, penne ai scampi*, and grilled fish eaten in *trattorie* on the spot. But the sheer effort required to tend such vineyards is not rewarded commensurately with a wine that is applauded throughout the world – or with prices which match the efforts. The intrepid wine growers of the Cinque Terre deserve to make great wine, not just good wine. Sadly, they do not. It is to their immense credit that they continue to grow grapes and make wine at all, seemingly against all the odds.

To gain a more intimate acquaintance with this unique wine land, it is necessary to strike into the vineyards on foot. Take the train from La Spezia or Lévanto to Riomaggiore, which, like the other typical villages, is sited where a narrow river valley has carved a steep aperture through the cliffs. Rising sharply from the waterfront, it looks down to the sea as well as up to the agricultural hinterland as the colourful houses climb steeply towards the vineyards and fields. Riomaggiore was probably settled in the 13th century; its parish church of San Giovanni Battista, remarkably large and self-important for such a small and remote village, dates from 1340, and attests to the town's former importance as a bastion against Saracen raiders.

The best-known (and trodden) footpath in the Cinque Terre links Riomaggiore with Manarola. It is poetically known as the '*Via dell'Amore*', but, inviting though this sobriquet sounds, it is actually the worst stretch of the coastal footpath, unless you particularly like strolling in high heels. Paved and fairly level, set into the rocky face below the vineyards, it is invariably extremely crowded; none the less, it is still worth the walk, simply to arrive at tiny Manarola, probably the most charming of all the 5 villages. Here, the harbour is so minuscule that the fishing boats have to be winched out of the water on to the promontory for protection.

From Manarola, the serious wine lover will wish to gain a perspective on the wine country by literally rising above and beyond, away from the colour and bustle of the popular sea villages. For just inland lies another world. Climb up the road that leads out of Manarola (following the signposted footpath no. 6) to Groppo for a visit to the important *cantina sociale*. It is a backbreaking effort simply to walk up the roads and footpaths, so one gains a sense at least of the labour that must be required to actually work the vineyards.

As we struggled up the hill from Manarola, we met an old barefoot woman emerging from the vineyards, her head wrapped in a scarf to protect her from the fierce midday sun. She stopped to admire our baby, Guy.

'He resembles you,' she said after examining me from head to foot. Then turning to Kim, she added shrewdly, 'It's better that way, no? Then everyone knows for sure who the father is.'

We talked about life in the Cinque Terre and the work in the vineyards.

'Yes. It is very hard. The only people you see working in the fields are the old ones like me, no? The young won't do it today. In 20 years' time all these vineyards will be gone, turned back to woods.' She pointed to an abandoned vineyard where the scrubby bush had already taken over to demonstrate her point.

But I don't think she is right. For at Groppo, the co-operative winery, founded in 1980, is a small but very modern installation which has some 250 grape growing members, plus another 400 or so members who 'believe in the cause'. It is common to deride wines from co-operatives and *cantine sociali* as being of little worth compared to estate bottlings, but this is a case where a co-operative of wine growers has banded together not only to safe-guard a historic wine that might otherwise have been lost, but also to protect an ancient way of life.

Investment in modern wine making equipment – cylindrical presses, temperature-controlled stainless steel fermentation vats – plus a policy that rewards quality through a system of selection of the best grapes for superior *cru* bottlings (*coste selezionate*) ensures that the wines are not just sound but very good. Furthermore, the co-operative winery has been able to ease the crippling workload in the vineyards through, for example, the installation of funiculars and *motorotaia* – mini-monorails – for the transport of men, tools and grapes at harvest time from one steep slope to the next or to the road for ease of collection. The *cantina* is also able to make use of helicopters to spray the vineyards collectively against pests. These are luxuries that the small *contadino*, working his tiny pocket handkerchief patch of vines, would never otherwise have been able to consider.

From Groppo, the *sentiero no. 6* continues into the higher mountains inland, but we suggest returning to Manarola to continue along the coastal footpath which leads through the vineyards to Corniglia. Unlike the other towns of the Cinque Terre, Corniglia does not sit with its toes lapping the water, but rather hangs cramped and brooding on a cliff promontory that juts out towards the sea far below. It is a maze of alleyways and typical narrow and tall houses clustered together, where life, it seems, carries on

Vernazza.

today as it has since medieval days. The 14th-century parish church is worth a visit.

The footpath from Corniglia to Vernazza becomes more rugged (though it is not difficult) and extends through both vineyards and olive groves, a reminder that the Ligurian coast is also a source of excellent and valuable olive oil.

It is well worth scrambling over this rather dilapidated cliff path not only for the stunning sea views that it affords all along the way but simply to arrive at Vernazza, for it is sheer magic to come around a bend and see the busy town with its fishing harbour colourfully spread out below. The old fortified town walls and castle still remain, reminders of when these towns were part of the powerful maritime Republic of Genoa.

Walk down now, down the steep steps to the little town itself, sit out on a shaded terrace and reward your efforts with a chilled glass of Cinque Terre together with a slice of *focaccia*, the dimpled salty bread made with good yellow Ligurian olive oil. Or else treat yourself to a glass of the rare sweet Sciacchetrà, to be sipped along with crunchy fennel-seed biscuits.

Monterosso al Mare is the largest of the Cinque Terre, and the only one with a sandy beach. Accessible by car, it is also one of the most popular. The old medieval centre of the town is almost entirely intact. It too retains parts of its old fortifications, castle, and towers, necessary for protection not only from the marauding Saracens but also from the rival Pisans to the south.

The Cinque Terre is a surprisingly tiny wine region, whose wine is not well-known or world-famous since it is rarely encountered outside its zone of production. Yet those of us who celebrate the cultivation of the grape in all its wide varieties should raise a glass to the wine growers here who do so not for glory, certainly not for great financial reward, but simply because their fathers did so, and their grandfathers before them, scratching a bare living from this inhospitable terrain, living the best they can off the fruits of land and sea.

Degustazione: Stop to Taste; Stop to Buy

1

COOPERATIVE 'AGRICOLTURA DI RIOMAGGIORE, MANAROLA, CORNIGLIA, VERNAZZA E MONTEROSSO' S.R.L.
FRAZIONE GROPPO
19017 RIOMAGGIORE SP
TEL: 0187/920435

WINES PRODUCED: Cinque Terre, Cinque Terre *coste selezionate*, Cinque Terre Sciacchetrà.
VISITS: open to all daily, working hours, for visits and direct sales.

THE NORTH-WEST

Guided visits by appointment. There is an almost evangelical air about this small but ultra-modern *cantina sociale*, for it has succeeded almost against the odds in reviving viticulture in a historic zone of production. The three *cru* wines, Costa de Serà di Riomaggiore, Costa da' Posa di Volastra, and Costa de Campu di Manarola, are vinified separately on successive days at the start of the *vendemmia*.

Produced in minuscule amounts, and rarely encountered outside the zone, they are worth seeking, for they demonstrate much greater character and individuality than the *normale*. Sciacchetrà, produced from semi-dried grapes, aged for 2 years in new oak *barrique*, is a remarkable dessert wine: only about 1000 bottles are produced each year, and it is correspondingly expensive, but definitely worth sampling.

Enoteca

1 LA CANTINA LEVANTESE
PIAZZA MASSOLA 3
19015 LÉVANTO SP

OPEN: daily 8–13h; 15–20h. Located by the Church of S. Andrea, this wine *cantina* sells own-produced Rosso e Bianco di Lévanto. The white, says the owner, is produced from the same grapes as Cinque Terre DOC, but vinified on the skins in the old traditional manner for a fuller, gutsier flavour. Wines from the co-operative, as well as *grappa*, are also on sale here.

Ristoranti

1 RISTORANTE ARISTIDE
VIA DISCOVOLO 138
19010 MANAROLA SP
TEL: 0187/920000

Closed Mon. Outstanding typical *trattoria* serving a vast array of *antipasti di mare*, good *primi piatti di mare* (*penne ai scampi, risotti*), and grilled fish. Just a few steps up from Manarola's tiny harbour, with a shaded outdoor terrace in summer.
Moderate

2 ALBERGO DUE GEMELLI
LOC. CAMPI
19017 RIOMAGGIORE SP
TEL: 0187/29043

One of the few hotels in the Cinque Terre, located 9 km south of Riomaggiore in the quiet wine hamlet of Campi, with a good local restaurant.
Moderate

---

3 TRATTORIA GRITTA
VIA VALLESANTA
19015 LÉVANTO SP
TEL: 0187/808593

Closed Wed. Reservations advisable in season.
Popular *trattoria* located right on the beach, serving good seafood pasta and *pesce alla genovese*.
Inexpensive to Moderate

Wine and Other Related *Sagre* and *Feste*

| 2nd Sun in May | Fish Festival | Camogli |
| Sept | Sagra dell'Uva | Riomaggiore |

E PER SAPERE DI PIÙ – ADDITIONAL INFORMATION

Assessorato al Turismo
via Fieschi 15
16121 Genoa
tel: 010/54852632

Agriturist Comitato Regionale
via T. Ivrea 11/10
16129 Genoa
tel: 010/5531878

Ente Provinciale del Turismo
Viale Mazzini 47
19100 La Spezia
tel: 0187/36000

THE NORTH-WEST

LOMBARDY

I Vini: THE WINES OF LOMBARDY   97

La Gastronomia   100

Le Strade dei Vini: THE WINE ROADS OF LOMBARDY
    The Oltrepò Pavese   100
    The Mountain Vineyards of the Valtellina   108
    Brescia Hills and the Lombardy Lakes   111

Le Sagre: WINE AND OTHER RELATED FESTIVALS   114

Additional Information   115

Salame, bread, and wine at the Castello di Luzzano.

Lombardy is Italy's richest and most sophisticated region. Milan, its capital city, is the national hub of finance, industry, and commerce, and a great city of art and culture. From the magnificent spiny gothic Duomo, third largest church in the world, to the Teatro La Scala, probably the world's most famous opera house; from the catwalks of Italy's greatest fashion empires to the exclusive Via Monte Napoleone: this is a city that exudes wealth, self-confidence, prosperity.

As befits a great cosmopolitan metropolis, Milan is international in a way that no other Italian city is (not even Rome). Restaurants here, for example, are more likely to offer French cuisine, *nouvelle cuisine*, Chinese, Brazilian, or regional *cucina* from Emilia-Romagna, Apulia or Tuscany than the local specialities of Lombardy. And those foods that are widely available have become so well-known – *ossobuco, costelleta alla milanese* – that they no longer seem regional, but rather have become part of a national Italian cuisine. When it comes to wine, too, the Milanese are equally catholic in their tastes, as happy enjoying an *aperitivo* of *vino bianco* from Friuli, a bottle of 'super-*vino da tavola*' from Tuscany (where many of the most famous estates are Milanese owned), a Californian Cabernet or a *flûte* of French Champagne. While, in most other parts of Italy, parochial attitudes remain to such a degree that it may be difficult to find wines from outside that particular locality, in Milan the opposite may be the case: local wines attract less interest than more fashionable wines from elsewhere.

Lombardy is not considered a wine region of great national importance. Few visitors will have come to the region solely in quest of local wines and foods. But that said, this is a region of great surprises, offering a range of overlooked wines that deserve to be better known. We make only the briefest dip into the wine regions of Lombardy as more obvious commitments take us elsewhere, but these zones offer scope for considerable further exploration and most enjoyable wine touring.

ORIENTATION

Lombardy is the fourth largest region in Italy, and consists of 9 provinces: Milan, Pavia, Cremona, Mantua, Sondrio, Bergamo, Como, Brescia, and Varese. Milan, the capital, has 2 airports: Linate (7 km east) and Malpensa (50 km north-west); and is well served by both extensive train and road networks. Bormio, Caspoggio, Chiesa and Santa Caterina are popular winter sports resorts in the Valtellina. Pavia, with its magnificent Certosa, is a good base for exploration of the Oltrepò Pavese. The Brescia hills and lake country can be explored from resorts on the Lombardy side of Lake Garda, or from bases on Lakes Como or Iseo.

Map Touring Club Italiano 1: 200 000 Lombardia.

I VINI: GLOSSARY TO THE WINES OF LOMBARDY

Wines of *Denominazione di Origine Controllata (DOC)*

Botticino DOC Wine commune just west of Brescia producing dry red wine from Schiava, Barbera, Marzemino. Minimum alcohol 12 degrees.

Capriano del Colle DOC *Denominazione* for both red (from Sangiovese, Marzemino, and Barbera), and white (from Trebbiano) wines from vineyards of Capriano del Colle, south of Brescia.

Cellatica DOC Another dry red wine from vineyards near Brescia, produced from Schiava, Barbera, and Marzemino. Minimum alcohol 11 degrees.

Colli Morenici Mantovani del Garda DOC Delimited wine zone extending over hills between Mantua and Lake Garda producing a full range of wines mainly for local consumption: red and *rosato* are produced from Rondinella,

Molinara, and Negrara and must reach 11 degrees; white is produced mainly from Garganega and Trebbiano; minimum alcohol 10.5 degrees.

Franciacorta DOC Important wine zone at southern tip of Lake Iseo, centred on wine town of Cortefranca, noted for its white and sparkling wines from Pinot Bianco (mainly) with some Pinot Grigio, Pinot Nero, and Chardonnay, and red wines from Cabernet Franc, Barbera, Nebbiolo, and Merlot.

Lambrusco Mantovano DOC Red wine from Lambrusco grapes grown in hill vineyards of Mantua.

Lugana DOC Dry white wine from vineyards south of Lake Garda mainly in Lombardy but overlapping also with Verona's vineyards of Bianco di Custoza. Produced from the Trebbiano di Lugana; minimum alcohol 11.5 degrees.

Oltrepò Pavese DOC *Denominazione* for broad range of 15 different wines from vineyards on the opposite (southern) flank of the Po river below Pavia. Source of basic red and *rosato* from blends of grapes; varietal reds (Bonarda, Barbera, Pinot Nero); special reds from smaller delimited zones (Buttafuoco, Barbacarlo, Sangue di Giuda); varietal whites (Cortese, Moscato, Riesling Italico, Riesling Renano).

Oltrepò Pavese Spumante Both DOC and non-DOC sparkling wines produced in this delimited vineyard mainly from Pinot Nero, Pinot Grigio, and Pinot Bianco by the laborious *metodo champenois* as well as by the Charmat or tank method. The trademark 'Classese' indicates wines produced from 85% Pinot Nero, 15% Pinot Grigio, by the *metodo champenois*, and aged for a minimum of at least 2 years.

Riviera del Garda Bresciano DOC Red and *rosato* wines (the latter is usually labelled as *chiaretto*) from vineyards between Brescia and Lake Garda made from Gropello, Barbera, Marzemino, and Sangiovese. Minimum alcohol 11 degrees; 12 degrees for Superiore.

San Colombano al Lambro DOC Local red wine from vineyards south-east of Milan around wine commune of San Colombano.

Tocai di San Martino della Battaglia DOC White wine from Tocai Friulano grown on vineyards south of Lake Garda around wine commune of San Martino della Battaglia. Minimum alcohol 12 degrees.

METODO CHAMPENOIS

The classic Champagne method of secondary fermentation in the bottle (as opposed to secondary fermentation in large stainless steel autoclaves as used in the Charmat or tank method) is still considered the finest method of turning still wines into sparkling. It is also the most costly and labour intensive. By this method, a blend of still wines from selected grapes (usually Pinot Nero, Pinot Bianco, Pinot Grigio, and/or Chardonnay) is bottled together with the addition of a small amount of sugar and yeast. The yeasts feed on the natural sugars, causing a slow secondary fermentation and producing, as a by-product, carbon dioxide which dissolves to give the wine its natural sparkle. However, in the process, the dead yeast cells and other solid matter remain and must be removed to render the wine crystal clear. This involves a skilled process of manual manipulation whereby the fine, sludgy sediment is gradually nudged into the neck of the bottle from where it can be expelled. This is usually achieved by placing the necks of the bottles in a freezing solution, thus trapping the sediment in the frozen wine; the bottles are opened, given a sharp tap, and the pressure expels the dirty block of ice. Then the bottles are topped up, in some cases with a mixture of old reserve wine and sugar, or in the case of bone-dry *pas dosé*, simply with more of the wine itself. Then they are recorked, wired down with a muzzle, and dressed in the elegant foil neck capsule and label. Such classic Italian sparkling wines are fine artisan-made products, and can compete with the very best in the world.

Valcalepio DOC *Denominazione* for both red and white wines from hill vineyards west of Bergamo. The red is a noteworthy Merlot-Cabernet blend, while the white, less widely encountered, is produced from Pinot Bianco and Pinot Grigio. Red Valcalepio requires minimum alcohol of 12 degrees and minimum 2 years' ageing in wood.

Valtellina DOC The basic *denominazione* for wines from mountainous vineyards in the province of Sondrio, made primarily from the Nebbiolo grape. Minimum alcohol 11 degrees; 1 year minimum ageing, 2 years for wines labelled Superiore. Some wines may be entitled to more specific sub-*denominazioni*: Grumello, Inferno, Sassella, and Valgella,

THE NORTH-WEST

terms that refer to historic *cru* zones. Wine made from semi-dried grapes (in a similar fashion to Amarone della Valpolicella) which reaches 14.5 degrees may be called Sfursat or Sforzato.

LA GASTRONOMIA: FOODS OF LOMBARDY

Lombardy is considered primarily an industrial region today, but outside the major cities the country remains wide, fertile, and varied. As such, it generously supplies the finest quality produce and products to the cities to feed appetites stoked up by strenuous efforts on the factory floors and in directors' boardrooms alike. However, Lombardy, unlike most other regions of Italy, does not live solely for and by its stomach. As always, food is important, but, one senses, primarily as a means, not as an end in itself. Here, the most serious concerns of the day are not what is for dinner, but rather how much money can we make.

Lombardy is more cosmopolitan and international than any other region of Italy, and this is reflected in the cities, at least, where international *haute cuisine* may compete with Italian *cucina creativa* (nowhere else in the country, I conjecture, could they get away with the *nouvelle cuisine* con), or even with American-style fast food. But in the country, fortunately, true home-cooked and local foods remain and reflect the variety of a region that ranges from the flat rice paddies of the Po to the snow-covered mountains of the Valtellina, from beautiful rolling lake country to the rugged hill vineyards south of Pavia. See page 101.

THE OLTREPÒ PAVESE

In Brief: The Oltrepò Pavese, Lombardy's most important wine zone, is less than an hour's drive south of Milan. Pavia lies just to the north of the zone, and, with its splendid Certosa, is one of the region's major attractions. The Consorzio is currently devising a signposted *Strada del Vino* to connect the disparate wine communes of the Oltrepò Pavese.

The word Oltrepò indicates that this zone lies on the opposite bank of the Po, for that formidable river has always served as a watershed of sorts, a

PIATTI TIPICI:
REGIONAL SPECIALITIES

Bresaola Air-dried fillet of beef from the Valtellina. Served raw in razor thin slices like *prosciutto crudo*.

Violini Similar air-dried goat's meat.

Pizzocheri The famous 'black pasta' of the Valtellina – homemade buckwheat noodles cooked with cabbage, potatoes, cheese, and garlic.

Zuppa pavese Meat broth, served with a poached egg floating on a round of fried bread.

Risotto alla milanese Arborio rice cooked in stock and flavoured with orange saffron. **Risotto alla certosina** Risotto made with freshwater fish and crayfish. **Risotto alla primavera** Risotto made simply with fresh spring vegetables.

Ossobuco Classic regional speciality: shin of veal (on the marrowbone) cooked slowly with wine until creamy and tender, and served with *gremolata* (grating of lemon peel, garlic, and parsley). The marrow itself is the best bit.

Costelleta alla milanese Ubiquitous veal cutlet, breaded and deep-fried.

Bollito misto Mixed trolley of boiled meats, usually served with famous fruit mustard of Cremona.

Polenta Cornmeal mush, staple of the north. **Polenta e osei** Polenta served with roasted small birds. **Polenta pasticciata** Polenta layered with cheese and butter and oven-baked.

Panettone The raisin-studded brioche-type Christmas cake of Milan.

Cheeses: *Gorgonzola* Creamy green-blue cheese made near Milan. *Mascarpone* Soft, creamy cheese to be eaten fresh, like very thick cream. *Taleggio* Strong, rind-ripened mountain cheese from Valsassina. *Grana padana* Lombardy's version of *parmigiano reggiano*, to be eaten both fresh and grated. *Formaggi di montagna* Rustic local mountain cheeses from alpine zones, often made from sheep's or goat's milk.

THE NORTH-WEST

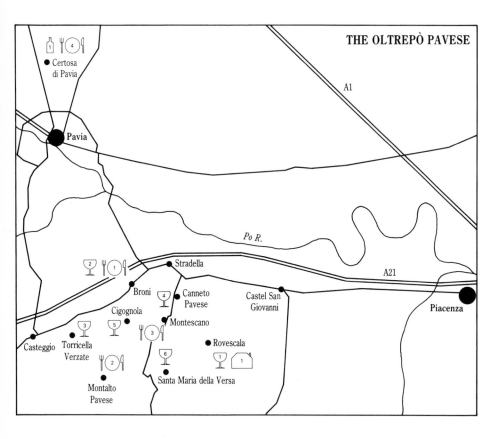

frontier delineating territories to be captured or recaptured. Indeed, this tiny triangular Lombardy wine zone lies like an isolated buffer between Piedmont to the west and Emilia-Romagna to the east, separated from Liguria by the Apennines. Its strategic location along the ancient Roman Via Emilia meant that it was much disputed over the centuries, and today virtually every hilltop is crowned with severe military castles which in the course of time have been transformed into country villas.

If any wines could be called the local tipple of the cosmopolitan Milanese, those of the Oltrepò Pavese could stake that claim. In truth, they are much loved locally, not just by citizens of northern Italy's greatest city, but also by those who live in other nearby urban areas such as Cremona and Parma. As a result, most of the considerable range of wines produced here is rarely encountered far from the zone of production, simply because the wines always find an eager and appreciative local market. The exceptions are the outstanding sparkling wines, from the *cantina sociale* of Santa Maria della Versa and other producers, which are widely distributed both nationally and internationally.

Therefore, the best way to gain a more intimate acquaintance with such distinctive but little-known wines as Buttafuoco, Barbacarlo and Sangue di Giuda, or with the sound varietals such as Bonarda, Barbera, Pinot, Riesling, Cortese, and Moscato, is to come to the zone and discover them for yourself.

The vineyards extend over 42 wine communes, but certain communes obviously have their own vinous specialities. Rovescala for example (located south of Castel San Giovanni) is most famous as the classic zone for Bonarda, one of the Oltrepò's most distinctive and important grapes (known elsewhere as Croatina), as well as for fine homemade *salame* and *coppe*, air-dried sausages that go well with this dense, slightly bitter wine. The commune's vineyards extend up to the former frontier between Lombardy and Emilia-Romagna, whose adjoining vineyards are known as the Colli Piacentini. Indeed, one of the zone's largest producers, the Castello di Luzzano, is located precisely along the Via Emilia (the castle itself was once the customs house). Thus, the estate's vineyards to the west of this historic byway are located in the Oltrepò Pavese DOC zone and produce notable Bonarda and Barbera, while those to the east are in the Emilian wine zone of the Colli Piacentini and produce specialities such as Gutturnio and Malvasia.

Santa Maria della Versa, south of Rovescala, has become the centre of the Oltrepò wine industry due to the prominence of its co-operative winery, the Cantina Sociale di Santa Maria della Versa. Founded in 1905, and with some 750 wine growing members, today it is one of the most important and highly respected co-operatives in the country, and rightly considered a source of considerable pride for the entire zone. It is most famous of all for its La Versa Brut sparkling wines, produced, since 1950, by the laborious *metodo champenois* secondary fermentation in the bottle. So important and successful is this wine that most of the vineyards surrounding Santa Maria della Versa are planted with both Pinot Nero (one of the classic grapes of Champagne) and Pinot Bianco, while a full range of both white and red table wines, and other sparkling wines, is also produced.

The vineyards meander further to the south through scores of other charming wine towns. Montalto Pavese affords notable views looking back to the valley of the Po and (on a clear day) the Alps to the north. Casteggio is another historic centre with an ancient vinous pedigree: fossilized vines have been found in this former Ligurian settlement that was later occupied by Hannibal. Canneto Pavese (located just below Stradella) is the famous source of two colourfully-named wines of the zone: Buttafuoco and Sangue di Giuda. The former (the name means 'sparks of fire'), produced from Barbera and Croatina, is an intense, full-bodied wine much enjoyed (like most reds locally) in a frothy *frizzante* version. Sangue di Giuda (Judas' blood) is also semi-sparkling, but this red wine also usually retains a certain residual sweetness.

The Oltrepò Pavese is a prolific wine zone, one whose potential for quality is immense and still not fully tapped or appreciated. It is also an area of quiet, totally unspoiled charm. As such, it deserves further exploration.

COLTURA BIOLOGICA

In Italy, there is an abiding and essential belief that natural foods are best so it is not surprising to find that a number of estates are run organically, utilizing the so-called *coltura biologica*. This means, for example, that all chemicals for pest control are eschewed. In some cases beneficial insects that eat harmful parasites are actually introduced into the vineyard when necessary. Chemical weedkillers are anathema, too, so the clearance of unwanted growth is achieved by manual labour. Natural fertilizers in the form of horse or cow manure are applied instead of chemical ones, while in some cases grass or beans are planted between the vines, then ploughed back in to nourish the soil.

In the *cantina* such an approach necessitates the minimum of intervention. Healthy grapes, carefully selected in the vineyard, which arrive in perfect shape after only the briefest periods, do not require excessive or heavy-handed use of sulphur. Stabilization is achieved not through the use of chemicals, but usually by mechanical means such as filtration. And if a little natural sediment should remain in the bottle, then so what?

'Organic wines' may sound rather cranky and off-beat, and admittedly not all are necessarily fine intrinsically. But in Italy, such wines are evidence of a preoccupation – indeed sometimes an obsession – with the genuine, the natural, the unadulterated. As such, they are well worth seeking and enjoying.

Degustazione: Stop to Taste; Stop to Buy

1

AZIENDA AGRARIA M. E G. FUGAZZA
CASTELLO DI LUZZANO
LOC. LUZZANO
27040 ROVESCALA PV
TEL: 0523/863277

WINES PRODUCED: Oltrepò Pavese
DOC: Barbera, Bonarda; Colli
Piacentini DOC: Gutturnio,
Malvasia; Barbera di Ziano;
Bonarda di Ziano; Romito anno 1°
red, Romito anno 1° white.
VISITS: daily, by appointment.
Maria Giulia and Giovanella
Fugazza have an estate of some 60
hectares straddling both the
Lombardy vineyards of Oltrepò
Pavese and the adjacent Emilian
vineyards of the Colli Piacentini.
The estate is run entirely on *coltura
biologica* lines and their philosophy
is to interfere as little as possible
throughout the grape growing cycle
and wine making process. Only the
best grapes are kept for the estate
wines which are at once faultlessly
made, yet genuine and full of
character.

2

AZIENDA AGRICOLA 'BARBACARLO' DA
LINO MAGA
VIA MAZZINI 50
27043 BRONI PV
TEL: 0385/51212

WINES PRODUCED: Oltrepò Pavese
DOC: Barbacarlo, Ronchetto,
Montebuono.
VISITS: visitors most welcome daily;
telephone call in advance advisable.
Famous estate producing 3
distinguished red wines from
different individual hill vineyards
planted primarily with Croatina,
Uva Rara, Ughetta, and Barbera.
Barbacarlo is the most famous but
the other 2 are also serious,
traditional red wines. Montebuono,
moreover, has the cachet of being
the wine that Napoleon enjoyed
after the battle of Marengo.
Some English spoken.

3

AZIENDA AGRICOLA MONSUPELLO DI
CARLO BOATTI
VIA SAN LAZZARO 5
27050 TORRICELLA VERZATE PV
TEL: 0383/86043

WINES PRODUCED: Monsupello
Rosso Oltrepò Pavese DOC,
Monsupello Bianco (Riesling),
Monsupello Spumante Brut
Classese; I Germogli Bianchi
(Pinot), Rosa (Pinot);
Bonarda *'vivace'*.
VISITS: daily, by appointment.
VIDE estate established in 1893
producing a range of excellent
medal-winning wines.
A little English spoken.

THE NORTH-WEST

4 AZIENDA AGRICOLA BRUNO VERDI
FRAZ. VERGOMBERRA 5
27044 CANNETO PAVESE PV
TEL: 0385/88023

WINES PRODUCED: Oltrepò Pavese
DOC: Sangue di Giuda; Riesling
Renano; Riesling Italico; Brut.
VISITS: daily, by appointment.
Direct sales weekdays 9–12h;
15–19h.

---

5 LUIGI VALENTI S.N.C.
VIGNETI DI MONTERUCCO
VALLE CIMA 22
27040 CIGOGNOLA PV
TEL: 0385/85151

WINES PRODUCED: Pinot; Riesling;
Buttafuoco; Sangue di Giuda; Rosso

Oltrepò Pavese; Classese.
VISITS: daily, working hours.
Appointment preferred.
Traditional production of a range of
wines of the Oltrepò.
Some English and French spoken.

---

6 LA VERSA
CANTINA SOCIALE DI SANTA MARIA
DELLA VERSA SPA
VIA FRANCESCO CRISPI 13
27047 SANTA MARIA DELLA VERSA PV
TEL: 0385/79731

WINES PRODUCED: Pinot Grigio;
Riesling Italico; Pinot Chardonnay;
Barbera; Bonarda; Rosso Oltrepò
Pavese; Moscato; and range of
sparkling wines.

VISITS: daily, working hours.
Appointment for guided visit.
For serious wine lovers, and the
technically-minded, it is well worth
taking the time to make an
appointment to visit this
super-modern *cantina sociale* for it
demonstrates how, utilizing the
most modern technologies,
outstanding wines can be made on a
large scale.

Enoteca

1 ENOTECA REGIONALE DI CERTOSA DI
PAVIA
VIA DEL MONUMENTO 5
27100 CERTOSA DI PAVIA PV
TEL: 0382/925893

Open Easter–Sept.
Regional *Enoteca* displaying
extensive range of Lombardy wines.
Adjacent to Vecchio Mulino
restaurant.

Ristoranti

1
RISTORANTE LIROS
QUARTIERE PIAVE 104
27040 BRONI PV
TEL: 0385/51007

Restaurant with rooms: specialities include *salami misti, pesce, filleti al pepe verde*, and a good selection of local wines. Music Sat and Sun.
Moderate

2
TRATTORIA CENTRO
PIAZZA VITTORIO VENETO 15
27040 MONTALTO PAVESE PV
TEL: 0383/870119

Closed Wed.
Typical Oltrepò *trattoria* serving

good local foods: homecured *salami* and *coppe*, homemade *pasta, brasato, coniglio, trippa, crostata*. Wines are exclusively from Montalto Pavese.
Inexpensive to Moderate

3
RISTORANTE 'AL PINO'
VIA PIANAZZA 11
27040 MONTESCANO PV
TEL: 0385/60479

Closed Tue eve, Wed. Reservations advised.
Outstanding restaurant with 2 suites with panoramic vineyard

views: traditional cuisine 'revisited': *insalata di lepre, torta di funghi, risotto con creste e spugnole, filetto al Barbacarlo*. Visits to wine *cantine* can be arranged.
English, French spoken.
Expensive

4
VECCHIO MULINO
VIA DEL MONUMENTO 5
27100 CERTOSA DI PAVIA PV
TEL: 0382/925894

Closed Sun eve, Mon.
Famous restaurant near the splendid Certosa di Pavia serving

genuine local foods of the zone: *coniglio in terrina, gnocchi, faraona, anatra all'aceto balsamico*, and an extensive selection of wines from the Oltrepò Pavese.
Moderate to Expensive

THE NORTH-WEST

Agriturismo

1 CASTELLO DI LUZZANO
(Address as above)

The Fugazza sisters have 3 former *mezzadria* apartments for rent on their lovely wine estate located along the old Via Emilia.

THE MOUNTAIN VINEYARDS OF THE VALTELLINA

In Brief: The Valtellina is located along the Adda valley that runs broadly east from the northern tip of Lake Como to the alpine resort of Bormio leading up to the Stelvio Pass. As such, it is a rugged mountainous zone which has only in recent years been opened up by the development of winter and summer sports venues. As a wine region, it is rare and undiscovered, and the wines are serious and worth seeking. There is a signposted *Strada dei Vini*, created by one of the zone's best-known and largest producers, Casa Vinicola Nino Negri.

The riviera road that follows Lake Como north from Lecco is dramatic, the peaks of the pre-Alps and jagged Alps reflected in the narrow waters. At the lake's tip, the broader valley of the Adda carves its way through the mountains, itself fed by smaller valleys running off to the north and south. One such valley, the Valmalenco, runs down into Sondrio, the region's capital and centre of a brief but remarkable wine zone.

This is a true mountain vineyard, planted at 600–800 metres above sea level and higher. In this rarefied atmosphere, the Chiavennasca grapes (the local name for a variety of Nebbiolo, great grape of Piedmont) bask in alpine sun that can be surprisingly fierce and direct, and thus ripen to produce considerable red wines which, though lacking in dense colour, are surprisingly full-bodied and finely perfumed.

There are 2 separate zones of production, the first and larger zone of Valtellina, and the smaller, more select delimited classic heartland of the Valtellina Superiore, whose wines are produced to much more stringent disciplines. Within the Valtellina Superiore, there are furthermore 4 separate historic sub-zones: Sassella (between Castione and Sondrio), Grumello (between Sondrio and Montagna), Inferno (between Poggiridente and Trevisio), and Valgella (between Chiuro and Teglio). The Nino Negri *Strada dei*

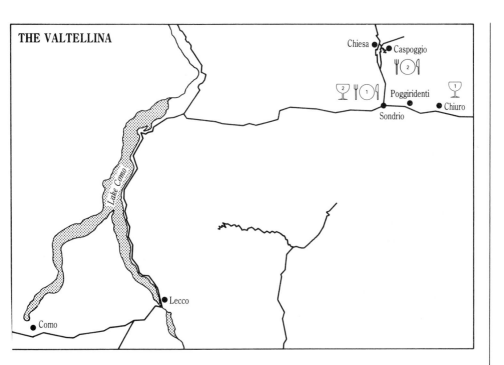

Vini broadly follows the SS38 from the point where the Sassella vineyards begin to the east until the finish of the Valgella zone, with 4 short circuits into the wine hills.

One other wine should be mentioned, Sfursat (or Sforzato), a wholly unique red table wine, made, like Recioto Amarone della Valpolicella, from grapes that have been laid out to dry on straw mats prior to pressing. This is an immense, rich, raisiny wine that is a real winter warmer, and a particularly fine accompaniment to hearty stews or game.

Such a wine might well be needed in this still isolated and severe mountain region. Yet the visitor in search of good country wines, robust but simple mountain foods – such as the rib-sticking and hearty buckwheat *pizzocheri*, or air-cured meats and cheeses – and stupendous alpine scenery winter and summer will not be disappointed.

Degustazione: Stop to Taste; Stop to Buy

1 CASA VINICOLA NINO NEGRI
VIA GHIBELLINI 3
23030 CHIURO SO
TEL: 0342/482521

WINES PRODUCED: Valtellina, Valtellina Superiore Inferno 'Botti d'Oro', Valtellina Superiore Sassella 'Botti d'Oro', Valtellina Superiore Grumello, Valtellina Superiore *cru* Fracia, Valtellina Superiore Riserva 'Nino Negri', Sfursat; Nino Negri Brut *metodo champenois*; Nino Negri Chiavennasca Bianco.

VISITS: Mon–Fri 8–12h; 14–18h. Appointment necessary for guided visits and wine tasting as well as for visits to the *cru* Fracia estate. Probably the zone's best-known and largest private winery is today part of the large Swiss-owned Gruppo Italiano Vini and as such serves as an ambassador for the wine zone as a whole. The winery, founded in 1897, is located in the 15th-century Castello di Quadrio in the heart of the old Chiuro village. English spoken.

---

2 ENOLOGICA VALTELLINESE SPA
VIA PIAZZA 29
23100 SONDRIO
TEL: 0342/212048

WINES PRODUCED: Valtellina Superiore, Valtellina Superiore Castel Grumello, Valtellina Superiore Paradiso Riserva,

Valtellina Sforzato.
VISITS: daily, working hours. Appointment advisable. Superlative co-operative winery producing a full range of wines from this rare mountain vineyard. English spoken.

Ristoranti

1 ALBERGO-RISTORANTE DELLA POSTA
PIAZZA GARIBALDI 19
23100 SONDRIO
TEL: 0342/211222

Closed Sun.
The oldest hotel in the valley is a historic venue which can boast among guests not only archdukes and emperors but Giuseppe

Garibaldi himself: the classic restaurant 'Da Sozzani' serves well-prepared and genuine foods of the zone, including *insalata di bresaola, polenta, funghi, capriolo al vino*, and a good selection of mountain cheeses as well as wines.
Moderate

2 RISTORANTE 'BAITA AL DOSS'
23020 CASPOGGIO SO
TEL: 0342/451352

Closed Mon out of winter season.
Located above this modest but
charming ski resort, a comfortable
winter inn serving the specialities
of the zone: *bresaola*, *pizzocheri*,
lepre con polenta and the wines of
the Valtellina.
Moderate

BRESCIA HILLS AND
THE LOMBARDY LAKES

In Brief: This broad, rather rambling hinterland between Lakes Garda,
Iseo, and Como is not a single wine zone, but throughout it notable wines
are produced that should not be overlooked. Visitors to any of the resorts
of the Lombardy lakes may therefore wish to strike out into the wine
hills. The western hills of Lake Garda yield plentiful wines that resemble
those of Bardolino, especially the delightful pink Chiaretto. Lugana is one
of the zone's best white wines, delicious with grilled lake fish.

Brescia, Lombardy's second industrial city, has some important Roman
ruins as well as Venetian *palazzi*. The gentle wine country of the Franciacorta, which extends mainly between Cortefranca and the southern flank
of Lake Iseo, is charming. Bergamo, especially the old, higher town, is a
fascinating and atmospheric medieval city.

Degustazione: Stop to Taste; Stop to Buy

1 AZIENDE AGRICOLE DEL LUGANA
CANTINA MARANGONA
25010 POZZOLENGO BS
TEL: 030/919379

WINES PRODUCED: Lugana, Lugana
Spumante Brut; Rovizzo (*vino
frizzante*); Primello (*vino novello*);
Sermano (*rosso da tavola*).

VISITS: daily, working hours.
Appointment necessary for groups.
Located at the base of the Sirmione
promontory on the southern flanks
of Lake Garda, this large estate
produces a good range especially of
white wines utilizing modern
technology.
English, some French spoken.

THE NORTH-WEST

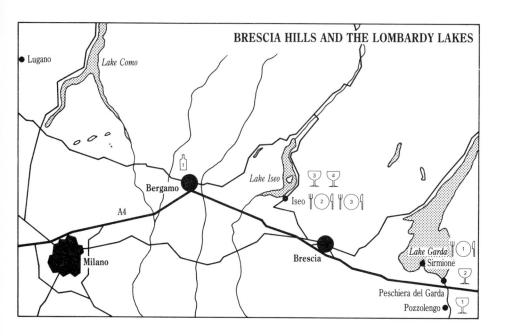

BRESCIA HILLS AND THE LOMBARDY LAKES

2

AZIENDA AGRICOLA ZENATO
VIA S. BENEDETTO 8
37010 SAN BENEDETTO DI LUGANA VR
TEL: 045/7550300

WINES PRODUCED: Lugana DOC;
Bianco di Custoza DOC; Bardolino
DOC; Valpolicella Classico DOC;
Amarone della Valpolicella; Soave
DOC; Chardonnay di Verona.

VISITS: daily, by appointment.
Lake Garda's vineyards extend over
the regions of both Lombardy and
Veneto: Zenato's winery, located
near Peschiera di Garda, virtually
straddles the border and produces a
highly-regarded range of these
delightful wines.
English spoken.

3

GUIDO BERLUCCHI & C. S.R.L.
PIAZZA DURANTI 4
25040 BORGONATO DI CORTEFRANCA
  BS
TEL: 030/984381

WINES PRODUCED: Cuveé Imperiale
Berlucchi Brut, Max Rosé, Pas

Dosé; Franciacorta Rosso e Bianco.
VISITS: daily 9–12h. Telephone
before coming.
Some of Italy's finest sparkling
wines are produced in Lombardy.
Visit the firm of Berlucchi to see
how they are made. Berlucchi also

produces a range of fine table wines, utilizing, for example, finishing in *barrique*.
English, French spoken.

---

4 AZIENDA AGRICOLA CA' DEL BOSCO
VIA CASE SPARSE 11
25030 ERBUSCO BS
TEL: 030/7267196

WINES PRODUCED: Franciacorta DOC: Bianco, Rosso; Chardonnay; Pinero; 'Maurizio Zanella'; Spumante Brut; Spumante Dosage Zero; Spumante Rosé; Spumante Crémant; Spumante Millesimato.
VISITS: daily 9–11h; 15–17h. Appointment essential.
Though a relatively new winery, Ca' del Bosco has already achieved worldwide recognition for its outstanding range of still and sparkling wines. At the forefront of the Italian *avanguardia*, the estate utilizes the utmost modern technology and takes on – sometimes beats – the French at their own game. The wines, despite their high prices, are always in great demand and are thus usually earmarked for customers in advance, so may not be available for purchase.
English spoken.

Enoteca

1 ENOTECA AL PORTICO
VIA ROMA 13
PONTE SAN PIETRO BG
TEL: 035/614257

Closed Sun eve, Mon.
Exceptional bar/*enoteca* in this small town on the Brembo river 7 km from Bergamo, serving a vast range of both Italian and French wines by the bottle or glass together with simple drinking snacks.
A little English spoken.

Ristoranti

1 TRATTORIA VECCHIA LUGANA
SS43
25019 SIRMIONE BS
TEL: 030/919012

Atmospheric old favourite: an elegant waterfront restaurant with outdoor terrace serving grilled lake fish. Located just outside this popular town famous for its Grotte di Catullo.
Moderate to Expensive

THE NORTH-WEST

2 RISTORANTE DA BERTOLI
VIA ISEO 29
25030 ERBUSCO BS
TEL: 030/7241017

Closed Mon.
Restaurant located out of town in the heart of the Franciacorta towards the lake, in a modern but classic setting: specialities include *risotti*, homemade *pappardelle*, *manzo all'olio* and a vast selection of wines, particularly from the Franciacorta.
Some English, French, German spoken.
Moderate to Expensive

---

3 RISTORANTE LE MASCHERE
VICOLO DELLA PERGOLA 7
25049 ISEO BS
TEL: 030/9821542

Closed Sun eve, Mon.
Located in the historic centre of this charming lakeside town, serving both classic and innovative *cucina: terrina di tinca tartufata, scaloppa di branzino al forno, petto di piccione coi funghi porcini, semifreddo di nocciole.*
Moderate to Expensive

Wine and Other Related *Sagre* and *Feste*

end Aug/early Sept	Rassegna dei Vini Oltrepò Pavese	Casteggio
2nd week of Sept	Fiera Millenaria	Mantua

E PER SAPERE DI PIÙ –
ADDITIONAL INFORMATION

Ufficio Turistico Regionale
via Marconi 1
20123 Milan
tel: 02/870016

Agriturist Comitato Regionale
Viale Isonzo 27
20135 Milan
tel: 02/5468387

Consorzio Vini DOC Oltrepò
   Pavese
Piazza San Francesco d'Assisi
27043 Broni
tel: 0385/51191

Consorzio Vini DOC Valtellina
via Valeriana
23100 Sondrio
tel: 0342/216433

Consorzio Vini DOC Bresciani
via Vittorio Emanuele II
25100 Brescia
tel: 030/45061

THE NORTH-EAST

Veneto
Trentino-Alto Adige
Friuli-Venezia Giulia

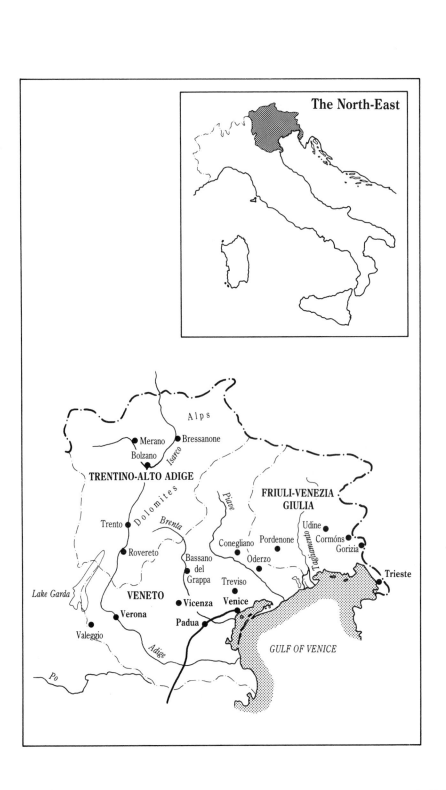

The North-East

Alps

Merano ● ● Bressanone
Bolzano ●
Isarco
TRENTINO-ALTO ADIGE

Dolomites

Piave

FRIULI-VENEZIA
GIULIA

Trento ● *Brenta*
Udine ●
Rovereto ● Conegliano ● ● Pordenone Cormóns ●
Bassano Oderzo ● *Tagliamento* Gorizia ●
del
Grappa ●
Treviso ●
Lake Garda Trieste ●
VENETO ● Vicenza Venice ●
Verona ●
Padua ●
Valeggio ●
Adige GULF OF VENICE

Po

VENETO

I Vini: THE WINES OF VENETO	120
La Gastronomia	123
Le Strade dei Vini: THE WINE ROADS OF VENETO	
The Vineyards of Verona	123
La Strada del Vino Bardolino	126
La Valpolicella: The Classic Heartland	136
Soave	151
La Strada del Vino Bianco di Custoza	156
La Marca Trevigiana: The Wine Hills of Treviso	159
La Strada del Vino Bianco	160
La Strada dei Vini del Piave	167
Colli Euganei: Villas, Hot Baths, and Wine	170
Le Sagre: WINE AND OTHER RELATED FESTIVALS	177
Additional Information	177

Villa Rizzardi, Negrar di Valpolicella.

The Venetian hinterland, the region known as the Veneto, extends in a broad arc over the north-eastern corner of the country. If today its capital city, Venice, stands apart, isolated on its lagoon and a historical (albeit beautiful and charming) anachronism, the Lion of St Mark still looks out benignly over the countryside it once dominated. Today the subtle influences of the Most Serene Republic of Venice – *La Serenissima* – remain: in municipal and religious architecture, splendid patrician villas, a style of cooking that is surprisingly simple and unostentatious, and in an overall

ORIENTATION

Veneto is made up of 7 provinces: Venice, Padua, Verona, Treviso, Vicenza, Rovigo, and Belluno. There are international airports at both Venice and Verona, and the region is well served by train, with a major west–east line linking Verona and Venice with Turin, Milan, or Trieste. The A4 *autostrada* extends across the region, skirting the bottom of Lake Garda to Verona, Vicenza, Padua, and Venice. This is a large region and, as elsewhere, for in-depth exploration of the wine country, the use of a car is essential.

Map Touring Club Italiano 1: 200 000 Veneto e Friuli-Venezia Giulia.

THE NORTH-EAST

feeling of well-fed contentment, even self-satisfaction, which extends from the shores of the Venetian lagoon to Lake Garda; from the broad flat valley of the Po way up to the snow-covered peaks of the Dolomites.

This, after all, is one of Italy's richest regions, and certainly one of her most important wine regions. Ranking fourth in overall production, no other region produces more wine entitled to *denominazione di origine controllata* status. The Veneto is the source of 3 of Italy's best-selling and most popular wines, Soave, Bardolino, and Valpolicella, as well as of vast amounts of simple table wines labelled varietally (Merlot del Veneto, Tocai del Veneto) and sold in two-litre screw-top bottles. Such bulk wines may represent the mainstay of the industry, yet this is also a region where wines of the highest quality are produced, handmade necessarily in minute quantities in traditional and *avanguardia* wineries alike.

Wine is produced throughout the region, but the two most important zones centre on Verona and Lake Garda, and on the eastern hills in the province of Treviso. A tour of wine regions can therefore be combined with holidays based in Venice or Verona, though some might opt to stay in any number of charming resorts on Lake Garda, or to hide out in delightful inland towns such as Bassano del Grappa and Asolo. The Colli Euganei, south of Padua, provides quiet unspoiled countryside, good local wines, and for those in need, thermal cures and hot baths.

I VINI: GLOSSARY TO THE WINES OF VENETO

Wines of *Denominazione di Origine Controllata (DOC)*

Bardolino DOC Red and pink *chiaretto* wines from terraced vineyards above Lake Garda produced from traditional Veronese blend of Corvina, Rondinella, Molinara, and Negrara. Classico zone above Bardolino itself produces the best wines. Minimum alcohol 10.5 degrees; wines that reach 11.5 degrees and which are aged for 1 year may be labelled Superiore. **Bardolino Novello DOC** Primeur wine vinified by carbonic maceration to be drunk within weeks or months of the *vendemmia*: fruity, fresh, grapey and one of the best examples of this increasingly popular type.

Bianco di Custoza DOC Light, dry white wine produced from vineyards west of Verona and south

LE VILLE VENETE

The boundaries of the Venetian Republic, until its fall in 1797, extended as far into the mainland as Bergamo (now in the region of Lombardy). Wealthy merchant patricians built splendid stately homes throughout the countryside of the Veneto, and today these gothic, Renaissance, baroque, and neo-classical villas remain as one of the most fantastic legacies from that bygone era. There are an estimated 3000 such stately homes, many of which are classified national monuments that can be visited. Those designed by the 16th-century architect Andrea Palladio are particularly noteworthy. Palladio came from Vicenza, and many of his finest examples are found in or around that gracious city, notably La Rotonda which was Thomas Jefferson's model for his Virginian mansion Monticello. Near Treviso, the Villa Barbaro at Maser is open to the public, and is famous for its cycle of frescoes by Veronese. The greatest concentration of villas, however, lies along the Brenta canal that connects Padua with Venice. Today, this rich procession of stately homes is best viewed by boat, *Il Burchiello*, which in season plies the canal daily either from Venice to Padua or vice versa. Further information from CIT or other travel offices.

of Lake Garda from Garganega, Trebbiano (di Soave and Toscano), Cortese, and Tocai Friulano. Minimum alcohol 11 degrees.

Breganze DOC Delimited vineyards north of Vicenza producing 6 different types of wine: Bianco (primarily Tocai), Rosso (primarily Merlot), Cabernet (both Franc and Sauvignon may be utilized), Pinot Bianco, Pinot Grigio, Pinot Nero, and Vespaiolo.

Colli Berici DOC Delimited vineyard extending over hills south of Vicenza producing 7 varietal wines: Cabernet (mainly Franc, though Sauvignon can be utilized), Garganega, Merlot, Pinot Bianco, Sauvignon, Tocai Italico, Tocai Rosso.

Colli Euganei DOC Delimited vineyard extending over volcanic hills south of Padua producing well-made white and red wines. DOC applies to 8 wines: Bianco (from Garganega, Serprina, and Tocai), Rosso (Merlot, Cabernet Franc, Cabernet Sauvignon, Barbera, and Raboso), Moscato (still, *frizzante*, and *spumante*), Pinot Bianco, Tocai Italico, Cabernet Franc, Cabernet Sauvignon, Merlot.

Gambellara DOC Delimited vineyards just east of Soave extending into the province of Vicenza: 3 wines made primarily from Garganega with a little Trebbiano di Soave: Bianco, Recioto di Gambellara (made, like Recioto di Soave, with semi-dried grapes in still, *frizzante*, and *spumante* versions), and Vin Santo (also made from semi-dried grapes, aged in wood for 2 years).

Lessini Durello DOC DOC zone for vineyards in Lessini hills next to Soave and Gambellara producing white wines from Durello grape.

Lison-Pramaggiore DOC Easternmost wine zone in Veneto, extending from east of the Piave river to the border with Friuli. DOC encompasses former zones of Tocai di Lison, and Cabernet and Merlot di Pramaggiore, and now applies to 12 varietal wines: Cabernet, Cabernet Franc, Cabernet Sauvignon, Chardonnay, Merlot, Pinot Bianco, Pinot Grigio, Refosco del Peduncolo Rosso, Riesling Italico, Sauvignon, Tocai Italico, Verduzzo.

Montello e Colli Asolani DOC Delimited vineyard extending over the Montello and Asolani hills south of Piave river and east and west of Montebelluno. DOC applies to 3 wines: Cabernet, Merlot, and Prosecco.

Piave DOC Vast wine zone centred on Treviso and extending along both sides of the Piave river valley, producing 8 varietal wines: Cabernet, Merlot, Pinot Bianco, Pinot Grigio, Pinot Nero, Raboso, Tocai Italico, and Verduzzo.

Prosecco di Conegliano-Valdobbiàdene DOC Still, *frizzante*, and *spumante* wines produced from the native Prosecco grape on delimited vineyards mainly between Conegliano and Valdobbiàdene. The wine may be dry, medium dry, or quite sweet, and is probably the Veneto's best sparkling wine. Wine from central classic zone near Valdobbiàdene may be labelled Cartizze.

Soave DOC Famous dry white wine from vineyards around medieval town of Soave located east of Verona. Produced from mainly Garganega, with Trebbiano di Soave, the best wines come from carefully tended hill vineyards in the Classico zone around Soave itself, not from high yielding vineyards on the plains. Minimum alcohol 10.5 degrees; 11.5 degrees for Superiore. **Recioto di Soave DOC** Sweet dessert wine made from semi-dried grapes: can be still or fully sparkling.

Valpolicella DOC Popular red wine produced from Corvina, Rondinella, Molinara, and Negrara from delimited vineyards mainly north of Verona. Classico zone extends over hills and valleys of Fumane, Negrar, Marano, Sant'Ambrogio, and San Pietro in Cariano. Minimum alcohol 11 degrees; 12 degrees and 1 year ageing for wines labelled Superiore. **Recioto della Valpolicella DOC** Sweet red dessert wine made from semi-dried grapes (see below). **Recioto della Valpolicella Amarone DOC** The dry version, known also simply as Amarone, is made from semi-dried grapes that are allowed to ferment out completely. Minimum alcohol 14 degrees for both Recioto and Amarone.

LA GASTRONOMIA: FOODS OF VENETO

The people of the Veneto are known as *I Polentoni* – the *polenta* eaters. Indeed, they are hugely proud of their fondness for this characteristic yellow cornmeal mush, the most distinctive feature of the cuisine of the Veneto. It is served with virtually every meal: freshly made and turned out on to a great wooden platter, cut into slices when cold, then grilled over an open fire, served *in umido* with meat and sauce, or deep-fried until crunchy.

Polenta reflects a cuisine that is mainly simple, unpretentious, and hearty. The products of sea, lake, river and land are all utilized in a cuisine that is ample, rarely fussy or over-elaborate, and always satisfying. *Risotti* in every variety – seafood, vegetable, or the sublimely simple Venetian *risi e bisi* – are the favourite start to the meal, not *pasta asciutta*. Seasonal produce is highly valued: asparagus from Bassano del Grappa, the favourite winter *radicchio* of Treviso, wild greens and mushrooms. See page 124.

THE VINEYARDS OF VERONA

Verona, one of the most beautiful cities in Italy, is the obvious centre for touring the wine regions that virtually surround it. An atmospheric mixture of ancient, medieval gothic, and Renaissance, its cobbled streets lead past the façades of still noble Venetian *palazzi* to fine old squares like the Piazza delle Erbe – the former Roman forum, today a lively everyday market

PIATTI TIPICI:
REGIONAL SPECIALITIES

Soppressa Large homemade *salame*, a typical drinking nibble of the region.

Risi e bisi Venetian *risotto* of *arborio* rice and fresh peas, usually quite soupy and liquid.

Bigoli Thick homemade spaghetti, usually served with simple sauce of anchovies, garlic and oil, with *ragù*, or with game or mushrooms in season.

Pasta e fagioli Hearty, thick bean and macaroni soup: warming winter fare.

Lasagne con fegatini Homemade egg noodles served with sauce made from chicken livers sautéed in wine.

Tortelli di zucca Pumpkin-filled ravioli-type pasta.

Baccalà alla vicentina Thick, creamy paste of dried salt cod beaten with onions, white wine, and milk. Speciality of Vicenza.

Stinco di vitello Enormous shin of veal, slow-cooked for hours with herbs and wine.

Fegato alla veneziana Thinly sliced calf's liver and onions.

Stracotto Beef cooked very slowly in thick sauce of wine, tomatoes, and herbs for hours until tender and falling apart.

Peperonata Characteristic *contorno* (side dish) of red peppers, tomatoes, onions, and aubergines stewed together in olive oil.

Pasta frolla Homemade shortbread cake from Verona.

Cheese *Asiago* Soft, mild mountain cheese from the Dolomites.

RECIOTO AND *AMARONE:* AGE-OLD CLASSICS

The production of these unique Veronese speciality wines harks back to Roman times or earlier, when the need to produce robust, intense, and immensely strong wines must have been a pressing one, since most wines were not bottled, and thus were particularly prone to spoilage. Recioto, the sweet version of the two, is also a reminder of the Roman predilection for sticky dessert wines, a style that may be somewhat out of favour with modern tastes, but which is none the less a classic.

The name Recioto comes from the word '*recce*', which in dialect means the ear (Italian, *orecchio*), signifying the top shoulders of the grape bunch, which have received greater exposure, and thus are richer in extract, concentration, and sugar. Once such selected grapes are harvested (before the main *vendemmia* and while their skins are still intact and the grapes are slightly higher in acid), they are carefully laid out on large wicker trays known as *tavoloni* (or else, these days, on smaller wooden pallets), then left to dry in great airy lofts for a period of some months, usually until some time after Christmas. This period is known as the *appassimento*, during which time the grapes slowly dry and concentrate their flavour and intensity, at the same time losing some 30–40% of their initial weight. Dry weather is essential during this period to ensure that the grapes do not rot. In fact, *Botrytis cinerea*, the beneficial noble rot so favoured for the production of wines such as Sauternes, may form on some grapes, adding further complexity and texture, though not all producers seek this.

Once the period of drying has been completed, the semi-dried *uve appassite* are very lightly crushed, and placed into small wooden fermentation vats. Winter temperatures are low, so the fermentation proceeds at an extremely slow but steady rate, for upwards of 50–60 days; gradually the concentrated sugars of the semi-dried grapes are either fermented out completely, resulting in dry Amarone (the name means 'the big bitter one'), an immense wine that can reach upwards of 17 degrees. Or else the fermentation stops, usually of its own accord, when the wine has reached a level of 13–14 degrees, leaving a residual sugar level of about 4–5 degrees to result in the classic sweet Recioto di Valpolicella or Recioto di Soave.

THE NORTH-EAST

spread out with typical canopied stalls selling fruit and vegetables – and the Piazza Bra, dominated by its famous Roman arena, best preserved of all Roman amphitheatres, and a magnificent summer setting for the annual open-air opera season.

The fertile hills to the north, north-east, north-west, and south-west have probably changed little over the centuries. Terraced vineyards are broken by lines of attentive cypress which loom like sentries on the hilltops, while elsewhere, the protruding turret of an ochre villa and the corduroy pattern of vineyards and roof tiles punctuate the pastoral vista. This is not a single wine region, but several, producing a variety of both plentiful and distinguished wines.

ENOTECA

Istituto Enologico Italiano SPA
Piazzetta Chiavica 2
37129 Verona
tel: 045/590366
Shop hours: 9–12h30; 15–17h. Closed Sun, Mon morning.

The Istituto Enologico Italiano, founded in 1968, is an important private organization which represents both domestically and internationally some 50 wine producers throughout Italy. Its principal objective is to promote and market Italian quality wines, and to this end it works closely with the estates that it represents through involvement in every stage of production.

The wine shop of the Istituto Enologico offers a full range of Italian wines, as well as olive oil, vinegar, and *pasta artigianale*. Tastings for groups or individuals may be arranged by appointment.

La Strada del Vino Bardolino

The Bardolino region, bordering the south-eastern corner of Lake Garda and extending into the rolling hills beyond, is about as perfect and idyllic a wine country as you will ever find. The vines thrive on grassy slopes and terraces, trained on old-fashioned *pergole* to spread dappled 'ceilings' of foliage, and creating grassy shaded corridors in which to stretch out after a long midday meal, or one glass of wine too many. By late summer, bunches of Corvina,

In Brief: The *Strada del Vino Bardolino* is a brief but lovely meander through wine country and charming lakeside towns. The circuit, which covers only the classic zone, can easily be completed in half a day or even a few hours, though most who are visiting the Lake Garda area will simply wish to join it at will, as a break from relaxing in towns such as Garda, Lazise, or Bardolino itself. Along the way there are some 40 *punti vendita* where the wines may be tasted and purchased, in a few cases along with tasty *spuntini*, or drinking nibbles. We include visiting details for a handful of producers whose wines we have enjoyed, but don't hesitate to stop at others wherever you see the distinctive sign, to discover your own favourite version of this most delightful wine. From Verona, the *Strada del Vino* can be joined at Cavalcaselle, near Peschiera.

Rondinella, Molinara, and Negrara grapes hang down invitingly, virtually begging to be picked. Fields of vines are interspersed with orchards of buff olive trees, while dark cypress punctuate the landscape. In the hills, rambling *aziende* and proud villas remind us that this is a long-established and prosperous land.

The wines produced from this region, Bardolino, Bardolino Classico (from the central heart of the district), and Chiaretto and Chiaretto Classico are totally in harmony with the region itself: mainly fresh, fragrant, uncomplicated wines that cry out to be drunk. Indeed, in its most vivid and freshest manifestation, that is as Bardolino Novello (Italy's first DOC *novello* wine), it is the very essence of wine at its most basic: grapey, fragrant, and quaffable. Chiaretto, a sort of pale red or dark pink version of Bardolino, is firm, full-bodied and delicious, a wine to be drunk in quantity, chilled, beside the lake with fried fish or *risotti*. Even the classic wines, vinified with grapes that have undergone greater selection and in some cases marketed under the name of a single vineyard, remain on the whole to be enjoyed not after periods of ageing, but above all while still fresh and fragrant, within the year, or at most within 2 or 3 years of production. That is not to say that they are one-dimensional: the best Bardolinos are indeed capable of complexity, but on the whole the wine's greatest asset is its delicacy, perfume, and vivacity.

As wine roads go, the *Strada del Vino Bardolino* is a most pleasant and welcome one. The distinctive road signs mark a well-trodden route around

THE NORTH-EAST

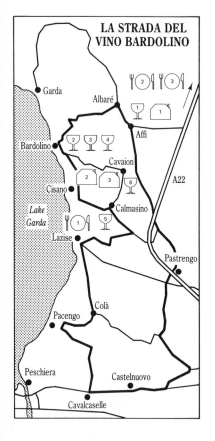

LA STRADA DEL VINO BARDOLINO

the lake and into the moraine hills, and producers are well used to thirsty wine tourists knocking on their back door for a bottle or two for a lakeside picnic, or a case to take back to their rented cottage or to the campsite. Indeed, as a quality wine, Bardolino is still an amazingly inexpensive bargain.

We join the *Strada del Vino* at Affi, for this is convenient for those heading into the wine country either as a diversion from the *autostrada* or as a day trip from Verona. However, those staying in the region or on the lake can pick it up elsewhere along the route.

Affi is typical of these inland villages of the classic zone, no more than a small hamlet clustered at the base of the great brooding prow of Monte Moscal, which rises dramatically above the lower-lying moraine hills, and leads the eye up towards the steeper mountain peaks of Monte Baldo and beyond. The Villa Poggi in Affi is a lovely 17th-century estate. The mulberry trees in the grounds are a reminder that here, and elsewhere in the region, the cultivation of silkworms was an important farm industry, especially in the 19th century.

From Affi, continue north, following the wine road signs as the road curves around the base of the cliff, then turn left to Bardolino itself, by way of Albaré. This short stretch of road is particularly stunning, for as it descends to the lake there are outstanding views of the cypress-lined road, the gentle rolling hills all covered with vines and olive trees, the little town of Bardolino itself, and beyond, of course, the wide, shimmering expanse of Lake Garda. Along this brief stretch, there are opportunities to taste and purchase both wine and olive oil (the signposted *Strada dell' Olio d'Oliva* parallels the wine road here). Just off this road there is the monastic complex of the Convento di San Colombano, which dates from 862. The monastery was itself a noted producer of wines in the Middle Ages, and the vineyards of these slopes are still highly prized today.

Bardolino is a lovely lakeside town, the hub of the wine industry and a major centre for tourists and visitors to the so-called Olive Riviera. Its romanesque church of San Severo, constructed in the 11th century, is considered the most important in the zone, while the church of San Zeno recalls the patron saint of the region.

The commune of Bardolino is the most important and largest producer of Bardolino Classico, and the surrounding vineyards of Calmasino, Costabella, San Colombano, and Val Sorda are all highly prized. The town, moreover, is the seat of the Consorzio for Bardolino, an organization that both safeguards standards of production and promotes the local wine. At the time of writing, the *Enoteca Permanente del Bardolino*, located on the waterfront, is in the process of being restored, but it is hoped that it has since reopened, for in the past it provided the best place to sample and/or purchase a wide range of wines from producers throughout the Bardolino zone, in an extremely pleasant and historic setting. As the eponymous centre for the wine industry, Bardolino hosts a lively 4-day wine festival (end of September), during which there is folk music, much wine drinking, sampling of local foods, arranged visits to producers along the wine road, and, as a grand finale, a fireworks display over the lake.

Those who go to Bardolino in the autumn may wish to take the '*Cura dell'Uva*', the 'grape cure', a programme whereby carefully controlled quantities of grapes are consumed 3 times a day as a means of cleansing and purging the body, as well as to absorb the rich concentration of minerals and other beneficial elements. Certain intestinal and other ailments, apparently, respond well to this treatment, administered under the supervision of doctors; but the grape cure can be taken simply as a means of promoting overall general health. For my part, though, I would still much prefer to partake of the grape in its traditional liquid form.

The signposted wine road extends back south, but an excursion must be made first north to the town of Garda itself, the busiest of all the little lakeside resorts. The rather sharp and dramatic hills that surround the town are riddled with ancient wine caves, hollowed out of the soft tufa, which have been used to conserve wine since at least the 8th century. Above all, though, come to Garda simply to stroll along the lakeside promenade, to watch the pleasure craft manoeuvring in and out of the busy little harbour, and enjoy a pizza or plate of grilled trout out of doors beside the lake, together with a cool bottle of Chiaretto Classico. Then continue along the wine route, back through Bardolino to little Cisano, a busy lakeside *frazione*. There is an interesting olive oil museum located on the main road which is worth a visit, while the Pieve di Santa Maria, with its strange hut-like façade, dates from the 12th century and is an important example of Verona's romanesque style

THE NORTH-EAST

SAN ZENO, PATRON SAINT OF VERONA

San Zeno, known as the smiling Moorish bishop of Verona, not only converted a large part of the population to Christianity in the 4th century AD, he also did much to further and encourage Veronese viticulture. At this time, as Imperial Rome was in its final decline, there was an economic and spiritual crisis not only here but throughout the Empire. San Zeno sought to encourage the dispirited people, and thus frequently travelled throughout the Veronese countryside, exhorting them to work by describing the fruits of their efforts as a symbol of their faith. Furthermore, he undertook minute studies, and detailed, described and illustrated the cultivation of the grape and the making of wine; he also encouraged the wine growers to keep their wines in the cellar where they would improve with age. After his death, the monastery he founded at San Colombano continued to cultivate the vine and produced wines of note throughout the Middle Ages. Today, an image of San Zeno is the trademark for the various Veronese DOC wine consortiums of Bardolino, Valpolicella, Soave, and Bianco di Custoza.

of architecture.

Next, follow the wine road signs inland to Calmasino, passing along the way a number of small private *aziende agricole*, including Colle dei Cipressi, sited magnificently below the distinctive line of cypress that dominates the hill. Below the church, the 17th-century Villa Belvedere, which overlooks the lake, has long been an important wine estate.

From Calmasino, descend to the lake once more and so arrive at the walled town of Lazise. Lazise was an important Venetian port, and the vernacular architecture attests to that bygone splendid age. Enter through the Porta del Leone, and visit the well-preserved 13th-century Scaligero castle, the old Dogana (customs house), and the military port. Or else simply come here for lunch or an ice cream, to sit by the water or at shaded tables in front of lovely pastel- and ochre-coloured restaurants and small hotels. The town has been noted for its wine since at least the 16th century.

The wine road passes next via the wine hamlet of Colà, to Pacengo, further down the coast, another typical small lakeside town, crowded in season or at weekends, its little harbour full of pleasure craft as well as small fishing boats. Like anywhere else along the shore, this is simply somewhere to lounge on whatever small patch of beach you can find, to watch the locals fishing for 'small fry' with enormous hand nets, or (what else?) to enjoy another cool, refreshing bottle of Bardolino or Chiaretto. Even the red wine, it should be noted, is often drunk well-chilled in summer, a quenching, light, and always refreshing tonic.

The wine circuit continues through Cavalcaselle and Castelnuovo, busy towns along the light-industrial urban sprawl out from Verona. These vineyards overlap with those of the Bianco di Custoza zone that extends further to the south. The *Strada del Vino Bardolino*, though, heads back north again into the moraine hills. For those with children, the Parco Zoo and Autosafari at Bussolengo may provide a welcome interlude from vineyard touring and wine tasting. Pastrengo is another well-known and fine wine town, located on somewhat higher ground, and noted for the production of both Bardolino and, in much smaller amounts, Bianco di Custoza, as well as a non-DOC wine known as Trebbianello di Pastrengo, drunk locally only. From Pastrengo, there are fine views down to the lake.

Degustazione: Stop to Taste; Stop to Buy

1 AZIENDA AGRICOLA F.LLI POGGI
VIA G. POGGI 7
37010 AFFI VR
TEL: 045/7235044

WINES PRODUCED: Bardolino Classico, Bardolino Chiaretto Classico; Bianco Valdadige; *olio d'oliva.*

VISITS: Mon–Sat morning 9–12h; 14–18h.
A good reliable source for well-made wines; located near the Villa Poggi and just off the A22 *autostrada.*
English spoken.

---

2 AZIENDA AGRICOLA LA ROCCA DI
OTTOLINI ATTILIO
VIA STRADA DI SEM 4
37011 BARDOLINO VR
TEL: 045/7210964

WINES PRODUCED: Bardolino Classico, Bardolino Chiaretto Classico; *vino bianco da tavola.*
VISITS: daily 9–12h; 15–19h.

Located off the hill road between Albaré and Bardolino, this small family producer makes sound quaffable wines that can be enjoyed by the bottle at shaded tables in the garden, served in season together with *spuntini* such as olives, *salami*, and bits of cheese.

THE NORTH-EAST

THE OLIVE RIVIERA

The gentle moraine hills that rise along the eastern edge of Lake Garda are conducive not only to the cultivation of the grape, but also, as is so often the case elsewhere, to that of its complementary crop, the olive.

This area is known as the *'Riviera degli Olivi'* – the Olive Riviera – in recognition not only of the large presence of olive trees and the excellent olive oil that they produce, but also of the mild Mediterranean climate found along these lovely shores. There is a *Strada dell'Olio d'Oliva* that at times parallels the *Strada del Vino Bardolino*. Olive oil producers, some of whom are also wine producers, offer their silky, green *'extra vergine'* oils for sale direct and they are among the finest in the country: thick, pungent, yet smooth, with that characteristic ever so slight hot-chilli prickle in the back of the mouth when new. Only the *extra vergine* oils of Tuscany surpass them in quality. At Cisano, the Oleificio Cisano del Garda has a small *'Museo dell'Olio'* which catalogues the history of olive oil making in the region, and has some old presses and grinding wheels on display. *Extra vergine* olive oil, *aceto balsamico*, and a good selection of local wines from a variety of properties are available for purchase.

Museo dell'Olio
Oleificio Cisano del Garda
37010 Cisano di Bardolino VR
tel: 045/7210356
Open: daily 8h30–12h30; 15–19h. Closed Sun afternoon.

---

3 AZIENDA AGRICOLA F.LLI GIRADELLI
VIA ZERBETTO 43
37011 BARDOLINO VR
TEL: 045/7211273

WINES PRODUCED: Bardolino Classico, Bardolino Chiaretto Classico, Bardolino Novello; *vino bianco da tavola*.
VISITS: daily 9–12h; 15–20h.

Located above Bardolino along the road to Albaré, the Giradelli family is noted both for medal-winning wines (the Chiaretto is outstanding) and for estate-bottled olive oil. The latter, however, quickly sells out to *conoscenti* who come to the farm direct to buy it in early winter.

4 AZIENDA AGRICOLA DEI CONTI
GUERRIERI RIZZARDI
PIAZZA PRINCIPE AMEDEO I
37011 BARDOLINO VR
TEL: 045/7210028

WINES PRODUCED: Bardolino
Classico, Bardolino Chiaretto
Classico, Bardolino *cru* Tacchetto;
Valpolicella Classico, Amarone
Classico; Soave Classico; Dògoli (dry
white wine produced from Moscato);
Castello Guerrieri.
VISITS: Mon–Fri 10–12h; 17–18h.
Sat 10–12h.
The Guerrieri Rizzardi family has
extensive estates in the classic
zones of Bardolino, Valpolicella,
and Soave, and the grapes are
cultivated entirely by *coltura
biologica*, utilizing no chemical
fertilizers or weedkillers. The range
of wines produced is impressive and
highly rated, especially the *cru*
wines from single vineyards, and the
superlative Castello Guerrieri, a
vino da tavola produced from
ancient local grapes grown in the
Bardolino region that undergo in
part a process of *appassimento*
similar to that carried out for the
production of Amarone. The ancient
historic *cantine* extend under the
old town walls of Bardolino. The
family villa at Poiega, near Negrar
in the Valpolicella, can also be
visited (see page 148).

5 AZIENDA AGRICOLA COLLE DEI
CIPRESSI
37010 CALMASINO VR
TEL: 045/7235078

WINES PRODUCED: Bardolino
Classico, Bardolino Novello,
Bardolino Chiaretto Classico;
Merlot; Bianco 'La Rocca'.
VISITS: Mon–Fri 9–12h30; 15–18h.
Appointment preferred.
This outstandingly beautiful estate
stands above Bardolino on moraine
hills overlooking the lake,
distinctively recognizable by the
rows of tall cypress in thick
formation. The Osele family have 26
hectares of vines which they
cultivate as naturally as possible,
and to a severely limited yield, to
produce a range of excellent quality
wines. Estate-bottled *olio extra
vergine d'oliva* is also produced in
limited quantity. Wines and oil can
be tasted and purchased; in
summer, *spuntini* may be served in
the pleasant tasting area if
previously arranged.
English spoken.

THE NORTH-EAST

Distilleria Artigianale

6 DISTILLERIA FRANCESCHINI BRUNO
VIA VILLA 12
37010 CAVAION VR
TEL: 045/7235059

VISITS: Mon–Sat 9–12h; 15–19h.
Tiny but highly-regarded family
operation producing superb *grappe*
from *vinacce* from Bardolino,
Valpolicella, and elsewhere
throughout Italy (some Tuscan
producers, for example, send their
vinacce here to be distilled). The pot
stills are tiny, so the *grappa* is
produced in minute quantities, but
this is the key to quality, says Bruno
Franceschini. Some *grappe* are aged
in wood, and thus acquire a rich,
walnut colour, though the Italian
taste is still primarily for *grappa
bianca* (clear). *Grappa* can be tasted
and purchased, and if time allows,
the distillery can be visited.
German spoken.

Ristoranti

1 RISTORANTE 'AL CASTELLO'
VIA PORTA DEL LION
37017 LAZISE VR

Located just below the famous walls
of the castle with pleasant shaded
terrace serving good *trota alla
griglia*, *pizze*, *tiramisù*.
Inexpensive

---

2 RISTORANTE 'STELLA D'ORO DA
MERZI'
LOC. PAZZON
37013 CAPRINO VERONESE VR
TEL: 045/7265066

Closed Tue.
Silvio and Bruna Merzi run a
wonderful old-style *ristorante
casalinga* in this quiet village on
the foothills of Monte Baldo:
home-cooked specialities of the
Veneto include *bigoli*, *stinco di
vitello*, *peperonata*, *stracotto*, *pasta
frolla*, served together with
own-produced Bardolino, Chiaretto,
and the famous *graspa di Merzi*.
Inexpensive

---

3 'DA CORRADO'
LOC. PAZZON
37013 CAPRINO VERONESE VR
TEL: 045/7265111

Closed Mon, Tue. Open evenings
only.
Giuseppe Fraccari offers a *menu
degustazione* together with an
extensive selection of wines from

Ristorante 'Stella d'Oro da Merzi', near Lake Garda.

some of the best small wine estates of Bardolino, Valpolicella, and Soave.
Moderate

Punti di Ristoro Agrituristico

1

AZIENDA AGRICOLA LA CASETTA
LOC. LA CASETTA
37010 AFFI VR
TEL: 045/7236352

OPEN: April–end Sept Tue–Fri eve only; Sat and Sun lunch and dinner. Other times by reservation.
Just off the wine road between Albaré and Affi, this well-organized farmhouse restaurant serves homemade *bigoli, grigiata mista* (assorted meats grilled over vine shoots), garden vegetables, together with jugs of fresh, own-produced Bardolino, on a large and pleasant canopied terrace.
Inexpensive

2 AZIENDA AGRICOLA VAL DEL TASSO
37010 CAVAION VR
TEL: 045/7150064

OPEN: Fri, Sat, Sun eve only, or by
reservation.
Really homely and simple *azienda
agristuristica* serving authentic but
basic foods, including *minestre di*

*fagiole, pasta e fagiole, carne salà,
speck, grigliata mista, polenta,* and
homemade *salame.* Lovely covered
terrace amidst the vineyards. Most
of the produce, including wine, is
home produced. Telephone for
reservations and directions.
Inexpensive

---

3 AZIENDA AGRICOLA CAMPORENGO
37010 CAVAION VR
TEL: 045/7280073

OPEN: Fri, Sat, Sun eve only, or by
reservation.
Another extremely welcoming
farmhouse *trattoria* set amidst the
vineyards of Bardolino near the
Adige river not far from the bridge

to Sant'Ambrogio di Valpolicella.
The *azienda* offers an excellent
complete menu – *bruschetta,
lasagne con fegatini, pollo in
squaseto, grigliata mista,* together
with own-produced wines and
grappa, served on a lovely outdoor
terrace.
Inexpensive

La Valpolicella: The Classic Heartland

Valpolicella, like Bardolino and Soave, is a name which is known throughout the world: indeed, simple, inexpensive bottles of uncomplicated, light
red Veronese wines labelled and sold as such have introduced millions to the
delights not only of Italian wine, but of drinking wine itself. This indeed is a
considerable achievement and one to be proud of. But it is important at the
outset to distinguish between such industrially-produced bulk wines, primarily made from grapes grown on the flatter plains towards Verona, and
those exceptional estate wines made from grapes whose production has been
severely limited, grown on historic, dry-stone terraced vineyards in the hills,
wines which count among the greatest of Italy. Indeed, it is not going too far
to state that Recioto Amarone, a unique and ancient wine, produced from
select hillside vineyards by a handful of dedicated producers, is without
question among the very greatest wines of the world.

Valpolicella is indeed an ancient wine that has been valued literally for
millennia. The region was settled in the 5th century BC by the Arusnati, a

In Brief: Unlike the vineyards of Bardolino, sited beside the beautiful shores and into the gentle moraine hills of Lake Garda, the Valpolicella is not, at first glance, an obvious tourist destination. The vineyards begin virtually at the outskirts of the city of Verona, which is ever growing and encroaching into the wine country, so that once self-contained wine hamlets are now populated with commuters. However, the 3 valleys that together make up the Valpolicella Classico, the traditional heartland of the wine country, Fumane, Marano, and Negrar, are all areas of splendid beauty and deserve lengthy and detailed exploration not only for the wines that are produced, but also for an insight into the culture of this quiet and hard-working region. There is no signposted wine road; we suggest a route which leads through the classic wine zone and gives a good introduction to the region, with details for visiting some of its most distinguished and famous wine producers. It should be noted that wine tourism in this zone is not yet well-established, so it is usually advisable to telephone in advance before visiting. Don't hesitate, however, to stop at any other *aziende* that you encounter along the way. You can dip into the Valpolicella in as little as half a day – or you can spend days getting lost along its myriad lanes.

Retica population whose religious and cultural capital was Tagus Arusnatium, sited near present-day Fumane. The poet Virgil praised the wine of 'Retico', which, according to Suetonius, was enjoyed by the Emperor Augustus. Martial and Pliny were also fond of it, while during the Middle Ages the wine was appreciated by the German emperor Henry VII as well as by the Doges of the Most Serene Republic of Venice.

How odd, then, that wines drunk by emperors and doges became so diluted and undervalued in the recent past that most were made and sold in bulk only, either to co-operative wine cellars, to the bars and restaurants of Verona where they were and are drunk as unbottled *vino sfuso*, or to the huge industrial firms that still dominate the Verona wine scene. As recently as the late 1960s, for example, Renzo Tedeschi, one of the region's top producers, did not bottle his wine himself, but continued to sell it in bulk. He was following the tradition of his grandfather, also named Lorenzo, who was known as 'Damigiana' Tedeschi because, at the turn of the century, he used to load up horse-drawn carts with 54-litre demi-johns which he then drove down to Verona to sell. The Boscaini family similarly recall those crazy

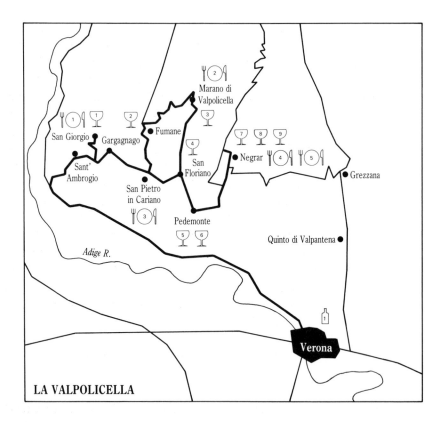

LA VALPOLICELLA

days, when a morning's entertainment consisted of racing horse carts loaded with wine down to market in Verona. And even as famous and historic an estate as Serègo Alighieri, possibly the oldest wine estate in continuous private ownership in Italy, was still selling its fine wine in bulk as recently as the mid-1970s.

For here, as elsewhere in Italy, grapes – and the wine they produced – were and still may be viewed much as any other agricultural crop, to be sold in bulk for cash as well as to be turned into wine for home consumption. The concept of 'fine wine' is a remarkably recent one: the main priority was quantity, not quality. To a large extent, this remains the case even today. Moreover, in the recent past, the system of *mezzadria* tenant farming, whereby the *padrone* took half the crop – always the best half, of course – may have left little incentive for the small wine grower.

However, after the devastation of phylloxera at the turn of the century, the present Count Pieralvise di Serègo Alighieri's grandfather began a school of viticulture in Valpolicella. In the past 20 years in particular, this school, now a state school under the direction of Dario Boscaini, has taught a new generation – the sons and daughters of local wine growers – the most modern developments relating to grape growing and wine making in the Valpolicella, Bardolino, Soave, and Bianco di Custoza zones. In particular, they have learned the essential lesson that is common throughout the best wine zones of the world, namely that improvement must come in part through the severe limiting of yields to produce higher quality grapes. As newer generations return to their family estates, knowledgeable about new trends in wine making not only here in their own zone, but worldwide, as far away as New Zealand and California, it is most probable that we shall see even better and more exciting estate wines emerging in the future.

Valpolicella Classico itself is a wine worthy of considerable attention, in spite of the scores of insipid, light, characterless wines that have debased the Valpolicella name. The principal grape varieties for Valpolicella are exactly the same as those cultivated in the vineyards of Bardolino, namely Corvina, Rondinella, Molinara, Negrara and some other minor varieties, but it is the terrain that makes all the difference between the two wines, especially the harsh, rocky, calcareous and granite hills upon which the finest classic vineyards of the Valpolicella are situated. The wines produced, especially those bearing the names of single-vineyard *vigneti* or *crus*, can be intense, vivid red wines which display marked and persistent fruity or floral aromas – cherries, violets, roses – combined with a finish that is always just a touch bitter.

Additionally, some wines are produced by a unique method known as *ripasso*, whereby they are refermented on the wine-drenched lees left over in the Recioto barrels once those great wines' fermentation has been completed. This age-old practice induces a secondary fermentation, adding an extra degree or so of alcohol, and at the same time intensifies bouquet and flavour as well as adding the unique, rich, raisiny aromas and textures of the dried Recioto grapes. Such wines as Masi's Campo Fiorin, Tedeschi's Capitel San Rocco Rosso delle Lucchine, Allegrini's La Grola, Boscaini's Santo Stefano, Quintarelli's Valpolicella Classico are about as far from mass-produced jug Valpolicella as you can get. Is it any wonder, then, that some producers prefer to eschew their rightful but much abused *denominazione*, and simply label such wines as *vino da tavola*?

For the visitor to the Valpolicella the region has much to offer. Yet, though easily accessible from Verona, it remains little visited, and is very much uncharted territory. The entire zone for Valpolicella is relatively large, but the classic heartland is manageable, and certainly repays detailed exploration. This principal zone extends over 3 valleys running north–south, the Fumane, Marano, and Negrar, their southern ends linked by the SS12, also known as the Via Valpolicella.

From Verona, find the SS12 north-west to Sant'Ambrogio di Valpolicella (this road leads eventually to Trentino-Alto Adige and the Brenner Pass). Sant'Ambrogio is not only an important wine town, it is also a key centre for one of the Valpolicella's other major industries, marble, as the scarred hills, numerous quarries, and endless lines of lorries laden with stone all attest. This beautiful pink Valpolicella marble has over the centuries been used to decorate not only the local churches and villas, but also palaces and monuments all over Europe. The wine of Sant'Ambrogio has been equally famous for centuries, especially the '*rosso vino della Grola*', a name which is recalled in the outstanding single-vineyard Valpolicella Classico 'La Grola' produced by the Allegrini family, one of the region's leading producers.

Just above Sant'Ambrogio, the medieval hill town of San Giorgio should be visited. Its Pieve, an ancient church dating from the 8th century, is probably the most important in the Valpolicella zone, a splendid example of Romanesque architecture, with its stern façade, simple interior, and lovely arched cloisters. San Giorgio, in fact, was an important religious centre for the ancient pagan Arusnati, as archaeological artefacts that have been unearthed testify. These, and much else of interest, may be viewed in the Museo della Pieve (open April–November Sundays only, or by appointment), which also has a reconstruction of a typical kitchen of the Valpolicella, with domestic implements and marble vessels.

From San Giorgio, return to Sant'Ambrogio, then follow the Via Valpolicella east towards San Pietro in Cariano. The main valleys of the classic zone are all situated to the left. Before reaching San Pietro, the small hamlet of Gargagnago is encountered. The winery of Masi is located just off the main road, while further into the hills, there is the historic Villa Serègo Alighieri.

San Pietro, and its *frazione* of San Floriano are both important wine centres, and the junction of two of the most important valleys, Fumane and Marano. To make a brief but lovely excursion into the wine hills from San Pietro, head out first to Fumane itself, follow the wine road over the hills, then across and down to Marano. Only by traversing this complex terrain can one gain an understanding of how different the exclusive hill vineyards are compared to the easy-growing, high-yielding vineyards on the flatter plains towards Verona. In the steep hills, the land is terraced, and held together by ancient dry-stone walls known as *marogne*. These stone walls, built and maintained by hand, formed into geometric criss-cross patterns, aid in soil drainage, add reflected light on to the vines, and help to maintain soil integrity. Such hill vineyards are labour-intensive, naturally, but so are any which are expected to yield great wine. Fumane and its surrounding communes are noted above all not only for the quality of the Valpolicella, but especially for the superlative, complex, and majestic sweet Recioto wines.

It remains a mystery still why one area is more suited to the production of sweet Recioto, and another to dry Amarone. The grapes may be selected and harvested identically, and placed in the same airy drying lofts to rest over the winter months. There are theories that west-facing vineyards receive a different quality of light that results not only in higher levels of sugar but also in a propensity, each year, for the fermentation to stop before all the sugar has been converted to alcohol, thus leaving a 4 or 5 degree residual sweetness. Or else it might be, in the case of Amarone, the presence, control or activation of the yeast *Saccharomyces bayanus* during the second phase of fermentation which occurs in spring as the temperatures warm. But still this essential and unexplained mystery remains. A grower pointed to his prized hill vineyard and shrugged. 'For decades we have made both Recioto and Amarone from this *campo*. The wines from this part are always dry, those from over there, right next to it, always remain sweet.'

Marano di Valpolicella, with its surprisingly large domed church, is the centre for numerous surrounding wine hamlets and communes of excellent renown. Just below Marano, for example, the small hamlet of Valgatara is the home of many fine producers, including the large family firm of Boscaini, the *azienda agricola* of Brigaldara, and Michele Castellani's La Bionda estate.

Michele Castellani is typical of many wine growers of the zone. Until only a few years ago, he sold all his wines in bulk. Yet the vineyards that the family had owned since the 15th century, particularly the hill site known as Ravazzol, were exceptional, and clearly capable of producing fine estate wines in their own right. Looking to the future, therefore, he recently took the bold decision to produce and market his own estate wines for the first time ever. The wines are indeed excellent and individual: I wonder how many other wine growers in the zone are simply waiting for a bolder, more forward generation to take over, and to reclaim the patrimony that is rightly theirs?

Returning to San Pietro, the wine tour continues through San Floriano, which has a most beautiful 12th-century Romanesque Pieve. San Floriano is

The Tedeschi family cellars at Pedemonte.

also the home of the important school of viticulture.

Nearby Pedemonte lies at the foot of the Negrar valley. If the wines of Marano are noted foremost for their big, forward, and rich style, then the finest wines from the narrower, higher Negrar are deemed to be initially more closed, yet ultimately more elegant and longer-lived.

Pedemonte is the home of one of the most highly rated family producers of Recioto, Amarone, and Valpolicella, the Fratelli Tedeschi, who produce true artisan-made wines in necessarily small quantities. Recioto Capitel Monte Fontana comes from a tiny 2-hectare patch of vines beneath the original family home: it is a wondrous wine of rare complexity, sweet certainly, but so rich in extract, flavour, and nuance that it can only be described as a *vino da meditazione*, to be enjoyed without the distraction of food or superfluous company. Renzo Tedeschi and other wine growers designate some of the best estate wines by the name '*capitel*', as in Capitel San Rocco or Roberto Anselmi's *cru* Soave Capitel Foscarino, recalling that here in the zone such *capitelli* – primitively decorated little wayside altars – would be placed between fields not only as a mark of ownership, but as a means of seeking divine protection in the vineyards.

That Negrar has been an important wine centre for many centuries is testified by the famous sculpted *carta lapidaria* on the tall bell-tower stating simply '*terris cum vineis*'. Indeed, today this important wine town encompasses the full gamut of the Veronese wine scene, from the Cantina Sociale di Valpolicella, a vast concern where many growers sell their grapes for cash, keeping only enough to make wines for home consumption, to the Azienda Agricola Giuseppe Quintarelli, the renowned and universally acclaimed 'king of Recioto', whose minute quantities of exquisite wines are truly hand-produced and rare works of art. The contrast between the industrial and the artisan could not be more marked: yet both are essential elements of the Veronese wine scene.

The Negrar valley continues beyond Negrar itself, to higher wine hamlets such as Torbe and Mazzano. That the wines from these zones have been prized for centuries has been documented historically. For example, the Mazzano vineyard was mentioned in a contract dated 1194, when the San Zeno Monastery leased land to one Musio di Panego, the rent for which was to be paid with a certain quantity of grapes produced in the best area of the fief indicated as Mazzano's vineyards. It was further stipulated that should the crop fail (hail then being as common a destroyer as it remains today), then the rent was to be paid with grapes from another hillside area of Torbe, identified now as the vineyards of Campolongo di Torbe. Today, Mazzano and Campolongo di Torbe are two of the finest vineyards in the Valpolicella for the production of two of Masi's *cru* Amarone.

The Valpolicella production zone continues well beyond this classic heartland, to Soave and beyond. One other valley that deserves further exploration is the Valpantena, a sub-zone located roughly between Quinto and Grezzana. The wines, which may be labelled as Valpolicella-Valpantena DOC, can be excellent.

Degustazione: Stop to Taste; Stop to Buy

1

MASI AGRICOLA SPA
37020 GARGAGNAGO DI
 VALPOLICELLA VR
TEL: 045/6800 588

WINES PRODUCED: Valpolicella Classico, Amarone Classico, Amarone 'Mazzano', Amarone 'Campolongo di Torbe', Recioto Classico 'Riserva degli Angeli', Recioto 'Mezzanella', Campo Fiorin (*vino di ripasso*), Serègo Alighieri Valpolicella Classico, Amarone Serègo Alighieri 'Vajo Armaron', Recioto Serègo Alighieri 'Casal de' Ronchi'; Bardolino Classico, Bardolino 'La Vegrona'; Soave Classico, Soave 'Col Baraca'; Masianco; Rosa dei Masi; Campociesa.

VISITS: by appointment, arranged directly or (preferably) through Masi's distributors.

Masi recently opened a new tasting area for both professionals and amateurs, a superb facility for learning about Masi's wines and much else besides.

Masi holds some 95 hectares of vineyards throughout the zone, and also purchases grapes from families who have supplied the company for generations (as with the *cru* Mazzano vineyard, owned and worked by the Fedrighi family with the full technical support of Masi). Additionally, Masi continues to play a leadership role in the region through viticultural experiments in

THE NORTH-EAST

CRU AS HISTORY

Italy is one of the oldest wine producing countries in the world with vineyards that have been cultivated continuously producing wines that have been drunk and praised literally for millennia. Yet due to the vagaries of its social, political, and economic history, Italy is only now emerging on the world wine scene as one of the 'new' producers of wines of world class.

The concept of fine Italian wine is a remarkably recent one. One of the most exciting and important developments, not only in the vineyards of Verona, but in Piedmont, Tuscany and elsewhere, is the recognition of 'cru' wines, that is, wines produced from exceptional named single vineyards. For unlike in France, where vineyards in Bordeaux and Burgundy, for example, were classified centuries ago into recognized *Grands* and *Premiers Crus*, there is little such tradition here (if there were, then there would be no need to borrow the French word).

Dr Sandro Boscaini, one of the great historians of the vineyards of Verona, believes that since Italy lacks a continuous tradition of classification of vineyards, constant research into the past is necessary. Therefore he studied historical documents such as medieval church or noble tithes, reasoning that, if a vineyard was historically documented long ago, that is, selected as superior above all others, then this was probably a sound basis for excellence that may still be valid today. Indeed, he discovered that the Mazzano and Campolongo di Torbe vineyards were highly valued in the 12th century, and today these same two vineyards produce wines that are the flagships of Masi.

In Piedmont, too, such historical research continues. In the Barolo zone, for example, certain vineyards have always been known to be superior, and indeed have been known to the growers by name. But the tradition in the past was primarily to blend wine from different vineyards throughout the zone to achieve a more uniform and harmonious result. However, in recent years, the concept of *cru* has become ever more important to the finest producers. The late Renato Ratti researched the region extensively, by examining past records and historical documents, talking to the older generation that still remembers things as they used to be, and basing his judgements on the quality of wines produced today: by so doing he was able to draw up a classification of the finest vineyards of Barolo (see page 40).

Whether or not everyone agrees with this list or that is not the issue: what is most important for the consumer is that such *cru* wines, made by the best producers, add a further and essential tier to our appreciation of Italian wines.

conjunction with the school of viticulture in Valpolicella, the development of new single vineyard *crus*, and the rediscovering and modernization of traditional wines, such as Campo Fiorin, credited as the first modern *vino di ripasso*.

Other important Masi estates include the outstanding Soave Col Baraca and Bardolino La Vegrona estates, which can be visited by appointment.
English spoken.

---

2 AZIENDA AGRICOLA ALLEGRINI
LOC. CORTE GIARA
37022 FUMANE DI VALPOLICELLA VR
TEL: 045/7701138

WINES PRODUCED: Valpolicella Classico, Valpolicella Classico 'La Grola', Recioto Classico della Valpolicella, Recioto della

Valpolicella Amarone 'Fieramonte'.
VISITS: Tue–Fri, by appointment.
One of the outstanding producers of Valpolicella, and the leading estate in the Fumane sub-zone, producing well-structured wines of power and elegance.
English, French spoken.

---

3 AZIENDA AGRICOLA LA BIONDA
37020 VALGATARA DI MARANO VR
TEL: 045/7701253

WINES PRODUCED: Valpolicella Classico 'Ravazzol', Recioto della Valpolicella Amarone; Soave 'Monteforte Costale'.
VISITS: by appointment, or arranged

through Masi.
The Castellani family have been wine growers in the region since the 15th century, though they have only recently begun to produce estate wines with the technical and commercial assistance of Masi.

---

4 AZIENDA AGRICOLA BRIGALDARA
37020 SAN FLORIANO VR
TEL: 045/7701055

WINES PRODUCED: Valpolicella

Classico, Valpolicella Classico 'Il Vegro' (*vino di ripasso*), Recioto della Valpolicella, Recioto della Valpolicella Amarone.

THE NORTH-EAST

THE SERÈGO ALIGHIERI ESTATE

During the arcane and baffling conflict between the Guelphs and the Ghibellines, the poet Dante had the misfortune to be on the wrong side, and thus found himself exiled from his native Florence on pain of being burned alive if ever caught returning. Thus, in 1304, the poet first came to Verona where he enjoyed the hospitality of the noble Scaligeri family, whom he assigned to *Paradiso* in *La Divina Commedia*. Dante lived out his life in exile and, after his death, his son transferred the family to a villa at Gargagnago in 1353, named on the deed as Casal de' Ronchi. Some two centuries later, in 1549, when the male line of the Alighieri family was extinct, Ginevra Alighieri married Conte Marc'Antonio Serègo, thus linking the families of Serègo and Alighieri. The wedding carriages still stand in splendour in the hall of the villa Serègo Alighieri.

The Serègo Alighieri family went on to become the most important noble family in the Valpolicella, and at one time held some 80% of what is now delimited as the Valpolicella Classico zone. The family were thus leaders in agriculture. Lands were planted not only with grapes but with maize (introduced to the region by Marc'Antonio, and soon to become, as *polenta*, a staple food for rich and poor alike), olives, and cherries, Valpolicella's other most famous crop.

Veronese viticulture, even on such a famous estate, was viewed much as any other cash crop: the *contadini* who worked the estate on the traditional *mezzadria* sharecropping basis brought the grapes in each year to the *cantina* where they were pressed and made into wine. The finest selected grapes, particularly from the Vajo Armaron and Casal de' Ronchi vineyards were put aside separately, dried in racks to make special wines for the family. But, as was the case with most wine growers in the region, the rest was sold in bulk.

However, today, some 20 generations later, this great and continuous wine heritage is resulting in some of the most exciting wines of the Valpolicella, produced on the estate and marketed with the assistance of Masi. Serègo Alighieri's Valpolicella Classico, for example, is a wine of considerable elegance and vivacity. Conte Pieralvise, mindful that cherry wood from the estate had always been used for ageing the wines in the past, came upon the idea of ageing the wine in new cherry wood barrels, an experiment, he believes, that gives the wine more life and enhances the distinctive flavour of cherries, a hallmark of authentic Valpolicella.

The other two wines of the estate also draw on a long and illustrious heritage. Casal de' Ronchi is a classic sweet Recioto, produced from the historic vineyards that surround the villa. Vajo Armaron is another wine of great historic significance, for it is now recognized as the probable original vineyard for the production of dry Amarone. Thus today, centuries old tradition and heritage linked with modern technology are resulting in wines worthy of an ancient and proud family.

Visits: The Villa Serègo Alighieri, located in Gargagnago di Valpolicella, is open to the public by appointment. Visits to the winery by appointment only, arranged through Masi (address above).

VISITS: weekdays, by appointment. The Cesari family estate consists of 15 hectares, 11 planted with vines, the remainder with olive trees for the production of estate-bottled *extra-vergine* olive oil. At one time the estate was planted mainly with mulberry trees for the cultivation of silk worms. Traditional production of well-structured, serious wines for ageing.

English spoken.

---

5 AZIENDA AGRICOLA F.LLI TEDESCHI
VIA G. VERDI 4/A
37020 PEDEMONTE DI VALPOLICELLA
VR
TEL: 045/7701487

WINES PRODUCED: Valpolicella Classico Superiore, Valpolicella Classico 'Capitel dei Nicalò', Recioto della Valpolicella Amarone 'Capitel Monte Olmi', Recioto della Valpolicella 'Capitel Monte Fontana', Capitel San Rocco Rosso delle Lucchine (*vino di ripasso*); Soave Classico, Soave 'Monte Tenda'; Capitel San Rocco Bianco; Bardolino; Bianco di Custoza.

VISITS: Mon–Fri 9–12h; 15–18h. Appointment preferred.
The Tedeschi family is widely recognized as one of the leading producers of a full range of Veronese wines. Wines such as Valpolicella 'Capitel dei Nicalò' and Capitel San Rocco Rosso delle Lucchine display how good the wines of Valpolicella can be, while the single *crus* Amarone 'Capitel Monte Olmi' and Recioto 'Capitel Monte Fontana' are outstanding wines of world class.

English spoken.

THE NORTH-EAST

6 AZIENDA AGRICOLA TOMMASI
VIA RONCHETTO 2
37020 PEDEMONTE DI VALPOLICELLA
VR
TEL: 045/7701266

WINES PRODUCED: Valpolicella Classico, Recioto della Valpolicella Amarone, Recioto della Valpolicella Classico; Bardolino Classico, Bardolino Chiaretto Classico; Soave Classico, Recioto di Soave Classico; Bianco di Custoza; Lugana; Vino Novello; Spumante. Also own-produced extra virgin olive oil and Amarone and Valpolicella wine vinegars.
VISITS: daily, working hours. No appointment necessary.
The Tommasi family has extensive vineyard holdings in the classic wine growing areas of Verona, and produce an impressive range of wines in their modern winery. English spoken.

---

7 AZIENDA AGRICOLA DEI CONTI
  GUERRIERI RIZZARDI
VILLA RIZZARDI POIEGA
LOC. POIEGA
37024 NEGRAR DI VALPOLICELLA VR
TEL: 045/7210028

WINES PRODUCED: Valpolicella Classico Superiore, Valpolicella Classico 'Villa Rizzardi Poiega', Recioto di Valpolicella Amarone Classico; Bardolino Classico Superiore, Bardolino Tacchetto, Bardolino Chiaretto Classico; Soave Classico, Soave Costeggiola; Bianco San Pietro; Dògoli; Castello Guerrieri; Aceto di Amarone.
VISITS: daily 10–12h; 17–18h.
The Guerrieri Rizzardi family produce an excellent range of wines exclusively from their own vineyards, cultivated biologically in the classic zones of Bardolino, Valpolicella, and Soave. Here at Poiega, just across the valley from Negrar in the heart of s the Valpolicella, the vineyards that surround the distinctive castle produce the prestigious *cru* Valpolicella 'Villa Rizzardi Poiega'. A visit here is a must not only for the estate's fine wines, but also to see its beautiful gardens, maintained today as they were when originally laid out by Luigi Trezza in 1780, designed to take advantage of the changing light throughout the day and planted with indigenous trees, shrubs, and flowers. The 'Teatro Verde', an amphitheatre made from yew hedges, and the neo-classical gazebo are particularly noteworthy.

8 AZIENDA AGRICOLA QUINTARELLI
GIUSEPPE
VIA CERÈ 1
37024 NEGRAR DI VALPOLICELLA VR
TEL: 045/7500016

WINES PRODUCED: Valpolicella
Classico Superiore (*vino di ripasso*),
Recioto di Valpolicella Amarone
Classico, Recioto di Valpolicella
Amarone Riserva, Recioto della
Valpolicella Classico, Amabile del
Cerè.
VISITS: weekdays, working hours;
appointment advisable.

Quintarelli is the undisputed 'king
of Recioto': at every level, the wines
are handmade with the utmost care,
from the growing and tending of the
vineyards at Monte Ca' Paletta, to
the hand drying of the grapes for
the *appassimento*, to the pressing
and fermentation of grapes, even to
the bottling and hand-written
labelling of the wines. These are
artisan-made wines – not designer
wines with a slick image, but wholly
traditional and of the highest
quality.

---

9 CANTINA SOCIALE DELLA
VALPOLICELLA
VIA BALLARIN
37024 NEGRAR DI VALPOLICELLA VR
TEL: 045/7500070; 7500295

WINES PRODUCED: Valpolicella
Classico Superiore, Recioto della
Valpolicella Amarone Classico,
Recioto della Valpolicella Classico;
Bardolino Classico; Soave Classico.
VISITS: Mon–Fri 8–12h; 14–18h.

The *cantina sociale* serves an
important role for many of the small
wine growers in the region who
have neither the modern wine
making equipment nor the
marketing expertise to make, bottle,
and sell their own wines. The wines,
especially those which have
undergone greater selection, are on
the whole well-made.
English spoken by appointment.

Ristoranti

1 TRATTORIA DALLA ROSA ALDA
37022 SAN GIORGIO DI VALPOLICELLA
VR
TEL: 045/7701018

Closed Mon.
This little village above
Sant'Ambrogio is well worth visiting

not only for the excellent *risotto ai
funghi*, *stracotto*, *brasato al
Amarone* and superb selection of
wines served on the terrace of this
friendly *trattoria*, but also for the
views across to Lake Garda, the
beautiful romanesque church, and

THE NORTH-EAST

ACETO DI AMARONE

Gianni opened yet another set of enormous wooden doors in the ancient *cantina* above Negrar. The wooden barrels looked the same as the small *barriques* used for the ageing of wine, but here they contained a rare and precious vinegar made from Amarone. In another hall, the barrels were arranged in a line, descending in size and age, the largest at one end and, 20 barrels or so later, two very small barrels, made of new oak, containing the oldest, produced from a mother vinegar that was over 100 years old.

As the precious vinegar is drawn from these last two, the barrels are replenished from the adjacent barrel, which is similarly replenished from the one above, and so on up the scale: it is in practice a sort of *solera* system like that used in the *bodegas* of Jerez de la Frontera, but here utilized for the production of *aceto di Amarone*.

Gianni prised open the bung of one of the final barrels, and plunged his huge little finger into the hole, pulled it up to show us, then licked it lustily. '*Ottimo!*' he pronounced, then motioned for us to do the same. We did. The vinegar was almost the colour of molasses, the aroma unbelievably rich, the flavour not at all sharp, but deep, round, rich, intense, like the wine from which it was made. Even 3 hours later, I could still smell that glorious vinegar on my hand.

the local museum tracing life in the Valpolicella.

Moderate

---

2 ANTICA TRATTORIA DA BEPI
37020 MARANO DI VALPOLICELLA VR
TEL: 045/7755001

Closed Tue.
Warm, welcoming local *trattoria* popular with wine growers: *cucina*

casalinga – agnello al Amarone, coniglio, griglia alla brace, polenta – and own-produced Valpolicella and Amarone.

Inexpensive

3 RISTORANTE MONTE DANIELE
VIA MONTE DALL'ORA 6
LOC. CASTELROTTO
37029 SAN PIETRO IN CARIANO VR
TEL: 045/7704949

Closed Mon.
Uninspired modern dining room with good views overlooking the vineyards of Valpolicella, serving the simple foods of the Veneto, together with a fine selection of wines from local growers.
Inexpensive to Moderate

---

4 PIZZERIA 'LE VIGNE'
37024 NEGRAR DI VALPOLICELLA VR

Open evenings only. Closed Tue.
Set amidst the vines, this traditional *pizzeria*, owned and run by the Guerrieri Rizzardi estate, also has a few rooms available, and so might make a peaceful base in the Valpolicella.
Inexpensive

---

5 TRATTORIA CAPRINI
37024 TORBE DI NEGRAR VR
TEL: 045/7500511

Closed Wed.
High up in the Negrar valley, amidst some of the region's finest *cru* vineyards, this simple *trattoria* serves homemade *pasta*, sausages, *salame*, grilled meats and *polenta*, accompanied by own-produced Valpolicella and Amarone.
Inexpensive

Soave

In Brief: Soave is located just off the main A4 *autostrada* and thus this famous wine town can be visited by those en route to Venice, as well as by those based in Verona. This is a compact vineyard, none the less beautiful for that.

Soave, like Valpolicella, is a wine that has found widespread fame and introduced millions to the pleasures of wine drinking. This success is due primarily to the efforts of the immense wine firms that dominate the Veronese wine industry today (for indeed industry it is, in every sense). The firm of Bolla, in particular, has done much to popularize Soave throughout the world. It may be easy to dismiss such mass-produced wines as of little

THE NORTH-EAST

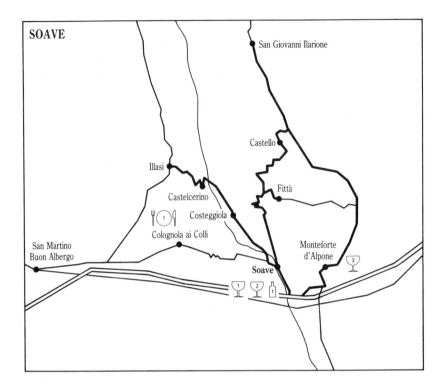

interest to the connoisseur, but it is important to note that they never would have achieved such popularity without an essentially sound base. Soave, even at its most neutral, is a good wine, strong, dry, clean, and with that pleasing, slightly bitter aftertaste which is its hallmark.

Yet the sheer quantity of grapes required for such world markets has meant that the Soave DOC zone has expanded ever further from its classic heartland in the hills, down over the plains that extend between Verona and Vicenza. Moreover, the small grape growers of the region have always found such ready markets for their produce, either from the large firms or at the *cantine sociali* of Soave or Colognola ai Colli, that over the decades many have seen little incentive to strive for quality at the expense of quantity. But today, as elsewhere in this historic Veronese wine region, new generations of wine makers are rediscovering their patrimony, and, especially in the classic zone between the communes of Soave and Monteforte d'Alpone, some outstanding wines are being produced. Wines such as Pieropan's Soave 'Vigneto Calvarino' or Anselmi's Soave 'Capitel Foscarino' are notable examples. Furthermore, a rare traditional dessert wine made from dried grapes,

Recioto di Soave, is also produced in the zone, albeit in minute quantities. Alongside the Recioto and Amarone of Valpolicella, this rare, sweet yet energetic nectar is considered one of the pinnacles of Veronese viticulture. For those who only consider Soave a jug wine, to be drunk out of open carafes or two-litre screw-top bottles, such wines come as a revelation.

Soave itself is easily reached from Verona, either directly via the SS11 or the A4 *autostrada*, or by way of the wine towns of San Martino Buon Albergo and Colognola ai Colli. The latter, like Soave itself, has its own communal *cantina sociale* and in autumn it is a heady sight to see tractors and even horse-drawn carts loaded with ripe grapes (mainly Garganega and lesser amounts of Trebbiano di Soave) brought in to be weighed, then dumped into vast, churning, below-ground-level screws. The grapes are quickly destemmed then lightly pressed, and the autumnal scent of fresh grape juice running freely into the vast stainless steel fermentation tanks is indeed intoxicating.

Soave itself is a fascinating and atmospheric medieval town, dominated by its medieval Scaligero castle and enclosed by its turreted town walls. Originally settled during the Stone Age, Soave was later an important Roman town, though it was probably during the 5th-century occupation by Swabian tribes that the town gained its name (through a philological corruption of Svevi to Soavesi). Its location along a main trade artery has meant that it has always been much fought over: in the 16th century the town achieved a famous victory over enemies of the Venetian Republic, and as a reward was granted the right to fly the standard of San Marco.

Soave boasts the oldest grape festival in Italy, officially begun in September 1929, an annual celebration of the Garganega vine, and an excuse for a raucous end-of-September party with folklore, cultural, and gastronomic displays. On the first Sunday in May, there is also a Soave Classico and Recioto festival of which the principal event is a pageant dedicated to the '*Magnifica Imperiale Castellana del Vin Bianco di Suavia*'.

To make a brief tour of the wine country, head out of Soave north into the surrounding hills, first to the wine hamlets of Costeggiola, Castelcerino, and Illasi. Or else strike across from Soave up the Alpone valley to Fittà, Castello, and San Giovanni Ilarione, a wine town noted not only for its Soave wines but also for a local wine made from the Durella grape. Then circle back south to Monteforte d'Alpone, located in the heart of the classic zone and surrounded by important vineyards.

RECIOTO DI SOAVE

Recioto di Soave is a most rare and wonderful wine, produced in minute quantity only by a handful of artisan wine makers in the classic zone. As in the production of Recioto di Valpolicella, the grapes, in this case mainly Garganega with some Trebbiano di Soave, are selected carefully, harvested, and spread out on wicker trays which are then placed in airy lofts to dry. They are inspected regularly, and any grapes that have turned mouldy are quickly discarded to ensure that they do not contaminate others. Dry weather is essential during this period of *appassimento*. Then, some time after Christmas, the semi-dried grapes, rich in concentrated sugar, are lightly pressed and slowly and carefully fermented until the desired balance between alcohol and residual sugar is reached. The finest examples, honeyed and luscious (some are aged in new oak *barriques*), count among the greatest sweet wines of Italy.

Degustazione: **Stop to Taste; Stop to Buy**

1
AZIENDA AGRICOLA PIEROPAN
VIA CAMUZZONI 3
37038 SOAVE VR
TEL: 045/7680044

WINES PRODUCED: Soave Classico, Soave Classico 'Vigneto Calvarino', Soave Classico 'Vigneto La Rocca', Recioto di Soave; Riesling Italico.
VISITS: weekdays, by appointment. The family firm of Pieropan is one of the most highly-regarded, producing not only fine 'straight' Soave, but superlative wines from named single vineyards. These wines, as well as those made by other committed producers, really are the 'great growths' of the region, as different from jug Soave as *Premiers* or *Grands Crus* wines from the Yonne are from Californian 'chablis'.

2
CANTINA DEL CASTELLO
CORTE PITTORA 5
37038 SOAVE VR
TEL: 045/7680093

WINES PRODUCED: Soave Classico Superiore, Soave Classico 'Monte Pressoni', Soave Classico 'Monte Carniga', Spumante Brut di Soave Classico, Recioto di Soave Classico Superiore.
VISITS: weekdays, by appointment 9–12h; 15–19h.

Traditionally made wines, in the historic 13th-century Palazzo dei

Conti Sambonifacio in the centre of Soave.

---

3 AZIENDA AGRICOLA ROBERTO ANSELMI
VIA SAN CARLO 46
37032 MONTEFORTE D'ALPONE VR
TEL: 045/7611488

WINES PRODUCED: Soave Classico 'Capitel Foscarino', Soave Classico 'Capitel Croce', Recioto dei

Capitelli; Realda (Cabernet Sauvignon).
VISITS: Mon–Fri 8–12h; 14–17h.
Appointment necessary.
Outstanding handmade *cru* wines of the highest quality.
English, French spoken.

Enoteca

1 ENOTECA DEL SOAVE
VIA ROMA 19
37038 SOAVE VR
TEL: 045/7681588

OPEN: daily except Wed 10–13h; 16–24h.

Taste and purchase the local wines, together with basic drinking snacks, in the simple *enoteca* located in the historic centre of the medieval village.

Ristorante

1 RISTORANTE ALBERGO POSTA VECIA
VIA STRÀ SS11
37030 COLOGNOLA AI COLLI VR
TEL: 045/7650243

Closed Aug.
Historic 16th-century coaching inn on the Verona–Vicenza road, with

an atmospheric dining room serving both local and national foods: homemade *pasta*, *porcini freschi*, *stinco di vitello al forno*, *selvaggina* and a good selection of wines.
Moderate

THE NORTH-EAST

La Strada del Vino Bianco di Custoza

In Brief: Another small, but lovely wine land located west of Verona and south of Lake Garda. Easily explored in a day or less, with lunch at Valeggio sul Mincio.

If, decades ago, Soave was the local carafe wine of Verona, such is the demand, especially internationally, for that pleasing white wine that today the Veronese quench their thirst with a far less well-known but equally excellent alternative, Bianco di Custoza. Indeed, in Verona, you don't ask for a '*vino bianco*' in a bar, you simply ask for a 'Custoza'.

The zone where this wine is produced lies to the west of Verona, coinciding in part with the zone for Bardolino, and indeed many wine growers produce both wines. It is a gentle, rolling land extending over the ripple of moraine hills south of Lake Garda, cultivated not solely with grapes, but with a mixture of crops such as wheat, corn, orchards, and, increasingly, kiwi.

Bianco di Custoza bears a definite family similarity to Soave, though the *uvaggio* of grapes utilized in its production is somewhat different: in addition to Garganega and Trebbiano di Soave (the latter is utilized in only small quantity), it is permissible furthermore to utilize Trebbiano Toscano, Cortese, and Tocai Friulano. On the whole, Bianco di Custoza seems to have a slightly fuller, fruitier taste than Soave and indeed is a wine capable of considerable distinction. Like Soave, it is meant to be consumed while still young and fruity and it remains pleasingly inexpensive, a wine to enjoy in quantity while touring or relaxing in the region.

The brief but pleasant signposted wine road leads through the vineyards, virtually from Verona's outskirts to the fine medieval town of Valeggio sul Mincio, itself well worthy of an extended visit. Take the SS11 west from Verona to Sona, and there turn off south to Sommacampagna, crossing over the *autostrada*. Sommacampagna is sited in a dominating position, the highest part of the zone, and for this reason numerous splendid villas were built here (especially during the 16th century) in order to enjoy panoramic views over both Verona and Lake Garda.

Custoza, the little town that has given its name to the wine zone, remains an important viticultural centre. The ultra-modern *cantina sociale* is a surprising sight, with its long row of enormous stainless steel fermentation tanks standing outside in the open air. This wine factory may look more like a petrol refinery (indeed, wines are pumped out irreverently from nozzles

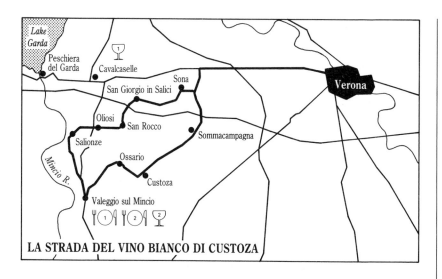

LA STRADA DEL VINO BIANCO DI CUSTOZA

with digital readouts), but the sound range of wine produced should not be shunned. For the production of good white wine requires modern technology: temperature-controlled stainless steel vats for fermentation and storage, and modern sterile bottling equipment to ensure that the wines are stable without the necessity for pasteurization. The *cantina sociale* at Custoza provides a market for the local growers to sell their grapes, while the ultra-modern plant ensures that the wines produced are on the whole superior than could be made by any except those who have the resources, knowledge and marketing ability to enable them to invest in such modern equipment themselves. On the negative side, as is usually the case, there is an inevitable levelling of quality.

Custoza was the scene of much fierce fighting during the war of Italian independence against the Austrians, especially during two savage battles, in 1848 and 1866. Today, there is a monument at Ossario where the remains of the dead soldiers from both sides lie finally in peace.

From Custoza, the wine road follows the sinuous Tione valley, first to Santa Lucia dei Monti, then on to Valeggio sul Mincio. Today a small but busy centre for the surrounding agricultural countryside, Valeggio was once a town of great strategic importance. Its castle, built on the slopes of Monte Ogheri and dominating the valley of the Mincio, changed hands many times over the centuries: once in control of the monks of San Zeno, it then became part of the powerful Scaligeri family, was taken by the Venetian Republic, and finally ceded to the commune of Valeggio. The fortified bridge that spans

the Mincio, though in part in ruins, remains a remarkable sight and still a
formidable barrier. But today the country is at peace, and it serves to link
Valeggio with its neighbouring hamlet Borghetto, separated by the wide,
lazy, lovely Mincio: from the bridge one looks down on waterside restaurants
as charming and inviting as any in the world, where the renowned specialities of the region (pumpkin pasta, freshwater fish) are served, together, of
course, with refreshing Bianco di Custoza.

The wine road completes the circuit to Sona by way of Salionze (the Villa
Tebaldi, constructed in the 19th century, is a notable monument), Oliosi,
San Rocco with its 15th-century Chiesetta di San Rocco, and San Giorgo in
Salici.

Degustazione: **Stop to Taste; Stop to Buy**

1

AZIENDA AGRICOLA ARVEDI DI EMILEI
VIA PALAZZO EMILEI 5
37010 CAVALCASELLE VR
TEL: 045/7553662

WINES PRODUCED: Bianco di
Custoza, Bianco di Custoza Brut;
Bardolino, Bardolino Chiaretto,
Bardolino Novello; Torre Gardello
(*vino frizzante*).

VISITS: Mon–Fri 9–12h; 15–18h.
Appointment appreciated.
Ancient noble family estate in a
lovely *villa veneta*, producing
highly-regarded range of modern
wines utilizing the latest
technologies: severe selection of
grapes, temperature-controlled
fermentation, use of *barriques*.
German, English, French spoken.

2

AZIENDA AGRICOLA FRATERNA
   PORTALUPI
LOC. TORRIONE
37067 VALEGGIO SUL MINCIO VR
TEL: 045/35283; 7945271

WINES PRODUCED: Bianco di
Custoza; Bardolino.
VISITS: by appointment.
Mixed farm, with a good reputation
for well-made wines with character.

Ristoranti

1 ANTICA LOCANDA MINCIO
VIA MICHELANGELO 12
LOC. BORGHETTO
37067 VALEGGIO SUL MINCIO VR
TEL: 045/7950059

Closed Wed eve, Thur.
Lovely traditional old favourite beside the Mincio serving *tortelli di zucca, fettucine ai funghi porcini, pesce alla griglia* and homemade desserts.
Moderate

2 TRATTORIA 'ARIANO'
LOC. ARIANO
37067 VALEGGIO SUL MINCIO
TEL: 045/7950979

Closed Mon eve, Tue.
Across Valeggio's famous bridge, this quiet family *trattoria* is

friendly and serves good homemade pasta – *spaghetti al torchio* and *maccheroncini alla boscaiola* – together with river fish, and homemade *salame* and *polenta*.
Inexpensive

LA MARCA TREVIGIANA: THE WINE HILLS OF TREVISO

Wine is produced throughout Veneto, but after the vineyards of Verona, the next most important region, in terms of both quantity and in some instances quality, is the province of Treviso, north of Venice. This is a vast source of the everyday table wines of Veneto, sold to bars and restaurants in *damigiane* or in two-litre screw-topped bottles, identified usually simply by the name of the grape, as in Merlot del Veneto or Tocai del Veneto. Such wines, produced in many instances in *cantine sociali*, are on the whole sound and well-made: they are simple everyday beverages to be consumed with food, as indispensable on the table as salt and pepper – and as noteworthy.

But this is not just a zone of bulk wines. As elsewhere, there is no shortage of private *aziende agricole* producing serious quality wines, in some cases outside the limitations imposed by *denominazione di origine controllata* (DOC). Such artisan-made wines, like Conte Loredan Gasparini's Venegazzù Etichetta Nera, a pungent and mouth-filling Cabernet/Merlot blend aged in oak, as well as others, are *cru* wines in every sense, worthy of comparison not just with the best of the region, but with the greatest wines from throughout the country.

THE NORTH-EAST

Within the Treviso province, therefore, a full range of wines is produced. In addition to both everyday and fine red and white wines, the region is further noteworthy as the source of one of Italy's most attractive and vivacious sparkling wines, Prosecco di Congeliano-Valdobbiàdene, and the superior Prosecco *cru* known as Cartizze.

Treviso itself, located only 32 km north of Venice, is a fascinating and picturesque town, surrounded by its 15th-century fortified ramparts and moat, and with numerous canals recalling its former allegiance to La Serenissima. The old section of the town, the *città antica*, is particularly atmospheric on warm summer evenings when anybody who is anybody makes a *passeggiata* to the Piazza dei Signori, the gathering point and hub for those who care to see and be seen. The Civic Museum is certainly worth a visit, for it contains paintings by prominent Venetian artists including Titian, Cima da Conegliano, Jacopo Bassano, Guardi, Tintoretto, and others.

Two signposted wine roads lead through the vineyards and wine hills of Treviso, the zone known as the Marca Trevigiana. Both begin in Conegliano, the region's principal wine town. This is a wine region, it should be stressed, that offers much more than just wine: travel these roads certainly to the source of much that is worth drinking, but also to visit villas or medieval churches, and simply to enjoy the beauty and harmony of the Veneto hinterland.

La Strada del Vino Bianco

In Brief: *La Strada del Vino Bianco* extends over the vine-covered hills between Conegliano and Valdobbiàdene, source of the sparkling wine Prosecco. All along the way there are *botteghe autorizzate*, displaying the distinctive logo, where wines can be tasted and purchased. This lovely wine road can be followed by those heading across to the Montello hills, or to Feltre, Asolo, or Bassano del Grappa.

Conegliano, the starting point for both signposted wine roads of the Marca Trevigiana, is a historic old wine town of considerable charm, best-known as the birthplace of Gian Battista Cima (known as Cima da Conegliano). The 14th-century Duomo, with its frescoes by Pozzoserrato and its arched porticoes, is located in an atmospheric medieval section of the town, lined with

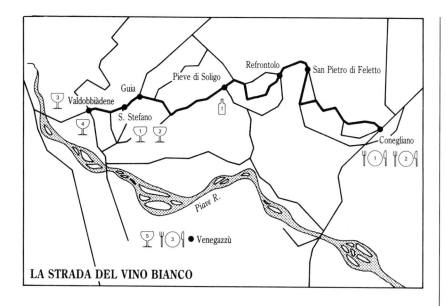

LA STRADA DEL VINO BIANCO

the *palazzi* of wealthy burghers. Climb up the steep, cobbled Calle Madonna della Neve to the Castello, and there sit out on the terrace to enjoy a glass of sparkling Prosecco and the splendid views across the rolling wine country up to the Dolomites. The Civic Museum is located in the castle and, in addition to works mainly from the school of Conegliano's famous son Cima, there is a separate permanent exhibition devoted to *'l'uva nell'arte'* – collections of silver, china, wood carvings, glass from Murano, all in homage to the grape. This museum is located in the castle tower, and it is worth a visit just for the view of the wine country from the very top terrace. As a wine town, Conegliano is also the home of one of the country's most important schools of viticulture and oenology, *La Scuola di Viticoltura e di Enologia*, as well as a centre for the production of wooden *botti* (large casks made principally from Slavonian oak), and, more recently, the smaller oak *barriques* that are in such fashion today in virtually every corner of Italy.

The *Strada del Vino Bianco* begins from the Castello. From here, the wine road climbs quietly into the rugged and steep hills. All along the way there are *botteghe autorizzate* where wines can be tasted and purchased, as well as small wine growers who are always more than happy to sell their product direct. However, much of the production of sparkling Prosecco remains in the hands of the large firms that dominate the industry, and thus there are perhaps fewer opportunities for visiting wine growers than one might expect. None the less, the drive from Conegliano to Valdobbiàdene via the wine road is a most pleasant meander.

San Pietro di Feletto is the first wine hamlet encountered, noteworthy for its ancient Pieve. There was a pagan temple on this site in antiquity, but the present structure dates originally from the 12th century. From here, there is a fine panorama of the surrounding vine-covered country. At Refrontolo it is worth the trouble to make the detour down to the old *molinetto*, a waterfall and still working waterwheel and -mill. This is a lovely, peaceful spot to have a picnic – some *soppressa* or *salame* purchased along the road, together with a bottle of fresh still or sparkling Prosecco, chilled in the cool, churning waters of the mill pond.

Further towards Valdobbiàdene, Pieve di Soligo is a rather smart, busy little centre, known primarily for its production of furniture, for its lovely old houses and *palazzi*, and for a rather stylish *enoteca*. Beyond Pieve di Soligo, the hills become even steeper, the geology more complex and confused. Here the vines are cultivated extensively, at Guia, Santo Stefano, and on to Valdobbiàdene itself. This area is the heart of the Prosecco Conegliano-Valdobbiàdene region, the zone where the finest, ripest, and most complex grapes are grown, grapes that produce wines that are exceptionally fruity, aromatic, and perfumed.

One particular section of these hills, just around the unassuming hamlet of Santo Stefano itself, is the classic *cru* zone known as Cartizze, an area from which the finest wines come, wines that are somewhat fuller, rounder, fruitier, and which should be drunk while still young and exceptionally fresh.

Neither Prosecco nor Cartizze are sparkling wines in the style of French Champagne, Saumur or others whose hallmark, in part, relies on a refreshing, zippy acidity. The Prosecco grapes are harvested when fully mature and they are not overly acid to begin with. Thus the wines, even when fermented to total dryness, maintain a round, rather soft and fruity character that is much loved. Partly to maintain this, the Charmat or tank method of production is preferred over the more elaborate *metodo champenois*. Not only is the former considerably less labour intensive and consequently cheaper; by allowing the secondary fermentation to take place very slowly in sealed stainless steel tanks, the inherent and essential fruity aroma of the Prosecco grape is intensified.

While there is no shortage of wine growers to visit on this brief wine road, it should be noted that some 90% of production lies in the hands of the large firms as well as the *cantina sociale* at Valdobbiàdene. The considerable *attrezzatura* – machinery – needed to produce sparkling wines is beyond the means of many small wine growers, so they may choose to sell most of their grapes direct to the larger concerns or the co-operative. However, to gain an insight into the wines and the region, it is essential to stop and visit the small growers, for their products can be among the most charming and individual.

One traditional but rather simple and rustic method of production may be encountered at the smaller private wine farms. After the initial fermentation, sweet grape must is added to the still wines which are then bottled and tightly corked. Yeast remaining in the wines begins to work, thus causing a secondary fermentation which gives off carbon dioxide in the process. Such wines thus become *frizzante* (rarely fully sparkling) and if a sediment of dead yeast cells remains, what does that matter? Obviously, such *metodo rustico* wines must be handled with care before drinking, to ensure that the sediment stays on the bottom, and is not poured out. But on an outdoor terrace in summer, perhaps with a handful of freshly picked cherries or some strawberries, they can be delightfully vivacious.

Valdobbiàdene is a small wine town nestled at the foot of the pre-Alps. It has a most pleasant and impressive central *piazza*, surrounded by the 14th-century Chiesa Arcipretale, bars, and shops selling wine, *soppressa*, and other good things to eat and drink. Many of the larger *spumante* firms are located here.

Beyond the *Strada del Vino Bianco*, the wine tourist can continue on, south past Montebelluna to Venegazzù and the wine estate of Conte Loredan Gasparini, or west, first by way of the wine zone of Montello e Colli Asolani on to Asolo itself, Robert Browning's favourite city, then to Bassano del Grappa, a fascinating medieval town, with its famous covered bridge. Bassano, of course, is the centre for the distillation of Italy's favourite firewater, *grappa*, and there are no shortages of tasting opportunities in local bars.

Degustazione: Stop to Taste; Stop to Buy

1 AZIENDA AGRICOLA CA' SALINA
VIA SANTO STEFANO 2
FRAZ. SANTO STEFANO
31049 VALDOBBIÀDENE TV
TEL: 0423/975296

WINES PRODUCED: Prosecco di Valdobbiàdene 'Ca' Salina', Prosecco di Valdobbiàdene *metodo rustico*; Chardonnay Spumante.
VISITS: daily 8–12h; 14–18h.

THE NORTH-EAST

Small family production of quality wines, produced from 6 hectares of grapes in the zone adjoining Cartizze. Welcoming tasting salon,

located on the main Valdobbiàdene–Santo Stefano road. English spoken.

---

2 AZIENDA AGRICOLA COLESEL
VIA COLESEL 1
FRAZ. SANTO STEFANO
31040 VALDOBBIÀDENE TV
TEL: 0423/900119

WINES PRODUCED: Prosecco di Valdobbiàdene, Cartizze.
VISITS: daily, working hours.

Azienda located in the heart of the Cartizze zone producing high-quality wines from 18 hectares of own vines. *'Colesel'* means 'little hill' in dialect, and is the name for a particular section of the Cartizze vineyard. English spoken.

---

3 CANTINA SOCIALE DI
VALDOBBIÀDENE
VIA PER SAN GIOVANNI 65
31049 VALDOBBIÀDENE TV
TEL: 0423/980266

WINES PRODUCED: Prosecco di Valdobbiàdene Superiore di Cartizze; Prosecco di

Valdobbiàdene; Marzemino.
VISITS: open daily for visits and direct sales. Appointment preferred but not essential.
One of the zone's major co-operatives, and an important and respected producer.

---

4 SPUMANTI VALDO SPA
VIA GARIBALDI 82
31049 VALDOBBIÀDENE TV
TEL: 0423/975541

WINES PRODUCED: Prosecco di Valdobbiàdene.
VISITS: daily, by appointment.
Family production of this favourite sparkling wine.

---

5 AZIENDA AGRICOLA CONTE LOREDAN
GASPARINI
VIA MARTIGNAGO ALTO 23
31040 VENEGAZZÙ DEL MONTELLO TV
TEL: 0423/871742

WINES PRODUCED: Venegazzù della

Casa, Venegazzù della Casa Etichetta Nera; Loredan Gasparini Brut *metodo classico champenois*.
VISITS: Mon–Fri 8h30–12h; 14–18h.
The Villa Gasparini wines are well-known and appreciated

throughout Italy, as well as abroad, most notably the fine Venegazzù Etichetta Nera, made from selected Cabernet Sauvignon, Cabernet Franc, Malbec, and Merlot grapes:

a sort of super claret from the Veneto. The sparkling wine is also a classic.

English, German spoken.

Enoteca

1 ENOTECA CONTE DEL MEDÀ
CENTRO BALBI VALIER
31053 PIEVE DI SOLIGO TV
TEL: 0438/840605

Fine selection of local, national, and international wines, for purchase or tasting by the glass or bottle together with simple drinking snacks such as *salame*, *prosciutto*, cheese, served in this rather elegant 'wine bar'.

Ristoranti

1 TRE PANOCE
VIA VECCHIA TREVIGIANA 50
31015 CONEGLIANO TV
TEL: 0438/60071; 62230

Closed Sun eve, Mon; Aug.
Located a few kilometres from Conegliano on the summit of a hill offering panoramic views of the Treviso countryside, this fine old house located in an ex-convent is an

elegant restaurant serving traditional *cucina* of the Veneto with seasonal menus that are changed monthly. Armando Zanotto, chef and proprietor, is the author of a remarkable book with 617 recipes for *radicchio*, the famous red lettuce of Treviso. French and a little German spoken.
Moderate

2 ALBERGO-RISTORANTE CANON D'ORO
VIA XX SETTEMBRE 129
31015 CONEGLIANO TV
TEL: 0438/34246

Restaurant closed Sat.
Hotel-restaurant located in a

16th-century *palazzo* in the historic centre of Conegliano near the railway station. Restaurant serves classic and local foods, and only wines from the region.
Inexpensive to Moderate

THE NORTH-EAST

LA GRAPPA

Grappa is the most distinctive of all Italian distillations. Whether taken as a post-prandial *digestivo*, a tot after a day on the ski slopes, or a dash in your *espresso* to 'correct' it, *grappa* is a characteristic flavour of the land.

Grappa, like French *marc*, is a distillation of the *vinaccia* or grape residue left over after the wine making process. Of course, there is *grappa*, and there is *grappa*. Specialist distillers take great care and produce true artisan handmade products that are eagerly sought by connoisseurs.

To make good *grappa*, a distiller tells us, you need to start with *vinaccia* of the highest quality, preferably wine-drenched and virtually straight from the presses or vats. Aromatic grape varieties are highly sought for so-called *monocru* distillations – *grappe* from, for example, Chardonnay, Nosiola, Traminer, Moscato, Müller-Thurgau and other single grape varieties. The *vinacce* are distilled usually in small pot-stills (some fired by direct flames) that need to be recharged after every batch; only the precious middle cut, that part of the distillation free of undesirable impurities, is kept.

While *grappa bianca*, clear *grappa*, is still overwhelmingly preferred in Italy, there is also a lesser following for *grappa gialla*, that is, *grappa* aged in oak barrels which contribute not only colour but more complex aromas, nuances, and smoothness. Artisan distilleries usually offer both types, the best examples bottled in fanciful and beautiful crystal flasks. While *grappa* is produced throughout the country's wine regions, its spiritual homeland is the alpine arc of northern Italy, and the town of Bassano del Grappa remains a traditional centre of production. The firm of Nardini, located on the town's famous bridge over the Brenta, is one of the country's famous producers.

Distilleria Bortolo Nardini SpA
Ponte Vecchio 2
36061 Bassano del Grappa VI
tel: 0424/27741
Visits: daily, by appointment.

3 RISTORANTE 'DA CELESTE'
VIA ARMANDO DIAZ 12
31040 VENEGAZZÙ DEL MONTELLO TV

Closed Mon eve, Tue.

Charming restaurant serving classic foods of the region: *risotti, baccalà alla vicentina, arrosti*, and good homemade desserts.
Moderate

La Strada dei Vini del Piave

In Brief: This signposted wine road starts, like the *Strada del Vino Bianco*, at Conegliano's castle, and explores a broad arc of the Piave valley between Conegliano and Treviso by way of Oderzo. The country is, frankly, rather flat, and much of the production of the high-yielding vineyards goes to the zone's large network of co-operatives. All the same, there are some fine individual wine estates to visit, and the country is never less than pleasant.

The wines of Treviso are known broadly as the wines of the Piave, for this important river that has its source high in the Alps cuts through the region, watering its rich and fertile valleys. In particular, mainly on the flatter plains on the left bank of the river between Conegliano and Oderzo, a broad range of sound to excellent red wines, primarily from Cabernet, Merlot, and the local Raboso, as well as lesser amounts of whites, principally from Tocai and Verduzzo, are produced.

The signposted wine road begins at Conegliano and leads first to Vazzola, then to San Polo di Piave, a river town noted for its freshwater eels and crayfish, both served in a pungent *salsa verde*. Oderzo, a larger ancient town that has been fought over, destroyed and rebuilt many times over the centuries, is today the centre for the wines of the Piave, and the home of the important Consorzio Cantine Sociali della Marca Trevigiana. The Consorzio co-ordinates and oversees the production and marketing of wines from the zone's numerous *cantine sociali*, and, in its co-operative wine store at Oderzo, undertakes the task of storing, ageing (in stainless steel and Slavonian oak *botti*), bottling and marketing wines from the various co-operatives. The symbol of such wines is a square seal showing two 'thumbs up' hands, one holding a glass of wine, the other a bunch of grapes.

While the serious wine connoisseur may tend to dismiss such co-operative

THE NORTH-EAST

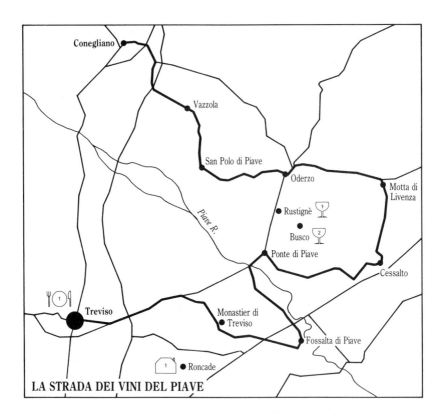

LA STRADA DEI VINI DEL PIAVE

produced wines, and while visits to *cantine cooperative* are generally of less interest than visits to private *aziende agricole*, it should be noted that the region's co-operatives, at Campodipietra, Musile di Piave, Zerman di Mogliano Veneto, Villorba, Caonada, Solighetto, San Giacomo di Veglia, Orsago, Codognè, Mareno di Piave, Tezze di Piave, Vazzola and Fontanelle are the source of abundant and generous everyday wines for the inhabitants of the region, many of whom purchase their *damigiane* or crates of two-litre bottles direct.

The *Strada dei Vini del Piave* continues from Oderzo east, first to Motta di Livenza, then circles back south to Cessalto, crosses the river at Ponte di Piave, and continues downriver to Fossalta, then to Monastier (where there is an ancient Benedictine abbey), and so finally arrives at Treviso.

Degustazione: **Stop to Taste; Stop to Buy**

1 AZIENDA AGRICOLA F.LLI MERCANTE
LOC. RUSTIGNÈ
31046 ODERZO TV
TEL: 0422/853744

WINES PRODUCED: Tocai, Verduzzo, Pinot, Sauvignon, Merlot, Cabernet Franc, Cabernet Sauvignon, Raboso.
VISITS: Mon–Fri 9–12h.

---

2 AZIENDA AGRICOLA LIASORA
ABBAZIA DI BUSCO
BUSCO DI PONTE DI PIAVE TV
TEL: 0422/752152

WINES PRODUCED: Tocai, Pinot Grigio, Buschino (*passito*), Pinot,

Merlot, Raboso.
VISITS: Mon–Sat, by appointment. Traditional production and the 'oldest *cantina* in the zone'.
English, German spoken.

Ristorante

1 HOTEL-RISTORANTE AL FOGHÈR
VIALE DELLA REPUBBLICA 10
31100 TREVISO
TEL: 0422/21687

Restaurant closed Sun.
Hotel-restaurant located near the door to the walled medieval part of

town, serving *cucina tipica veneta* with particular reference to the specialities of Treviso, together with the local wines of the region.
English, French, German spoken.
Moderate

Azienda Agricola Agrituristica

1 CASTELLO DI RONCADE
VIA ROMA 133
31056 RONCADE TV
TEL: 0422/708736

WINES PRODUCED: Merlot del Piave, Cabernet del Piave, Tocai del Piave; Pinot Grigio, Sauvignon, Chardonnay, Riserva Villa Giustinian.

VISITS: open to the public 'always'. Baron Vincenzo Ciani Bassetti's moated *castello* dominates the town of Roncade and is the source of a range of quality wines of the Piave. The estate is also a welcoming *azienda agrituristica*, with rooms and apartments for rent.

THE NORTH-EAST

COLLI EUGANEI: VILLAS, HOT BATHS, AND WINE

In Brief: This compact, little-known wine region lies just south of Padua and can easily be explored in a day or two. For those visiting Venice or Padua, it thus provides a peaceful and relaxing interlude. Others may wish to relax in thermal spa towns such as Montegrotto or Abano, important tourist destinations in their own right. Though there is a signposted wine road, it is not at all easy to follow. We have therefore devised one route through this complex maze of hills, but don't hesitate to deviate from it.

South of Padua, a weird steep chain of hills erupts above the flatter plains to the north and south. These are the Colli Euganei, a series of rounded, contorted, at times bizarrely-shaped mounds that resulted from volcanic activity rippling down from the alpine foothills of the Dolomites hundreds of thousands of years ago. But the volcanoes never broke the surface here: rather, their power, their energy, and their heat was diffused into deep underground streams which found outlets throughout the hills, making them a unique and prized thermal source. Indeed, for millennia, the so-called 'terme Euganei' have been visited by those in need of a therapeutic cure. Romans built their villas here, and Pliny the Elder wrote of the healing properties of the waters. And where the Romans settled, they naturally planted the vine.

As a spa centre, the region flourished not only during the Roman era, but also throughout the Middle Ages. Petrarch, for example, lived at Arquà and cultivated both the vine and the olive. Today, the region remains as popular as ever, as a centre not simply for those in need of a cure, but for anyone interested in natural beauty, tranquillity, a long and rich history, and gastronomy and wine.

As wine regions go, it must be admitted that the Colli Euganei is strictly a minor one. The zone's wines are usually mentioned in passing, as of local interest only. True, most of its production is drunk within the region, in the spa towns themselves, certainly, and rarely further afield than Padua. However, the Colli Euganei region has benefited from DOC since as long ago as 1963, and its range of wines has a long and impressive tradition. It deserves to be better known.

For example, out of all the Tre Venezie wine regions, the Colli Euganei is the only zone where Moscato is entitled to a *denominazione di origine*

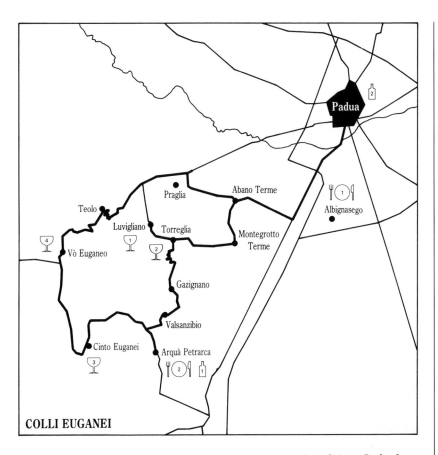

COLLI EUGANEI

controllata. Moscato is an ancient grape, first introduced into Italy from Turkey by the Romans. This was one of the first areas where it was cultivated, and here it has remained ever since. Indeed, the Moscato wines produced, both from the Moscato Bianco and Moscato Fior d'Arancio, usually semi-sweet, often sparkling, are among the region's best.

In addition to Colli Euganei Moscato, there are a number of wines entitled to the zonal DOC: Colli Euganei Bianco, Colli Euganei Rosso, Colli Euganei Pinot Bianco, Colli Euganei Tocai, Colli Euganei Cabernet, and Colli Euganei Merlot. The production is about half-and-half between red and white. The Cabernet wines, in particular, are capable of considerable distinction.

The wine traveller to the zone clearly has a wide range from which to slake his thirst. In truth, though, he or she will probably not be here solely in search of wine. Rather, for those visiting Venice or Padua, or who have

THE NORTH-EAST

come for a vacation or cure in Montegrotto Terme or Abano, the Colli Euganei is simply a lovely, compact, and little-known area in which to relax. The fact that it is also a wine region of not inconsiderable note is a singular bonus.

Padua must be the starting point for a tour of the Colli Euganei. It is one of our favourite towns in the Veneto, and is certainly worthy of extended exploration. Historic Padua remains today as in the past an important religious, cultural, and commercial centre for the region. Its university is one of the oldest in Europe, founded in 1222 by the Emperor Frederick II, and Galileo Galilei was once a professor there. The city's greatest monument is the Capello degli Scrovegni, an intimate chapel decorated by Giotto with a magnificent series of some 38 frescoes depicting the life of Christ. There is much to see in Padua: the Basilica del Santo; the cathedral; the Chiesa degli Eremitani, with its fragments of frescoes by Mantegna; the lovely and peaceful Prato della Valle, a fine municipal garden surrounded by medieval *palazzi*; or the Caffè Pedrocchi, one of the most famous cafés in Europe.

From Padua, head into the hills to taste wine and to relax. Leave the city south via the Prato della Valle, and find the road to Montegrotto Terme. Montegrotto today sprawls together with its sister spa town of Abano: both have been thermal centres for literally millennia. Their importance in antiquity is evident from the fact that Abano was named after Aponus, a Roman god of healing, while Montegrotto derives from Mons Aegratorum, 'Mount of the Infirm', the name of this ancient healing sanctuary and the site of the legendary oracle Geryon. Today, Montegrotto and Abano, together with Galzignano and Battaglia Terme, attract millions who come to bathe in the natural hot springs as well as to benefit from the famous *fango* or hot mud cures. Almost every hotel in these spa towns has a thermal swimming pool (naturally heated to about 33° C), and there are scores of additional health and beauty treatments on offer.

The entire zone of the Colli Euganei is cultivated with vines, and though there are signposted wine roads, virtually every road through this confused system of hills leads eventually into the vineyards, or to a wine producer or two. From Montegrotto Terme, we suggest first heading out to Torreglia, a town famous not only for wine but for a cherry liqueur made from the prized locally-grown *marasche* cherries. The firm of Luxardo is world famous for its Maraschino liqueur, and the distillery can be visited. The firm also additionally produces a range of highly-regarded table wines.

From Torreglia, next find little Luvigliano, centre today for the local wine industry, and the headquarters of the Consorzio, or official union of wine growers for the region. Here, the 16th-century Villa dei Vescovi, designed by Giovan Maria Falconetto, demonstrates particularly well the classic Venetian harmony between domestic architecture and the surrounding countryside which makes the region so pleasing to the eye. The *azienda agricola* of the Villa dei Vescovi is probably the best place to come and taste the wines of the Colli Euganei, at outdoor tables in the gardens overlooking the villa. The Serprino wine (local name for the Prosecco grape), well-chilled, *frizzante*, and just a touch sweet, is particularly refreshing together with a plate of homemade *soppressa*, local breads, and cheese.

From Luvigliano, return to Torreglia, then find the road to Galzignano, another major spa centre and formerly a popular watering hole for the Venetian and Paduan nobility, as the many villas in the area attest. The most remarkable, located outside Galzignano past the little village of Valsanzibio, is the Villa Barbarigo, built in the 17th century, noted not only for its architecture, but even more for the splendour of its baroque Italianate gardens, with its stately tree-lined avenues, maze, grottoes, and numerous statues.

From Valsanzibio, next travel on to Arquà Petrarca, a tiny hamlet where the poet Francesco Petrarch came in 1370 and lived until his death some 4 years later. Petrarch is one of Italy's most important literary figures of the Renaissance, credited, along with Dante, as the father of the Italian language, for he wrote many of his sonnets and *canzoniere* in the vernacular, not in the formal Latin of the church or court. His pure and elevated unrequited love for his Laura is legendary. Today, the Casa Petrarca is a museum devoted to his life. It contains, among other items, the chair in which the great man was sitting when he died, a box containing one of his ribs, numerous manuscripts and

Petrarch's house, Arquà.

visitors' books (signed by Byron and Mozart, among others), and even – my God! – the poet's embalmed cat, encased behind glass in a hollow in the wall. The museum certainly deserves a visit, not least because it is an authentic and well-preserved house dating from over 600 years ago.

Arquà, though only a small hamlet, is deservedly one of the most important venues for visitors to the Colli Euganei. As a result, the local wines have gained a minor renown, especially the so-called Bianco d'Arquà. Taste it, and other own-produced wines at the *Enoteca 'Da Loris'*, located just a few steps from the poet's house, where wines can be enjoyed at outdoor tables together with simple drinking snacks.

To continue the wine tour, leave Arquà on the back road to climb up to Monte Fasolo, an impressive hill about 300 metres high. The road becomes just a dirt track, but take courage and continue on. Notice the complexity of the terrain – here sandy and loose, there riddled with large chunks of limestone, or there again almost pure white chalk. These steep, sunbaked hill vineyards clearly produce grapes considerably superior to those grown on the flatter, lusher plains down below, and it is evident that this is a quality vineyard capable of producing exceptional wines. The Fattoria Monte Fasolo, a private *azienda* where wines are made from grapes grown on 3 different estates, provides another opportunity to taste and purchase this incredibly varied and interesting range. The deep, rich, oak-aged *riserva* wines are particularly noteworthy.

From Monte Fasolo, find the road down to Cinto Euganei, then return to Padua or Abano by way of Vò Euganeo, where one of the zone's two wine co-operatives is located, and Teolo. Just off this road, before Abano, the Benedictine monastery of Praglia can be visited.

Degustazione: Stop to Taste; Stop to Buy

1 VILLA DEI VESCOVI
VIA DEI VESCOVI 33
35038 LUVIGLIANO DI TORREGLIA PD
TEL: 049/5211222

WINES PRODUCED: Colli Euganei DOC: Moscato, Pinot Bianco, Colli Euganei Bianco, Tocai Italico, Cabernet, Merlot, Colli Euganei Rosso; Serprino, Fior d'Arancio Moscato, Prosecco, Raboso.
VISITS: daily 8–19h.
A must stop on any tour: own-produced wines from the Vescovi estate, together with a range of *buone cose* from the region: homemade marmalade, cheese, honey, liquor, olive oil, *soppressa*. Wines can be tasted or enjoyed by

the glass or bottle, served together with *soppressa, salame, formaggi,* and bread at pleasant outdoor tables overlooking the vineyards and the old villa of the Bishops.

---

2 LUXARDO
35038 TORREGLIA PD
TEL: 049/511032

LIQUORI AND WINES PRODUCED: Maraschino cherry *liquori*; full range of Colli Euganei DOC wines.
VISITS: Mon–Sat 9–12h30.
Famous firm specializing in production of Maraschino cherry liquor, produced on the premises from locally grown fruit, the *marasche* cherry. Visits to the distillery to see the copper stills, and wooden ageing vats. Also production of highly-regarded table wines, as well as exceptional *maraschino* marmalade.

---

3 FATTORIA MONTE FASOLO
VIA MONTE FASOLO
35030 CINTO EUGANEI PD
TEL: 0429/94130

WINES PRODUCED: Colli Euganei DOC: Cabernet, Pinot, Tocai, Rosso, Moscato; Marzemino; Merlot; Sauvignon; Pinot Grigio; Moscato Rosa Spumante; Chardonnay Brut; Pinot Spumante *metodo champenois.*

VISITS: Mon–Sat 8h30–12h; 15–18h30. No appointment necessary.
Fattoria, located high in the dramatic hills above Arquà, offers an impressive range of medal-winning wines produced from grapes grown on three different estates. Full range of wines available for tasting in the atmospheric cellars.

---

4 VILLA SCERIMAN
VIA DEI COLLI 68
35030 VÒ EUGANEO PD
TEL: 049/9940123

WINES PRODUCED: Colli Euganei DOC: Cabernet, Merlot, Pinot Bianco, Tocai, Moscato; Fior d'Arancio, Pinello, Prosecco.
VISITS: daily except Mon 8–12h; 15–19h.
Wines and simple *merenda* of *salame* and cheese in the 15th-century Villa Sceriman.
English, German, French spoken.

THE NORTH-EAST

Enoteche

1 ENOTECA 'DA LORIS'
VIA VALLESELLE 7
35032 ARQUÀ PETRARCA PD
TEL: 0429/718188

WINES PRODUCED: Colli Euganei
Moscato; Pinello Brut Spumante;
Moscato Rosa Spumante; Moscato
Fior d'Arancio; Cabernet; Bianco
d'Arquà.

OPEN: daily 9–12h30; 15–18h.
Own-produced wines are available
for purchase, or served by the glass
or bottle on a pleasant shaded
terrace of this historic hill town,
together with *soppressa*, cheese, and
typical breads.

---

2 ENOTECA 'DA SEVERINO'
VIA DEL SANTO 44
35100 PADUA
TEL: 049/30581

OPEN: 9–13h30; 16–21h. Closed
Sun.
Padua's second 'basilica', just up

the road from Il Santo, serving a
wide range of wines by the glass in
an atmospheric stand-up setting.
Superlative range of wines from
throughout Italy, and a rare chance
to taste the elusive Clinton.

Ristoranti

1 TRATTORIA DA BRUTTO RUGGERO
LOC. SOLBORO
35100 ALBIGNASEGO PD
TEL: 049/8010700

Really simple, rustic *trattoria*
located not far from Padua, serving
seasonal foods of the Veneto: *risi e
bisi*, *bigoli*, *grigliata mista*, and
own-produced wines.
Inexpensive

---

2 TRATTORIA 'IL GIARDINETTO'
35032 ARQUÀ PETRARCA PD

Closed Mon.
Good family *trattoria* with pleasant

shaded terrace serving local foods –
bigoli, *fettucine*, *spezzatino d'asino*,
baccalà alla vicentina, and
own-produced wine of Arquà.
Inexpensive to Moderate

POLIPI AND FIOR D'ARANCIO

We love to simply wander through Padua's two main squares, the Piazza delle Erbe and the Piazza della Frutta, where the fruit and vegetable markets take place daily. This is one of the best markets that we know, always full of lively activity, as well as the colours and smells of the finest produce from the Veneto and further afield. At one end of the Piazza delle Erbe there is a stall that sells freshly-cooked *polipi* – baby octopus. Steaming from the cauldron, chopped up quickly and seasoned with a little olive oil, parsley, and lemon, it is delicious eaten with toothpicks while standing up. After enjoying this simple Paduan market food, go into the adjoining covered market and cleanse your palate with a tumbler or two of Moscato Fior d'Arancio from the wine stall there: the flowery, fresh, sweet taste of the wine goes extremely well with the rather oily, rich after-flavour of the *polipi*.

Wine and Other Related *Sagre* and *Feste*

mid-April	VINITALY (Italy's most important wine trade fair)	Verona
Easter	Sagra del Recioto	Negrar
1st Sun in May	Festival of Soave Classico	Soave
end Sept	Sagra dell'Uva	Bardolino
end Sept	Sagra del Vino	Soave
early Oct	Festa dell'Uva	Fumane

E PER SAPERE DI PIÙ –
ADDITIONAL INFORMATION

Ente Provinciale per il Turismo
via C. Montari 14
37100 Verona
tel: 045/25065

Ente Provinciale per il Turismo
Riviera Mugnai 8
35100 Padua
tel: 049/25024

Agriturist Comitato Regionale
Corso Monteverdi 15
30174 Mestre VE
tel: 041/987400

Ente Provinciale per il Turismo
Palazzo Scotti
via Toniolo 41
31100 Treviso
tel: 0422/47632

Associazione Vini Veronese DOC
Camera di Commercio
Corso Porta Nuova 96
37100 Verona
tel: 045/591077

TRENTINO-ALTO ADIGE

The tap room of the welcoming Neustift abbey.

I Vini: THE WINES OF TRENTINO-ALTO ADIGE   181

La Gastronomia   183

Le Strade dei Vini: THE WINE ROADS OF
TRENTINO-ALTO ADIGE

    Trentino Wine Country   183

    Wines and Wine Gardens of the Südtirol
    (Alto Adige)   193

      *Südtiroler Weinstraße – La Strada Altoatesina
      del Vino*   195

      Eisacktal (Isarco) Valley   204

      Etsch (Adige) Valley from Bozen to Meran   205

Le Sagre: WINE AND OTHER RELATED FESTIVALS   206

Additional Information   207

Trentino-Alto Adige is an autonomous region that extends from the watershed of the Alps that border Austria, south along the valleys of the Adige and its tributaries, to just below the northern tip of Lake Garda and the Veneto. As a scenically beautiful but somewhat introverted alpine land, a natural corridor from northern Europe to the south, and a disputed border zone where many of the population speak German as their first language (and a tiny section still speak Ladin, an ancient Romansch tongue), it is one of the most unusual but interesting regions of Italy.

Indeed, though grouped as a single entity, Trentino and Südtirol (the historic name for the northern Alto Adige) are really two very different regions. Both found themselves under the rule of the Hapsburgs for some centuries, but the southern Trentino province always managed to maintain its separate cultural identity and language. During World War I, Italy entered on the side of the Allies primarily with the aim of reclaiming the two regions, which it did. But whereas the inhabitants of Trentino welcomed this development, those of the Südtirol were less than enthusiastic, and the problem was further aggravated through the insensitive Fascist policy of encouraging Italians, primarily from the south, to settle in the region.

Today the region has settled into a not unhappy coexistence; if Italians who travel north to the Südtirol may feel as if they are in another country (particularly in outlying rural areas where Italian is hardly spoken, and where women wear dirndl dresses, men loden coats), what of it? In effect, they are, for everything including food, architecture, language, folk customs, and wine, stems from Austro-Germanic traditions.

Trentino-Alto Adige is not one of Italy's larger wine regions, but what is produced is of remarkably high and even quality (as an indication, in Südtirol some 80% of production is entitled to controlled *denominazione* status, indicated as either DOC or QbA). Such wines, their labels and names often written in German, find a ready export market in Austria, Switzerland, and Germany especially. But the rest of the world is beginning to discover them, too.

Trentino and Südtirol are both regions of great attraction, centres where many come year after year to enjoy the spectacular mountain scenery, summer walking, winter sports, farmhouse tourism, and the charms of lovely, unspoiled upland villages and hamlets. The wine tourist, no less, will find ample reasons to return to this unique region of Italy again and again.

ORIENTATION

Trentino-Alto Adige is an autonomous region comprising 2 separate provinces, German-speaking Bolzano (Bozen) in the north and Italian-speaking Trentino in the south. The region has historically served as a corridor linking Italy with northern Europe by way of the Brenner Pass. The A22 *autostrada* leads north from Trento to Bolzano and Bressanone (Brixen), and finally into Austria. The region is furthermore well situated on a principal rail line linking Brenner–Bolzano–Trento–Verona with the rest of northern Europe via TEE trains to Innsbruck and Munich. Verona's Villafranca airport is the most convenient, but international visitors may find it easiest to fly to Munich, then rent a car. It should be noted, moreover, that both Munich and Innsbruck are only hours away, and the region is extremely popular with German-speaking tourists.

Map Touring Club Italiano 1: 200 000 Trentino-Alto Adige.

I VINI: GLOSSARY TO THE WINES OF TRENTINO-ALTO ADIGE

Wines of *Denominazione di Origine Controllata (DOC)*

Alto Adige (Südtiroler) DOC
Large regional *denominazione* applying to some 19 different wines of every style produced throughout the Alto Adige vineyard: dry white, sweet white, rosé, red, and sparkling. Wines are all varietally labelled: Cabernet (both Sauvignon and Franc), Chardonnay, Lagrein (produced in two versions: red Dunkel and rosé Kretzer), Malvasia (Malvasier), Merlot, Moscato Giallo (Goldenmuskateller), Moscato Rosa (Rosenmuskateller), Müller-Thurgau (Riesling-Sylvaner), Pinot Bianco (Weißburgunder), Pinot Grigio (Ruländer), Pinot Nero (Blauburgunder), Riesling Italico (Welschriesling), Riesling Renano (Rheinriesling), Sauvignon, Schiava (Vernatsch), Sylvaner, Traminer Aromatico (Gewürztraminer).

Caldaro or **Lago di Caldaro (Kalterersee) DOC** Popular red wine produced from grapes grown around the Lago di Caldaro, primarily Schiava Grossa, with some Pinot Nero and Lagrein. Minimum alcohol 11 degrees. Wines from selected grapes exceeding this minimum may be labelled Superiore or Auslese.

Casteller DOC Basic red wine of Trentino, made generally from Schiava Grossa and Gentile, Merlot and Lambrusco. Minimum alcohol 11 degrees.

Colli di Bolzano (Bozner Leiten) DOC Red Schiava wine from hills around Bolzano. Minimum alcohol 11 degrees.

Meranese di Collina (Meraner Hügel) DOC Light Schiava wine from steep hill vineyards mainly to the north of the popular spa town of Merano. Minimum alcohol 10.5 degrees.

Santa Maddalena (St Magdalener) DOC Südtirol's best (certainly best-known) red wine, produced from varieties of Schiava grown on hill vineyards above Bolzano, mainly around the village of Santa Maddalena. Minimum alcohol 11.5 degrees. Round, warm, pleasant bitter aftertaste.

Sorni DOC Rare, little encountered wine from vineyards around town of Sorni, north of Trento. Red wines are made from Schiava, Teroldego, and Lagrein; white is mainly from local Nosiola.

THE NORTH-EAST

Terlano (Terlaner) DOC
Denominazione for 7 different wines produced from grapes grown in vineyards south-west of Bolzano mainly in the communes of Terlano (Terlan), Andriano (Andrian), Nalles (Nals), Appiano (Eppan), Caldaro (Kaltern) and San Genesio: Pinot Bianco (Weißburgunder) di Terlano, Chardonnay di Terlano, Müller-Thurgau di Terlano, Riesling Italico (Welschriesling) di Terlano, Riesling Renano (Rheinriesling) di Terlano, Sylvaner di Terlano, Terlano (Terlaner). Wines from Terlano, Andriano and Nalles may be labelled Classico.

Teroldego Rotaliano DOC Great Trentino red from Teroldego grapes grown on the Campo Rotaliano between San Michele all'Adige and Mezzolombardo. Minimum alcohol 11.5 degrees; 12 degrees for wines labelled Superiore.

Trentino DOC Large regional *denominazione* covering most of the vineyards of Trentino, and applying to some 20 different wines: Bianco (Chardonnay/Pinot Bianco), Cabernet (both Franc and Sauvignon can be specified), Chardonnay, Lagrein, Marzemino, Merlot, Moscato Giallo, Moscato Rosa, Müller-Thurgau, Nosiola, Pinot Bianco, Pinot Grigio, Pinot Nero, Riesling Italico, Riesling Renano, Rosso (primarily Cabernet/Merlot), Traminer Aromatico, Vin Santo (made from semi-dried Nosiola grapes).

Valle Isarco (Eisacktaler) DOC
Delimited vineyard following Isarco (Eisack) valley north-east of Bolzano up to and beyond Bressanone. The *denominazione* applies to 5 wines: Müller-Thurgau, Pinot Grigio (Ruländer), Sylvaner (Silvaner), Traminer Aromatico (Gewürztraminer), Veltliner. Wines from vineyards around Bressanone may cite this fact on the label (either Bressanone or Brixner).

Valdadige (Etschtaler) DOC
Large zonal *denominazione* for red and white wines produced from grapes grown almost the length of Adige valley. Valdadige Rosso is made from Schiava, Lambrusco, Merlot, Pinot Nero, Lagrein, Teroldego and other grapes, and must reach a minimum 11 degrees of alcohol. Valdadige Bianco is a blend of Pinot Bianco, Pinot Grigio, Riesling Italico, Müller-Thurgau, Trebbiano Toscano, Nosiola, Vernaccia, Sylvaner and/or Veltliner and must reach a minimum of 10.5 degrees of alcohol.

Above: Pasticceria in Asti

Right: Bread shop

Below: Castiglione Falletto, in the heart of the Barolo vineyard

Above: Radda-in-Chianti, Tuscany

Right: Harvest time in Soave

Below: Courtyard of Villa Rizzardi, Negrar di Valpolicella

Above: Lakeside resort of Garda

Left: Courgette flowers

Below: Grapes laid out on *graticci* for the production of Vin Santo

Above: The vineyards of the Collio, looking across the frontier to Yugoslavia

Right: Vineyards of Bozen (Bolzano)

Below: Vin Santo is traditionally served and enjoyed with crunchy almond biscuits – *cantuccini di Prato*

Above: Autumn vinescape, Carmignano

Left: Prosciutti home-cured on the Barbi estate, Montalcino

Below: Ovuli mushrooms, a great autumn delicacy

Above: Damigiane

Right: A quiet moment at a wine festival

Above: Castello di Vicchiomaggio in the heart of the Chianti Classico

Left: Sangiovese grapes

Below: The *vendemmia* – grape harvest

LA GASTRONOMIA: FOODS OF TRENTINO-ALTO ADIGE

The Alto Adige (Südtirol) was for centuries the southern flank of the Austrian Tyrol, while the Italian-speaking province of Trento, like much of northern Italy, was occupied by the Hapsburgs for lengthy periods. Thus, the dominant feature of the cuisines of these two allied but definitely separate provinces is a character that is Austrian in flavour, and more central European in outlook than Mediterranean.

Hearty, warming mountain foods, dumplings, *gulasch*, and pickled vegetables; German-style sausages, home-cured and -smoked bacon (*Speck*); delicious and varied breads made with mixtures of wheat, rye, and barley flours; and exquisite pastries and fruit-filled strudels: these are foods that are little different from those found across the Brenner Pass in Austria. But there are subtle differences, as well. For though the Alto Adige is definitely Austrian in outlook, the younger generation at least are more ready to consider themselves Italian, and look south, too, for inspiration. In Trentino, moreover, influences from the Imperial Hapsburgs are intermingled with those of Venice, and though the food still retains an essentially Germanic character it does so with an Italian accent. Dumplings are eaten, like *pasta*, as first courses, while *risotti, polenta, gnocchi* and other such foods remain popular. See page 184.

TRENTINO WINE COUNTRY

In Brief: There is no signposted wine road through the province of Trentino, but this is none the less accessible and eminently satisfying wine country. Though linked with the German-speaking Südtirol, Trentino is a separate and important wine region in its own right: the vine is cultivated extensively, from the northern shores of Lake Garda, up through the Adige valley to the south and north of Trento, the region's capital. Trento is a fine, historic city, while Rovereto and San Michele all'Adige are two important wine towns, but the entire region repays in-depth exploration.

For those entering Italy by way of the Brenner Pass, Trentino is the first taste of Italy (after passing through the German-speaking Südtirol); on the

PIATTI TIPICI:
REGIONAL SPECIALITIES

Speck Home-cured and -smoked bacon, a typical Südtirol drinking snack.

Carne salà Raw beef marinaded in wine, vinegar and spices: a delicious first course or drinking snack of Trentino.

Canederli Large bread dumplings, boiled then lightly fried in melted butter.

Polenta smalzada Buckwheat polenta, mixed with butter, anchovies, and cheese.

Strangolapreti 'Priest stranglers' – *gnocchi* dumplings usually made with spinach and cheese.

Minestra di orzo Hearty barley and vegetable soup.

Weinsuppe Wine soup, made with wine, eggs, spices and milk.

Gröstl Potato cake made with *Speck* and onions.

Crauti Sauerkraut.

Tiroler Speckknödelsuppe Bacon dumpling in homemade broth.

Tafelspitz mit Kren Boiled beef with horseradish.

Zwiebelrostbraten Roast or braised beef and onions served with gravy and dumplings.

Dampfknüdeln Steamed sweet fruit dumplings.

Apfelstrudel Thin layered pastry filled with apples and spices.

Cheeses: *Grana trentino* Parmesan-type eaten fresh or grated. *Cioncada* Smooth cow's milk cheese.

other hand, for those travelling north from Lake Garda or Verona, Trentino, though still Italian-speaking, is undoubtedly and vividly coloured by the Austrian heritage and influence that remains.

Differences in food, for example, are one way that we mark the crossing of cultural if not political boundaries. Come to Trento, the region's capital, and sit down at a table in the Locanda Port'Aquila by the old Castello del Buon

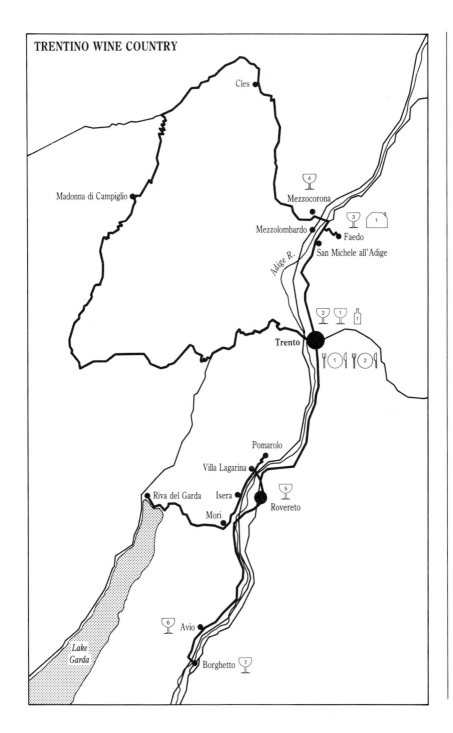

Consiglio (former residence of the prince-bishops who ruled the province), and you will be left in no doubt that you are in an autonomous region with a separate heritage from the rest of Italy. For in this simple bastion of authentic *cucina trentina* you will be served *canederli* (German-style dumplings fried in butter and eaten as a *primo piatto*), hearty *minestra di orzo* (barley soup), and smoked meats served with sauerkraut and (to complicate the cultural mix) *polenta*. These hearty mountain foods are washed down with the full-bodied house Teroldego Rotaliano, an exceptional, deep red wine produced from vineyards to the north of the city on the ancient Campo Rotaliano.

After such a hearty feast, stroll over to the Piazza del Duomo and have a *caffè* or a *gelato* in the square overlooking the impressive gothic Duomo. The Council of Trent was held here between 1546 and 1563 in a futile attempt to reconcile the differences between Protestants and Catholics following Martin Luther's Reformation Proclamation. Some 400 years later, Hitler and Mussolini met in Trento to discuss the division between them of the rest of Europe. Today Trento is a fine, vibrant university town; though ancient, with its frescoed arches and 15th- and 16th-century mansions lining the Via Belenzani, it is a town above all which feels young and vital.

The wine country of Trentino lies both to the north and south of the region's capital, and thus Trento serves as a convenient starting point for those either heading north to the Südtirol or the Dolomites, or south, back towards Lake Garda and Verona.

Some 18 km north of Trento, San Michele all'Adige is an important Trentino wine town, the home not only of numerous wine growers, but also of the Istituto Agrario Provinciale, one of Italy's leading schools of viticulture and oenology, and itself a leading wine producer. Founded in 1869, while the region was still part of the Austrian Tyrol, the Istituto is not only the oldest school of viticulture in Italy but one of its most important. Wine growers from all over northern Italy send their sons and daughters to San Michele all'Adige to learn about the newest developments in clonal selection, training methods, cultivation, and wine making. This important institute, together with the schools of oenology at Conegliano, Asti and elsewhere, are partly responsible for the great renaissance in quality Italian wines in recent decades.

To gain a perspective on the Trentino vineyard, drive up from San Michele all'Adige, beyond the flatter plains up to the little wine hamlet of Faedo. Along the way, the steep road winds past carefully tended, terraced vineyards, some neatly marked by a single rose bush at the end of each row. The vines are trained in the traditional *pergole trentina*, fanned out at a favourable angle not just to gain maximum exposure, but also to keep the ground below cool, and to encourage the circulation of air.

For, indeed, in summer the Trentino province enjoys blistering hot days and very cold nights, factors that contribute to the development of fresh fruit flavours and aroma, particularly important for the production of quality white wines. This is a prolific and varied wine region: the Trentino DOC applies to 20 different wines, mainly produced from single grape varieties. Though quality red wines are produced, especially the superlative Teroldego Rotaliano which benefits from its own DOC, the region is noted foremost for its exceptional dry white wines.

'The more aromatic the grape variety,' explained Mario Pojer, of the small but highly regarded Azienda Agricola Pojer & Sandri, as he poured us a sample, 'the higher the vineyard. Down on the plains we have Schiava, the local native red grape, and it does very well. In the middle altitudes – between 300 and 400 metres – we have planted Chardonnay and, recently, Sauvignon Blanc. This Müller-Thurgau, though, comes from our very highest vineyards above Faedo, situated at up to 750 metres.'

The wine was outstanding: very fresh, very aromatic, but with a strong, steely backbone that comes from a high level of fruity acidity. Müller-Thurgau elsewhere makes soft, rounded wines, but Pojer's is a strong, bone-dry, full-bodied wine to enjoy with food.

'Our wine making tradition in Trentino is different from that in the nearby Südtirol, which has always enjoyed access to the ready markets of Switzerland, Austria, and Germany, where tastes are quite different. We have always had to look south, so our wines are probably more Italian in character: strong and dry, but with the freshness and acidity that comes from high hill vineyards and aromatic grape varieties.'

Faedo itself is a fine, atmospheric hill village, with an old church consecrated in the 14th century and narrow, claustrophobic alleys. The vineyards cease not far above, but from up here there are splendid views of the entire Adige valley, and across to the western Brenta Dolomites.

From Faedo, return to San Michele all'Adige, then cross the Adige river to the important wine towns of Mezzocorona and Mezzolombardo. The latter is an industrial and commercial centre, as well as a notable wine town. Its 16th-century castle is well preserved. The flatter plain around Mezzocorona and Mezzolombardo leading up towards the western mountains is the home of Trentino's most famous – and best – red wine, Teroldego Rotaliano, a wine of surprising depth of colour, richness, and flavour. The Campo Rotaliano,

THE NORTH-EAST

favoured vineyard for Teroldego, lies principally on the scoured gravel plains where the Noce river enters the mighty Adige.

Other red grape varieties also do well in the Trentino vineyard, especially Merlot, Cabernet, and the local, attractively fruity Marzemino. The vineyards continue north up the Noce valley to the wine town of Cles, located above Lake Santa Giustina. From there, continue around to Madonna di Campiglio, an alpine resort and a good starting point for exploring the beautiful Brenta Dolomites.

Returning once more to Trento, it should be mentioned that the capital is a noted wine town in its own right. The favourite everyday beverage is Casteller, an easy quaffing red produced from Schiava mainly, with some Merlot, grown on vineyards to the north and south of the city. Just south of Trento, moreover, are located the large wineries that are an important feature of the Trentino wine scene. Notably, the *cooperative* winery of Càvit produces an extensive and well-made range of table wines and sparkling wines that are enjoyed not just in Italy but internationally as well. Indeed, the sparkling wines of Trento are among the region's most famous. At the private firm of Ferrari, the Lunelli brothers ferment Chardonnay and some Pinot Nero grapes grown on chalk soil to the north of Trento into still base wines that then undergo the laborious *metodo champenois* process of secondary fermentation in the bottle. Such wines as Ferrari Brut de Brut rank among the finest that Italy produces and really can compare with the best sparkling wines from anywhere, France included.

South of Trento, the vineyards continue down the Adige valley almost uninterrupted until they merge with those of the Veneto, north of Verona. The next great Trentino wine centre of note is Rovereto, a stylish Venetian town, controlled by the Republic of San Marco when the rest of Trentino was still ruled by the prince-bishops of Trento. The impressive castle, built in the 14th century, pre-dates the Venetians, though later it was enlarged by them. A reminder of its more recent turbulent past is exhibited in the Museo Storico della Guerra, housed in the castle, which has some 30 rooms devoted to the history of World War I. And each evening at sunset, the town's *Campana dei Caduti*, the largest bell in Italy, tolls a sombre commemoration to the victims of wars throughout history and the world.

The Conti Bossi Fedrigotti family has been in Rovereto since 1692, and began making wine from grapes grown in its own vineyards more than 200 years ago. However, as was the case elsewhere in Italy – and in many cases still is – for most of that time wine was viewed simply as another agricultural product to be made and sold in bulk by the vat or *damigiana*. It was only in 1961 that the decision was made to concentrate on the production of quality estate-bottled wines. The decision proved to be a farsighted one, for the Bossi Fedrigotti's most prestigious vineyard, Foianeghe, a patch of well-exposed basaltic terrain south of Rovereto, was planted with Cabernet and Merlot long before these French varieties became ultra-fashionable elsewhere in Italy. Foianeghe may be the Bossi Fedrigotti's most famous flagship, but the range of wines produced – no fewer than 11 – reflects the diversity and quality of the southern Trentino vineyard.

Trentino's wine country extends well south of Rovereto, and can be enjoyed while driving down towards Verona on the N12. Another aristocratic wine estate, that of the Marchesi Guerrieri Gonzaga, produces a fine range of quality wines. Their Tenuta San Leonardo is located just off this road between Vò and Borghetto (near the Ala-Avio exit from the *autostrada* and just above Trentino's border with the Veneto).

An alternative tour through the Trentino wine country crosses the Adige river at Rovereto. There, either explore the nearby wine hamlets to the north, such as Isera, Villa Lagarina, and Pomarolo. Or head south through Mori (passing by the way the vineyard of Foianeghe), then circle around to the northern shore of Lake Garda to arrive, finally, at Riva del Garda. The vineyards along the way, from Mori to above Lake Garda, are most famous for the production of Vin Santo, a classic traditional *passito* wine made from semi-dried Nosiola grapes. Rare, difficult to find, it should be tried when in the region.

Degustazione: Stop to Taste; Stop to Buy

1

CÀVIT CANTINA VITICOLTORI
VIA DEL PONTE 31
38100 TRENTO
TEL: 0461/922055

WINES PRODUCED: Pinot Grigio; Pinot Bianco; Chardonnay; Traminer; Nosiola; Marzemino; Teroldego Rotaliano; Merlot; Cabernet; Pinot Nero, and others, including a range of sparkling wines.

VISITS: guided visits by appointment for groups only.

Individuals may visit the large and spacious shop for tasting and purchase during office hours.
The largest co-operative society of the region, and one of its most important producers, with more than 5000 member wine growers. The full range of wines of Trentino are produced here, utilizing the most modern and advanced viticultural methods.
English, German spoken.

THE NORTH-EAST

2 SPUMANTE FERRARI
F.LLI LUNELLI SPA
VIA PONTE DI RAVINA 15
38040 TRENTO
TEL: 0461/922500

WINES PRODUCED: Ferrari Brut,
Ferrari Brut Rosé, Ferrari Brut de
Brut (vintage), Giulio Ferrari
Riserva del Fondatore *metodo
champenois*; *grappe trentine*.
VISITS: Mon–Fri 9–12h; 15–18h.
Telephone for an appointment.
One of the leading sparkling wine
producers in Italy, producing a
range of superlative wines
primarily from Chardonnay and
Pinot Nero grapes grown on their
own vineyards, rendered sparkling
exclusively by the classic *metodo
champenois* process of secondary
fermentation in the bottle followed
by lengthy ageing on the lees.
Come here to see the fascinating
process in the ancient and vast
underground cellars at Ravina.
English, German, and some French
spoken.

---

3 AZIENDA AGRICOLA POJER & SANDRI
LOC. MOLINI
38010 FAEDO TN
TEL: 0461/650342

WINES PRODUCED: Müller-Thurgau
di Faedo; Chardonnay di Faedo;
Nosiola di Faedo; Traminer di
Faedo; Schiava di Faedo; Pinot
Nero di Faedo; Vin dei Molini; Faye
Chardonnay; Sauvignon Blanc;
Spumanti *metodo classico*; *grappe*;
acquavite di frutta.
VISITS: Mon–Fri working hours.
Telephone call in advance
appreciated.
Pojer & Sandri has established
itself as a small 'boutique' winery
producing white wines of the
highest quality from grapes
cultivated around the *azienda* at
Faedo at levels of between 250 and
750 m above sea level. The wines
are noted primarily for their
elegance and steely balance, which
maintains the fruit and varietal
characteristics of the grapes
together with a firm underlying
backbone of acidity. Such is the
demand that the entire production
is usually sold out by the January
following the vintage: therefore
wines may not be available for
purchase, but Fiorentino Sandri
and Mario Pojer are happy to
receive visitors for a tour of the
ultra-modern winery, and tasting if
time permits.
German spoken.

4 FRATELLI DORIGATI S.D.F.
VIA DANTE 5
38016 MEZZOCORONA TN
TEL: 0461/605313

WINES PRODUCED: Chardonnay;
Pinot Grigio; Teroldego; Lagrein
Kretzer; Cabernet; Grener; Rebo.

VISITS: Mon–Sat morn.
The wines are made by traditional
methods from grapes in part grown
by the family, and in part acquired
from small growers in the zone.
German spoken.

---

5 AZIENDA AGRICOLA CONTI BOSSI
    FEDRIGOTTI
VIA UNIONE 43
38068 ROVERETO TN
TEL: 0464/24950

WINES PRODUCED: Foianeghe Rosso;
Foianeghe Bianco; Merlot;
Marzemino; Cabernet; Teroldego
della Vallagarina; Chardonnay;
Traminer Aromatico; Pinot Bianco;
Schiava Rosato; Moscato.
VISITS: Mon–Sat morning 8–12h;
14–18h for direct sales.
The Bossi Fedrigotti family has
been making fine wines in Trento

since at least the 18th century, and
today continues to produce a fine
and extensive range. The 2 best
wines are named after the privileged
hill site opposite the town of
Rovereto where the grapes grow:
Foianeghe. Foianeghe Rosso is a
richly flavoured, well-structured
wine of some elegance, and a minor
classic. Foianeghe Bianco is
produced from Chardonnay,
together with a small amount of
Traminer Aromatico.
English spoken.

---

6 AZIENDA AGRICOLA VALLAROM
38060 VÒ SINISTRO DI AVIO TN
TEL: 0464/64297

WINES PRODUCED: Chardonnay,
Pinot Nero, Cabernet Sauvignon,
Sauvignon, Marzemino.

VISITS: daily, by appointment.
Forward-thinking producer
utilizing modern methods to
produce a fine range of varietals.
French, German spoken.

---

7 MARCHESE ANSELMO GUERRIERI
    GONZAGA
TENUTA SAN LEONARDO S.A.S.
LOC. SAN LEONARDO
38060 BORGHETTO A/A TN
TEL: 0464/65004

WINES PRODUCED: Trentino DOC:
Cabernet, Merlot, Pinot Bianco;
S. Leonardo dei Campi Sarni
(Cabernet Sauvignon, Cabernet
Franc, and Merlot); Villa Gresti dei

THE NORTH-EAST

Campi Sarni
VISITS: Mon–Fri, by appointment, for guided visits of the cellars and wine museum. Wines can be purchased from a shop on the estate. The Tenuta San Leonardo is located on the old road from the Brenner Pass and Austria, and was the site of a hospice and walled monastery in the 13th century. Today the Guerrieri Gonzaga family work a small but prestigious wine estate producing wines primarily from Cabernet and Merlot, grown organically and vinified in Slavonian oak casks. The cellars, located in part in those of the ancient monastery, as well as a small wine museum, are well worth a visit.
English spoken.

Enoteca

1 ENOTECA LUNELLI
LARGO CARDUCCI 12
38100 TRENTO
TEL: 0461/982496

OPEN: 8h30–12h; 15–19h15. Closed Sun, Mon morn.
Outstanding *enoteca* located in the historic centre of the city, displaying and selling an extensive selection of wines from not only Trentino but throughout Italy. The Lunelli's own Ferrari wines are of course highlighted.
French, some English and German spoken.

Ristoranti

1 LOCANDA PORT'AQUILA
VIA CERVARA 66
38100 TRENTO
TEL: 0461/30420

Closed Sun.
Long-established and popular *trattoria* beneath the castle walls, serving well-prepared Trentino foods such as *canederli smalzadi*, and smoked meats with *polenta* and *crauti*, together with house Teroldego by the carafe.
Inexpensive

2 RISTORANTE CHIESA
PARCO S. MARCO
38100 TRENTO
TEL: 0461/985577

Closed Sun.
Located in an 18th-century palace, this traditional restaurant serves not only authentic foods of the

region, but also a *menù storico*, with recipes from cinquecento Trentino. Local and national wines.

English spoken.
Expensive

Punto di Ristoro Agrituristico

1

AZIENDA AGRITURISTICA 'MASO
  NELLO'
38010 FAEDO TN
TEL: 0461/650384

Closed Mon. Reservations advisable.
Cristina Arman runs a warm family *azienda agrituristica* in an isolated farmhouse located high in

the massif above the little wine town of Faedo. Typical foods of the region include: *canederli, carne salà, gnocchi, trippa, coniglio con polenta*, together with own-produced wines.
Accommodation available.
Inexpensive

WINES AND WINE GARDENS OF THE SÜDTIROL (ALTO ADIGE)

The Südtirol, as Alto Adige is known to almost everyone in the region, even today remains considerably more Germanic than Italian. While most young people are now comfortably bilingual in both tongues, many of the older generation steadfastly continue to speak German only. Towns, wines, streets, squares: all have names in both German and Italian, but it has certainly been our experience that the Teutonic forms are those that are most frequently encountered. We therefore utilize mainly German names in our coverage of this unique region and give the Italian equivalents where necessary. If this seems overly confusing and at times inconsistent, believe me, it is!

The Südtirol vineyard was already well in place by the time the region became part of the Roman Empire in 15 BC. During the Dark Ages, the Bavarians took over the region, and viticulture continued under the patronage of the Church. The Bishop of Friesing, for example, first acquired vineyards near Bozen (Bolzano) in 720, and eventually more than 40 German bishoprics and monasteries owned vineyards in Südtirol. By the time the region became part of Austria in 1363, therefore, the history of viticulture, and the appreciation of Südtirol wine, was well established.

After more than 500 years as part of Austria, the shock of finding itself suddenly ceded to Italy after 1919 was a profound one, the reverberations of which clearly have not yet died out. From a wine point of view, too, the region found itself cut off from its principal home market, and reduced in status from one of Austria's premier wine zones to an Italian minor curiosity. Naturally, viticulture suffered: it is a wonder it did not die out completely. Today, traditional markets, primarily Austria, Switzerland, and Germany, have been re-established and exports now account for some 60% of production, a remarkably high proportion.

Those wines that do not find their way abroad are as likely as not to be drunk on the spot by locals as well as by the millions of German-speaking tourists who descend on the region each summer and winter by way of the Brenner Pass. In mountain resorts, or by the lovely Kalterersee (Lago di Caldaro), it is rare to hear Italian spoken. We should remember, after all, that from Bozen it is but a few hours up the autobahn to Innsbruck and then Munich.

The principal wine zones of Südtirol are the Eisack (Isarco) valley that leads from Bozen towards the Brenner Pass; the vine-covered hills around Bozen itself; the Etsch (Adige) valley north from Bozen to Meran (Merano); and the vineyard zone to the south of Bozen, known as the Überetsch, particularly around the Kalterersee. The latter zone has one of Europe's loveliest signposted wine roads, the *Südtiroler Weinstraße (Strada Alto-atesina del Vino)*.

Bozen is the capital of the Südtirol, and as such it is the place to begin a tour of the region's vineyards. Nestled at the confluence of three rivers – the Etsch (Adige), Eisack (Isarco), and Talfer (Talvera) – underneath the great terraced, vine-covered brow of the Ritten hills and St Magdalena, Bozen is the focus of the region's wine industry. Not only do the region's rivers converge here from their sources high in the Alps, it is also a natural convergence for wines from the various Südtirol regions. Positioned on the main north–south axis that led from northern Europe to Rome, it has always been an important market centre, and it remains so today. Indeed, Bozen can fairly be called one of the great wine towns of Italy.

As a city it is stylish and atmospheric. The Waltherplatz, its central square, is a broad, open space lined with linden trees and surrounded by rather grand baroque merchants' houses. Across the way, the spiny sandstone gothic cathedral is dominant, with its shiny polychrome tiled roof. In one apse, there is a gothic portal called the 'wine door', decorated with vine shoots and grapes to commemorate the special licence granted to the church to sell wine in 1387.

This is a town simply to meander in. Stop at a street stall for a *Würstl und brot*, served Austrian-style with a good dab of mild mustard. Or find your way to the cobbled Obstplatz, a beautiful outdoor fruit and vegetable market that impressed both Goethe and Mozart. Here there are stalls selling not just the usual splendid array of fruit and vegetables but also such Süd-tiroler specialities as *Speck* and *Schuttelbrot* alongside *salame* and *pane casereccio*.

THROUGH HILL VINEYARDS IN SEARCH OF WINE

A fine and rewarding walk from the Bozen city centre into the wine country begins along the Talfer river, and leads past the squat 13th-century Mareccio castle, surrounded by its vines. Continue past the castle to where the promenade meets the road, turn right, and, 200 yards later, find the Oswaldpromenade that leads directly into the steeply terraced vineyards of the Ritten. The path is fairly steep, but there are plenty of benches along the way, and the walk gives a dramatic prospect of Bozen and her vineyards. Notice the arduous methods of training the vines on *pergole*, and consider the backbreaking effort required to work such steeply terraced vineyards, and, at harvest time, to transport the grapes down or up to the wine cellars. It is a good hour's climb from here to St Magdalena itself, but the righteous will be rewarded with a pitcher of the blessed St Magdalener wine, own-produced by the Eberle family, who have a welcoming *Gasthof* where the promenade emerges at the crest of the hill. Enjoy this easy-to-quaff soft red wine together with a platter of thinly sliced *Speck*, or a bowl of *Südtiroler Weinsuppe*.

Südtiroler Weinstraße – La Strada Altoatesina del Vino

In Brief: The 37-km signposted wine road starts on the outskirts of Bozen and leads through vineyards and charming half-timbered wine villages and hamlets. Throughout this popular zone there is no shortage of friendly family-run hotels, restaurants, *Gasthöfe*, *Buschenschanke*, or bed and breakfast in private homes (*Zimmer mit Frühstück*). Most serve own-produced wines, while there are ample opportunities to visit and purchase wines direct.

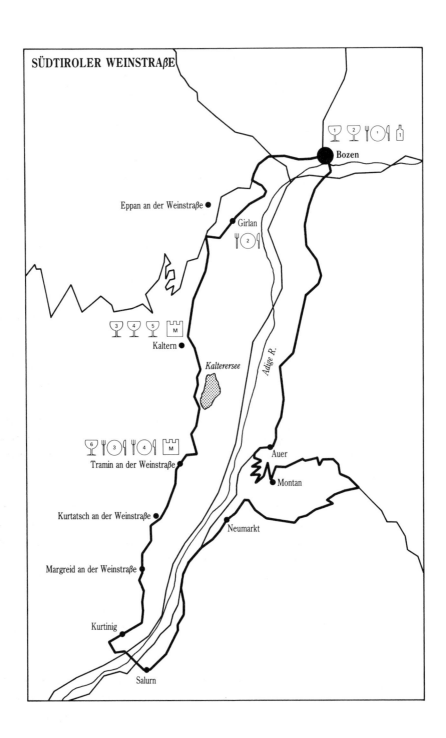

SÜDTIROLER WEINSTRAßE

Bozen

Eppan an der Weinstraße

Girlan

Kaltern

Kalterersee

Adige R.

Tramin an der Weinstraße

Auer

Montan

Kurtatsch an der Weinstraße

Neumarkt

Margreid an der Weinstraße

Kurtinig

Salurn

To begin a tour of the *Südtiroler Weinstraße*, leave Bozen over the Talfer-brücke, and follow the Drususallee which leads out to the wine suburb of Gries. Not only is Gries the home of many of Bozen's well-known wine growers and producers, it can also lay claim to one of Südtirol's best red wines. For the native Lagrein grape, particularly when grown on the red porphyry cliffs of Gries and Moritzing, is capable of producing particularly fine wines in two contrasting styles, either full-bodied red, Lagrein Dunkel, or light, easy-drinking rosé Lagrein Kretzer. The name Kretzer comes from the Tyrolean word for a type of plaited basket used to filter the crushed grapes as a sort of rustic method of making rosé wine.

At Gries, the well-signposted *Weinstraße* soon begins to climb into the thick of the vine-covered slopes in the direction of Girlan (Cornaiano). This hill is dominated at the top by the impressive Schloß Sigmundskron (Castel Firmiano), built in 1473 for the archduke Sigmund, and commands spectacular views of the Etsch (Adige) valley leading north to Meran. This hill vineyard is a particularly favoured zone for full-bodied, spicy wines from the Ruländer (Pinot Grigio).

Girlan is the first town on the wine road, and an important source of a range of highly-regarded wines. Nearby Eppan an der Weinstraße (Appiano) is also a wine town of some note, as well as an important and popular tourist centre, an atmospheric medieval town with many interesting old houses and buildings. Eppan claims within its immediate vicinity some 22 castles, and there is a 'Burgenweg' castle footpath linking many of them. The most notable is Schloß Hocheppan (Castel Appiano), which has a lovely chapel containing 13th-century frescoes.

The wine road continues its brief meander south, always leading through the vine-covered slopes, next to the most important wine town of Kaltern (Caldaro). It is a charming little place, with its delightful Südtirolese architecture, its pastel-coloured houses with shutters, and its broad Markt-platz opposite the town Rathaus. It is reminiscent not so much of any other wine town in Italy, but rather of those charming hill towns nestled on the lower slopes of the Vosges mountains in French Alsace, or else, perhaps, a secret, lakeside wine village by Austria's steamy Neusiedlersee. As a wine town, it is the home of both prestigious private producers as well as large-scale *Winzergenossenschaften* (wine co-operatives), many located down along the atmospheric Kellereistraße.

Kaltern also yields one of the most popular and best-known wines of the Südtirol. For from grapes grown around the town, and the slopes above and around the lake to which it has given its name, the lovely crater-like

Kalterersee, comes the wine of the same name, Kalterersee (or Lago di Caldaro). Light, fruity, rather soft and rounded, this is a red wine that is wholly un-Italian in character, lacking in profound colour, body, alcohol, and tannin. Yet here, in the alpine setting of this northern wine country, munching on crunchy *Schuttelbrot*, or gnawing on a thick piece of *Speck*, it is delicious, a light, easy-to-drink wine that can be consumed in quantity. Is this the reason for its perennial popularity with the hordes of Germans, Swiss, and Austrians who come to this idyllic spot year after year for their summer holidays? The German term *Auslese* may be utilized on a bottle of Kalterersee: but this does not signify a sweet wine, rather that the grapes utilized to make it have been selected for particular ripeness.

To gain a perspective of the wine country and surrounding valleys, take the cable car above Kaltern up to the Mendola Pass. There is a lovely gothic church on top, and splendid panoramas of the Südtirol countryside.

If Kaltern is today the most famous wine town on the *Südtiroler Weinstraße*, the next town, Tramin an der Weinstraße (Termeno), may lay claim to even greater international recognition, as the original home of the famous Gewürztraminer grape variety. This fickle and difficult grape which produces such distinctive wines in Alsace is capable of considerable dis-

Kalterersee (Lago di Caldaro).

tinction here, too, particularly in vineyards around the village itself as well as neighbouring Kurtatsch (Cortaccia). In particular, the famous 'Kolben-hof' above Tramin produces wines of special richness and spice, though in general a Südtirol Gewürztraminer is not as overblown or obviously aromatic as typical versions from Alsace. Tramin has a lovely town church with the highest bell-tower in the region, stretching up a remarkable 93 metres. There is also a fine little folk museum, and countless family-run *Gasthöfe* and restaurants, usually serving their own wines. In the hills just above the town, the isolated church of St Jacob im Kastelaz is surrounded by vines, and has some beautiful frescoes.

The wine road continues, next, to Kurtatsch, a small hill hamlet whose wines are not as famous as those of neighbouring Tramin but which can be none the less very good indeed. It is a quiet village, less obviously touristic than those that preceded it, but worthy of exploration for its lovely unspoiled and rather grand wine growers' manors.

By the time Margreid (Magrè) is reached, the wine road has swung down from the hills towards the flatter plains where fruit orchards (especially apples) compete with vines. Margreid itself is a splendid little wine hamlet with some notable vernacular architecture. Men in characteristic blue aprons cluster together here and there gossiping in Tyrolese German, and it cannot help but give the sense that here life has changed little, in spite of the political upheavals of this century alone. As a final wine-related curiosity, Margreid boasts the oldest vine in the region, ancient, gnarled, serpent-like, winding its way across the façade of the Augustin house.

Kurtinig (Cortina) may still be on the wine road, but today this quiet old village is surrounded by apple orchards, as is Salurn (Salorno), the southern-most German-speaking village. Cross the invisible frontier into Trentino to return to the Italy that we are more familiar with. Or else, linger for a while yet in this other Italy, and circle north back towards Bozen through wine towns such as Neumarkt (Egna), with its fine medieval arcades, Montan (Montagna), and Auer (Ora). The latter is an excellent starting point for exploration of the Dolomites.

Weinproben/Degustazione: Stop to Taste; Stop to Buy

1 WEINGUT EBERLEHOF
ST MAGDALENA 26
39100 BOZEN
TEL: 0471/978607

WINES PRODUCED: Klassische St Magdalener; Südtiroler Lagrein Dunkel; 'Blaterle' (white table wine); Sekt (*metodo champenois* sparkling wine).

VISITS: weekdays, working hours or by appointment.

Family-produced classic St Magdalener and other wines can be purchased at the Weingut or else sampled and purchased at the Gasthof Eberle.

German spoken.

_____

2 WEINGUT UND WEINKELLEREI ALOIS
LAGEDER
DRUSUSALLEE 235
39100 BOZEN
TEL: 0471/920164

WINES PRODUCED: Südtiroler DOC:
Chardonnay, Weißburgunder,
Terlaner, Ruländer, Rheinriesling,
Gewürztraminer, Lagrein Kretzer,
Grauvernatsch, Blauburgunder,
Merlot, Cabernet; Eisacktaler DOC
Müller-Thurgau; Terlaner DOC
Sauvignon; Kalterersee Auslese;
Bozner Leiten DOC; *crus:*
Weißburgunder 'Haberlehof',

Ruländer 'Benefizium Porer',
Terlaner 'Lehenhof'; Spumante
Brut Alois Lageder.

VISITS: Mon–Fri 9–12h30; 15–20h.
One of the most important
producers of the zone, both for its
vast range and for its superlative
quality. Visits daily at the above
hours to the 'Vinotheque' where not
only the full Alois Lageder range is
displayed and available for
purchase, but also a selection of the
best wines from throughout Italy.
German, English, French spoken.

_____

3 WEINGUT WEINKELLEREI CANTINA
VINI KETTMEIR
KELLEREISTRAßE 4
39052 KALTERN AN DER WEINSTRAßE
BZ
TEL: 0471/963135

WINES PRODUCED: Kalterersee
Auslese; St Magdalener; Südtiroler
Chardonnay, Gewürztraminer,

Ruländer, Müller-Thurgau,
Cabernet Sauvignon, Lagrein
Kretzer.

VISITS: daily, by appointment.
Large well-known private winery
producing a full range of Südtirol
wines.

German spoken.

_____

4 GROSSKELLEREI GENOSSENSCHAFT
KELLEREISTRAßE
39052 KALTERN AN DER WEINSTRAßE
BZ
TEL: 0471/963149

WINES PRODUCED: Kalterersee
Auslese 'Hochleiten'; Südtiroler
DOC: Grauvernatsch;
Weißburgunder; Gewürztraminer;
Goldenmuskateller; Lagrein

Dunkel; Blauburgunder; Cabernet.
VISITS: Mon–Sat 8–12h; 14h30–19h.
Large, welcoming tasting room just
off the *Weinstraße* for this

important co-operative wine cellar.
Wines can be enjoyed by the glass
or bottle, and are available for
purchase.

---

5 KELLEREIGENOSSENSCHAFT BARON
JOSEF DI PAULI
BAHNHOFSTRAßE 10
39052 KALTERN AN DER WEINSTRAßE
BZ
TEL: 0471/963359

WINES PRODUCED: Kalterersee
Auslese 'Bichlhof'; Kalterersee
Auslese 'Planitzinger'; St
Magdalener; Südtiroler DOC:
Gewürztraminer; Ruländer;

Rheinriesling; Grauvernatsch;
Merlot; Lagrein Kretzer;
Rosenmuskateller;
Goldenmuskateller.
VISITS: Mon–Sat 8h30–12h;
14h30–18h30.
Another large co-operative wine
cellar, with shop where wines can
be tasted and purchased. Also shop
near the Südtiroler Weinmuseum.

---

6 J. HOFSTÄTTER – WEINGUT
WEINKELLEREI CANTINA VINI SRL
RATHAUSPLATZ 5
39040 TRAMIN AN DER WEINSTRAßE
BZ
TEL: 0471/860161

WINES PRODUCED: Südtiroler DOC:
Blauburgunder, Kolbenhofer,
Chardonnay, Gewürztraminer,
Pinot Bianco, Riesling Renano,
Cabernet Sauvignon.

VISITS: Mon–Fri 8h30–12h; 14–18h.
The Hofstätters have 38 hectares of
vineyards in the Südtirol, and
make an impressive and highly
respected range of wines utilizing
modern techniques. Tramin is the
original home of Gewürztraminer
and the Hofstätter Kolbenhof
example is among the best.
German, Italian spoken.

WINE AND FOLK MUSEUMS

M SÜDTIROLER WEINMUSEUM
GOLDGASSE 1
39052 KALTERN AN DER
WEINSTRAßE BZ
TEL: 0471/963168

OPEN: April–Sept Tue–Sat
9h30–12h; 14–18h.
Fine, important little wine
museum sited in a vaulted *Keller*
tracing viticulture in the

THE NORTH-EAST

Südtirol, with exhibits demonstrating training methods, old tools, containers for the harvest and a good collection of wooden presses, barrels, and fermentation vats.

TRAMINER DORFMUSEUM
AM RATHAUSPLATZ
39040 TRAMIN AN DER WEINSTRAßE
    BZ
TEL: 0471/860132

OPEN: April–Nov Tue–Fri 10–11h; 16–18h; Sat 10–11h. This small wine and folk museum has the usual collection of old implements, but is worth visiting to see the old home *Schnapskessel*, a small copper alembic that was once a common feature of Südtirol upland farms for the distillation of soft fruits. Upstairs there is an old Tyrolean kitchen, with a fireplace in which *Speck* and sausages were hung up to smoke. Pictures of Franz Josef and other military regalia are demonstrations of traditional allegiance to Austria in this nationalistic backwater.

Weinkellerei/Enoteca

1 WEINKELLEREI/ENOTECA GANDOLFI
DRUSUSALLEE 349
39100 BOZEN
TEL: 0471/920335

OPEN: Mon–Sat 8–12h; 14h30–18h30.
Vast *enoteca/cantina* located along the Drususallee near the start of the *Südtiroler Weinstraße*: more than 1000 different Italian wines, as well as gastronomic specialities such as olive oil, wine vinegars, and foods.
German spoken.

Restaurants/Ristoranti

1 GASTHOF EBERLE
ST MAGDALENA
39100 BOZEN
TEL: 0471/26125

Located right at the end of the Oswaldpromenade in the famous wine town of St Magdalena, this welcoming family-run *Gasthof* offers good Tyrolese specialities and a range of own-produced wines. Accommodation available.
Inexpensive to Moderate

2 RESTAURANT
   MARKLHOF-BELLAVISTA
   VIA BELVEDERE
   39050 GIRLAN AN DER WEINSTRAßE
   BZ
   TEL: 0471/52407

Closed Mon.
Traditional Tyrolese house located in a splendid position overlooking the vineyards and Etsch valley near Schloß Sigmundskron (Castel Firmiano). Typical specialities include *Tiroler Speckknödelsuppe*, game, and wild mushrooms. Pleasant outdoor terrace in summer.
Moderate

---

3 HOTEL ARNDT
   39040 TRAMIN AN DER WEINSTRAßE
   BZ
   TEL: 0471/860336

Set amidst the vineyards, located actually on the *Weinstraße*, this friendly family hotel-restaurant serves good home cooking: *Leberknödelsuppe, Tafelspitz mit Kren und salsa verde, Tiroler Zwiebelrostbraten, Hausgemacht Apfelstrudel*, and a good selection of local wines.
Inexpensive to Moderate

THE BUSCHENSCHANK

Südtirol is primarily a wine region made up of small growers, many of whom make wine primarily for their own consumption as well as to sell to passers-by. One tradition that remains very much alive in the region is the *Buschenschank*, whereby each year wine growers set up tables in their garden, terrace or cellar following the harvest, and there serve the new season's wine, together with simple drinking snacks: pretzels, *Speck*, cheese, homemade breads and the like. This particular institution continues a tradition begun in the 18th century when the Austrian emperor decreed that wine growers could legally sell both wine and food on their premises provided that it was produced by themselves. Usually a bunch of fir branches or a straw wheel is hung over the door to signify that such places are open.

A full list of Südtirol *Buschenschanke* is available from the *Agriturismo* office listed at the end of the chapter. Or ask in local tourist offices when in the area, particularly during the autumn.

THE NORTH-EAST

4

HOTEL WINZERHOF
39040 TRAMIN AN DER WEINSTRAßE
TEL: 0471/860183

Friendly family hotel-restaurant set amidst the vines near the famous Kolbenhof above the village. Restaurant serves authentic Südtirol foods and wines, and there is a *Spargelkarte* (asparagus menu) in season. Terrace has splended views over the vine-covered valley.
Inexpensive to Moderate

OTHER SÜDTIROL WINE REGIONS

Eisacktal (Isarco) Valley

Just north of Bozen, the Eisack river carves its way dramatically through a steep vertical gorge as it plummets south from the Alps and the Brenner Pass to empty into the Etsch (Adige). This valley corridor is the great thoroughfare that connects Italy with Innsbruck and Munich, a historic avenue that was traversed by Roman legions, barbarians from the north, troops of the Holy Roman Empire, and the Hapsburgs who annexed the region as a natural continuation of their own Tyrol.

Today, the Eisack valley is Italy's most northerly wine growing district, devoted primarily to the production of white wines grown on alpine vineyards. Around Klausen (Chiusa), Brixen (Bressanone), Vahr, and Neustift, vineyards extend up to altitudes of 600–800 metres, producing refreshing wines from a range of grapes: Sylvaner (by far the most prevalent, accounting for some 70% of production), Gewürztraminer, Ruländer, Müller-Thurgau, and Veltliner. The wines are not labelled with the more general Südtiroler *denominazione* but rather are entitled to their own Eisacktaler (Valle di Isarco) DOC. Brixen is a lovely old Tyrolese town, atmospheric with its twin baroque towers of the cathedral, and its wide, open, ordered Rathausplatz. A stop at the tap room of the great abbey of Neustift is a must for any wine lover travelling into or from Italy via the Brenner Pass.

Restaurant/Ristorante

HOTEL-RESTAURANT BRÜCKENWIRT
39042 NEUSTIFT BEI BRIXEN BZ
TEL: 0472/36692

Closed Wed.
Just opposite the Neustift abbey, beside a delightful covered wooden bridge, this comfortable family hotel-restaurant serves good local foods: *Neustifter Weinsuppe, Tiroler Speck, Knödelsuppe, Klosterschmaus*.
Inexpensive to Moderate

STIFTKELLER NEUSTIFT/ ABBAZIA DI NOVACELLA: THE MONASTIC TRADITION

During the Dark Ages, the Church kept viticulture alive in the Südtirol. Wine was needed for the celebration of Mass, and it was, of course, also an important trading commodity. Today such monastic wine traditions continue, notably at the Benedictine Klosterkellerei of Muri-Gries, and at the Stiftskellerei Neustift, north of Brixen. Neustift, a centre for Augustinian monks founded in the 12th century, served as an important hospice, a place of refuge for pilgrims en route to the Holy City who had just braved the Brenner Pass. The circular, fortified Chapel of St Michele was consecrated in 1199, after the Church of the Holy Sepulchre in Jerusalem. Today, for 10 days every year (end of May/early June), it is the venue for an important wine tasting open to the public. The Abbey Church is an incredible, overblown neo-baroque creation, enlarged in the 18th century.

The vineyards extend behind the abbey itself, and a varied range of well-made wines is produced. They can be sampled together with typical Tyrolese drinking snacks – *Speck*, pretzels, bread, cheese – in the atmospheric vaulted tap room.

Stiftskellerei Neustift Cantina
Neustift/Abbazia di Novacella
Vahr/Novacella N. 1
39042 Brixen BZ
tel: 0472/36189
WINES PRODUCED: Sylvaner; Müller-Thurgau; Gewürztraminer; Kalterersee; Blauburgunder; Lagrein Dunkel.
Tap Room: Mon–Sat 10–19h.

Etsch (Adige) Valley from Bozen to Meran

While the Eisack valley leads north-east to the Brenner Pass, the Etsch valley leads north-west, from Bozen to the popular spa town of Meran. This too is a notable wine zone. Near Bozen, the wine commune of Terlan

THE NORTH-EAST

produces some superlative white wines, principally from Weißburgunder and Chardonnay.

Meran itself was the capital of the Tyrol during the Middle Ages, and the counts resided in the 15th-century castle. Though Innsbruck later took on the mantle of the region's capital, Meran enjoyed a particularly splendid *belle époque* in the 18th and 19th centuries as a holiday resort and health spa where Europe's nobility and aristocrats came to relax. Meran, after all, enjoys a particularly mild and beneficial climate; it is a thermal spa; and the popularity of the grape cure made it a vital stop for those jaded creatures who had partaken of too much good food and drink during the year. Today, the spas and the grape cure remain, and it is still a particularly popular and lovely town.

The vineyards of Meran extend on the steep slopes mainly to the north of the town, particularly over the Küchelberg. They are primarily planted with Vernatsch (Schiava), the native red grape that is the principal workhorse of the Südtirol, which elsewhere is used to produce St Magdalener and Kalterersee and here results in the light but tasty wine known as Meraner Hügel. Just to the east of Meran, Schloß Rametz was planted with Blauburgunder (Pinot Noir) as long ago as 1860.

Beyond Meran to the north-west lies the Vinschgau (Val Venosta), a wide green valley dotted with small agricultural hamlets and ancient castles. Once a wine region of importance, today its vineyards have declined considerably: however, a full and interesting range of wines continues to be produced and should be sampled if in the region. Grape varieties include Blauer Portugieser, Vernatsch, Weißburgunder, Müller-Thurgau, Ruländer, and Gewürztraminer. This is a region of small family *Höfe* (upland farms), and there are plenty of opportunities for farmhouse holidays.

Wine and Other Related *Sagre* and *Feste*

April	Bozner Weinkost	Bozen
April/May	Festa del Vino	Trento
end May/June	Neustifter Weinverkostung	Neustift
end Aug	Großer Festumzum	Kaltern
Sept	Sagra del Vino	Rovereto
Sept/Oct	Traubenkur	Kaltern; Meran

E PER SAPERE DI PIÙ –
ADDITIONAL INFORMATION

Azienda per la Promozione
Turistica del Trentino
Corso 3 Novembre 132
38100 Trento
tel: 0461/895111

Ufficio Provinciale per Il Turismo
Piazza Parrocchia 11/12
39100 Bozen
tel: 0471/993808

Agriturist Comitato Regionale
via Brennero 23
38100 Trento
tel: 0461/824211

Südtiroler Bauernbund/Unione
Agricoltori e Coltivatori Diretti
Südtirolesi
Brennerstraße 7
39100 Bozen
tel: 0471/972145

The Südtirol is probably the most
highly developed region for
farmhouse holidays. There are
literally scores of private houses
offering rooms for rent, as well
as *Buschenschanke*: Write and
ask for the booklet *Erholung
am Südtiroler Bauernhof
(Agriturismo nel Südtirolo)*.

THE NORTH-EAST

FRIULI-VENEZIA GIULIA

I Vini: THE WINES OF FRIULI-VENEZIA GIULIA   209

La Gastronomia   212

Le Strade dei Vini: THE WINE ROADS OF
FRIULI-VENEZIA GIULIA
    Il Collio: *La Strada del Vino*   213
    Isonzo   220
    Colli Orientali del Friuli   222
    Grave del Friuli   223
    Aquileia   223
    Latisana   224
    Carso   224

Le Sagre: WINE AND OTHER RELATED FESTIVALS   226

Additional Information   227

Gostilna Dvor, San Floriano del Collio.

Friuli-Venezia Giulia is an autonomous region located in the far north-eastern corner of Italy, extending beyond the Veneto up to the national borders with Yugoslavia and Austria. As a border zone, it has historically been a much fought over crossroads; today it presents a culture that is a rather odd fusion of central European, Venetian, Italian, and Slovenian.

Venetian influence was maintained over the region until the fall of the Republic in 1797. Then, under the Hapsburgs, the port of Trieste gave the Austro-Hungarians a window to the sea. Following the Napoleonic wars, the entire region became part of the Austrian Empire. When Italy was finally unified in 1866, Friuli became part of the new nation, but much of Venezia Giulia remained under the influence of Austria. Thus, during World War I, the region was the scene of much fierce and bloody fighting as the Italians struggled, eventually successfully, to gain control and possession of Trieste, Gorizia, and Capodistria. But again, during World War II, the region suffered more profound destruction as the scene of fierce fighting. In the final days of the war, Tito's partisans arrived in Trieste in an attempt to claim that city. Though the Allies resisted, most of the province, half of the city of Gorizia, and all of Capodistria (Istria) were lost to Yugoslavia.

As a wine region, Friuli-Venezia Giulia is best-known for its superlative range of dry white wines, considered by many to be the finest in Italy, as well as for some excellent and individual red wines. There are 7 separate DOC wine zones, each producing an outstanding and varied range of wines, the majority of which are labelled varietally, that is, by the name of the single grape variety used in their production. The 7 wine zones are Collio, Colli Orientali, Isonzo, Aquileia, Latisana, Carso and Grave del Friuli. We include below a tour of the wine road of the Collio, a small but particularly lovely zone that produces some of the region's best wines. However, the remaining areas are all worthy of extended exploration in their own right.

ORIENTATION

Friuli-Venezia Giulia is an autonomous region comprising 4 provinces: Gorizia, Trieste, Udine, and Pordenone. The region is easily accessible from Venice or Trieste, while some may wish to dip into the wine country as a break from beach holidays in Adriatic resorts. The region, though apparently out on a limb from our point of view, is ideally placed and indeed exceedingly popular with visitors from Austria, Yugoslavia, and other central European parts.

Map Touring Club Italiano 1: 200 000 Veneto e Friuli-Venezia Giulia.

I VINI: GLOSSARY TO THE WINES OF FRIULI-VENEZIA GIULIA

Wines of *Denominazione di Origine Controllata (DOC)*

Aquileia DOC Delimited wine zone established in 1981 applying to 13 wines made from grapes grown on vineyards stretching from Aquileia north to Palmova. White wines are Tocai Friulano, Pinot Bianco, Pinot Grigio, Riesling Renano, Sauvignon, Traminer Aromatico, Verduzzo Friulano. Reds and *rosato* are Merlot, Cabernet, Cabernet Franc, Cabernet Sauvignon, Refosco dal Peduncolo Rosso, Rosato.

Carso DOC Recently granted DOC status for vineyards on finger of land formed by the province of Trieste extending into Yugoslavia. DOC applies to 3 wines: red Carso (70% Terrano, a strain of Refosco), red Carso Terrano (from vineyards planted mainly with Terrano in the communes of Trieste, Aurisina, Sgónico, and Monrupino), and white Carso Malvasia.

Colli Orientali del Friuli DOC Prestigious vineyard north of the

Collio delimited in 1970 for the production of 15 mainly varietal wines: whites are Tocai Friulano, Verduzzo Friulano, Ribolla, Pinot Bianco, Pinot Grigio, Sauvignon, Riesling Renano, Picolit, Malvasia Istriana, Traminer Aromatico; reds and *rosato* are Merlot, Cabernet, Pinot Nero, Refosco dal Peduncolo Rosso, Rosato.

Collio DOC Tiny but prestigious vineyard delimited in 1968, located north of Gorizia on the Yugoslavian border up to Dolegna del Collio. Source of outstanding wines from the following grapes: whites are Riesling Italico, Tocai Friulano, Malvasia, Pinot Bianco, Pinot Grigio, Sauvignon, Traminer, Collio (the only non-varietal, made from blend of Tocai, Ribolla, and Malvasia), plus Riesling Renano, Ribolla, and Chardonnay; reds are Merlot, Cabernet Franc, Pinot Nero, Cabernet Sauvignon, Rubino.

Grave del Friuli DOC Friuli's largest delimited vineyard by far, established in 1970 and encompassing vineyards mainly across the provinces of Udine and Pordenone. Today zone produces 7

varietal wines – Tocai Friulano, Pinot Bianco, Pinot Grigio, Verduzzo Friulano as whites, and Merlot, Cabernet, and Refosco as reds. Other wines are currently under consideration for elevation to DOC status: Pinot Nero, Riesling Renano, Sauvignon, Traminer Aromatico, Chardonnay, and Rosato.

Isonzo DOC Small delimited vineyard that extends along the gravelly Isonzo river valley: noted foremost for Cabernet and Merlot, though a number of wines are entitled to the DOC: Tocai Friulano, Sauvignon, Malvasia Istriana, Pinot Bianco, Pinot Grigio, Verduzzo Friulano, Traminer Aromatico, Riesling Renano.

Latisana DOC Another small delimited vineyard extending along the Tagliamento river valley north and south of Latisana. DOC currently applies to 7 wines: (whites) Tocai Friulano, Pinot Bianco, Pinot Grigio, Verduzzo Friulano; (reds) Merlot, Cabernet, and Refosco.

Principal Grape Varieties of Friuli

Malvasia Istriana Native Istrian strain of the ancient Malvasia

grape, producing pale, fresh, light white wines.

Picolit Rare, famous grape with exceptionally minuscule yields that produces delicately scented sweet dessert wine.

Pinot Bianco Second most widely cultivated white variety producing light, firm white wine when young that can acquire deeper, rounder nuances with bottle age.

Pinot Grigio This dark, almost copper-coloured grape is vinified both *in bianco* and with brief skin contact to result in both clean and lighter styles as well as deeper, rounder wines that stand up well to food.

Ribolla Gialla Ancient traditional variety of Friuli, particularly popular in vineyards around Gorizia and Udine, producing refreshing lemon-yellow wine.

Riesling Italico This is the lesser variety of Riesling, grown primarily in Collio to produce dry white wines with some scent.

Riesling Renano The true, or Rhine, Riesling is entitled to DOC in 4 of Friuli's 6 wine zones, and is capable of producing wines of some considerable class, combining perfume, body, and acidity.

Sauvignon Though elsewhere in Italy this French variety is a newcomer, it has long been established in Friuli and makes wines that demonstrate its characteristic pungency allied in the best cases with delicacy and elegance.

Tocai Friulano Outstanding indigenous grape variety and the most widely planted in Friuli. In some parts, especially Collio and Colli Orientali del Friuli, it produces full-bodied wines with extreme delicacy and length that reach the zone's highest pinnacle.

Traminer Aromatico The spicy grape variety that originated in the Südtirol (and found greater fame in French Alsace) is not widely planted, but can produce some finely scented wines.

Verduzzo Friulano Another typical indigenous grape variety, utilized to produce dry white table wines, as well as, in a Ramandolo version, full, dark, sweet dessert wines.

Cabernet Franc The French variety was introduced to Friuli almost a hundred years ago, and is now widely planted to produce red wines with a characteristic grassy pungency that is locally much appreciated.

Cabernet Sauvignon Cabernet

THE NORTH-EAST

Sauvignon, generally considered the superior Cabernet variety, is being planted increasingly in the zone to produce somewhat bigger wines that are capable of withstanding some barrel and bottle age. Wine is generally full-bodied but not aggressively tannic.

Merlot Another widely planted French variety, particularly in Grave del Friuli vineyards. Produces good, everyday quaffing reds as well as, with Cabernet Sauvignon, some distinguished wines capable of improving with bottle age.

Pinot Nero The great grape of Burgundy and Champagne is not widely planted in Friuli, but is utilized to produce sound red and *rosato* wines, as well as white and sparkling wines.

Refosco dal Peduncolo Rosso Friuli's best indigenous red grape variety, the Refosco produces excellent red wine with its own particular character: dense garnet, full-bodied, and with a characteristic bitter finish.

LA GASTRONOMIA: FOODS OF FRIULI-VENEZIA GIULIA

Friuli-Venezia Giulia even today maintains an identity that is closer to central Europe than the Mediterranean. In terms of food, this means that lard is used in cooking, not olive oil, and mountain-cured smoked hams, sausages, and *salame* are enjoyed together with dumplings, boiled and pickled vegetables, and the ever-present staple *polenta*. Yet lighter influences from Venice and the Dalmatian coast are also evident. The seafood of Trieste is legendary, especially in the local fisherman's stew known as *broeto*. And spicy Slovenian-style grilled meats are also popular.

PIATTI TIPICI:
REGIONAL SPECIALITIES

Prosciutto di San Daniele
Italy's greatest raw air-cured
ham, surpassing even that of
Parma.

Prosciutto di cinghiale
Air-cured wild boar ham.

Cjalzon Typical local *ravioli*-type
pasta filled with variety of
stuffings, usually mixtures of
cheese and vegetables.

**Gnocchi con ciliegie; con
susine**
Unusual dumpling filled with
cherries or plums, and cooked in
butter to be eaten as a *primo
piatto*.

Broeto Classic fish stew, made
with whatever is freshest, cooked
in wine and vinegar, and served
with *polenta*. Speciality of
Trieste.

Jota Dense sauerkraut, bean and
pork soup: speciality of Trieste
and Gorizia.

Musetto con brovada Boiled
pork sausage served with sour
turnips.

Gulasch; gulyas
Paprika-flavoured soupy meat
stew.

Cevapcici Ground meat skewers,
served with spicy chilli sauce and
raw onions.

Stinco Shin of pork or veal on
the bone, slow cooked in one
piece in wine.

Strucolo Strudel pastry, usually
fruit filled.

Cheese: *Carnigo* Fresh, creamy
mountain cheese.

Il Collio: *La Strada del Vino*

In Brief: There is a brief signposted *strada del vino* that leads through
the vine-covered hills of the Collio, up to and around the border with
Yugoslavia. This circuit, beginning from Cormòns, can easily be covered
in a day, but as the region itself is rather out on a limb, it would be a
shame not to spend more time here, relaxing in the wine country, in the
mountains, or along the Adriatic coast.

THE NORTH-EAST

In the far north-east corner of Italy, a low ripple of hills rises from the flatter plains of the Isonzo river valley, steadily up towards the Julian Alps and the border with Yugoslavia. This is the Collio, a historic vineyard that extends well beyond that frontier, formed seemingly arbitrarily by politicians during more turbulent times in the earlier part of this century.

Indeed, wine towns and hamlets such as San Floriano, Plessiva, Dolegna del Collio, and others nestle against the *confine di stato* – the border –

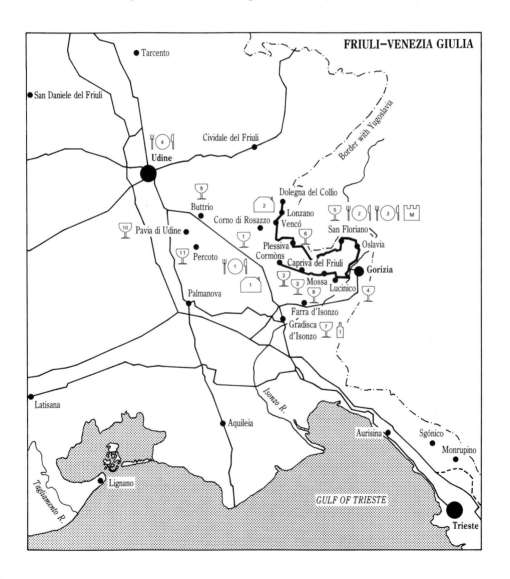

overlooking similar vine-covered hills on the other side. Today, the greater part of the Collio hills actually lies in Yugoslavia, and the wines there, we have been told by Italian growers, are produced from the same grapes, in the same manner, and can be equally exceptional.

Road signs are written in both Italian and Slovenian, a *trattoria* is a *gostilna* (what different images each conveys!), but on the whole one does not sense that there is a strong undercurrent of nationalism here, as one may feel in Südtirol. True, in one or two pockets, Slovenian remains a principal language and is even taught to youngsters in school. But today the inhabitants mainly think of themselves as Friulans first and Italians second.

Cormòns, the important economic and cultural centre of the Collio, is located less than 10 km from today's border. As the home of some of the zone's most famous wine growers and an important *cantina sociale*, it is the place to begin a tour of the *strada del vino*. The history of Cormòns follows that of the rest of the region: caught between the patronage of the Patriarch of Aquileia and the Counts of Gorizia during the Middle Ages, the city was briefly occupied by the Venetians in the 16th century, then passed into the control of the Hapsburgs until the end of World War I. During World War II its citizens fought bravely for the liberation of Italy, then suffered as their neighbouring communities were divided by the new frontier.

From Cormòns, begin a circuit of the wine country by heading east towards Gorizia, first to the wine town of Capriva del Friuli. Capriva, located on the flatter plains above the Isonzo valley, is a small but busy agricultural town. Its tall bell-tower with a characteristic onion dome looks decidedly central European, and was constructed in 1784 during the Austrian occupation. Beyond the town itself, the vine-covered hills soon begin, and there are a number of fine wine estates located here, notably Azienda Agricola Villa Russiz, Azienda Agricola Russiz Superiore, and Azienda Agricola Schiopetto.

THE VINEYARD OF THE WORLD

As a poignant tribute to its turbulent past, the Cantina Produttori Vini di Cormòns conceived a unique project, the 'Vineyard of the World'. Hundreds of different vines from every corner of the earth were gathered and planted around the winery outside Cormòns, and in 1985, they bore their first fruit to produce a unique wine, *Il Vino Della Pace*, the Wine of Peace, bottles of which, decorated with labels by eminent artists, have been sent to every civil and religious head of state in the world.

THE NORTH-EAST

Villa Russiz, today owned by the Cerruti Institute, was once the property of Barone Ritner Von Zahoni, whose daughter married Count La Tour-en-Voire. It was Count La Tour who, in the middle of the last century, first imported French and German grape varieties to the zone.

Wine growers not only in the Collio, but throughout Friuli, generally produce a remarkable range, as many as 10 or 12 different wines, usually from single grape varieties that are entitled to the DOC of their zone of production. Collio, for example, has some 16 wines entitled to bear the DOC. Thus, one might seek a Collio or Colli Orientali Tocai, for example, or an Isonzo Cabernet, or a Pinot Grigio from Grave del Friuli. This simple method of labelling wines by both the zone and grape variety has certainly been a boon for the consumer, for the general standard is very high indeed and such wines rarely disappoint. The technology to produce clean, full-bodied dry white wines of character, as well as some superb reds, is certainly well in place, and though the region as a whole produces a meagre 2 per cent of the national output of wine, it is a very important percentage in terms of quality.

It should be noted, however, that as elsewhere in Italy, forward-thinking wine growers – in many cases from a new younger generation – have in recent years begun to experiment, blending together atypical grape varieties – Tocai with Sauvignon, Chardonnay with Picolit – and in some cases ageing the blends in new oak *barriques* to result in exciting new wines of great individuality. The older generation may shake their heads at such developments, and prefer to continue sipping their favourite Ribolla Gialla or Tocai. But it cannot be doubted that such new wines and wine makers are now an important and exciting feature of the Friuli vineyard.

From Capriva, continue through the wine towns of Mossa and Lucinico, almost to the outskirts of Gorizia itself. Gorizia is a fascinating ancient town, first settled in 1000 AD, and once the seat of the powerful Counts of Gorizia, whose estates covered a vast area including parts of Carinthia, Slovenia, Istria, and Friuli. When Gorizia came under the rule of the Imperial House of the Hapsburgs, the local wines found great favour at the royal court, a fact which led to the expansion of the wine country during the 16th century.

The principal factors that make the Collio vineyard so very favourable include the fact that these low-lying, mainly south-facing hills are sheltered from north winds by the mountains that surround the zone, while the nearness to the Adriatic tempers the climate. The hills themselves mainly consist of rich marl terrain, while closer to the river the soil is scoured gravel.

The wine road rises above the river valley just before Gorizia, and climbs the slopes of Monte Calvario towards Oslavia and San Floriano. Monte Calvario today may be mainly covered with woods and vines, but during World War I it was the scene of some of the bitterest and fiercest fighting. Indeed, some 60,000 men fought and died here and there is a great Sacrario at Oslavia dedicated to their memory.

Such reminders cannot help but make one feel uneasy, especially while wandering around border country. San Floriano, located high up overlooking the hills, is just a brief stone's throw from today's frontier. Indeed, most of the road signs here are written in both Italian and Slovenian. The name of the local *cantina sociale* is Vini Steverjan, Steverjan being the old Slovenian name for the town. But while such borders seem so arbitrary to us, it should be noted that the inhabitants on both sides are allowed to travel freely back and forth, apparently as far as 15 km each way, with no need of border formalities.

The Conti Formentini have been in San Floriano since 1520: today the family remains one of the important wine producers of the Collio, and runs a fine hotel-restaurant located in the ancient castle. There is also a small but interesting wine museum.

From San Floriano, the *strada del vino* skirts the border, following it around to Dolegna through unspoiled little wine hamlets like Plessiva, Ruttars, Vencó, and Lonzano. The views, on one side across the border to the hills of Yugoslavia and the Julian Alps, on the other down the Collio to the broad Isonzo plain, are quite stunning.

Dolegna del Collio is a busy, self-contained wine town, and an agricultural centre especially for the fine fruits that the region is equally famous for, plums, cherries, and other soft fruits. Such fruits are transformed traditionally into clear, potent spirits such as *slivovitch* and other such fruit brandies. Enjoy them at your peril!

Degustazione: Stop to Taste; Stop to Buy

1

CANTINA PRODUTTORI VINI DI
  CORMÒNS
VIA MARIANO 31
34071 CORMÒNS GO
TEL: 0481/61798

WINES PRODUCED: Collio DOC:
Pinot Bianco, Merlot, Tocai

Friulano, Malvasia *secco*,
Sauvignon, Collio, Riesling Renano,
Pinot Nero, Blaufrankisch,
Cabernet Sauvignon. Isonzo DOC:
Merlot, Cabernet Franc, Pinot
Grigio, Sauvignon, Verduzzo
Friulano, Traminer. Also a range of

THE NORTH-EAST

sparkling wines and table wines.
Numbered bottles of the unique
Vino della Pace may be available
VISITS: open daily, working hours.
Kiosk for direct sales open
9–12h30; 15–19h. Closed Wed
afternoon; Sun.

This most impressive co-operative
society is the largest in the
province of Gorizia, and an
important producer of a fine range
of wines from Collio and Isonzo,
which have over the years won
many awards. The co-operative has
more than 200 members, and the
wine making facilities are
extremely modern and up-to-date.
German, French spoken.

Stop to taste; stop to buy.

---

2 AZIENDA AGRICOLA VILLA RUSSIZ
RUSSIZ INFERIORE 5
34070 CAPRIVA DEL FRIULI GO
TEL: 0481/80047

WINES PRODUCED: Collio DOC:
Pinot Grigio, Pinot Bianco,
Sauvignon, Tocai, Riesling,
Malvasia, Ribolla; Silvaner; Pinot
Nero; Rosso de la Tour; Merlot;
Cabernet; Picolit.

VISITS: Mon–Fri, by appointment.
Villa Russiz was one of the first
wine properties founded in the
prestigious Collio zone as a means
of supporting the A. Cerruti
orphanage. Today the estate
produces an impressive and
highly-regarded range of wines.
English spoken.

---

3 AZIENDA AGRICOLA RUSSIZ
SUPERIORE S S
LOC. RUSSIZ SUPERIORE 1
34070 CAPRIVA DEL FRIULI GO
TEL: 0481/80328

WINES PRODUCED: Tocai,
Pinot Bianco, Pinot Grigio,
Sauvignon, Riesling, Merlot,
Cabernet, Roncuz, Verduzzo.
VISITS: Mon–Fri 8–12h; 14–17h.
English, German spoken.

4 AZIENDA AGRICOLA CONTI ATTEMS
VIA G. CESARE 46
34070 LUCINICO GO
TEL: 0481/390206

WINES PRODUCED: Collio DOC:
Pinot Grigio, Sauvignon, Tocai
Friulano, Riesling Italico, Merlot,
Cabernet Sauvignon. Isonzo DOC:
Pinot Bianco, Cabernet; Rosato
Attems.

VISITS: Mon–Fri 8–12h; 14–17h.
Appointment advisable.
A full range of wines of Collio,
produced entirely from the estate's
own grapes, as well as wines from
the neighbouring zone of Isonzo.
English, German, French spoken.

---

5 VINI STEVERJAN
LOC. BUCUJE 6
34070 SAN FLORIANO DEL COLLIO GO
TEL: 0481/884192

WINES PRODUCED: Collio DOC:
Pinot Bianco, Pinot Grigio,
Sauvignon, Tocai Friulano,
Traminer Aromatico. *Vini da
tavola*: Chardonnay, Ribolla Gialla,
Rosso.

VISITS: open for direct sales
Mon–Fri 8–12h; 13–17h.
Steverjan is the ancient Slovenian
name for San Floriano. This is an
exceptional wine growing
environment, and the local growers
have banded together to form this
small co-operative producing
well-made wines with modern
technology.

---

6 AZIENDA AGRICOLA GRADNIK
LOC. PLESSIVA 5
34071 CORMÒNS GO
TEL: 0481/60737

WINES PRODUCED: Tocai, Ribolla
Gialla, Chardonnay, Sauvignon,
Pinot Bianco, Pinot Grigio,
Traminer, Picolit di Cormòns,
Cabernet Franc, Merlot.
VISITS: daily, by appointment.
The late Gradmir Gradnik was one
of the great wine makers and
personalities of the Collio. The

estate, today administered by his
daughter Wanda, is located on the
frontier with Yugoslavia and
continues to produce an exceptional
range of wines, entirely from its
own grapes. While varieties such as
Sauvignon and Chardonnay are
cultivated throughout the region, it
is the traditional wines of the
Collio, such as Gradnik's Tocai and
Ribolla Gialla, that we consider
most outstanding.

THE NORTH-EAST

MUSEO DEL VINO

MUSEO DEL VINO
ANTICA AZIENDA AGRICOLA DEI
   CONTI FORMENTINI
VIA OSLAVIA 5
34070 SAN FLORIANO DEL COLLIO
   GO
TEL: 0481/884131

WINES PRODUCED: Collio DOC:
Cabernet Franc, Pinot Bianco,
Pinot Grigio, Tocai Friulano,
Malvasia, Sauvignon.
OPEN: Mon–Fri 8–17h; Sat and
holidays 14–19h.
Small wine museum in the
cantina of this famous and highly
respected wine producer:
collection of barrels, carts,
ploughs, presses, and other tools.
Possibility of purchasing from the
full range of Formentini wines, as
well as grape seed oil and wine
vinegar. The *selezioni cru* wines
are outstanding, but even the
'straight' bottlings are very good.
The Formentini estate is a
complete tourist centre, with a
hotel-restaurant in the castle,
and 9-hole golf course (see below).

OTHER FRIULI WINE ZONES

Isonzo

The Isonzo wine region is situated south of Gorizia, along the flatter plains of the Isonzo river valley towards the sea and the lagoon of Grado. The wide river has over millennia scoured the river valley, leaving a varied and rich sedimentary soil riddled with gravel and pebbles. This ancient vineyard has been cultivated since before Christ, for the local inhabitants, the Aeneti, first imported the vine from Greece. Gradisca d'Isonzo, an old Venetian outpost which retains a 15th-century fortress and town walls built by the Republic of San Marco, is today an important regional centre and the home of the *Enoteca Permanente 'La Serenissima'*, a showcase not only for the wines of Isonzo, but for all of Friuli.

ENOTECA REGIONALE

1

ENOTECA PERMANENTE DELLA
    REGIONE FRIULI-VENEZIA GIULIA
'LA SERENISSIMA'
VIA C. BATTISTI
34072 GRADISCA D'ISONZO GO
TEL: 0481/99217

OPEN: Tue–Sun 10–13h; 16–23h.
This regional *enoteca*, located in
the historic 15th-century Palazzo
dei Provveditori Veneti, provides
an excellent opportunity to taste
and purchase the best table
wines, *spumante*, and *grappe* of
the Friuli-Venezia Giulia region.
Wines are only admitted to the
prestigious 'Regional Wine
Collection' after several selections
carried out by official committees
and the annual competition
known as the 'Gran Premio Noé'.
There is always a good selection
of open wines for tasting
(including the rare Picolit),
together with simple snacks,
meat, cheese, bread. Wines can
furthermore be purchased at
prices only marginally higher
than at the *aziende* themselves.
German spoken.

Degustazione: Stop to Taste; Stop to Buy

7

MARCO FELLUGA SRL
VIA GORIZIA 121
34072 GRADISCA D'ISONZO GO
TEL: 0481/99164

WINES PRODUCED: Collio Tocai,
Pinot Bianco, Pinot Grigio,
Sauvignon, Riesling, Ribolla,
Chardonnay, Merlot, Cabernet,
Pinot Nero, Refosco, Carantan.
VISITS: Mon–Fri 8–12h; 14–17h.
Another highly-considered estate
producing top-notch wines.
English, German spoken.

8

VINNAIOLI JERMANN
VIA MONTE FORTINO 17
34070 VILLANOVA DI FARRA GO
TEL: 0481/888080

WINES PRODUCED: Vintage Tunina,
Vinnae, Engelwhite, Tocai Italico,
Pinot Bianco, Pinot Grigio,
Sauvignon, Chardonnay, Traminer
Aromatico, Riesling Renano,
Moscato Rosa, Red Angel, Cabernet,
grappa.
VISITS: weekdays working hours, by
appointment.
Silvio Jermann is considered one of
Friuli's outstanding and innovative
wine makers. Eschewing zonal

THE NORTH-EAST

DOC qualifications, his wines speak for themselves. Vintage Tunina is an exceptional wine produced from selected Chardonnay, Sauvignon, Malvasia, Ribolla, Tocai, Picolit and other white grapes. Vinnae is a fine example of Ribolla Gialla, while Engelwhite is produced from Pinot Nero vinified *in bianco*. These are indeed wines of the highest quality and demonstrate the potential of the region. English spoken.

Colli Orientali del Friuli

The Colli Orientali, or Eastern Hills of Friuli, is probably the next best known of Friuli's 7 wine zones after the Collio. The area covered by the DOC extends beyond the Collio, to the north and west of Dolegna, and encompasses such important wine towns as Cividale del Friuli (a fine, atmospheric medieval town, and former capital of the Lombard duchy, with cobbled streets and a 'devil's bridge' over the Natisone river); Tarcento; Corno di Rosazzo; and Buttrio.

The Colli Orientali del Friuli DOC applies to a range of some 15 different wines, 10 white, 4 red, and a *rosato*. It is, moreover, the only zone where the rare and famous Picolit is entitled to DOC. In the 18th and 19th centuries, this wine was enjoyed in all the imperial and royal courts of Europe, and was long hailed as the greatest wine in Italy. Today, floral abortion has caused yields from this fickle indigenous grape to dwindle to virtually nothing, but small trickles of wine continue to be made at great expense.

Degustazione: **Stop to Taste; Stop to Buy**

9

AZIENDE VITIVINICOLE VALLE DI L. VALLE & C. S.A.S.
VIA NAZIONALE 3
33042 BUTTRIO UD
TEL: 0432/674289

WINES PRODUCED: Colli Orientali del Friuli DOC: Pinot Grigio, Merlot, Refosco, Cabernet, Ribolla Gialla, Riesling Renano, Tocai

Friulano, Verduzzo Ramandolo, Picolit. Collio DOC: Traminer, Pinot Bianco, Sauvignon.
VISITS: weekdays, by appointment. Large, modern firm located on the state road Udine–Trieste, producing a range of respected wines from the Colli Orientali del Friuli and Collio.

Grave del Friuli

As the name suggests, Grave del Friuli is a wine zone made up of mainly gravelly, stony soil. It is, by quite a long way, the largest of Friuli's 7 wine zones, extending over the provinces of Udine and Pordenone. The Grave del Friuli DOC covers 7 varietal wines, 4 white and 3 red, and the wines produced, by both small private wine growers and large merchants and co-operatives, can rank among the region's finest and most interesting.

Udine is the capital of Friuli, and today this important city remains a stylish regional centre. Originally settled by the Magyars, ruled later by the Patriarchs of Aquileia, Udine belonged to Venice from 1420 onwards, and much of the city, particularly around the Piazza della Libertà, retains the unmistakable atmosphere of the lion of San Marco.

Degustazione: Stop to Taste; Stop to Buy

10

AZIENDA AGRICOLA F.LLI PIGHIN
VIALE GRADO 1
33050 PAVIA DI UDINE UD
TEL: 0432/675444

WINES PRODUCED: Grave del Friuli DOC: Pinot Grigio, Sauvignon, Chardonnay, Cabernet Sauvignon, Merlot. Collio DOC: Pinot Grigio, Sauvignon, Chardonnay, Pinot

Bianco, Cabernet, Merlot.
VISITS: weekdays, by appointment.
A full and impressive range of wines, produced entirely from the Pighin family's own vineyards in the Collio and Grave del Friuli regions.
English, German spoken.

Aquileia

Aquileia, today only a small agricultural settlement above the lagoon of Grado, was in Roman times the important port for Rome's Adriatic fleet and one of the largest cities in the Empire. Abandoned after the barbarian invasions, it rose to prominence again during the Middle Ages under the powerful Patriarchs of Aquileia. Today, the town boasts extensive Roman ruins that attest to its former splendour, as well as an important roman-esque basilica, decorated with outstandingly beautiful mosaic pavements.

The vine was planted at Aquileia before even the Romans, and the wines produced were praised by Pliny and enjoyed at the court of Augustus. Today the Aquileia DOC can be utilized for the production of some 13 wines. It

THE NORTH-EAST

applies to a relatively small wine area, stretching from the coastline inland to the fortified town of Palmanova, constructed by the Venetians in 1593 with fortified walls that form a symmetrical 9-pointed star.

Distilleria Artigianale

11

DISTILLERIE NONINO
VIA AQUILEIA 104
PERCOTO UD
TEL: 0432/676332

VISITS: Mon–Fri, by appointment. The Friuli region is not only a noted wine region, it is also the traditional centre for distillation of *grappe* and fruit spirits. The

Nonino family are true artisan-distillers, and produce an extensive and highly regarded range of *grappe* primarily from selected *vinacce* of single grape varieties from the vineyards of Aquileia, Collio, Colli Orientali, Grave del Friuli, and Carso. English, French spoken.

Latisana

The wide old Tagliamento river winds down through Friuli, past San Daniele del Friuli, a small mountain town noted for its superlative air-cured *prosciutto crudo*, through Latisana, once an important river port and a link between Venice and Trieste, before finally emptying into the Adriatic at Lignano. The southern part of this narrow spit makes up the wine zone known as Latisana, a small coastal vineyard that produces 7 DOC wines. For those holidaying at the resorts of the Lignano complex that stretches along the Adriatic coast and the Marano lagoon, these easy-drinking, plentiful wines will quench the thirst most ably.

Carso

The Carso, the coastal region that extends from above Trieste around into Yugoslavia, is an area of strange limestone formations, underground rivers, and caves. The most notable wines of this relatively new DOC zone are produced from Terrano, a strain of the indigenous Refosco grape, and from Malvasia, another ancient grape cultivated in the zone for literally centuries. To tour the vineyards of the Carso, head into the hills just north of Trieste, first to Monrupino, then to Sgónico, and around to Aurisina near the coast.

Ristoranti

1
TRATTORIA 'AL GIARDINETTO'
VIA G. MATTEOTTI 54
34071 CORMÒNS GO
TEL: 0481/60257

Closed Mon eve; Tue.
Typical specialities of Friuli,
displaying the influences of central
Europe, including *gulasch*,
kaiserfleish, *gnocchi di susine*,
salsiccia friulana, accompanied by
an intelligent selection of the wines
of Friuli.
English, German spoken.
Inexpensive to Moderate

2
GOSTILNA DVOR
VIA CASTELLO 5
34070 SAN FLORIANO DEL COLLIO GO
TEL: 0481/884035

Closed Thurs.
Really basic, atmospheric
Slovenian tavern, serving *cevapcici*
and other grilled meats, *gnocchi
con ciligie, lo stinco*, and wines of
'Steverjan' outdoors in shaded
terrace in summer.
Very Inexpensive

3
CASTELLO FORMENTINI
34070 SAN FLORIANO DEL COLLIO GO
TEL: 0481/884034

Closed Mon; Jan, Feb.
Fine luxury hotel-restaurant
located in the 15th-century castle of
the noble Formentini family which
dominates the hilltop of San
Floriano. Hearty specialities of the
region together with outstanding
range of wines from the Antica
Azienda Agricola dei Conti
Formentini. 9-hole golf course and
swimming pool.
Moderate to Expensive

4
RISTORANTE ASTORIA ITALIA
PIAZZA XX SETTEMBRE 24
33100 UDINE
TEL: 0432/290869

Open daily.
Wine growers' favourite, serving
local and classic foods, together,
mainly, with the wines of Friuli.
The restaurant is located in a hotel
in the historic centre of town near
the Duomo, but it is run separately.
Moderate

THE NORTH-EAST

Agriturismo

1

TRATTORIA 'AL CACCIATORE'
CENTRO AGRITURISTICO 'LA SUBIDA'
LOC. MONTE 22
34071 CORMÒNS GO
TEL: 0481/60531

Closed Tue; Wed.
This *trattoria rurale* set in a
splendid restored traditional
Friulan house, is the centrepiece of
the Sirk's *centro agrituristico*
complex and serves the authentic
foods of the country: *prosciutto di
cinghiale, strudel con le ciliegie, lo
stinco*, together with an intelligent
selection of wines from local
growers, and *slivovitch* and other
aquavitae.
Moderate

2

CENTRO AGRITURISMO FATTORIA
FAMILIA AMBROSI
LOC. LONZANO
34070 DOLEGNA DEL COLLIO GO
TEL: 0481/61045

Open Sat and Sun evenings only or
by reservation. Closed during the
vendemmia (end Sept–early Nov).
Local foods of Friuli – *minestra di
orzo*, homemade *prosciutto* and
salame, and grilled meats, together
with home produced Collio wines in
this friendly family-run farmhouse
inn.
Inexpensive

Wine and Other Related *Sagre* and *Feste*

April	Gran Premio Noé	Gradisca d'Isonzo
May	Festa del Vino e delle Fragole	Faedis
early Sept	Rassegna dei Vini Cormònesi	Cormòns
Sept	Festa del Vino	San Floriano

E PER SAPERE DI PIÙ – ADDITIONAL INFORMATION

Azienda Regionale per la
Promozione Turistica
via G. Rossini 6
34100 Trieste
tel: 040/60336

Agriturist Comitato Regionale
via Savorgnana 26
33100 Udine
tel: 0481/60214

Consorzii Tutela Vini DOC
Aquileia e Latisana
via Vittorio Veneto 65
33100 Udine
tel: 0432/297068

Consorzio Tutela Vini DOC Colli
Orientali del Friuli
Viale della Stazione
33043 Cividale del Friuli UD
tel: 0432/730162

Consorzio Tutela Vini DOC Collio
via Duca d'Aosta 113
34170 Gorizia
tel: 0481/87127

Consorzio Tutela Vini DOC
Grave del Friuli
Corso Vittorio Emanuele 47
33170 Pordenone
tel: 0434/381290

Consorzio Tutela Vini DOC
d'Isonzo
Palazzo Locatelli
34071 Cormòns GO
tel: 0481/61833

THE CENTRE

Tuscany
Umbria
Emilia-Romagna
The Marches

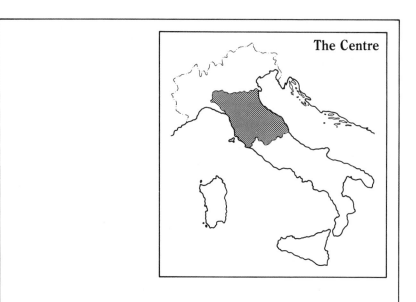

The Centre

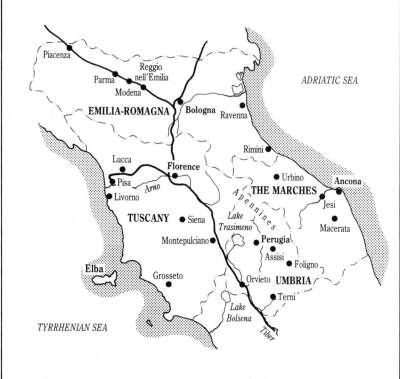

Piacenza

Reggio
nell'Emilia

Parma

Modena

EMILIA-ROMAGNA

Bologna Ravenna

ADRIATIC SEA

Rimini

Lucca

Florence

Pisa *Arno*

Livorno

Urbino

THE MARCHES **Ancona**

Jesi

Siena *Lake
Trasimeno* *A p e n n i n e s*

Macerata

TUSCANY

Montepulciano

Perugia

Assisi Foligno

Elba Grosseto

Orvieto **UMBRIA**

Terni

*Lake
Bolsena*

TYRRHENIAN SEA *Tiber*

TUSCANY

Marzocco.

I Vini: THE WINES OF TUSCANY 234

La Gastronomia 238

Le Strade dei Vini: THE WINE ROADS OF TUSCANY

Florence and Siena: Ancient Rivals Connected by a Prestigious Wine Land 242

The Chianti: *Il Mondo del Gallo Nero* 247

Carmignano: Etruscan Tombs, Medici Villas, and Outstanding Wine 276

● Montalcino: *Terra di Brunello* 286

● Montepulciano and its Noble Wine 300

The Rufina and Pomino: Noble Wines from a Majestic Land 307

San Gimignano, '*Città delle Belle Torri*' 313

The Maremma: Hot Springs, Warming Wines, and Etruscan Ruins 318

Le Sagre: WINE AND OTHER RELATED FESTIVALS 326

Additional Information 328

Tuscany, land of Michelangelo, Leonardo, Botticelli, Dante, Petrarch, Machiavelli, and so many other great names is undoubtedly still Italy's cultural and artistic heartland. The Italian language as spoken in Tuscany is the purest in a nation notorious for its multifarious dialects. And the Tuscan landscape – steep hills covered with silver-grey olive trees, both mixed and specialized viticulture, and dense woodlands punctuated throughout with isolated medieval castles and rambling old farmhouses – is even today the background of a Renaissance painting.

Virtually the entire region is wine country. The classic zone between Tuscany's two greatest cities, Florence and Siena, historically served as a buffer zone between those two great rivals; indeed, an ancient political organization, the Lega del Chianti, gave its name to the region's most famous wine. Today Chianti is not only produced in this élite Classico heartland, but in 6 other sub-zones as well. From south of Siena, in the isolated and steep hill country around the walled town of Montalcino, comes possibly Italy's greatest red wine, Brunello di Montalcino. Montepulciano with its 'noble wine' is another nearby zone of fame and repute, while smaller areas stake their claims for the attention of the wine lover: Carmignano, a tiny but prestigious vineyard in the Montalbano hills west of

THE CENTRE

Florence; San Gimignano, famous for its white Vernaccia and its incredible medieval towers; the Rufina, isolated, majestic wine country in the foothills leading up to the Apennines; and the Maremma, Tuscany's deep south, known for exceptional red wines from the Morellino grape as well as for Etruscan ruins and remarkable thermal springs.

If the Florentines initiated the Renaissance in the 14th century, Tuscany stands today at the very forefront of an Italian wine renaissance that has both rediscovered its ancient and prestigious patrimony, and looks to the future. Traditional wines such as Chianti Classico have been improved beyond recognition by modern vinification techniques and improvements in the vineyard, while new ideas and energies in zones such as Montalcino mean that today's wines are reaching a potential hardly even dreamed of just a decade or two ago. Nowhere else in the country is there more forward-thinking experimentation – in both the vineyard and the *cantina* – nor a greater profusion of modern, new styles of wine for today's consumer.

Tuscany is a region that has always attracted visitors from throughout the world. There is so much the region has to offer – art, culture, medieval cities, splendid unspoiled countryside, and not least exceptional wines and basically simple but always satisfying local foods – that those of us in love with the region find ourselves yearning to return year after year.

ORIENTATION

Tuscany comprises 9 provinces: Florence, Arezzo, Grosseto, Livorno, Lucca, Massa Carrara, Pisa, Pistoia, and Siena. The most convenient international airport is Pisa Galileo Galilei, but air, rail or road connections with the region from either Milan or Rome are possible. Florence is on the main Paris–Rome rail line. The A1 north-south *autostrada* runs from Milan to Rome via Florence; the A11 connects Florence with Pisa, Livorno, and the north-west.

Map Touring Club Italiano 1: 200 000 Toscana.

LA MEZZADRIA

The *mezzadria* was a system of feudal sharecropping common in many parts of Italy, but particularly prevalent in Tuscany and Umbria. It was based on a supposedly even distribution of the crops whereby the landowner supplied the land and a dwelling to the *contadino*, who in turn gave half his produce – grapes, wheat, olives, chickens, vegetables, whatever – to the *padrone* and kept the remainder for himself. No wages were paid; instead, after the crops had been brought in, the farmer would receive, for example, a certain number of *barile* of wine and oil, or, say, a number of *staia* of grain in exchange for his labours. These old measuring containers, stamped with the insignia of the landowner's family, can be seen on many farms and estates today, piled up in a corner or used as planters for geraniums.

In medieval times, certainly, when the peasantry of the rest of Europe had the status of mere serfs or slaves, and even to a certain extent in more recent times, *mezzadria* gave the Italian *contadino* direct rights over and an interest in the land that he worked. But it was a system open to abuse on both sides. Based as it was on antiquated notions of patronage, of lord and master on the one hand, grateful dependant on the other – the *contadino* who tipped his hat to the *padrone*, and delivered to him his best *prosciutto* and *salame* every Christmas – it is not surprising that, since the last war, it has been gradually phased out. Today, in many cases, those who formerly worked under this system are employed on the same lands, but as salaried agricultural workers. They may no longer be entitled to keep a share of their crops, but instead they receive a steady weekly wage, and enjoy health care, old age pensions, and other such benefits. Yet as the old retainers retire, will there be a new younger generation to replace them, when they can find ready and usually better paid work in factories and industry?

Meanwhile, the former sharecroppers' cottages, dotted throughout the countryside, have been or are being restored and renovated, and throughout Tuscany especially, as well as elsewhere, a new industry of *agriturismo* is now emerging as these are let out to city dwellers and *stranieri* from northern Europe and North America.

THE CENTRE

I VINI: GLOSSARY TO THE WINES OF TUSCANY

Wines of *Denominazione di Origine Controllata (DOC)* and *Denominazione di Origine Controllata e Garantita (DOCG)*

Bianco di Pitigliano DOC White wine produced from mainly Trebbiano Toscano with some Grechetto, Malvasia, and Verdello, grown on volcanic tufa vineyards of Pitigliano, Sorano, Manciano and Scansano in the province of Grosseto. Minimum alcohol 11.5 degrees.

Bianco Pisano di San Torpe DOC White Trebbiano Toscano (mainly) wine from hill vineyards in the provinces of Pisa and Livorno, overlapping with the zone for Chianti Colli Pisane. Minimum alcohol 11 degrees. **Vin Santo Pisano DOC** *Passito* dessert wine from the same zone.

Bianco Valdinievole DOC White wine made from Trebbiano Toscano, Malvasia, Vermentino, Canaiolo in vineyards around Montecatini Terme, Buggiano, Uzzano, and surroundings. Minimum alcohol 11 degrees.

Bianco Vergine Valdichiana DOC White wine from provinces of Arezzo and Siena produced from Trebbiano Toscano and Malvasia. Minimum alcohol 11 degrees.

Bolgheri DOC Wine zone on the Tuscan seaboard south of Livorno, primarily around Castagneto Carducci, noted primarily for outstanding *rosato* and red wines from Sangiovese, Canaiolo, and some Cabernet, as well as for Trebbiano whites.

Brunello di Montalcino DOCG Great red wine from Brunello grapes (a superior clone of Sangiovese Grosso) grown in the commune of Montalcino in the province of Siena. Minimum alcohol 12.5 degrees; minimum ageing 4 years in wood. Wines that undergo 5 years' ageing may be labelled Riserva.

Candia Colli Apuani DOC Little encountered white wine produced from Vermentino and Albarola grapes grown in the Apuani hills in the province of Massa Carrara.

Carmignano DOC Tiny wine zone west of Florence extending into the Montalbano hills producing 3 outstanding wines. Red Carmignano is produced from Sangiovese and Canaiolo (as well as lesser grapes) with the addition of up to 10% Cabernet. Minimum alcohol 12.5 degrees, minimum ageing in wood 2 years; 3 years overall for Riserva. Rosato Carmignano (known also as Vin Ruspo) is a good robust *rosé* produced from the same grapes. The DOC also applies to Vin Santo, a dessert wine made from semi-dried *passito* grapes, some examples of which are superlative.

Chianti DOCG Red wine produced in provinces of Florence, Siena, Arezzo, Pisa, and Pistoia, from recognized and amended (in 1984) formula of Sangiovese (mainly), Canaiolo, and small amounts of Trebbiano Toscano and Malvasia. Minimum alcohol 12 degrees (12.5 degrees for Chianti Classico). Wines aged for minimum of 3 years may be labelled Riserva. In addition to 'straight' Chianti, the wines may come from the following 7 sub-zones:

Chianti Classico The classic heartland, between Florence and Siena. Symbol for members' consortium is the *gallo nero* – black rooster.

Chianti Colli Aretini Wine zone east of Florence along Arno valley in province of Arezzo.

Chianti Colli Fiorentini Wine zone over hills mainly south and east between Val d'Arno and Val di Pesa.

Chianti Colline Pisane Wine zone south-east of Pisa, centred on Casciana Terme.

Chianti Colli Senesi Chianti produced from vineyards throughout much of the province of Siena.

Chianti Montalbano Dramatic hill zone west of Florence encompassing the Carmignano vineyard, and extending across to Vinci.

Chianti Rufina Tiny, but prestigious, wine zone east of Florence in foothills of the Apennines above the Sieve valley.

Colline Lucchesi DOC Red and white wines produced in hills around Lucca, Capannori, and Porcari.

Elba DOC Island vineyards producing both Sangiovese based red (minimum alcohol 12 degrees) and Trebbiano Toscano based white (10 degrees).

Montecarlo DOC Undervalued white wine produced from Trebbiano (mainly) with the addition of Sémillon, Pinot Grigio, Pinot Bianco, Sauvignon, and Roussanne, from vineyards around Montecarlo, Altopascio, Capannori, and Porcari, east of Lucca; also lesser amounts of Sangiovese based red. Minimum alcohol 11.5 degrees.

Montescudaio DOC Wine zone in province of Pisa around communes of Montescudaio and Val di Cecina producing Sangiovese based red (minimum alcohol 11.5 degrees), Trebbiano based white (11.5 degrees), and Vin Santo.

Morellino di Scansano DOC Hill vineyards south of Grosseto around communes of Scansano, Manciano, Magliano in Toscana, and others, producing rich, undervalued Sangiovese based wine. Minimum alcohol 11.5 degrees. Riserva wines must reach 12 degrees and be aged for at least 2 years, 1 of which must be in wood cask.

Moscadello di Montalcino DOC Sweet, sometimes *frizzante* white wine produced from Moscato Bianco grapes grown in the vineyards of Montalcino. Rare concentrated *liquoroso* version is also produced.

Parrina DOC Tiny delimited vineyard around sea commune of Orbetello in southern province of Grosseto: produces both Sangiovese based red (minimum alcohol 12 degrees), and Trebbiano based white (11.5 degrees).

Pomino DOC Tiny but outstanding historic wine zone encompassed by Chianti Rufina, producing red wine from Sangiovese and Canaiolo, with the addition of Cabernet and Merlot, white wine from Chardonnay, Pinot Bianco, and Trebbiano, and Vin Santo from semi-dried *passito* grapes.

Rosso di Montepulciano DOC New *denominazione* for red wine produced from similar *uvaggio* of grapes as Vino Nobile di Montepulciano but to less stringent ageing requirements.

VINI DEL PREDICATO

Vini del Predicato are quality wines made outside the current scope of DOC but to extremely rigorous and stringent regulations as laid down by member producers. There are currently 4 categories of wines that may qualify: Predicato del Bitùrica (mainly Cabernet or Cabernet-based blends); Predicato del Cardìsco (Sangiovese); Predicato del Muschio (Chardonnay and Pinot Bianco); and Predicato del Selvànte (Sauvignon). For the consumer such designations are important for they not only serve as an indication of the style but give an alternative (and more stringent) guarantee of quality than DOC.

Centine !

Rosso di Montalcino DOC Wine produced from Brunello grape in the same Montalcino zone of production, but to less stringent requirements, notably only 1 year obligatory ageing.

Val d'Arbia DOC Wine zone overlapping part of southern Chianti Classico and extending into Montalcino for the production of Trebbiano based white as well as Vin Santo.

Vernaccia di San Gimignano DOC White wine from Vernaccia grapes grown in vineyards around commune of San Gimignano.

Minimum alcohol 12 degrees. Wines labelled Riserva require not less than 1 year ageing.

Vino Nobile di Montepulciano DOCG Distinguished red wine from vineyards entirely within the commune of Montepulciano, produced from Prugnolo Gentile (a clone of Sangiovese Grosso), Canaiolo, and tiny amounts of Malvasia and Trebbiano Toscano. Minimum alcohol 12 degrees; minimum age 2 years. Riserva wines must age for at least 3 years; Riserva Speciale need 4 years' ageing or more.

VIN SANTO

When guests or friends drop in on one another in Tuscany, the traditional wine of hospitality is Vin Santo, offered together with a plate of small, crunchy almond biscuits such as the famous *cantuccini di Prato*. While gossip and chatter is exchanged, the little biscuits are dunked into the usually sweet, amber Vin Santo to soften them, then munched together with the wine.

The name Vin Santo means 'holy wine' and is attributed to different stories. Some say that Vin Santo was originally brought to central Italy from the Greek island of Xantos; others that it resembles the sweet wines of that island. Another version is that the wine is so-called because it was traditionally, and in some cases still is, bottled at Easter during the *settimana santa*. Or else, more probably, this most exquisite wine was drunk by discerning prelates and priests during religious rituals.

Even in its own region (and in neighbouring Umbria where it is also much enjoyed), Vin Santo remains one of the most undervalued wines of Italy. For the best, made by unique and traditional methods that have changed not at all over the centuries, can rank among the great sweet wines of the world.

THE CENTRE

The traditional production of Vin Santo is unique. During the harvest, the best white grapes – usually Trebbiano Toscano, Malvasia, San Colombano, Grechetto – are laid out in attics on cane mats known locally as *graticci* or *stuoie*. These are then stacked in layers on wooden pedestals called *castelli*, and left to dry usually until at least Christmas or later (around Monte- pulciano, the grapes may remain on the *stuoie* until well into the new year). In the process, they shrivel and concentrate their sugar content, becoming rich, sweet, and raisin-like.

The dried, shrivelled grapes must be selected by hand, then lightly crushed and pressed.

Finally, the ugly, shrivelled grapes are selected by hand (those which have been affected by grey mould or attacked by insects are discarded), they are lightly crushed and pressed, and the sugar-rich *mosto* is placed in small 50- or 100-litre wooden barrels known as *caratelli*. The *caratelli* contain the dregs and lees of pre- ceding vintages, a rich yeasty sludge that is known as the *madre*, and it is this which gives each Vin Santo its unique character. The *caratelli* are sealed with wax or cement and then left in the attics for up to 4 years or longer, during which time the wine suffers the freezing cold of winter and the terrible heat of summer, the long, slow fermentation ceasing and recommencing in fits and starts. The wine which emerges from this brutal sojourn is both glorious and virtually indestructible: and, given the time, care, and selection necessary to produce it (almost always in minuscule quantities) it remains one of the greatest bargains in the wine world.

LA GASTRONOMIA: FOODS OF TUSCANY

Tuscany, home of the Italian Renaissance, is not a region of great outward sophistication. Rather, its greatest hallmark is simplicity and purity, attributes which pertain equally to its architecture, style of living, and not least *cucina*. In Renaissance *palazzi* or rambling *aziende* alike, in grand *ristoranti* and humble Tuscan *trattorie*, it is the simple foods of the country above all which continue to captivate.

Fresh, seasonal vegetables dressed simply in pure virgin olive oil; wild mushrooms freshly gathered from the woods and served over homemade noodles; meats simply grilled over a wood fire; white beans cooked in an old Chianti *fiasco*: these are true foods of the country, served without fuss or pretension. But such apparent simplicity can be deceptive. For the preparation of pure and unadorned Tuscan dishes takes great culinary skill, developed, implemented, adjusted, modified over a period of centuries to suit the uncompromising taste of refined palates. For Tuscans know better than most that sublime simplicity is often the hallmark of great artistry.

PIATTI TIPICI:
REGIONAL SPECIALITIES

Crostini di fegatini Rounds of toasted bread spread with a chicken liver, capers and anchovy paste.

Fettunta Unsalted Tuscan bread, toasted over an open fire, rubbed with garlic, then doused liberally with virgin olive oil and seasoned with salt and pepper.

Finocchiona Large Tuscan *salame* flavoured with wild fennel seeds.

Pinzimonio Platter of raw vegetables served simply with the finest virgin olive oil and salt.

Migliaccio 'Pancake' of fresh blood and seasonings, eaten with grated cheese: popular wine festival fare.

Pappa al pomodoro Typical, heavy bread soup made with fresh tomatoes, basil and olive oil.

Ribollita Characteristic hearty cabbage, bean and bread soup, reboiled to further thicken and concentrate the flavours.

Panzanella Delicious Florentine summer salad of stale bread soaked in ice water, mixed together with chopped tomatoes, cucumber, onions and fresh herbs, and dressed in olive oil and vinegar.

THE CENTRE

Pappardelle alla lepre
Wide homemade noodles served
with pungent sauce of stewed
hare.

Pinci Homemade fat
spaghetti-type noodles from
province of Siena.

Bistecca alla fiorentina
Tuscany's most famous dish:
T-bone steak of *vitellone* (meat
half-way between beef and veal),
cooked over a wood fire and
seasoned simply with salt,
pepper, and a little olive oil.
Invariably sold by weight (*per
etto*); can be (and usually are)
enormous.

Arrosto girato Chicken, rabbit,
beef, lamb or game birds,
spit-roasted over a wood fire.

Scottiglia Rich stew made with
different varieties of meat,
together with wine, tomatoes and
herbs, usually served on slices of
toasted bread.

Rosticianna Highly-seasoned
pork ribs, grilled over a wood fire:
favourite street food at wine
festivals.

Cinghiale Wild boar.

Panforte Famous, flat spiced
cake from Siena.

Castagnacci Characteristic
desserts made from chestnut
flour.

Cantuccini Hard almond
biscuits to be dipped into Vin
Santo.

Cheese: *Pecorino* Sheep's milk
cheese, available either *dolce*
(mild) or *piccante* or *stagionato*
(aged and hard). Best comes
from the *crete Senese* around
Pienza.

TUSCAN *OLIO EXTRA VERGINE D'OLIVA*

Just as the vine is an enduring feature of the Tuscan country, so is the olive
tree. Indeed, their complementary products, wine and olive oil, together with
bread and salt, have been the basis of the local diet for millennia. After the
great freeze of January 1985, which left the region's olive groves almost
totally devastated, old plants have rejuvenated, replanted olive groves have

Terracotta orci, *the traditional storage containers for Tuscan* olio extra vergine d'oliva.

come into production, and most estates are now producing quality *olio extra vergine d'oliva* again, the famous dense green olive oil of Tuscany, stored in the traditional *orciaia* in great terracotta urns. Such oils are to industrially-produced oil what great estate-bottled wines are to *vino sfuso*.

The best, like the best wines, come usually from select hill zones such as the Chianti Classico, Carmignano, Montalcino, and Lucca. Here, the small trees yield only tiny amounts of fruit – perhaps just 5–10 kg per tree – compared to the vast crops from, for example, the oak-sized olive trees of Apulia. But the olives from these smaller plants render an oil that is considerably finer, intensely fruity yet somehow less fatty, and exquisitely elegant.

The production of such artisan-made *olio d'oliva* demands the greatest care. The olives are harvested by hand using a rake-like instrument (they are never allowed to ripen until they fall off the tree as is the case elsewhere), then they are carefully transported to the *frantoio*. The washed fruit is ground into a paste by heavy granite mill-stones, then this paste is layered, and pressed once only to extract both oil and vegetable water. The oil is simply separated from the vegetable water in a centrifuge, and it is then ready to be consumed (it may or may not be filtered prior to bottling). *Olio extra vergine d'oliva*, the best quality, indicates oil that has a very low acidity – no more than 1 per cent.

Each year there is great excitement when the new oil is available. Unlike most wines, extra virgin olive oil is best when fresh from the *frantoio* for it then maintains all its fruitiness, and also leaves a rather sharp, hot prickle in the back of the throat that is much loved (this diminishes with age). When such new oil is available, there is no better way to enjoy it than simply dribbled generously on to a slice of Tuscan bread, seasoned with salt and pepper, and accompanied by a glass of good red wine.

FLORENCE AND SIENA: ANCIENT RIVALS CONNECTED BY A PRESTIGIOUS WINE LAND

Tuscany today is so beautiful and peaceful that it is hard to imagine that centuries ago an internecine struggle took place that was to decimate families, villages, and cities. For the city-states of Florence and Siena found themselves on opposing sides of the arcane Guelph–Ghibelline struggle and were thus almost constantly at odds and at war with one another. At its most basic, the Guelphs, supported by Florence, were the champions of the papacy while the Ghibellines, with whom the Sienese allied themselves, supported the Holy Roman Empire over the central medieval argument of right of investiture. But the struggle was much more complex and twisted than this, and at times was reduced to no more than a vicious and un-dignified dog-fight between the rival cities. Even within Florence itself, the Guelphs split into two rival factions, the more liberal Whites and the arch-conservative Blacks; the poet Dante, a White, was exiled from his beloved native city by Boniface VIII.

A principal battleground for this long-standing conflict took place over the rugged hills of the Chianti that served as a buffer zone between Florence and Siena. Villages and towns were mainly settled on top of high hills for protec-tion, and individual fortified estates and hamlets were created almost wherever there was a strategic rise in the terrain. The name Chianti is probably of Etruscan origin, and it came to refer first not to the wine, but to an important political organization, the Lega del Chianti, that was formed in the 13th century when the communities of Castellina, Radda, and Gaiole banded together under Florentine jurisdiction. Their symbol was a black cockerel on a field of gold, and this, centuries later, was adopted as the trademark for the Consorzio Gallo Nero.

If, even today, a rivalry of sorts remains – or at the least, a certain antipathy – between long-standing Florentine and Sienese families, both cities are among the most popular and important tourist destinations in all of Italy. For central Tuscany is considered the cradle of humanism, fantas-tically rich in medieval and Renaissance art, sculpture, and architecture: Florence and Siena lie at the very heart of Italian culture and identity.

This central Tuscan heartland lies, too, at the very epicentre of the Italian wine renaissance: indeed, here as much as anywhere in the nation is evi-dence not only of a reclamation of an ancient vinous heritage that extends back centuries, but also of the discovery and extension of new frontiers, as improved viticulture – the plantation of superior clones as well as new grape varieties; innovative wine making techniques – and the development of new styles of wine look forward to the next millennium.

Florence and Siena have so much to offer every visitor, not least the wine lover. Florence and its commune, in addition to parts of the Chianti Classico, can boast the prestigious vineyards of the Chianti Rufina, Pomino, and Carmignano, while Siena claims the vineyards of Montalcino, Montepulciano, and San Gimignano. While there are no shortages of restaurants and *enoteche* in both Florence and Siena, ensuring that none need go thirsty or hungry, we must particularly single out the Cantinetta Antinori for the opportunity to taste, in an elegant Renaissance setting, the full range of wines from probably Italy's leading and most forward-thinking producer; the *Enoteca Pinchiorri*, Florence's leading restaurant, which boasts one of the best-stocked cellars in Italy if not the world; and of course the *Enoteca Permanente* in Siena, Italy's only national wine library, and a repository for an intelligent selection of wines from all of Italy's 20 regions. These wines can all be tasted by the glass or bottle in the imposing Fortezza, in effect enabling the Italian wine lover and wine tourist to undertake a most enjoyable journey throughout the land without ever having to leave his or her seat.

FLORENCE

Degustazione: Stop to Taste; Stop to Buy

MARCHESI L. & P. ANTINORI
PALAZZO ANTINORI
PIAZZA DEGLI ANTINORI 3
50100 FLORENCE
TEL: 055/298298; 282202

WINES PRODUCED: Santa Cristina estate: Santa Cristina, Chianti Classico Villa Antinori Riserva, Chianti Classico Riserva Tenute Marchese Antinori; Tignanello; Solaia. Péppoli estate: Chianti Classico Péppoli. Badia a Passignano estate: Chianti Classico Badia a Passignano. Castello della

Sala estate: Orvieto Classico *secco* and *abboccato*; Cervaro della Sala; Borro della Sala; Muffato della Sala (late harvest dessert wine made with grapes affected by *muffa nobile*). Belvedere estate: Vigneto Scalabrone Bolgheri *rosato*. Other wines: Galestro; Antinori Extra Brut; Villa Antinori Bianco; San Giocondo (*vino novello*).

VISITS: tastings of the full range of Antinori wines by the glass or bottle in the Cantinetta Antinori (see below). Visits to the estates are

THE CENTRE

not usually available to the general public, but professionals and serious wine lovers should apply to the public relations office at the above address as far in advance as possible.

Marchese Piero Antinori is rightly considered one of the most forward-thinking wine makers in Italy today, not only for his extensive range of classic Tuscan wines, but moreover for his leadership in the development of new styles of wine, and his considerable marketing skills.

The Palazzo Antinori, a 15th-century mansion in the heart of Florence, is the headquarters for a vast wine empire that dates back at least 6 centuries and which today comprises 5 different estates: Santa Cristina, Péppoli, Belvedere, Badia a Passignano, and Castello della Sala. Though pioneers of a new generation of super-*vini da tavola*, the Antinori also believe very much in the vinous patrimony of Tuscany, and this is evident, for example, in the contrast between Chianti Classicos such as Péppoli, Villa Antinori Riserva, or the *barrique*-aged Badia a Passignano. One of the most fascinating wines is the Tenute Marchesi Antinori, made only in the best years, with a selection of grapes from all 3 estates.

Tignanello first, then Solaia, have inspired an entire generation of new Tuscan wine makers and served as models for the new so-called *super-Toscani*, while new wines are constantly being developed for changing markets. English, French, German spoken.

———

MARCHESI DE' FRESCOBALDI SPA
VIA S. SPIRITO 11
50125 FLORENCE
TEL: 055/218751

WINES PRODUCED: Tenuta di Pomino: Pomino Bianco, Pomino *cru* 'Il Benefizio', Pomino Rosso, Pomino Vin Santo. Tenuta di Nipozzano: Castello di Nipozzano Chianti Rufina; Montesodi Chianti Rufina; Mormoreto.
VISITS: the Frescobaldi estates are not open to the general public, but wine professionals and serious wine lovers may be able to visit by prior arrangement.

The headquarters for this immense family empire remain in the Palazzo Frescobaldi in Florence, and serious wine lovers are advised to arrange visits as far in advance as possible. The aristocratic Frescobaldi have been wine growers since 1300. The Castello di Nipozzano is still a favourite family summer retreat, and recent guests there have included Prince Charles.

In addition to the Frescobaldi

estates in the Rufina, there are also notable estates located in other zones, comprising 850 hectares of specialized vineyards on nine wine estates in all. The important Castelgiocondo estate at Montalcino is the most recent addition to the Frescobaldi portfolio.

English, French, German spoken.

Ristoranti

CANTINETTA ANTINORI
PALAZZO ANTINORI
PIAZZA DEGLI ANTINORI 3
50100 FLORENCE
TEL: 055/292234

Closed Sat, Sun.

This stylish wine bar/*trattoria* is located in the 15th-century Palazzo Antinori, and is most notable as the best place in which to sample the full range of Antinori wines by the glass or bottle (including rare and prestigious wines such as Cervaro della Sala, Tignanello, Solaia, Muffato della Sala). Drinking snacks are available to accompany the wines, which can be enjoyed at the bar, while full meals based on traditional Tuscan foods are served at tables.

Moderate to Expensive

ENOTECA PINCHIORRI
VIA DI GHIBELLINA 87
50122 FLORENCE
TEL: 055/242777

Closed Sun, Mon lunch, August.

Probably the best restaurant in town, serving *cucina novella* as well as modern interpretations of traditional Tuscan foods, most noteworthy for the wine lover for the altogether exceptional cellar which has reserves of not only the best wines of Tuscany and Italy, but from throughout the world.

Very Expensive

IL CANTINONE DEL GALLO NERO
VIA S. SPIRITO 6R
50100 FLORENCE
TEL: 055/218898

Closed Mon.

Dark subterranean drinking den serving a good choice of reasonably priced Chianti Classico and *riserva* wines together with simple but authentic drinking foods and Tuscan dishes: *fettunta, ribollita, pappa al pomodoro, crostini.*

Inexpensive

THE CENTRE

RISTORANTE DINO
VIA GHIBELLINA 51/R
50122 FLORENCE
TEL: 055/241452

Closed Sun eve, Mon.
Renaissance *palazzo* with vaulted
dining rooms not far from Santa

Croce serving traditional and
historic Tuscan foods such as *risotto
della Renza, stracotto del Granduca,
garretto ghibellino*, accompanied by
a noteworthy and extensive
selection of wines.
Inexpensive to Moderate

Siena

ENOTECA ITALICA PERMANENTE

ENOTECA ITALICA PERMANENTE
FORTEZZA MEDICEA
53100 SIENA
TEL: 0577/288497

OPEN: daily 15-24h.
Siena's *Enoteca Permanente* is the
only one of its kind in all Italy,
and thus should be considered a
must for the wine tourist in
Tuscany. For here, in the historic
Medici fortress, is the rare
opportunity to wander through
all of Italy in a bottle. There is a
permanent exhibition of some

250 wines from every corner of
the country, a selection that is
renewed each year. Thus rare
wines, impossible to find outside
their zone of production, can be
sampled by the glass or bottle at
pleasant tables inside or on the
terrace in summer, or else
purchased to take away. From
time to time, professional
organizations arrange special
exhibitions, tastings, and
conferences, many of which are
open to the public.

Ristorante

AL MANGIA
PIAZZA DEL CAMPO 43
53100 SIENA
TEL: 0577/281121

Closed Mon.
Siena's Il Campo is one of the
town's main attractions, so it is
most pleasant to sit at outdoor
tables overlooking the piazza at

this old-established restaurant,
serving both regional and national
foods, including: *cannoli de ricotta e
spinaci ai funghi porcini, cinghiale
in umido, filetto di manzo al
dragoncello.*
English, French spoken.
Moderate

noteca
ermanente,
iena.

THE CHIANTI:
IL MONDO DEL GALLO NERO

In Brief: The Chianti Classico country extends over the rugged and beautiful hills between Florence and Siena. As such, it can be easily and most enjoyably dipped into by anyone travelling between those two cities. The signposted *strada del vino* roughly follows the Via Chiantigiana (N222) and carves through the heart of the wine country, but the wine lover will wish to divert from this central axis to explore the myriad small roads and dirt tracks leading from one small wine community to another. Greve, Radda, and Gaiole are probably the 3 most important communities that everyone will wish to visit; they offer plenty of opportunities for visiting wine estates, wine tasting, wine purchasing in private *enoteche*, and enjoying local foods. Indeed, this is one of the best developed zones in Italy for wine tourism.

While our suggested tour can be completed in a long day, it should probably serve as the basis for a number of smaller tours, with appointments to visit wine producers made in advance. It is essential for visitors who wish to explore the region in greater detail, as well as to locate individual properties, to acquire the detailed map of the *zona di produzione del Chianti Classico*, available from tourist offices or the Consorzio

THE CENTRE

Gallo Nero. This marks the secondary roads and tracks as well as all the names of the *fattorie* and *aziende agricole*.

Agriturismo – farmhouse tourism – is extremely well developed in the zone, as many wine producers have converted disused buildings and former sharecroppers' cottages into self-contained villas (in some cases with swimming pools and other leisure facilities) for short- or long-term rentals. A holiday on a wine estate is undoubtedly the best way to gain an intimate knowledge of the region, as well as a most enjoyable way to explore central Tuscany. There are also some good farmhouse restaurants on wine estates.

Just twenty years ago, and for centuries previously, the countryside between Florence and Siena had a profoundly different character from today. For even that recently, the aristocratic estates, *fattorie*, and smallholdings were almost completely given over to traditional mixed farming, and thus a variety of cultivation was the dominant feature in place of the specialized vineyards that characterize this most important Tuscan wine zone today. The promiscuous cultivation of the past was a direct legacy of the *mezzadria* system of sharecropping where each smallholding had to be virtually self-sufficient. Thus, 3 or 4 rows of vines were planted up trees or other living supports, then there might be a few rows of olive trees, then a patch of grain, a few rows of sunflowers, a vegetable garden, and then some more vines.

The economic crises of the 1950s and 60s saw a mass exodus from the land to the cities, and thus put an end to this antiquated but none the less charmingly aesthetic agricultural system of cultivation. In fact, whole estates were abandoned, and much of rural Tuscany went into considerable decline. Wine production in the Chianti Classico of course continued, but on the whole it was carried out by merchants who purchased and blended wines on an industrial scale, usually with neither care nor selection for quality, and the wines were vinified to be drunk young, preferably from a wicker-covered *fiasco* that became the enduring image not just for Chianti, but indeed for Italian wine the world over.

Even if the wine was not great, this lovely zone of rolling and majestic hills leading up to the Monte dei Chianti continued to exercise its enduring charm. Foreigners – English, Germans, Dutch, Swiss, Americans – purchased properties and began to reclaim vineyards; and Italians from elsewhere

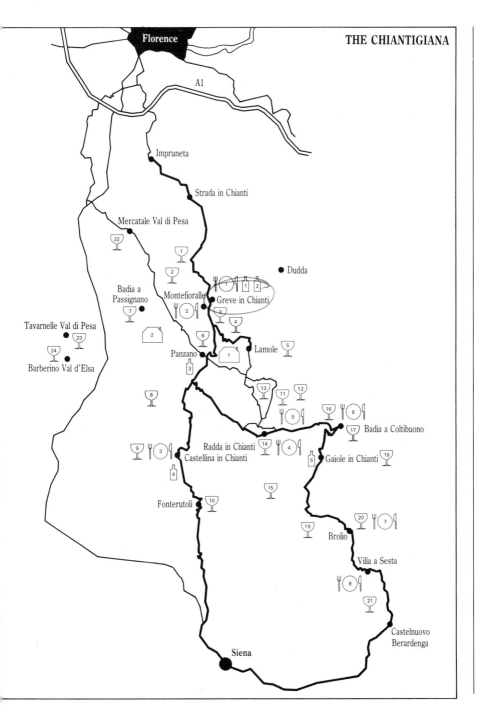

THE CHIANTIGIANA

Florence

A1

Impruneta

Strada in Chianti

Mercatale Val di Pesa

Dudda

Badia a
Passignano

Montefioralle

Greve in Chianti

Tavarnelle Val di Pesa

Panzano

Lamole

Barberino Val d'Elsa

Radda in Chianti

Badia a Coltibuono

Castellina in Chianti

Gaiole in Chianti

Fonterutoli

Brolio

Villa a Sesta

Castelnuovo
Berardenga

Siena

THE CENTRE

who had made their fortunes in other sectors – commerce, manufacturing, entertainment – came too, first undoubtedly for the charm and pleasures of owning a farmhouse in Tuscany, then, more so, for the not inconsiderable challenge of making fine if not great wine.

Investment in the Chianti Classico in recent years has thus been substantial, literally changing the face of the land over the last few decades. Not only were the old mixed plantings uprooted and replaced with well-ordered specialized vineyards; the old, tired wooden fermentation vats and *botti* were disposed of, and in their place came gleaming stainless steel tanks with temperature control, and new oak *botti* and French *barriques*. Consultant oenologists – many of whom have since become international superstars, flying by helicopter from estate to estate – were employed to advise on quality as well as on the development of new modern styles of wine.

In addition to bringing investment to the zone, the new owners brought much more: a new and exciting mentality and – these high-fliers from other sectors – the determination to succeed at the highest level. Moreover, unlike the ancient landed gentry whose only income came from the land, the new owners were in many cases able to inject large sums of money into their pet projects without necessarily requiring an immediate return on capital.

When Giampaolo Pacini, a successful marketing consultant from Prato, decided in the early 1970s to purchase an estate in the Chianti Classico, for example, there was no shortage of properties on the market. He and his wife eventually chose Capaccia, then an abandoned 12th-century medieval *borgo* located in a commanding position 500 metres above sea level, overlooking Radda in Chianti and the neighbouring estates of Monte Vertine and Castello di Volpaia.

As recently as the 1950s this lovely medieval collection of stone cottages and outbuildings had been lived in and worked by a small rural community of several families. Capaccia was renowned then, recalls an old worker, for its superb wines and beautiful women. But by the 1970s everything had been abandoned, the houses were left in ruins and in need of total restoration, and the vineyards and olive groves were overgrown and in disrepair. Pacini, together with his wife and young family, set to the task with considerable energy and enthusiasm, first replanting the vineyards, then, with the advice and guidance of consultant oenologist Vittorio Fiore, installing new equipment in the winery, and only finally restoring the houses to create an enviable weekend and summer retreat.

Signor Pacini himself had trained as an oenologist as a young man, for his

'DESIGNER WINES'

In a country that prides itself almost more than anything else on its sense of style, fashion, and above all individuality, it is probably not surprising that such factors also enter into the world of wine. The rules for DOC and DOCG, after all, emanate from bureaucrats in Rome and there is a deep-seated resentment at being told what can or can't be done by such professional mandarins. Thus, the anomaly today is that some of Italy's greatest wines do not qualify for *denominazione di origine controllata* status, but are labelled and sold as humble *vini da tavola*. Nowhere is there a greater profusion of such wines than in Tuscany where they are sometimes known collectively as '*i super-Toscani*' – the super-Tuscans.

Just as there are changes of taste in high fashion, so does *chic* influence the development of styles of wine. Grape varieties popular in France and the New World, in particular Cabernet Sauvignon, Chardonnay, Sauvignon, are currently enjoying a considerable vogue in Italy, too, and are increasingly being planted in Tuscany to replace traditional but little-known (internationally) varieties. Sangiovese, one of Italy's greatest red grapes, is the exception, and some producers are making either pure varietal, or Sangiovese/Cabernet blends that are outstanding. The current taste – indeed obsession – for wines (both red and white) aged in 225-litre new French oak *barriques* continues, utilized sometimes even when the particular wood tastes and perfumes that such receptacles impart clearly do not suit the wine in question.

Of course, design and fashion have their price – they always do. Such wines, bottled in heavy 'antique' Bordeaux bottles with deep punts in the bottom, given fanciful names and minimalist labels, can fetch prices that may seem to have little to do with the quality of what is actually inside. But make no mistake, the best of such wines are artisan-made products of the highest quality and truly do represent the pinnacle of Italian wine.

father had been a wine merchant in Prato. At Capaccia, his intention from the outset was not only to produce good or even very good wine, but to create a great wine. Like many of the new generation of wine growers in Tuscany, Marchese Piero Antinori's Tignanello served as both model and inspiration of what could be achieved. This meant, naturally, that though the production of Chianti Classico was of importance, the real goal was to create a super-Tuscan table wine. Thus was born Querciagrande, produced from 100% Sangioveto from extremely limited yields, fermented in stainless steel at controlled temperature, and aged in *barriques* made with oak from the French Limousin and Massif Central forests.

Of course, not all those making good wines in the Chianti Classico are newcomers. Indeed, the roll-call of ancient family names and their estates reads like a list of some of the zone's greatest wines: Antinori (Santa Cristina, Péppoli, Badia a Passignano), Mazzei (Castello di Fonterutoli), Cappelli (Montagliari), Strucchi Prinetti (Badia a Coltibuono), Castelbarco Albani Masetti (Castello di Uzzano), Manetti (Fontodi), Ricasoli-Firidolfi (Castello di Brolio and Castello di Cacchiano) and many others.

Chianti Classico itself has improved beyond all recognition within the last decade, and must now rank as one of the great red wines of Italy. Not everyone may agree with the merits of the Chianti DOCG discipline (which grants similar DOCG status not just to the élite wines of the Classico and Rufina, but also to Chianti produced from other sub-zones to much less stringent guidelines), but the new rules have undoubtedly improved the wine. Previously, the formula for the production of Chianti had allowed the inclusion of up to 30% white grapes in the *uvaggio*, supposedly to soften the rather harsh and austere character of Sangiovese. However, under the revised regulations, the reduction of white grapes to a mere mandatory 2–5% (some producers utilize none at all) together with the right to utilize such supplementary grapes as Cabernet Sauvignon, Merlot, and Pinot Nero

GALESTRO

When the Chianti discipline was revised to reduce – in some cases virtually eliminate altogether – Trebbiano Toscano and Malvasia from the Chianti *uvaggio*, the producers were left with a problem: what to do with the surplus white grapes? One answer was the invention of a new type of wine, Galestro. This *vino bianco da tavola dei Colli della Toscana Centrale* is one of the only wines in Italy to have a *maximum* alcohol level restriction set at only 10.5 degrees. Vinified for freshness and lightness, usually slightly *frizzante*, it is pleasant, refreshing, zesty beverage wine that can be downed in quantity, particularly on hot summer days and nights.

has unquestionably led to the production of wines with greater structure, scent and potential for ageing. Yields in the Classico were also reduced from 115 *quintali* per hectare to 75 *quintali*, and it is now forbidden to 'correct' wines with grape must or wine from other areas or regions.

Chianti Classico, and especially the selected *riserve* wines that have undergone at least 3 years' ageing from the harvest, have thus emerged as serious, well-structured wines of class and elegance, as far removed from the frivolous jug Chiantis sold in wicker flasks as can be imagined. Is it any wonder that this once charming symbol of Italian wine is now almost universally despised within its zone of production?

There are more than 800 wine growers in the Chianti Classico and about 250 of them bottle and sell their own wines. The Consorzio Chianti Classico is, moreover, one of the most forward-thinking of such organizations, and is serving not only to promote the wines of the zone but positively to improve standards both today and for the future. Looking ahead to the year 2000, the Consorzio Chianti Classico is currently undertaking extensive experiments in the vineyard, to improve, for example, such aspects as clonal selection, systems of training, and plant density. As research in the *cantina* proceeds at a similar pace, it is certain that in future years we shall see even more outstanding and better-made wines emerging.

The Chianti Classico is thus one of the most exciting areas for the wine traveller, for it is only by visiting the zone and sampling wines on the spot that one can hope to keep abreast with the ever new developments that are taking place. Much of the charm of travelling this timeless wine region lies in simply exploring it serendipitously and at one's own pace. Although we suggest a broad route below that covers most but not all of the principal wine communes, we therefore advise you to devise your own itinerary, and literally to get off the beaten track and hunt down new or old favourite estates and wines.

From Florence, leave the *autostrada* at Firenze Certosa and follow the road first to Impruneta, a market town famous above all for its terracotta pottery, then find the start of the signposted *strada del vino* that leads to the heart of the wine country. Strada in Chianti is the first significant wine town encountered, probably so named because of a Roman road that formerly passed nearby. But it is Greve that is undoubtedly the most important in this northern section of the Chianti Classico.

Greve, a rather sprawling market town lying along the river of the same name, is dominated by its irregular 17th-century *piazza*, Il Mercatale, which is itself surrounded by pleasant arcades and terraced balconies. North

Giovanni di Verrazano.

Americans may be surprised to find in the square a statue of Giovanni di Verrazano, for the explorer who is credited with the discovery of New York Bay and much of the east coast of America was born nearby in the castle of the same name, today an important wine estate. Greve's impressive square is the site of a lively Saturday market, while the zone's most important wine festival, '*Il Mostro Mercato del Chianti Classico*', takes place here each September. One interesting development at the festival in recent years is the auctioning of new wines *en primeur*, that is, selling the wines while still in cask in the wine growers' cellars, as is done in Bordeaux. This is significant in that Italian wine, unlike French, is generally not released until it is ready to drink, even if that means, in some cases, that the wines must stay in *botte*, *barrique* or bottle for upwards of 5–10 years. An *en primeur* market will undoubtedly help the top quality wine growers with their cash flow, but whether this creation of an investment element in fine Italian wine is a good thing or not for the general consumer may be open to debate.

The importance of '*Il Mostro Mercato*', however, has traditionally been more than just commercial, for Greve has always served as a centre where the people from the surrounding communities and isolated hill estates come down each week to exchange opinions and compare ideas, as well as to discuss political and economic problems. These meetings, the so-called *riunioni di Greve*, continue to be important even today, and the greatest such annual gathering is the yearly wine fair.

For indeed, this part of the Chianti Classico, like many other parts of the zone, is characterized foremost by its collection of lonely hill communities and isolated fortified, aristocratic estates. Just in the vicinity of Greve lie 3 such important wine estates – Vicchiomaggio, Verrazzano, and Uzzano – which can all be visited and which graphically demonstrate the way the zone was settled centuries ago as isolated fortresses struggled against one another. For British visitors, the Castello di Vicchiomaggio is undoubtedly of most interest, for it is owned by an Englishman, John Matta. Not only does Vicchio-

John Matta, beside an old-style vine trained up a tree.

maggio produce some of the best and highly-reputed wines of this part of the Classico, there is also a farmhouse restaurant on the estate (by reservation only), a Tuscan cooking school, and farmhouse apartments for rent.

Matta believes wholeheartedly in Chianti Classico, and thus concentrates his considerable efforts primarily on the creation of a range of fine estate wines that proudly bear the *denominazione*. To achieve this, he has classified his vineyards to produce 3 *cru* wines, San Jacopo (a fresh, lighter Chianti ideal for summer drinking), Vigna Petri Riserva (not released until at least the fourth year after the harvest, a deep, round, well-balanced Chianti), and Prima Vigna.

Prima Vigna is a fascinating wine, Matta's most serious and profound, and a complex wine of considerable structure and stature which gains in character through a year's ageing in French oak *barrique* (20% new each year). What is most amazing, though, is that Prima Vigna, as the name

THE CENTRE

suggests, comes from the oldest vines on the estate, with an average age of over 50 years per plant. These old vineyards were of course already on the estate when Matta's family acquired it in 1965, and thus they are still cultivated in the old, haphazard promiscuous style, that is, in isolated patches trained up trees.

Matta showed us this ancient part of the vineyard, and we marvelled at the contorted shapes of the thick vines entwined into the very fabric of their living supports.

'This is how all of Tuscany looked 20 years ago. These vines yield only minuscule amounts of grapes – perhaps just 2 or 3 bunches per plant – and they take up a great deal of ground so it is hardly an economical system today,' explained Matta. 'But it would be a tragedy to dig them up. Not only are they part of the history of the estate, these old vines consistently produce fruit that is riper, more concentrated in extract, and more complex than grapes from our other vineyards. That is why Prima Vigna is such an exceptional wine.'

Numerous excursions can be made from Greve into the surrounding countryside. Nearby Montefioralle (which boasts the house of Amerigo Vespucci) is a charming fortified hill hamlet. Back roads can be taken, south to estates such as Rignana which has a renowned farmhouse *trattoria*, east to Dudda, or west across the wine country to Badia a Passignano, once one of the most important and richest religious communities in Tuscany. Today the massive medieval crenellated abbey of the Vallombrosan monks is still owned by the Church, but its extensive vineyards have passed into private hands, and there are only a handful of monks still living on the premises. But in the vaulted, silent cellars of the abbey lie many hundreds of French oak *barriques*, for this is the repository for two of Tuscany's most famous and prestigious wines, the Marchesi Antinori's rare Tignanello and Solaia.

From Greve, the Via Chiantigiana continues south to Panzano, though an excursion can be made off left to Lamole, another characteristic fortified hill village dominated by the Castello di Lamole. Along the way, such important estates as Vignamaggio (most famous as the birthplace of Mona Lisa Gherardini, the enigmatic young woman immortalized by Leonardo da Vinci) and Pile e Lamole are encountered. The latter's Lamole di Lamole Chianti Classico is a wine of exceptional grace.

Panzano is today one of the larger communities in the zone, though much of it sprawls outside the walled confines of the medieval village that was once an important market centre. Little remains of the 12th-century castle that was razed by the Ghibellines in 1260 in one of the many continual struggles between Florence and Siena that wracked this now peaceful land. Panzano has a good private wine shop, the *Enoteca del Gallo Nero*, while one of its best-known wine estates, Montagliari, runs a popular farmhouse *trattoria* open to the public by reservation.

The Via Chiantigiana continues to Castellina in Chianti, dominated by its medieval fortress and remaining stout fortifications. Castellina, like both Radda and Gaiole, was a judicial and commercial centre in the Lega del Chianti, and once marked the much disputed frontier between the Republics of Florence and Siena. Today this pleasant hill town remains an important centre for the surrounding isolated small communities. From Castellina, the Via Chiantigiana leads south through Fonterutoli, where the noble Mazzei family produce a distinguished range of wines, and so eventually arrives at Siena.

However, for those with more time to spare, it is essential to strike out from Panzano across the hills to reach the town of Radda in Chianti. For if the Chianti Classico is the heart of the Tuscan Chianti country, then Radda, together with Gaiole, is the true heart of the Chianti Classico itself. Historically the two towns, together with Castellina, were the powerful founding members of the Lega del Chianti, but today they are most important (for the wine lover) in that they arguably form the central core of the most prestigious wine zone, with a greater concentration of top estates than anywhere else. Radda, with its fortified aspect and splendid Palazzo del Podestà adorned with colourful coats of arms, is still reminiscent of the stirring era when it was the capital of the Lega, as well as of those darker times when the town was sacked and destroyed, first by the Sienese in 1230, then by Charles d'Anjou in 1268, then again in 1478. Today it continues to serve as a focus for surrounding communities, isolated estates, small farms, and restored medieval hamlets.

The hill vineyards that rise above and around Radda are among the highest in the Chianti Classico zone, and whereas the terrain of the northern part of the wine region is characterized by the stony, calcareous terrain known as *galestro*, here the fundamental underlying feature is volcanic tufa: these factors in part result in wines that may be initially more austere, but are ultimately more profound and have the greatest capacity for ageing. Of course, here as elsewhere, it is a question not just of terrain, but of priorities in both the vineyard and the *cantina*: decisions to restrict yield to result in grapes with higher levels of sugar and extract; whether or not to utilize, for example, Cabernet Sauvignon in the *uvaggio*; methods of vinification – traditional, with lengthy maceration, or modern, at controlled temperature with *rimontaggio* 2 or 3 times a day; and, of course, whether or not to age the wine in large Slavonian oak *botti* or in small French oak *barriques*. Indeed, the variables are countless, and this is one reason why Chianti Classico presents itself in such a bewildering array of different styles. Some

TIGNANELLO: MODEL FOR A NEW GENERATION

When Marchese Piero Antinori and his renowned oenologist Giacomo Tachis first conceived of the creation of this now classic wine in the late 1960s, there was considerable dissatisfaction with the Chianti discipline as well as with the poor image of Chianti. For under the then existing regulations, the Chianti discipline required the use of inferior grapes, including a large proportion of white varieties, grapes which Antinori deemed were unsuitable for the production of great red wines capable of conservation. Inspired by the considerable success of Sassicaia, a pure Cabernet produced from grapes grown on a family estate near Livorno belonging to his uncle, Marchese Incisa della Rocchetta, Antinori decided to see what could be produced from his finest vineyard, the Tignanello site, located on his Santa Cristina estate. Following precepts common wherever great wine is made – severe pruning and thinning out of bunches to reduce yields and increase quality, rigorous control of the various phases of vinification, and selection of only the best vats for final assembly – Antinori produced a new wine from selected clones of Sangiovese, Tuscany's great red grape, together with the addition of some Cabernet Sauvignon and Cabernet Franc. Tignanello was aged for about 20 months in French oak *barrique* followed by further finishing in the bottle. Yet, since it was made outside then existing Chianti DOC regulations, it was only entitled to the humble *vino da tavola* designation. Despite this lowly *denominazione*, Tignanello was an immediate success, and it has been produced every year since 1975 with the exception of the poor 1984.

Today, when virtually every estate in Tuscany aspiring for quality accolades has French oak in the *cantina* and the profusion of super-*vini da tavola* increases every year, we should pay homage to their inspiration, for even today, Tignanello remains one of the finest examples of its type: an intense, muscular wine of immense breed and class which manages to achieve greatness without compromising its Tuscan *tipicità*.

of the best estates in or around Radda include Podere Capaccia, Castello di Volpaia, Vignavecchia, and Monte Vertine.

From Radda, find the road across the hills that leads to Badia a Coltibuono. This impressive stone compound, with its bell-tower built in 1160, consists of a church, former convent, farmhouse, and extensive cellars surrounded by vineyards, pine trees, and chestnut woods. There are signposted walks through the woods above the estate. The lands surrounding the abbey of Coltibuono were exchanged in 1141 for the Castello di Brolio, a deal struck between the Ricasoli family and the Vallombrosan monks who had settled there. The monks of the abbey are thought to have been the first to cultivate vines in this part of the Chianti, though today the estate's aristocratic owners, the Strucchi-Prinetti family, cultivate vineyards located 16 km to the south around Monti in Chianti. The Badia a Coltibuono range of wines is superlative, and the *riserve* wines in particular are among the most long-lived of the wine zone. Old vintages can be purchased at the shop near the entrance to the estate; there is also a well-known cookery school run by Lorenza de' Medici, and a simple farmhouse restaurant serving good local foods.

Gaiole in Chianti came under Florentine jurisdiction in 1308, and the numerous castles and parish churches which encircle the small wine community bear witness to the village's agricultural and commercial prosperity over the centuries. Indeed, so rich in ancient monuments is this particular corner of the Chianti Classico that there is a signposted *Strada dei Castelli del Chianti* which makes an interesting diversion from more single-minded wine touring. Gaiole is also surrounded by a number of prestigious wine estates, notably to the north Riecine (a tiny but highly-regarded estate owned by Englishman John Dunkley and his Italian wife Palmina) and Capannelle (the source of prestigious super-Tuscan table wines that eschew the Chianti *denominazione*), and to the south, the Castello di Ama, Giorgio Regni's Fattoria Valtellina, and the ancient angular 12th-century Castello di Meleto. As a contrast to the private wine estates, there is a large local co-operative, Agricoltori Chianti Geografico, located just outside Gaiole, which produces a good range of wines.

Our wine tour continues south on the N484, next to the famous Castello di Brolio, an important national monument (open to the public) and home of the noble Ricasoli family since the 12th century. The stout castle stands in a dramatic hilltop position, regally surveying its surrounding vineyards, olive groves, and dense woodlands of oak and chestnut, while below lies the immense winery complex that is at the hub of an important international company.

THE CENTRE

Of course, the historic role of the Ricasoli family in the production of Chianti was an immense one. The wines of Brolio had been exported and enjoyed throughout Europe since at least the 17th century, but it was during the mid-19th century that Barone Bettino Ricasoli, later dubbed the 'Iron Baron' when he became Prime Minister of Italy after Cavour, perfected the so-called 'recipe' for Chianti which in substance remains even today. 'From Sangioveto the wine takes the main component of its bouquet as well as its vigorous quality; Canaiolo softens the tone of the first without taking anything from its bouquet; and Malvasia, which could be omitted for those wines intended for ageing, tends to slightly dilute the product resulting from the first two, making it lighter and suitable for everyday drinking,' wrote the Baron in a letter in 1874.

South of Brolio, we enter into the far south-eastern corner of the Chianti Classico vineyard, lying mainly within the commune of Castelnuovo Berardenga. This zone enjoys a microclimate that is considerably warmer and more fertile than the higher reaches of Gaiole and Radda, for the sandy-limestone land here adjoins the so-called *terra calda* of the volcanic *crete Senese* which extends down further south almost to Montalcino. This is particularly mineral-rich terrain, and wines from Villa a Sesta, Pagliarese,

The Pagliarese 'Casa del Vin Santo'.

and Berardenga Felsina reflect a warmer, more full-bodied a.... ....
acter. But these more fleshy, immediately appealing wines have the capacity
to age, too. We tasted, for example, a 1968 from the Pagliarese estate that,
though brown around the edges, was still full of warm, deep fruit and more
profound, complex bottle nuances, all the more remarkable considering that
it was made at a time when about 20% white grapes was included in the
traditional *uvaggio*. The Pagliarese estate offers a particularly warm
welcome for the wine tourist: wines can be tasted and purchased, in summer
there is a farmhouse restaurant (by reservation), and there are lovely
farmhouse apartments for rent.

The fortified town of Castelnuovo Berardenga itself actually lies outside
the delimited border of the Chianti Classico: in the past it was of strategic
importance for its proximity to the border between the Republics of Florence
and Siena. Allied to the latter, Castelnuovo was the headquarters for the
Sienese troops, though little remains today of the castle from which it takes
its name, built by the Sienese in 1386. From Castelnuovo Berardenga, the
quickest road to Siena is the N73.

Degustazione: **Stop to Taste; Stop to Buy**

1

CASTELLO VICCHIOMAGGIO
50022 GREVE IN CHIANTI FI
TEL: 055/854079

WINES PRODUCED: Chianti Classico
San Jacopo, Chianti Classico Vigna
Petri Riserva, Chianti Classico
Prima Vigna; Ripa delle Mimose
(Chardonnay); Ripa delle More
(Sangiovese).
VISITS: daily, by appointment.
Vendita diretta 'always open'.
The first *castello* on this site was
built in AD 957 by the Lombards,
and took its present form,
dominating the Greve countryside,
during the Renaissance. Today,
owned by Englishman John
Matta, Vicchiomaggio produces a

range of *cru* Chiantis as well as
innovative modern *vini da tavola*,
entirely from the vineyards that
surround the castle. John Matta is
an enthusiast, and Vicchiomaggio
is one of the most welcoming and
informative estates for the
Anglo-Saxon to learn more about
the wines and land of the Gallo
Nero.

Vicchiomaggio has a number of
renovated apartments available for
letting, there is a rural *ristorante*
on the estate for groups and
individuals by prior arrangement,
and there is also a Tuscan cookery
school with lessons in English.
English spoken.

2 FATTORIA DI VERRAZZANO
CASTELLO DI VERRAZZANO
50022 GREVE IN CHIANTI FI
TEL: 055/854243

WINES PRODUCED: Chianti Classico, Chianti Classico Riserva; Il Sassello; Brut Nature; Vin Santo; *vino bianco, vino rosato da tavola; grappa.*

VISITS: tasting room open Mon–Fri 8–17h; weekends *punta di vendita* on main road open 10–19h. Cellar visits and tastings including simple drinking snacks, by appointment at least 3 days in advance.

The imposing castle of Verrazzano, located in a dominating hilltop position outside Greve, is private and cannot be visited, but there is a most welcoming tasting room where the wines of the estate can be sampled and purchased. The vineyards of Verrazzano are located at between 300 and 450 metres on stony calcareous *albarese* terrain. They are cultivated entirely by *coltura biologica*, using no chemical weedkillers or fertilizers, and selection is rigorous, resulting in deep, intense wines capable of considerable ageing.
English, German spoken.

---

3 CASTELLO DI UZZANO
VIA DI UZZANO 5
50022 GREVE IN CHIANTI FI
TEL: 055/854032-3

WINES PRODUCED: Chianti Classico, Chianti Classico Riserva; Il Fresco di Governo, Vigna Niccolò da Uzzano, Vino Bianco Chardonnay.
VISITS: Mon–Fri 8–18h; Sat 8–12h. *Punta di vendita* on main road before entrance into Greve 'always open'. Tastings with Tuscan meals available by previous arrangement. Highly-regarded wines from this splendid aristocratic estate dating from the 13th century.
Apartments available for rent.
English, German, French, Dutch spoken.

---

4 FATTORIA VIGNAMAGGIO
50022 GREVE IN CHIANTI FI
TEL: 055/853559

WINES PRODUCED: Chianti Classico Vignamaggio, Chianti Classico Vignamaggio Riservá.

VISITS: daily, by appointment. *Vendita diretta* at Il Cenobio. Vignamaggio is a villa built at the beginning of the 15th century by the Gherardini family, whose most famous member was the young

Lisa: her enigmatic smile was immortalized by Leonardo against a Tuscan backdrop that seems little different from the scene at Vignamaggio today. Chianti Classico Riserva is robust, full-bodied wine that improves with some bottle age.

Il Cenobio is a small private hotel in the grounds of the estate. English spoken.

---

5 ANTICHE FATTORIE FIORENTINE
VIA DI LAMOLE
50022 GREVE IN CHIANTI FI
(ADMINISTRATION: VIA DI GAVILLE
66, 50063 FIGLINE VALDARNO)
TEL: 055/9501063

WINES PRODUCED: Chianti Classico Lamole Riserva, Chianti Classico Lamole di Lamole, Chianti Classico Salcetino, Chianti Marsilio Ficino.
VISITS: Mon–Fri by appointment for minimum of 10 persons.
Traditional wines in this ancient estate with *cantina* dating from 1400.
English spoken.

---

6 FATTORIA DI MONTAGLIARI
VIA DI MONTAGLIARI 29
50020 PANZANO FI
TEL: 055/852014

WINES PRODUCED: Chianti Classico Montagliari, Chianti Classico Montagliari Riserva, Chianti Classico La Quercia; Bianco della Lega; Brunesco di San Lorenzo (*barrique*); Vin Santo di Montagliari; Spumante; *grappa*.

VISITS: daily, by appointment.
Giovanni Capelli is one of the few remaining producers still utilizing the traditional Tuscan *governo* method of production whereby semi-dried grapes are utilized to induce a secondary fermentation. The well-made wines are best sampled in the adjoining Trattoria del Montagliari.
English, French spoken.

---

7 AZIENDA AGRICOLA POGGIO AL SOLE
BADIA A PASSIGNANO
50020 SAMBUCA VAL DI PESA FI
(COMMERCIAL OFFICE: VIA DEI
BASTIONI 7, 50125 FLORENCE)
TEL: 055/6812690

WINES PRODUCED: Chianti Classico, Chianti Classico Riserva; Vino Rosso; Vino della Signora; Vin Santo 'Riserva Personale'.
VISITS: by appointment.
Estate overlooking the

Vallombrosan abbey of Badia di Passignano, to which the land belonged for nearly 1000 years. Today some 7 hectares are given over to specialized viticulture, supplemented by a further 6

hectares of traditional mixed culture. Award-winning Chianti, as well as a rare and unusual Gewürztraminer (Vino della Signora), and estate olive oil.

---

8 ISOLE E OLENA
VIA OLENA 15
50021 BARBERINO VAL D'ELSA FI
TEL: 055/8072763

WINES PRODUCED: Chianti Classico; Cepparello; Chardonnay; Vin Santo.

VISITS: by appointment.
Highly-regarded family producer making excellent range of wines utilizing both new techniques and age-old tradition.
English, Spanish spoken.

---

9 PODERI CASTELLARE DI CASTELLINA
LOC. CASTELLARE
53011 CASTELLINA IN CHIANTI SI
TEL: 0577/740362

WINES PRODUCED: Chianti Classico Castellare, Chianti Classico Castellare Riserva; Castellare Bianco Val d'Arbia; Spartito di Castellare (Sauvignon); I Sodi di San Niccolò; Vin Santo San Niccolò;

grappa; *olio d'oliva*; *aceto di Sangioveto*.
VISITS: open for *vendita diretta* daily.
Quality wine estate utilizing modern equipment for the production of both classic and innovative wines.
English, French spoken.

---

10 CASTELLO DI FONTERUTOLI
LOC. FONTERUTOLI
5301200 CASTELLINA IN CHIANTI SI
TEL: 0577/740476

WINES PRODUCED: Chianti Classico Castello di Fonterutoli, Chianti Classico Riserva 'Ser Lapo'; Concerto di Fonterutoli.

VISITS: daily, working hours.
Telephone before coming.
This highly rated wine producer is one of the oldest aristocratic estates in the Classico, property of the Marchesi Lapo Mazzei since 1435.
English, French spoken.

11 FATTORIA DI MONTE VERTINE
53017 RADDA IN CHIANTI SI
TEL: 0577/738009

WINES PRODUCED: Monte Vertine
(*rosso*); Il Sodaccio (*rosso*); Le
Pergole Torte (*rosso*); Bianco di
Monte Vertine; Vin Santo.
VISITS: Mon–Fri, working hours.
Appointment appreciated.

Meticulous winery producing range
of red and white super-Tuscan
wines of the highest quality.
The Fattoria has a small Museo
della Civiltà Contadina
Chiantigiana, as well as
agriturismo apartments for letting.
English, German, French, Spanish
spoken.

---

12 PODERE CAPACCIA
LOC. CAPACCIA
53017 RADDA IN CHIANTI SI
TEL: (Podere) 0577/738385;
    (Administration) 0574/23395

WINES PRODUCED: Querciagrande;
Chianti Classico; Chianti Classico
Riserva.
VISITS: daily including weekends
8–12h; 14–17h.
Highly-regarded estate best known
for its super-Tuscan *vino da tavola*
Querciagrande, produced from
100% Sangioveto aged in new oak

barrique. Chianti Classico is also
excellent and has won awards.
Giampaolo Pacini, the owner, is a
renowned gastronome: wine
seminars and Tuscan lunches (for
professionals) may be arranged in
advance (at least 15 days). While
the *vendita diretta* is open
throughout the week, the Pacini
family are on the estate most
weekends, and are always happy to
meet and receive serious wine
lovers.
English spoken at weekends.

---

13 CASTELLO DI VOLPAIA
LOC. VOLPAIA
53017 RADDA IN CHIANTI SI
TEL: 0577/738066

WINES PRODUCED: Chianti Classico,
Chianti Classico Riserva;
Coltassala (Sangioveto/Mammolo);
Balifico (Sangioveto/Cabernet);
Torniello (Sauvignon Blanc);
Bianco Val d'Arbia; Vin Santo.
VISITS: by appointment. Charge for

visit and *degustazione*.
Volpaia is a 12th-century *borgo*
that remains intact, dominated by
its stern castle. The wines of the
estate are well known and highly
regarded, and there is furthermore
a schedule of cultural activities, as
well as *agriturismo* in restored
houses in the ancient *borgo*.
English, French spoken.

THE CENTRE

14 FATTORIA VIGNAVECCHIA
SDRUCCIOLO DI PIAZZA 6
53017 RADDA IN CHIANTI SI
TEL: 0577/738090

WINES PRODUCED: Chianti Classico
Vignavecchia, Chianti Classico
Vignavecchia Riserva; Canvalle
(*barrique*).
VISITS: *punta di vendita* with
tastings open Mon–Sat.
Appointment necessary only for
groups.
Fine traditional Chianti produced
by the Beccari family, whose
grandfather, Odoardo Beccari, the
Florentine explorer, botanist, and
zoologist, after a lifetime touring
the world, returned to the family
estate at Radda in 1876 and
devoted himself to agriculture. His
passion for collecting led him to
start the Vignavecchia *enoteca*
which has bottles of wine dating
back to the year of his return.
 Farmhouse apartments available
for letting.
German spoken.

---

15 FATTORIA DI AMA
LOC. AMA
53010 GAIOLE IN CHIANTI SI
TEL: 0577/746031–4

WINES PRODUCED: Chianti Classico
'Castello di Ama', Chianti Classico
crus: 'Vigneti di San Lorenzo',
'Bellavista', 'La Casuccia'; Colline
di Ama (Trebbiano e Malvasia),
Sauvignon, Chardonnay, Pinot
Grigio; Rosato del Toson d'Oro; Vin
Santo di Ama; Acquavite 'Castello
di Ama'.
VISITS: Mon–Fri by appointment.
Ama is a characteristic medieval
fortified *borgo* that once formed
part of the Florentine line of
defence against the Sienese along
with the castles of Monteluco at
Lecchi and Campi at Tornano. The
vineyards of this historic estate are
located in what is considered by
many to be one of the best areas of
the Chianti Classico, and the wines
of Ama were already exported
throughout Europe in the 18th
century. Today, rigorous care in the
vineyard, and selection vineyard by
vineyard, results in both classic,
traditional Chianti *riserva* as well,
unusually, as a fine selection of *cru*
white wines. While the estate can
only be visited by appointment,
parts of the ancient *borgo* of Ama
are open to the public.

---

16 BADIA A COLTIBUONO
53015 GAIOLE IN CHIANTI SI
TEL: 0577/749498

WINES PRODUCED: Chianti Classico,
Chianti Classico Riserva,
Sangioveto di Coltibuono,

Coltibuono Rosso, Coltibuono Bianco, Coltibuono Rosato, Coltibuono Vin Santo, *grappa*; *extra vergine olio d'oliva, aceto di vino*, Coltibuono honey.
VISITS: *vendita diretta* near the entrance to the complex where wine and food products can be purchased. Visits and tastings by appointment only: visits to the abbey, cellars, and gardens can be arranged for minimum groups of 5, with discounts for larger groups of over 20; English-speaking guides are available. In addition to the restaurant on the premises, there is also a residential cookery school with classes conducted in English. Badia a Coltibuono is an 11th-century monastery whose vineyards were originally cultivated by the monks of Vallombrosa who did much to further viticulture in the upper Chianti. Today this impressive medieval estate is the villa of the Stucchi-Prinetti family, who produce a highly-regarded range not just of wines, but also other food products such as estate bottled olive oil, wine vinegar, and honey.

The vineyards of the estate are mainly located about 16 km away around the village of Monti in Chianti, an area prized for producing wines capable of long-term ageing. Rigorous vineyard maintenance, and extremely low yields from vines aged between 20 and 45 years are cited as the reasons for the characteristic intensity and complexity, especially of the *riserve* wines and the super-Tuscan *barrique*-aged Sangioveto di Coltibuono. Badia a Coltibuono, incidentally, maintains an abundant stock of old vintages for sale in the shop, dating from 1958. English spoken.

---

17 AZIENDA AGRICOLA RIECINE
53013 GAIOLE IN CHIANTI SI
TEL: 0577/749527

WINES PRODUCED: Chianti Classico, Chianti Classico Riserva; 'La Gioia di Riecine' (red and white super-*vino da tavola*).
VISITS: Mon–Fri 10–12h; 15–17h30. Appointment necessary.
Englishman John Dunkley and his Italian wife Palmina have established a fine reputation for their Chianti produced on this small specialist wine farm. A maximum of only 25,000 bottles a year is produced, entirely from grapes grown on their own land. The 'Gioia di Riecine' red *vino da tavola* is aged in *barrique*, while the white is fermented in small wooden barrels.
English spoken.

THE CENTRE

18

AZIENDA AGRICOLA CAPANNELLE
LOC. CAPANNELLE
53013 GAIOLE IN CHIANTI SI
TEL: 0577/749691

WINES PRODUCED: Capannelle
(*barrique*); Capannelle Chardonnay.

VISITS: Mon–Fri by appointment.
Impeccable super-Tuscan wines
made in an ultra-modern *cantina*.
English spoken.

19

CASTELLO DI CACCHIANO
53010 MONTI IN CHIANTI SI
TEL: 0577/747018

WINES PRODUCED: Chianti Classico
Castello di Cacchiano, Chianti
Classico Castello di Cacchiano
Riserva; Vin Santo; *vino rosso
toscano*.
VISITS: working hours Mon–Fri.

Appointment preferable.
This outstandingly sited historic
castle has been the property of the
Ricasoli-Firidolfi family since 1150.
Today Baronessa Elisabetta and
her family continue to produce
outstanding Chianti Classico by
traditional methods.
English, French spoken.

20

CASA VINICOLA BARONE RICASOLI
CANTINE DI BROLIO
53013 GAIOLE IN CHIANTI SI
TEL: 0577/749710

WINES PRODUCED: Brolio Chianti
Classico Riserva, Brolio Chianti
Classico, Ricasoli Chianti Classico;
Brolio Vin Santo; Torricella;
Ricasoli Galestro.
VISITS: Mon–Fri 8–17h.
Appointment necessary only for
groups.
The Castello di Brolio was acquired
by the Ricasoli family in 1076,
according to a document signed by
Pope Gregory VII, when they

purchased it from the monks of
Vallombrosa in exchange for lands
close by. The fortified castle, a
national monument that is open to
the public, is located on the old
main route between Rome and the
north, and its strategic position
made it the scene of countless
struggles and battles, especially
between Florence and Siena.

The immense modern winery is
located below the castle and is well
organized for visits and tours.

Apartments available for letting.
English, French, German spoken.

21 FATTORIA PAGLIARESE
VIA PAGLIARESE 4
53019 CASTELNUOVO BERARDENGA SI
TEL: 0577/359070

WINES PRODUCED: Chianti Classico
Pagliarese, Chianti Classico
Pigiatello, Chianti Classico
Riserva; Camerlengo (Sangiovese
aged in *barrique*); Vin Santo;
Bianco Val d'Arbia.
VISITS: open daily, all year;
appointment not essential but
appreciated.
The Pagliarese estate dates back to

1242, when it was built by the
Sienese Republic as defence against
the Florentines. Today the
Sanguineti family work some 27
hectares of vineyards, and produce
an impressive and highly regarded
range of wines. There is an *enoteca*
on the estate where all the wines
may be tasted and purchased, as
well as estate olive oil, and acacia
honey.
   Farmhouse apartments available
for letting.
English, French, German spoken.

22 CASTELLI DEL GREVEPESA
FATTORIE E COLTIVATORI DIRETTI
   RIUNITI
VIA GREVIGIANA 34
50024 MERCATALE VAL DI PESA FI
TEL: 055/821101; 821196

WINES PRODUCED: Chianti Classico
Castelgreve, Chianti Classico
Castelpesa, Chianti Classico
Lamole, Chianti Classico Panzano,
Chianti Classico Montefiridolfi,
Chianti Classico Vigna Elisa,
Chianti Classico Sant'Angiolo Vico
L'Abate; Val Greve (*vino bianco da
tavola*); Maggese (*rosso giovane*);

Moraiolo (*vino aromatizzato*); Otto
Santi Vin Santo; *grappe*.
VISITS: Mon–Fri 8h30–12h; 14–17h.
Appointment necessary for guided
visits.
The largest *cantina* in the Chianti
Classico, made up of 160 member
estates, the Grevepesa co-operative
has a well-earned reputation for the
excellence of its selected wines from
both historic sub-zones (Lamole,
Panzano, Montefiridolfi) and
individual *cru* sites (Vigna Elisa,
Sant'Angiolo Vico L'Abate).
English, German, French spoken.

23 FATTORIA DELL'UGO
50028 TAVARNELLE VAL DI PESA FI
TEL: 055/8074032

WINES PRODUCED: Chianti; Bianco
Toscano; Il Rugo; Vin Santo.

VISITS: daily, working hours.
Appointment preferable.
An old favourite: excellent Chianti,
produced by the Amici Grossi family
for 6 generations. Chianti, as well as
Il Rugo, produced from Sangiovese

THE CENTRE

and Cabernet Sauvignon, are aged in the ancient 17th-century *cantina* of the villa, the latter in small oak *barriques*. Also estate olive oil and *aceto di vino*.

Farmhouse accommodation available.

English spoken.

---

24 FATTORIA PASOLINI DALL'ONDA
BORGHESE
50021 BARBERINO VAL D'ELSA FI
TEL: 055/8075019

WINES PRODUCED: Chianti; Chianti Riserva; Montepetri Bianco dei Colli della Toscana Centrale; Terra del Palazzo Bianco e Rosso; Novello di Toscana.

VISITS: daily, by appointment.
The Pasolini family have estates at Barberino Val d'Elsa as well as at Montericco in Emilia-Romagna, and have been producing wines since 1573.
English, French spoken.

LE DONNE DEL VINO

Wine, its production and consumption, has traditionally been a male preserve, but the times they are a-changing, even in Italy. Indeed, today a great many of the country's important quality estates are directed or owned by women, and the daughters of wine growers are now taking their rightful place alongside wine growers' sons as the torch passes to a new generation. Therefore, a national association of women associated with wine – *Le Donne del Vino* – was established in 1988 and comprises female producers, restaurateurs, *sommeliers*, oenologists, and wine journalists. As such, it provides a forum where women can meet and bring their particular perspectives to bear on the world of wine. A principal aim is to raise the awareness of the female consumer and to improve the image of Italian quality wine through public tastings, round tables, conferences and discussions.

Further information from:
L'Associazione Nazionale Donne del Vino
c/o via Speronari 4
201123 Milan
tel: 02/808698

Enoteche

1 ENOTECA DEL GALLO NERO
PIAZZETTA S. CROCE 8
50022 GREVE IN CHIANTI FI
TEL: 055/853297

OPEN: 9h30–12h30; 15h30–19h30.
Closed Wed.
The best and most comprehensive
enoteca in the zone and the only one
that exhibits wines from all the
commercial producers of Chianti
Classico. Large, well displayed
selection not only of Chianti, but of
other Tuscan wines, including
Brunello di Montalcino, Vino Nobile
di Montepulciano, Vernaccia di San
Gimignano, Vin Santo, and
super-Tuscan *vini da tavola*.

---

2 CANTINETTA DI GREVE IN
CHIANTI
CLUB ESPORTATORI VINI CHIANTI
CLASSICO
VIA IV NOVEMBRE 8
50022 GREVE IN CHIANTI FI

OPEN: 9–13h; 15–19h30. Closed
Mon.

This small *cantinetta* run by
enthusiasts specializes in wines
from about 70 small to tiny *fattorie*
and *aziende*: the names of most of
them may not be easily familiar, so
ask for advice: some of these wines
can be superlative.

---

3 ENOTECA DEL CHIANTI CLASSICO
VIA G. VERRAZZANO 8-10
50020 PANZANO IN CHIANTI FI
TEL: 055/852003

OPEN: daily 8h30–13h; 15h30–
19h30.
Impressive selection of Chianti
Classico from varying *annate*, as
well as wines from throughout
Tuscany. Small selection of food
specialities, including olive oil,
aromatic vinegars, honey. Tastings
may be arranged by appointment.
A little English and German
spoken.

---

4 BOTTEGA DEL VINO
CANTINA ORLANDI
VIA DELLA ROCCA 13
53011 CASTELLINA IN CHIANTI SI
TEL: 0577/740500

OPEN: Mon–Sat 9–13h; 15–19h30.
Small but select display of some of
the finest Tuscan wines, not just
Chianti Classico, but also Brunello,
Vino Nobile, Vernaccia di San
Gimignano, and super-Tuscan *vini
da tavola*. Tasting possible.
English spoken.

THE CENTRE

5 CANTINA ENOTECA MONTAGNANI
VIA B. BANDINELLI 9
53013 GAIOLE IN CHIANTI SI
TEL: 0577/749517

OPEN: daily 8–13h; 15–20h.
Fine range of Chianti Classico and
super-Tuscan *vini da tavola*.
A little French spoken.

Ristoranti

1 RISTORANTE-ALBERGO GIOVANNI DA
    VERRAZZANO
PIAZZA MATTEOTTI 28
50022 GREVE IN CHIANTI FI
TEL: 055/853189

Closed Sun eve, Mon.
Popular restaurant-hotel located in
the heart of the Chianti region in
the old market square of Greve,

serving typical foods on the balcony
terrace in season, including
homemade *pappardelle, panzanella,
ribollita, trippa, stracotto al Chianti*
together with a wide selection of
Chianti Classico. Hotel has
pleasant rooms overlooking the
square.
Inexpensive to Moderate

2 TAVERNA DEL GUERRINO
CASTELLO DI MONTEFIORALLE
50022 GREVE IN CHIANTI FI
TEL: 055/853106

Open Thur–Sun only.
Come to this steep, cobbled, fortified
hamlet above Greve to enjoy
spectacular views of the Tuscan

countryside, as well as simple,
homely foods such as *ribollita,
spaghetti*, grilled meats, and
excellent own-produced Chianti
Classico. Apartments available for
letting.
Inexpensive

3 ANTICA TRATTORIA LA TORRE
PIAZZA DEL COMUNE
53011 CASTELLINA IN CHIANTI SI
TEL: 0577/740236

Closed Thur.
Classic Tuscan *trattoria* located in

the medieval *piazza* of this popular
wine town, serving foods such as
minestre toscane, grilled meats and
roasts cooked over a wood fire, and
in season, *funghi* and game.
Inexpensive to Moderate

4 RISTORANTE 'LE VIGNE'
PODERE 'LE VIGNE'
53017 RADDA IN CHIANTI SI
TEL: 0577/738640

Closed Tue.
Charming restaurant in an old
house surrounded by the vineyards

THE *FIASCO*

One of the most enduring images of Italian wine is the straw-covered Chianti *fiasco*. This humble, homely receptacle came not only to represent Chianti on a thousand *trattoria* tables in Tuscany and throughout the world, it was transformed into a very symbol of the fun and easy times that uncomplicated, honest wine can bring to us.

Empoli, still today an important glass manufacturing centre along the Arno valley west of Florence, was once the focus of this particular cottage industry, and scores of women worked at home, utilizing local reed from the river to cover the bottles and to build up the thick base by hand. My friend Giuliano remembers that as a boy he used to accompany his father there from time to time to visit an old aunt who would re-weave all their bottles for them, and also repair any damaged wicker *damigiane*.

Of course, in those days, Chianti *was* uncomplicated, an on the whole honest wine with little pretension, rarely considered more than a beverage to accompany meals, not a precious object in need of age or special care. Indeed, the very shape of the *fiasco* precluded such wines from ever being 'laid down'.

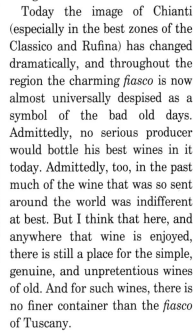

Today the image of Chianti (especially in the best zones of the Classico and Rufina) has changed dramatically, and throughout the region the charming *fiasco* is now almost universally despised as a symbol of the bad old days. Admittedly, no serious producer would bottle his best wines in it today. Admittedly, too, in the past much of the wine that was so sent around the world was indifferent at best. But I think that here, and anywhere that wine is enjoyed, there is still a place for the simple, genuine, and unpretentious wines of old. And for such wines, there is no finer container than the *fiasco* of Tuscany.

Fiaschi.

of the Fattoria Vignavecchia: Luca Vitali and Elena Damiani serve *cucina tipica toscana*, including homemade *pasta, ribollita,* *acquacotta, cinghiale in umido, torta al formaggio 'Le Vigne'.* English spoken.

Inexpensive

---

5 ALBERGO-RISTORANTE 'LA VILLA MIRANDA'
VILLA A RADDA
53017 RADDA IN CHIANTI SI
TEL: 0577/738021

Established in 1842, this extremely popular wayside inn has a restaurant serving *chiantigiana* specialities such as *ravioli con nostra ricotta, arrosto girato.* Also a shop selling local produce and wines. Open all year.

Inexpensive to Moderate

---

6 RISTORANTE BADIA A COLTIBUONO
53013 GAIOLE IN CHIANTI SI
TEL: 0577/749424

Closed Mon, Nov.
Simple, friendly *trattoria* in the grounds of the Badia, serving satisfying basic foods: *tortelle allo* *zio Carlo, pollo alla Gianetto, carne ai 7 sapori,* and the full range of wines of the estate. You can also come here for *panini* and a glass or two of wine if you don't feel like a full meal.

Inexpensive to Moderate

TUSCAN COOKERY SCHOOLS

Food and wine are such an integral part of the Tuscan experience that it is not surprising that a number of wine estates have begun cookery schools where the preparation of regional and local foods can be learned and enjoyed together with the estate's wines. Lorenza de' Medici, for example, holds cooking classes at her family estate, the 11th-century Badia a Coltibuono near Radda. Englishman John Matta also offers a range of serious 'hands on' cooking classes at his Vicchiomaggio estate, under the direction of Paolo Paroli. Such courses are not only a means of learning about Tuscan foods, they are an opportunity to share in and experience a hospitable way of life and gracious living.

Further course details from Badia a Coltibuono and Castello di Vicchiomaggio, addresses above.

7 RISTORANTE DA GINO
LOC. BROLIO
53013 GAIOLE IN CHIANTI SI
TEL: 0577/747194

Closed Tue.
Good simple *cucina casalinga*

below the Iron Baron's castle:
homemade *tagliatelle ai funghi,
vitello al forno, rosticianna,* and
(of course) the wines of Brolio.
Inexpensive

---

8 BOTTEGA DEL TRENTA
VILLA A SESTA
53019 CASTELNUOVO BERARDENGA SI

This rustic *trattoria* serving simple
foods and wines is a wine growers'
favourite.
Inexpensive

Punti di Ristoro Agrituristico

1 TRATTORIA DEL MONTAGLIARI
VIA DI MONTAGLIARI
50020 PANZANO FI
TEL: 055/852184

Closed Mon.
Just outside Panzano on the Greve
road, Giovanni Cappelli's farmhouse
trattoria is deservedly popular,
serving simple Tuscan foods in a

relaxed rustic atmosphere. Outdoor
tables in summer. Open by
reservation only, though if passing
take pot luck and see if a table is
available. Apartments and rooms
available for rent (even for a single
night).
Moderate

---

2 CANTINETTA DI RIGNANA
FATTORIA DI RIGNANA
LOC. RIGNANA
50022 GREVE IN CHIANTI FI
TEL: 055/852065

Closed Mon, Nov.
It is essential to book in advance for
this restaurant on the wine estate
of Rignana. Well-proven

specialities include *crostini in 16
modi, cannelloni con sugo e ricotta
di Rignana,* grilled meats, and
Chianti Classico from the estate.
Located down a country track
(signposted) roughly between Badia
a Passignano and Panzano. Rooms
available for rent.
Inexpensive to Moderate

THE CENTRE

CARMIGNANO:
ETRUSCAN TOMBS, MEDICI VILLAS,
AND OUTSTANDING WINE

In Brief: The small but prestigious wine zone of Carmignano lies just 20 km to the west of Florence, on the lower slopes of Montalbano, overlooking the plains of Prato and Pistoia. Compact and easily reached, it has all the elements for successful wine touring: welcoming estates producing outstanding wines; beautiful countryside; historic and cultural points of interest; and a concentration of excellent restaurants serving local foods and wines.

A full day tour of the region might begin from either Prato or Florence and lead through the wine country with visits to wine producers, to the Etruscan Tomba di Montefortini, the Medici villas of Poggio a Caiano or Artimino (the latter has a superb Etruscan Archaeological Museum), and a stop along the way for lunch, before finally arriving at the town of Vinci, birthplace of Leonardo, where there is a fascinating museum with replica models made from his drawings.

In 1480, at the height of the Florentine Renaissance, the city's great leader and patron Lorenzo de' Medici (later known by the honorific 'Il Magnifico') purchased a country villa at Poggio a Caiano. Lorenzo, head of Florence's most powerful banking family, was himself a lyric poet of considerable renown, and loved nothing more than to retire to the peace of the Tuscan countryside. Later Cosimo I de' Medici, Granduca di Toscana, declared a delimited zone of this Carmignano countryside to be royal property, and constructed some 40 km of stone walls to enclose the so-called Barco Reale as a royal hunting preserve and woodland. Another Medici, Ferdinando I, commissioned the architect Buontalenti to construct a hunting lodge and villa at Artimino, and there in 1594 installed the entire Granducal court.

The Medici, *nouveaux riches* who liked to model themselves on aristocratic landowners, cultivated great agricultural estates that included, naturally, vineyards. But long before they made this compact and lovely country their private realm and pleasure ground, the wines of Carmignano had enjoyed great renown. Archaeological evidence indicates that vines were certainly cultivated in the zone by the Etruscans, who had important settlements at Artimino and Comeana. Later, the lands were passed on by Julius Caesar to

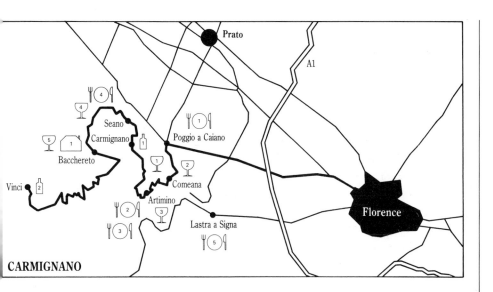

CARMIGNANO

his veteran soldiers who established estates here. Other historical documents indicate that during the 9th century the estate of Capezzana, for example, was devoted almost precisely to the same activities as it is today, the cultivation of the vine and olives, a remarkable 1200 years of continuity. In the 14th century, the wines of Carmignano and Artimino were deemed to be excellent by the epicurean Bartoloni.

Carmignano wines, of course, received a particular boost by being given, as it were, the royal seal of approval in 1716 when they were included in Granduca Cosimo III's Il Bando, a granducal decree that identified the exact delimited zones for production of Carmignano (corresponding more or less with the Medici's Barco Reale) and established fixed rules of production. The Bando is often cited as Italy's first legislative example of *denominazione di origine controllata*.

Carmignano had thus long established an identity that set it apart from the other wines of Tuscany, and so it remains today. It is not simply a question of the exceptional terrain in this steep limestone balcony of hills overlooking the plains of Prato and Pistoia, it is also the result of a long tradition of viticulture and wine making. For example, the Medici, in the tradition of gentlemen farmers, loved to experiment with agriculture, and introduced more than 100 different foreign grape varieties to the zone, including a number from France. Many of these survive in isolated pockets today. At Capezzana, itself once a Medici villa, there are a number of

THE CENTRE

Artimino. historic grape varieties still in cultivation, including, for example, Occhio di
Pernice, a type of black muscat still used in minute quantities in the wine,
as well as enjoyed as a table grape. It is seems likely, therefore, that the
mixture of grape varieties used in the production of Carmignano wine
always differed somewhat from the traditional blend used for the production
of Chianti.

Carmignano lost its historical identity and heritage when, earlier this
century, it was incorporated into the Chianti wine zone of Montalbano.
However, through the efforts of its leading producers, this was rectified in
1975, when it was granted its rightful *denominazione di origine controllata*.
One difference that was established at that time was the inclusion in its
permitted *uvaggio* of Cabernet Sauvignon, in combination with Sangiovese,
the traditional mainstay of the Tuscan vineyard, Canaiolo, Trebbiano and
Malvasia. Not only does Cabernet, the aristocratic grape of the Médoc, recall
the past cultivation of foreign grape varieties by the Medici, it furthermore
gives the robust red wines of Carmignano a particular structure, elegance,
and firmness. Indeed, Carmignano was the first DOC in Tuscany to be
permitted to utilize this much-loved and universally acknowledged
thoroughbred. It is interesting to note that now the revised DOCG rules
relating to Chianti permit the further addition of Cabernet to the traditional

blend, a recognition of how successfully the French grape blends with San-giovese.

The wine growing region of Carmignano is characterized by the fact that most of its limited production is in the hands of only a small number of *fattorie* and *aziende*, perhaps a reflection of the zone's aristocratic past when relatively large estates were worked by tenant farmers. Further evidence of the prevalence of the system of *mezzadria* is recalled by another DOC wine of the zone, Vin Ruspo. The name signifies 'stolen wine', for in the old days, when the tenant farmers harvested the grapes to take to the *padrone*, they used to store a barrel or two of grapes overnight at their own farms. Then, before delivering the grapes the next morning to the *cantina*, they would first draw off a few *damigiane* of the free-run grape juice. This 'stolen' grape must, tinged a pale to dark pink from its overnight contact with the skins, then fermented on its own accord into a *rosato* wine that was deemed to be most refreshing, none the less so, no doubt, for its liberal provenance. The owners of the properties apparently all knew of this practice, but generally turned a blind eye to it. Today Vin Ruspo is produced in the same way, that is, by drawing the juice off the grapes after a night's contact on the skins. Produced thus from the same superior and ripe grapes as Carmignano itself, it is a particularly robust and full-bodied rosé.

To reach the Carmignano zone, leave Florence on the old Pistoia road (SS66) to Poggio a Caiano. Or else, from Prato, find the road to Poggio a Caiano. This is the logical starting point for a tour of this compact region, for it is sited on the fringe of the wine country, where the plains begin to rise into the hills of Montalbano. Lorenzo de' Medici commissioned the architect Giuliano da Sangallo to rebuild the Villa Poggio a Caiano in the style of a classic country house set amidst lovely natural gardens. The villa, which is open to the public, is entered by gracefully sweeping twin staircases, and is decorated grandly with frescoes by 16th-century masters, including Pontormo, del Sarto, and Allori. The gardens extend down to the little Ombrone river, and are simply a lovely place to stroll about and relax in. As a footnote to Medici intrigue, Francis I and Bianca Cappello were poisoned here in 1587.

From Poggio a Caiano, next find the road out of town into the hills that lead to the nearby wine hamlet of Comeana, noted foremost for its impressive Etruscan tombs. The Tomba di Montefortini, located in the grounds of the wine estate of the Fattoria di Calavria, dates from the 7th century BC. This is a wholly intact rectangular tomb that was for a personage of considerable, perhaps even semi-divine importance, judging from the richly

THE CENTRE

decorated artefacts that have been recovered, including rare objects of Egyptian origin. It forms part of an immense circular burial mound some 11 metres high and 60 metres in diameter that is currently being excavated and which predates it by a century. There is also another smaller Etruscan tomb nearby, the Tomba di Boschetti, beside the village cemetery.

The principal Etruscan settlement, however, was not at Comeana itself, but above the town, in the steep hills of nearby Artimino where an extensive necropolis has been discovered. Artimino, a tiny fortified medieval hill town, is best known for the Medici Villa Reale 'La Ferdinanda', known also as the 'villa of a hundred chimneys', which from its commanding position on the hills overlooks the entire Carmignano vineyard. Today the villa is owned by the Fattoria di Artimino, one of the zone's largest producers. It is open to the public, and there is an important Etruscan archaeological museum in the basement which should be visited.

From Artimino, the wine tour continues next to the eponymous wine town itself. Carmignano was a much sought prize during the frequent struggles between Florence, Prato and Pistoia in the Middle Ages, and was destroyed and subjugated by Florence finally in 1237. Today, it is the seat of the Congregazione del Vino Carmignano, which each year organizes a rigorous public tasting to determine only those select wines that are entitled to the Congregazione's neck band, one reason why the standard of this wine is so uniformly high. Whether this function will still be needed once Carmignano is granted DOCG status (which automatically requires mandatory tasting) is not yet clear, but this important body will still continue energetically to promote the interests of its wine growing members. One aim is the re-establishment of a communal *enoteca* in the town hall, which it is hoped will be open before too long. Carmignano's Church of San Michele is famous for its 'Visitation' by Pontormo, a vivid and striking example of the weird Florentine Mannerism that succeeded the Renaissance.

Carmignano itself is located on top of a steep hill overlooking the plains. Descend next to Seano, then find the road that climbs up to Capezzana. This is the steepest, most dramatic part of the wine zone, and it is also the most renowned. For the Tenuta di Capezzana, property of the noble Contini Bonacossi family, is not only rightly regarded as the zone's most outstanding, it has furthermore for many years served to represent the entire Carmignano wine zone, and to help it gain an international profile. The range of wines produced today at Capezzana is superlative, including not only two renowned Carmignano wines, 'Villa di Capezzana' and 'Villa di Trefiano', but also the highly-acclaimed super-Tuscan *vino da tavola* Ghaie delle

Tenuta di Capezzana.

Furbe, produced with the classic Bordeaux *uvaggio* of Cabernet Sauvignon, Cabernet Franc, and Merlot. Conte Ugo claims that he was the first to introduce the grapes of Bordeaux to the Carmignano vineyard: the cuttings, he recalls, were filched, no less, on a visit to his friend Baron Eric de Rothschild's estate, Château Lafite.

The wine road next winds down from Capezzana and around to Bacchereto. Leonardo da Vinci's grandmother lived in the hamlet, and her old house has been turned into a charming farmhouse restaurant, run by the owners of the Fattoria di Bacchereto, a notable wine estate located on the fringe of the Barco Reale in yet another Medici hunting estate. Not only is Bacchereto the source of fine Carmignano wines, the estate is also a most welcoming *azienda agrituristica*, with both farmhouse apartments and rooms to rent for a most idyllic and lovely retreat.

From Bacchereto, rejoin the road from Carmignano that leads over the wooded slopes of Montalbano. Near the summit the small romanesque church of San Giusto is built out of green and white marble from Prato. From here, we leave the Carmignano wine zone, and re-enter the zone of Chianti Montalbano (Galestro, the new-style Tuscan white wine, is also produced from grapes grown in this area), finishing at the small town of Vinci. There, housed in the historical medieval castle of the Conti Guidi family, the Museo Leonardo da Vinci contains almost 100 fascinating models of mechanisms, machines, and inventions created from the original drawings of the great Renaissance man. Below the castle there is a small private *enoteca* and wine museum, while just outside the town, at Anchiano, the house where Leonardo was born has been restored and can be visited.

THE CENTRE

Degustazione: Stop to Taste; Stop to Buy

1

FATTORIA AMBRA
VIA LOMBARDA 85
LOC. COMEANA
50042 CARMIGNANO FI
TEL: 055/486488

WINES PRODUCED: Carmignano,
Carmignano Riserva; Barco Reale;
Vino Bianco.
VISITS: daily, by appointment.
Carmignano itself is a tiny wine
zone, and within it, the Fattoria
Ambra, located between Poggio a
Caiano and Comeana, is one of the
smallest properties with only 2
hectares of vineyards given over to
the production of Carmignano and
Carmignano Riserva. But it is as
indicative of the zone as of this
dedicated property run by the
Rigoli family that the small
amounts of wine produced achieve
such quality and excellence.
English, French spoken.

2

FATTORIA DI CALAVRIA
VIA MONTEFORTINI
LOC. COMEANA
50042 CARMIGNANO FI
TEL: 055/879041

WINES PRODUCED: Carmignano,
Carmignano Riserva, Vin Ruspo,
Vin Santo; Barco Reale; *vino da
tavola rosso e bianco.*
VISITS: daily, by appointment.
Punta di vendita open Thur and Sat
9–12h.
The Fattoria di Calavria dates from
1500 and today remains the
property of the original family of
the Conti Michon Pecori of
Florence. The large estate produces
fine Carmignano in the best years,
as well as a robust and refreshing
Vin Ruspo, but the outstanding
wine for us is the estate's
exceptional traditionally produced
Vin Santo, one of the best examples
we have tasted. Visit in November
and early December to see the
Trebbiano, Malvasia, and San
Colombano grapes laid out on cane
mats stacked in wooden '*castelli*' in
the loft above the *cantina*, as well
as the tiny oak *caratelli* in which
this traditional wine is left to
mature for at least 4 years. The
new season olive oil, stored in the
orciaia in immense terracotta urns,
is also exceptional.

The Fattoria has within its
grounds the remarkable Tomba
Etrusca di Montefortini, which is
open to the public.

Farmhouse accommodation
available for letting (preferably
long stays).
French spoken.

3 FATTORIA DI ARTIMINO
VIA 5 MARTIRI 29
50040 ARTIMINO FI
TEL: 055/8718072

WINES PRODUCED: Carmignano, Carmignano Riserva, Carmignano 'Villa Medicea', Vin Ruspo, Vin Santo di Carmignano; Barco Reale; Chianti Montalbano; Vino Bianco 'Artimino'; Spumante 'Artimino Brut'.
VISITS: daily, by appointment.
Punta di vendita open daily at the winery in the centre of the old medieval village, as well as at the bar of the Hotel Paggeria Medicea. Artimino is one of this small wine zone's 2 large producers. The estate's winery is located under the walls of the medieval village, and a full and extensive range is produced. The *riserve* wines are particularly worth seeking, and are best sampled in either the Ristorante Biagio Pignatta (owned by the estate and adjacent to its Hotel Paggeria Medicea), or in the famous Da Delfina, located just outside the village walls.

4 TENUTA DI CAPEZZANA
VIA CAPEZZANA 100
50042 CARMIGNANO FI
TEL: 055/8706005; 8706091

WINES PRODUCED: Carmignano 'Villa di Capezzana', Carmignano 'Villa di Capezzana' Riserva, Carmignano 'Villa di Trefiano', Vin Ruspo, Vin Santo; Ghiaie della Furba; Barco Reale; Chardonnay; Capezzana Bianco; Chianti Montalbano.
VISITS: Mon–Fri 9h30–11h30; 15–17h. Appointment necessary, preferably at least two days in advance. *Punta di vendita* open daily working hours.
The Nobil Casa di Contini Bonacossi is the leading producer in the Carmignano zone. For many years now, Conte Ugo has worked to gain greater recognition not just for Capezzana, but for the zone as a whole.

While Capezzana is best known for its premium wines, it is also the source, in the region, for large quantities of well-made wines for everyday drinking, including the lighter Barco Reale, Capezzana *rosso* and *bianco*, Chianti Montalbano, and *vino sfuso*. There is also a traditional olive oil mill on the estate producing outstanding *olio extra vergine d'oliva*.
English, French spoken.

THE CENTRE

5 FATTORIA DI BACCHERETO
LOC. BACCHERETO
50042 CARMIGNANO FI
TEL: 055/8717191

WINES PRODUCED: Carmignano,
Carmignano Riserva, Carmignano
cru Vigna di Sanctuario (aged in
part in *barrique*), Vin Ruspo, Vin
Santo; Barco Reale; Chianti
Montalbano; *vino rosso sfuso*.
VISITS: daily, by appointment.
Punta di vendita open Tue and
Thur 16–19h or at the Cantina
di Toia (see below).
Originally another Medici hunting
lodge located on the edge of the
Barco Reale (parts of the old royal
wall are still standing on the
estate), Bacchereto is an extensive
mixed estate of nearly 200 hectares
(including woodlands), though
there are just 4.5 hectares of vines
in the Carmignano zone. The
Bencini Tesi family make
outstanding wines and also run a
fine *agriturismo* complex that
includes the Cantina di Toia
restaurant, farmhouse rooms and
apartments for rent, and courses
in ceramics, cooking, and yoga.
There is a traditional *frantoio* on
the estate for the production of *olio
extra vergine d'oliva*, and estate
honey is also produced.

Enoteche

1 ENOTECA DI CARMIGNANO
PALAZZO COMMUNALE
50042 CARMIGNANO FI

The communal *enoteca* is currently
closed, but the Congregazione 'plans
to reopen it soon'.

———

2 ENOTECA LEONARDO
CANTINA DEL CASTELLO DI VINCI
50053 VINCI FI
TEL: 0571/56028

OPEN: 10h30–12h30; 15h30–18h30;
closed Mon and Thur morning, all
day Tue and Fri.

Own-produced Chianti Montalbano,
vino da tavola and *olio d'oliva* and a
small *museo della civiltà contadina*
underneath the castle which houses
models of Leonardo's sketched
inventions.

Ristoranti

1

HOTEL-RISTORANTE HERMITAGE
VIA GINEPRAIA 112
50046 POGGIO A CAIANO FI
TEL: 055/877244; 8777045

Restaurant closed Fri, Sun eve.
Friendly modern hotel with

restaurant serving both local and
national foods: *crespelle alla
fiorentina, panzerotti, bistecca alla
fiorentina* and own-produced
Chianti.
Inexpensive to Moderate

2

RISTORANTE 'DA DELFINA'
VIA DELLA CHIESA 1
50040 ARTIMINO FI
TEL: 055/8718074

Closed Mon eve, Tue.
One of the most outstanding
restaurants in Tuscany: famous
traditional country *trattoria* serving
deceptively simple foods – *crostini
vari, tagliatelle alle ortiche, faraona*

*con olive e pinoli, stracotto di
Carmignano* – in a lovely setting
overlooking the hills of this small
but prestigious vineyard. Carlo
Cioni, son of the legendary Delfina,
has always lived in Artimino and
knows the land and its foods
intimately.
Moderate to Expensive

3

HOTEL PAGGERIA
 MEDICEA – RISTORANTE BIAGIO
 PIGNATTA
VIALE PAPA GIOVANNI XXIII
50040 ARTIMINO FI
TEL: 055/8718081 (HOTEL); 8718086
 (RESTAURANT)

Restaurant closed Wed, Thur lunch.
The Fattoria di Artimino owns the
Villa 'La Ferdinanda', and runs an

exclusive hotel in the adjoining
residence once used by servants and
pages, as well as a most welcoming
and friendly restaurant serving
good local foods: *ribollita, minestra
di verdura, carne alle brace* and a
selection of *riserve* wines from the
Fattoria.
Moderate

4

ALBERGO LA BUSSOLA – RISTORANTE
 DA GINO
SS66
CATENA
51039 QUARRATA PT
TEL: 0573/743128

Closed Mon.
On the fringe of the Carmignano
vineyard, along the main
Florence–Pistoia route, this
authentic Tuscan *trattoria* serves

THE CENTRE

traditional foods: homemade *prosciutto* and *salame, penne ai funghi, tagliatelle alla lepre, bollito,* and homemade ice cream.

Inexpensive to Moderate

5
ANTICA TRATTORIA SANESI
VIA ARIONE 33
50055 LASTRA A SIGNA FI
TEL: 055/8720234

Closed Sun eve, Mon.
Just outside the Carmignano

vineyard on the opposite bank of the Arno, but worth a detour for about the best *bistecca alla fiorentina* in this hectic, friendly, typical Tuscan eating house.

Inexpensive to Moderate

Punto di Ristoro Agrituristico

1
CANTINA DI TOIA
50040 BACCHERETO FI
TEL: 055/8717135

Closed Mon, Tue.
This welcoming rustic *trattoria* forms part of Fattoria di Bacchereto's impressive *agriturismo* complex (rooms and apartments are also available for letting, even for single nights).

Located in the ancient home of Lucia di Zoso, maternal grandmother of Leonardo da Vinci, it serves simple but authentic foods of the region: *focaccine al forno,* homemade *pasta, minestrone d'orzo, stracotto al Carmignano* together with wines from the estate.

Moderate

MONTALCINO: *TERRA DI BRUNELLO*

In a nation seemingly obsessed with fashion and labels, Brunello di Montalcino can rightly claim to be Tuscany's, indeed Italy's, first 'designer wine'. It was the personal invention more than 100 years ago of Ferrucio Biondi-Santi and, over the last decades in particular, it has remained at the forefront of a quality-led expansion which has seen massive investment and the establishment of this relatively small Tuscan outpost as possibly Italy's greatest red wine region (alongside the Barolo vineyards of Alba).

Previously, the wines of Montalcino had enjoyed some renown as robust Tuscan heavyweights, but like those of the rest of the region they were the products of rustic tradition and country wine making techniques, and were

In Brief: Montalcino lies some 32 km south of Siena and 200 km north of Rome. As Italy's premier red wine zone, and the source now of not only prestigious Brunello di Montalcino but also lighter and less expensive Rosso di Montalcino, it is an area that no keen wine lover visiting Tuscany will wish to miss. Montalcino itself is a fine, rather austere fortified hill town, while the wine country that surrounds it is a mixture of vineyards, dense woodlands, and olive groves. The zone itself is quiet and friendly, and would make a good base for a 'wine and walking' holiday in southern Tuscany as there are ample footpaths through woods and vineyards. In autumn, the gathering of *funghi* and chestnuts is a popular pursuit. *Agriturismo* is well-developed, and there are many opportunities for renting farmhouses or rooms as well as eating in farmhouse *trattorie*.

usually produced from blends of local red and white grapes vinified together.

What Biondi-Santi did was to undertake lengthy experiments on the Greppo estate to identify and isolate the superior Brunello grape, a clone of Sangiovese Grosso. Considering that clonal selection has only in recent decades been perceived elsewhere as of primary importance to quality in the vineyard, this achievement alone was remarkably ahead of its time. The Sangiovese grape, it had previously been deemed, was too austere and tannic to be vinified alone, but Biondi-Santi furthermore undertook oenological experiments to devise a traditional vinification and lengthy ageing discipline that allowed the wine to mellow, develop, and eventually achieve greatness with age.

Ferrucio Biondi-Santi thus not only managed to create fine, indeed great wine; more importantly, he and his heirs should also be credited with the creation of the marketing concept of Italian wine as a fine and precious commodity. For while elsewhere – in the Chianti, Alba, Valpolicella, for example – wines that today we consider among Italy's finest were even as recently as 20 years ago being sold primarily in bulk by the vat or demi-john, Biondi-Santi's Brunello di Montalcino was already appreciated by a select Italian *conoscenti* at the turn of the century, and collectors sought rare and old bottles as virtually the only Italian wine worthy of investment and speculation.

A prerequisite of great wine, of course, is the capacity not only to age gracefully, but positively to improve (and correspondingly to increase in

THE CENTRE

LA GRAPPA DI ROBERTO: REMEMBRANCE OF TIMES PAST

It was the day after Christmas, and Giuliano and Littorio invited us to spend the day with their friend Roberto, a successful textile factory owner, who was planning to distil a *damigiana* of Brunello wine. Roberto calls himself '*il grappaiolo a tempo perso*', for in virtually every spare moment, he indulges himself in his favourite passion of distilling.

In times past, the home distillation of *grappa* was an important farm event throughout the country. The *contadini* would assemble their homemade alembics in the woods, near to a stream since a source of water is necessary for cooling the snake-like condenser. The pungent, potent liquors that they managed to coax out of such contraptions – made with wine-drenched *vinacce*, with soft fruits, or, as in this case, with wine itself – may have been exquisite or they may have been virtually poisonous: but they certainly would have tasted all the better for the fact that they were made at the State's expense.

The alembic was assembled, charged with the demi-john of robust, dense wine, and the gas fire was lit underneath. We stood around for some hours, talking, and sampling tots of Roberto's *grappa gialla* – *grappa* that had aged in tiny artisan-made oak casks containing no more than 5 or 10 litres. There was a loud cheer when the first dribble of clear liquor finally piddled forth, and we all huddled together, anxious to sample the magical wine essence. Though such home distillation is apparently still technically illegal, the authorities, we understand, turn a blind eye at that made only for personal use. However, I'm sure that there would be a loud cry of protest if they were to legalize it completely, for then the *grappa* would no longer have quite that same particular '*contrabbando*' savour.

In truth, to me, the raw colourless spirit that emerged directly from Roberto's still was barely potable: but the men we were with waxed lyrical, their eyes misty, not only from the searing alcohol but also out of nostalgia for the remembrance of times past, and the re-connection with generations-old rural roots which today many had moved so far away from.

value) over lengthy periods of time, and in this respect Brunello di Montalcino was singularly successful, with the best vintages lasting well over 50 years. Biondi-Santi's wines were thus – and still are – able to command prices that by any standard, including comparison with the most prestigious *grands crus* from Bordeaux and Burgundy, are simply staggering. Indeed, old bottles remain among the most expensive in the world today.

The rest of the wine growers of this prestigious zone south of Siena have

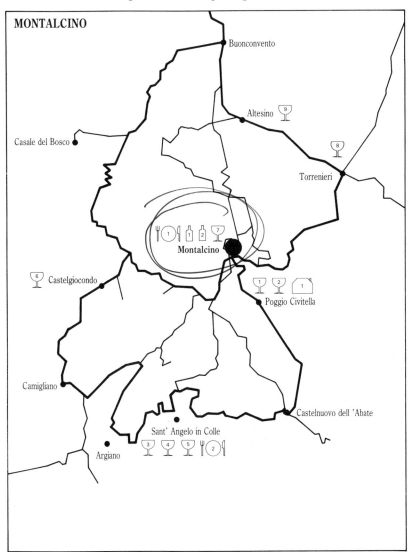

undoubtedly benefited from the considerable marketing expertise of the Biondi-Santi family, who continue to produce some of the best – and certainly the most expensive – wines of the zone. There are now about 70 wine growers who bottle and sell their own wines, though of this number over half own less than 5 hectares of vineyards. The region, once an important source of fuel in the form of wood and charcoal, remains today some three-quarters covered by woodlands and olive groves.

Though the vineyards that extend over the commune of Montalcino are arguably Italy's most prestigious, the zone remains wonderfully accessible and welcoming. By no means entirely given over to viticulture (there are, for example, extensive tracts of uncultivated barren 'moonscape' – the *crete Senese* – to the west, as well as the large tracts of dense woodland), the vineyard zone can be roughly divided into 3 sub-zones that produce wines of broadly differing characteristics. To the north and east of Montalcino, for example, a fairly heavy clay and chalk terrain tends to result in wines that are perfumed and elegant; Altesino, Caparzo, Val di Suga are 3 noteworthy quality estates that fall within this zone. The vineyards to the south, on the other hand, towards Sant'Angelo in Colle, are influenced by the milder proximity of the sea and give very rich and robust wines; Villa Banfi, with its immense space-age winery, as well as Col d'Orcia, owned by Cinzano, are leading estates here. A third sub-zone, nearest Montalcino in the direction of Monte Amiata, an extinct volcano over 1700 metres high, has the highest vineyards and as such, it yields wines that are lean, rich in tannin, and have the greatest capacity for ageing, traditionally Brunello's premier asset; Biondi-Santi's Il Greppo and the Fattoria dei Barbi are the flag-bearers of this sub-zone.

As elsewhere in Tuscany, there is a mix of old traditional families who have been making wines for literally centuries and new firms (often with businessmen owners from Milan and elsewhere) that have brought considerable investment as well as new ideas to the region.

The Fattoria dei Barbi, one of Montalcino's leading estates, has been in the possession of the Colombini-Cinelli family for over 200 years, though this aristocratic Sienese clan can trace their lineage in the zone back to the 16th century at least. Today, as in the past, it carries on the traditions of a typical Tuscan farm, and is an immense, virtually self-sufficient estate of over 400 hectares, producing not only wine, but also fine olive oil, handmade *pecorino* and *ricotta* cheese from its own flocks, and Tuscan *prosciutto*, *salame*, and sausages from own-raised pigs. There is, moreover, a fine farmhouse *trattoria* on the estate where these products and other typical

Sienese foods can be sampled, alongside the wines of the Barbi-Colombini.

'The Barbi farm has always passed on to the women of the family,' explained Donatella Colombini-Cinelli, who currently directs this substantial undertaking. 'Originally, some centuries ago, this land was probably considered the worst when the estate was split up because it was located on the highest part of the zone. But fortunately for us today, this is where the best wines are produced.'

The *cantina* at the Fattoria dei Barbi is one of the most distinctive and charming we have ever visited, for it definitely shows the influence of the women of the family. Whereas most wine cellars are at best functional if atmospheric, the *cantina* at Barbi is positively homely: there are plates and paintings on the walls, works of art and sculpture, collections of domestic implements, even comfortable armchairs, perhaps placed there to allow the owners to relax and meditate on the development of this or that vintage when tasted direct from the barrel.

The wines, however, are traditional, and like most Brunellos, muscular and manly, not particularly feminine at all. Indeed, it was a pleasure to taste a range of the Barbi Brunellos to gain an understanding of how this unique wine evolves. The 1988 drawn from the barrel, for example, was an inky purple; thickly concentrated in the glass, with a perfumed, fruity nose and an immense concentration of tannin in the mouth. This was a traditionally vinified wine, still closed and mute; on tasting it, one can well understand why the Brunello discipline requires a minimum of 4 years' ageing in *botte*: it will need at least that time and longer to soften its initially aggressive and harsh nature, but there was sufficient extract and fruit to warrant Donatella's belief that it could turn out to be the 'harvest of the century'. The 1983 Brunello di Montalcino *cru* Vigna del Fiore we tasted next demonstrated clearly how this most austere grape evolves with age: the wine was garnet with brown tinges, and had a complex, warm, peppery, spicy nose; it was still very fresh, though, and the rich tannins that are the hallmark of Brunello had already softened considerably and were no longer overly aggressive. We next tasted a much older wine, Barbi's 1971 *riserva* which demonstrated the very particular taste and perfume of mature Brunello: garnet with brown edges, a profound and complex tarry, leathery nose, and in the mouth, complex, austere, and extremely long: a truly wondrous *vino da meditazione*.

These days, it must be said that wine drinkers' tastes are changing. Or to put it another way, few have the money, or for that matter the opportunity, to purchase such mature and rare vintage wines, while those that may have no shortage in liquid funds rarely have the patience to lay aside such 'liquid assets' until ready to drink. Other styles of wine, therefore, are emerging.

One forerunner was Barbi's now famous Brusco dei Barbi. This wine was developed for a very clear and specific reason. After Donatella's grandmother died, her widower grandfather found that he was often taking his meals alone, and thus inevitably dined on the cold meats and cheese of the farm. Brunello di Montalcino was too important a wine to drink on such everyday occasions, but he wanted all the same a big, powerful wine to accompany these simple foods. So he created Brusco dei Barbi, a traditional red Tuscan wine made utilizing the ancient *governo* process of adding partially dried grapes to the wine to induce a secondary fermentation, and at the same time to accelerate development and contribute fruity flavours and aroma.

Brusco dei Barbi, while still an immense, gutsy wine that is man enough to cut the fat of Tuscan salted meats and *salame*, is not a wine that requires lengthy ageing before it is ready to drink. Others have also felt the need to produce wines that can be enjoyed much earlier than Brunello di Montalcino, and thus a relatively recent DOC, Rosso di Montalcino, was created for Montalcino's second wine, produced similarly from the Brunello grape, but legally requiring only 12 months of ageing prior to release. The advantage for the wine producer is clear, namely that the immense amounts of space and capital required for the lengthy ageing of Brunello di Montalcino are not tied up; thus cash-flow is aided and the wine producer gets a more

Montalcino.

immediate return on his investment. For the wine drinker, this younger version of the venerable Brunello demonstrates the same noble family pedigree, but at a much less prohibitive cost.

There are more fundamental differences in philosophy at stake, too. For many modern wine producers here feel that the ageing disciplines for Brunello are too lengthy, and consequently rob the wines of their essential and attractive fruity perfumes and elegance. Over-ageing in *botte*, they claim, can result in tired, woody, old-style wines which today's consumer simply does not want. The Rosso di Montalcino discipline, therefore, gives them the opportunity to produce not simply a second-rate or lighter wine, but a more supple, fresher style that can be none the less of considerable stature, richness, and importance in its own right. As elsewhere in Tuscany, the clash between old values and styles and modern ideas and innovations is one of the region's most fascinating aspects.

The town of Montalcino is one of the great wine towns of Italy. Driving here from Florence or Siena in autumn or winter, you may well find yourself locked in dense fog virtually the whole tortuous way. But as you climb into the wine country from Buonconvento, you should emerge finally from the damp darkness into a glorious, sunny cloudscape, the towers and walls of this fortified Sienese stronghold floating above the *nebbia* and glowing warmly against a deep blue sky. Under such circumstances, Montalcino may seem rather remote and rarified; indeed, it is probably these qualities that enabled it to hold out for so long as the final bastion of the Sienese Republic, under constant siege from the Florentines, the French army sent by Pope Clement VII, and Spanish troops sent by the Holy Roman Emperor Charles V. Indeed, after Siena itself fell, some 2000 inhabitants of that proud Republic retreated to Montalcino, re-established the Sienese Republic in exile, and held out against the Medici for another 4 years.

The medieval town of Montalcino today remains unspoiled and atmospheric. Her famous 14th-century Rocca, the stout and immense castle where the townspeople retreated in times of siege, is today the site of Montalcino's best *enoteca*, where a fine selection of the wines of the commune can be sampled by the glass or bottle (and are also available for purchase) together with simple Tuscan drinking snacks, served in a remarkable historic setting. Indeed, no wine lover visiting Tuscany will wish to miss this superlative 'wine library', probably second only to Siena's *Enoteca Permanente*. The Palazzo Communale, located in the town's main square, dates from the 13th century and is the seat of the Consorzii for both Brunello and Rosso di Montalcino, while the local museum has a collection of Sienese paintings as

THE CENTRE

Enoteca 'La Fortezza', *Montalcino.*

well as Renaissance ceramics. Some 9 km outside Montalcino, on the road that leads to the Greppo and Barbi estates, lies the Sant'Antimo abbey, which many consider one of Italy's most beautiful – certainly most peaceful – romanesque buildings. This partially ruined complex was, apparently, founded by the Emperor Charlemagne himself.

The wine lover wishing to gain a more intimate acquaintance with the Brunello countryside (having sampled the products in the *Enoteca 'La Fortezza'*) can strike out at random in virtually any direction. Head out to the south, past Il Greppo and Barbi to the abbey, then, at Castelnuovo dell' Abate, find the road across country to Sant'Angelo in Colle. Either return to Montalcino via Poggio Civitella, or explore the extensive wine country further west, via Argiano, Sant'Angelo Scalo, and around to Camigliano. A good circuit to the north-east and west heads out from Montalcino first in the direction of Torrenieri, then forks north to Buonconvento. Return to Montalcino via Casale del Bosco, Castiglione del Bosco, and Castelgiocondo.

Degustazione: Stop to Taste; Stop to Buy

1

AZIENDA AGRARIA 'IL GREPPO' DI
  BIONDI-SANTI
53024 MONTALCINO SI
TEL: 0577/848087

WINES PRODUCED: Brunello di Montalcino, Brunello di Montalcino Riserva and Gran Riserva; Rosso di Montalcino; *olio extra vergine d'oliva.*
VISITS: Mon–Fri 8–12h; 14–18h. Appointment necessary. Charge for *degustazione*
The legendary and most famous

estate in Montalcino, still producing exceptionally immense and long-lived wines. The history of Brunello begins at 'Il Greppo' which has bottles in the cellar dating from over 100 years ago. Less venerable but still prestigious – and expensive – examples may be offered for sale.

Farmhouse accommodation available.
English spoken.

THE WOODCUTTER

Montalcino today is synonymous with fine and expensive wine, and businessmen from Milan and elsewhere may have invested great sums in farms and wineries. However, the zone itself remains essentially humble and hard-working. As recently as a generation ago, for example, one of the principal occupations was that of the *boscaiolo* or woodcutter. There were once more than 800 families who worked the dense woods of Montalcino. Each autumn they cut logs and slabs of turf and constructed their *capanna*, a woodcutter's simple one-room hut where they lived until the end of July. A fire smouldered constantly on the dirt floor (there was no chimney), and the basic diet was *polenta* – cornmeal mush flavoured with aged *pecorino* cheese and chillies. Days were spent gathering wood for fuel, bark for tanning leather, special roots for pipe making, and small branches to smoulder into charcoal, until recently still a principal fuel for cooking.

Ilio Raffaelli was born in a *capanna* and spent the first 25 years of his life as a woodcutter's son. He has now reconstructed a *capanna* in the woods of the Barbi estate, and he conducts guided walks through the land he knows and loves so well.

'Without doubt, it was a hard life,' he says. 'But for us it was no worse than for many. Remember, 30 years ago it was a hard life for all Italians except the very rich. Those woodcutters that worked hard could eventually succeed in buying their own house.'

Visits: Guided walks and visits by appointment with Fattoria dei Barbi (address below).

2 FATTORIA DEI BARBI
53024 MONTALCINO SI
TEL: 0577/848277

WINES PRODUCED: Brunello di Montalcino, Brunello di Montalcino Riserva, Brunello di Montalcino *cru* 'Vigna del Fiore'; Rosso di Montalcino; Brusco dei Barbi; Bruscone dei Barbi; Sole dei Barbi;

Chianti Colli Senesi; Vin Santo.
VISITS: Mon–Fri 9–13h; 15–18h.
Weekends 14h30–17h30.
This large Tuscan estate carries out organic farming wherever possible for the production not only of its wines, but also for the other products of the farm. Wine production is traditional, but in

THE CENTRE

addition to the excellent range of Brunellos, there are some exciting new wines that are also being developed. Bruscone dei Barbi is a similar wine to Brusco dei Barbi but aged in new oak *barriques*, while Sole dei Barbi is an exceptionally elegant, classy, new-style wine that is more international in taste.

The cellars date from the 17th century, and contain more than 120 Slavonian *botti*. In addition to being one of the leading wine estates of Montalcino, the Fattoria dei Barbi is also a producer of fine olive oil, meats and *salame*, and sheep's milk cheese, all of which find their way on to the generous tables of the Taverna dei Barbi (see below).

Farmhouse accommodation available for letting.

English, French spoken.

3

AZIENDA AGRARIA LISINI
53020 SANT'ANGELO IN COLLE SI
TEL: 0577/864040

WINES PRODUCED: Brunello di Montalcino, Brunello di Montalcino Riserva; Rosso di Montalcino; Vin Santo; *grappa di Brunello*.
VISITS: by appointment.

Another old local wine making family who inherited this famous Brunello estate in the mid-1800s, renowned for its rich traditional wines of the highest quality. The *cantina* dates from 1300, though the villa was built in 1700.

4

TENUTA COL D'ORCIA SPA
53020 SANT'ANGELO IN COLLE SI
TEL: 0577/864064

WINES PRODUCED: Brunello di Montalcino, Brunello di Montalcino Riserva; Rosso di Montalcino.

VISITS: Mon–Fri, by appointment. One of the zone's leading traditional producers, owned by the great Piedmont vermouth firm of Cinzano.

English, French spoken.

5

CASTELLO BANFI
VILLA BANFI SRL
53020 SANT'ANGELO SCALO SI
TEL: 0577/864111; 864127

WINES PRODUCED: Brunello di Montalcino, Brunello di Montalcino Riserva; Centine Rosso di

Montalcino; Chianti Classico; Tavernelle Cabernet Sauvignon; Santa Costanza Novello dei Colli di Toscana; Moscadello di Montalcino, 'B' Moscadello di Montalcino Liquoroso; San Angelo Pinot Grigio; Fontanelle Chardonnay

della Toscana; Fumé Blanc della Toscana; *grappa di Brunello*.
VISITS: weekdays 9–16h.
Appointment necessary.
The space-age winery of Castello Banfi was created in 1978 as the flagship of the American Mariani brothers' Villa Banfi empire, whose remarkable success was based on exporting Italian wine to the US, and which has other important wineries at Strevi and Gavi in the Piedmont. The Montalcino estate, developed and directed by one of Italy's leading oenologists, Ezio Rivella, is massive: over 800 hectares of vineyards planted not only with classic Tuscan varieties for the production of Brunello and Rosso di Montalcino, but also with other native and international varieties to result in a remarkable gamut of both traditional and modern wines under the Banfi label. The castle which appears on the Brunello label is currently being refurbished and when open should have a visitors' reception where the full range of wines can be tasted and purchased.
English, French, German spoken.

---

6 TENUTA DI CASTELGIOCONDO
LOC. CASTELGIOCONDO
53024 MONTALCINO SI
TEL: 0577/848492
ADMINISTRATION: MARCHESI DE'
   FRESCOBALDI, FLORENCE
TEL: 055/218751

WINES PRODUCED: Castelgiocondo Brunello di Montalcino; Campo ai Sassi Rosso di Montalcino; Vergene 'Predicato del Selvànte' (Sauvignon Bianco).

VISITS: by appointment, made through the Frescobaldi head office in Florence.
This 13th-century castle and wine estate is the latest addition to the extensive Frescobaldi portfolio, though the estate's well-made wines had previously been marketed by them.
English, German, French spoken.

---

7 AZIENDA AGRICOLA VAL DI SUGA
53024 MONTALCINO SI
TEL: 0577/848701

WINES PRODUCED: Brunello di Montalcino, Brunello di Montalcino Riserva, Brunello di Montalcino *cru* 'Vigna del Lago'; Rosso di Montalcino; Rosso del Merlot.

VISITS: by appointment. *Punta di vendita* open daily, working hours.
This modern estate is Milanese-owned alongside two other estates, one in Montepulciano, the other in Chianti Classico. Dr Enzo Tiezzi, former president of the Brunello

consortium, oversees all three of them. Val di Suga has 23 hectares of specialized vineyards located just north of Montalcino, as well as a further 14 hectares planted in the southern zone near Sant'Angelo in Colle. The winery is purpose-built and brand new, and thus provides a striking contrast to more traditional estates. However, the most modern equipment – small stainless steel fermentation vats and new Slavonian oak *botti* – is important for the new style of Brunello that Tiezzi is seeking: sleek, well made wines that above all have perfume, finesse, and elegance.

8

TENUTA CAPARZO
LOC. TORRENIERI
53028 MONTALCINO SI
TEL: 0577/848390

WINES PRODUCED: Brunello di Montalcino, Brunello di Montalcino 'La Casa'; Rosso di Montalcino; Spumante di Brunello Brut Rosé; Ca' del Pazzo (Cabernet Sauvignon and Brunello); Le Grance (Chardonnay); *grappa di Brunello.*
VISITS: daily, by appointment.
Modern, forward-thinking estate owned by a consortium of Milanese professionals who purchased the property in 1965. A range of outstanding wines is produced utilizing both traditional and innovative techniques in the ultra-modern purpose-built winery. Caparzo has received considerable attention recently not only for its elegant, concentrated Brunellos, but also for its oak fermented Le Grance Chardonnay, demonstrating that the zone is also capable of producing white wines of the highest quality.

9

AZIENDA AGRICOLA ALTESINO
PALAZZO ALTESI
LOC. ALTESINO
53028 MONTALCINO SI
ADMINISTRATION: C/O ALZAIA
  NAVIGLIO GRANDE 70, 20144 MILAN
TEL: 0577/806208

WINES PRODUCED: Brunello di Montalcino, Brunello di Montalcino Riserva; Rosso di Montalcino; Palazzo Altesi (Sangiovese Grosso from *cru* Montosoli vineyard aged in *barrique*); Alte d'Altesi (Sangiovese Grosso/Cabernet Sauvignon); Bianco di Montosoli.
VISITS: daily, by appointment.
Another of Brunello's forward-thinking and leading Milanese-owned estates. The owners have completely renovated

the 15th-century palace, and the winery is the most up-to-date, for the production of modern wines

that combine structure with elegance.
English spoken.

Enoteche

1 ENOTECA 'LA FORTEZZA'
PIAZZALE FORTEZZA
53024 MONTALCINO SI
TEL: 0577/849211

OPEN: summer 9–13h; 14h30–20h; winter 9–13h; 14–18h. Closed Mon except from 15 July–15 Sept.
Historic *enoteca* located in the 14th-century La Rocca fortress: all of the region's 70 producers who bottle their wine are represented and a range of wines (up to 30 in

summer) is available for tasting by the glass or bottle. Simple drinking snacks – local *salame, prosciutto* and *pecorino* – are served, and there are pleasant outdoor tables in the fortress courtyard in good weather. Most of the wines on display are from the most recently released years but older vintages may also be available. Wine tastings can be arranged for groups.
French spoken.

---

2 CAFFÈ FIASCHETTERIA ITALIANA
PIAZZA DEL POPOLO 6
53024 MONTALCINO SI
0577/849043

Closed Thur.
Montalcino's central hang-out is a stylish *belle époque* bar serving a

good range of Brunello and Rosso di Montalcino by the glass or bottle together with the usual bar snacks and nibbles. There is also an adjoining *cantina* with a good selection of wines for purchase.

Ristoranti

1 LA CUCINA DI EDGARDO
VIA S. SALONI
53024 MONTALCINO SI
TEL: 0577/848232

Closed Wed out of season.
Small, classy little restaurant in

the old part of town serving local foods as well as French-inspired creative cuisine: *pâté*, homemade *pinci, brasato al Brunello* and an exceptional selection of local wines.
Moderate

THE CENTRE

2 'IL POZZO'
PIAZZA DEL POZZO 2
53020 SANT'ANGELO IN COLLE SI
TEL: 0577/864015

Closed Tue.
Bar-*ristorante* in the centre of the

wine town serving *cucina
casalinga: zuppa di pane, pinci,
scottiglia, coniglio ripieno*, and a
good selection of Brunello and
Rosso di Montalcino.
Inexpensive

Punto di Ristoro Agrituristico

1 TAVERNA DEI BARBI
FATTORIA DEI BARBI
53024 MONTALCINO SI
TEL: 0577/848277

Closed Wed.
Authentic farmhouse *trattoria*
serving local foods of Montalcino
prepared to traditional recipes by

English cook Mary Bailey, almost
entirely with produce and products
from the Barbi estate, including
homemade *salame, prosciutto*,
sausages, *pecorino*, and of
course the full range of Barbi
wines.
Inexpensive to Moderate

MONTEPULCIANO AND ITS NOBLE WINE

In Brief: The hill town of Montepulciano is located in southern Tuscany
near the region's border with Umbria, and conveniently not far off the A1
autostrada. As such, it can be dipped into by those travelling north or
south, or by those based by Lake Trasimeno. Alternatively, this quiet, less
visited zone makes a pleasant base in itself, while the nearby spa town of
Chianciano Terme is conveniently located for those who have over-
indulged: Chianciano, the locals proudly boast, is where you come if you
are in need of a '*fegato sano*' – a healthy liver.

Montepulciano is often grouped together with Montalcino, two southern
Tuscan hill towns famous for their respective wines. In fact, historically
they were more often than not at odds with one another. For whereas
Montalcino was staunchly Sienese, Montepulciano was one of Florence's
principal and long-standing allies. The Marzocco, the quizzical stone lion
that is the symbol of Florentine dominions, stands proudly on its stone
pedestal at the entrance to the town, its paw placed on a blank shield, an

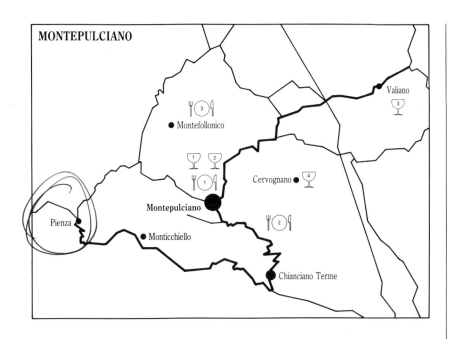

MONTEPULCIANO

Valiano

Montefollonico

Cervognano

Montepulciano

Pienza

Monticchiello

Chianciano Terme

indication that the town was not subjugated by force.

If today the wines of Montepulciano and Montalcino continue a rivalry of sorts (both were early recipients of select DOCG status), those of the former can certainly boast the longer pedigree. For whereas Brunello di Montalcino was only created by Feruccio Biondi-Santi in the 1870s, Vino Nobile di Montepulciano was drunk and praised for centuries before that, the first documented mention dating from the 8th century. And it was in the 17th century that Francesco Redi, the great poet, imbiber, and author of *Bacco in Toscana*, wrote that 'Montepulciano of all wines is king.' Perhaps this led to the local wines gaining the cachet of nobility, or possibly the name came from the fact that Vino Nobile di Montepulciano was often made and drunk by the noble and aristocratic Poliziani, as the inhabitants of this once fashionable town are known.

The delimited vineyards for Vino Nobile di Montepulciano are all located within the commune of Montepulciano, itself encompassed within the larger wine zone of Chianti Colli Senesi. The wine is produced from a similar *uvaggio* of grapes – primarily Prugnolo Gentile (a clone of Sangiovese), Canaiolo Nero, Mammolo and others – and, indeed, Vino Nobile has been considered little more than a variation of Chianti, rarely worth the higher price that its supposed noble pedigree commands, say its detractors. That

THE CENTRE

judgement, though, is unfair, for the wine zone is particular: this far southern Tuscan vineyard has a fertile, sandy-clay terrain that results generally in wines that are more delicate, fruity, and feminine than, say, the more austere wines of the Chianti Classico.

Montepulciano itself is a town of not inconsiderable charm. The stately Renaissance palaces that line the Via di Gracciano del Corso as it climbs up towards the Piazza Grande are evidence of its former power and prosperity. And below many of them, hollowed out of the soft tufa rock upon which Montepulciano sits, are the wine cellars and *cantine* upon which part at least of this prosperity was based. The Piazza Grande is a spacious, open square, particularly pleasant after the claustrophobia of Montepulciano's medieval alleys and streets. The façade of the cathedral remains rough-cast and unfinished, but the inside is calm and peaceful and worth visiting for the fine triptych of the Assumption painted by the Sienese master Taddeo di Bartolo. The Palazzo Comunale in the square apes Florence's Palazzo Vecchio, while the Palazzo Contucci, once the town fortress, is today the wine *cantina* of the Contucci family, producers of solid, traditional Vino Nobile di Montepulciano. The *cantina* is open to the public and the wines can be tasted and purchased.

One of the town's most important wine producers is located in the Palazzo Avignonesi, opposite the Marzocco, a grandiose edifice designed by the architect Vignola and in the Avignonesi family's possession since the 15th century. For much if not all of that period, the Avignonesi have made wine from their extensive vineyard holdings, and stored and aged it in the 12th-century cellars below the palace (themselves probably hollowed out by the Etruscans as tombs some two-and-a-half millennia ago). In the past, however, like many aristocratic landowners throughout Tuscany and indeed the rest of Italy, the Avignonesi considered wine to be little more than a basic agricultural commodity, and sold it mainly in bulk by the vat or demi-john. Even as recently as the mid-1970s, the concept of 'fine wine' as a precious commodity was still relatively unknown here.

However, when Ettore Falvo married into the family, bringing with him equally extensive and prestigious vineyard holdings from La Selva near Cortona, a conscious decision was taken to concentrate on quality in a quest to reclaim and re-establish a great vinous patrimony. Thus, in addition to the traditional native grapes – Prugnolo Gentile, Canaiolo Nero, and Mammolo for the production of Vino Nobile di Montepulciano – new plantations of Cabernet and Merlot were added and, at La Selva, white grapes such as Chardonnay and Sauvignon were experimented with to replace the rather neutral and less fragrant Trebbiano Toscano, Grechetto, and Malvasia. Today, the most modern vinification techniques and equipment are utilized (especially the ageing of both red and white wines in new French oak *barriques*) to result in a range of fine, well-made wines that represent some of the best of the zone, if not the region.

The Avignonesi Vino Nobile di Montepulciano is undoubtedly a fine traditional wine, full and fragrant, and with the characteristic and rather austere body of tannin that will allow it to age gracefully. But the most exciting wines that we tasted were atypical: I Grifi, a super-Tuscan *vino da tavola* made from Prugnolo Gentile and Cabernet; Marzocco, a *cru* Chardonnay fermented *sur lie*; a 100% Merlot that was as silky and elegant as a classed growth St-Emilion; an outstanding Sauvignon tasted from the *barrique*, reminiscent of a really good Pouilly-Fumé; and a Sauternes-like dessert wine fermented in new oak from Chardonnay and Sauvignon affected by *muffa nobile*.

These are unquestionably superlative wines. But, with the exception of Avignonesi's Vino Nobile, they are not particularly Italian in style.

Ettore Falvo shrugged unapologetically. 'The French are the masters,' he told me unequivocally. 'We used to produce a Bianco Vergine della Valdichiana but, quite frankly, Trebbiano and Malvasia, the local white grapes, will never produce great wine. I don't think there is any point in slavishly following tradition if it does not result in excellence.'

An iconoclast, perhaps? Yet Falvo is proudest of all of what is undoubtedly the most quintessentially traditional of all Tuscan wines: Vin Santo. This unique wine is produced from selected grapes (in this case primarily Grechetto, Trebbiano and Malvasia) which are laid out to dry on cane mats known locally as *stuoie* from October until as late as March. This lengthy drying process – considerably longer than that carried out on most farms in other zones – is critical for the final quality. Little flecks of *muffa nobile*, the fungus known as *Botrytis cinerea*, develop on some of the bunches, further intensifying flavours, sugar levels, and glycerine. The raisin-like grapes are finally lightly crushed, and the honeyed, sugar-rich must is placed in tiny new oak *caratelli* of 50 litres which are sealed with cork and then melted wax and left in the airy *vin santeria* to age for a full 6 years, a remarkably lengthy sojourn. During this time, they are not touched, the wax seal is never opened, nor are they ever racked. Only about 1600 bottles of this unique wine eventually emerge, but the Avignonesi Vin Santo is rightly considered one of the greatest dessert wines of Italy, if not the world.

Falvo makes Vin Santo for the passion of it. Such tiny quantities of wine

The drying of Prugnolo Gentile grapes for the production of the rare Vin Santo, Occhio di Pernice.

are never viable from a commercial point of view, for there is simply too little of it to go round even for favoured customers. The time and effort that it takes to produce this most traditional wine, too, is rarely commensurate with the financial rewards that it fetches, even at the staggering prices that Avignonesi's always commands. Yet still the wine is produced, seemingly out of the sheer love of it. Falvo also makes an even more rare Vin Santo, Occhio di Pernice, from black Prugnolo Gentile grapes that undergo the same process. So limited is this wine that only about 300 half-bottles a year are ever produced, to be shared jealously with friends, family, and perhaps the luckiest and most privileged customers.

The Vino Nobile wine country extends mainly down the tufa-rich slopes of the eponymous town. To the south and west of Montepulciano, vineyards extend over the hills towards Chianciano Terme, Monticchiello, and Pienza, a beautiful medieval town, the birthplace of Pope Pius II, and a centre for exceptional *pecorino* cheese. To the north and east, the wine country follows the slopes down towards the Val di Chiana (too flat, low, and fertile for the cultivation of grapes), then, past Montepulciano Stazione and the *autostrada*, the vineyards begin again where the land rises around Valiano and continue to the borders with Umbria and the Tuscan province of Arezzo. The vineyards in the latter sub-zone, in particular, have in recent years seen considerable investment, and are now producing wines of real quality. In addition to Avignonesi's Fattoria Le Capezzine located here, the Tenuta Trerose is a serious estate producing not only fine Vino Nobile, but also some attractive modern white wines utilizing state-of-the-art technologies. We witnessed there, for example, a vineyard planted automatically by lasers, as well as an amazing automated '*barriqueria*'.

The wine country of Montepulciano, like that of much of Tuscany, is a fascinating blend of the old and new: long-standing noble families who have made wine literally for centuries, and upstarts who have invested in the region with capital made in other sectors; old-style wines such as traditional Vino Nobile di Montepulciano and Vin Santo, and new wines made from non-Tuscan grapes – Cabernet, Merlot, Chardonnay, Sauvignon – fermented and aged in new French oak. This clash between the old and new creates its own dynamism, and indeed demonstrates how wine growers here, as elsewhere, are moving forward at speed, while maintaining roots in their centuries-old patrimony.

Degustazione: Stop to Taste; Stop to Buy

1

AVIGNONESI S.N.C.
VIA DI GRACCIANO NEL CORSO 91
53045 MONTEPULCIANO SI
TEL: 0578/757872

WINES PRODUCED: Vino Nobile di Montepulciano, Vino Nobile di Montepulciano Riserva; I Grifi; Chianti Colli Senesi; Il Marzocco (Chardonnay fermented in *barrique*), Terre di Cortona (Chardonnay); Vin Santo; *grappa di Vino Nobile.*
VISITS: Mon–Fri, by appointment. Wine shop open Mon–Sat 9–13h; 16–20h.
One of the leading producers of

Vino Nobile di Montepulciano, as well as of modern, well-made wines from non-typical varieties.

The full range of Avignonesi wines is available for purchase in the wine shop, also located in the Palazzo Avignonesi, and a range of wines is usually open for tasting (not the rare Vin Santos, which are strictly rationed and not even usually available for sale). The historic 12th-century cellars below the palace can be visited on request.
English spoken.

2

AZIENDA AGRICOLA CONTUCCI
PALAZZO CONTUCCI
VIA DEL TEATRO 1
53045 MONTEPULCIANO SI
TEL: 0578/757006

WINES PRODUCED: Vino Nobile di Montepulciano, Vino Nobile di Montepulciano Riserva; Bianco della Contessa; Il Sansovino; Chianti Colli Senesi; Vin Santo.
VISITS: daily, working hours.
Long-established traditional family

producer with cellars located in 13th-century Palazzo Contucci in the historic heart of old Montepulciano near the cathedral. The ancient *cantina* was once the town's fortress; today it is the site of the working winery, open to all for visits, tastings, and direct sales. Il Sansovino, a sort of young Vino Nobile produced entirely from Prugnolo Gentile, is noteworthy. French and some English spoken.

THE CENTRE

3 TENUTA TREROSE
LOC. VALIANO
53045 MONTEPULCIANO SI
TEL: 0578/724018; 0577/848701

WINES PRODUCED: Vino Nobile di
Montepulciano, Vino Nobile di
Montepulciano Riserva; Salterio
(Chardonnay/Sauvignon fermented
in *barrique*); Vin Santo.
VISITS: by appointment.
Tenuta Trerose forms part of the
Milanese-owned wine complex of 3
estates under the direction of Dr
Enzo Tiezzi. The lovely golden
yellow 16th-century Villa

Belvedere belies a winery that is
rigorously modern and up-to-date
and which has in recent years seen
considerable investment. Trerose
Vino Nobile di Montepulciano is
vinified traditionally, but about
20% of the wine is aged in new oak
barriques to result in a wine of sleek
elegance. Salterio is a new-style
barrique-aged Tuscan white wine
produced from about 80%
Chardonnay, 20% Sauvignon. A
new vineyard has recently been
planted with Cabernet Sauvignon.

---

4 PODERE BOSCARELLI
VIA DI MONTENERO 28
LOC. CERVOGNANO
53045 MONTEPULCIANO SI
TEL: 0578/767277

WINES PRODUCED: Vino Nobile di
Montepulciano; Boscarelli (*vino da*

tavola); Chianti Colli Senesi.
VISITS: daily, working hours.
Appointment preferred.
Traditional family production of
good Vino Nobile di Montepulciano
as well as special *vino da tavola*
aged in *barrique.*

Ristoranti

1 ALBERGO-RISTORANTE IL MARZOCCO
VIA DI GRACCIANO
53045 MONTEPULCIANO SI
TEL: 0578/757262

Friendly family-run hotel opposite
the Marzocco, with a decent

restaurant serving basic
pensione-style cooking. Rooms are
large and airy, all with private
facilities.
Moderate

---

2 FATTORIA PULCINO
SA146
53045 MONTEPULCIANO SI
TEL: 0578/776905

Closed Mon in winter.
Just outside Montepulciano, along
the road to Chianciano Terme, this
basic farmhouse restaurant serves

foods of the *fattoria*, including grilled meats, suckling pig, and

homemade wines.
Inexpensive

---

3 RISTORANTE LA CHIUSA
VIA DELLA MADONNINA 88
53040 MONTEFOLLONICO SI
TEL: 0577/669668

Closed Tue except in summer.
Famous elegant country restaurant

serving refined Tuscan cooking as well as *cucina creativa*, utilizing primarily own-grown or -raised produce and products. A few rooms available.
Expensive

THE RUFINA AND POMINO: NOBLE WINES FROM A MAJESTIC LAND

In Brief: The Rufina wine zone lies about 20 km north-east of Florence in the steep balcony of hills that climbs towards the upper reaches of the Apennine range that separates Tuscany from Emilia-Romagna. As such, though in proximity to the city, it is an area of wild grandeur and beauty, and has long been a favourite retreat for nobles and wealthy Florentine families alike. This small wine zone is the source not only of Chianti Rufina, but also of superlative wines from the tiny delimited vineyard of Pomino. A tour through these vineyards can be completed in a day.

Chianti, confusingly for the consumer, can be produced in 7 different sub-zones. The central heartland, the Chianti Classico, is rightly regarded as the most important, and its symbol, the *gallo nero* or black cockerel, is viewed by many as a necessary and essential guarantee of quality. However, just north of the Classico zone lies a much smaller but equally prestigious vineyard that is little visited, but which makes wines that are every bit as excellent: the Rufina.

The Rufina is the smallest of the Chianti sub-zones, and takes its name from the small market town of Rufina that lies along the Sieve river. The vineyards lie mainly on the steeper slopes that lead up towards the jagged peaks of the Apennines, but this is by no means a single-minded, wholly specialized wine zone. As elsewhere, the long-standing heritage of the *mezzadria* has left a tradition of mixed farming, so that vineyards compete with woodlands, olive groves, fields of grain, vegetable gardens, and the

THE CENTRE

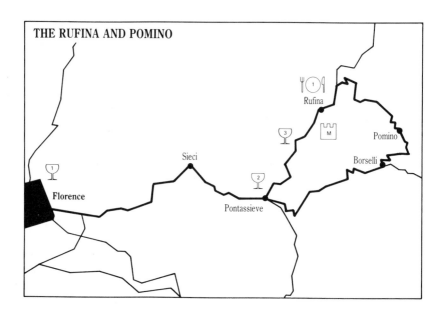

THE RUFINA AND POMINO

Rufina

Pomino

Sieci

Borselli

Florence

Pontassieve

raising of livestock.

For those familiar with the countryside of the Chianti Classico, the Rufina comes as a striking contrast, for this is an austere and grandiose land that is steep, majestic, even rather forbidding. The proximity of the Apennines results in a cooler microclimate, and the rugged hill vineyards generally yield grapes that result in leaner, rather tannic wines of considerable structure and stature. These are big, robust wines that need lengthy ageing and which correspondingly are among the longest lived of all Chiantis.

To gain a general view of the wine country, leave Florence on the N67 which is a continuation of the Lungarno and follows the Arno to Pontassieve before branching north eventually through the Passo di Muraglione and into Emilia-Romagna. The bottling and shipping headquarters of the Marchesi de' Frescobaldi are located along this road at Sieci, before Pontassieve. This important wine town has particularly specialized in the bottling and shipping of basic table wines from central and southern Italy.

The Frescobaldi are undoubtedly the most important and leading wine producers in the Rufina. Their flagship is the exceptional Castello di Nipozzano estate, located in the steep hills past Pontassieve off the road to Borselli. The aristocratic Frescobaldi proudly proclaim the fact that they have been *viticoltori* since 1300; over the course of centuries, they have been much more as well: renowned politicians, bankers, statesmen, soldiers, artists, poets, musicians. Today, with some 850 hectares of specialized vine-yards located on 9 different wine estates, they are probably the largest private family wine grower in Italy, possibly even Europe.

The Castello di Nipozzano, which dates from the 11th century, as well as other Frescobaldi estates, were clearly marked on a 15th-century map now on display in the Uffizi Gallery, indicating that this noble family was already important in those times. Indeed, wine has been made continuously by the family for literally centuries, and the Frescobaldi are proud to boast 'our own wines from our own vineyards', indicating that their full and extensive range is produced entirely from their own-grown grapes.

The Nipozzano estate today, as in the former days of *mezzadria*, is largely self-sufficient. The workers live on the estate as part of an extended agri-cultural family community, and indeed, in some cases generations have worked the land. The extensive vineyards that surround the castle are certainly among the Frescobaldi's most prestigious and highly valued. Cas-tello di Nipozzano Riserva is a Chianti Rufina produced in the best years only, matured in oak cask and *barrique* for a minimum of 2 years, followed by at least a year in bottle prior to release. The wine is an exceptional example of fine reserve Chianti: always well-structured, and, in the best vintages, in need of upwards of a decade to reach its peak.

Two other exceptional wines from the Nipozzano estate should be men-tioned. The *cru* Montesodi is a Chianti Rufina produced from a 10-hectare vineyard of old selected vines located 350 metres above sea level. The tradi-tional Chianti blend is boosted with the addition of about 10% Cabernet Sauvignon, and the wine is subsequently aged in French oak *barrique* (50% new each year) for 20–22 months. Mormoreto, from a larger 19-hectare vineyard on the Nipozzano estate, is produced from 90% Cabernet Sauvig-non and 10% Cabernet Franc, and qualifies as one of the élite Predicato di Bitùrica wines. It too undergoes lengthy finishing in *barrique*. These are both immensely powerful and concentrated wines of great quality and class. Their massive extract and high tannin content means that they both require considerable time to reach their peaks. Montesodi must rank as one of the greatest Chiantis, while Mormoreto is possibly more appealing to inter-national tastes.

To continue the wine tour, carry on to little Borselli and there find the road that leads first to Pomino, then across to the Sieve valley and Rufina. This is quite simply a stunning drive through a majestic land dominated above by the ever-present high corona of mountains, its dense woodlands criss-crossed with vineyards and grassy meadows.

THE CENTRE

Pomino itself is only a tiny hamlet, but the wines from this remote hill vineyard were singled out as exceptional in 1716 when they were included in Granduca Cosimo III's Il Bando. In modern times, the Pomino vineyard was elevated to DOC status in 1983 and today produces remarkable red and white wines as well as Vin Santo. Not surprisingly, it is the omnipresent Frescobaldi who hold a virtual monopoly on its production.

These wines truly do deserve their own particular *denominazione* for they are unique. Over 100 years ago – long before it was fashionable – an ancestor of the Frescobaldi who had been living in France returned to Pomino and there planted a range of different French grapes, including the now ultra-chic Cabernet Sauvignon and Chardonnay. Thus, when Pomino was granted its own DOC, these non-Tuscan grape varieties were allowed to form parts of the *uvaggio*. Pomino Rosso, for example, is vinified from 60% Sangiovese, 20% Cabernet Sauvignon, 10% Merlot, and 10% Pinot Nero. Not surprisingly, this elegant, soft and well-rounded wine is very French in style. Similarly, Pomino Bianco is produced from a blend of Chardonnay and Pinot Grigio. In particular, the Pomino Bianco *cru* 'Il Benefizio', produced only in the best years, comes from a 22-hectare single vineyard planted up to 700 metres in altitude. The wine, fermented in new oak *barrique* and aged at least a year prior to release, is exceptionally full-bodied and well-structured. I consider it one of the most successful *barrique*-aged Italian Chardonnays that I have tasted. The Pomino *denominazione* also applies to Vin Santo. This most traditional and ancient wine is also noteworthy for, unlike in other zones where the grapes are harvested then laid out or hung up to dry in airy lofts, here the grapes are left on the vine until as late as December, an indication of how dry and well-ventilated this high mountainous zone is.

The Pomino estate is of particular interest to the social historian as well as the wine lover. This was a large estate once worked by some 40 *contadini* and their families along the lines of the *mezzadria*. Here at the Pomino winery, it is possible to see how this age-old system of sharecropping worked in practice, for there are still in place the 40 large wooden *tine* – open-topped wooden fermentation vessels – one for each family. The grapes were delivered to the winery in containers known as *bigoncie*: each *tina* could hold some 90 *bigoncie* at a time. Then, once the wine was made, it was measured out in small wooden barrels known as *barili*. For each *barile* of wine measured out and poured through an opening in the floor beneath the vat that led to the *padrone*'s underground *cantina*, a *barile* was given in turn to the *contadino* to take back home for his own use.

From Pomino, the road leads down to the Sieve valley and eventually to

Rufina itself, a pleasant enough little wine town dominated by the Villa Poggio Reale. This beautiful 16th-century Renaissance edifice was designed by Michelangelo and now houses a communal wine museum, the Museo della Vite e del Vino.

Further down the valley towards Florence lies the Fattoria di Selvapiana. This is one of the most important and highly regarded estates in the Rufina, renowned especially for its dense, concentrated *riserve* wines. Selvapiana has a direct sales outlet on the N67 road. This road was traditionally the route from Tuscany over the mountains to Romagna, and it was well served with post houses where travellers could sleep and eat, and horses could be changed. One such inn, the Locanda della Malcantone, was located on what is now the Selvapiana estate, and in the 18th century it was a noted *osteria* serving the wines of the Rufina. However, at that time it acquired a rather ghastly reputation when a number of travellers died mysteriously in their sleep. Night watches were posted, and the culprit was discovered to be an enormous poisonous spider which was itself eventually caught, killed, and displayed in the Specola Museum of Florence.

Degustazione: Stop to Taste; Stop to Buy

1 MARCHESI DE' FRESCOBALDI SPA
VIA S. SPIRITO 11
50125 FIRENZE
tel: 055/218751

(see Florence entry page 244)

---

2 TENIMENTI RUFFINO
VIA ARETINA 42/44
50065 PONTASSIEVE FI
TEL: 055/8302307

WINES PRODUCED: Chianti Classico, Chianti Classico Riserva Ducale; Brunello di Montalcino 'Il Greppone Mazzi'; Cabreo 'Predicato del Muschio' (Chardonnay), Cabreo 'Predicato di Bitùrica' (Cabernet/Sangiovese); Tondo dal Nero (Pinot Nero); Libaio (Chardonnay/Sauvignon Blanc).
VISITS: by appointment.

It is confusing that the Tenimenti Ruffino has its headquarters in Pontassieve in the zone for Chianti Rufina: in fact, the Folonari family's various estates are located mainly in the Chianti Classico as well as in the zone of Montalcino. The family firm may once have built its success primarily on bulk table wines bottled in the straw *fiasco*, but today it is noted foremost for *vini pregiati* of the very highest quality. The Folonari have been instrumental in the development of

THE CENTRE

the *Vini del Predicato* scheme, and the Cabreo wines are among the finest examples.

English, French, German spoken.

---

3 FATTORIA DI SELVAPIANA
VIA SELVAPIANA 3
50065 PONTASSIEVE FI
TEL: 055/8304848; (*PUNTA DI VENDITA*) 8314779

WINES PRODUCED: Chianti Rufina, Chianti Rufina Riserva, Chianti Rufina Riserva *cru* Bucerchiale; Rosato della Val di Sieve; Bianco della Val di Sieve (Pinot Bianco); Vin Santo.
VISITS: daily, by appointment 1 or 2 days in advance. *Punta di vendita* (located south of Rufina on N67) open Mon–Sat 9–12h; 15–19h or by appointment.

One of the most highly regarded properties in the Rufina, producing an exceptional range of wines that are particularly well suited to lengthy conservation. The Fattoria is located in a Renaissance villa. At the *punta di vendita* there is generally a good selection of older vintages available for sale.

English, French, German spoken.

MUSEO DEL VINO

MUSEO DELLA VITE E DEL VINO
VILLA POGGIO REALE
VIA PIAVE 5
50068 RUFINA FI
TEL: 055/839003

Open mornings only.
Located in the town's famous 16th-century villa, and the centre for the promotion of the wines of the Chianti Rufina zone.

Ristorante

1 RISTORANTE-ALBERGO DA GRAZZINI
VIA PIAVE 14
50068 RUFINA FI
TEL: 055/839027

Closed Wed.
Hotel-restaurant serving local foods and wines.
Inexpensive to Moderate

SAN GIMIGNANO, *'CITTÀ DELLE BELLE TORRI'*

In Brief: San Gimignano, one of Tuscany's loveliest and best preserved medieval towns, is also one of its most popular, especially in summer and at weekends. Be that as it may, no visitor to the region will wish to miss visiting this remarkable 'medieval Manhattan', and sampling the famous Vernaccia wines on the spot. The wine country which surrounds San Gimignano is altogether more quiet. Easily reached from either Florence or Siena, the zone could provide an alternative base for touring the region.

The approach to San Gimignano, whether from Poggibonsi, Certaldo, or Volterra, inevitably leads through the vine-covered hills, giving tantalizing glimpses of a remarkable medieval skyline rising above the classic Tuscan landscape. Only some 14 towers remain today out of the legendary 70 that once punctuated this tiny medieval city in the 14th and 15th centuries. Even now the effect of those that remain – the tallest, the Torre della Rognosa, is over 50 metres high – is still most striking, indeed somewhat dizzying, to say the least.

And yet we read that in the past most Tuscan towns were built thus, the towers serving not only as manifestations of municipal power, but indeed as private domestic residences, affording the medieval inhabitants a unique and bizarre high-rise tenement perspective. Of course the towers themselves, like modern skyscrapers today, were awesome symbols of power and prosperity for the richest aristocratic and merchant families. They were also necessary places of refuge during the Guelph and Ghibelline struggles that wracked most of Tuscany, for opposing families burnt down each other's towers, or subjected them to siege, so that clusters of mini-fortresses had to group together by clan for protection and were connected to one another with ladders and ramps. During times of strife, apparently, the inhabitants were not even able to venture outside. Nowhere else in Tuscany is the absurdity of that tragic and pointless civil faction more graphically demonstrated.

San Gimignano is rightly a focus of attention for the visitor to Tuscany, and the wines produced from the surrounding countryside undoubtedly benefit from this, shall we say, rather 'high profile'. But even in medieval

THE CENTRE

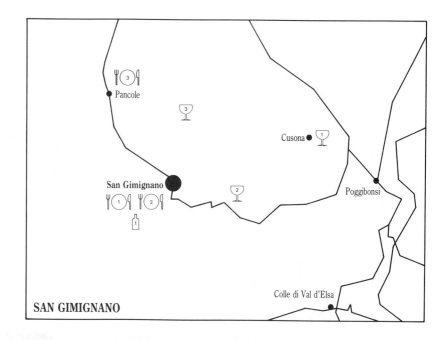

SAN GIMIGNANO

times, when the town's aspect was perhaps considered less unusual, her wines were already deemed excellent. Lorenzo de' Medici, apparently, was a great fan of Vernaccia di San Gimignano, while Michelangelo is claimed to have said that the wine 'kisses, licks, bites, tingles, and stings'. More recently, the pedigree of Vernaccia di San Gimignano was recognized in 1962 when it was the first wine in Italy to be granted DOC status.

Vernaccia di San Gimignano can rightly be acclaimed as Tuscany's best native white wine. In a region overwhelmingly known for its reds, it is the one traditional *denominazione* capable of producing white wine of real character and individuality – even if that character is not necessarily in keeping with what today's so-called international palate is clamouring for. Elsewhere in Tuscany, the ubiquitous Trebbiano Toscano is utilized to produce neutral, clean, but on the whole rather boring white wines. In other parts of the region, Chardonnay and Sauvignon have been planted and the wines produced, often aged in French oak *barrique*, have been widely acclaimed as worthy of comparison with similar wines from France, California, or Australia. But Vernaccia – the name probably comes from the Latin *vernaculus*, thus indicating its native provenance – is a true indigenous varietal of real character and quality, capable of producing wines that compromise not one jot to international tastes.

*an
'imignano.*

Surprisingly, Vernaccia is little grown elsewhere than in these highly-valued vineyards that extend around San Gimignano, south towards Siena as well as to the north and west. There are about 170 producers, and naturally styles of wine vary considerably. However, traditionally, the wine was vinified in part on the skins, then aged in oak *botte* for a year or two, resulting in a gutsy, full-bodied (and sometimes slightly oxidized and woody) white wine of force and character, one, incidentally, capable of standing up well to the robustly flavoured foods of the region. Today, although such styles of wine can still be found, particularly from the smaller peasant producers who make wine mainly for their own and local consumption, the largest and best wine makers – some of whose families have been land-owners in the zone for centuries – have invested in modern technology, and are producing cleaner, fresher, fruitier white wines that none the less demonstrate the varietal *tipicità* of the Vernaccia. Clonal selection in the vineyard, restriction of yields, and the identification of top *cru* vineyards for special bottlings have resulted in a range of white wines of real character that deserve to be better known.

Of course, the best place to indulge in such further research is in San Gimignano itself. The town is literally riddled with cellars, and virtually every shop, no matter what its principal activity, seems to display boxes and

THE CENTRE

cartons of wine to sell to passers-by and visitors. The best place to sample wines is the *Enoteca 'Il Castello'* located in the atmospheric Palazzo Gonfiantini. Then, after climbing the towers, strike out into the surrounding wine country, and drive through tiny, quiet wine hamlets such as Pancole, Cusona, Cortenanno and scores of others to sample and purchase the wines at the source.

Degustazione: Stop to Taste; Stop to Buy

1

FATTORIA CUSONA
LOC. CUSONA
53036 SAN GIMIGNANO SI
TEL: 0577/950028

WINES PRODUCED: Vernaccia di San Gimignano, Vernaccia di San Gimignano *cru* San Biagio, Vernaccia di San Gimignano Riserva, Spumante di Vernaccia; Chianti; Sodole; Vin Santo; *acquavite di Vernaccia*.
VISITS: daily, by appointment.

The Conti Guicciardini-Strozzi are one of the oldest noble families of San Gimignano: today they produce a Vernaccia that is thoroughly modern, fermented *'in bianco'* (off the skins) at controlled low temperatures to result in a fully fragrant, strong and clean dry white wine. Also source of good Chianti Colli Senesi, as well as *barrique*-aged Sodole.
English spoken.

2

SOCIETA AGRICOLA PIETRAFITTA S.R.L.
LOC. CORTENNANO
53037 SAN GIMIGNANO SI
TEL: 0577/940332

WINES PRODUCED: Vernaccia di San Gimignano, Vernaccia di San Gimignano Riserva; Chianti Colli Senesi; Bianco dei Colli della Toscana Centrale; Rosato; Vin Santo.
VISITS: by appointment.
In AD 961, Pietrafitta was a fortified farm belonging to the Castello dei

Fosci. Today, the estate produces a good range of wines, including the particularly distinctive, traditional Vernaccia Riserva; not released until the second year after its production, it spends some 5–6 months in oak, and it is a particularly full-bodied and robust white wine that can accompany a range of foods, including even game.

Honey and olive oil are also produced and sold on the estate. English spoken.

3 FATTORIA PONTE A RONDOLINO
LOC. CASALE
VIA CASALE 19
53037 SAN GIMIGNANO SI
TEL: 0577/940143

WINES PRODUCED: Vernaccia di San
Gimignano, Vernaccia di San
Gimignano Riserva, Vernaccia di
San Gimignano 'Terre di Tufo',
'Vigna Peperino'.

VISITS: daily, working hours for
direct purchases. Visits and
tastings for professionals only, by
appointment.
Teruzzi e Puthod Vernaccia is well
known abroad, but the '*cru*' wines
deserve particular attention, as
they rank among the finest serious
white wines of central Italy.
English, French, German spoken.

Enoteca

1 ENOTECA 'IL CASTELLO'
PALAZZO GONFIANTINI
VIA DEL CASTELLO 20
53037 SAN GIMIGNANO SI
TEL: 0577/940878

OPEN: daily 9–24h; closed Thur
night only.
San Gimignano has literally
countless shops, *enoteche*, bars and
the like, all offering the wines of
San Gimignano for either tasting or
purchase. Many producers
themselves have an outlet in the
medieval town centre for

vendita diretta. However, this
atmospheric *enoteca*, located
just off the Piazza della Cisterna, is
the best in town, offering an
excellent selection of Vernaccias
from the major producers as well as
other Sienese wines both for
purchase and to enjoy by the glass
or bottle in the vaulted courtyard of
this ancient palace. Simple typical
drinking snacks – *crostini*, *fettunta*,
salsicce, *focaccine* – are served. The
12th-century *cantina* holds a
selection of *riserve* and old bottles.

Ristoranti

1 RISTORANTE LE TERRAZZE
PIAZZA DELLA CISTERNA 23
53037 SAN GIMIGNANO SI
TEL: 0577/940328

Closed Tue; Wed lunch.
The restaurant of the Hotel La

Cisterna is San Gimignano's most
famous, as much for the traditional
Tuscan *cucina* as for the views of
the surrounding countryside from
the lovely old terraced dining room.
Moderate to Expensive

THE CENTRE

2 TRATTORIA 'LA MANGIATOIA'
VIA MAINARDI 5
53037 SAN GIMIGNANO SI
TEL: 0577/941528

Closed Fri.
It is advisable to book at this
favourite rustic *trattoria* run by

enthusiasts serving good *cucina
casalinga: pappardelle ai funghi
porcini, gnocchi deliziosi, cinghiale,
grigliate*, and gutsy own-produced
Vernaccia.
Inexpensive to Moderate

---

3 HOTEL LE RENAIE – RISTORANTE
LEONETTO
LOC. PANCOLE
53037 SAN GIMIGNANO SI
TEL: 0577/955044

Closed Tue.
Lovely hotel-restaurant located in

the heart of the Vernaccia wine
country not far outside medieval
San Gimignano, serving typical
foods, and in season *piatti con
tartufi e funghi*.
German, French spoken.
Inexpensive to Moderate

THE MAREMMA:
HOT SPRINGS, WARMING WINES,
AND ETRUSCAN RUINS

In Brief: The Maremma, a fertile area of drained marshlands, is located
in the far southern corner of Tuscany in the province of Grosseto, bordering the sea and the region of Latium. One of Tuscany's undiscovered
and least visited zones, it offers rare treats and rewards for the wine
lover, notably in the form of Morellino di Scansano, a rich, warming red
wine of elegance and class. The vineyards extend around charming,
unspoiled medieval villages and centre on the amazing hot springs of
Saturnia, a dip into which is an experience not to be missed. Saturnia is
equidistant from Florence and Rome. The entire zone is particularly rich
in Etruscan remains.

From Grosseto, the road leads into the high, rolling hills that rise above the
flatter now-drained marshes of the Maremma to the quiet medieval wine
town of Scansano. Yet, though there are isolated fields of vines here and
there, this does not seem on first impression a single-minded or specialized
wine region. Vineyards compete with grazing lands, the cultivation of wheat

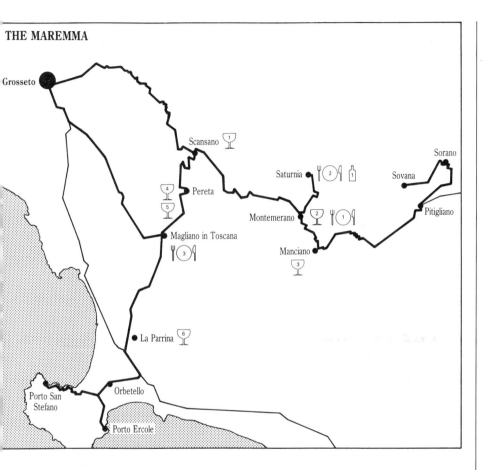

THE MAREMMA

and other cereals, flax, hemp, and olives. Even in winter, wide, expansive fields are already a deep, lush green and in place of the tall cypress of central Tuscany, there are stately oak trees. Herds of sheep and goats roam over the meadows.

Scansano itself, located on a sheltered spur that overlooks the steep valley, gives its name to the region's most important and significant wine, Morellino di Scansano, the only DOC wine in Tuscany other than prestigious Brunello di Montalcino entitled to be produced entirely from the aristocratic Sangiovese grape (though this is not obligatory: up to 15% of other black grape varieties can be optionally included). New investment in the zone, coupled with innovative wine making techniques (the use of *barriques*, of course) and careful selection, means that the best examples are capable of complexity, longevity, and elegance. Morellino di Scansano

THE CENTRE

Montemerano.

remains today one of the most undervalued wines of central Italy, and is certainly worth seeking and sampling when in the region.

The delimited wine zone is rather disparate, not compact and specialized, and extends over 7 communes: Scansano itself, Grosseto, Campagnatico, Magliano in Toscana, Roccalbegna, Semproniano, and Manciano. The nature of the mixed terrain here, plus a history of extensive *mezzadria* share-cropping, means that many wine growers still only cultivate small patches, and thus do not make or bottle wines themselves except for home consumption. So the *cantina cooperativa* at Scansano plays an important role in the production not just of Morellino di Scansano, but also of the region's best white, Bianco di Pitigliano, and other wines. The ultra-modern winery is computer controlled and the wines are well-made, if not overly exciting. The co-operative's Morellino di Scansano Riserva, however, made from grapes that have undergone greater selection, is particularly worth sampling.

From Scansano, continue through the majestic country to Montemerano, another fine medieval fortified hill town located just below the hot springs of Saturnia. Montemerano can serve as a base from which to enjoy the hot baths, as well as a place to come to purchase wine and eat in the fine old olive mill that producer Erik Banti has converted into an excellent Tuscan *enoteca-trattoria*.

Saturnia, according to legend, was the very first place in the Italian peninsula to be settled, by no less than the god Saturn himself. Even in the dead of winter, when the earth is locked in frost, it is amazing to come to this sheltered, isolated, forgotten corner of Tuscany. Of course, you can stay and swim in the Terme di Saturnia, a super deluxe hotel and the only commercial establishment that makes use of the hot springs. But that is really only for the lily-livered and pampered. The place to seek is where the waters simply boil forth from the bowels of the earth at some 100°F, cascading wildly over white, sulphur-covered rocks as they have since ancient days. In January, when steam billows forth on crisp cold days, it is astonishing to see people walking around outside in robes or swimsuits, wallowing under the cascades, or plastering themselves with thick, dank mud. There is a natural atmosphere of hedonism and sybaritic pleasure, and you would be well advised to discard your inhibitions and join in.

Afterwards, hair damp and smelling strongly of sulphur, repair to the little hill town of Saturnia itself and seek out the *Enoteca Bacco e Cerere* where you can enjoy warming, crystal goblets of Morellino di Scansano Riserva together with a range of tasty, home-produced drinking snacks.

The wine country continues south to Manciano, a former Sienese stronghold located on a commanding hilltop ledge overlooking the surrounding countryside in all directions. From Manciano it is an interesting excursion across to Pitigliano, once an important Etruscan centre, perched precariously on a high spur of tufa. This soft rock is riddled with ancient tombs and private wine cellars, while the town above still maintains its rather grim medieval aspect, with old, crumbling houses and alleyways. Tufa, of course, is a volcanic sub-soil much loved by the vine, and it is especially beneficial for the production of fine white wines. So it is not surprising to find that the Maremma's best white comes from this zone, Bianco di Pitigliano, a rather fresh, bracing example made from the traditional and most prevalent grape varieties of central Italy: Trebbiano Toscano (mainly), Malvasia, Verdello, and Grechetto. Indeed, virtually this same formula is utilized to great effect in the neighbouring vineyards of Orvieto in Umbria, and those of Lake Bolsena across the border in Latium.

From Pitigliano, continue through the carved-out gorge to visit nearby Sorano and Sovana. Sorano, like Cìvita di Bagnoreggio, is a small, high-perched medieval town whose soft tufa understructure has been under-

mined by land erosion, and which has consequently been gradually abandoned over the last decades. Yet its former strategic importance is recalled by
its imposing 12th-century castle and medieval fortifications. Sovana, like
Pitigliano an Etruscan centre, is today only a tiny village, but in the Middle
Ages it was the stronghold of the powerful Aldobrandeschi who dominated
the zone, and the birthplace of Pope Gregory VII. Just outside the town
there is a well-preserved Etruscan necropolis.

Alternatively, wine tourists at Saturnia may wish to return to Scansano,
then find the road south to Magliano in Toscana for further exploration of
the vineyards of Morellino di Scansano. Pereta is another fortified medieval
hill town located on a tongue of land extending over the valley, while
Magliano in Toscana, still surrounded by its fine set of medieval walls, was
an important Sienese township, laid out first by the Aldobrandeschi, then
completed by the Medici who later assumed power. Once an Etruscan settlement (there are important ruins nearby), today Magliano is perhaps most

*Hot springs
at Saturnia.*

famous for an ancient, gnarled olive tree, known as the '*olivo della strega*' or witches' olive under which pagan and magical rituals were once carried out. The tree, according to carbon dating, is some 3000 years old.

From Magliano, either continue back towards Grosseto, or else go down to explore the flatter coastal plains. Nearby Orbetello is a typical lagoon town, located on the narrow tongue of land separating the natural lagoons of Ponente and Levante, and the near-island of Monte Argentario. Located along the old Aurelian Way, Orbetello was settled by the Romans in 273 BC, but even earlier than this, it served as the Etruscans' principal coastal port, and remains from that period can still be seen under the waters of the lagoon below the modern breakwater. Today it is an area of considerable touristic interest (particularly the resort towns of Porto Ercole and Porto San Stefano) and a natural oasis for wildfowl and wildlife protected under the auspices of the Worldwide Fund for Nature.

This strange and rather isolated corner of Tuscany was once contested by France and Spain during the 16th century, with the latter ultimately emerging as victors. The Spaniards ruled under a military *Presidio*, and left behind their influences even after their departure in the early 18th century. For example, though viticulture was undoubtedly practised much earlier by both the Etruscans and Romans, the Spanish furthered the cultivation of the vine on the slopes of Monte Argentario, as well as on the hills of the mainland, and it was they who gave the name Parrina to the local wine, derived from the Spanish word '*parra*', signifying vines trained on *pergole*. The Alicante grape was also introduced into the zone, and is still used to produce a good local red wine.

The Parrina DOC today applies to white (mainly), red, and *rosato* wines produced on just a few private *aziende* located in this protected maritime oasis. The white is rather pleasing, produced from Trebbiano Toscano, Malvasia, and Ansonica, a variety that originated in Sicily. The best-known producer is the Fattoria La Parrina whose labels recall that this is the modern version of the ancient wine of the Etruscans.

Degustazione: Stop to Taste; Stop to Buy

1 CANTINA COOPERATIVA DEL
'MORELLINO DI SCANSANO'
LOC. SARAGLIOLO
58054 SCANSANO GR
TEL: 0564/507288

WINES PRODUCED: Morellino di Scansano, Morellino di Scansano Riserva; Bianco di Pitigliano; Seragiolo (*vino novello*); La Rasola

THE CENTRE

Moscato Giallo; San Bruzio Pinot Brut; *bianco e rosso da tavola*.
VISITS AND DIRECT SALES: Mon–Fri 8h30–12h30.
This modern, well-equipped *cantina*

cooperativa was founded in 1977 and is the source of good Morellino di Scansano, especially the Riserva aged in Slavonian oak.

---

2 ERIK BANTI VITICOLTORE
PIAZZA SOLFERINO 9
58050 MONTEMERANO GR
TEL: 0564/602778

WINES PRODUCED: Morellino di Scansano, Morellino di Scansano 'carato' (*barrique*-aged), Morellino di Scansano *cru* Aquilaia, Morellino di Scansano *cru* Ciabatta; Alicante; *grappa*.
VISITS: Mon-Sat, by appointment.
Erik Banti is one of the leading producers in the zone as well as one

of its most animated and energetic characters. His *barrique*-aged Morellino is particularly silky and elegant, while the *cru* wines also deserve attention. The best place to sample them is in the Antico Frantoio, the *enoteca-trattoria* that Erik has recently opened in the centre of this charming medieval town.
English, French, German, Danish spoken.

---

3 AZIENDA AGRICOLA LA STELLATA
VIA FORNACINA 18
58014 MANCIANO GR
TEL: 0564/620190

WINES PRODUCED: Bianco di Pitigliano 'Lunaia'; 'Il Doccio' *vino*

bianco da tavola.
VISITS: daily, telephone in advance.
Small highly-regarded farm producing distinctive white wines of character.
A little English spoken.

---

4 FATTORIA LE PUPILLE
LOC. PERETA
58051 MAGLIANO IN TOSCANA GR
(POSTAL ADDRESS: AUGUSTO GENTILI, VIA MAZZINI 112, 56100 PISA)
TEL: 0564/505129; 050/501980

WINES PRODUCED: Morellino di Scansano, Morellino di Scansano Riserva; 'Saffredi' (*vino da tavola*

principally from Cabernet Sauvignon).
VISITS: daily, 8–12h. Afternoons by appointment.
Pupille's outstanding Morellino di Scansano Riserva, vinified traditionally and aged in French oak *barriques*, is well-known in Britain and is one of the standard-

bearers for this little-known wine zone. The farm is located between Pereta and Magliano and has been in Augusto Gentili's family since the end of the last century. English, French spoken.

---

5 AZIENDA AGRARIA MANTELLASSI
    EZIO
LOC. BANDITACCIA 26
58051 MAGLIANO IN TOSCANA GR
TEL: 0564/592037

WINES PRODUCED: Morellino di Scansano, Morellino di Scansano Riserva; Vino Alicante; Vino Bianco di Pitigliano; Vino Spumante 'Nonna Beppina'; Vino Bianco Lucumone; *vino da tavola bianco*.
VISITS: daily, working hours. No appointment necessary.

Ezio Mantellassi and his 3 sons cultivate about 22 hectares of specialized vines utilizing organic precepts on their farm located about 4 km outside Magliano on the road to Scansano. Most of the production is Morellino di Scansano (a small proportion of which is aged with considerable success in small French *barriques*).
English spoken.

---

6 FATTORIA LA PARRINA
LOC. LA PARRINA
58010 ALBINIA GR
TEL: 0564/862636

WINES PRODUCED: Parrina Rosso, Parrina Bianco, Rosato di Albinia.

VISITS: daily, by appointment. About the only source for the wines of the minute, rarely encountered Parrina DOC.
English spoken.

Enoteca

1 ENOTECA BACCO E CERERE
58050 SATURNIA GR
TEL: 0564/601235

OPEN: 9–13h; 16–20h. Closed Tue. Repair to this welcoming *enoteca* in the centre of Saturnia after a dip in the hot cascades for a warming glass (or bottle) of Morellino di Scansano, accompanied by simple drinking snacks: locally-cured *prosciutto*, *pecorino*, vegetables preserved in olive oil. Good selection of wines for sale, as well as homemade preserves, vegetables, honey, oil, and other local products.

Ristoranti

1

ANTICO FRANTOIO
PIAZZA SOLFERINO 7
58050 MONTEMERANO GR
TEL: 0564/602615

Open evenings only (mid-day on holidays – telephone to check).
Closed Thur, Feb.
Wine producer Erik Banti has converted an old olive mill into a welcoming Tuscan *trattoria* and *enoteca* serving simple but well presented local foods: *crostini di polenta al tartufo bianco, acquacotta, maltagliati alla frantoiana, stracotto all'Alicante*. A small number of rooms are available for accommodation. Erik's wines can be purchased from the *enoteca*.
Moderate

2

TERME DI SATURNIA
58050 SATURNIA GR
TEL: 0564/601061

Open all year.
This super deluxe spa hotel has superb facilities in addition to the famous thermal baths. Come here to swim, then enjoy lunch in the excellent Villa Montepaldi Restaurant which serves good seafood, game, and produce and products from the Villa Montepaldi farm.
Hotel **Expensive**
Restaurant **Moderate**

3

RISTORANTE AURORA
VIA CHIASSO LAVAGNINI 14
58051 MAGLIANO IN TOSCANA GR
TEL: 0564/592030

Closed Wed in winter.
Just outside the medieval walls of this typical wine town, a good local *trattoria* serving specialities of the Maremma: *crostini bianchi, pappardelle con anatra, scottiglia d'agnello, tordi all'uva*.
Moderate

Wine and Other Related *Sagre* and *Feste*

late May	Mostra Mercato del Vino	Pontassieve
end May/June	Festa del Vino	Carmignano
end May/June	Mostra Mercato del Vino	Montespertoli
mid-June	Mostra Mercato del Vino	Vinci;
		Cerreto-Guidi
early July; mid-Aug	Palio	Siena

VINO SFUSO:
PURCHASING 'OPEN WINE'

Many who drink wine habitually in Italy as a beverage to accompany meals (and, it seems, who doesn't?) go direct to the *fattoria* or *azienda* to purchase it in bulk as *vino sfuso* or 'open wine', sold in large cane-covered *damigiane* of 54 litres or in smaller 25-litre containers. The wine is inexpensive, and it can be good or very good or absolutely awful: it is always, so the farmer insists, *'tutto genuino'*, that is, made without chemicals, additives, or other alchemy.

Of course, wine purchased in bulk must be transferred to smaller vessels once home, a 54-litre *damigiana* being just a little too heavy to place in the middle of the dining room table, even if amounts may be drawn from it in prodigious quantity. Country superstition deems that this should only be done when the moon is on the wane, a new moon apparently causing the wine to begin to re-ferment. Be that as it may, and whenever, the usual method is to siphon the wine into clean 1.5-, 2-, or 5-litre bottles. Since the wine is likely to be drunk soon, the bottles are not sealed even with anything so permanent as a crown cork (the type used on bottles of fizzy drinks). Rather, as in the days of the Romans, a thin layer of a special odourless oil known as *olio enologico* is simply poured into the top of each bottle, thus sealing it from oxygen, a twist of paper is put over the top to keep out insects, and the bottles are then stored standing upright. Prior to drinking, the oil is siphoned off, the remaining dregs tamped up with a bit of cotton wool, then the very last bit removed with a dextrous two-handed flick into the sink.

end August	Bravio delle Botti	Montepulciano
mid-Sept	Sagra dell'Uva	Pitigliano
mid-Sept	Mostra Mercato del Vino	Greve
	Chianti Classico	
last Sun in Sept	Festa dell'Uva	Scansano
late Sept/early Oct	'Bacco Artigiano'	Rufina
last Sunday in Oct	Sagra del Tordo	Montalcino
early Dec	Antica Fiera di Carmignano	Carmignano

E PER SAPERE DI PIÙ –
ADDITIONAL INFORMATION

Ente Provinciale per Il Turismo
di Firenze
via A. Manzoni 16
50121 Florence
tel: 055/2478141

Ente Provinciale per Il Turismo
di Siena
via di Città 5
53100 Siena
tel: 0577/47051

Ente Provinciale per Il Turismo
di Grosseto
via Monterosa 206
58100 Grosseto
tel: 0564/22534

Associazione Agriturist Toscana
Piazza S. Firenze 3
50122 Florence
tel: 055/287838
Write for useful handbook to
farms offering farmhouse
accommodation: *Ospitalità in
Campagna.*

Consorzio Gallo Nero
via de' Serragli 146
50124 Florence
tel: 055/229351

Consorzio Chianti Putto
Lungarno Corsini 4
50123 Florence
tel: 055/212333

Consorzii dei Vini di Montalcino
(Brunello e Rosso)
Palazzo Comunale
53024 Montalcino SI
tel: 0577/848246

UMBRIA

I Vini: THE WINES OF UMBRIA	330
La Gastronomia	332
Le Strade dei Vini: THE WINE ROADS OF UMBRIA	
Orvieto: Umbria's 'Liquid Gold'	334
Torgiano: *Il Mondo di Giorgio Lungarotti*	344
Montefalco: 'Sacramental' Wines on Umbria's Balcony	349
Le Sagre: WINE AND OTHER RELATED FESTIVALS	355
Additional Information	355

Orvieto's Duomo.

Umbria, the 'green heart of Italy', is usually over-shadowed by its more famous neighbour Tuscany to the north. Italy's only land-locked region is an altogether gentler, quieter, and less-visited land, but it has much to offer none the less. Rich in Etruscan and Roman remains, still starkly medieval with its collection of fine old hill towns – Orvieto, Gubbio, Spoleto, Assisi, Perugia and others – and the noted homeland of scores of important religious figures, notably Saint Francis, Saint Benedict and Saint Clare, Umbria today offers the visitor peace and tranquillity, and the chance to experience a slower pace of life in a rural countryside that is simply heavenly.

As throughout central Italy, there are few places where the vine does not grow. However, this is not a single-minded or wholly specialized region, and the land still is primarily made up of mixed farms that recall the days of self-sufficiency and the *mezzadria*. Orvieto's wines have been praised and enjoyed literally for centuries, while today, two relatively new regions are commanding most attention worldwide as the source of exciting wines: the Torgiano vineyards south of Perugia and, to a lesser degree, the vineyards of Montefalco south of Foligno. However, wherever the visitor in Umbria finds himself, it is unlikely that he will go thirsty.

THE CENTRE

ORIENTATION

Umbria, located between Tuscany and Latium along the Tiber valley west of the Apennines, comprises 2 provinces: Perugia and Terni. Perugia's S Egidio airport is at present for domestic flights only, but international connections to the region can be made from either Rome or Milan. The western part of the region is served by the Florence–Rome railway line, though only local trains stop at Orvieto. The Ancona–Rome railway line stops at Narni, Terni, Spoleto, Foligno (with connections to Perugia). By car, the A1 *Autostrada del Sole* extends through the region, with a spur motorway to Perugia, and an exit at Orvieto.
Map Touring Club Italiano 1: 200 000 Umbria & Marche.

I VINI: GLOSSARY TO THE WINES OF UMBRIA

Wines of *Denominazione di Origine Controllata (DOC)*

Colli Altotiberini DOC Delimited vineyard in the far north of the region, on slopes above the upper Tiber valley around Città di Castello for the production of red, white and rosé wines. Red is the most distinctive, produced from Sangiovese and Merlot with a minimum alcohol of 11.5 degrees.

Colli Perugini DOC Vineyards extending along the Tiber valley between Perugia and Todi for the production of red and rosé (both mainly from Sangiovese) and white (mainly Procanico) wines.

Colli del Trasimeno DOC Vast, sprawling vineyard that extends over the hills above Lake Trasimeno for the production of red and white wines. Red is produced from Sangiovese with Ciliegiolo, Gamay, Malvasia, and Trebbiano, and has a minimum alcohol of 11.5 degrees. White is from a blend of Procanico (mainly) with Malvasia, Verdicchio, Verdello, and Grechetto. Minimum alcohol 11 degrees.

Montefalco DOC Delimited vineyards around Montefalco and surrounding communes, producing 2 distinctive wines. Rosso di Montefalco, from Sangiovese, together with no more than 10% Sagrantino, as well as with smaller

THE ETRUSCANS

The exact origins of the Etruscans are lost in time, and it is unclear whether or not they were an indigenous people, or, as the Greek historian Herodotus claimed, they came to the Italian peninsula from Asia Minor. What is certain is that by 700 BC the Etruscans had risen to become the greatest civilization in central Italy, with an influence that extended throughout much of present-day Umbria, Latium, and Tuscany (the region to which they gave their name). They banded together in a confederation of independent and autonomous city-states (including Volsinii, Tarquinii, Caere, Vetulonia, Populonia, Veii, Rusellae, Chiusi, Cortona, Perugia, and Arezzo) and were clearly a complex and developed civilization, as the remains of sculpture, funerary objects, elaborate jewellery, beautiful and complex ceramic ware (notably the black *bucchero*) and other artefacts recovered from tombs testify. The Etruscans, moreover, cultivated the vine extensively throughout their dominions, and probably introduced into central Italy the practice of training vines up trees or other living supports as a means of freeing the land below for other crops. This ancient method of so-called promiscuous cultivation remains throughout the region even today.

amounts of Trebbiano Toscano, Malvasia, Merlot, Barbera, and Montepulciano, is a robust and full-bodied table wine of great potential. Sagrantino di Montefalco is even more distinctive: produced entirely from the Sagrantino grape, either vinified dry, or else made into a rare sweet *passito* wine by semi-drying the grapes as for the production of Recioto; minimum alcohol 14 degrees, minimum ageing 1 year.

Orvieto DOC Famous white wine from vineyards around Orvieto and surrounding communes, produced from Procanico, Verdello, Grechetto, Drupeggio, and Malvasia. Minimum alcohol 11.5 degrees. Wines labelled Orvieto Classico come from the historical heart of the wine zone.

Torgiano DOCG Delimited vineyard extending south of Perugia to the medieval town of Torgiano, and the source of Umbria's greatest wines (from the Lungarotti estate). Torgiano Bianco is produced from Trebbiano with a high proportion of the distinctive Grechetto; minimum alcohol 11.5 degrees. Torgiano Rosso is from

Sangiovese, Canaiolo, Ciliegiolo, and Montepulciano; minimum alcohol 12 degrees. Wines aged for at least 3 years may be labelled Riserva.

MUFFA NOBILE

Muffa nobile is the Italian name for a rare fungus (*Botrytis cinerea*), known to the French as *pourriture noble*, to the Germans as *Edelfäule*, and the prosaic English as 'noble rot'. In the Orvieto vineyard, these conditions occur in certain select pockets only, particularly around Lake Corbara, where in autumn early morning mists rising from the lake combine with hot, dry afternoons to encourage the formation of *Botrytis*. The fungus pierces the grapes' skin and extracts water content, causing natural sugar and flavours to be concentrated, glycerine content to be increased, and in the process imparting rare and intense flavours, bouquet, and texture. Such affected grapes may stay on the vine even as late as December and are harvested literally grape by grape. It is obviously not only hugely expensive to produce such wines, it is also extremely risky. Prolonged rain in winter can turn 'noble rot' into simple grey rot, and thus ruin the entire crop. And in Orvieto, not only is it necessary to frighten away hungry birds, there is also the further threat of *cinghiale* – wild boar – who are apparently quite partial to these unpromising-looking but extra-sweet grapes. Barberani's Calcaia, Decugnano dei Barbi's Pourriture Noble, and Antinori's Muffato della Sala demonstrate how great and unique such sweet wines can be.

LA GASTRONOMIA: FOODS OF UMBRIA

Italy's only land-locked region presents a cuisine that probably differs little from that served over the centuries, based on produce and products that every self-sufficient smallholding would always have on hand: fresh garden vegetables, extra virgin olive oil, wild *funghi* and greens, home-cured meats and *salame*, and of course game such as hare, wood pigeon, songbirds, wild boar – whatever is available. This is fertile, verdant, rich land, still locked in its rural traditions, but it demonstrates the sheer bounty and generosity of Italy. Even that most sophisticated, most expensive foodstuff of all, the truffle (both black and white), is found in abundance in the region and used liberally in both humble *trattorie* and grand *ristoranti* alike.

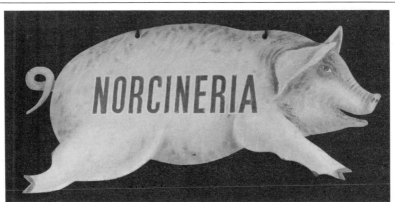

Norcineria.

NORCINERIE:
THE PORK BUTCHERS OF NORCIA

Umbria is famous not only for its tasty black pigs that feed on a diet of acorns and black truffles, but also for the particular expertise of its pork butchers, especially those from Norcia, where the age-old traditional art of utilizing virtually everything from the pig (except its squeak) is still carried out to great effect for the production of scores of different types of *salame, prosciutto crudo e cotto*, fresh spicy *salsicce* for grilling, little sausages preserved in olive oil, and much else. So successful and renowned are the pork butchers of Norcia, that many have left their home province to set up shops throughout Italy and the world: the word *norcineria* has now come to denote a pork butcher's shop anywhere in Italy.

PIATTI TIPICI:
REGIONAL SPECIALITIES

Umbrici Large, handmade noodles, usually served with garlic and oil sauce.

Stringozzi Thin homemade noodles, often served with wild mushrooms or truffles.

Salame di cinghiale Wild boar *salame*.

Zuppa di lenticchie Lentil soup.

Palomba Wood pigeon.

Fagiano Pheasant.

Porchetta Umbrian fast food: suckling pig stuffed with garlic, pepper and herbs, and spit-roasted – usually purchased from street or market stalls stuffed in rolls.

Scottadito Means literally 'burn fingers' – baby lamb chops (sometimes kid) grilled over a wood fire, to be picked up and eaten with the fingers.

Tartufato; alla norcina Truffled; served with black truffles.

Cheese: *Pecorino* Sheep's milk cheese, either fresh and mild or aged and sharp.

ORVIETO: UMBRIA'S 'LIQUID GOLD'

In Brief: Orvieto is located just off the main A1 *Autostrada del Sole*, and can therefore most conveniently be visited either in its own right as part of a tour of Tuscany and Umbria, or on the way to Rome and the south. Indeed, located on the main north-south railway line, it is even within reach of Rome or Florence for a day trip.

The wine country of the classic zone extends west around the nearby artificial Lake Corbara as well as to the north of Orvieto. There is not as yet a signposted *strada del vino* but the Consorzio Tutela Vino Orvieto Classico plans to initiate this project shortly. There are, however, a number of welcoming producers who can be visited. Orvieto itself is worthy of exploration, and has no shortage of hotels, good restaurants, and opportunities for farmhouse tourism.

The tufa mesa upon which Orvieto is built rises sheer above the valley floor, topped by its magnificent Duomo. This tufa outcrop resulted from volcanic activity in past millennia which left not only a remarkable geological formation, but also a mineral-rich tufa and balsatic terrain that from time immemorial has been a propitious habitat for the vine.

The site of Orvieto was almost certainly inhabited by Iron and Bronze Age settlers. But it was the Etruscans who developed the city, known to them probably as Volsinii, into one of the principal centres of the Etruscan Confederation. In the 3rd century BC, the Romans, who had successfully

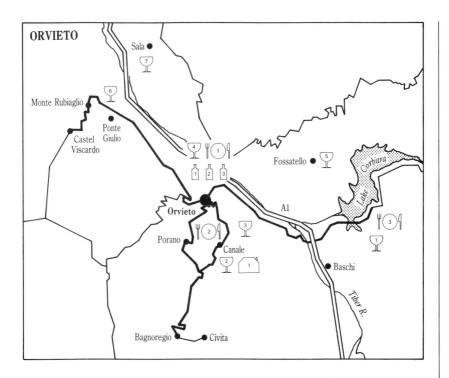

been subduing this highly developed civilization, finally entered the city and took it with minimal resistance. Some of the local inhabitants left to found the new settlement of Volsini Novi (present-day Bolsena) south on the shores of Lake Bolsena. The Romans called the old city 'Urbs Vetis', and perhaps the name of Orvieto is derived from this. Under the conquerors, the city continued to prosper as an important trading centre on the principal route from Rome to the north.

The Etruscans cultivated the vine extensively in Etruria, and were well-versed in the production of wine. Archaeological evidence in Orvieto indicates, furthermore, that they tunnelled into the soft tufa by hand to create ingeniously practical wine *cantine* on 3 floors. They brought the harvested grapes from the outlying vineyards up to the town, and pressed them on the floor closest to ground level. The *mosto* then ran down stone channels by gravity to the second floor where it fermented in earthenware vessels. Finally, the wine, when finished, was transferred again by gravity to the third, lowest floor, which enjoyed a cool, constant temperature that was ideal for the conservation of wine. The Romans continued this practice, and the well-made wines of Orvieto enjoyed considerable renown, and were traded extensively via the river port of Palianum (numerous Roman amphorae have recently been discovered there).

Indeed, it can be fairly said that it was the natural tufa habitat which led to the centuries-old fame of the wine of Orvieto. Not only does this volcanic soil continue today to nourish the vines and provide a particularly fertile microclimate for the cultivation of the grape; from ancient times right up until the most recent decades, when the scientific technologies of oenology were still little known, the cool tufa caves provided an almost perfect natural wine making environment. In the cool, moist atmosphere fermentation proceeded at a slow, steady rate, resulting in fragrant white wines that were probably far superior to those produced elsewhere at the time. Since the temperature remained at an even, low temperature (between 11° and 14° Centigrade winter and summer), moreover, the fermentation often ceased naturally, and the wines retained a slight residual sweetness that was – and is – most delicious.

It is interesting to note that today in wineries up and down the peninsula, the greatest development in the production of quality white wines lies in the control of fermentation by maintaining low temperatures to preserve above all fruit and aroma. To achieve this end, the use of expensive refrigeration equipment and computer controlled stainless steel fermentation vessels may be necessary: yet virtually the same conditions can be achieved naturally (if less conveniently) in the cool tufa caves of Orvieto.

If it is true that in the past the white wines made in such cool caves were far superior to those produced elsewhere, it is also indisputable that they were best enjoyed in the locality where they were produced. The problem, of course, was that the wines of Orvieto often retained that certain residual sweetness, so, once removed from their stable subterranean environment, they had the propensity to referment. Modern refrigeration and filtration equipment have on the best estates replaced pasteurization (which unarguably alters the character of wine) as a means of rendering such wines stable for export. But even today, they still taste best on the spot.

In medieval times Orvieto's fame resulted primarily from its role as the occasional residence of various popes, who either retired to the town in summer, or else retreated there when the Vatican was under threat of siege. As at Châteauneuf-du-Pape in the French Rhône valley, papal patronage ensured fame and popularity for the local tipple, and Orvieto's wine naturally benefited as a result.

So valued was Orvieto's 'liquid gold' in times past that artists even stipulated it in their contracts. Luca Signorelli, for example, who completed the magnificent collection of frescoes in the Capella Nuova of the Duomo, insisted that he be given as much Orvieto wine as he wanted. Pinturcchio, on the other hand, was sacked for 'consuming too much gold, too much blue, and too much wine'.

Today, Orvieto Classico continues to be produced by traditional methods in its historic zone of production. The permitted grape varieties are Trebbiano Toscano (known locally as Procanico), Verdello, Grechetto, Drupeggio, and Malvasia. In practice, quality-conscious producers in the classic zone tend to rely less heavily on the rather bland if prolific Procanico, and instead are increasing the percentage of the low-yielding but distinctive Grechetto, which elsewhere in Umbria makes outstanding varietal wines. The Consorzio is also, we understand, considering the possibility of introducing Chardonnay into the permitted *uvaggio*.

The greater proportion of Orvieto produced today is *secco*. The best, especially wines that benefit from rigorous selection or which are produced from superior *cru* vineyards, are characterized foremost by a full but easy equilibrium, a harmony of scent, flavour, and alcohol that makes Orvieto a wine that you can enjoy again and again without it ever cloying. The *amabile* wines, to my way of thinking, are often even more attractive, usually only slightly sweet, and delicious as an *aperitivo*, or simply in mid-afternoon at an outdoor table in the Piazza del Duomo.

The town of Orvieto itself remains today an atmospheric medieval hill town completely dominated by its splendid Duomo. Begun in the late 13th century, construction of the cathedral continued over a further 300 years. It is most notable for its magnificent façade, credited to Lorenzo Maitani, depicting in sculpted bas-relief scenes from the Old and New Testaments. The exterior mosaics, particularly in late afternoon when the setting sun highlights the façade, are most striking. The Duomo was constructed to commemorate the Miracle of Bolsena; the precious relic is housed in the Capella del Corporale, decorated with frescoes mainly by the Orvietan master Ugolino di Prete. The Capella Nuova, however, is the Duomo's most famous and stunning centrepiece, containing a breathtaking cycle of frescoes by Fra Angelico and Signorelli.

Other sites of interest in Orvieto include the Pozzo di San Patrizio, a remarkable and immense well commissioned by Pope Clement VII to safeguard the city against siege; the medieval quarter; the Palazzo del Capitano which is currently being restored from its state of dilapidation (Orvieto's colourful market takes place in the square here every Saturday); the

THE CENTRE

National Etruscan Archaeological Museum; and, below the town, the Etruscan necropolis.

A tour of Orvieto's vineyards can be undertaken from virtually any road leaving the city. Orvieto Scalo is the home of the zone's largest and most important co-operative, CO.VI.O. The road to Lake Corbara leads to the ultra-modern winery of Barberani, which is open for visits without appointment. From Lake Corbara, it is but a short drive to the lovely fortified hill town of Todi.

Leaving Orvieto by way of the road to Bagnoregio leads past a ruined 12th-century Benedictine abbey (now tastefully restored as a luxury hotel) to Le Velette, the immense, private wine estate of the Bottai family, with over 100 hectares of specialized vineyards. The estate is located along an ancient Roman road that linked Orvieto to Bolsena, and it enjoys particularly splendid views overlooking Orvieto itself. From Le Velette, continue on through Bagnoregio to visit the weird, ruined, near ghost town of Cìvita, then return to Orvieto by way of Porano where there is a painted Etruscan tomb. The views of Orvieto, especially at Sette Camini, are stunning.

As is the case throughout Umbria, the Orvieto wine zone is not wholly intensive or single-minded: vines are grown alongside grain, olives, sunflowers, tobacco, as well as meadows for animals. This is a carry-over from old methods of self-sufficient farming, when every smallholding had to produce everything for itself, essentials such as wine, oil, bread, vegetables and meat. Perhaps as a result, the land is gentler, more pleasing to the eye than many intensively cultivated wine zones. To the north of Orvieto, the wine roads lead to hamlets such as Ponte Giulio where the extensive cellars of Luigi Bigi can be visited, to Castel Viscardo, and to Monte Rubiaglio. Beyond, at the far north of the Orvieto Classico zone, the Castello della Sala is owned by the famous Tuscan Antinori family who produce not only fine Orvieto Classico, but a range of superlative white wines that are among the most exciting in the country.

Domenica Muzi.

CÌVITA DI BAGNOREGIO

Cìvita is a town that has been dying since the mid-17th century when an earthquake obliterated much of the land around it, turning it into a virtual island above a canyon. Then, after World War II, the Germans blew up the old bridge connecting it to the 'mainland', and the process was further accelerated as the pinnacle of tufa upon which it precariously sits has gradually begun to crumble away. Earlier this century there were still some 650 people living here; at the time of writing there are only 25 original inhabitants left. Most of them, in their late 60s, 70s, or older, pass the time talking to the tourists who cross over the footbridge that connects this bizarre time capsule with Bagnoregio. The people of Cìvita in the past lived off the land, but tending the steep, schistous terrain has little appeal for today's young. 'It is backbreaking labour,' explained Domenica Muzi, who tends her vineyards below Cìvita with the help of her mule, Lisa. 'The young people today won't do it.' Each year she harvests her grapes, and with the help of Lisa carries them back up to Cìvita where she makes wine in a remarkable three-storey *cantina*, hollowed out of the soft tufa. The *cantina*, located beside the church, dates back to the 3rd century AD, she told us. Domenica sells her wine to the visitors who make their way here. The wine, fermented in small wooden barrels or in *damigiane*, is a delicious tonic after the long climb up the narrow footbridge: appley-tart, albeit oxidized, served cave-cool in stout tumblers to the music of braying mules and donkeys.

THE CENTRE

Degustazione: **Stop to Taste; Stop to Buy**

1

BARBERANI
AZIENDA AGRICOLA VALLESANTA
LOC. CERRETO
BASCHI
05018 ORVIETO TR
(ADMINISTRATION: VIA ALBANI 14,
  ORVIETO)
TEL: 0763/41820; 0744/950113

WINES PRODUCED: Orvieto Classico *secco* and *amabile*, Orvieto Classico *cru* 'Castagnolo' (*secco*), Orvieto Classico *cru* 'Pulicchio' (*amabile*), Orvieto Classico 'Calcaia' (*muffa nobile*); Pomaio (Sauvignon/Semillon/Grechetto fermented in *barrique*); Lago di Corbara (Sangiovese/Barbera/Cabernet Franc); Foresco (Cabernet/Sangiovese).
VISITS: Mon–Fri, working hours without appointment.
The Barberani family produces an outstanding range of Orvietos entirely from grapes grown in their own vineyards. The old cellars used to be located in the historic centre of Orvieto itself, but the new, ultra-modern winery was built above the shores of Lake Corbara in 1986. If not as picturesque as the old, hand-dug tufa caves, here the wines are produced utilizing the most modern temperature-controlled technology. Select *cru* wines are outstanding, including the rare 'Calcaia' produced from grapes affected by *muffa nobile*.

For those who don't have time to visit the winery, the Barberani have a direct sales outlet opposite the Duomo (Cantina Barberani, via Maitani 1, open 9–19h30 including Sundays and holidays).
English, French spoken.

2

AZIENDA AGRICOLA LA CACCIATA
LOC. LA CACCIATA 6
FRAZIONE CANALE
05010 ORVIETO TR
TEL: 0763/90192; 92881

WINES PRODUCED: Orvieto Classico; Rosso della Cacciata; *rosato da tavola*; *vino spumante*.

VISITS: daily, by appointment.
Avv. Belcapo produces traditional wines of Orvieto at La Cacciata as well as fine estate olive oil. La Cacciata is also run as a most welcoming *azienda agrituristica*.
Some English, French, German spoken.

3

TENUTA LE VELETTE
LOC. LE VELETTE
05010 ORVIETO TR
TEL: 0763/29090

WINES PRODUCED: Orvieto Classico *secco* and *amabile*; *rosso da tavola*.
VISITS: Mon–Sat by appointment.

The Bottai family have been at Le Velette since 1850, but grapes have been grown on the estate for 1000 years at least (there was an ancient monastery located here, and the monks dug out part of the extensive *antica cantina* underneath the villa). Today this vast estate produces the classic wines of the zone. Experimentation in the vineyard (clonal selection, methods of training, and plantation of grape varieties such as Riesling and Chardonnay under the auspices of the local wine *consorzio*) as well as in the cellar (use of *barriques* for ageing), demonstrate that this is a forward-looking estate. English spoken.

---

4 COOPERATIVA VITIVINICOLA CO.VI.O.
VIALE 1 MAGGIO 75
05010 ORVIETO STAZIONE TR
TEL: 0763/90296

WINES PRODUCED: Orvieto Classico (*secco*, *amabile*, and *muffa nobile*).

VISITS: Mon–Thur (except during the *vendemmia*) 9–12h; 15–17h. The region's largest *cantina cooperativa* produces a good range of wines. Come here to taste and purchase them direct.

---

5 AZIENDA AGRICOLA DECUGNANO DEI BARBI
LOC. FOSSATELLO DI CORBARA
05019 ORVIETO TR
TEL: 0763/24055

WINES PRODUCED: Orvieto Classico, Orvieto Pourriture Noble.
VISITS: daily except weekends and holidays 8–12h; 14–18h. Appointment necessary.
An outstanding estate producing wines of character and *tipicità*.

---

6 CASA VINICOLA LUIGI BIGI
LOC. PONTE GIULIO
05018 ORVIETO TR
TEL: 0763/26224

WINES PRODUCED: Orvieto Classico, Orvieto Classico *cru* Torricella, Orvieto Classico *cru* Vigneto Orzalume; Marrano (Grechetto fermented in *barrique*).
VISITS: Mon–Thur (excluding the *vendemmia*) 8–12h; 13–17h.
Bigi is one of the largest wineries in the Orvieto zone, and forms part of the Swiss-owned Gruppo Italiano Vini (GIV). However, it has a high reputation for quality wines, especially the *cru* wines produced from greater selection which demonstrate how fine a wine Orvieto Classico can be.

THE CENTRE

7 AZ AGRARIA M.SI L. & P. ANTINORI
CASTELLO DELLA SALA,
LOC. SALA
05016 FICULLE TR
TEL: 0763/86051

WINES PRODUCED: Orvieto Classico *secco* and *abbocato*; Cervaro della Sala; Borro della Sala; Muffato della Sala.

VISITS: daily, by appointment (telephone the above number or else Antinori's public relations office in Florence: 055/298298). The Castello della Sala, a 14th-century castle built by the infamous Monaldeschi family, today forms part of the great Antinori collection of estates and is the centre above all for the production of white wines of the highest quality. Both styles of Antinori's Orvietos are excellent examples of the *denominazione*, but the greatest wines are produced outside DOC regulations: Cervaro della Sala, from Grechetto and Chardonnay fermented in new oak *barriques* on the lees; Borro della Sala from Procanico and Sauvignon Blanc; and Muffato della Sala, a remarkable late-harvest wine made from Semillon, Sauvignon, Grechetto, Riesling and other grapes affected by *Botrytis cinerea*. English spoken.

Enoteche

1 CANTINA FORESI
PIAZZA DEL DUOMO 2
05018 ORVIETO TR

Closed Tue in winter; Jan. This little *enoteca* has outdoor tables overlooking the cathedral where you can enjoy the Foresi family's own Orvieto – *secco*, *amabile*, or *spaccato* ('half and half') – by the glass or bottle, together with simple drinking snacks (home-produced *salame*, *prosciutto* and *pecorino* cheese).

Cantina Foresi, Orvieto.

bove: The fishing quay at Gallipoli

elow: Mediterranean seafood, the
iet of the south

ight: The *fortezza*, Montalcino

Left: Villa Reale 'La Ferdinanda', Artimino

Below: The *'vinsanteria'* at the Frescobaldi Pomino estate

Below: Barili – the old measuring
containers of the *mezzadria*

Right: Sagrantino grapes laid out to dry
for the production of Paolo Bea's rare
Sagrantino di Montefalco *passito*

Foot: Orvieto

Main picture: Urbino

Inset: The Orvieto Duomo

Above: Vineyards of the Colli Lanuvini, south of Rome

Left: Trulli and vineyards near Alberobello

Below: Nemi, in the Colli Albani, is famous for its exquisite wild strawberries

Above: Sun-dried tomatoes, a speciality
of the Mezzogiorno

Right: Lecce

Below: The Palestra, Pompeii

Left: The Greek Doric temple at Metaponto, Basilicata

Above: The bare landscape of Basilicata

Below: Sicilian landscape near Alcamo

2 ENOTECA 'VINO VINO'
VIA LOGGIA DEI MERCANTI 21
05018 ORVIETO TR

OPEN: 9h30–13h; 16–20h. Closed
Tue.

Extensive selection of all the best
Orvietos, including *cru* and *muffa
nobile* wines together with a
selection of wines from elsewhere in
Italy.

---

3 ENOTECA LA LOGGIA
VIA LOGGIA DE' MERCANTI 6
05018 ORVIETO TR
TEL: 0763/44371

OPEN: daily except Wed afternoon
10–13h15; 16–20h30.
Small *enoteca* with selection of
mainly white wines not just from

Orvieto and Umbria (Barberani
and Lungarotti), but also from
throughout the country. The most
remarkable purchases, however,
are the fruit preserves, handmade
by Laura Punzi in the minuscule
adjoining kitchen.

Ristoranti

1 RISTORANTE 'COCCO'
VIA GARIBALDI 4
05018 ORVIETO TR
TEL: 0763/42319

Closed Fri.
Simple family *trattoria* beside the

Palazzo Comunale serving *cucina
casalinga: tortellini alla certosina,
risotto alla norcina, bistecca alla
Cocco*.
Inexpensive to Moderate

---

2 HOTEL-RISTORANTE LA BADIA
LOC. LA BADIA
05019 ORVIETO TR
TEL: 0763/90276

Remarkable hotel-restaurant
converted from 12th-century
Benedictine monastery, located
about 5 km south of Orvieto.
Moderate to Expensive

---

3 VISSANI
LOC. CIVITELLA DEL LAGO
BASCHI
05018 ORVIETO TR
TEL: 0744/950396

Closed Wed.

Famous temple of *cucina novella*,
acclaimed by some as one of the
greatest restaurants in Italy.
Located beside Lake Corbara, not
far from the Barberani winery.
Very Expensive

THE CENTRE

Punto di Ristoro Agristuristico

1 AZIENDA AGRICOLA LA CACCIATA
(address above)

The Belcapo family run one of the most welcoming *azienda agrituristica* that we have visited. Apartments and rooms (all with private facilities) available for letting, and meals served either in the rural *trattoria* or with the family around their own dining table. The farm is also a centre for horse riding.

Inexpensive

The Belcapo family.

TORGIANO: *IL MONDO DI GIORGIO LUNGAROTTI*

In Brief: Torgiano, located just 10 km south of Perugia and 15 km south of Assisi, gives its name to a small but prestigious vineyard. There is only one major producer, but none the less the zone provides all the elements for a successful and enjoyable wine excursion: visits to the impressive cellars of Cantine Lungarotti, a superb and informative wine museum that is one of the best in Italy if not Europe, the adjoining Osteria del Museo where the superlative range of Lungarotti wines can be tasted and purchased, and finally an outstanding and elegant hotel-restaurant, Le Tre Vaselle. Easily visited either from Perugia or nearby Assisi, Torgiano can itself serve as a base for further exploration of Umbria.

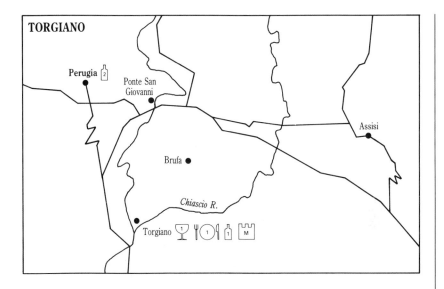

Torgiano, today a small wine town located on an elevated tongue of land at the confluence of the Tiber and Chiascìo rivers, was originally a fortified medieval settlement built on the remains of a Roman settlement destroyed by the Goths in the 6th century. It was an important strategic post not only because it commanded the Perugian territories up to the plain of Assisi, but because the rich and fertile lands provided agricultural produce and products for the nearby cities.

Wine, of course, has always been one of those principal products. Excavations have revealed numerous fragments of amphorae, pitchers, wine making utensils, stone tanks and tubs dating from Roman times and earlier, indicating the long and continuous practice of viticulture in this select vineyard. However, as elsewhere throughout central Italy, the zone of Torgiano was cultivated from medieval times up until the decades after World War II in the mixed, promiscuous fashion which still exists today in many parts of Umbria as well as Tuscany.

In the decades after World War II, Giorgio Lungarotti undertook the not inconsiderable task of changing centuries of agricultural practice through the plantation of specialized viticulture. This, combined with the most modern wine making technology, has created what must now be regarded as one of the great wine zones of Italy; indeed, through his virtually single-handed efforts, the zone was rewarded with elevation to DOC status in 1968, and in 1989 to select DOCG status.

THE CENTRE

CASTAGNE E MOSTO: CHESTNUTS AND STILL-FERMENTING WINE

In autumn, after the season of *funghi* comes the time for gathering chestnuts. In mid-October everybody is out at weekends, rummaging through the woods amongst the fallen leaves, collecting sacks and bags full of bright shiny *castagne*.

These are invariably taken home, slit with a knife, and roasted over an open fire in the special long-handled *padella* with holes in it. The chestnuts, once done, are placed in a serviette or cloth, sprinkled with a little wine, then wrapped up quickly, crunched together and left to soften for a few minutes.

Roasted chestnuts are traditionally eaten together with the new year's still-fermenting young wine. If you are visiting a wine producer, he will simply go down into the cellar and draw off a jug or two of *mosto*. This still-frothing, cloudy and sweet, partially-fermented wine is delicious with the soft, creamy, always slightly burnt chestnuts. It tastes of the old year washed down by the new yet to come.

The delimited wine zone of Torgiano extends south from the outskirts of Perugia, at Ponte San Giovanni through Brufa (the former medieval walled village of Castel Grifone) to below Torgiano itself. While there are some small growers producing wine mainly for their own use, to all intents and purposes, commercial production is entirely in the able hands of the Lungarotti family.

The success of the zone is firmly based on two wines, both of which bear the Torgiano DOC: red Rubesco and white Torre di Giano. These are wines that are entirely typical of Umbria, produced from grapes native to the zone. The former is mainly a blend of Sangiovese with some Canaiolo (the classic basis for Chianti), together with smaller amounts of Ciliegiolo and Montepulciano. The latter is made from Trebbiano and Grechetto (two principal components of, for example, Orvieto). Yet, on this prestigious terrain, and in particular on select vineyards such as Monticchio for Rubesco and Il Pino for Torre di Giano, the wines display a character, elegance, and incredible depth of flavour and complexity that is unique to the zone. They are true, individual expressions of their particular habitat and must rank alongside the greatest wines of Italy.

Such is the potential of this as yet under-developed wine zone that the

THE *BANCO D'ASSAGGIO*

The *Banco d'Assaggio*, one of the most important annual wine events in Italy, takes place each year in Torgiano. Conceived and initiated originally by Giorgio Lungarotti in 1980, it has established itself as one of the most important national tastings of Italian wine and is now jointly administered by various public bodies. The judges comprise wine technicians, oenologists, and wine journalists from throughout the world, thus ensuring not only that international tastes are represented, but also that the results of the *Banco d'Assaggio* receive widescale publicity. The samples of wine – some 700–800 – are all tasted anonymously: a notary assigns to each bottle a code that only he knows. The wines are then grouped together by broad categories (red DOC wines, *metodo champenois* sparkling wines, white table wines, etc) and they are tasted by two separate commissions. It is a particularly severe test and, after no less than 5 days of critical examination, 5 wines eventually emerge as top of each category, a significant and noteworthy achievement for the winners.

Lungarotti team has also demonstrated how successfully international grape varieties can thrive on this rich, mainly sandstone and limestone ridge. Indeed, varietal wines produced from Cabernet Sauvignon (Cabernet di Miralduolo), Chardonnay (Chardonnay di Miralduolo, Chardonnay Vigna I Palazzi), and Pinot Grigio are worthy of comparison with the best from France and the New World. San Giorgio is a sleek super-*vino da tavola* produced from Sangiovese and Cabernet Sauvignon aged in new French *barrique*. The winery even produces a sparkling wine that is one of the best in Italy, Lungarotti Brut, made from Chardonnay (90%) and Pinot Noir (10%) by the classic *metodo champenois*.

Torgiano itself is a small and intimate wine town. Parts of the 13th-century town fortifications remain, as well as an isolated guard tower, built from the local yellow sandstone. On a clear day, the views from the guard tower across the wide plain to Assisi are remarkable. Torgiano's relative prosperity in the past is further indicated by the baroque mansions that line its streets, such as that of Graziani-Baglioni, which dates from 1696 and today houses the Lungarotti's important Museo del Vino. For those who would like a closer examination of the vineyards there is a hillside path from Torgiano which leads into the heart of them.

THE CENTRE

Degustazione: **Stop to Taste; Stop to Buy**

1 CANTINE LUNGAROTTI
06089 TORGIANO PG
TEL: 075/982348

WINES PRODUCED: Rubesco, Rubesco Riserva *cru* Monticchio; Torre di Giano, Torre di Giano Riserva *cru* Il Pino; Chardonnay; Pinot Grigio; Cabernet Sauvignon; San Giorgio; Castel Grifone; Spumante Champenois; Vin Santo; *grappe*.
VISITS: Mon–Fri 8–13h; 15–18h. Appointment preferable.

Umbria's leading wine estate is well known internationally through the fame and excellence of wines such as Rubesco and Torre di Giano. The estate, though enormous, is still under family control, and traditional methods continue alongside the most modern technology.

It is worth visiting the Lungarotti cellar both to learn about the impressive range of wines and also about the history of viticulture at the important Museo del Vino. Moreover, though the range of Lungarotti wines is well-known internationally, the special *cru* wines are made in minute quantities, and thus are not usually encountered elsewhere. Come to the Osteria del Museo to taste them by the glass as well as to purchase them direct.

English, French, German spoken.

MUSEO DEL VINO

MUSEO DEL VINO
PALAZZO BAGLIONI
06089 TORGIANO PG

OPEN: 9–13h; 15–19h.

The Lungarotti *Museo del Vino* is one of the most important in the country, with some 20 rooms of archaeological, historical, artistic, folkloric and technical displays relating to wine and viticulture. This is not simply a collection of barrels and old farming tools, but a serious attempt to place wine within its broader historical and cultural context.

Enoteche

1 OSTERIA DEL MUSEO
PALAZZO BAGLIONI
06089 TORGIANO PG

OPEN: same hours as the *Museo del Vino*.

The full range of Lungarotti wines can be tasted and purchased in the *osteria* adjoining the wine museum.

2 ENOTECA PROVINCIALE
VIA ULISSE ROCCHI 18
06100 PERUGIA
TEL: 075/24824

OPEN: Tue–Sat 9h30–13h30;
16–20h; Sun 9h30–13h30.
Located behind the cathedral in the
historic centre of Perugia, this

important regional *enoteca* offers
tastings and direct sales of wines
from throughout Umbria. Small
snacks – *bruschetta, tartine con
tartufo*, cheeses – are served
together with wines by the glass.
English spoken.

Ristorante

1 RISTORANTE-ALBERGO LE TRE
VASELLE
VIA GIUSEPPE GARIBALDI 48
06089 TORGIANO PG
TEL: 075/982447

Outstanding luxury hotel-
restaurant tastefully restored
from an ancient *palazzo* in the
centre of the old village. The
elegant restaurant serves both

traditional and regional foods, as
well as *cucina creativa: fettucine
rosa con salsa basilico e pecorino,
pappardelle al tartufo nero, filetto di
manzo con salsa Rubesco*,
accompanied by a full selection of
Lungarotti wines (including old
vintages), as well as the best from
other parts of Italy.
Expensive

MONTEFALCO: 'SACRAMENTAL' WINES ON UMBRIA'S BALCONY

In Brief: Montefalco is a small, still relatively unknown wine zone
centred on the eponymous hill town and its surrounding *frazioni*, located
12 km south of Foligno. The small town itself, known as the *'Ringhiera
dell'Umbria'*, deserves to be visited in its own right, not only for its
extensive views of the surrounding countryside, but also for the San
Francesco church, which contains a remarkable collection of frescoes
and paintings. As a wine zone, moreover, Montefalco is an ancient vineyard which in the last decade has seen considerable reinvestment, and
which can rightly now be regarded as one of the most important in
Umbria.

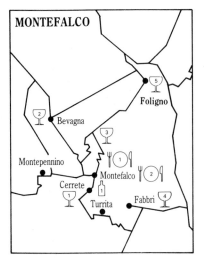

The roads that lead into central Umbria are not overly steep, but the climb up to the lower slopes of the Apennines is a steady one. By Montefalco, we have arrived at a uniquely strategic point along the old Roman Via Flaminia which once linked the Tyrrhenian and Adriatic seas. From the top of the bell-tower above the old Palazzo Comunale (take care when climbing the rickety wooden staircase, for the bell sounds every quarter of an hour) the views over the surrounding countryside are astounding, especially in early morning when an eerie mist hangs over the lower valleys stretching across to Foligno, Assisi, and Perugia. Montefalco is known as the *'Ringhiera dell'Umbria'*, Umbria's balcony, because of its commanding, lofty position and the extensive views that it affords.

During the Middle Ages, this strategic position was the natural site for a fortified castle, called Il Coccorone, which served as a refuge for the people of the surrounding countryside during the barbarian invasions. The town took its present name in the mid-13th century and became an important political, artistic, and spiritual centre, and the home of the Papal Rector, Jean d'Amiel. Lorenzo Maitani, later the architect of Orvieto's magnificent Duomo, was commissioned by the Vatican to strengthen and rebuild the town walls, which remain intact today, and the small community's churches were decorated with magnificent collections of frescoes. That of San Francesco, today a museum, is particularly worthy of a visit, containing Gozzoli's Life of Saint Francis, as well as works by Perugino, Tiberio d'Assisi, and the local Francesco Melanzio.

It is probable that the vine has been cultivated in and around Montefalco since the earliest times. The wines were cited by Pliny in AD 50, and documented thoroughly during the Middle Ages when they were produced not only by religious orders, but also on large feudal estates such as that at Fabbri. But even up to the very recent past, the wines of Montefalco, though uniquely traditional, were known and drunk locally only. However, the granting of DOC status for Rosso di Montefalco and Sagrantino di Montefalco in 1980 has brought enormous investment into the region, and the wines now produced in this tiny zone are among the best that Umbria has to offer. Indeed, it would not be going too far to state that these wines will not only become better known internationally, they may also come to be considered among the great red wines of Italy.

Sagrantino is certainly the most distinctive. This indigenous, low-yielding grape variety is found nowhere else but in this zone, and it is capable of producing red wine of the highest quality. Though it has apparently been cultivated here for centuries, the origin of the name is unclear, though it is thought that it may be a corruption of Sacramentino, indicating a wine that was used for sacramental purposes. Today, two types of wine are produced, Sagrantino *secco*, a robust, well-structured dry table wine with a persistent bouquet of blackberries, and Sagrantino *passito*, a rare, unique sweet *vino da meditazione* made from partially dried Sagrantino grapes in a style similar to Recioto della Valpolicella.

Of course, this being Italy, the granting of DOC was not welcomed universally as a harbinger of better things. Older folks inevitably say that it has led to a diminishing of character in the wines, as some of the new larger firms have planted new vineyards along the flatter plains towards Bevagna. In truth, the wines of the zone have picked themselves up from obscurity and have moved with the times. If that means there has been an evolution of sorts, so be it. At least it means that the rest of us are now able to enjoy these most interesting and exciting wines.

Paolo Bea is typical of the small-scale farmers who have always grown grapes and produced wines in the region. Indeed the Bea family have historical documents tracing the family as *viticoltori* as far back as 1700. Today, he works just 1 ½ hectares of specialized vineyards to produce wines of the highest quality. To Bea, the granting of DOC status to the zone has, if anything, debased the historical patrimony of the wines of Montefalco. For the Sagrantino, says Bea, was in the past only ever produced in its sweet *passito* form; the Sagrantino *secco*, he feels, is a modern invention which enables the incomers to produce this famous wine far more easily than by the laborious traditional methods.

Indeed, it is a wonderful privilege to witness how this rare wine is made at the Antica Azienda Paolo Bea. The Sagrantino grapes destined for the *passito* wine (it is only made in the best years) are left on the vine until as late as November. At that time, they are hand-harvested only by Bea, his wife, and son Giampiero (architect of the commune). In this way the family are able to maintain the most rigorous selection, even discarding berry by berry. These Sagrantino grapes are then carefully transported back to the house, where they are laid out in the domestic attic on cane mats known locally as *camorcanne*. There the grapes slowly dry and shrivel, concentra-

THE CENTRE

ting their grape sugars, but losing much of their liquid in the process.

Fermentation takes place in late December or early January. The semi-dried Sagrantino grapes, removed from their stalks and lightly crushed, are placed in small vats to ferment for about a week. At this point, there is so little juice that the mass resembles a sort of semi-solid sludge or '*sugo*'. The grapes are then very lightly pressed and transferred to barrels to continue their slow but steady fermentation, which generally ceases when the wines have reached about 16 degrees, leaving behind a considerable residual sweetness. In a good year, Bea makes no more than 500 bottles of Sagrantino *passito*. Concentrated, with an amazing, deep bouquet of blackberries, sweet in the mouth yet not overly so, this is a rare *vino da meditazione*, indeed, a true artisan wine, handmade on the smallest scale but of the highest quality. It is no wonder that these few bottles are reserved by customers even years in advance.

The wine-drenched Sagrantino lees, incidentally, are not wasted. For the Bea family have always followed tradition by transferring their normal red wines into the barrels containing the residue left after the pressing of the semi-dried grapes, a practice similar to the *ripasso* process by which the best Valpolicellas are produced. Thus Bea's Rosso di Montefalco gains rounder, richer flavours and an immense structure that comes from the raisiny character of the semi-dried grapes, and the extra degree or so of alcohol from the secondary fermentation that this induces. Those who might have considered Rosso di Montefalco a sort of lightweight version of Sagrantino should taste Bea's immense and exceptional wines. While Sagrantino in both its *secco* and *passito* versions is 100% varietal, Rosso di Montefalco is based on a blend that consists primarily of Sangiovese (65–75%), together with no more than 10% Sagrantino, as well as with smaller amounts of Trebbiano Toscano, Malvasia, Merlot, Barbera, and Montepulciano.

One other wine from this exceptional, little-known vineyard deserves special mention, Grechetto, made from another indigenous Umbrian grape. At Orvieto, this low-yielding, temperamental variety is deemed to add considerable character to that delightful white wine, and indeed quality-conscious producers include a higher proportion of it in their *uvaggio*, usually at the expense of the neutral Procanico. Here at Montefalco, though, some producers are making 100% Grechetto wines which, when vinified by modern methods, can demonstrate exceptional structure, scent, and class. Though at present Grechetto is classified as humble *vino da tavola*, we consider that it may emerge as one of the great white wines of Italy, demonstrating class, character, and elegance while maintaining its Umbrian *tipicità*.

The wine country of Montefalco sprawls down the slopes of Umbria's balcony to include surrounding communities and hamlets such as Cerrete, Turrita, Camiano, Montepennino, San Marco, Fabbri. Bevagna, located on the lower, flatter *pianura* below Montefalco is a notable wine centre, an ancient Roman staging town along the Via Flaminia, and today a quiet medieval town.

Degustazione: Stop to Taste; Stop to Buy

1 ANTICA AZIENDA AGRICOLA PAOLO
BEA
VIA CERRETE 8
06036 MONTEFALCO PG
TEL: 0742/790128

WINES PRODUCED: Rosso di Montefalco, Sagrantino Passito di Montefalco; *rosso vino da tavola*.
VISITS: daily, working hours. Telephone in advance.
The Bea family farm is typical of central Italian smallholdings in that a number of activities continue to be carried out: specialized wine making, of course, but also the raising of livestock, as well as cultivation of fruits, grain, olives and other such crops. In this way, there is a natural symbiosis with the land. The vineyards are cultivated organically, without the use of artificial weedkillers and the animals of the farm provide organic manure for fertilizer.

The wines of the farm are made wholly by traditional methods, in necessarily minute quantities. Olive oil may also be available for sale as well as handmade fruit preserves.

Giampiero Bea, architect of the commune of Montefalco, is a most hospitable guide, and interested visitors are welcome provided they telephone first. The farm also practises *agriturismo* with a few rooms available for rent. Some English spoken.

---

2 AZIENDA AGRICOLA F.LLI ADANTI
LOC. ARQUATA 37
06031 BEVAGNA PG
TEL: 0742/62295

WINES PRODUCED: Rosso d'Arquata; Bianco d'Arquata; Grechetto; Sagrantino di Montefalco, Rosso di Montefalco.

VISITS: daily, by appointment. One of few large producers from this select vineyard known internationally for its fine range of wines produced in the modern style.

3 TENUTA 'VAL DI MAGGIO' DI
ARNALDO CAPRAI
LOC. TORRE DI MONTEFALCO
06036 MONTEFALCO PG
TEL: 0742/62433

WINES PRODUCED: Rosso di Montefalco, Sangrantino di Montefalco; Grechetto.
VISITS: daily, by appointment. Well-made wines from this large estate located between Montefalco and Foligno.

---

4 AZIENDA AGRICOLA ROCCA DI
FABBRI
LOC. FABBRI
06036 MONTEFALCO PG
TEL: 0742/790318

WINES PRODUCED: Rosso di Montefalco, Sagrantino *secco* and *passito*.
VISITS: daily, by appointment. The medieval Rocca di Fabbri is today the setting for an ultra-modern winery producing new-style wines.

---

5 ENOPOLIO DI FOLIGNO
CONSORZIO AGRARIO PROVINCIALE
PERUGIA
CANTINA DI FIAMENGA
VIA FIAMENGA 17/A
06034 FOLIGNO PG
TEL: 0742/20386

WINES PRODUCED: Rosso di Montefalco, Sagrantino di Montefalco; Grechetto.
VISITS: daily, working hours. The Foligno wine co-operative is probably the largest producer of these hard-to-find wines, and is a sound and reliable source.

Enoteca

1 ENOTECA DI METELLI BERNARDINO
PIAZZA DEL COMUNE 10
06036 MONTEFALCO PG
TEL: 0742/79292

OPEN: daily 8–13h; 15–20h. Extensive selection of the wines of Montefalco: Rosso di Montefalco, Sagrantino di Montefalco *secco* and *passito*, and Greccheto. There is usually a selection of open wines that can be tasted. Signor Metelli is a great enthusiast, and will help arrange appointments to visit producers.

Ristoranti

1

RISTORANTE 'COCCORONE'
LARGO TEMPESTIVI
06036 MONTEFALCO PG
TEL: 0742/79535

Closed Wed.
Exceptional family *trattoria* just off the main square serving *stringozzi ai funghi, pappardelle al Sagrantino, faraona in salmi, scottadito* and good selection of local wines.
Moderate

2

HOTEL-RISTORANTE NUOVO MONDO
VIALE DELLE VITTORIA 7
06036 MONTEFALCO PG
TEL: 0742/79243

Modern hotel-*ristorante* on the outskirts of town. Restaurant serves authentically prepared Umbrian *cucina: tagliatelle al Sagrantino tartufato, risotto alla Nuovo Mondo, stringozzi, scottadito.*
Inexpensive to Moderate

Wine and Other Related *Sagre* and *Feste*

April	Festa del Vino	Montefalco
May	Sagra della Bruschetta	Bagnaia
June	Grande Festa Regionale del Vino	Orvieto
June	Sagra del Vino	Bevagna
August	Mostra Mercato	Torgiano
October	Fiera di Tartufo	Gubbio

E PER SAPERE DI PIÙ – ADDITIONAL INFORMATION

Ufficio Regionale Turismo
Corso Vannucci 30
06100 Perugia
tel: 075/6962483

Associazione Regionale Agriturist
via Tuderte 30
06100 Perugia
tel: 075/30174

Consorzio Tutela Vino Orvieto
Classico e Orvieto
Corso Cavour 36
05018 Orvieto TR
tel: 0763/43790

THE CENTRE

EMILIA-ROMAGNA

Colli Piacentini.

I Vini: THE WINES OF EMILIA-ROMAGNA 357

La Gastronomia 361

Le Strade dei Vini: THE WINE ROADS OF
EMILIA-ROMAGNA

    The Colli Piacentini 363

    Parma–Reggio–Modena–Bologna 365

    The Romagna Hills 367

Le Sagre: WINE AND OTHER RELATED FESTIVALS 370

Additional Information 371

Emilia-Romagna is the belly of Italy. The region stretches like a broad girth nearly from the western Ligurian coast all the way across to the eastern Adriatic, from the wide, flat Po valley in the north, to the rugged Apennines in the south. This is not only a great agricultural zone, and the source of fine fruit, wheat for pasta, dairy products, fresh and processed meats, and much else (an estimated 30% of what the nation eats comes from here), it further-more boasts perhaps the greatest regional culinary tradition in all of Italy. It is no wonder, then, that the regional capital is sometimes known simply as 'Bologna the Fat'.

The Romans built the Via Emilia in 187 BC, a straight thoroughfare which bisects the region and connects its major cities: Piacenza, Parma, Reggio nell'Emilia, Modena, Bologna, and Rimini. The vine is cultivated virtually all along its 250-km length, and the region is a prodigious source of everyday beverage and quality wines alike. Lambrusco is probably the only one that is a household name, and even at that, its reputation is not an enviable one: the sweet, fizzy, industrially-produced soda-pop wines in screw-top bottles that have flooded the export market – and incidentally introduced generations to the simple pleasures of the fermented grape – may hardly be our idea of what fine wine is all about. But be reassured: Lambrusco in its own homeland is another proposition altogether and a truly fine accompaniment to the always rich foods of the region. Above all it is such everyday wines – wines that can be enjoyed at the table without fuss or pretension – that Emilia-Romagna so generously supplies.

Starting from the north along the Via Emilia, we briefly touch base in three zones: the Colli Piacentini, the vineyards of Reggio-Modena-Bologna, and the Romagna hills. But for those in search of good food and wine, the region deserves far more extended exploration.

ORIENTATION

Emilia-Romagna comprises 8 provinces: Piacenza, Parma, Reggio nell' Emilia, Modena, Bologna, Ferrara, Ravenna, and Forlì. The region's Adriatic coastal resorts (especially Riccione, Rimini, and Ravenna) are extremely popular with both Italians and foreign tourists alike, while the principal inland towns along the Via Emilia all have much to offer.

Bologna's international Guglielmo Marconi Airport is probably the most convenient, though Rimini's Miramare airport is also well served internationally, particularly in summer by the charter airlines. Piacenza is probably best reached from Milan. The region's strategic central location means that it is particularly well served by both rail and road routes. By rail, for example, the region is connected with Turin–Milan and the eastern Adriatic; there are convenient northern rail routes to Verona, Padua and Venice; and the major Naples–Rome–Milan line connects via Bologna. Similarly, the A1 *autostrada* continues from Milan to Bologna before turning south across the Apennines to Florence, while the A14 extends on to Rimini and the eastern Adriatic. Most of the wine country can be explored off the Via Emilia.

Map Touring Club Italiano 1:200 000 Emilia-Romagna.

I VINI: GLOSSARY TO THE WINES OF EMILIA-ROMAGNA

Wines of *Denominazione di Origine Controllata (DOC)* and *Denominazione di Origine Controllata e Garantita (DOCG)*

Albana di Romagna DOCG First Italian white wine to be awarded select DOCG status: produced from Albana grapes grown in the provinces of Forlì, Ravenna and Bologna, and available in dry (mainly) as well as *amabile*, and *passito* versions. Albana di Romagna Spumante is usually produced by the Charmat method, in medium-sweet and sweet versions. Minimum alcohol 11.5 degrees.

Bianco di Scandiano DOC White wine from the province of

Reggio-Emilia produced from Sauvignon (at least 85% – this grape is known locally as Spergola), together with Pinot Bianco, Malvasia, and Trebbiano. Produced in dry, *semi-secco*, and *dolce* versions, as well as still, *frizzante* and fully sparkling. Minimum alcohol 10 degrees.

Cagnina DOC Local red wine from the Romagnan vineyard produced from Terrano grape: light, usually sweetish though sometimes dry. Minimum alcohol 11.5 degrees.

Colli Bolognesi DOC – Monte San Pietro – Castelli Medioevali DOC Delimited vineyard with two

---

LAMBRUSCO

The ubiquitous Lambrusco has, quite wrongly, come to be associated by many with the worst of Italian wines. True, much of the industrially produced export versions are little more than alcoholic soda-pop. But real Lambrusco as produced and enjoyed in the region is a unique and important wine that should not be dismissed.

Lambrusco has been produced in the zones of Modena and Reggio since Roman times at least – possibly even earlier, since the method of training the vines up trees is a direct legacy of the Etruscans. Today in the zone, the production of this almost always semi-sparkling red wine continues to be carried out by natural traditional methods on small private *aziende*. Here, wines made to be drunk at home or sold locally are produced with a natural secondary fermentation in the bottle. If a slight sediment remains afterwards, it matters little. For Lambrusco is a robust country wine to be enjoyed with gusto, not to be sniffed at delicately or examined hypercritically.

The vast bulk production of Lambrusco, though, is carried out in immense private wineries and *cantine sociali*, with the secondary fermentation taking place in sealed vats by the Charmat method. None the less, this too is a natural process, and the lively red froth that erupts when the bottle is uncorked (real Lambrusco DOC is never sealed by a metal screw-top) is always most vivid and enjoyable.

While export Lambrusco is usually semi-sweet to sweet, in the region itself, the dry version, foaming wildly and low in alcohol, is preferred as the perfect complement to wash down in quantity the rich, sometimes overly heavy foods of Emilia-Romagna.

sub-zones respectively south-west and south of Bologna producing a range of wines mainly drunk by the Bolognese themselves: Barbera, Bianco (Albana/Trebbiano), Cabernet Sauvignon, Merlot, Pignoletto, Pinot Bianco, Riesling Italico, and Sauvignon.

Colli di Parma DOC Delimited wine zone in the Parma hinterland producing 3 wines: Rosso (Barbera/Bonarda/Croatina); Malvasia (dry and sweet, often *frizzante* or fully sparkling); Sauvignon (usually slightly *frizzante*).

Colli Piacentini DOC Large, important zone adjoining Lombardy's Oltrepò Pavese producing a range of distinctive wines: Barbera, Bonarda, Gutturnio, Malvasia, Monterosso Val d'Arda, Ortrugo, Pinot Grigio, Pinot Nero, Sauvignon, Trebbianino di Val Trebbia, Val Nure.

Lambrusco di Sorbara DOC; Lambrusco Grasparossa di Castelvetro DOC; Lambrusco Salamino di S. Croce DOC 3 separate delimited zones in the province of Modena for the production of Lambrusco, a frothy red wine from the Lambrusco grape made in both dry and sweet versions. Minimum alcohol 11 degrees.

Lambrusco Reggiano DOC The largest Lambrusco zone by far, and the most widely exported: this always sparkling, dry to semi-sweet red wine is produced from varieties of the Lambrusco grape grown mainly on the plains throughout the province of Reggio. Minimum alcohol 10.5 degrees.

Montuni del Reno DOC Newly delimited zone in the province of Bologna for the production of white wine from Montuni grapes (mainly) produced in *secco*, *semi-secco*, and *amabile* versions, as well as still, *frizzante* and fully sparkling. Minimum alcohol 10.5 degrees.

Pagadebit DOC White wine from the indigenous Pagadebit grape grown in the Romagnan vineyard. Name comes from the fact that this early ripener is a heavy cropper and thus has traditionally helped to *'pagare i debiti'* – pay the bills. Minimum alcohol 11.5 degrees.

Sangiovese di Romagna DOC Red wine from the Sangiovese di Romagna grape (different from the Tuscan clone Sangiovese Grosso) grown in the provinces of Forlì, Ravenna, and Bologna over a vast area. Can be drunk young, though the best wines improve with age and can reach considerable distinction. Minimum alcohol 11.5 degrees.

THE CENTRE

ACETO BALSAMICO

Aceto balsamico is one of the great products of Emilia-Romagna. It has been produced in the zones of Modena and Reggio-Emilia since at least the 11th century on small farms and large noble estates alike in the *acetaia*, usually a dry, airy attic where wooden casks of varying sizes are passed on from generation to generation. Indeed, so precious was *aceto balsamico* that it often formed part of a woman's dowry.

Though this exquisite essence is usually translated as 'aromatic' or 'balsamic vinegar', it is as far from that mundane substance vinegar as can be imagined. The real product – and it must be stressed that widely available commercial balsamic vinegars bear no relation – is so special, so rare, so prized, so unbelievably expensive that it must be viewed almost more as an alchemic elixir.

Aceto balsamico tradizionale is produced from grape must which, at the first sign of fermentation, is immediately filtered then boiled down in large uncovered copper cauldrons. The thick cooked must is then poured into the first of a series of wooden casks in which the *aceto balsamico* matures. These casks contain a centuries-old *madre* or fermenting culture unique to each farm. Over a period of years – upwards of 50 or more in some cases – the *aceto balsamico* ages progressively in a battery of different casks, all of varying sizes and made from different woods – oak, cherry, mulberry, ash, locust, juniper, each contributing its own aromas and flavours. As the *aceto* is drawn from one barrel, that one is topped up with *aceto* from the next up the scale, and so on, so that a process of continual dynamic ageing results. The product that finally emerges is unbelievably concentrated, viscous, and aromatic – so precious, so strong is this pure *aceto balsamico tradizionale* that only a few drops are needed to transform magically a dressing or a sauce. Just as well, since a tiny flagon containing just 10 cl may cost upwards of 100,000 *lire*.

Azienda Agricola Pedroni
Rubbiara di Nonantola MO
tel: 059/549019
Italo Pedroni is not only one of the leading producers of *aceto balsamico tradizionale di Modena*, he is also a restaurateur. His Antica Osteria restaurant in Rubbiara serves many dishes made with his own *aceto balsamico*. Telephone the farm for an appointment to visit the *acetaia*.

Trebbiano di Romagna DOC
Prolific white wine from Trebbiano di Romagna grape grown in the provinces of Bologna, Forlì, and Ravenna. Trebbiano di Romagna

Spumante Brut is a dry sparkling wine usually produced by the Charmat method. Minimum alcohol 11.5 degrees.

LA GASTRONOMIA: FOODS OF EMILIA-ROMAGNA

Think of classic Italian food, and you are immediately transported to Emilia-Romagna. This is the land, after all, of Parmesan cheese and *prosciutto di Parma, lasagne al forno, tagliatelle al ragù* (known better elsewhere as '*alla bolognese*', *tortellini, mortadella* (the pale, unrecognizable American version is known as 'baloney' after Bologna), *zampone* and much else. It is hardly possible to eat badly in Emilia-Romagna, but this is not a region for those watching their waistlines.

PIATTI TIPICI: REGIONAL SPECIALITIES

Mortadella Famous finely minced and cooked meat sausage of Bologna: the larger the sausage, the better (they can reach enormous proportions).

Prosciutto di Parma Quite simply the finest, sweetest raw air-cured ham in the world.

Piadina Sort of dry bread-like pancake cooked on a griddle over a wood fire and eaten with cheese and cured meats – the classic drinking snack of Romagna.

Tagliatelle al ragù Handmade and cut egg noodles served with the classic long-simmered meat and tomato sauce. This dish may be served throughout Italy, but the real thing, as served in its homeland is still exceptional.

Tortellini Stuffed pasta inspired, believe it or not, by Venus' navel – small, crescent-shaped, stuffed with mixture of ground pork, *prosciutto, mortadella*, herbs and spices (usually nutmeg), served either *in brodo*, that is, in rich

THE CENTRE

homemade broth, or in a cream sauce, or *al ragù*.

Tortelli di ricotta e spinaci Large pasta stuffed with *ricotta* cheese and chopped spinach.

Pasticcio di tortellini Stuffed pasta pie – an immense meal in itself, though invariably served as a first course.

Lombato di vitello Veal escalope layered with *prosciutto di Parma* and Parmesan cheese, breaded and deep-fried.

Coniglio arrosto Rabbit roasted with wine, garlic, olive oil, and herbs.

Zampone Stuffed pigs' trotters, boiled and served with lentils. Speciality of Modena.

Cheeses: *Parmigiano reggiano* Real Parmesan cheese (as opposed to other undelimited hard *grana*-type cheeses) is produced only in zones of Parma and Reggio. It is indispensable not only for grating, but also for eating fresh when young.

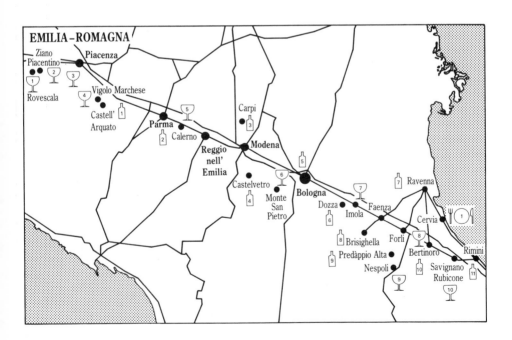

THE COLLI PIACENTINI

In Brief: The Colli Piacentini are a series of wine hills south of Piacenza, virtually contiguous with those of the Lombardy vineyards of the Oltrepò Pavese, extending in a broad arc over the foothills of the Piacentine Apennines roughly from Ziano Piacentino around to Castell' Arquato. A fine range of wines is produced in the zone which are entitled to the Colli Piacentini DOC, most notably the excellent red Gutturnio, produced from Barbera and Bonarda in both dry and sweet versions as well as still and *frizzante*. The Malvasia wines, particularly dry *frizzante* examples from the zone of Ziano Piacentino, are also delightful.

Piacenza is the northernmost town along the Via Emilia. Its strategic position just south of the natural frontier of the Po meant that it has traditionally served as the first line of defence of the Emilian plain, a role it played as a Roman fortified camp. The city was devastated in the last war, and it has since grown into a considerable industrial centre. But the old historic centre still retains its medieval atmosphere.

Castell'Arquato is one of Emilia-Romagna's loveliest medieval fortified villages, a steep town of winding alleys and old houses. It too was originally a Roman fortified camp in the foothills of the Apennines: today it is the best place to sample the wines of the zone in the welcoming *Enoteca Communale*.

Degustazione: Stop to Taste; Stop to Buy

1

AZIENDA AGRARIA M. E G. FUGAZZA
CASTELLO DI LUZZANO
LOC. LUZZANO
27040 ROVESCALA PV
TEL: 0523/863277

WINES PRODUCED: Colli Piacentini DOC: Gutturnio, Malvasia; Barbera di Ziano; Bonarda di Ziano; Romito anno 1° red, Romito anno 1° white.
VISITS: daily, by appointment.
Castello di Luzzano is located on the road that once formed a border defence between Emilia-Romagna and Lombardy. In addition to their noteworthy wines produced in the vineyards of the Oltrepò Pavese, Maria Giulia and Giovanella Fugazza also have vineyards that extend over the wine hills of the Colli Piacentini. The Gutturnio and Malvasia wines from the Romito estate near Ziano are particularly excellent.

THE CENTRE

2 AZIENDA AGRICOLA MOLINELLI
GIANCARLO
VIA DEI MILLE 21
29010 ZIANO PIACENTINO PC
TEL: 0523/863230

WINES PRODUCED: Colli Piacentini:
Gutturnio, Malvasia, Barbera,

Bonarda; Müller-Thurgau; Vino
Molinelli.
VISITS: daily, appointment not
necessary.
Traditional family production of
the classic wines of the Colli
Piacentini.

---

3 AZIENDA AGRICOLA ZERIOLI SRL
LOC. POZZOLO 253
29010 ZIANO PIACENTINO PC
ADMINISTRATION AND SALES: VIALE
IL PIACENTINO 22, 29100 PIACENZA
TEL: 0523/37200

WINES PRODUCED: Colli Piacentini:
Gutturnio, Barbera, Bonarda,
Sauvignon, Pinot Grigio, Ortrugo,
Malvasia; Zerioli Spumante Brut
metodo champenois.
VISITS: Mon–Fri 9–12h; 15–18h.
By appointment.
English, French spoken.

---

4 AZIENDA AGRICOLA PUSTERLA
29010 VIGOLO MARCHESE PC
TEL: 0523/896105

WINES PRODUCED: Chardonnay;
Colli Piacentini Monterosso Val
d'Arda; Colli Piacentini Gutturnio.
VISITS: daily, working hours.
Wines of the Colli Piacentini,
produced entirely from own-grown

grapes. Vigolo Marchese, located
7 km from Castell'Arquato, has a
notable romanesque parish church.
To reach the *azienda agricola*, leave
Vigolo Marchese on the road
towards Chiavenna, then, after less
than a kilometre, the distinctive
tower of the estate will be on your
right.

Enoteca Communale

1 ENOTECA COMMUNALE DI
CASTELL'ARQUATO
ANTICO PALAZZO DEL PODESTÀ
PIAZZA DEL MUNICIPIO
CASTELL'ARQUATO PC
TEL: 0523/803208; 803161

OPEN: Feb–Oct daily, 10–12h;
15–18h.

The wines of the Piacenza province
(Monterosso Val d'Arda, Gutturnio,
Barbera, Malvasia, Ortrugo,
Sauvignon, Pinot, Moscato, and
Bonarda) are displayed for tasting
and purchase in the communal
enoteca located in the historic centre
of the fascinating medieval

town. Arrangements can be made to visit wine producers direct. Each March, the first of the new wines from the preceding harvest are presented for tasting.

PARMA-REGGIO-MODENA-BOLOGNA: *TERRA DEL LAMBRUSCO*

In Brief: The vast plains of the Po valley extend all along the Via Emilia, and from Parma down to Bologna and beyond. In this central Emilian heartland, the vine is grown extensively, both on the delimited wine hills of the Colli di Parma DOC and the Colli Bolognesi DOC and in between, in the flatter plains which are the source of great quantities of Lambrusco in all its varying guises.

Degustazione: Stop to Taste; Stop to Buy

5

AZIENDA AGRICOLA MORO
VIA PATRIOTI 47
42040 CALERNO DI SANT'ILARIO
  D'ENZA RE
TEL: 0522/679190

WINES PRODUCED: Lambrusco Pjcol Ross, Lambrusco Reggiano; Il Morone; Rinaldo Brut.
VISITS: daily except Sun and holidays 8h30–12h; 14h30–18h. No appointment necessary.
There are literally hundreds of producers of Lambrusco in the Reggio-Emilia hinterland. Come to the *azienda* of Rinaldo Rinaldini to learn about and taste the real thing. Lambrusco Pjcol Ross is produced from the rare Lambrusco Peduncolo Rosso sub-variety (Pjcol Ross in dialect), and gains its froth from secondary fermentation in the bottle. It is dry, full of body and acid, and demonstrates how good this much maligned wine can be. Calerno is also in the centre of the zone for the production of Parmigiano-Reggiano.
French spoken.

6

TENUTA BISSERA DI BRUNO NEGRONI
VIA MALVEZZO 2
40050 MONTE SAN PIETRO BO
TEL: 051/412442

WINES PRODUCED: Bianco dell'Abbazia; Sauvignon Colli Bolognese di Monte San Pietro; Rosso della Bissera Colli Bolognesi di Monte San Pietro (Montepulciano); Sparvo (*vino*

THE CENTRE

frizzante); Bruno Negroni Spumante Brut.
VISITS: daily, by appointment.
The Colli Bolognesi south of Bologna are a series of lovely wine hills that are the source of much good drinking for the thirsty burghers of that great city. The Negroni family have particularly specialized in the production of fine white wines and sparkling wines utilizing modern techniques of fermentation at controlled temperatures and cold sterile bottling.
Some English spoken.

Enoteche

2 ENOTECA ANTICA OSTERIA
FONTANA
VIA FARINI 24/A
43100 PARMA
TEL: 0521/286037

OPEN: daily except Sun and holidays 9–15h; 16h30–21h.
Vast selection of wines of Parma and Piacenza, as well as from elsewhere throughout Italy and also France and California. At midday traditional *piatti parmigiani* are served including *tortelli verdi, pissareii con funghi e fagioli, braciole con formaggio e carciofi, semifreddo della casa.*
English, French spoken.

---

3 CARPI A TAVOLA
VIA CARLO MARX 83
41012 CARPI MO
TEL: 059/696072

OPEN: 9–13h30; 17–20h. Closed Sun and Mon.

Extensive *enoteca* with fine selection of wines from throughout Italy, as well as prepared foodstuffs to take away, including homemade pasta.
English, French spoken.

---

4 CASA DEI LAMBRUSCHI
SOTTERRANEI CASTELLO DI
LEVIZZANO
CASTELVETRO MO
TEL: 059/790221

Communal *enoteca* under the castle of Levizzano. For visits and tasting telephone to make an appointment.

THE ROMAGNA HILLS

In Brief: The Via Emilia continues from Bologna down to Rimini along the rich, verdant Po valley, a great source, here in particular, for a profusion of fine fruit. But to the south, the outline of the Apennines is never far off, and in the foothills of the mountains the wine hills of Romagna ripple down almost to the coast. This is probably Emilia-Romagna's greatest wine zone for both serious reds and whites, as well as for vast quantities of everyday beverage wines.

A signposted wine road begins at Dozza near Imola (where the *Enoteca Regionale*, housed in the dungeons of the splendid Rocca Sforzesca, is located), and winds its way south through charming little wine villages, hamlets, and larger towns along the Via Emilia: Faenza, Predappio Alta, Bertinoro, Savignano sul Rubicone, and scores of others. Along the way, in addition to wine producers who welcome visitors for tastings and direct sales, there are the 'Ca' de Be' drinking houses to ensure that no one need go thirsty.

Degustazione: Stop to Taste; Stop to Buy

7

VILLA MONTERICCO
VIA MONTERICCO 9
40026 IMOLA BO
TEL: 0542/40054

WINES PRODUCED: Albana di Romagna, Albana *da dessert*; Sangiovese di Romagna; Trebbiano di Romagna.

VISITS: daily, by appointment
The Pasolini dell'Onda family produce a fine range of wines on the Montericco estate as well as in central Tuscany.
English, French spoken.

8

FATTORIA PARADISO
VIA PALMEGGIANA 285
47032 BERTINORO FO
TEL: 0543/445044

WINES PRODUCED: Albana di Romagna Dolce 'Vigna del Viale', Albana di Romagna Secco 'Vigna dell'Oliva'; Barbarossa di Bertinoro; Pagadebit di Romagna; Sangiovese di Romagna.

VISITS: daily 9–12h; 15–19h.
Appointment appreciated.
VIDE member and one of the zone's leading producers and standard-bearers. Impeccably made wines as well as apartments and rooms for rent in this lovely *agriturismo* complex. Small wine museum.

THE CENTRE

9 PODERE DAL NESPOLI
VIA STATALE
NESPOLI FO
TEL: 0543/989637

WINES PRODUCED: Sangiovese di
Romagna; Trebbiano di Romagna;

Albana Amabile; Pagadebit di
Romagna.
VISITS: daily 8h30–12h;
14h30–18h30
Highly-regarded wines on an estate
in the heart of the Romagna hills.

---

10 TENUTA DI SAVIGNANO
VIA MATTEOTTI 62
47039 SAVIGNANO SUL RUBICONE FO
TEL: 0541/943446

WINES PRODUCED: Sangiovese di
Romagna Superiore; Trebbiano di
Romagna; Ribanobianco *(vino da*

tavola); Il Gianello *(vino da tavola)*.
VISITS: Mon–Fri 8–12h; 15–18h.
Traditional family production
entirely from own grapes.
Picnic-rest area near Castello di
Ribano with lovely views.
French, German spoken.

Enoteche

5 BOTTEGA DEL VINO OLINDO
FACCIOLI
VIA ALTABELLA NO. 15/B
40126 BOLOGNA
TEL: 051/223171

OPEN: daily from midday until 1 or
2 a.m.
Long-established private *enoteca*

located by the Torre Asinelli with
an extensive selection of local
wines, served together with simple
thirst-inducing snacks such as
salumi, cheese, *panini*. More
substantial foods can be arranged
in advance.
French, some English spoken.

---

6 ENOTECA REGIONALE
EMILIA-ROMAGNA
ROCCA SFORZESCA
40050 DOZZA BO
TEL: 0542/678089

OPEN: daily except Mon 10–12h;
15–18h
Emilia-Romagna's regional *enoteca*
is located in the dungeon of the
town's medieval fortress and is

dedicated to the promotion, display,
and tasting of the wines of
Emilia-Romagna. In addition, the
enoteca organizes tastings,
conventions, and round tables for
consumers and professionals. The
castle itself is also open to the
public and houses the *Museo della
Civiltà Contadina*.

THE 'CA' DE BE' DRINKING HOUSES

The 'Ca' de Be' drinking houses of Romagna, under the auspices of the Ente Tutela Vini di Romagna, are atmospheric *enoteche* of the highest order which no wine lover or wine tourist will wish to miss. Like secular churches devoted to the service and enjoyment of the fruits of the vine, they serve not only the full range of Romagna wines, but also drinking snacks such as the classic *piadina* (a sort of dry bread pancake cooked over a wood fire), cured meats and *salame*, as well as, in some cases, more substantial foods.

They are generally open from mid-afternoon until about midnight and are at their liveliest in the evenings.

7
CA' DE VÉN
VIA CORRADO RICCI 24
48100 RAVENNA
TEL: 0544/30163

OPEN: 10–14h; 17–23h. Closed Mon.
Situated in the historic heart of the important provincial capital near the tomb of Dante, serving a full range of Romagna DOC and DOCG wines together with typical foods such as *piadina con prosciutto o formaggio, crescione alle erbe*.
English, French, German spoken.

8
IL GUFO
OSTERIA ENOTECA
BRISIGHELLA FO
TEL: 0546/85102

9
CA' DE SANZVES
PIAZZA CAVOUR 18
47010 PREDAPPIO ALTA FO
TEL: 0543/922410

OPEN: 15h30–24h. Closed Mon.
In addition to serving wines and simple foods of Romagna, this 'House of Sangiovese' also a small wine museum.

10
CA' DE BÉ
PIAZZA DELLA LIBERTÀ
47032 BERTINORO FO
TEL: 0543/445303

THE CENTRE

11 CHESA DE VEIN
VIALE DANTE 18
47037 RIMINI FO
TEL: 0541/54180

Ristorante

1 TRATTORIA CASA DELLE AIE
VIA DELLE AIE 5
48015 CERVIA RA
TEL: 0544/927631

Closed Wed. Essential to book.
Trattoria installed in 18th-century
country house some 15 miles south
of Ravenna, owned and run by the
Ministry of Fine Arts, and serving
simple but faithfully prepared
Romagnese foods, especially meats
cooked over the open wood fire,
together with local wines.
Inexpensive to Moderate

Wine and Other Related *Sagre* and *Feste*

March	Mostro Mercato del Vino	Castell'Arquato
June	Festa dei Vini	Montalbo (Ziano)
end Aug	Sagra del Porcino	Castel del Rio
early Sept	Sagra dei Vini dei Colli Bolognesi	Calderino di Monte S. Pietro
Sept	Festa dell'Uva e dei Vini Tipici Locali	Ziano Piacentino
end Oct	Settimana del Tartufo	Castel di Casio
mid-Nov	Fiera di San Martino	Bomporto

E PER SAPERE DI PIÙ –
ADDITIONAL INFORMATION

Ente Provinciale di Turismo
via Marconi 45
40122 Bologna
tel: 051/237414

Ente Provinciale di Turismo
Corso Canalgrande 3
41100 Modena
tel: 059/237479

Ente Provinciale di Turismo
Piazza Duomo 5
43100 Parma
tel: 0521/33959

Ente Provinciale di Turismo
via San Siro 17
29100 Piacenza
tel: 0523/34347

Ente Provinciale di Turismo
Piazza Battisti 4
42100 Reggio-Emilia
tel: 0522/43370

Associazione Agriturist Regionale
via Delle Lame 15
40123 Bologna
tel: 051/233321

Ente Tutela Vini Romagnoli
Corso Garibaldi 2
48018 Faenza FO
tel: 0546/28455

Consorzio Tutela Lambrusco
Viale Martiri Della Libertà 28
41100 Modena
tel: 059/235005

Consorzio per la Tutela del
    Lambrusco Reggiano
c/o Camera di Commercio
Piazza Della Vittoria 1
42100 Reggio-Emilia
tel: 0522/33841

THE CENTRE

THE MARCHES

I Vini: THE WINES OF THE MARCHES   373

La Gastronomia   375

La Strada del Vino: THE WINE ROAD OF THE
MARCHES
    The Castelli di Jesi and Cònero:
      Ancona's Hinterland   376

Le Sagre: WINE AND OTHER RELATED FESTIVALS 383

Additional Information   384

Urbino.

The Marches can fairly be called '*Italia in una regione*' – Italy in one region, for this often overlooked Adriatic locality encapsulates many of the most characteristic features of the nation: sea and mountains; an inspired regional cuisine utilizing the produce of both; art and culture in centres such as Urbino, Jesi, Loreto, Pesaro. Even Italy's national problems are encapsulated in the Marches: industrial pollution and environmental problems which threaten the prosperity of the traditional tourist and fishing industries, and, as elsewhere, an exodus from the land by the region's youth.

The wine scene in the Marches, similarly, can be called '*Italia in una bottiglia*', for the region as a whole mirrors the patterns which, over the past decades, have characterized Italian wine both at home and abroad. The phenomenal success of the Marches' most famous wine, Verdicchio dei Castelli di Jesi, was achieved in tandem with the super-popularity of Italian wines from elsewhere, notably Soave, Frascati, old-style *fiasco* Chianti, wines which sold as much on price as on a carefree image of wine as a non-serious commodity to be drunk gaily, carelessly, and preferably in great quantity.

But Verdicchio's very success, in a sense, created problems for the serious wine producer, striving – like producers elsewhere – to demonstrate to the world that Italy is capable also of making wines of the highest quality. The wine lover who comes to the Marches, therefore, will find much more of interest than merely that quenching and popular seafood wine: this is the home, too, of serious and full-bodied whites from select single vineyard sites of the Castelli di Jesi and Matelica, as well as of *barrique*-aged reds of considerable class and distinction.

The Marches remains deservedly popular mainly for the traditional pleasures of its Adriatic resorts. But those who venture into the rugged hinterland – the wine hills that rise towards the Apennines – will find a quieter world where the living is good and the wine flows freely. The Marches is a wine region that is always satisfying, and which deserves greater exploration.

ORIENTATION

The Marches is located along the eastern Adriatic coast between the regions of Emilia-Romagna to the north and the Abruzzi to the south. The Apennine range separates the region from Tuscany and Umbria to the west. There are 4 provinces: Ancona, Pesaro, Macerata, and Ascoli Piceno.

The nearest international airport is at Rimini, north of Pesaro in Emilia-Romagna. Ancona's Falconara airport is the most convenient for connections with Rome or Milan. The region lies on the main Milan–Bologna–Lecce rail line, while there are also direct services between Rome and Ancona. The A14 motorway extends down virtually the entire Adriatic coast south of Bologna. Within the region itself, the terrain is characterized by steep river valleys cutting down perpendicularly from the Apennines to the Adriatic.

Map Touring Club Italiano 1:200 000 Umbria & Marche.

I VINI: GLOSSARY TO THE WINES OF THE MARCHES

Wines of *Denominazione di Origine Controllata (DOC)*

Bianchello del Metuaro DOC
Sharp dry white wine made from local Bianchello grape (known locally as Biancame) grown along the catchment basin of the Metauro valley that extends down from near Urbino. Minimum alcohol 11.5 degrees.

Bianco dei Colli Maceratesi DOC Dry white wine from large zone extending across the province of Macerata produced mainly from Trebbiano Toscano, together with Maceratino, Malvasia Toscana, and Verdicchio. Minimum alcohol 11 degrees.

Falerio dei Colli Ascolani DOC
Dry, sometimes sharp white wine
made from Trebbiano Toscano
(mainly) together with Verdicchio,
Malvasia, and Pinot Bianco grown
in the hills of Ascoli Piceno.
Minimum alcohol 11.5 degrees.

Lacrima di Morro d'Alba DOC
Rustic, gutsy country red wine from
province of Ancona centred on wine
town of Morro d'Alba, produced
from Lacrima grapes with some
Montepulciano. Minimum alcohol
11 degrees.

Rosso Cònero DOC Outstanding
red wine produced from hill
vineyards around Ancona and the
Cònero promontory, from
Montepulciano grapes with up to
15% Sangiovese. Minimum alcohol
11.5 degrees.

Rosso Piceno DOC Quality red
wine from large zone stretching
from the lower slopes of the
Apennines to the Adriatic in the
provinces of Ancona, Macerata, and
Ascoli Piceno. Wine can be produced
from Sangiovese (not less than 60%)
together with Montepulciano (not
more than 40%), with some
Trebbiano and Passerina. Minimum
alcohol 11.5 degrees.

**Sangiovese dei Colli Pesaresi
DOC** Red wine produced mainly
from Sangiovese grapes grown to
the north and south of Pesaro.
Minimum alcohol 11.5 degrees.

**Verdicchio dei Castelli di Jesi
DOC** Famous dry white wine from
hill zone primarily in the province of
Ancona around the so-called Castelli
di Jesi wine towns that extend
around Jesi itself. Produced from
the indigenous and characterful
Verdicchio grape (together,
optionally, with small amounts of
Trebbiano Toscano and Malvasia).
Minimum alcohol 11.5 degrees. The
Classico zone, the historical
heartland, comprises all but the
north-west of the delimited
vineyard.

Verdicchio di Matelica DOC
Tiny but prestigious inland wine
zone for the production of fine white
wines from the Verdicchio grape,
grown around the towns of
Matelica, Camerino, Fabriano and
others. Minimum alcohol 12
degrees.

Vernaccia di Serrapetrona DOC
Ancient traditional red sparkling
wine, usually sweet or *amabile* as
well as dry, produced from
Vernaccia di Serrapetrona grapes
together with up to 15% of
Sangiovese, Montepulciano, and
Ciliegiolo. Minimum alcohol 11.5
degrees.

SPUMANTE DELLE MARCHE

The Marches has long been the source of fine but little-known sparkling wines. In particular, the Verdicchio grape lends itself exceptionally well to serve as the base wine for transformation into sparkling by both the Charmat tank method and by the more laborious classic *metodo champenois*. Such wines are the favoured *aperitivo* in the region, and are increasingly finding favour internationally, too. The *Associazione Spumante Marchigiano* serves to safeguard quality as well as to promote the sparkling wines of the zone.

LA GASTRONOMIA:
FOODS OF THE MARCHES

The Marches remains today little spoiled by the influences of outsiders or tourists so the true foods of the region come from land and sea based on age-old traditions of self-sufficiency. Indeed, the *marchiagiani* are noted trenchermen, with such foods served in great abundance. Every coastal village has its fishing fleet which brings in a stupendous and varied catch from the Adriatic. Fish may be simply grilled or fried, or else it goes into the pot for the great speciality of the Marches, *brodetto*. Inland, hearty foods consist of game casseroles, roasted or grilled meats, homemade pasta, and innovative vegetable dishes utilizing the best from home and market gardens. In a region where fish and meat take equal pride of place, it is just as well there is such a fine choice of outstanding wines, both white and red.

PIATTI TIPICI:
REGIONAL SPECIALITIES

Antipasti di mare Varied and usually outstanding array of mixed seafood and shellfish appetizers.

Vincigrassi Fresh pasta sheets layered with bechamel sauce mixed with cream, black truffles, diced *prosciutto*, and chicken livers.

Brodetto Outstanding fish soup

made in some versions with up to 13 different varieties of fish and shellfish, usually cooked in wine and vinegar and flavoured with garlic, onion, parsley, and saffron.

Sarde alla marchigiana
Sardines baked with rosemary, lemon, parsley, and breadcrumbs.

Porchetta Spit-roasted suckling pig, usually stuffed with wild fennel, rosemary, plenty of garlic, and black pepper.

Coniglio in porchetta Rabbit treated as above, that is, stuffed with wild fennel, rosemary, garlic, salt and pepper, then roasted over an open fire.

Oca in potacchio Goose slow-cooked in a pot with white wine, olive oil, rosemary, garlic, and tomato. Chicken, pheasant, or guinea fowl can all be prepared in this typical manner.

Misticanza Salad made from wild leaves and greens.

Tartufi The Marches is one of Italy's principal zones for the gathering of both white and black truffles. They should not be missed if in the region during autumn and winter.

Cheese: *Pecorino di Monterinaldo* Sheep's milk cheese flavoured with wild herbs.

THE CASTELLI DI JESI AND CÒNERO: ANCONA'S HINTERLAND

In Brief: The vineyards of the Castelli di Jesi extend inland from Ancona mainly along the Esino valley over a series of low-lying hills about 200–350 metres above sea level. The Rosso Cònero zone extends over the slopes of Monte Cònero, the mountain south of Ancona which dominates and overlooks a particularly lovely stretch of coast known as the Riviera del Cònero. These relatively small wine regions can be most profitably and enjoyably dipped into by those relaxing along this lovely stretch of the Adriatic coast.

Ancona, the regional capital of the Marches, was a Greek colony, founded in the 4th century BC. Located just above the Cònero promontory where the coast makes a sharp bend, it was named after the Greek *ankòn*, or elbow. From its earliest days, this fine natural harbour served as a trading post for

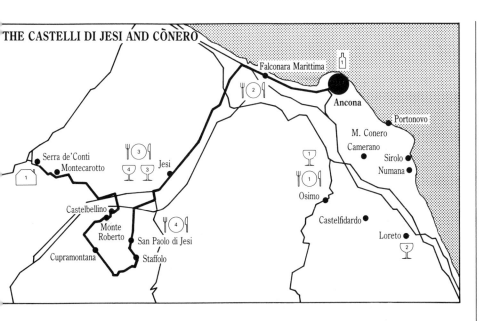

THE CASTELLI DI JESI AND CÒNERO

the ancients – first the Greeks, then the Romans – and it is certain that wine was one of the commodities most in demand. Proof of its importance is evident in the scores of *amphorae* that have been recovered from the sea bottom.

To emphasize this lengthy and historic connection with the vine, a special bottle was devised for the Marches' now most famous wine, Verdicchio dei Castelli di Jesi: the so-called *amphora* – known also as the Lollobrigida for its suggestive curves, or even simply as the 'sexy bottle'. Without a doubt, the *amphora* contributed greatly to Verdicchio's runaway success, and to its popularity in *ristoranti* up and down the Adriatic coast, as well as in *trattorie* in Rome, Soho, or Greenwich Village alike. Moreover, this was no mere marketing gimmick: the wine was (and usually still is) well-made, sound and relatively inexpensive.

The Verdicchio grape, however, has the potential for much more than simply slaking the thirst of the mainly undiscriminating masses. Fortunately for the serious wine lover, there were those few dedicated wine growers and producers who realized that this distinctive indigenous grape variety, when grown on select sites in the classic zone to severely limited yields, had the potential to produce some of the most exciting, richly textured white wines of Italy.

One such firm is the Azienda Vinicola Umani Ronchi, which is the wholly

THE CENTRE

owned concern of the Bianchi-Bernetti family. In the early 1980s, Dr Massimo Bernetti, the company's director, took what was at the time the courageous decision to concentrate on quality through the creation of a range of selected single-vineyard wines.

'The market was ready for this development,' he explains. 'Fifteen years ago it was impossible to sell Verdicchio in anything but the *amphora*. If you had suggested producing a *cru* Verdicchio, or a Rosso Cònero aged in *barrique*, people here would have thought you were crazy.'

The Bianchi-Bernetti family today owns some 80 hectares of vineyards in the classic zone of the Castelli di Jesi in 4 different municipalities: Montecarotto, Moie, Monteschiavo, and Serra de'Conti. This again is typical of the zone, for in these foothills below the Apennines the risk of hail is always great, and thus growers have traditionally spread their holdings.

This spread of vineyards allowed Dr Bernetti to experiment with wines produced from the various sites. Thus was born the *cru* Casal di Serra, which comes from the single vineyard of that name located at Serra de'Conti. As elsewhere throughout Italy, the first requisite for quality was to restrict yield drastically through intensive, careful pruning. For example, the DOC discipline for Verdicchio Classico dei Castelli di Jesi allows a maximum harvest of 150 *quintali* of grapes per hectare: the Casal di Serra vineyard yields less than half that amount.

In Umani Ronchi's winery at Castelbellino, one of the charming hilltop Castelli di Jesi towns, there is all the modern equipment that is today *de rigueur* for the vinification of quality white wines. The Vaslin presses, for example, are capable of working at extremely soft and delicate levels. But for Casal di Serra, the crushed Verdicchio grapes are simply pumped into them, then, with no additional pressure whatsoever, the free-run juice percolates through to be collected, resulting in an extremely low *resa* of no more than 50% of the weight of the grapes. The unfiltered grape must is then placed in refrigerated vats to enable the solid matters to precipitate, then it is transferred to small temperature-controlled stainless steel fermentation vats where the fermentation occurs at a temperature of between 16 and 18 degrees.

'We have found that these small stainless steel vats of about 120 hectolitres contribute much greater perfume and character than larger ones,' explained Dr Bernetti. 'Of course, they are also much more expensive. With Casal di Serra, after the principal fermentation, we transfer the wine to temperature-controlled autoclaves where the final sugars continue to ferment very slowly for another 5 or 6 months to reach a natural alcohol level of about 12.5 degrees. This slow fermentation is crucial to the develop-

Verdicchio vinescape near Monteschiavo.

ment of the character of the wine. Casal di Serra is never bottled before May or June, and then we hold the wine in bottle for at least another 2 months.'

The result is certainly successful: very bright lemon yellow with notable green tinges; an intensely ripe – even overripe – tropical fruit nose; and very long, opulent flavours and texture, balanced by the cleansing bitter-almond finish of the Verdicchio.

Given the commitment to quality and innovation, it is perhaps inevitable that the *barrique* would find its way into the cellars of Umani Ronchi. Indeed, the latest development is Le Busche, a single-vineyard wine from a 3-hectare site at Montecarotto. Produced from 90% Verdicchio, 10% Chardonnay, the must is steeped on the skins for a brief period, then it is fermented on the lees in 225-litre barrels made with oak from the Allier and Tronçais forests. Two-thirds of the barrels are new each year.

It was fascinating to taste the new wine from the *barrique*. The Verdicchio had much more colour than the Chardonnay, and was heavier, richer, and fatter. The Chardonnay, on the other hand, was undoubtedly leaner, more elegant and classy. After fermentation and subsequent assembly, the wine undergoes a further period of finishing in the bottle for up to 10 months until it is deemed ready for release. The wine is indeed exceptional: yellow-gold and heavy in the glass; a fat, buttery, toffee nose that mixes with the attractive creamy fruit of the Verdicchio; and an explosion of ripe fruit and wood in the mouth.

Other quality firms in the zone are also concentrating on such select or *cru* wines: those whose special selection wines particularly deserve to be singled

THE CENTRE

out include the Monte Schiavo *cantina cooperativa*, Fazi-Battaglia, Garofoli, and Mario & Giorgio Brunori.

The Castelli di Jesi wine country is a delight to explore. From Ancona, come first to Jesi, an impressive medieval town still almost wholly enclosed by its 14th-century fortifications. Jesi was the birthplace of the Holy Roman Emperor Frederick II in 1194: by all accounts, it was a humble and rude start; his mother, Costanza of Sicily, was suddenly taken short while travelling south, and forced to squat under an awning in the town marketplace. In medieval times, Jesi gave protection to the cluster of fortified hilltop towns that virtually surround it and which thus came to be known collectively as the Castelli di Jesi. These wine towns are mostly tiny medieval villages that remain wholly unspoiled and charming. Cupramontana, Castelbellino, Monte Roberto, Staffolo, Serra de'Conti, Montecarrotto are all worth visiting.

Closer to Ancona, the Cònero promontory is an impressive wooded mountain that rises directly from the coast then sprawls down over a broader inland hinterland. This brief stretch of coast, known as the Riviera del Cònero, is particularly lovely, and resorts such as Portonovo, Sirolo and Numana are all popular.

The broad flanks of the Cònero promontory are by no means wholly devoted to viticulture, for the Marches remains primarily a land of mixed farming, a carry-over from the days when each smallholding had to be virtually self-sufficient. Moreover, the concept of wine as a precious commodity is a relatively new one here. Yet today, this zone is the source of a fine red wine that deserves to be considered among the élite of Italian wines: Rosso Cònero, produced from the Montepulciano grape, with the optional addition of up to 15% Sangiovese.

Even as recently as a decade ago, this wine was hardly ever even bottled, but was enjoyed locally only and almost always in the year of production. Nobody believed that it had the potential, with age, for greatness. It came as a revelation even to the quality wine producers themselves to discover how much finer, softer, more complex the Montepulciano could become after, say, 2 or 3 years in Slavonian *botte*. A number of producers have now furthermore begun producing wines from selected single vineyards, some aged in new oak *barriques* with remarkable results.

Wine towns of note in the Rosso Cònero zone include Castelfidardo (birthplace of the accordion, still its major local industry), Camerano, and Osimo, a former Roman town, sited high on a hill with views across to the sea and down the Musone valley.

Degustazione: Stop to Taste; Stop to Buy

1 AZIENDA VINICOLA UMANI RONCHI
SS16
60028 OSIMO SCALO AN
TEL: 071/7108019; 7108050

WINES PRODUCED: Verdicchio dei
Castelli di Jesi Classico, Verdicchio
dei Castelli di Jesi Classico 'Villa
Bianchi', Verdicchio dei Castelli di
Jesi Classico *cru* 'Casal di Serra',
Verdicchio Spumante Brut; Le
Busche (Verdicchio/Chardonnay
fermented in *barrique*); Rosso
Cònero *cru* 'San Lorenzo', Rosso

Cònero *cru* Cùmaro (*barrique*);
Bianchello del Metauro;
Montepulciano d'Abruzzo.
VISITS: Mon–Fri, by appointment.
One of the zone's leading producers.
The winery is located along the
main coast highway SS16 just south
of the Ancona Sud exit from the
autostrada and there is an adjoining
restaurant-*enoteca* where the wines
can be tasted and purchased.
English spoken.

2 CASA VINICOLA GAROFOLI
VIA DANTE ALIGHIERI 25
60025 LORETO AN
TEL: 071/977658

WINES PRODUCED: Verdicchio dei
Castelli di Jesi Classico, Verdicchio
dei Castelli di Jesi Classico *crus*
Serra Fiorese, Macrina; Verdicchio
dei Castelli di Jesi Classico
Spumante Brut; Rosso Cònero,

Rosso Cònero *cru* Piancarda.
VISITS: daily, by appointment.
The Garofoli brothers are
traditionalists dedicated to quality,
and their selected *cru* wines are
outstanding: but even the Garofoli
normale Verdicchio still remains
one of the best examples of its type.
English, French spoken.

3 BRUNORI MARIO & GIORGIO S.N.C
VIALE DELLA VITTORIA 103
60035 JESI AN
TEL: 0731/207213

WINES PRODUCED: Verdicchio dei
Castelli di Jesi Classico, Verdicchio

dei Castelli di Jesi Classico *cru* 'San
Nicolò'.
VISITS: daily, by appointment.
Highly-regarded family production
of artisan-made wines.

THE CENTRE

4 MONTE SCHIAVO COOP. AGR. ARL.
VIA VIVAIO
60030 MONTESCHIAVO DI MAIOLATI
SPONTINI AN
TEL: 0731/700385; 700297

WINES PRODUCED: Verdicchio dei Castelli di Jesi Classico *crus* 'Pallio di San Floriano', 'Coste del Molino', 'Colle del Sole', Verdicchio dei Castelli di Jesi Classico Spumante Brut 'Vigna Tassanare'; Rosso Cònero; *vino frizzante*.

VISITS: daily, by appointment. Open working hours for direct sales. Technically advanced co-operative winery with a reputation for producing 'boutique wines' of the highest quality. The *cru* 'Pallio di San Floriano', produced from late-harvested grapes affected by *muffa nobile*, is particularly noteworthy.
English, French spoken.

Enoteca

1 ENOTECA DEI VINI REGIONALI
ENTE SVILUPPO MARCHE
VIA ALPI 20
60124 ANCONA
TEL: 071/8081

Centre for the promotion of the wines of the Marches.

Ristoranti

1 RISTORANTE 'LA CANTINETTA DEL
CÒNERO'
SS16
60028 OSIMO SCALO AN
TEL: 071/7108019

Closed Sat.
Simple *trattoria* located on the SS16

directly in front of the Umani Ronchi winery serving excellent *antipasti* and fresh grilled fish, together with the full range of Umani Ronchi wines, including the top *crus*.
Inexpensive to Moderate

---

2 VILLA AMALIA
VIA DEGLI SPAGNOLI 4
60015 FALCONARA MARITTIMA AN
TEL: 071/912045

Closed Tue.
Regional and creative *cucina*,

especially seafood, in this classy *ristorante-locanda* with rooms. Meals served on pleasant outdoor veranda in season.
Moderate to Expensive

3 HOTEL-RISTORANTE FEDERICO II
VIA ANCONA 10
60035 JESI AN
TEL: 0731/543631

De luxe hotel-restaurant complex, aimed at business and conference users as well as tourists. Exceptional facilities and a well-regarded restaurant serving local foods.
English, French, German spoken.
Expensive

---

4 RISTORANTE NATALE BALDI
VIA BORGO S. MARIA 32
60038 SAN PAOLO DI JESI AN
TEL: 0731/779202

Closed Mon. Essential to book. *Rigatoni alla contadina, gnocchi all'anatra, oca in potacchio*, and own-produced Sangiovese and Verdicchio.
Inexpensive

Agriturismo

1 AZIENDA AGRITURISTICA MORO
BELLO
LOC. SERRA 27
60030 SAN MARCELLO AN
TEL: 0731/267060

Verdicchio DOC, homemade cheese, and apartments and rooms for rent.

Wine and Other Related *Sagre* and *Feste*

| July | Sagra del Vino | Numana |
| early Oct | Festa dell'Uva | Cupramontana |

THE CENTRE

E PER SAPERE DI PIÙ –
ADDITIONAL INFORMATION

Ente Provinciale per il Turismo
via Marcello Marini 14
60100 Ancona
tel: 071/201980

Associazione Regionale Agriturist
Corso Mazzini 64
60100 Ancona
tel: 071/201751

Consorzio Tutela del 'Verdicchio
   Classico dei Castelli di Jesi'
   DOC;
Consorzio Tutela del 'Rosso
   Cònero' DOC
Piazza XXIV Maggio 1
60124 Ancona
tel: 071/28971

THE MEZZOGIORNO

Latium
Abruzzi and Molise
Campania
Apulia
Basilicata
Calabria

The Mezzogiorno

Lake Bolsena

Viterbo

Rome

APENNINES

Tiber

L'Aquila Pescara
Chieti

ABRUZZI

Frosinone

MOLISE

Isernia Campobasso

Foggia

LATIUM

CAMPANIA

ADRIATIC SEA

Caserta

Naples

Ischia

Mt Vesuvius

Capri

Avellino Melfi
Salerno

Potenza Matera

Bari

APULIA

Táranto

Brindisi

Lecce

Otranto

Gallipoli

BASILICATA

TYRRHENIAN SEA

*GULF OF
TÁRANTO*

CALABRIA

Cosenza

Catanzaro

IONIAN SEA

Réggio di Calabria

*STRAITS OF
MESSINA*

LATIUM

Typical wine cantina *at Castel Gandolfo.*

I Vini: THE WINES OF LATIUM   388

La Gastronomia   391

Le Strade dei Vini: THE WINE ROADS OF LATIUM
     The Colli Albani: Wine Hills and Villas of Rome   392
     Montefiascone: *Bonum Vinum Est! Est!! Est!!!*   402

Le Sagre: WINE AND OTHER RELATED FESTIVALS   404

Additional Information   404

Latium is the region that encompasses Rome, the nation's capital, and its environs. All roads may lead to the vast, sprawling Eternal City, but the Roman countryside itself remains remarkably unspoiled and rural. The region is a large one: somewhere, as it passes from the Tyrrhenian Sea below Tuscany's Argentario peninsula through Rome itself to the border with Campania, a definitely marked transition takes place, and we know that we have entered the Mezzogiorno, the southern land of the midday sun.

Of course, the ancient Romans established the great vineyards not just of Italy but also of Europe, so it might be logical to assume that Latium today remains a great wine region. In ancient times, certainly, there were scores of named wines from Rome and its environs. But Rome has always been a cosmopolitan city, and even in times past, the best wines from as far afield as Gaul, the Rhenish Palatinate, and the Danube were drunk and enjoyed by wealthy patricians and nobles alike. Undoubtedly, then as now, there was a certain snob value to drinking wines transported from afar at great cost and effort.

But the Roman Campagna, especially the lovely hills just south of Rome known as the Colli Albani, was a favourite retreat, and the local wines such as Frascati, Marino, Castelli Romani (the Romans knew them as Albanum, Labicanum, Praenestinum and scores of others) have been enjoyed literally for millennia. These lovely hills remain just as popular today and make a pleasant interlude from city sightseeing. Elsewhere, the vine is cultivated throughout the region, notably in the plains of Aprilia (the rather drab and flat Pontine marshlands reclaimed by the Fascists, and today the vast source

THE MEZZOGIORNO

of varietal wines such as Trebbiano and Merlot di Aprilia), and around the hills of Lake Bolsena, source of the curiously named Est! Est!! Est!!!

ORIENTATION

Latium is a volcanic, mountainous region stretching from its northern border with Tuscany, south to the Garigliano river, which marks the boundary with Campania. Rome is a provincial capital, as well as the capital of the region and nation; there are additionally 4 further provinces: Viterbo, Rieti, Frosinone, and Latina.

Rome's Fiumicino is the country's principal international airport. There are rail connections with every part of the country as well as with most European destinations. The A1 *Autostrada del Sole* connects Rome with Florence and the north as well as with Naples and the south. While a car is essential for exploring the countryside, driving in Rome itself is only for masochists.

Map Touring Club Italiano 1:200 000 Lazio.

I VINI: GLOSSARY TO THE WINES OF LATIUM

Wines of *Denominazione di Origine Controllata (DOC)*

Aleatico di Gradoli DOC Rare red dessert wine from Aleatico grapes grown around the north-west shores of Lake Bolsena. Minimum alcohol 12 degrees. **Aleatico de Gradoli Liquoroso** Unusual fortified dessert wine from the same grape with a minimum alcohol of 17.5 degrees.

Aprilia DOC Prolific vineyard on the plains of Aprilia for the production mainly of bulk varietal wines from Merlot, Sangiovese, and Trebbiano. Minimum alcohol 12 degrees.

Bianco Capena DOC White wine produced from Trebbiano, Malvasia, and Bonvino on large zone of vineyards north of Rome around wine communes of Capena, Fiano, Morlupo, and Castelnuovo di Porto. Minimum alcohol 11.5 degrees.

WINE IN ANTIQUITY

The ancient Romans' fondness for the fruits of the vine is well documented. During the Roman Republic viticulture was probably the richest and most productive form of agriculture (during the later years of the Empire competition with wines from further afield created a drastic domestic economic crisis as landowners saw the value of their efforts plummet on a flood of cheap imports).

The Roman *cantina* in ancient times was remarkably sophisticated and well-organized. There were, of course, strict regulations and prohibitions relating to wine production. In a well equipped farm, the grapes were brought from the fields and placed in large stone vats where men and women pressed them with their bare feet. The grape must, coarsely filtered through wicker baskets, ran down stone channels into terracotta *dolia*, immense fermentation urns that were often buried below the ground. After fermentation, the wines were fined with beaten egg whites (still used today for the same purpose) or with fresh goat's milk. Then the wine was racked into different *dolia* where it stayed until the spring festival of *Vinalia*.

Even after the libations to the gods at this important annual event, the best wines were not yet ready to drink. For, like the great wines of today, the best of antiquity were deemed to improve with further and considerable ageing – even up to 20–25 years or longer in terracotta *amphorae*. The aged wines became very concentrated, high in alcohol, and bitter in taste, but prior to drinking, they were mixed by an *arbiter* with water, or with flavourings such as aromatic herbs or honey.

In other cases, wines were made from grapes that had been semi-dried before pressing (as Recioto and Vin Santo continue to be made today); condensed wines were made by boiling the grape must to reduce it to a concentrated syrup; and even sparkling wines were made by fermentation in cold, sealed vats. It is probably fair to surmise that the many different styles and types of wine available in Roman times have probably not even been surpassed today.

THE MEZZOGIORNO

Cerveteri DOC Delimited vineyard along the northern Latium seaboard below Civitavecchia producing both red from Sangiovese, Montepulciano, Canaiolo, Barbera, and Cesanese (minimum alcohol 12 degrees), and white from Trebbiano, Malvasia, Verdicchio, Tocai, Bellone, and Bonvino (minimum alcohol 11.5 degrees).

Cesanese del Piglio DOC; Cesanese di Affile DOC; Cesanese di Olevano Romano DOC Red wine from the Cesanese grape grown south-east of Rome in 3 different wine zones in the provinces of Frosinone and Rome. The wine can be made in 4 different styles of varying dryness: *secco, asciutto, amabile,* and *dolce,* as well as still, *frizzante,* or fully sparkling. Minimum alcohol 12 degrees.

Colli Albani DOC Dry (mainly) white wine produced from varieties of Malvasia and Trebbiano, from Alban hill vineyards around Albano, Ariccia, and Castel Gandolfo. Lesser amounts of *amabile* also produced. Minimum alcohol 11.5 degrees.

Colli Lanuvini DOC Wine zone centred on the towns of Lanuvio and Genzano di Roma, extending over the hills south almost to

Aprilia for the production of undervalued white wine from Malvasia, Trebbiano, Bellone, and Bonvino. Minimum alcohol 11.5 degrees.

Cori DOC Tiny wine zone around town of Cori east of Velletri for the production of both red wine from Montepulciano, Nero Buono di Cori, and Cesanese (11.5 degrees), and white wine from Malvasia and Trebbiano, made in 3 styles: *secco, amabile, dolce* (11 degrees).

Est! Est!! Est!!! di Montefiascone DOC Dry white wine produced from Trebbiano Toscano, Malvasia, and Rossetto grapes grown on hill vineyards around Lake Bolsena in province of Bolsena. Minimum alcohol 11 degrees.

Frascati DOC Dry (mainly) white wine from varieties of Malvasia and Trebbiano grown in communes of Frascati, Grottaferrata, and Monteporzio Catone. Minimum alcohol 11.5 degrees, 12 degrees for Superiore. Sometimes available in traditional medium-sweet *cannellino* or *amabile* versions.

Marino DOC Dry white Castelli wine made from varieties of Malvasia and Trebbiano, together with Bonvino around town of Marino. Minimum alcohol 11.5 degrees.

Montecompatri Colonna DOC
Another Castelli Romani dry white from vineyards in the north of the zone around Colonna, Montecompatri, Zagarolo, and Rocca Priora, made from varieties of Malvasia and Trebbiano. Minimum alcohol 11.5 degrees, 12.5 degrees for Superiore.

Orvieto DOC This famous white wine comes from vineyards mainly centred in Umbria, but the wine country spills over briefly into Latium's province of Viterbo (see page 331).

Velletri DOC Large delimited wine zone in the south of the Castelli Romani for the production of both red wine (from Sangiovese, Montepulciano, and Cesanese; minimum alcohol 11.5 degrees), and dry white (from Malvasia and Trebbiano; minimum alcohol 11.5 degrees).

Zagarolo DOC Delimited wine zone in the far north-east of the Castelli Romani for the production of dry white wine from varieties of Malvasia and Trebbiano, together with Bellone and Bonvino. Minimum alcohol 11.5 degrees; 12.5 degrees for Superiore.

ENOTECA

1

ENOTECA TRIMANI
VIA GOITO 20
00100 ROMA
TEL: 06/497971

Closed Sun.
There is no time or space to explore the myriad wine shops of Rome, but this famous *enoteca* deserves to be singled out as the source of the very best wines not only of Latium but from throughout Italy.

LA GASTRONOMIA:
FOODS OF LATIUM

In Latium it is not the foods that are eaten so much as the manner in which they are enjoyed that is most important. In city centre restaurants with outdoor terraces, or in simple *osterie* in the wine hills alike, families, friends, acquaintances, business folk gather for long extended lunches which reflect an all-consuming passion not only for the joys of food and drink but for living

THE MEZZOGIORNO

itself. *La vita breva, buon divertimento* – life is short, enjoy yourself – could be the motto that sums up life in the region.

Though the excesses of the ancient Romans are legendary, the foods encountered in the Latium countryside today have developed out of poorer popular rural traditions, and are all the more delicious for that. This is a region, after all, where as they say in dialect *'la piu se spenne, peggio se magna'* – the more you spend, the worse you eat. Indeed, food, no more than wine, is not meant to be fussed over: it is there to be enjoyed with full gusto. See page 393.

THE COLLI ALBANI:
WINE HILLS AND VILLAS OF ROME

In Brief: The Colli Albani or Alban Hills, whereon lie Rome's best-known vineyards, are about 20 km south-east of the city. As such they have always served as a favourite playground for citizens of the Eternal City.

For visitors, it is possible to tour the Colli Albani in a single day's excursion from Rome, but to do so is to miss the essential charm and beauty of the zone. That said, the very popularity of the area with Romans as well as foreign visitors means that the wine towns are invariably extremely crowded, especially at weekends or holidays.

Those who wish to experience the real beauty and tranquillity of this Roman hinterland are advised to stop for a few days at wine grower Ernesto Lercher's welcoming Azienda Agrituristico 'Tre Palme' in the much quieter adjoining Colli Lanuvini.

The Colli Albani, a series of gentle volcanic hills to the south of Rome, have for over two millennia served as a retreat, to escape the cares of the busy city and the world. The road south, the famous Appian Way, led through the hills to Naples and finally Brindisi, so the zone lay very much along a well-trodden path. During the centuries when Rome was surrounded almost entirely by low-lying malaria-infested swamps and marshlands, the cooler, higher hills of the Colli Albani served as a literal retreat in times of epidemic. The Roman aristocracy and wealthy have always come here, especially in summer. Cicero had a villa at ancient Tusculum near Frascati, and even today the Pope himself continues to find relaxation and solace at the immense Villa del Papa in Castel Gandolfo.

PIATTI TIPICI: REGIONAL SPECIALITIES

Bruschetta Roman garlic bread; slice of country bread toasted over a wood fire, rubbed with garlic, and soaked in virgin olive oil.

Porchetta Suckling pig stuffed with a pungent mixture of herbs, garlic, and pepper, roasted in a *forno di legno* (wood-fired oven), and sold from shops, street stalls, or vans, together with *pane casereccio* (homemade bread, also cooked in the wood *forno*).

Supplì al telefono Little balls of *risotto* stuffed with *mozzarella* cheese, coated in breadcrumbs, and deep-fried. When bitten into, strings of melted cheese stretch like telephone wires, hence the name.

Bucatini all'amatriciana Elbow macaroni served with a fiery sauce of tomatoes, *pancetta* or *guanciale* (cured pork belly or cheek) and hot chilli peppers.

Fettucine Thin, homemade egg noodles, usually served either simply with butter and freshly grated cheese, *alla romana* with a sauce of tomatoes, ham, and chicken giblets, or *alla papalina* with peas, ham and eggs.

Spaghetti alla carbonara Spaghetti tossed with *pancetta*, grated *pecorino* and raw egg which cooks from the steam of the hot pasta.

Gnocchi alla romana Semolina dumplings baked with cheese and butter.

Spaghetti aglio e olio Simplest of all pastas, and the Romans' favourite for a midnight feast: chopped garlic and chilli peppers, fried in abundant olive oil, and poured over *al dente* spaghetti.

Abbacchio Milk-fed baby lamb, a Roman favourite.

Fritto misto alla romana Mixed fried platter of meats, offal and vegetables.

Coda alla vaccinara Rich flavourful oxtail and wine stew.

Budino de ricotta Cheesecake made with fresh *ricotta*.

Cheeses: *Pecorino romano* Salty sheep's milk cheese, both for eating and for grating. *Ricotta* Found throughout Italy, but some of the best fresh *ricotta* comes from farms in the Latium countryside.

THE MEZZOGIORNO

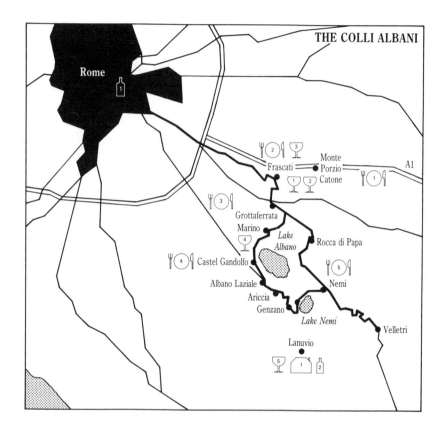

The Colli Albani themselves are extinct volcanoes, their concave craters long filled in to create the two splendid lakes of Albano and Nemi. The almost black, potassium-rich soil here provides a fertile bed for the cultivation of grapes, as well as of fine vegetables, fruit, and flowers, products which all find a ready market in the sprawling metropolis below. But it is for wine above all that the Colli Albani is most famous, almost entirely white: forceful, clean, and strong, and which goes so well with the robust, forthright foods of the region.

Much of it, made in large *cantine cooperativi* or by small private growers alike, is never even bottled, but drunk on the spot in charming wine taverns and *osterie*. Indeed, it is the sort of beverage to lubricate simple feasts of succulent *porchetta* and coarse homebaked *pane casereccio*. Rarely will you find a wine–food combination that can beat this basic Roman repast: the cave-cool, gutsy wine, drawn out of the wood or demi-john into litre carafes, more than a match for the pungent, garlic-and-rosemary infused meat.

Admittedly, the wine on its own may be neither elegant nor particularly noteworthy. But you don't come to these timeless wine hills to analyse, sniff and spit, or to pontificate about wine: you come simply to drink it.

Frascati, of course, is the most famous wine of the Colli Albani, but in truth there seems little to choose between it and the other whites of the zone, Marino, Montecompatri Colonna, Velletri, Zagarolo and the larger zonal *denominazioni* of Colli Albani, Colli Lanuvini, and Castelli Romani. All are produced primarily from varieties of Malvasia, together with Trebbiano Giallo and Toscano, and smaller amounts of other grapes such as Greco, Bellone, Bonvino, Cacchione and others.

In the past, most of the wines were made by somewhat rustic methods, to say the least, often pressed and vinified on the skins to result in deep yellow to gold wines that were at best full-bodied and powerful, at worst decidedly coarse and oxidized. However, the large *cantine cooperativi* and private firms that now dominate the Castelli Romani wine scene and which export such wines throughout the world are today able by modern methods to produce white wines that are impeccably well-made: light, clean as a whistle, usually rather dry and soft. All too often, they can be rather dull, neutral, and nondescript as well. Cold fermentation, ultra-filtration of grape musts, sterile bottling all have their roles to play in the production of good white wines, and such technological advances mean that really bad bottles should only rarely be encountered. However, such methods carried to extremes on grapes grown for quantity not quality must inevitably result in wines that display little regional or varietal character.

The marketing men who have to sell such wines may delight in the fact that their brands may broadly and consistently taste the same, whether sampled in Rome or in New York or Tokyo, and indeed there is something to this. But for my money, I'd still prefer any day to come direct to the source, to sample the genuine wines of the zone on the spot, with all their character – and in many cases all their faults and rusticity – gloriously and un-apologetically intact. Nowhere is this simple pleasure more enjoyable and accessible than in the Colli Albani.

To reach this favourite wine zone from Rome, leave the city on the ancient Via Tuscolana (N215) which leads south eventually to arrive at Frascati. If approaching the zone from the A2 *autostrada*, exit at Monte Porzio.

Frascati has always been one of the most popular and fashionable resorts of the Castelli Romani, as the 13 towns and villages of the Colli Albani are collectively known. From ancient times, through the Middle Ages, even up to today, it has been surrounded by the villas of Rome's wealthy and most

THE MEZZOGIORNO

privileged. Nearby ancient Tusculum was the birthplace of Cato the Censor (who wrote an early treatise on wine growing and wine making, *De Agricultura*), as well as the home of Cicero, Lucullus, Pompey, Tiberius and many other illustrious personages from the classical era. After the fall of Rome, a medieval collection of huts built from brushwood (*frascata*) grew up near the ancient site, and over the subsequent centuries the famous from Rome, under the patronage of popes, cardinals, and princes, began once more to build their splendid Renaissance and baroque villas, the finest of which is the Villa Aldobrandini that still dominates the town. And today, here in Frascati and in the other towns of the Castelli Romani, the privileged classes of Rome continue this tradition, hiding out in their modern and luxurious villas hardly visible behind their protective walls and electronically controlled gates.

For those families enclosed within their own grounds, the Colli Albani may really be a place of peace and relaxation. But for the rest of us, Frascati's Piazza Marconi on a weekend is a riot of noise, colour, and the screeching and honking of a million – so it seems – mopeds, motorbikes, and Fiats. Then you may well ask, where is the tranquillity, the relaxed bucolic peace that is the essence of the zone? It is there, believe me, but you may have to search for it. Start by exploring the medieval streets of the old town to hunt out one of numerous simple, genuine wine *cantine*, take your paper-wrapped packet of *porchetta* and a loaf of bread there, and order a carafe (or two) of cool, golden wine. This is what people have been coming here to do for centuries, after all.

From Frascati, continue to Grottaferrata, famous both for its wines (also entitled to the Frascati DOC), and for its fine Byzantine abbey, founded in 1004 by the Basilian monk Saint Nilo of Rossano, and fortified in 1473 by Pope Julius II. The view from the abbey terrace over the slopes of the Colli Albani to the Roman Campagna is splendid.

The N216 from Grottaferrata leads next to Marino, whose wines are probably the best-known after Frascati's. A lively wine festival, the *Sagra dell'Uva*, takes place on the first Sunday in October, and during this time the town's fountain flows with wine. Marino, and its neighbour Castel Gandolfo, are located on the rim of a long-extinct volcanic crater which has filled in to form Lake Albano. Both are popular resort towns, though the recreational opportunities at both Lake Albano and nearby Lake Nemi are fairly limited. Castel Gandolfo is most famous, of course, as the summer residence of the Pope, and on Sundays in particular, the streets of the tiny town are packed.

Carry on along the lake road to Albano Laziale, bombed severely during the last war, though today once again one of the most popular tourist centres of the Castelli Romani. The town is actually located along the Via Appia Antica, as well as on the Via Appia Nuova (N7), so access to and from Rome has been easy for centuries. Albano is one of the oldest of the Castelli Romani, its name derived from ancient Alba Longa, founded, according to legend, in 1150 BC by Aeneas' son Ascanius. In the 2nd century AD it probably increased in importance as a staging post along the Appian Way. The Villa Communale, at the entrance to Albano, overlooks the Roman Campagna and was once owned by Pompey. The *cisternone*, a massive reservoir hewn out of solid rock, dates from this period, and served as a source of water not only for the town's inhabitants but also for thirsty Roman legions.

Charming little Ariccia is next reached on the N7, another ancient village once surrounded by villas, now by vineyards and chestnut groves. Its most famous product, however, is *porchetta*; the inhabitants are noted for producing the best local version, and there are many shops and stalls from which to sample it. Neighbouring Genzano is located on the lip of another volcanic crater, this one filled in to create the lovely, smaller Lake Nemi. Genzano is famous for its annual flower festival, the *Infiorita*, which takes place after Easter in the week of Corpus Cristi. During this time the main avenue of the town is carpeted with flowers arranged in amazing pictorial patterns and intricate designs.

Small, deep, circular Lake Nemi was known in ancient times as the Mirror of Diana because a sacred grove and temple stood on its north-east side, reflected in the still, dark waters. The woods that covered the volcanic slopes (today they are covered with greenhouses for the cultivation primarily of flowers) were considered sacred to the goddess. During Roman times, an emperor, either Claudius or Caligula, had two full-scale galleys constructed, decorated elaborately with bronze, marble and other precious objects. After the fall of Rome, these enormous hulks remained at the bottom of the lake for centuries until the well-preserved hulls were eventually recovered in 1929, and lodged in two huge buildings by the lake's edge. After such a lengthy underwater sojourn, their return to the light of day was tragically short-lived, for the German army blew them up during the retreat in 1944. The remains were collected, and can be viewed in the lakeside museum. The medieval town of Nemi itself lies above the lake, a secret little hamlet dominated by its impressive castle. Nemi is most famous for its delicious wild strawberries, celebrated in a *Sagra delle Fragole* each June.

From Nemi, a tour of the wine hills can circle back to Rocca di Papa, at

680 metres above sea level the highest of the Castelli Romani. Otherwise, continue south to Velletri, not one of the 13 Castelli Romani, but none the less an important wine commune in its own right. It is noted not only for its typical white wine, but also for good local red wine produced mainly from Sangiovese and Montepulciano grapes, also entitled to the Velletri DOC.

The Castelli Romani are always popular venues for day-tripping Romans, even out of season. The hectic sprawl of Frascati into Grottaferrata into Marino, the hundreds of motorcycles, mopeds, and scooters, the traffic jams in summer, may hardly suggest an idyllic retreat from the city.

However, those in search of real peace, tranquillity, and exceptional foods and wines, need look no further than the adjoining Colli Lanuvini, the wine hills that centre on the nearby medieval town of Lanuvio, and which overlook not Rome but the plains that lead down to Aprilia, Anzio, and Latina. Lanuvio itself is much less visited than the better-known towns above, but it is no less charming. At weekends, the wines from this tiny, overlooked zone can be sampled and purchased from the *Enoteca Communale* located in the medieval tower in the town's main square.

Just outside Lanuvio, on the Tre Palme farm in the small hamlet of I Muti, Ernesto Lercher makes wine in the traditional fashion, as it has been made for centuries. The vineyards are cultivated entirely by organic methods, and the wine is produced as simply and naturally as possible. Vinified in part on the skins to utilize natural yeasts, and racked and bottled unfiltered according to the phases of the moon, the wine that results is gutsy, deep yellow, perhaps even slightly oxidized, and with a delicious, liquorice, bone-dry finish that makes it an excellent accompaniment to the foods of the region.

Lercher and his family are originally from the Südtirol, and they came to these wine hills south of Rome for the sheer passion of working the land together as a family unit. In the house that they built themselves, they offer not only their superb wines, but also accommodation in rooms or apartments, and delicious homemade foods mainly from their own-grown produce served on a terrace overlooking the vineyards. This is *agriturismo* – farmhouse tourism – at its best, and for any who have not yet sampled this unique form of holiday, it is an experience not to be missed.

Degustazione: Stop to Taste; Stop to Buy

1

CANTINE COLLI DI CATONE SPA
VIA FRASCATI 31/33
00040 MONTE PORZIO CATONE RM
TEL: 06/9449113

WINES PRODUCED: Frascati Superiore Colli di Catone, Frascati Superiore *cru* 'Colle Gaio'.
VISITS: Mon–Fri, by appointment.
Antonio Pulcini is a noted producer of traditional Frascati. His *cru* 'Colle Gaio', produced from severely limited yields of the superior Malvasia del Lazio grown on an exceptional 3-hectare vineyard, is one of the finest wines of the zone. The wine is macerated on the skins for 3 days prior to an extremely long, slow fermentation at controlled temperatures to result in a white wine of outstanding depth and concentration. The winery is located between Frascati and Monte Porzio.
Some English spoken.

2

VILLA SIMONE
VIA FRASCATI-COLONNA 29
00040 MONTE PORZIO CATONE RM
TEL: 06/3603575

WINES PRODUCED: Frascati Villa Simone, Frascati *cru* 'Vigneto Filonardi', Frascati Cannellino Villa Simone.
VISITS: daily, by appointment.

Piero Constantini produces outstanding wines, including the rare old-style, medium-dry Frascati Cannellino. The single vineyard Filonardi has been planted with a high density of low-yielding vines treated by organic precepts.
Some English spoken.

3

FONTANA CANDIDA
VIA VANVITELLI 20
00044 FRASCATI RM
TEL: 06/9420066

WINES PRODUCED: Frascati, Frascati Superiore, Frascati Superiore 'Santa Teresa'.

VISITS: Mon–Fri, by appointment. The best-known private producer, and a source of always reliable wines of character. Some 10 million bottles a year of Frascati are produced.

4

AZIENDA VITIVINICOLA PAOLA DI MAURO
VIA COLLE PICCHIONI 46
00040 FRATTOCCHIE DI MARINO RM
TEL: 06/9356329

WINES PRODUCED: Marino 'Colle Picchioni', Marino 'Colle Picchioni' Etichetta Oro; 'Colle Picchioni' Rosso (Merlot, Cesanese,

THE MEZZOGIORNO

Sangiovese, Montepulciano); 'Colle Picchioni' *cru* Vigna del Vassallo (Merlot, Cabernet Sauvignon, Cabernet Franc, Sangiovese); Le Vignole (Malvasia del Lazio, Trebbiano, Sauvignon, fermented in *barrique*).
VISITS: Mon–Fri, by appointment. Highly-regarded small-scale artisan

winery producing both white and red wines of the highest quality. Paola di Mauro's superlative Marinos gain their character in part through vinification with brief skin contact. The reds, especially the *cru* Vigna del Vassallo, have a great capacity for ageing.
English spoken.

---

5 AZIENDA AGRICOLA 'TRE PALME' LOC. I MUTI
VIA MUTI 42
00045 GENZANO DI ROMA RM
TEL: 06/9370286

WINES PRODUCED: Colli Lanuvini 'Mutino'; red *vino da tavola*.
VISITS: daily; no appointment necessary.

In addition to the traditional Colli Lanuvini 'Mutino', Ernesto's red is worth sampling, while other farm products include superlative homemade marmalade and preserves, olive oil, and vegetables, all of which are served in the farmhouse *trattoria* by reservation.
English, German spoken.

Enoteca

2 ENOTECA COMMUNALE
TORRE MEDIOVALE
00045 LANUVIO RM

OPEN: Sat 17–19h; Sun 9h30–12h; 16–19h.
This charming town *enoteca*, open weekends only, is located in the

medieval tower and is manned by enthusiastic pensioners. Good selection of the wines of the Colli Lanuvini, as well as a small collection of old farm and wine-making equipment.

Ristoranti

1 HOSTARIA FONTANA CANDIDA
VIA DI FONTANA CANDIDA 19
00040 MONTE PORZIO CATONE RM
TEL: 06/9449614

Closed Mon eve, Tue.

The Micara family has for many years run this welcoming, typically Roman *osteria*, located conveniently beside the Monte Porzio exit of the *autostrada*. Foods include *fettucine*, *crespelle di mare, vitello arrosto alle noci* together with a good selection of wines not only from Fontana Candida, but from elsewhere in the zone as well as throughout Italy. Meals served on the veranda in summer.

Moderate

---

2 CANTINA VIGNA VERDE AIOMONE
VIA MICHELANGELO GAITANI 8
00044 FRASCATI RM

Just one of scores of typical underground wine taverns – a rustic, dark drinking den serving strong, local wines by the carafe together with simple snacks.

Very Inexpensive

---

3 RISTORANTE 'AL VIGNETO'
VIA DEI LAGHI KM 4500
00040 MARINO RM
TEL: 06/9387034

Closed Tue.
Bustling traditional *trattoria* set amidst the vineyards of Marino serving *antipasti di mare, fettucine caserecce, bucatini all'amatriciana, abbacchio alla cacciatora, coniglio in porchetta*, and fresh fish, together with good local Marino.

Inexpensive to Moderate

---

4 HOTEL-RISTORANTE PAGNANELLI
00040 CASTEL GANDOLFO RM
TEL: 06/9360004

Friendly family hotel-restaurant located on the main road, and overlooking the lake. Restaurant serves simple foods, including trout and meats grilled over an open fire.

Inexpensive to Moderate

---

5 TRATTORIA DEI CACCIATORI DA
TIBERIO
PIAZZA UMBERTO 1
00040 NEMI RM
TEL: 06/9368096

Closed Tue.
The proprietors have changed, but the food is still good in this simple hunter's *trattoria* in the heart of old Nemi: *pappardelle alle lepre, fettucine ai funghi, abbacchio alla cacciatora, fragoline di Nemi.*

Inexpensive

THE MEZZOGIORNO

Punto di Ristoro Agrituristico

1

AZIENDA AGRITURISTICA 'TRE PALME'
(see address above)

The farmhouse *trattoria* of this wonderful oasis is open to all by reservation: Adele Lercher serves both local and Tyrolese specialities, while daughter Tabita makes the sweets. Rooms available for letting by the night or week.
Inexpensive

MONTEFIASCONE: *BONUM VINUM EST! EST!! EST!!!*

In Brief: Northern Latium borders southern Umbria and Tuscany, and so may be explored by those based in either region. The wine country around Lake Bolsena can easily be reached, for example, from either Orvieto or the southern Tuscan seaboard. Alternatively, Bolsena, located on the lake of the same name, makes a suitable base for exploration of wine lands and Etruscan ruins.

The little wine town of Montefiascone is located along the Via Cassia, the ancient Roman road that led from the north of Italy all the way down through the country to Rome itself. Thus, in ancient, medieval, and even modern (pre-*autostrada*) times, travellers from northern Europe descended on the Eternal City by means of this route.

Once, during the 12th century, a German bishop named Johannes Fugger was travelling south to Rome along the Via Cassia, presumably on ecclesiastical business. This pre-Reformation prelate was clearly a man who enjoyed the excesses of the table and, not one to waste time, he therefore sent his trusted servant Martin ahead of him to scout out the inns along the way which served the best wines. Martin's brief was to sample the wines, and to mark the doors of the best taverns with the Latin word '*Est*' ('it is', indicating that the wine was up to scratch).

Martin took to his task with considerable gusto, and the bishop's journey was a pleasant one as he travelled south in a drunken haze from one *osteria* to the next. At each, Martin's discreetly printed '*Est*' ensured that he need not waste his noble tastebuds on inferior *vinum*. The gates of Rome were almost in sight when Bishop Fugger arrived in the town of Montefiascone. But here, Martin, in an overzealous fit, had been so carried away with the

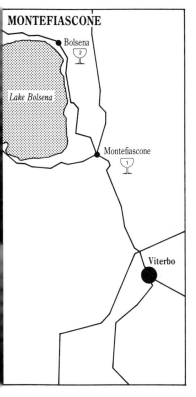

MONTEFIASCONE

Bolsena

Lake Bolsena

Montefiascone

Viterbo

wine that he scrawled the triple superlative '*Est! Est!! Est!!!*' on the tavern's door before presumably falling asleep in a drunken stupor.

Bishop Fugger never made it to Rome: so delicious was the wine (goes the story) that he stayed there until his death (untimely) from over-indulgence. Faithful Martin erected a tombstone that can still be seen in the churchyard of the romanesque Chiesa di San Flaviano. The poignant epithet reads:

Est. Est. Propter Nimtum
Est Hic Jo. Defuk Dominus
Meus Mortuus Est

Roughly translated, this means: 'Because of too much Est! Est!! Est!!! my master, Johannes Fugger, died here.' I consider that in the long history of the Church, there have been many worse causes for which to lay down one's soul to eternity.

Montefiascone itself is a rather charming medieval town, sleepy, somewhat run-down and little visited. The octagonal cathedral was erected in the 16th century, and there are still remains of the fortress that housed a number of popes.

Charming though I find the story of Bishop Fugger and his admirable devotion to the fruits of the vine, it has to be said that the wine Est! Est!! Est!!! di Montefiascone is really not all that great, great, great. On the other hand, it does not deserve to be wholly dismissed, simply because it cannot live up to the rather fanciful story of its derivation.

In fact, this confused volcanic terrain is singularly suited to the production of white wines, and the vineyards surrounding Lake Bolsena can be seen as an extension of the vineyards of Umbria's Orvieto zone, and Tuscany's Bianco di Pitigliano. These wines may none of them be world-beaters, but for easy, everyday drinking, they can be very satisfying all the same.

THE MEZZOGIORNO

Degustazione: Stop to Taste; Stop to Buy

1 CANTINA SOCIALE DI
MONTEFIASCONE
VIA CASSIA
01027 MONTEFIASCONE VT
TEL: 0761/86148

WINES PRODUCED: Est! Est!! Est!!!;
vino rosso da tavola.
VISITS: daily, working hours for
direct sales.

---

2 VILLA SEIANO
LOC. VILLA SEIANO
01023 BOLSENA VT
TEL: 0761/225870

WINE PRODUCED: Est! Est!! Est!!!
VISITS: by appointment, normally
Saturday morning.

Wine and Other Related *Sagre* and *Feste*

early June	Sagra delle Fragole	Nemi
end September	Festa dell'Uva	Lanuvio
1st Sun in Oct	Sagra dell'Uva	Marino
Corpus Cristi	Infiorita	Genzano

E PER SAPERE DI PIÙ – ADDITIONAL INFORMATION

Ente Provinciale per il Turismo
via Parigi 11
00185 Rome
tel: 06/461851

Ente Provinciale per il Turismo
Piazzale dei Caduti 16
01100 Viterbo
tel: 0761/226161

Consorzio Tutela Vini DOC
Frascati
via Matteotti 12/a
00044 Frascati RM
tel: 06/9420022

Azienda Autonoma Soggiorno e
Turismo
Piazza Marconi 1
00044 Frascati RM
tel: 06/940331

Associazione Agriturist Regionale
Corso Vittorio Emanuele 101
00186 Rome
tel: 06/6512342
(Note: this address is also that of
the national head office for the
Agriturist organization.)

ABRUZZI AND MOLISE

I Vini: THE WINES OF ABRUZZI AND MOLISE   406

La Gastronomia   407

Le Strade dei Vini: THE WINE ROADS OF
ABRUZZI AND MOLISE

    The Abruzzi   409

    Molise   411

Le Sagre: WINE AND OTHER RELATED FESTIVALS   412

Additional Information   413

Trebbiano grapes.

The Abruzzi and Molise have for centuries been Italy's most isolated zone. Originally a single Roman province, they were rejoined in 1860 and only officially separated again into 2 distinct regions in 1963. But they are still connected by geography and their history of remote isolation. The Apennine range is at its highest here and effectively cuts both areas off from the rest of the country, particularly to the north. Indeed, the Gran Sasso forms a towering and formidable barrier nearly 3000 metres high, and this has only recently been breached by the Gran Sasso tunnel and the completion of the Rome–L'Aquila *autostrada*. Even still, both the Abruzzi and Molise remain areas of great majestic unspoiled beauty: grandiose peaks, verdant valleys carved by roaring streams, and above all pasturelands for the traditional rearing of sheep and goats.

As everywhere else throughout Italy, the vine is cultivated in both regions. The wines of the Abruzzi have in recent years gained some attention, possibly helped by the fact that this is one of the country's few regions to have a single, simplified regional *denominazione di origine controllata* that applies to just 3 types of wine: Montepulciano d'Abruzzo, Montepulciano d'Abruzzo Cerasuolo (*rosato*), and Trebbiano d'Abruzzo. The wines of Molise, on the other hand, are rarely seen outside the region, let alone internationally. Therefore, there are two ways to sample them: either at the *Enoteca Permanente* in Siena, or by coming to the region itself. But make no mistake: this would be no great sacrifice. The very fact that both the Abruzzi and Molise remain undiscovered and well off the beaten track would be reason enough to come here.

THE MEZZOGIORNO

ORIENTATION

The Abruzzi and Molise are located on the Adriatic coast, roughly level with Latium but separated by the great spine of the Apennines. Abruzzi comprises 4 provinces: Teramo, Pescara, Chieti, and L'Aquila; Molise consists of 2: Isernia and Campobasso. Pescara's Pasquale Liberi airport is served by international flights, and also connects with regular domestic flights. Both regions lie along the main Milan–Bologna–Lecce rail line, while Pescara connects directly with Rome. The A24 *autostrada* which links Rome with Pescara has probably done more to open up the region than anything else, and the mountains are now popular venues for walking and winter sports. The A14 Bologna–Taranto *autostrada* which extends virtually the length of the Adriatic has also opened up both the Abruzzi and Molise. Be that as it may, this is still on the whole undiscovered country.

Map Touring Club Italiano 1: 200 000 Abruzzi & Molise.

I VINI: GLOSSARY TO THE WINES OF ABRUZZI AND MOLISE

Wines of *Denominazione di Origine Controllata (DOC)*

Biferno DOC Red, *rosato*, and white wines from delimited zone in Molise mainly along the Biferno river valley that traverses the region from its deep inland interior to the Adriatic coast. Red and *rosato* are produced from Montepulciano (60–70%) with Trebbiano Toscano (15–20%) and Aglianico (15–20%). Minimum alcohol 11.5 degrees. White is produced from Trebbiano Toscano (65–70%) with Bombino (25–30%) and Malvasia (5–10%). Minimum alcohol 10.5 degrees.

Montepulciano d'Abruzzo DOC Dense red wine produced in all 4 provinces from the Montepulciano grape with up to 15% Sangiovese. Quality can range from rustic country wine for local drinking only to fine wines suitable for conservation. Minimum alcohol 12 degrees. **Montepulciano d'Abruzzo Cerasuolo DOC** Same grapes grown throughout the region are utilized to produce light and popular *rosato*.

Pentro di Isernia DOC Delimited

vineyard in Molise province of Isernia for the production of red, *rosato*, and white wines. Red and *rosato* are produced from Montepulciano and Sangiovese. Minimum alcohol 11 degrees. White is produced from Trebbiano Toscano (60–70%) and Bombino (30–40%). Minimum alcohol 10.5 degrees.

Trebbiano d'Abruzzo DOC
Sound dry white wine produced throughout the region, mainly from hill vineyards planted with Trebbiano d'Abruzzo, Trebbiano Toscano, and other local grape varieties. Minimum alcohol 11.5 degrees.

THE TRANSHUMANCE

The raising of sheep and goats has long been a traditional mainstay of the Abruzzi and Molise. However, in these isolated and high zones where winter comes early and stays long and hard, there has for centuries been an annual migration when, before the coming of the first snows, the shepherds take their flocks over the mountain passes, down to the lusher, warmer, fertile pastures of Apulia. It is recorded that in the 17th century more than 5 million head of sheep were transhumed annually, and the men stayed away from home for months on end. If, today, shepherds may transport their flocks by truck or lorry, the old pastoral paths and sheep trails remain across the mountains, and they have given rise to popular activities such as trekking and hiking, especially in the Gran Sasso massif and throughout the Abruzzi National Park.

LA GASTRONOMIA: FOODS OF ABRUZZI AND MOLISE

As befits these two isolated mountainous regions located along the Adriatic coastline, the cuisine of Abruzzi and Molise is distinguished foremost by its simplicity born out of poverty. These are the foods of fishermen, hunters, herdsmen – people who had the ingenuity to turn meagre pickings into delicious regional specialities, usually highly piquant through the liberal use of the *peperoncino* chilli.

Indeed, such is the ingenuity of the people of the Abruzzi that the province

THE MEZZOGIORNO

of L'Aquila, a remarkable landlocked area centred on its medieval market town located in the Gran Sasso basin, is famous for supplying good and great chefs throughout the world.

PIATTI TIPICI: REGIONAL SPECIALITIES

Calcioni alla molisana *Ravioli*-like pasta stuffed with *ricotta* cheese and minced meat.

Maccheroni alla chitarra Egg pasta handmade by rolling out strips then passing them over a wooden frame with guitar-like steel wires to cut them. Usually served with *ragù* or with chilli-spiked tomato and *guanciale* (cured pork cheek) sauce.

Brodetto The classic Adriatic stew, here made with the daily catch, spiked, of course, with *peperoncino*.

Scrippelle 'mbusse Pancakes served in rich chicken broth. Some consider that *scrippelle* are the forerunners of French *crêpes*.

Virtù Famous soup made with 7 types of vegetables, 7 types of greens, and 7 types of pasta.

Coniglio alla molisana Rabbit Molise-style, that is, cut into pieces, skewered with sausage and herbs, then grilled over an open fire.

'Ndocca 'ndocca Hearty peasant stew made with pig's offal, ribs, and *guanciale*, cooked together with vinegar, chillies, and herbs.

Cheeses: *Pecorino* This great land of herdsmen yields not surprisingly a wealth of sheep's milk cheeses, soft and creamy, or hard and aged. *Scamorza* Bland cow's milk cheese that is best grilled. *Caciocavallo* Distinctive sack-shaped sheep's milk cheese eaten fresh or grilled.

THE ABRUZZI

In Brief: The Abruzzi is one of the most mountainous regions in Italy, and viticulture is not its most dominant agricultural activity. None the less, grape growing is still an important feature and table grapes as well as wine grapes are widely cultivated. About two-thirds of the viticultural crop goes to the region's 40 co-operative wineries. Half the crop is Montepulciano grapes for the production of the region's best red wine. Such wines have a lengthy historical pedigree, too: the poet Ovid was a native of the Abruzzi and sang their praises loudly.

Unusually, whereas most regions have a profusion of delimited vineyards with mainly provincial or local geographical indications, the Abruzzi chose to request a single regional DOC to apply to its 3 wines: Montepulciano d'Abruzzo, Montepulciano d'Abruzzo Cerasuolo, and Trebbiano d'Abruzzo. From the consumer's point of view, this has led to ease of recognition combined with the fact that the wines, whether produced in co-operative wineries or on private estates, are generally of a high standard. However, the region's terrain varies considerably, so there is an argument that more specific indications may eventually be warranted. The red wines in particular are of a quality that deserve more specific indications of provenance, and it is likely that in the future we may see, for example, more precise *denominazioni* for zones such as Torano Nuovo, or for provincial areas such as Chieti. Be that as it may, the Abruzzi remains as yet one of the great undiscovered regions of Italy, not least from a wine point of view. We include the addresses of 2 of the region's better-known private estates.

Degustazione: Stop to Taste; Stop to Buy

1 AZIENDA AGRICOLA ILLUMINATI DINO
C. DA SAN BIAGIO 18
64010 CONTROGUERRA TE
TEL: 0861/856631

WINES PRODUCED: Trebbiano d'Abruzzo; Montepulciano d'Abruzzo, Montepulciano d'Abruzzo Riserva 'Zanna', Montepulciano d'Abruzzo Cerasuolo; Nicolino (*vino frizzante fermentazione naturale*); Ciafre' (*riserva bianco*); Diamante d'Abruzzo (*spumante metodo champenois*).
VISITS: weekdays, working hours, without appointment.
German spoken.

THE MEZZOGIORNO

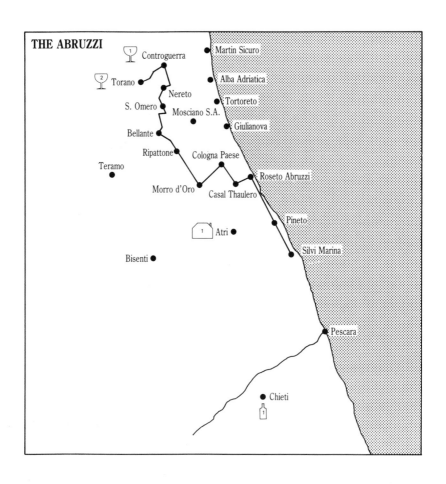

THE ABRUZZI

Controguerra
Torano
Nereto
S. Omero
Mosciano S.A.
Bellante
Ripattone
Teramo
Morro d'Oro
Casal Thaulero
Atri
Bisenti

Martin Sicuro
Alba Adriatica
Tortoreto
Giulianova
Cologna Paese
Roseto Abruzzi
Pineto
Silvi Marina
Pescara
Chieti

2 AZIENDA AGRICOLA PEPE EMIDIO
VIA CHIESI 10
64010 TORANO NUOVO TE
TEL: 0861/856493

WINES PRODUCED: Montepulciano
d'Abruzzo; Trebbiano d'Abruzzo.
VISITS: daily, by appointment.
Traditional production with
minimum intervention results in
characterful and forthright wines of
Abruzzo. The estate practises
agriturismo, so some
accommodation may be available.
English, some French and German
spoken.

Enoteca

1 ENOTECA TEMPLI ROMANI
VIA PRISCILLA 13
66100 CHIETI
TEL: 0871/69277

OPEN: Mon–Sat (except Thur afternoon) 9–13h; 16–20h.
Vast selection of local wines, as well as the best from throughout the country.
Some English spoken.

Agriturismo

1 AZIENDA AGRARIA VILLA FERRETTI
VILLA FERRETTI 10
64032 ATRI TE
TEL: 085/87202

Rooms for rent, camping, and farmhouse *punto di ristoro* serving

own-produced Montepulciano d'Abruzzo, *salame*, *olio*, bread and cheese. Located about 15 km from the Adriatic near the former Roman town of Atri.

MOLISE

In Brief: Molise is the second smallest region in Italy (only the Valle d'Aosta is smaller), with a population of less than half a million. Wine production is minuscule, but it should be noted none the less.

The most important area is the province of Campobasso, and in particular the vineyards of the Biferno valley which comprise the region's principal DOC. The area between Larino and Guglionesi is considered the best zone for the cultivation of Montepulciano and Sangiovese grapes for the hearty Biferno red wine.

The Pentri were an ancient tribe of the Samnites, best-known for their fierce resistance against Roman rule. Today, they have given their name to Molise's second DOC wine, Pentro di Isernia (known also simply as Pentro), from the province of Isernia. The vineyards are cultivated around Agnone in the valley of Verrino, as well as to the south-west of Isernia in the valley of Volturno.

At present, there are no exporting firms in Molise, but Majo-Norante has almost single-handedly put the wines of the region on the vinous map of Italy.

THE MEZZOGIORNO

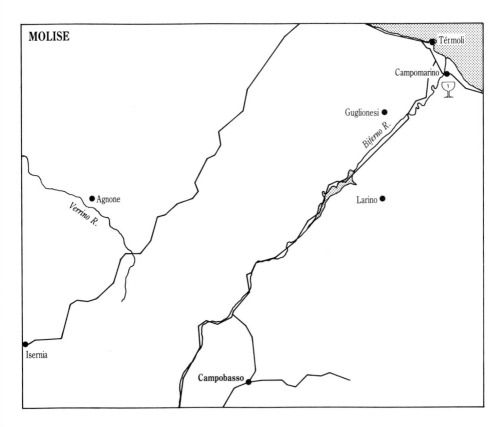

Degustazione: **Stop to Taste; Stop to Buy**

1 CANTINA DI MAJO-NORANTE
CONTRADA RAMITELLO 4 SS16
86042 CAMPOMARINO CB
TEL: 0875/57208

WINES PRODUCED: Ramitello *rosso*,
bianco; Molì Biferno *rosso, rosato,*
bianco.

VISITS: Mon–Fri by appointment.
Located on the coast near the
regional border with Apulia.
English spoken.

Wine and Other Related *Sagre* and *Feste*

early August	Mostro Interregionale di Vini	Montepagano
mid-August	Sagra del Vino, Salsiccia e Pecorino	Torano Nuovo
early Sept	Sagra della Porchetta	Campli
mid-Sept	Festa della Vendemmia	Corropoli

E PER SAPERE DI PIÙ –
ADDITIONAL INFORMATION

Ente Provinciale di Turismo
Piazza Santa Maria di Paganica
67100 L'Aquila
tel: 0862/25149

Ente Provinciale di Turismo
via Spaventa 29
66100 Chieti
tel: 0871/65231

Ente Provinciale di Turismo
via N. Fabrizi
65100 Pescara
tel: 085/22707

Ente Provinciale di Turismo
via del Castello 10
64100 Teramo
tel: 0861/51357

Ente Provinciale di Turismo
Piazza della Vittoria 14
86100 Campobasso
tel: 0874/95662

Ente Provinciale di Turismo
via Farinacci
86170 Isernia
tel: 0865/59590

Associazione Agriturist Regionale
via Catullo 39
65100 Pescara
tel: 085/61544

Associazione Agriturist Regionale
via Cavour 18
86100 Campobasso
tel: 0874/92912

THE MEZZOGIORNO

CAMPANIA

The town of Tufo, still in ruins even today.

I Vini: THE WINES OF CAMPANIA   415

La Gastronomia   418

Le Strade dei Vini: THE WINE ROADS OF CAMPANIA
    The Avellino Hills   418
    Falernum, Wine of Ancient Renown   427

Additional Information   430

Below the still active volcano lies a hotbedded country that is more vivid, more full of life, more exciting and dangerous than virtually anywhere else in Italy. Naples, the old crumbling Bourbon capital, of course dominates the region, the Amalfi coast remains as popular as ever, while the islands of Capri and Ischia, set like glittering paste in the rather murky Bay of Naples, still exercise their charms and attractions for Italian and foreign visitors alike.

Campania is one of the ancient wine regions of Italy, for the Campania Felix, as it was known to the Romans, served as their granary and vineyard and supplied those basics – bread and wine – to the capital of an Empire. Today the countryside outside Naples remains dominated by agriculture, a traditional mixture of grain, vegetables, vines and the raising of livestock such as cows, pigs and water buffalo. Admittedly, the region's wines collectively may no longer rank in the modern nation's first division – indeed the great majority do not even qualify for DOC status and are rarely seen outside their locality of production. But in one instance a trio of wines from the Avellino hills – Taurasi, Fiano di Avellino, and Greco di Tufo – continue to be produced which are as worthy of the zone's ancient patrimony as they are to take their place in the splendid legion of the great wines of Italy today.

Naples at any time of the year is one of the craziest and most hectic cities in the world, while in season the Amalfi coast drive is clogged with cars, exhaust fumes, and noise, and the Sorrentine peninsula is virtually inaccessible by sheer weight of numbers. But outside the over-populated and over-popular areas, the Campania countryside continues to exist at a slower pace, and the people are among the friendliest that you will meet anywhere.

ORIENTATION

Campania is located south of Latium on the shin of the Italian boot. The region consists of 5 provinces: Avellino, Benevento, Caserta, Naples, and Salerno. Naples is not only the regional capital, but the undoubted capital of the entire Mezzogiorno. The city's Capodichino airport serves the region, connecting with both international and domestic flights. Indeed, all communications centre on Naples, including rail and road. It lies on the principal north–south rail line that extends from Milan all the way along the west coast to Reggio-Calabria and Messina. There are local services to Pompeii and to Avellino.

Be warned: driving in Naples and its surroundings is not for the faint-hearted. That said, exploration of the Campania countryside requires a car. The region is well served by the A1 *Autostrada del Sole* that runs virtually the length of the country. The A16 *autostrada* cuts across the country, via Avellino, to Apulia, so that the Avellino wine zone could be dipped into by any heading in that direction.

There are frequent ferries from Naples and Sorrento to Capri and Ischia, both wine producing islands of note in their own right.

Map Touring Club Italiano 1: 200 000 Campania & Basilicata.

I VINI: GLOSSARY TO THE WINES OF CAMPANIA

Wines of *Denominazione di Origine Controllata (DOC)*

Capri DOC Red and white wines produced on, and almost wholly drunk by visitors to, this famous island. White is made from Falanghina and Greco grapes and goes well with local seafood. Red is produced from Piedirosso. Minimum alcohol for both is 11.5 degrees.

Falerno DOC The ancient Roman's favourite tipple, Falernum, produced today in red, *rosato*, and white versions from vineyards north of Mondragone near the coast. Red comes from Piedirosso and can be robust and full-bodied. White is crisp, full-bodied from the indigenous Falanghina grape from which the word Falernum was derived.

POMPEII

At about midday on 24 August AD 79 Mount Vesuvius erupted, sending flames rocketing into the air and belching forth clouds of black, poisonous gases which blocked out the sun and made day darker than night. Then, bits of red-hot pumice, blackened stone, and molten volcanic ash rained down on the surrounding communities for 3 whole days. Pompeii, a prosperous city of 20,000 inhabitants, was buried under a 5–6-metre blanket of death and total destruction.

Today Pompeii has been excavated by archaeologists, and the ancient city is revealed once more, frozen in time underneath its hardened blanket of ash. Like visitors from a time machine, we can walk its streets (still rutted from the tracks of chariots), peer into the courtyards of fine and extensive houses and villas, marvel at paintings and mosaics, and browse amongst the shops whose façades still beckon with pictures of wine *amphorae* or baskets of fruit. There are of course monumental temples, theatres, and the amphitheatre, but more interesting still are those buildings that reveal everyday life in the ancient city: bakeries, laundries, public baths and latrines, *tabernas*, shops that once sold hot drinks (precursors of the modern Italian bar), a brothel decorated with vividly lewd scenes. And there are the contorted plaster casts moulded from the void of decomposed organic matter that reveal more graphically than anything else the horror of that day, frozen in the grimaces, the pain, the clenched fists of the victims.

Today, as in the past, vines grow in the rich volcanic ash of Vesuvius, and wine nourishes the soul of a people whose spirit seems virtually indestructible, no matter what the adversity or natural or man-made tragedy.

Pompeii.

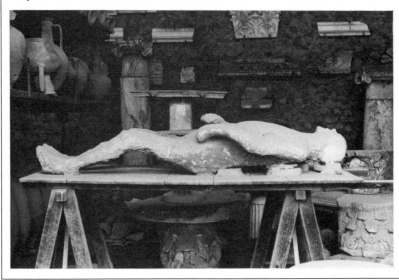

Fiano di Avellino DOC The best white wine of the region, and one of the great white wines of Italy: produced from at least 85% Fiano, the indigenous grape of Campania, the remainder made up of Greco, Coda di Volpe, and Trebbiano, all grown in the hill vineyards of Avellino. Minimum alcohol 11.5 degrees.

Greco di Tufo DOC Another distinguished white wine of the Avellino hills, produced from Greco grapes (80% at least), and Coda di Volpe. Minimum alcohol 11.5 degrees.

Ischia DOC Red and white island wines that are rather more distinguished than those of neighbouring Capri: white is produced from the local Forestera grape (65%) together with Biancolella and has a minimum alcohol of 11 degrees. Red is produced from Guarnaccia, Piedirosso, and Barbera. Minimum alcohol 11.5 degrees.

Solopaca DOC Red and white wines from the province of Benevento: white is produced from Trebbiano Toscano, Malvasia, and Coda di Volpe; red is produced from Sangiovese, Aglianico, and Piedirosso.

Taurasi DOC Campania's world-class red, produced from Aglianico grapes (together with optional small proportions of Piedirosso, though the leading producer utilizes none) grown in the Avellino hills. This is a wine that requires lengthy ageing before it is ready to drink: it cannot be released by law with less than 3 years' ageing, and 4 years' for wines labelled Riserva. Minimum alcohol 12 degrees.

Taburno; **Aglianico di Taburno DOC** Delimited zone of Taburno hills near Avellino for the production of red and *rosato* wines from the Aglianico grape.

Vesuvio DOC Red, *rosato*, and white wine produced from grapes grown in the mineral-rich volcanic ash of Vesuvius. Red and *rosato* are produced from Piedirosso; white is produced from Coda di Volpe. The best-known is the white labelled as Lacryma Christi del Vesuvio, and is made in dry, medium, and sweet versions.

THE MEZZOGIORNO

LA GASTRONOMIA: FOODS OF CAMPANIA

Plum tomatoes, *mozzarella*, dried pasta, pungent garlic, bread and wine: these are the 'poor' staples of Campania, foods from the wretched alleys of Naples which have gone out and conquered the world. It may be a truism that great cuisines are born out of poverty: in Campania such foods are a celebration not just of a people's ingenuity at making something palatable out of humble ingredients, they are a celebration of the bounty and goodness of life itself.

Indeed, here, where tomatoes ripen under a splendid sun that almost always shines, what more is needed than the simplest salad, sliced up and layered with moist *mozzarella*, dusted with fresh herbs, and bathed in olive oil? Pizza may now be served throughout the world in many hundreds of varieties, but in its homeland it is still enjoyed best *'alla marinara'*, that is with the bread dough spread with no more than olive oil, garlic, fresh tomatoes, and salt and pepper, and cooked in a *forno di legno* – a wood-fired oven. Nowhere else in the world will you find fruit or vegetables with such richness of flavour and perfume. Meats when they are eaten (which is not regularly) are simply grilled, and any variety of seafood and shellfish – preferably caught or gathered yourself – can be sautéd in abundant garlic and olive oil and served over pasta, or else deep-fried or simply grilled. These and others may be foods born out of poverty and necessity: but today when we are all seeking the purer, genuine flavours from another age, they are all the more satisfying. See page 419.

THE AVELLINO HILLS

In Brief: The Avellino wine hills extend over the province of Avellino, whose capital lies about 50 km due east of Naples. The area suffered greatly from the earthquake of 1980 and has not yet recovered. Even before that disaster, though, it was never developed for tourism. However, serious students of Italian wine may wish to make a visit to the masters of Campania, Mastroberardino, whose rebuilt winery is located in Atripalda near Avellino, as well as to explore further this fascinating, down-at-heel, but extremely friendly wine country.

PIATTI TIPICI: REGIONAL SPECIALITIES

Lampasciuoli Highly-prized, bitter, wild onion-like tuber, usually boiled, then marinated in oil and served as *antipasto*.

Pomodori secchi Sun-dried tomatoes. Usually eaten as *antipasto* together with *mozzarella*.

Salame napoletane Usually quite tough, hard, and spicy, highly seasoned with salt, pepper, garlic, and sometimes chillies.

Mozzarella in carrozza *Mozzarella* sandwiched between bread and deep-fried.

Spaghettini alle vongole The classic pasta of Campania: thin spaghetti served with tiny clams sautéed in plenty of olive oil and garlic.

Maccheroni General term for long pasta, not simply for the tube-like variety we know as such.

Parmigiana di melanzane Great layered casserole of sliced aubergine, *mozzarella*, tomatoes and basil, baked in an oven. A virtual meal in itself.

Involtini Meat balls made from minced pork or beef, mixed together with spices, raisins, pine nuts, garlic, and herbs, then fried and simmered slowly in tomato sauce.

Cheeses: *Mozzarella di bufala* The real thing comes only from Campania, made with the milk of water buffalo. *Fior di latte* Mozzarella made with cow's milk. *Provolone* Large round sheep's milk cheese sometimes smoked (*affumicato*). *Cacioricotta* Hard, aged *ricotta* cheese. *Caciocavallo* Classic cheese of the south, made usually from sheep's milk.

At 7.23 p.m. on 24 November 1980 a devastating earthquake struck the provinces of Avellino, Potenza, Naples, and Salerno. It lasted 80 seconds and measured 6.8 on the Richter scale. In its aftermath, more than 200,000 people were left homeless and there were more than 3000 fatalities. In the 33 aftershocks that rebounded and added further destruction, Avellino's medieval centre was almost razed to the ground, and was described in an eyewitness report as 'a ghost town lying amid piles of rubble'. The family

THE MEZZOGIORNO

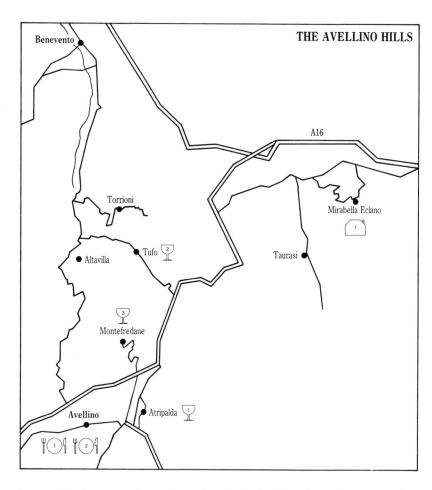

home of Avellino's leading wine maker Antonio Mastroberardino, a rambling old patrician palace in the centre of Atripalda, was destroyed but fortunately nobody was killed. In the old tufa cellars, 4 immense Slavonian *botti* of wine and 38,000 bottles of Taurasi Riserva were lost. 'More, much more than any material loss,' remembers his son Carlo Mastroberardino, then a 16-year-old. 'The earthquake changed all our lives: an event like that gives you such a different perspective on how small, how helpless and insignificant we all are. In a sense we have been rebuilding not just our livelihoods but our lives ever since.'

In the nearby hill town of Tufo, Michele Buonomo, cellarmaster of the Azienda Agricola Di Marzo, was watching television in his sitting room overlooking the village square when the earthquake struck. It destroyed the

Michele Buonomo.

church completely and profoundly damaged every house in the village. If the earthquake had struck half an hour earlier during evening mass there would have been many dead. Today, the façade of the church is all that remains; the bar and post office were destroyed too, robbing the community and its surroundings of their centre. More than a decade later, they have still not yet been rebuilt.

Buonomo and his wife spent 7 years living with friends and family. It did not take that long to rebuild their house: rather the bureaucracy which led to delays in compensation, the inefficiency, and the inevitable graft, greed and corruption which siphoned off much of the large sums of money sent by a shocked world resulted in virtually another tragedy in itself. Today, Tufo and scores of towns like it, are still in a shambles, with piles of rubble everywhere, houses propped up or abandoned, people living makeshift lives, waiting for normality to return, if ever.

When the earthquake struck that year, the grape harvest had already been completed. Yet, amazingly, Mastroberardino and Buonomo separately remember how just days after the disaster the workers, many homeless and living outside in freezing winter temperatures, were back in the *cantine* ready to continue the necessary wine making tasks at what was traditionally one of the busiest times of the year. This was not simply out of the need to reassert normal daily activity in a world literally turned topsy-turvy: it was also out of pressing economic necessity and the realization that if the

THE MEZZOGIORNO

wines were not made, then a year's income would be lost at a time when clearly money was going to be needed more than ever. For viticulture has been an important way of life – indeed one of the only decent ways of making a living in this desperate poverty-stricken region – for literally millennia.

The vine has been planted on the mountainous slopes of Avellino since time immemorial. The ancient Greeks introduced both Aglianico (*Vitis hellenico*) and Greco to the zone, but the temperamental Fiano (called *Vitis apianum* by Pliny because of honey bees' apparent fondness for the super-sweet grapes) was here even earlier, a true indigenous variety found nowhere else. Under the Romans, the vineyards of the so-called Campania Felix quenched the thirst of an Empire. Today these same ancient grapes yield a trio of wines that are certainly Campania's finest. Indeed, it would not be going too far to say that the Mastroberardino's Greco di Tufo, Fiano di Avellino, and Taurasi (made entirely from Aglianico) may rank among the great wines not only of Italy, but of the world.

The Mastroberardino family trace their wine heritage back to 1580 when an antecedent named Berardino was a Master of Wine (thus Mastroberardino) in nearby Naples. Soon after, the family established themselves in Atripalda, and the oldest parts of the family cellars were carved out by hand from the soft volcanic tufa in 1720. Angelo Mastroberardino founded the present company in 1878, though international markets had already been established in the early 19th century. After World War II, however, the winery lost virtually all its old markets, the Germans had destroyed every single cask of wine in the cellars during their retreat, and the company was left virtually bankrupt.

Since then, Antonio Mastroberardino and his family have rebuilt the company not by adapting to international tastes, but by constructing a winery based firmly on the ancient patrimony of viticulture in the region, a courageous decision given the fact that wines such as Taurasi and Greco were at the time – are even to a large extent today – virtually unknown internationally compared to Italian wines such as Chianti or Barolo.

The Fiano grape, even in the region itself, was virtually non-existent. For over the years and centuries, its perennial low yields, combined with a malady known as floral abortion, led the growers of the region to grub up this historic grape and replace it with easier, more prolific varieties. After the war, only isolated vines remained here and there, planted haphazardly amongst rows of other varieties. Mastroberardino, however, believed that this most ancient grape should not be allowed to disappear, and thus he carefully nurtured the old vines and from them propagated new. In 1952 he was thus able to harvest 50 kg of Fiano grapes and made 30 bottles of Fiano. Today the production of this rare wine is still severely limited, resulting in little more than 5000 cases a year, but the wine repays such dedication: intensely concentrated, elegant and harmonious, it is unique and unlike any other white wine of Italy. Moreover, like Greco, it has the rare ability to benefit from bottle age for upwards of 10 or 15 years.

Such dedication is to be admired and applauded, especially in a world where uniform international tastes seem increasingly to dictate all. 'The world does not need another Chardonnay or Cabernet Sauvignon. But Greco, Taurasi, and Fiano are unique. They cannot be produced anywhere else. It is our duty to safeguard them,' says Mastroberardino.

There is, significantly, no *barrique* to be seen in the newly rebuilt super-modern, earthquake-proof winery, for the Mastroberardinos do not believe in pandering to the latest fashions in wine. 'Besides,' adds Carlo, 'we don't believe that the taste of new oak would be right for these wines.' At the same time, it should perhaps be pointed out that the wines of Avellino, precisely because of their unique character that is so markedly different from wines produced elsewhere, may not be immediately attractive to the newcomer. Taurasi is a notoriously slow developer. Indeed, it is aged for at least 3 years before it is released and a minimum of 4 for the *riserve* and *cru* 'Radici', and even then, the wine improves dramatically after up to a decade's bottle age or more. Greco di Tufo has a creamy, rich, opulent character that is almost completely at odds with the vogue for light, crisp, neutral white wines that are found elsewhere. It too is a wine that demands thought and consideration, and which takes time to develop.

Mastroberardino is the leading producer in the zone, and virtually the only one whose wines will be encountered outside Campania. As such, any wine lover visiting Campania will undoubtedly wish to visit the winery in Atripalda. Although it and the neighbouring town of Avellino, like the entire region, remain severely damaged by the earthquake and thus are grim to say the least, the intrepid wine traveller may wish to explore the region's hinterland further.

Avellino itself was the centre for the indigenous Irpini, a fierce barbarian tribe which was only subdued by the Romans in 80 BC with the passing of the Edict of Silla; even today this region is therefore known as Irpinia. The Irpino Museum in Avellino documents the zone's history from prehistoric times.

As for the zone as a whole, like a visit to Pompeii, a tour of these vine-covered hills and small wine villages is a sadly moving experience – indeed,

THE MEZZOGIORNO

far more so than Pompeii, for here the suffering continues even today. One is eavesdropping again on pain, human courage and resilience. Even before the tragedy of the earthquake, this was a region locked hopelessly in rural poverty, crumbling and depressing. And yet come all the same to Tufo, not as a *voyeur* but to visit an ancient and historic wine town, and to marvel at the amazing tufa *cantina* of Di Marzo, one of the most fascinating and remarkable that we have seen anywhere. The Greco di Tufo produced in this antiquated, museum-like cavern is astounding, all the more so given the devastation that still remains above ground.

Other important wine towns include Montefusco, Torrione, Altavilla, and of course Taurasi itself, an old Roman town that once controlled the valley (today little remains from that classic era when Taurasia was the 'city of towers').

Avellino may be only some 50 km from Naples, but when you are here it feels more like a million miles from anywhere. The region, of course, is isolated from Naples by the broad barrier of Vesuvius which dominates Campania. The slopes of Vesuvius, rich in deep, volcanic ash, have long been fertile ground for the vine. Indeed, local legend has it that this was one of the earth's first vineyards: for when the Archangel Lucifer fell from grace, he clutched a piece of Paradise with him on his descent into the Bay of Naples. When God saw this, He cried and where His tears fell on the slopes of Vesuvius, there grew the first vines. Or so say the priests. Today Lacryma Christi del Vesuvio (both red and white) remains one of the principal DOC wines of Campania.

The story points to an ecclesiastical origin of this historic vineyard, when such wines were made for the celebration of mass. However, it is certain that the slopes were planted with vineyards even earlier than the Roman era. An ancient winery has recently been discovered and excavated on the outskirts of Pompeii. The archaeologists, significantly, consulted Antonio Mastroberardino in their attempts to understand the excavations, and there is even talk now of replanting the vineyard as part of the archaeological reconstruction, perhaps even making wine from the grapes. Indeed, nowhere else in the world do history and tradition in the vineyard provide such a close and continuous link over the centuries.

Degustazione: Stop to Taste; Stop to Buy

1 AZIENDA VINICOLA
MASTROBERARDINO
VIA MANFREDI 45
83042 ATRIPALDA AV
TEL: 0825/626123

WINES PRODUCED: Taurasi, Taurasi Riserva, Taurasi *cru* 'Radici'; Greco di Tufo, Greco di Tufo *cru* 'Vigndangelo'; Fiano di Avellino, Fiano di Avellino *cru* 'Vignadora', *cru* 'Radici di Lapio'; Lacryma Christi del Vesuvio Bianco, Lacryma Christi del Vesuvio Rosso; Lacrimarosa d'Irpinia (*rosato*); Plinius.

VISITS: Mon–Sat morning, by appointment.

The Mastroberardino family own about 100 hectares of vineyards and control another 100 through family and long-standing contracts. After the earthquake of 1980, the old winery was completely rebuilt, though the oldest parts of the cellars remain intact and serve as bottle store for Taurasi Riserva. The winery is now among the most modern in Italy, and boasts state-of-the-art technology, including ultra-filtering operations, computer-controlled fermentation in stainless steel, and an almost wholly automatic computer-controlled bottling line.

In addition to the classic trio of Greco di Tufo, Fiano di Avellino, and Taurasi, new wines are being developed, such as Plinius, a remarkable full-bodied white wine vinified *in bianco* from the black Aglianico.

The family residence above the winery is in the process of being completely rebuilt, and Carlo Mastroberardino hopes in due course to open an *enoteca* for tastings and direct sales, and a restaurant.

English spoken.

---

2 AZIENDA AGRICOLA DI MARZO
VIA G. DI MARZO 11
83010 TUFO AV
TEL: 0825/998022

WINES PRODUCED: Greco di Tufo; *rosso vino da tavola* (Aglianico).

VISITS: daily. Telephone Michele Buonomo before coming.

The Di Marzo family have been important landowners in the Greco area since 1642, though the winery was founded in 1827 (the family also founded and still work a sulphur factory in the area). Today, in earthquake-ravaged Tufo, this winery seems almost from another era, an ancient, ramshackle *cantina* hollowed out of tufa on several storeys snaking beneath the streets of the medieval hill village.

The white Greco di Tufo is fermented in concrete or wood, and

THE MEZZOGIORNO

the free-run juice is blended with a little press wine to give it more body, for this is a full, opulent, old-style white that is fascinating and delicious. The red *vino da tavola* is another traditional wine, made from the noble Aglianico, but raspingly tannic in youth and definitely something of an acquired taste.

---

3 AZIENDA VITIVINICOLA 'VADIAPERTI'
VIA VADIAPERTI
FRAZ. ARCELLA
83030 MONTEFREDANE AV
TEL: 0825/36263; 607270

WINES PRODUCED: Fiano di Avellino; Greco di Tufo.
VISITS: weekdays, after 16h, or by appointment.

Another source of these two rare and difficult-to-find wines. The search for them is definitely worth the trouble because they are not mere historical curiosities but wines produced under the most extreme conditions and of the highest quality.
English, French spoken.

Ristoranti

1 HOTEL JOLLY
VIA TUORO CAPPUCCINI 97/A
83100 AVELLINO
TEL: 0825/25922

Apparently this modern chain is the only decent hotel in the area: the restaurant is uninspired, but serves good *antipasto, spaghetti al vecchio Napoli, scaloppine al Greco di Tufo*, together with the full range of wines from Mastroberardino.
English spoken.
Hotel **Expensive**; Restaurant **Moderate to Expensive**.

---

2 RISTORANTE 'MALAGA'
VIA F.SCO TEDESCO 347
83100 AVELLINO
TEL: 0825/626045

Closed Tue.
The menu of this popular restaurant is based entirely on fish: *insalata di mare, spaghetti alle vongole, linguine agli scampi, pesce acqua pazza, grigliata mista*, and local wines.
A little English spoken.
Moderate

Agriturismo

1 PODERE 'LA TAVERNETTA'
LOC. MARTINELLI
83036 MIRABELLA ECLANO AV
TEL: 0825/431284

Farmhouse camping, and
own-produced wine, vegetables,
salame, cheese, and conserves.

FALERNUM, WINE OF ANCIENT RENOWN

In Brief: The vineyards of ancient Rome's most famous wine, Falernum, are in production once more for its modern version, Falerno. The wine zone lies along the coast just below the regional border with Latium, on the ancient Via Appia north of the town of Mondragone. This is quiet, peaceful country, a pleasant interlude between the crazy, hectic bustle of Rome and Naples, where the incongruous sight of water buffaloes amidst vines seems somehow to be in perfect harmony.

Salvatore Avallone, of the Fattoria Villa Matilde, has a most pleasant *agriturismo* complex on the winery estate with apartments around a communal swimming pool, popular in summer with English visitors and friends.

Falernum is one of the most famous wines of antiquity. In his epigrams, Martial wrote of drinking it to soothe the pain and loneliness after his lover deserted him. The poet Virgil, who settled in Campania, also enjoyed Falernum and once wrote *'Nec cellis ideo contendere Falernis'*, a statement of the futility of attempting to compete against Falernum wine, which at the time was considered pre-eminent by the Romans. The Scuola Medica Salernitana described *'Vinum album Phalanginum'* thus: *'Si bona vina cupis, quinque haec laudantur in illis: fortia, formosa, fragrantia, frigida, fresca'*, so naming the 5 virtues of Falanghina wine as strength, beauty, fragrance, freshness, and a slightly sparkling quality.

The name Falernum was derived from the ancient indigenous Falanghina grape. Undoubtedly in Roman days, Falernum, like all Roman quality wines, was aged and concentrated: a dense, sweetish beverage that was meant to be mixed by the *arbiter* in the typical decorated terracotta mixing bowls with honey, spices, resins and water before drinking. It was among the most famous and prized of all wines of its time. Yet, as recently as a

THE MEZZOGIORNO

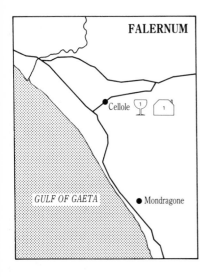

quarter of a century ago, the ancient grape variety from which it was produced, the Falanghina, was on the point of extinction. Phylloxera had virtually wiped out the plant at the turn of the century, and growers had replanted with easier-to-grow, higher-yielding vines.

Dottore Avallone, a lawyer and classical scholar from Naples, continually came across references to Falernum in his studies, and his passion for the past as well as for wine led him to attempt to recover this ancient patrimony. Hence he purchased Villa Matilde, an old wine estate in the heart of the historical Falernum vineyard north of Mondragone on the Campanian seaboard. There, like Antonio Mastroberardino and his work with the Fiano grape, Avallone nurtured existing Falanghina vines and at the same time propagated new plants, thus safeguarding for posterity this historic vine. Today Falanghina is planted elsewhere in Campania, but it thrives best on the plains of its traditional homeland.

Fortunately for Avallone, as well as for curious students of the grape, such efforts have proved worth while. There is little point, after all, in preserving grape varieties that give wines of little more than mere historical interest. Falerno Bianco, produced entirely from the Falanghina grape, is a white wine of considerable character and elegance; vinified by modern methods, it none the less manages to escape the blandness and uniform neutrality that has been the fate of so many other Italian whites. For example, though temperature controlled fermentation is of course a necessity, the grape must is not ultra-filtered. Rather, natural precipitation at low temperatures results in a clean must that retains more of the integral varietal character of the Falanghina.

At Villa Matilde, a red Falerno is also produced, from Aglianico and Piedirosso. The best wines (both *riserva* and *cru*) ferment in part in small 250-litre barrels made from Slavonian, not French, oak. 'We felt that the pronounced woody flavours of *barrique* are not right for our wine,' explained Salvatore Avallone. The results are full, powerful red wines that combine finesse and delicacy.

Such dedication to making historic wines with passion and utilizing modern, sound viticulture techniques has recently been rewarded with elevation to DOC status for both Falerno white and red, a recognition based not simply on prestigious lineage, but on the quality of wines being made in the zone today by the best properties.

The Falerno vineyard extends a short way from the northern Campanian seaboard north of Mondragone into the gentler hills above. Located roughly half-way between Rome and Naples off the ancient Via Appia, it is a quiet, lovely zone that can be explored en route between those two great cities. To the north, across the border in Latium there are interesting sea towns such as Gaeta and Terracina to explore. Mondragone itself is an old Roman town, and the centre, among other things, for the production of *mozzarella di bufala*. The main reason for coming to the zone, though, is simply to enjoy the peace and tranquillity of the Campania Felix, the great vineyard and granary of ancient Rome, to relax in countryside where patricians once built villas, and to drink an ancient wine restored once more to a fitting pedestal.

Degustazione: **Stop to Taste; Stop to Buy**

1

FATTORIA VILLA MATILDE
SS DOMIZIANA KM 4799
81030 CELLOLE CE
TEL: 0823/932088

WINES PRODUCED: Falerno Bianco, Falerno Rosato, Falerno Rosso, Falerno Rosso Nobile Riserva.
VISITS: Mon-Sat, working hours. No appointment necessary for direct sales.
What began as a hobby for classical scholar Dottore Avallone has become a well-tended winery of considerable renown. Today the family works some 70 hectares of specialized viticulture. About 70% of the wine produced is Falerno Bianco from the Falanghina grape, produced in the extremely modern winery. The Falerno Riserva Rosso, however, is also worthy of serious consideration.

Located along the coastal *superstrada*, the Fattoria has a *punta di vendita* open working hours, and Salvatore Avallone is always interested to meet serious wine lovers and show them the winery and vineyards.
English spoken.

Agriturismo

1

Villa Matilde has 3 apartments on the Fattoria estate that are available for rental in season by the week or month. Telephone or write to the above address.

THE MEZZOGIORNO

E PER SAPERE DI PIÙ –
ADDITIONAL INFORMATION

Ente Provinciale per il Turismo
via Partenope 10a
80121 Naples
tel: 081/95662

Ente Provinciale per il Turismo
via Due Principati 5
83100 Avellino
tel: 0825/35169

Ente Provinciale per il Turismo
Palazzo Reale
81100 Caserta
tel: 0823/322233

Associazione Agriturist Regionale
via S. Lucia 90
80132 Naples
tel: 081/412374

APULIA

I Vini: THE WINES OF APULIA   432

La Gastronomia   437

Le Strade dei Vini: THE WINE ROADS OF APULIA
  From Bari to Brindisi: In the Land of the *Trulli*   437
  The Salentine Peninsula: Italy's Ancient,
  Well-worn Heel   445

Le Sagre: WINE AND OTHER RELATED FESTIVALS   456

Additional Information   456

Alberobello.

Though Apulia today may seem very far out on a long, lanky limb, it should be recalled that this was once one of Europe's great gateways – the departure and entry along the Via Appia to and from the eastern Mediterranean and the Levant (from Otranto, on a clear day, you can see Albania). Cities such as Bari and Lecce retain a somewhat cosmopolitan feel about them, and the influences of a multi-chequered past.

Vines are everywhere. This is Europe's single largest vineyard, contributing a massive annual 15% or more of the entire Italian wine output. Most of this wine has traditionally served as *vino da taglio* – strong, highly coloured 'cutting wine' to blend with insipid, thinner, lighter table wines from the north or from France. The vermouth industry of Turin has always been one important customer, for the robust but neutral white wines of Apulia serve as an excellent base for that aromatized *aperitivo*. However, these markets have shrunk appreciably over recent years, and much Apulian wine has merely spilled over into the EEC's already flooded surplus 'wine lake'.

Yet, as in the rest of Italy, there are new attitudes to wine making emerging even in this deepest outpost. The best wine growers are taking advantage of new viticultural techniques (primarily new methods of training vines, allied with severe reduction of yields and the picking of grapes at their moment of optimal acidity), as well as modern technology in the *cantina* to produce a range of premium wines that are remarkably varied and excellent in quality.

Apulia today is an exciting region, with its potential only just beginning to be realized and appreciated, not just as a wine zone of quality, but as an area

THE MEZZOGIORNO

of great charm, history, and natural beauty. Surprisingly, tourism is not yet highly developed, though the region is increasingly popular with northern Italians, understandably so. There are literally miles of clean, unspoiled beaches; the weather is almost always reliable; there is much of cultural and historic interest; the regional table is varied and colourful; and the local wines always slip down very well indeed.

ORIENTATION

Apulia comprises not only the heel of the Italian boot but a good deal of its calf as well, extending north as far as the Gargano peninsula. It is made up of 5 provinces: Bari (the region's capital), Brindisi, Foggia, Lecce, and Taranto. To reach this furthest outpost there are international flights direct to Brindisi's Casale airport, as well as domestic connections to both Brindisi and Bari. By rail, the major east coast line extends south from Bologna to Bari and Brindisi via Ancona, Pescara, and Foggia. By car, the A14 *autostrada* connects the region via the Adriatic coast with Bologna and points north, while the A16 connects Bari with Naples.

Brindisi is still the gateway to the eastern Mediterranean and there are regular ferries to Yugoslavia and Greece. Apulia therefore makes more than a pleasant stop-over for any heading in those directions.

Map Touring Club Italiano 1: 200 000 Puglia.

I VINI: GLOSSARY TO THE WINES OF APULIA

Wines of *Denominazione di Origine Controllata (DOC)*

Aleatico di Puglia DOC Sweet red wine from the Aleatico grape (minimum 85%) and other local varieties produced throughout the region. Minimum alcohol 13 degrees plus 2 degrees residual sugar. A fortified *liquoroso* version is also produced.

Alezio DOC Red and *rosato* wines produced from Negro Amaro grapes with some Malvasia Nera in the province of Lecce mainly around the wine commune of Alezio near Gallipoli. Minimum alcohol 12 degrees; 2 years' minimum ageing for Riserva.

OLIVE OIL IN GALLIPOLI

The Salentine peninsula is a great source not only of abundant and generous wines, but also of olive oil. In the last century in particular, Gallipoli was the major port for its export all over Europe and the world. Indeed, the old town is still riddled with ancient hand-dug caves, for there were once some 35 subterranean olive oil mills in the medieval centre producing this precious commodity. These mills were each worked by 4 men and 1 or 2 donkeys (to turn the heavy mill-stones), who all lived and ate together underground for some 6 months of the year, working the mills non-stop 24 hours a day and rarely emerging into the sunlight. The reconstructed mill in the Palazzo Granafei demonstrates graphically how the mills functioned, as well as what a grim and brutal existence it must have been. Even as recently as 30 years ago such mills were still in operation.

At the height of production in the last century, the quays of Gallipoli were awash with thousands of barrels of oil to be transported by ship above all to Great Britain, Russia, France and elsewhere. The oil served not for culinary purposes, but primarily as a fuel for lighting (olive oil, apparently, burns very cleanly and leaves no deposit), and as a lubricant to ease the wheels and gears of the Industrial Revolution.

Antico Frantoio
Palazzo Granafei
73014 Gallipoli LE
OPEN: April–Oct daily
9–12h; 17–21h.
Weekends out of
season.

Reconstructed olive oil mill, Gallipoli.

THE MEZZOGIORNO

Brindisi DOC Red and *rosato* wines produced from the Negro Amaro grape in the province of Brindisi around the wine communes of Brindisi and Mesagne. Minimum alcohol 12 degrees. At least 12.5 degrees and 2 years' ageing for wines labelled Riserva.

Cacc'e Mmitte di Lucera DOC Obscure but colourfully named red wine from the province of Foggia (in dialect signifies 'drink your fill and fill again'), produced from blend of grapes including Troia, Montepulciano, Sangiovese, Malvasia Nera, Trebbiano Toscano, and Bombino. Minimum alcohol 11.5 degrees.

Castel del Monte DOC Outstanding delimited zone in the province of Bari for the production of red, *rosato*, and white wines. Castel del Monte Rosso is from Troia, together optionally with Bombino Nero, Montepulciano, and Sangiovese. Minimum alcohol 12 degrees; wines with minimum alcohol of 12.5 degrees and aged for at least 3 years (1 in wood) may be labelled Riserva. Castel del Monte Rosato is well-known and is produced from Bombino Nero, together optionally with Troia and Montepulciano. Minimum alcohol 11.5 degrees. Castel del Monte Bianco may be produced from Pampanuto with Trebbiano Toscano, Bombino Bianco, and Palumbo. Minimum alcohol 11.5 degrees.

Copertino DOC Red and *rosato* wines produced from Negro Amaro grapes with some Malvasia Nera, Malvasia di Brindisi, Montepulciano, and Sangiovese in the province of Lecce mainly around the wine communes of Copertino, Galatina, and Lequile. Minimum alcohol 12 degrees; wines with minimum alcohol of 12.5 degrees and aged for at least 2 years may be labelled Riserva.

Gioia del Colle DOC Relatively recent wine zone south of Bari around Gioia del Colle and surrounding communes of the Murge for the production of red and *rosato* (from Primitivo, Montepulciano, and Sangiovese), white (mainly from Trebbiano Toscano), and Primitivo di Gioia (from Primitivo).

Gravina DOC Dry white wine produced from Malvasia del Chianti, Greco di Tufo, and Bianco d'Alessano from vineyards around commune of Gravina in the interior of the province of Bari. Minimum alcohol 11 degrees.

Leverano DOC Red, *rosato*, and white wines produced in the province of Lecce around the wine communes of Leverano and parts of Copertino and Arnesano. Leverano Rosso and Rosato are produced from Negro Amaro grapes, with the optional addition of Sangiovese, Montepulciano and Malvasia. Minimum alcohol 12 degrees; wines with minimum alcohol of 12.5 degrees and aged for at least 2 years may be labelled Riserva. Leverano Bianco, one of few DOC white wines from the Salento, is produced from Malvasia Bianca with the optional addition of Bombino Bianco and Trebbiano Toscano. Minimum alcohol 11 degrees.

Locorotondo DOC Clean, popular dry white wine produced from Verdeca and Bianco d'Alessano grapes grown around the wine communes of Locorotondo, Cisternino, and parts of Fasano. Minimum alcohol 11 degrees.

Martina; Martina Franca DOC Similar to the above, from the same blend of grapes grown in the adjoining wine communes of Martina Franca, Alberobello, and Castellana Grotte.

Matino DOC The southernmost DOC of the Salento peninsula, applying to red and *rosato* wines from the traditional Negro Amaro, with the optional addition of Malvasia Nera and Sangiovese. Minimum alcohol 11.5 degrees.

Moscato di Trani DOC Sweet dessert wine from Moscato Bianco and Moscato Reale grapes grown in the province of Bari. Minimum alcohol 15 degrees. A fortified *liquoroso* version is also produced.

Nardò DOC Red and *rosato* wines produced from the Negro Amaro grapes with Malvasia Nera in the province of Lecce mainly around the wine commune of Nardò. Minimum alcohol 12 degrees; wines with minimum alcohol of 12.5 degrees and aged for at least 2 years may be labelled Riserva.

Ortanova DOC Red and *rosato* wines produced in the province of Foggia mainly from Sangiovese, with the optional addition of Troia, Montepulciano, Lambrusco, and Trebbiano Toscano. Minimum alcohol 12 degrees.

Ostuni DOC Red and white wines from the hinterland around and inland of the 'white city'. Ostuni Bianco is produced from local grapes such as Impigno, Francavilla, Bianco d'Alessano, and Verdeca. Minimum alcohol 11 degrees. Ostuni Ottavianello is more interesting, a light red wine produced from the obscure Ottavianello grape (minimum

90%), together with optional addition of other local grapes. Minimum alcohol 11.5 degrees.

Primitivo di Manduria DOC The famous early-ripening, high-in-sugar Primitivo grape produces a range of immense table wines as well as sweet dessert and fortified wines that are noteworthy, particularly from vineyards around the town of Manduria east of Taranto. Normal version has a minimum alcohol of 14 degrees and comes in both dry and *amabile* styles. Wines with a minimum alcohol of 15 degrees may be labelled Dolce Naturale, Liquoroso Dolce Naturale (sweet fortified), and Liquoroso Secco.

Rosso Barletta DOC Red wine from northern Apulia around town of Barletta, produced mainly from Troia grapes together with optional addition of Montepulciano, Sangiovese, and Malbec. Minimum alcohol 12 degrees. When aged not less than 2 years (1 in wood) it may be labelled Invecchiato.

Rosso Canosa DOC Red wine from northern Apulia around town of Canosa di Puglia, produced from a blend of Troia, Montepulciano, and Sangiovese grapes. Minimum alcohol 12 degrees; wines with 12.5 degrees and minimum ageing

of 2 years (1 in wood) may be labelled Riserva.

Rosso di Cerignola DOC Red wine from northern Apulia around wine communes of Cerignola, Stornara, and Stornarella, produced mainly from blend of Troia and Negro Amaro grapes. Minimum alcohol 12 degrees.

Salice Salentino DOC Probably the best-known *denominazione* of the Salento peninsula, applying to fine red and *rosato* wines produced mainly from Negro Amaro grapes, with the optional addition of Malvasia Nera. Minimum alcohol 12.5 degrees; minimum ageing 2 years for wines labelled Riserva.

San Severo DOC Red, *rosato*, and white wines from the northern province of Foggia. San Severo Rosso and Rosato are produced from Negro Amaro, with the optional addition of Malvasia Nera and Sangiovese; minimum alcohol 12.5 degrees. San Severo Bianco is produced from Bombino Bianco and Trebbiano Toscano; minimum alcohol 11 degrees.

Squinzano DOC Red and *rosato* wines produced mainly from the Negro Amaro grape with Malvasia Nera and Sangiovese in the provinces of Lecce and Brindisi mainly around the wine communes of Squinzano, San Pietro Vernotico, and Torchiarolo. Minimum alcohol 12.5 degrees; 13 degrees and minimum ageing 2 years (6 months in wood) for wines labelled Riserva.

LA GASTRONOMIA: FOODS OF APULIA

While most of Italy's Deep South is mountainous and impoverished, Apulia, by contrast, is a relatively verdant paradise and one of the richest agricultural regions in Italy. Vast fields of wheat on the plains of Foggia, immense harvests of olives and grapes, the cultivation of a profusion of vegetables and fruits, fish from the coast, and meat and dairy products from herds grazing in the uplands of the Murge: these produce and products not only find their way northwards to feed the nation, they are also utilized with generous abundance in what is undoubtedly one of the most colourful of all regional kitchens. See page 438.

FROM BARI TO BRINDISI: IN THE LAND OF THE *TRULLI*

In Brief: The inland countryside between Bari and Brindisi, known as the Murge, is one of the most charming wine zones in the south of Italy. Castel del Monte, Alberobello, Ostuni, Locorotondo, and Martina Franca are all wine towns of note that have much to offer the visitor. Visitors may wish to spend time along the Adriatic coast, as well as visiting Bari itself, while the zone can also be sampled en route by those heading for Greece via Brindisi's ferry port.

There are unique opportunities for *agriturismo* in *trulli* houses set amidst the vineyards.

To view Italy's Deep South as all one uniform sun-baked land is erroneous: in many ways, Apulia, the far-off heel of the Italian boot, stands apart from Campania, Calabria, and Basilicata. Bari, the region's pre-eminent city, has been an important commercial port since at least the days of the Roman Empire; today this bustling, busy and relatively prosperous town is known

THE MEZZOGIORNO

PIATTI TIPICI:
REGIONAL SPECIALITIES

Antipasti pugliese Only Piedmont surpasses Apulia in the vast array of *antipasti* offered by the humblest local *trattorie* or grand restaurants alike: an array of vegetables preserved in oil or vinegar and herbs, fried foods, marinated seafood and shellfish, and bits of olives, air-dried sausage, meats, and different breads.

Purea di fave con cicoria; n'capriata Favourite broad bean purée, mixed with abundant virgin olive oil, and always served with raw chicory.

Orecchiette Handmade 'ear-shaped' pasta made from a variety of different wheats: the favourite characteristic pasta in the region. **Orecchiette con cima di rape** Served with boiled turnip greens seasoned with olive oil and chilli pepper.

Cavatelli; cavatieddi Another characteristic pasta: rather like a handmade shell macaroni. Served *con la ruca* (with rocket), as well as with *cima di rape*, or with tomato sauce, or *ragù*.

Panzerotti alla barese Deep-fried stuffed *ravioli*-like pasta: speciality of Bari.

Ostriche alla Tarantina Oysters from Taranto bay, opened on to the half-shell, coated with breadcrumbs and olive oil, and baked in a hot oven.

Zuppa di pesce Favourite seafood medley served anywhere along the coast from the day's catch.

Tiella d'agnello Lamb and vegetable hotpot: a *tiella* is a characteristic terracotta cooking pot originally introduced by the Spaniards, used to stew any combination of meats and vegetables together in wine and herbs.

Cheeses: *Bocconcini* 'Little balls' of fresh cow's milk *mozzarella*. *Caprini* Small goat's milk cheeses. *Formaggio fresco* Fresh cow's or sheep's milk cheese. *Cacioricotta* Hard aged *ricotta* cheese for grating.

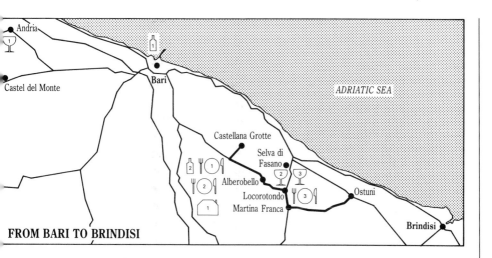

FROM BARI TO BRINDISI

not wholly facetiously as the 'Milan of the Mezzogiorno'. Geographically, too, the mountains which dominate most of the south have curved away towards the nation's toe, leaving flatter, fertile plains that can be cultivated easily. South of the Gargano Massif – the spur-like promontory that juts out into the Adriatic – the mountains give way to rich, flat plains covered in fields of wheat, grain, and vines, while between Bari and Brindisi, the uplands of the Murge are no more than a series of gentle limestone hills thickly covered with vineyards.

Yet even this is not the classic Mediterranean landscape that one might expect. For the countryside of the Murge, sprouting chips of limestone teeth, littered with boulders, and criss-crossed with a patchwork of dry-stone walls, resembles not so much the sunbaked south but rather, dare I say, the north of England, even the Scottish Highlands (in 100 years' time, when the greenhouse effect will have warmed the earth sufficiently to turn Great Britain into a major wine growing country).

Even the weird, whitewashed bee-hive dwellings, the *trulli*, that appear throughout the countryside, with mysterious and magical symbols painted on their pointed conical roofs, look more like the primitive stone dwellings of Celtic peoples, rather than those we stereotypically imagine would be more suited to southern Italians. However, these *trulli*, originally refuges and storehouses in the fields, do make sense here: for the thick tufa walls of these virtually windowless dwellings insulate them from the scorching heat of the summer, and the surprisingly bitter cold of winter. So much so that even new houses in the zone, particularly around Alberobello and Locorotondo, are constructed in this bizarre fashion.

Bari is both capital and trading centre. Perhaps most famous for its Chiesa di San Nicola, which boasts the remains of Saint Nicholas – Santa Claus, the patron saint of children – it is a lively commercial port, and hosts every September the *'Fiera del Levante'*, an important national trade fair that recalls its historic links with the eastern Mediterranean. Within Bari's provincial confines, in the hinterland that rises above the city, notable wines are produced. Inland and north-west of that great maritime city, on the foothills of the Murge south of Andria, lie the vineyards of Castel del Monte, which extend around one of Apulia's greatest monuments.

Constructed in the 13th century, the Castel del Monte is a massive octagonal stone castle built originally by the Holy Roman Emperor Frederick II as a defence against papal troops attacking from the north. Once the threats of invasion were subdued, it became his favourite private hunting lodge: it was here that the philosopher-warrior wrote a treatise still regarded as a standard work on falconry. In homage to this, the zone's best-known wine producer, the Azienda Vinicola Rivera, produces a notable red wine called 'Il Falcone'.

The vineyards of the Murge continue considerably to the south of Bari. This is rugged, confused limestone terrain, most vividly demonstrated at Castellana Grotte where rivers have plunged underground to scour out and carve a weird series of caverns, rich in phantasmagoric formations and limestone stalactites and stalagmites. These caverns are well worth a visit, and provide a cool respite in summer.

Above ground, vineyards continue to dominate the countryside, and virtually surround the whitewashed village of Alberobello nearby. Consisting almost entirely of conical *trulli* dwellings (there are more than 1000), it is undoubtedly one of the most remarkable sights in the region, and should not be missed. The locals, taking advantage of their unique heritage, have created something of a tourist town here, and will gladly invite you into their houses. But, even so, the charm remains.

The vineyards surrounding Alberobello and neighbouring communes may be entitled to either the Martina Franca or the Locorotondo DOC. Many growers in the zone belong to the latter's now famous co-operative winery. The wine industry in Apulia continues to be dominated by *cantine cooperativi*, many of which still sell their wines in bulk to blenders in the north. But, in recent years in particular, the emphases and priorities of wine growers here have had to change radically. The *cantina sociale* of Locorotondo, for example, was founded in 1932, and for decades existed quite happily by supplying base wines to the huge vermouth firms in the Piedmont. However, as the markets for that aromatized wine declined, something needed to be done to safeguard the interests of the co-operatives' 1500 wine growing members.

Thus, a courageous decision was taken in the last decade to concentrate on the production and commercialization of quality table wines. This could only be achieved, deemed the co-operative's dynamic president Dr Giuseppe Pirelli, firstly through convincing the member growers to reduce yields drastically to result in better-quality grapes, secondly through massive investment in the latest technologies for the production of white wine, and thirdly through the vigorous and aggressive marketing of the resulting wines not just nationally but even internationally. Today the *cantina sociale* of Locorotondo is one of the most remarkable and up-to-date co-operative wineries in the country, with modern presses capable of working at extremely delicate and soft levels, sophisticated filters to ensure ultra-clean must prior to fermentation, a battery of some 40 immense temperature-controlled, computer-operated stainless steel fermentation vats, and an impressive, high-speed, cold-sterile bottling line. The main production is Locorotondo DOC, a clean, well-made white wine produced from the traditional varieties of Verdeca and Bianco d'Alessano; the wine, if never great, none the less demonstrates the potential of this zone to produce sound, fruity wines of character – at very reasonable prices. The Locorotondo *cru* 'Cummersa' is particularly promising, while experiments in newer, mainly light young styles of wine are also being undertaken.

Locorotondo itself is a magical, secret little hill village overlooking the vineyards and *trulli* country, its historic centre a circular maze of tiny alleys, and tall, narrow, whitewashed townhouses. The latter are known as '*cummerse*' (thus the name of the above *cru*), and are built, like *trulli*, by traditional dry-stone construction methods.

Just south of Locorotondo lies the lovely 18th-century baroque town of Martina Franca, which gives its name to a similar, sound dry white wine. The town itself seems from another age: rather elegant, somehow old-world, and very unspoiled. On Sundays or on warm evenings, the men of the town congregate by the central piazza, dressed immaculately in suits and hats for the ritual *passeggiata*, the serious activity of simply gathering to walk and talk, seeing and being seen by all who matter.

From Martina Franca, come next to Ostuni, the startling, dreamlike '*città bianca*' – the white city – that has such suggestive Moorish overtones. Built

THE MEZZOGIORNO

on 3 separate hills, it is a steeply ascending and descending maze of cobbled streets, an Escher-like optical illusion, the whitewashed houses and streets shimmering against the deep blue of sky and sea. Ostuni is the source of sound Ostuni Bianco, as well as the more distinctive Ostuni Ottavianello, an attractive light red wine produced from the Ottavianello that goes well with the gutsy lamb dishes of the zone.

In ancient days, the Roman Appian Way ended at Brindisi, for the natural port here provided the gateway to the Middle East and Constantinople. Today only one of the twin Roman columns that marked the end of this famous imperial road remains intact, but Brindisi is still an active and important port. Like all such working towns, it is, admittedly, rather grimy and workmanlike, but it still serves as the ferry port for those departing to Corfu or Patras. Outside the city itself, Brindisi's hinterland is the source of some exceptional red wines entitled to the Brindisi DOC. Such wines, produced primarily from Negro Amaro, are similar in style and stature to the best red wines of the Salentine peninsula of which the vineyards are an extension. That the people of this area are fond of the odd tipple is evidenced by the fact that throughout Italy the standard colloquial phrase meaning 'to have a drink' or 'to make a toast' is *'fare un Brindisi'*.

Degustazione: Stop to Taste; Stop to Buy

1

AZIENDA VINICOLA RIVERA
VIALE ALTO ADIGE 139
70031 ANDRIA BA
TEL: 0883/82862

WINES PRODUCED: Castel del Monte Rosso, Rosato, Bianco, Castel del Monte 'Il Falcone' Riserva; Sauvignon di Puglia; Pinot Bianco di Puglia.
VISITS: Mon–Fri, by appointment. Historic vineyards surrounding Frederick II's octagonal

13th-century castle for the production of modern and famous wines. The Rivera winery is large and up-to-date, and it is highly regarded not only for its extremely popular Castel del Monte Rosato, and its rich, full-bodied 'Il Falcone' Riserva, but also for fragrant well-made white wines from atypical grapes such as Sauvignon and Pinot Bianco.
English, French spoken.

2 CANTINA SOCIALE COOPERATIVE DI
LOCOROTONDO
VIA ALBEROBELLO 155
70010 LOCOROTONDO BA
TEL: 080/711644

WINES PRODUCED: Locorotondo,
Locorotondo *cru* 'Cummersa',
Locorotondo Spumante; Olimpia;
Roccia; *vino novello.*
VISITS AND DIRECT SALES: Mon–Fri

8–13h; 15h30–18h.
Apulia's most famous co-operative
winery has a *vendita diretta* located
in its old premises just outside the
town. But the new, ultra-modern
winery nearby is definitely worth a
visit. Call in advance to make an
appointment, or else ask at the
office if you can be shown around.

---

3 CANTINE BORGO CANALE
CONTRADA CANALE DI PIRRO 23
72015 SELVA DI FASANO BR
TEL: 080/799351

WINES PRODUCED: Locorotondo;
Martina Franca; Agorà (*vino*

frizzante).
VISITS: daily, by appointment.
Small private winery producing
well-made wines of character by
modern methods.

Enoteche

1 VINARIUS
VIA M. DI MONTRONE 87/89
70124 BARI

OPEN: Mon–Sat 8–14h; 16–21h.
In the old walled historic centre of

Bari, near the Teatro Petruzzelli,
this *enoteca* has a selection of more
than 1000 wines. Wines can be
tasted as well as purchased.

---

2 ENOTECA PUGLIA
LARGO MARTELLOTTA 84
70011 ALBEROBELLO BA
TEL: 080/721034; 725558

OPEN: summer daily 9–20h. Out of
season weekends only or by
appointment.

Antonio Pezzolla, himself a trained
oenologist, has gathered an
extensive and important collection
of wines from throughout Puglia in
his *enoteca* located in the *trulli* zone
of Alberobello.

THE MEZZOGIORNO

Ristoranti

1

RISTORANTE 'IL POETA CONTADINO'
VIA INDEPENDENZA 21
70011 ALBEROBELLO BA
TEL: 080/721917

Closed Fri.
Atmospheric and lively restaurant serving both local and creative foods. Specialities include *antipasti alla contadina, purea di fave con cicoria, cavatelli ai cima di rape,* and good grilled fish.
Moderate

2

RISTORANTE 'IL GUERCIO DI PUGLIA'
LARGO MARTELLOTTA
70011 ALBEROBELLO BA
TEL: 080/721816

Closed Wed.
Stupendous array of *antipasta* *pugliese*: vegetables preserved in olive oil, *salame*, mussels and other shellfish, fried foods, as well as good homemade *orecchiette*.
Inexpensive

3

RISTORANTE CASA MIA
VIA PER CISTERNINO
70010 LOCOROTONDO BA
TEL: 080/711218

Closed Tue; November.
Cucina pugliese and local wines from the nearby *cantina sociale*.
Inexpensive

Agriturismo

1

AZIENDA AGRICOLA GUIDOTTI
CONTRADA CANALE DI PIRRO
72015 ALBEROBELLO BA
TEL: 080/721442

The Rotolo family have a charming *trullo* house for rent by the night or week amidst the vineyards of the Canale di Pirro. They themselves are wine growers and members of the *cantina sociale* of Locorotondo. They are most proud, however, of their superb oyster mushrooms cultivated in plastic tunnels on their nearby Masseria. These mushrooms, grilled over an open fire, and seasoned with good Apulian olive oil, are as tasty and meaty as steak.

THE SALENTINE PENINSULA: ITALY'S ANCIENT, WELL-WORN HEEL

In Brief: The Salentine peninsula, like an Italian Florida, enjoys the influence of two lovely seas, the Adriatic and the Ionian. As far from anywhere else in the country as can be imagined, it is a zone of considerable charm, solitude, and beauty. Lecce, the provincial capital, is a fine old city with its own unique form of intricate baroque architecture, while towns such as Gallipoli and Otranto not only have vivid pasts, but are today popular tourist destinations.

As a wine zone, the Salentine peninsula produces a range of wines that deserves to be better known, especially superlative *rosatos*, as well as some of Apulia's best reds. The finest are well-made wines that go some way to belie the region's reputation for producing only baked, concentrated wines of immense power.

There are opportunities for *agriturismo* on wine growers' estates in the zone.

Down, down, down: down to the very heel of Italy in search of wine. How far away it seems: yet any impressions that this is a remote and forgotten land are quickly dispelled. Lecce, the provincial capital, is a small, charming city that is positively dynamic and throbbing with energy. Its bizarre and unique form of baroque architecture has to be seen to be believed: so soft is the local tufa stone that it can literally be carved with a knife. Thus, the Spanish heritage of the 16th and 17th centuries left behind a profusion of the most lavish, intricate, and sometimes outrageous decorations and carvings on religious and domestic architecture alike.

Lecce was an important Roman town, and the ancient amphitheatre remains in the centre of the old city. But long before even the earlier Greek occupation, the peninsula was inhabited by the mysterious civilization of Messapica. It was probably the Messapicans who first cultivated the grape here, for examples of their beautiful intricate ceramic ware – double-handled wine vases, cups, mixing bowls, *amphorae* – have been unearthed at many sites.

The Salentine peninsula is a rich, fertile plain carpeted almost entirely with vineyards, enormous olive groves, and citrus plantations. Throughout the peninsula stand commanding *masserie* – farmhouses grouped around agricultural buildings and stalls for beasts – which once constituted self-

THE MEZZOGIORNO

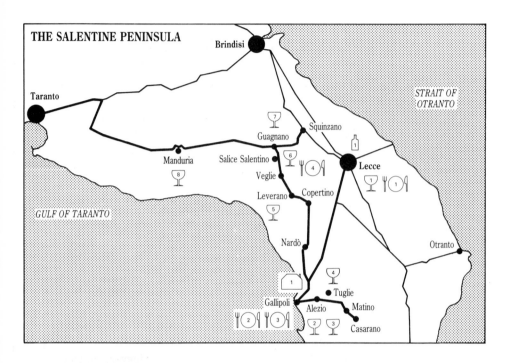

contained, self-sufficient agricultural communities. In the not-far-off days of lawlessness, and when this vulnerable peninsula was prey to maurauders and pirates, these farms were fortified, so that today they stand like shimmering white or pink mini-fortresses, palm-lined oases in a desert of vines.

Few will have arrived way down here just for the wine, but make no mistake, this *is* a zone for intrepid oenophiles. Without any exaggeration at all, the best pink wine in Italy comes from this far-flung vineyard (Mino Calò's Rosa del Golfo), while the zone is also the source of powerful but serious, complex red wines produced from the surprisingly fine Negro Amaro grape. Yet this is a wine region, above all, to be explored and enjoyed with wholehearted gusto and a certain sense of adventure, for the bewildering array of wines produced here and rarely encountered outside the zone make for most enjoyable sampling: Primitivo di Manduria, Salice Salentino, Copertino, Squinzano, Leverano, Alezio, Matino, Nardò.

In truth, the terrain differs little from one community to the next, and so many different names are bound to confuse the consumer. The best place to

Fish market, Gallipoli.

gain a further acquaintance with the wines of the Salento is in Raffaele Rollo's *Enoteca Internazionale* in Lecce, but wine explorers will certainly wish to strike out from the provincial capital into the heart of the wine country.

We suggest heading first to Gallipoli. Founded by the Greeks, the old city juts out on a spit into the warm Ionian Sea and the chaotic, medieval warren seems to have changed little over the centuries. Come down to the old fish market by the harbour to view the vivid array of the freshest fish and shellfish just off the boats, then afterwards repair to any number of small, basic *trattorie* for a feast from the sea accompanied by a jug or bottle of the forthright, full-bodied pink wines of the zone. The intricately-carved, baroque cathedral should not be missed, while the nearby restored underground olive oil mill is a reminder that this town is literally riddled with such caves.

Carlo Coppola's family has cultivated the 'Li Cuti' vineyard outside Gallipoli since 1499, the year when Laura Cuti married Orsino Coppola, bringing the land with her as a dowry. Coppola, like many wine growers in the zone, used to produce grapes primarily to be utilized for powerful *vino da taglio* – 'cutting wine' to send to the north for blending. However, as the market for such wines has shrunk in recent years, he decided instead to concentrate on one of the zone's primary new growth industries, tourism, retaining only about 8 hectares of the best specialized vineyards, and turning the rest into an impressive *agriturismo* complex. Coppola's wines, especially the *rosato* 'Li Cuti' and old vintages of the exceptional fortified Santo Stefano, are well-made, and can be sampled and purchased in the tavern of 'La Masseria' located north of Gallipoli at Torre Sabea.

Gallipoli makes a good base for exploration of the wine communes of the Salento. Just inland lies the town of Alezio, centre for the production of the delimited wine of the same name, and once a Messapican stronghold, as the local town museum evidences. The town's Via Garibaldi is riddled with wine *cantine* and this is where the wine lover should head. The best producer here is the Azienda Vinicola Rosa del Golfo, named after its most famous wine, the *rosato*, which has been widely acclaimed nationally and internationally. Mino Calò eschews the Alezio *denominazione*, preferring to market Rosa del

THE MEZZOGIORNO

Golfo as simply a *vino da tavola*. This is because he believes that the discipline, which allows the harvesting of up to 140 *quintali* of grapes per hectare, is still much too lax to result in wines of quality (his vineyards by contrast only ever yield a maximum of 90–100 *quintali*).

Rosa del Golfo is produced by an old traditional method known as *lacrima*. This consists of simply destemming and crushing the Negro Amaro (90%) and Malvasia Nera (10%) grapes, then placing them in vats to steep for about 14–16 hours, depending on the year. After this period, the free-run juice is allowed to percolate off and is collected without the utilization of any pressure whatsoever.

'This traditional *lacrima* system is extremely costly,' explained Calò, 'as the wine that results represents a *resa* of only about 25–30% of the initial weight of the grapes. However, in my opinion, lengthy contact on the skins is the only way to make a *rosato* of real excellence, with vivid colour, extract, and structure.'

After the grape must is collected, it is refrigerated to clarify it naturally, then fermentation lasts for 14–15 days at a controlled temperature no higher than 20 degrees. The result is a fine, full-flavoured *rosato* that is at once exceedingly elegant and long. Indeed, the *cru* Scalieri Mazzì is possibly the finest pink wine that I have ever tasted.

Calò is an ambitious wine maker, eager to ensure that the wines of the Salento – and his in particular – receive the recognition that they have hitherto lacked. It is not surprising, therefore, to discover that new French *barriques* have even found their way down here. They are utilized in part for the production of his best red wine, Quarantale, a classy Negro Amaro/Malvasia Nera blend that demonstrates again the potential for quality in the zone.

Further south of Alezio, the small town of Matino, where the 15th-century Marquis del Tufo built a castle, gives its name to the southernmost DOC of the peninsula which applies to similar *rosato* and red wines. If you make it this far down, it is worth continuing on to Casarano to visit the church of Casarenello with its stunningly beautiful Byzantine mosaics (you may have to hunt out the caretaker for the key to this tiny church). How did such intricate and finely-detailed work arrive in such an out-of-the-way place? This is a reminder, though, that the peninsula was for centuries not out on a limb, but along the route to the Middle East, and thus able to benefit from a constant diversity of influences and sophistication.

North of Gallipoli, the wine country continues virtually without break, both along the coast and throughout the interior hinterland. All around the peninsula's coastline, there are stout guard towers built by Charles d'Anjou to guard against invasion by the Turks. During the last war, these were supplemented with less aesthetic concrete bunkers as a defence against the expected invasion by the British that never materialized here.

Nardò is a rather crumbling old town on the flat Salento plain, with some remains of ancient Messapican and Roman fortifications as well as notable baroque buildings. The Piazza Salandra, a long, broad, tree-lined promenade lined with galleries and baroque balconies, is the place where the whole town turns out on warm evenings and at weekends. The *cantina sociale* is the main producer of similar Negro Amaro/Malvasia Nera red and *rosato* wines entitled to the Nardò DOC.

The Negro Amaro, grown apparently nowhere else but in Apulia, is not a household name, but it can be a very satisfying grape none the less, with a particular vegetal character that is most distinctive and not at all unpleasant; but is it just coincidence that it reminds me of the flavour and bouquet of many inexpensive Chiantis? Apulia has long been the source, after all, of blending wines that are much utilized in Tuscany – quite legally – to 'correct' light wines or lesser vintages. Only with the advent of DOCG has this practice been eliminated in the Chianti Classico and Rufina zones.

Copertino has a fine baroque church, the Chiesa della Madonna della Neve, an immense, well-preserved Angevin castle, and sound red and *rosato* wines, also produced by the town's co-operative winery. Neighbouring Leverano is notable for the fact (unusual here) that the *denominazione* applies not only to red and *rosato* wines, but also to some good clean whites, produced primarily from Malvasia Bianca, Bombino, and Trebbiano Toscano. The Conti Zecca's Donna Marzia range of wines is highly regarded, produced not just from local grape varieties but also from international stars such as Chardonnay. Véglie is not yet entitled to its own *denominazione*, but it too is surrounded by some prestigious vineyards (Mino Calò cultivates 22 hectares in this commune) it is also the home of the 16th-century Franciscan Convento della Favano.

Salice Salentino, a rather sleepy one-street town, is probably the best known *denominazione* of the Salentine peninsula, certainly the best-known internationally. This is mainly because of one winery, the Antica Azienda Vinicola Leone de Castris, which stands behind the immense white walls of a Spanish-style palace. The oldest part of this vast wine empire dates from 1500, for the Leone de Castris family, originally Spanish soldiers in service under the viceroys who ruled from Naples, settled in the region and from an early time began to acquire extensive vineyard holdings.

The fame of this ancient winery is based primarily on a remarkable aged *rosato* known as 'Five Roses'. The family have made this wine since 1923, when it was known as Rosato Stravecchio del Salento. However, during World War II, an American general in charge of procuring food and drink for US forces stationed in Italy enjoyed the wine immensely, and suggested that it could sell well in North America, given a suitable English name. As the farm from which it was produced was called '*Cinque Rose*', this was translated to 'Five Roses' and the wine has subsequently enjoyed considerable success internationally. Instead of the 3–4 years' ageing it was previously given, the wine now receives only one in deference to modern tastes, but it is still a full-bodied wine of considerable stature, a rosé capable of standing up to the most robustly-flavoured foods.

This is by no means the only wine produced in the modern and immense Leone de Castris winery. Indeed, this family-run concern is at the forefront of the Apulian wine renaissance, and has been instrumental in developing new styles of wine, especially lighter, fruity, in some cases *frizzante* wines utilizing modern technology. And the robust Salice Salentino reds, especially the *barrique*-aged *cru* 'Donna Lisa', are serious wines that deserve wider recognition.

From Salice, a wine tour can continue to Guagnano (where Dr Cosimo Taurino produces fine wines, notably the exquisite, highly-rated and expensive 'Il Patriglione' Brindisi DOC), and to Squinzano, a wine town and *denominazione* which ought to win an award simply for its delicious name.

The road across the peninsula, however, connects its two major cities, Lecce and Taranto, by way of Manduria. Taranto was a Spartan colony founded in the 8th century BC, and was one of the largest cities of Magna Grecia, but smaller Manduria still boasts remains of the even older Messapican civilization in its ancient dry-stone fortifications and necropolis. Manduria is the source of a remarkable Apulian wine, Primitivo di Manduria. This unique early-ripening grape claims to be the progenitor of California's trendy Zinfandel, but here it has for decades been grown for its remarkable potential to achieve natural alcohol levels in excess of 18 degrees, thus making it the ideal partner to blend with weaker, insipid wines of the north. Around Manduria, however, the Primitivo is proudly bottled in its own right, as an immense dry table wine, sweet dessert wine, or sweet, fortified port-like wine. After you have become accustomed to these wines, insist friends from Apulia who will drink nothing else, any other wine tastes like water.

Lecce.

Degustazione: Stop to Taste; Stop to Buy

1 AZIENDE AGRICOLE VALLONE
(OFFICE) VIA XXV LUGLIO 5
73100 LECCE
TEL: 0832/28041

WINES PRODUCED: Vigna Flaminio Brindisi Rosso e Rosato; Salice Salentino Rosso e Rosato; Sauvignon del Salento; Bianco del Salento 'Le Viscarde'; Rosso del Salento 'Graticciaia'.
VISITS: daily, by appointment, for professionals only.
Another serious winery producing a fine range of premium wines from grapes grown on 3 estates: Iore (Salice Salentino DOC), Flaminio (Brindisi DOC), and Castelserranova. The Tenuta Flaminio, located on SS16 km 923, near Brindisi, is the most important and also serves as the winery and *cantina* for the entire operation, though the administration remains in Lecce. While the Salice Salentino and Vigna Flaminio wines are noteworthy, the most remarkable we have tasted is the Rosso del Salento 'Graticciaia', produced from semi-dried grapes: an immensely powerful and rich heavyweight rather like an Apulian Amarone. English spoken.

THE MEZZOGIORNO

2 AZIENDA AGRICOLA ING. NICCOLÒ
COPPOLA
VIA GARIBALDI 89
73011 ALEZIO LE
TEL: 0833/281014

WINES PRODUCED: 'Li Cuti' Rosso e
Rosato Alezio DOC; *vino bianco da
tavola*; Santo Stefano *vino
liquoroso*.
VISITS: daily, by appointment (or
ask at the bar of 'La Masseria' – in

season there are certain 'open days'
each week).
Carlo Coppola's main occupation
nowadays is the immense 'La
Masseria' *agriturismo* complex (see
below), but he still produces some
good wines from vineyards in the
family since the 15th century. The
best place to sample them is in the
friendly bar of 'La Masseria'.

------

3 AZIENDA VINICOLA ROSA DEL GOLFO
VIA GARIBALDI 56
73011 ALEZIO LE
TEL: 0833/281045

WINES PRODUCED: Rosa del Golfo,
Rosa del Golfo *cru* Scaliere Mazzì;
Portulano; Quarantale; Bianco
Bolina; *grappa del Rosa del Golfo*;
aceto del Rosa del Golfo.
VISITS: daily, by appointment.
Mino Calò's winery is without

doubt one of the jewels of the
Salentine peninsula, still run on a
small artisan scale (only about
150,000 bottles a year are
produced), but utilizing the most
modern technologies to result in a
range of fine well-made wines. In
addition to the famous Rosa del
Golfo, don't miss the opportunity to
sample the excellent Quarantale.

------

4 AZIENDA VINICOLA CALÒ
VIA MASSERIA VECCHIA 1
73058 TUGLIE LE
TEL: 0833/366244
ADMINISTRATION AND *ENOTECA*: VIA
F. TURATI 7, 20010 ARLUNO MI,
TEL: 02/9017047.

WINES PRODUCED: 'Mjère' Alezio
Rosso DOC, 'Mjère' Alezio Rosato
DOC, 'Mjère' Bianco del Salento
Verdeca; 'Vigna Spano' Rosso
Riserva.
VISITS: daily, by appointment.

The Azienda Vinicola Calò (not
related to the Azienda Agricola Rosa
del Golfo) has been run by Michele
Calò and his family for some 35
years, but the seat of the business
as well as an *enoteca* are now
located near Milan. None the less,
the Calòs, alternating between
Arluno and Tuglie, continue to
cultivate about 7 hectares of
vineyards (Negro Amaro, Malvasia
Nera, Verdeca) and make an
excellent range of wines bearing the

distinctive 'Mjère' label (the name is local dialect for the Latin *merum*

indicating '*vino genuino*'). English spoken.

---

5 AZIENDA AGRICOLA CONTI ZECCA
SOC. COOP.
VIA CESAREA
73045 LEVERANO LE
TEL: 0832/925613

WINES PRODUCED: Donna Marzia Bianco, Rosso, Rosato, Chardonnay,

Chiaretto; Leverano DOC: Vigna del Saraceno Bianco, Rosso, Rosato.
VISITS: daily, by appointment.
The Donna Marzia range of wines is highly regarded and enjoys good distribution throughout Apulia and further afield.

---

6 ANTICA AZIENDA AGRICOLA
VITIVINICOLA LEONE DE CASTRIS
VIA DE CASTRIS 50
73015 SALICE SALENTINO LE
TEL: 0832/731112

WINES PRODUCED: 'Five Roses' Rosato del Salento; Salice Salentino Rosso and Rosato, Salice Salentino *cru* 'Donna Lisa'; Imago (Chardonnay); Ursi (*vino frizzante*); Locorotondo; *vino spumante del Salento*.
VISITS: Mon–Sat 8h30–12h30. Appointment necessary (telephone Dott. Pinto).
The immense Spanish-style winery of Leone de Castris is a significant monument in this otherwise rather

sleepy town. 40 years ago the grapes were still brought in to the *cantina* by horse, but today there is all the modern equipment necessary for the production of premium wines, albeit on a large scale. 'Five Roses' made Leone de Castris' name nationally and internationally, while Salice Salentino Rosso is one of the better known of the myriad wines that come from the Salentine peninsula. As well, the white wines of Leone de Castris, produced utilizing modern technology to preserve fruit, aroma, and acidity, are noteworthy.
English, some French spoken.

---

7 AZIENDA AGRICOLA TAURINO
SS605
73010 GUAGNANO LE
TEL: 0832/724495

WINES PRODUCED: Rosso del

Salento; Salice Salentino Rosso, Salice Salentino Rosato; Brindisi Rosso 'Il Patriglione' Riserva.
VISITS: daily, working hours, by appointment.

THE MEZZOGIORNO

Dr Cosimo Taurino's Salice Salentino wines were the first Apulian wines we ever tasted, and they have remained firm favourites ever since. This is a serious estate winery totally dedicated to the production of quality wines. 'Il Patriglione' Brindisi Riserva is one of the great red wines of Italy. English, French, German spoken.

---

8 AZIENDA VINICOLA GIOVANNI
SOLOPERTO
SS7/TER PER TARANTO
74024 MANDURIA TA
TEL: 099/8794286

WINES PRODUCED: Primitivo di Manduria 14°, 17°, 20°; *vino da tavola rosso, rosato, bianco*.
VISITS: Mon–Sat 8–12h30; 16–18h. Telephone call advisable.

Primitivo di Manduria is a wine unique to Apulia which should be tried when in the region. While this indigenous grape continues to be cultivated widely to serve as bulk *vino da taglio*, Soloperto is one of the leading estates dedicated to producing the wines in bottle in varying degrees of strength. English, French spoken.

Enoteca

1 ENOTECA INTERNAZIONALE
VIA C. BATTISTI 23
73100 LECCE
TEL: 0832/22832

OPEN: Mon–Sat 8h30–13h30; 16–21h.
Cav. Rag. Raffaele Rollo is a professional *sommelier* and an

expert on Apulian wines. His shop stocks an extensive range of the best (as well as other wines from throughout the world), and he will delight in explaining them to you as well as help in arranging visits to wineries.

Ristoranti

1 GRAND HOTEL
VIALE ORONZO QUARTA 28
73100 LECCE
TEL: 0832/29405

Stylish Art-Nouveau hotel near the train station with a friendly (if chaotic) restaurant serving good local foods.
Moderate

2 RISTORANTE MARECHIARO
LUNGOMARE MARCONI
73014 GALLIPOLI LE
TEL: 0833/476143

Closed Tue.
Located directly on the water,
serving (naturally) a superb array
of the freshest fish and shellfish:
*insalata di mare, farfalle al
salmone, orecchiette Marechiaro.*
Moderate

---

3 TRATTORIA 'IL MARINAIO'
VIA MICETTI 13
73014 GALLIPOLI LE
TEL: 0833/471773

Closed Wed.
Tucked away in a little alley, this
local restaurant is another good
source of superb seafood pasta,
grilled fish, and local wines.
Inexpensive to Moderate

---

4 ALBERGO RISTORANTE 'VILLA DONNA
LISA'
VIA SEN. LEONE DE CASTRIS
73015 SALICE SALENTINO LE
TEL: 0832/732222

Open all year.
The Leone de Castris family have
recently opened this 4-star
hotel-restaurant around the corner
from the winery. The comfortable
restaurant serves good national and
international foods, together, of
course, with the full range of Leone
de Castris wines.
Moderate

Agriturismo

1 'LA MASSERIA'
AZIENDA AGRICOLA ING. NICCOLÒ
COPPOLA
LOC. TORRE SABEA
73014 GALLIPOLI LE
TEL: 0833/281014; 22295

Open all year.
Carlo Coppola's immense
agriturismo complex offers
accommodation in small
apartments, rooms, or on the large
camp site. There are good facilities,
and direct access to the beach, but
be warned, in high season the place
is literally jam-packed. The tavern
of the Masseria is a good place to
sample Coppola's wines, while the
on-site restaurant serves
exceptional pizza.

THE MEZZOGIORNO

Wine and Other Related *Sagre* and *Feste*

Easter	Settimana Santa	Taranto
early May	Sagra di San Nicola	Bari
Sept	Fiera del Levante	Bari
last week of Sept	'Te lu Mieru' (wine festival)	Carpignano Salentino

E PER SAPERE DI PIÙ – ADDITIONAL INFORMATION

Ente Provinciale per il Turismo
Piazza Moro 33a
70122 Bari
tel: 080/228855

Ente Provinciale per il Turismo
via Cristoforo Colombo 88
72100 Brindisi
tel: 0831/222126

Ente Provinciale per il Turismo
via Monte S. Michele 20
73100 Lecce
tel: 0832/54117

Ente Provinciale per il Turismo
Corso Umberto 113
74100 Taranto
tel: 099/21233

Ente Provinciale per il Turismo
via San Emilio Perrone 17
71100 Foggia
tel: 0881/23650

Associazione Agriturist Regionale
via G. Petroni 23
70124 Bari
tel: 080/365025

BASILICATA

Melfi, with the extinct Monte Vulture volcano in the distance.

I Vini: THE WINES OF BASILICATA   458

La Gastronomia   458

La Strada del Vino: THE WINE ROAD OF
BASILICATA
    The Hill Vineyards of Vulture   460

Le Sagre: WINE AND OTHER RELATED FESTIVALS   467

Additional Information   467

Basilicata is Italy's poorest, most desolate and sparsely populated region, a land that has been sadly left behind as the rest of the Mezzogiorno has tried to pull itself up towards the 21st century. More than 90 per cent of the land is mountainous and there is little work save agriculture, the ceaseless attempt to scrape a bare living from the meagre land which has been carried out since time immemorial. In the country, the people live, on the whole, in ancient, claustrophobic hilltop villages, clustered together for protection and warmth. This is inhospitable terrain where even nature conspires against man. Potenza, the regional capital, was badly damaged by the 1980 earthquake (which followed on the great earthquakes of 1273, 1694, 1806, and 1930). In the region's second city, Matera, people still huddle together in primitive *sassi* dwellings: little more than caves carved out of the soft volcanic tufa. Yet, on the Ionian coast at Metaponto, the splendid remains of a Greek Doric temple dating from the 7th century BC stand as a cruel reminder of a grander golden age long passed.

It is not surprising to find that the vine is cultivated, even way down south here in Basilicata (or Lucania as the region is also known). Indeed, where in Italy is it not? Yet what is remarkable is that, almost totally against the odds, this bare land produces not simply *vino da pasto* to quench the local thirst, but undoubtedly one of the nation's greatest red wines, Aglianico del Vulture. This fact alone makes the region worthy of our attention: indeed, for those of us who enjoy seeking the vine and its fruits in the most unlikely places, a journey to Basilicata is a rare and rewarding experience.

THE MEZZOGIORNO

ORIENTATION

Basilicata extends like a broad strap across the foot of the Italian boot, spanning it from Tyrrhenian coast to Ionian coast, dominated by the horny spine of the Apennine range, and squeezed successively between Campania, Apulia, and Calabria. Basilicata has 2 provinces: Potenza and Matera. There are no direct flights to the region, but airports at Naples, Bari, Lamezia Terme or Reggio Calabria could all be utilized. By rail, Potenza can be reached from Naples, while the south coast is accessible from Reggio Calabria–Taranto. By road, the Vulture region is accessible off the A16 *autostrada* that spans the country east–west from Naples to Bari.

Map Touring Club Italiano 1: 200 000 Campania & Basilicata.

I VINI: GLOSSARY TO THE WINES OF BASILICATA

Wines of *Denominazione di Origine Controllata (DOC)*

Aglianico del Vulture DOC Basilicata's only DOC applies to outstanding dry red wine produced from the Aglianico grape grown mainly on the eastern flanks of Monte Vulture in the province of Potenza. Minimum alcohol 12.5 degrees. Wines aged for 3 years may be labelled Vecchio; wines aged for at least 5 years may be labelled Riserva. The DOC may also apply to sweet sparkling wines produced from the same grape, but such wines are rarely encountered outside the zone.

LA GASTRONOMIA: FOODS OF BASILICATA

Basilicata is the land of the pig and the *peperoncino*. In the past – and even still today – every family kept a pig, and the annual ritual of the pig slaughter and sausage- and *salame*-making was an important and heady one, for such home-cured products, usually highly spiced, served as provisions over winter when fresh meats might not be available. The pig, of

PIATTI TIPICI:
REGIONAL SPECIALITIES

Lucaneca; luganega The famous sausage of Basilicata (eaten and enjoyed since Roman times and now popular throughout Italy): available both fresh or dried, usually sold in a long continuous coil, and highly spiced with red chillies and pepper.

Soppressata Highly spiced large blood sausage, sometimes preserved in oil.

Fusilli al rape Homemade twisted noodles served with turnip greens sautéed in olive oil and chilli peppers.

Strascinati alla potentina Ravioli-like pasta filled with *ricotta*, ham, egg, and parsley, and served with meat sauce and grated salted *ricotta*.

Ciambotta Vegetable medley of peppers, aubergine, tomatoes, herbs, stewed in olive oil.

Funghi al forno Fresh mushrooms (preferably *funghi porcini*) baked with olive oil, chopped garlic, chopped parsley and chilli peppers.

Frittata con gli asparagi selvatici Egg omelette made with fine, tender wild asparagus.

Agnello ai funghi Lamb baked with *funghi porcini* or *funghi cardoncelli*, white wine, and olive oil.

Cheeses: *Caciocavallo* Classic semi-hard southern *formaggio* made by suspending pairs of cheeses saddle-like astride a pole to drain. Here it is often eaten grilled like meat. *Buttiro* Sheep's milk cheese with hard crust and creamy interior. *Pecorino* The classic sheep's milk cheese in Basilicata is often aged and flavoured with peppercorns or chillies.

course, is the great mainstay of peasant cuisine, a diet based on self-sufficiency which has traditionally had to make little taste like a lot. Pasta made simply from ground durum wheat and water (no egg) is the staple here, seasoned with little other than olive oil, perhaps some home-grown greens and a liberal dose of *peperoncini* – fresh or dried hot chilli peppers.

THE MEZZOGIORNO

Indeed, chillies are one way of giving zesty flavour to foods at little expense, one reason for their popularity here. It is said, furthermore, that the chilli also helped keep malaria at bay in the days before quinine. Even today, the foods of Basilicata are nothing if not devilishly hot.

THE HILL VINEYARDS OF VULTURE

In Brief: The vineyards of Vulture extend over the communities that spread over the foothills of the extinct eponymous volcano in northern Basilicata. The wine zone is little visited, and hardly developed from a tourist point of view. Perhaps best reached by those travelling along the *autostrada* from Naples to Bari, it is a region that can be dipped into by intrepid wine travellers en route between those two points. Melfi, with its impressive 11th-century Norman castle, is the centre, though Rionero, a rather drab agricultural town, can also serve as a base. The twin Lakes of Monticchio, filled-in craters of Monte Vulture, are lovely and deserve visiting. There are opportunities, furthermore, for *agriturismo*.

The hill vineyards of Vulture are among the least visited and most remote in all of Italy's varied wine country. They produce poor Basilicata's single DOC wine, Aglianico del Vulture, which none the less is undoubtedly if surprisingly one of the great red wines of Italy. Majestic bare hills ripple down from the slopes of the ancient, extinct volcano of Monte Vulture, and small towns such as Rionero, Barile, Melfi, Ripacandida, Venosa, Ginestra, and others huddle on top of hills. This is not a specialized wine region, manicured into ordered ranks of vines: indeed its most striking feature is the very lack of specialized viticulture. Tiny squares of ancient, gnarled vines are planted here and there amidst groves of olives, patches of wheat and tobacco, perhaps a vegetable garden, or some terrain left for the grazing of sheep or goats. The vines, traditionally either free-standing or trained up cane poles 'tepee' style, are cultivated almost entirely by hand by impoverished *contadini*, women wrapped in black shawls summer and winter, men prodding along a stubborn donkey, still the beast of burden here, and often the only aid to easing the crushing workload.

Winter comes early to this mountainous land and lasts long. Indeed, they say here that there is no spring or autumn in the province of Potenza: just a few months of hellishly hot summer before the cold, long months of winter

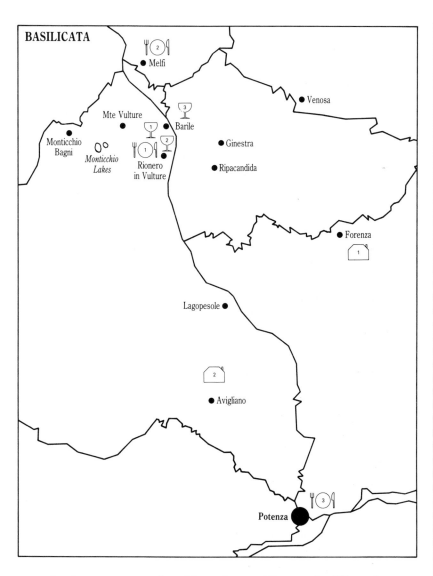

set in. It often snows as early as November, and Potenza itself has winters as cold as alpine Bolzano. This certainly belies the myth that the Mezzogiorno is all sun-baked.

However, the wine produced from this strange and unique vineyard is altogether exceptional. The Aglianico grape, brought to the region by the ancient Greeks, is one of the greatest noble black grapes of Italy (ranking alongside the élite Nebbiolo and Sangioveto). Moreover, on these mountain-

FREDERICK II OF SWABIA

The Hohenstaufen Frederick II of Swabia succeeded to the imperial throne when he was just 25 and was crowned at Melfi, in Basilicata, in 1215. As Holy Roman Emperor, Frederick II tried to consolidate his Italian possessions and territories, and to this end he built or renovated castles throughout the peninsula to serve as bases for his struggles, primarily against the papal and Lombard forces. In the Vulture zone alone, Frederick II had, in addition to his favourite castle at Melfi, additional fortified castles at Lagopesole and San Gervasio, while in nearby Apulia, the octagonal Castel del Monte was but another in his considerable line of defences.

Frederick II, though, was no mere warrior: he was by all accounts a man of rare and varied talents, and intellectually one of the most enlightened leaders of his era. He spoke German, Latin, Greek, Arabic, French, and Italian. He founded the university of Naples and a school of medicine at Salerno, patronized the arts and literature, and wrote poems in the vernacular Italian, as well as the definitive treatise on the art of falconry.

Born in a tent at Jesi, in the heart of the great vineyards of the Marche, with possessions at Melfi (Aglianico del Vulture), Castel del Monte (a great Apulian vineyard), and elsewhere – is it just coincidence that this great philosopher-warrior always seemed to rest his boots where the wine was good?

ous vineyards that reach heights of 750 metres above sea level, the late-ripening vines are extremely low-yielding, perhaps giving only 2 or 3 bunches per plant. But, in the best years when they ripen sufficiently, they are capable of yielding grapes of the highest quality. Indeed, the wine that can result, Aglianico del Vulture, has immense colour, body, tannin, yet allied with delicacy, finesse – yes, even elegance.

It is as if here in deepest, backward, rural Italy these rare grapes are yielded almost by haphazard chance, and certainly on the whole unappreciated by those who grow them. Yet, as elsewhere, the history of viticulture in the region is a long and illustrious one; moreover, though today the zone seems isolated and by-passed by the 20th century, in times past this part of southern Italy was far from out on a limb. Horace was born in the little wine hamlet of Venosa. And the impressive Norman castle at

Melfi, rebuilt by the Swabian Emperor Frederick II, attests to the prosperity and strategic importance of the area during the Middle Ages.

Somewhere along the way, though, a great vinous patrimony was lost or misplaced. Growers sold their grapes only to be made into powerful *vino da taglio* – cutting wine – to boost insipid, weaker wines from the north. Or else the Aglianico grapes were carted off to nearby Apulia and made into wine there (this practice still continues today). Those who grew grapes as they always had done, here and there in patches in the bare, stony land together with other crops, saw them only as another fruit to sell for cash, not the potential source of greatness in a glass.

There is hardly any tradition of estate wine making in the Vulture zone. The activities of growing grapes and making wine have always been and still remain quite separate. Thus, Donato d'Angelo, probably the leading and best-known producer of Aglianico del Vulture, owns no vineyards himself. The family business was started just 50 years ago by his grandfather in an old garage in the centre of Rionero, a rather crumbling old wine town severely damaged by the earthquake that hit Campania and northern Basilicata in 1980.

Donato d'Angelo himself is a young man with a broader outlook; he is a trained oenologist and a stickler for quality who refuses to compromise. He purchases all of his grapes from growers whom the family has worked with

Donato d'Angelo.

over the last 5 decades – those peasant farmers who scratch this bare land and struggle to make a living from it. But he pays them well for their efforts, for he wants only the ripest, quality grapes in top condition. Over-production, he says, quite simply is not a problem: these ancient vines grown on steep slopes yield so little. The harvest, which begins in late October and lasts into November, is always one of the very latest in Italy. Indeed, high up on this knife edge of the vine's feasibility, even this late the grapes do not always ripen sufficiently. In such years, d'Angelo refuses to produce the dry, aged Aglianico del Vulture, and makes instead a rather bewildering array of sweet and sparkling wines that are for local consumption only. Good and unusual though they can be, especially with the chilli-spiked local foods, these are not wines that d'Angelo is proud

THE MEZZOGIORNO

of in an international context.

The hill communities of Vulture, like the rest of the impoverished south, have seen in recent years the acceleration of a process whereby the youth abandon their homelands to seek fortunes elsewhere – in the north of Italy, or abroad. Quite simply, the grinding poverty of a life on this harsh land holds little or no appeal for the young, and who can blame them? In the 1960s, for example, Rionero was a bustling town of 18,000 inhabitants. Today little more than half that number remain. The *contadini* who work the steep hill vineyards and supply grapes to d'Angelo and other *case vinicole* are on the whole as ancient as the land. Who, I wonder, will replace them when they are gone, and what will become of the land? It is more than probable that wine makers such as d'Angelo may in future have to buy and cultivate land as the only means of maintaining an adequate supply of the rare and precious Aglianico grapes.

For those who come to the region (and, it must be said, few do, for tourism is virtually non-existent here), Melfi serves as the probable starting base. The town achieved notable fame in the 11th century when Norman mercenaries led by Tancred de Hauteville (known to Italians as Altavilla) and his 12 sons met there to found the County of Melfi, the beginning of the establishment of a Norman kingdom that was to rule all of southern Italy and Sicily. Today the stout, multi-sided Norman castle, later expanded and renovated by Frederick II, then again in the 14th century by Charles I d'Anjou, dominates this small medieval market centre. Melfi's Duomo is another fine example of this rather austere style of Norman architecture.

Near Melfi, Barile and Rionero in Vulture are the two most significant wine communities of the zone, though apart from this most important commodity, they have little to offer the visitor. In Barile, notice the scores of private *cantine* dug into the volcanic hillsides, the traditional stores for the small peasant wine growers who, in addition to selling their grapes to the large wine houses, also of course retain enough to make wine for their own home consumption. As well as red wine made from the aristocratic Aglianico, the locals also enjoy white wines made from both Malvasia and Moscato, the latter a rustic but refreshing sweet wine that is particularly well-conserved in these cool, hand-dug caves. Barile, incidentally, is famous for its Good Friday procession during which the local inhabitants enact the passion and crucifixion of Christ.

While viticulture takes place over the hills and slopes of numerous surrounding communities, it is generally agreed that the finest grapes come from the steep hill vineyards planted above Rionero and Barile in the rich, fertile volcanic ash of Monte Vulture. Indeed Monte Vulture, which reaches a height of 1326 metres, is the dominant feature of this remote corner of Basilicata. Its slopes have been inhabited since Paleolithic times and archaeological excavations have unearthed the remains of prehistoric elephants and hippopotami. The extinct volcano actually has 7 separate peaks, and its two major craters have filled in to create the lovely twin Lakes of Monticchio. This is a fine, unspoiled area of great natural beauty, well worth exploration. Nearby Monticchio Bagni is a minor spa town with sulphur baths.

East of Melfi, the wine country continues through Venosa, birthplace of the Roman Horace: the remains of a *tepidarium* are somewhat hopefully displayed as the natal house of the poet, while the town's massive castle and Duomo attest to its importance in medieval times. Forenza, another high mountain wine commune, has opportunities for *agriturismo* on the farm of a local wine grower.

South of Rionero, the massive Norman castle of Lagopesole dominates the countryside en route to the provincial capital of Potenza. This once marked the frontier between the realms of Byzantine-Greco Apulia and the Longobardian realms of Salerno.

Degustazione: Stop to Taste; Stop to Buy

1 CASA VINICOLA D'ANGELO
VIA PROVINCIALE
85028 RIONERO IN VULTURE PZ
TEL: 0972/721517

WINES PRODUCED: Aglianico del Vulture, Aglianico del Vulture Riserva; 'Il Canneto'.
VISITS: Mon–Fri, appointment preferable.
Donato d'Angelo is the leading producer of Basilicata's most famous wine. The winery, located on the outskirts of Rionero, is modern and well maintained, and the wines are made with considerable skill and care.

The fashion for *barrique* has even found its way to this far-flung vinous corner of Italy. Thus, in addition to traditional Aglianico del Vulture, d'Angelo also makes a *barrique*-aged wine called 'Il Canneto', named after the cane stakes used to support the vines. More international in character than Aglianico del Vulture, combining the soft, silky vanilla flavours of new oak while maintaining the unique varietal characteristics of this rare grape, 'Il Canneto' is a worthy contender in Italy's super-*vini da tavola* stakes. English spoken.

THE MEZZOGIORNO

2 CASA VINICOLA ARMANDO MARTINO
VIA LAVISTA 2/A
85028 RIONERO IN VULTURE PZ
TEL: 0972/721422; 721745

WINES PRODUCED: Aglianico del
Vulture; 'Carolin' (*vino novello*);

'Vulcanello' (*bianco e rosato*); *vino
spumante*.
VISITS: Tue–Sat 9–13h; 16–18h.
Appointment preferable.
Another respected producer of this
rare and undervalued wine.

---

3 AZIENDA VITIVINICOLA
   PATERNOSTER
VIA NAZIONALE 23
85022 BARILE PZ
TEL: 0972/770224

WINES PRODUCED: Aglianico del
Vulture; Vini Spumanti.
VISITS: Mon–Sat, by appointment.

The Azienda Vitivinicola
Paternoster is the oldest winery in
the zone, established in 1925, and a
highly-respected producer not only
of fine Aglianico but also of quality
sparkling wines by the Charmat
method.
A little English spoken.

Ristoranti

1 HOTEL-RISTORANTE 'LA PERGOLA'
VIA LAVISTA 27/31
85028 RIONERO IN VULTURE PZ
TEL: 0972/721819

Closed Tue.
The best hotel-restaurant in the

zone: *antipasti, cavatelli ai funghi,
ziti alla lucana, agnello ai funghi*,
and good selection of the wines of
Vulture. Hotel has 43 rooms all
with private facilities.
Inexpensive

---

2 HOTEL-RISTORANTE 'DUE PINI'
PIAZZALE STAZIONE
85025 MELFI PZ
TEL: 0972/21031

Good, clean alternative to the above
in town famous for its 11th-century

castle. Restaurant serves simple,
spicy foods of the region: *fusilli al
rape, scallopine alla pizzaiola,
caciocavallo alla brace*.
Inexpensive

---

3 TAVERNA ORAZIANA
VIA ORAZIO FLACCO 2
85100 POTENZA
TEL: 0971/21851

Closed Fri, Aug.
Good regional restaurant in the
provincial capital serving local
foods such as *strascinati alla*

potentina, luganega alla brace, agnello ai funghi, and selection of Aglianico del Vulture.

Inexpensive to Moderate

Agriturismo

1 AZIENDA NATALE-SANTOIANNI
LOC. CONTRADA MALANDRINO
CORSO GRANDE 222
85020 FORENZA PZ
TEL: 0971/943001; 943216

5-room apartment available on farm producing Aglianico del Vulture, as well as cheese, *salame*, and oil.

---

2 PUNTO DI RISTORO 'PIETRA DEL
    SALE'
MONTE CARUSO
85021 AVIGLIANO PZ
TEL: 0971/87189

Located high in the wooded Mount Caruso above Avigliano, this rustic *punto di ristoro agrituristico* serves simple foods – *prosciutti e salame paesane*, grilled meats and *luganega* sausage, homemade cheese and local wines – at outdoor tables from May until the end of September. Located 5 km from Castel Lagopesole and 1.5 km from Santuario della Madonna del Carmine. Telephone above number for reservations and directions.

Inexpensive

Wine and Other Related *Sagre* and *Feste*

October	Sagra dei Funghi	Various towns throughout the region.

E PER SAPERE DI PIÙ – ADDITIONAL INFORMATION

Ente Provinciale per il Turismo
via Cavour 15
85100 Potenza
tel: 0971/21839

Ente Provinciale per il Turismo
via Deviti de Marco 9
75100 Matera
tel: 0835/221758

Associazione Regionale Agriturist
via XX Settembre 39
75100 Matera
tel: 0835/214565

THE MEZZOGIORNO

CALABRIA

I Vini: THE WINES OF CALABRIA	469
La Gastronomia	471
Le Strade dei Vini: THE WINE ROADS OF CALABRIA	
Cirò: Wine of the Ancient Olympians	473
Greco di Bianco, 'the Best Wine in the World'?	478
Le Sagre: WINE AND OTHER RELATED FESTIVALS	481
Additional Information	482

Fattoria San Francesco, Cirò.

The wide, steep instep of Italy sweeps around from Apulia, the nation's relatively well-heeled heel, to Calabria, the poor, bruised, forgotten toe. Though this is the southernmost point of the mainland, the region is rugged, even alpine in the extreme, dominated by the harsh granite massif of the Sila and isolated mountainous Aspromonte which extend steeply upwards from what is the longest coastline in Italy. Indeed the stark grandeur of the mountains, the beauty of the still unspoiled beaches of the Ionian and Tyrrhenian seas, stand in stark contrast to the squalor, the poverty, the crumbling abandoned inland villages and the haphazard and ghastly development of the coastal towns.

Calabria remains one of the poorest regions in Italy and has seen a virtual mass exodus as native sons have travelled north to the factories of Florence, Milan, or Turin, or else across to America in search of work. Yet Calabrians have a great sense of their roots, and a deep, abiding love of their homeland. Thus, many hope to return and send money home to build new houses where they plan eventually to retire. These homes, unfinished concrete tenements, dominate most of the villages along the coast: concrete columns and rusted, twisted steel bars rise from each, waiting for the next instalment of money, and the addition of another floor.

Calabria, once an integral part of Magna Grecia, is of particular interest to the oenophile primarily because of its ancient pedigree. Wines from this timeless land were drunk by the victors of the ancient Olympic games, no less. If today they are perhaps less noteworthy, they deserve our attention even so, not least because the region's tourism is finally being developed and more and more visitors are coming here.

ORIENTATION

Calabria, the toe of the Italian boot, comprises 3 provinces: Catanzaro, Cosenza, and Reggio Calabria. There are domestic and charter flights to Lamezia Terme and Reggio Calabria. The main north–south rail line extends from Rome to Reggio Calabria, while there is a coastal rail line from Reggio Calabria around to Taranto. The A3 *autostrada* extends south from Naples to Reggio Calabria, a distance of nearly 500 km. Reggio Calabria and Villa San Giovanni are connected with Sicily by frequent ferries across the narrow Straits of Messina.
Map Touring Club Italiano 1: 200 000 Calabria.

I VINI: GLOSSARY TO THE WINES OF CALABRIA

Wines of *Denominazione di Origine Controllata (DOC)*

Cirò DOC Calabria's most famous wine, produced in red, *rosato*, and white versions. Red and *rosato* are produced from Gaglioppo grapes together with small amounts of Greco and/or Trebbiano. Minimum alcohol 13.5 degrees; wines aged for at least 3 years may be labelled Riserva. White Cirò is produced from Greco grapes, together with a small optional addition of Trebbiano. Minimum alcohol 12 degrees.

Donnici DOC Hill vineyards near Cosenza for the production of red and *rosato* wines from the Gaglioppo, Greco Nero, Malvasia, Mantonico, and Pecorello grapes.

Minimum alcohol 12 degrees.

Greco di Bianco DOC
Outstanding and rare dessert wine (formerly known as Greco di Gerace) made from Greco grapes grown in white tufa soil around towns of Bianco, Caraffa, and Bovino near the tip of the toe of the Italian boot. Produced from grapes left to shrivel in the outdoor sun, the wine reaches a minimum alcohol content of 17 degrees.

Lamezia DOC Red wine produced from Nerello, Gaglioppo, and Greco Nero grapes grown in wine communes around the town of Lamezia Terme, notably at

MAGNA GRECIA

The first Greek settlers to the Italian peninsula came in about the 9th century BC and over the next few hundred years they established major centres throughout what is now Apulia, Basilicata, Calabria, Campania, Sicily, and further afield. They called this fertile land 'Enotria' – the land of vines – because of its suitability to grape growing, but later the region as a whole became known simply as Magna Grecia, signifying that it was not merely a colony of Greece, but an integral extension of the Hellenic world. In Calabria, important former Greek cities include Crotone (Croton), Sibari (Sybaris), Reggio Calabria (Rhegium), Cirò (Crimisa) and many others. Outside the region, Taranto (Taratum), Naples (Neapolis), Ancona, Syracuse, Agrigento (Acragas), and Catania (Catana) are all cities of Greek origin.

The Greeks brought classical civilization to the Italian peninsula, and left behind an artistic and cultural legacy that the Romans often copied if rarely equalled (Reggio Calabria's Museo Nazionale has a splendid and important collection of Greek artefacts, including the famous bronzes of Riace, recovered from the sea bed in 1972). However, it could be said that the Greeks' most significant contribution was the introduction of the systematic cultivation of the vine and the olive tree, whose respective products have been the cornerstones of Italian daily life down the centuries.

Sambiase near the hot baths known as the Terme di Caronte. Minimum alcohol 12 degrees.

Melissa DOC Delimited vineyard adjacent to Cirò producing both red (from Gaglioppo and Greco Nero; minimum alcohol 11.5 degrees) and white (from Greco) wines.

Pollino DOC Sturdy red wine from the province of Cosenza produced from the usual blend of Gaglioppo and Greco Nero. Minimum alcohol 12 degrees, 12.5 degrees for wines labelled Superiore.

Sant'Anna di Isola di Capo Rizzuto DOC Mouthful of a delimited wine zone near ancient Croton by the town of Isola di Capo Rizzuto: red wine produced from Gaglioppo together with other local black and white grape varieties. Minimum alcohol 12 degrees.

Savuto DOC Red and *rosato* wines from the provinces of Catanzaro and Cosenza produced mainly from Gaglioppo, Greco Nero and other local black grapes. Minimum alcohol 12 degrees; if wine reaches 12.5 degrees and has minimum 2 years' ageing, it may be labelled Superiore.

LA GASTRONOMIA: FOODS OF CALABRIA

Think of Calabria, and the dishes that come to mind are great platters of seafood and vegetable *antipasti*, dried pasta served with garlicky arrays of seafood and shellfish, and enormous grilled swordfish steaks, as meaty and tasty as giant T-bones. These foods reflect the maritime aspect of Calabria today and the fact that most tourists to the zone stay on or near the coast.

However, Calabria, in spite of its enormous coastline, has traditionally looked inward. Centuries of invasion from marauding pirates coupled with epidemics of malaria from the coastal lowlands drove the people literally into the mountains. And so today, in the harsh uplands and mountain zones, the cuisine still reflects the nature of the terrain. Here, the grazing of goats and sheep remains a traditional activity for the production of fine mountain cheeses, while wild foods – game in profusion, mushrooms, and wild greens – all find their way into the cooking pot. Sea and mountains: this is the essential duality of Calabria.

PIATTI TIPICI: REGIONAL SPECIALITIES

Alici al gratin Fresh anchovies baked with olive oil, garlic, and breadcrumbs, and served as an *antipasti*.

Mustica Paste made from tiny salted anchovy fry, olive oil, and great quantities of *peperoncini* chillies – said to be Arab in origin, *mustica* is remarkably similar to Korean fish and chilli pastes. Eaten here as part of *antipasti* array, usually spread on bread.

Macco di fave Thick, almost solid broad bean soup dressed with olive oil, grated *pecorino* cheese, and chilli pepper.

THE MEZZOGIORNO

Spaghetti ai frutti di mare
Spaghetti or other similar dried
pasta served with shellfish (squid,
clams, mussels, langoustines, etc)
which have been fried in garlic,
copious amounts of olive oil, and
wine.

Maccheroni con le sarde Pasta
with sauce made from mashed
sardines, olive oil, raisins, and
pine nuts.

Pesce spada Swordfish,
traditionally grilled in steaks.

Capretto arrosto Roast kid, a
speciality of the mountains.

Melanzane a scapece Grilled
aubergines marinated in vinegar.

Ficchi ripieni Dried figs stuffed
with chopped walnuts and
almonds, then baked in thick
syrup flavoured with cloves and
cinnamon.

Cheeses: *Caciocavallo* Today this
hard, tasty cheese is made all
over the south, but it originally
came from Calabria. *Pecorino*
Sheep's milk cheese, often
flavoured with peppercorns or
chillies: aged *pecorino* is the
cheese usually utilized for
grating.

Cirò Marina.

CIRÒ: WINE OF THE
ANCIENT OLYMPIANS

In Brief: The southern Ionian instep and toe of the Italian boot boasts some of the oldest vineyards on the peninsula, most notably those of Cirò. Today, this isolated, poor, depressed zone is attracting visitors not mainly for the wine, but for some of the most beautiful and unspoiled beaches in the Mediterranean. The Ionian Sea is unpolluted, there are few of the beach restrictions found in other Italian seaside resorts, and nudism is popular; couple that with good, inexpensive seafood and sound local wines and it is probably fair to conjecture that this still mainly undiscovered zone may one day become a minor mainstream holiday destination. Just inland from the sea lies another world, for the stark mountains of the Sila rise dramatically, presenting terrain as poor, harsh, inhospitable, and majestic as any in Italy.

It is unlikely that any but the maddest and most intrepid wine tourists would come all the way down here just for the wine: it is good, it has the most ancient pedigree, yes, but frankly it is not distinguished enough – with the exception of certain *riserva* reds – to rise above the level of good holiday drinking.

Driving around Italy's instep, from Apulia through Basilicata to Calabria, the flatter coastal plains are rich and fertile in contrast to the scrubby hill terrain that leads up to the mountains. But with the exception of lands around Metaponto, with its splendid Greek temple, there are surprisingly few vineyards. Rather, the terrain is cultivated with enormous, gnarled, pitted olive trees, and lush, irrigated orange groves, while the hills are given over to the grazing of sheep and goats.

By Cirò Marina, however, we re-enter the kingdom of the grape, for the land is carpeted almost entirely with vines, trained low by the bush *alberello* system, along wire *spaliere*, or by the high-trained, high-yielding *tendone*. This is clearly a specialized vineyard, one with antecedents that go back literally millennia. In the midst of the wine country, out by Punta Alice, a spit marking the point where the deep Gulf of Taranto ends and the land turns south towards the pointed toe of Reggio Calabria, lie the remains of an ancient Doric temple dedicated to the god Apollo. This was the site of Crimisa, a Greek town of considerable importance, and the source of one of antiquity's most famous wines.

THE MEZZOGIORNO

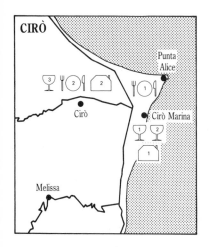

For Magna Grecia was considered an integral part of Greece itself. Thus, city-states such as nearby Croton sent their favourite sons across the sea to Olympia to pit their strength and prowess in the games which our modern Olympics attempt to emulate. Magna Grecia enjoyed considerable success in these ancient trials: one of Croton's most famous sons was the wrestler Milon, who was apparently never beaten in competition. Such victorious athletes were naturally fêted grandly on their return to Magna Grecia with, according to history, copious libations of the wine of Crimisa.

Such vinous antecedents should not be dismissed, remote though they undoubtedly are. True, the wine that Milon and his tutor Pythagoras enjoyed was unlikely to be even remotely similar to the wines of Cirò today. But the ancient Greeks were among the shrewdest and most discerning topers in history, and in many cases vineyards that they established thousands of years ago still produce superlative wines (how ironic that the wines of modern Greece itself have been relegated to such lowly status). Moreover, the Greeks brought the vine to these lands, so it is probable that Calabria's wines of antiquity were produced from the same grape varieties as those of today, including Gaglioppo (Calabria's predominant black grape variety) and Greco (utilized for Cirò Bianco).

Cirò Marina sounds rather grand, but don't come to this far-flung vinous outpost expecting to see yachts and motor launches – not yet, anyway. The town, like most which extend along the Calabrian coast, is frankly grubby, a poor village that lives by fishing, wine, and only lately tourism. The '*marina*' aspect refers to the fact that previously, particularly throughout the Middle Ages, all the towns along the Calabrian coast were sited not by the sea but in the hills above as protection from marauders and invaders. Even today the watchtowers that were erected around the coast to warn of invading Turkish pirates remain in place (Britain's Martello towers are direct copies of these). However, in recent years, peace coupled with improvements in communications has led these tough people down from the hills to settle by the sea. Cirò Marina, therefore, is simply the maritime counterpart of the older, inland hill town of Cirò.

The vineyards of Cirò extend mainly between the communities of Cirò, Cirò Marina, and Melissa (which is also entitled to its own *denominazione*).

Cirò DOC can be red, white or *rosato*, though holidaymakers to Calabria are probably most familiar with Cirò Bianco, for it is the region's only white wine of note with relatively wide distribution, and the usual accompaniment to the great feasts of seafood and shellfish which are served in local restaurants. Cirò Bianco is produced entirely from the Greco grape, at best fresh, clean, and with the particular and pleasing bitter-orange aftertaste of that traditional and distinctive varietal. However, like most white wines from the Mezzogiorno, it does have the propensity to oxidize, so it is always advisable to drink it as young as possible.

Cirò Rosso, and particular *riserva* bottlings from the best producers (including Ippolito and San Francesco), can be a wine of considerable stature with plenty of body and perfume, produced from the beefy Gaglioppo grape lightened with the addition of only a little Greco and Trebbiano. Today, improvements in both the vineyard and the *cantina* (in particular the use of stainless steel fermentation vats and the control of temperature during fermentation) means that these are indeed well-made, stable wines which ought to be tried given the opportunity (they are only rarely encountered outside the region).

If Cirò Marina, like the rest of the Calabrian coast, is rather tatty, the old hill town of Cirò itself is positively grim and foreboding. None the less, it is essential to strike into the hills to gain a higher perspective on this poor, overlooked region. Drive up here, ignoring the trash beside the road, the rusting cars, the goats grazing in the garbage, simply to gain an impression of the clustered, claustrophobic medieval hill village, and to look back, beyond the horrendous, ghastly, crumbling sprawl, out to the coast and the timeless beauty of the Ionian Sea.

Then drive beyond Cirò itself, into the bare mountains, for an even more startling contrast: the land is an arid, rugged moonscape, harsh, timeless, threatening. It is not hard to imagine that these mountains and the neighbouring Aspromonte are the hideaways for the brutal kidnappers and criminals who continue to terrorize the north of Italy, and who unfairly give such an unsavoury name to the people of Calabria.

Antonio Ippolito.

Degustazione: Stop to Taste; Stop to Buy

1

AZIENDA VINICOLA VICENZO
   IPPOLITO
VIA TIRONE 118
98072 CIRÒ MARINA CZ
TEL: 0962/31106

WINES PRODUCED: Cirò Classico
Riserva, Cirò Classico, Cirò Bianco,
Cirò Rosato.
VISITS: daily, by appointment.
The Azienda Vinicola Ippolito is
one of the oldest in Cirò, and indeed
Vicenzo Ippolito, father of current
directors Antonio and Salvatore,
was probably the first to bottle and
commercialize the wine. Previously
it had been mainly sold in bulk as
high-strength cutting wine to
producers in northern Italy and
France. But Vicenzo saw the
potential in marketing the wine as
a privileged nectar of antiquity
('the gods of Olympus are our oldest
clients' states a publicity brochure),
and indeed, the wine has even been
supplied to modern Italian Olympic
teams. Today, tradition allied with
modern computer-controlled wine
making equipment results in a
range of excellent wines.

2

CAPARRA & SICILIANI
BIVIO SS106
88070 CIRÒ MARINA CZ
TEL: 0962/31217

WINES PRODUCED: Cirò Rosso
Classico; Cirò Rosato; Cirò Bianco.
VISITS: daily, working hours.
Well-regarded co-operative winery
located just outside Cirò Marina.
English spoken.

3

AZIENDA AGRICOLA FATTORIA SAN
   FRANCESCO
CASALE SAN FRANCESCO
88071 CIRÒ CZ
TEL: 0962/32228

WINES PRODUCED: Cirò Classico
Riserva, Cirò Classico 'Ronco dei
Quattro Venti', Cirò Bianco, Cirò
Rosato; Pinot Chardonnay
Spumante.
VISITS: Mon–Fri 8h30–12h30;
15–18h. Sat 9h30–13h30.
The old convent of San Francesco is
the atmospheric location for a
well-run family winery located up
the hill just off the road before
reaching Cirò Superiore itself. Here
the Siciliani have an extensive
agricultural estate and work some
100 hectares of specialized
vineyards, producing not only some
of Cirò's finest wines but also
superb extra virgin olive oil and
handmade *pecorino* cheese. While
the San Francesco convent is
currently the administrative seat of

the estate, the winery itself is located in Cirò Marina. However, the wines can be purchased here, and the traditional olive oil mill can be visited (working Nov–early Jan).

Ristoranti

1

HOTEL-RISTORANTE 'IL GABBIANO'
PUNTA ALICE
88070 CIRÒ MARINA CZ
TEL: 0962/31338

Friendly family hotel located directly on the beach at Punta Alice, with an excellent restaurant serving seafood pasta, fresh fish and shellfish.
Moderate

2

RISTORANTE IL CAMINO
LOC. CAPPELLA
88071 CIRÒ SUPERIORE CZ
TEL: 0962/32197

Closed Wed. Advisable to book. Located in the hills above Cirò Marina, a good local restaurant serving not just the fruits of the sea, but also the authentic foods of the harsher mountainous terrain: *antipasto cirotano, pesce alle brace, coniglio, capretto, tordi*. Good selection of local wines.
Inexpensive to Moderate

Agriturismo

1

LA PAGODA
LOC. ACUTETTO
88072 CIRÒ MARINA CZ
TEL: 0962/31112

Holiday complex on a farm: *villette* and bungalows, bar, *pizzeria*, tennis courts, and own-produced Cirò DOC, cheese, eggs, and poultry.

2

AZIENDA AGRARIA SAN VINCENZO
CASALE SAN VINCENZO
88071 CIRÒ CZ
TEL: 0962/32171

Apartments to let on the estate of a producer of Cirò DOC wine, oil, honey, eggs, and chickens.

THE MEZZOGIORNO

GRECO DI BIANCO, 'THE BEST WINE IN THE WORLD'?

In Brief: This compact wine region lies virtually at the tip of the Italian boot. We doubt many wine tourists will penetrate this far, but those intrepid few who do will be rewarded with a veritable nectar, Greco di Bianco, one of the great dessert wines of Italy, some say the world.

As on other parts of the Ionian coast, the beaches here are beautiful and unspoiled, though tourists are gradually discovering this long over-looked and isolated outpost.

The wine roads of Italy lead to some curious places, none more so than the wine hills of Bianco, located on the underside of the rugged Aspromonte, nearly at the tip of the bulging digit of the Italian foot. There is no easy way to reach this worn-out land: indeed, Milan is closer to London than it is to Reggio Calabria, the provincial capital. Around the Ionian seaboard through interminable half-finished villages, their concrete, rust-stained columns a stark parody of the fragmented classical temples that litter the coast; or else way down the A3 *autostrada*, a concrete cemetery, say some, for countless victims of the ruthless 'Ndrangheta, Calabria's vicious Mafia equivalent: when you finally make it to Bianco, you know that you have arrived for there really is nowhere else to go.

Just up from the remains of a Greco-Roman villa, we struck into the hills between the tiny towns of Bovalino and Bianco until we arrived at a ram-shackle, haphazard old farm. There were mangy dogs scratching around the yard, and a cat nursing her litter of kittens. A black-haired boy no more than 12 years old emerged from the furry drapery that served as a front door. I had telephoned a few days earlier so I expected to be expected.

'Is this the Azienda Agricola of Umberto Ceratti?' I asked.

The boy thumped himself on the chest. '*Io sono Umberto Ceratti*,' he answered in a surprisingly deep voice (it turned out that the farm and the boy were both named after his grandfather).

As we stepped out of our van, I noticed two dark-skinned men by the half-cracked door of a shed. They were grinning at us hugely, seemed not unfriendly; they motioned us to come, and through the door we could see the flames of a large fire. It was late November and bitterly cold outside. But Umberto motioned us away.

'Moroccans,' he told me, as if in explanation. 'Here for the olive harvest.'

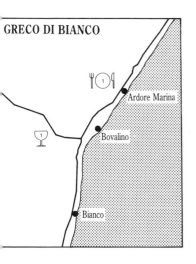

GRECO DI BIANCO

Ardore Marina

Bovalino

Bianco

Of course, we had come to see the *cantina* and to taste the Greco di Bianco, a rare dessert wine that is almost impossible to find but which none the less has been hailed as one of the great wines of Italy.

Umberto was more direct. 'Here,' he said, showing us an equally ramshackle and rudimentary winery, littered with wooden crates, a tiny hand press, and a half-dozen or so fibreglass fermentation vats. 'Here,' he said, reaching up to thump me soundly on the back, 'we make the best wine in the world.'

In an adjoining part of the cellar, the boy's grandmother, a tough old peasant in her 70s or 80s, sat in front of a disc of glowing ashes, busy drawing red *vino da tavola* from a vat to be bottled for a local wedding the next day. She quietly confirmed the boy's assertion: 'Our Greco di Bianco is the best wine in the world.'

Pasquale, Umberto's father, who arrived later from his principal occupation as director of the local post office in nearby Caraffa, was also adamant that I was aware of the apparently indisputable: 'The *best* wine,' he stressed, 'not just in Italy, but in *tutto il mondo* – the whole world.' He then reached down to squeeze our baby son Guy's cheeks so hard that he made him cry.

I have to say that given the situation (and considering the competition: the world after all is a rather large place) this statement of fact seemed all the more remarkable. However, he then thrust in front of me a photocopy from a book that settled the question beyond any doubt: *Courvoisier's Book of the Best*, edited by Lord Lichfield ('the cousin, no less,' he reminded me, 'of the *Regina Elisabetta*'). In this apparent bible for the international set, Ceratti's Greco di Bianco is singled out as 'one of the world's best sweet apéritif wines': presumably *'the'* wine to be seen drinking in the Caffè Alemagna di Roma, while dressed, of course, in your designer outfits by Armani. Its very scarcity, and the fact that so few people have heard of it, only adds to its snob appeal in this guide to what is 'in'. Nor is the Queen's cousin the only one who has praised Ceratti's wine: Italian wine experts Burton Anderson and Nicolas Belfrage have been almost equally enraptured with it.

I am basically one who shies away from such hype, but for all of the inflated hullabaloo, I have to admit that the wine really is exceptional, all the more so given its rather unlikely provenance. Moreover, Pasquale

THE MEZZOGIORNO

Ceratti himself did not seek such accolades and seemed genuinely baffled at how he had received them.

Ceratti may be a part-time wine maker, but it is his passion, and, like any whose aim is quality, he takes the utmost care and attention at every stage of the process. The Greco grapes that are grown on the stark chalk-white terrain are cultivated entirely organically, fertilized with manure from horses kept for that purpose. Following traditional practices which elsewhere have been abandoned, he grows beans, for example, between the vines, then turns them back into the ground to add nourishment and humus to the soil. Ceratti moreover ensures that the yields are strictly limited, pruning back severely in spring, and thinning out the bunches further in summer.

After the *vendemmia* the selected grapes are laid out on straw mats and left outside in the shade to dry and shrivel in the hot Calabrian autumn for 15–30 days. Then, unbelievably, these raisin-like grapes are transferred to wooden slatted crates which are each individually immersed in a vat of boiling water for a few seconds only, 'just long enough to sterilize them'. I have never heard of such a bizarre process used anywhere else in the world. The grapes are next pressed and the sugar-rich must is transferred to fibreglass vats where it is simply left to ferment extremely slowly (with 3 rackings), reaching finally an incredible 17 degrees of alcohol naturally before being bottled some time the following summer.

We sampled the wine from chipped tumblers, warming ourselves in front of that glowing disc of hot ashes together with the Nonna Ceratti. She squinted in the dark, looking to us for confirmation of the obvious. '*Si, è vero,*' I said. '*È squisito.*' The wine was indeed exquisite: raisiny rich as are all such *passiti* wines, yet finely, delicately perfumed, and with the characteristic but sublime bitter-orange twist of the Greco grape in the finish which kept it from cloying.

Only some 6000 bottles are made in that basic home winery each year, and almost the entire production – with the exception of small amounts sent to those few select outlets in Rome and elsewhere – is sold direct at the farm for what seems to me a pittance (about 8000 *lire* a bottle at the time of writing). It is perhaps ironic that 'the best wine in the world' is carted off mainly by an army of undiscriminating holidaymakers from the vast Eurocamp at the bottom of the road. For yes, mass tourism has even penetrated into this deepest southern outpost.

Degustazione: **Stop to Taste; Stop to Buy**

1 AZIENDA AGRICOLA UMBERTO
   CERATTI
VIA DEGLI UFFIZI 5
89030 CARAFFA DEL BIANCO RC
TEL: 0964/913073

WINES PRODUCED: Greco di Bianco;
Mantonico; red *vino da tavola.*
VISITS: daily 6–20h. Telephone first.
In addition to the exceptional Greco
di Bianco, Pasquale Ceratti also
makes a similar dessert wine from
local Mantonico grapes, as well as
decent red table wine. Ceratti and
his wife run the local post office in
Caraffa, but there is usually
someone on hand to show you round
or sell a few bottles of this rare
nectar.

Hotel-Ristorante

1 EURO HOTEL
SS106
89037 ARDORE MARINA RC
TEL: 0964/61024

Handy hotel-restaurant near the
tiny but prestigious Bianco
vineyard on the main road facing
the sea: friendly Italo-American
owners and a decent restaurant
serving mainly fish.
Inexpensive to Moderate

Wine and Other Related *Sagre* and *Feste*

| early autumn | Sagra del Maiale | Towns throughout the region |
| mid-Sept | Sagra del Vino di Cirò | Cirò Marina |

THE MEZZOGIORNO

E PER SAPERE DI PIÙ –
ADDITIONAL INFORMATION

Ente Provinciale per il Turismo
Centro Mancuso
via F. Spasari
88100 Catanzaro
tel: 0961/29823

Ente Provinciale per il Turismo
via Tagliamento 15
87100 Cosenza
tel: 0984/27821

Ente Provinciale per il Turismo
via D. Tripepi 72
89100 Reggio Calabria
tel: 0965/98496

Associazione Regionale Agriturist
via XX Settembre 42
88100 Catanzaro
tel: 0961/45084

THE ISLANDS

Sicily
Sardinia

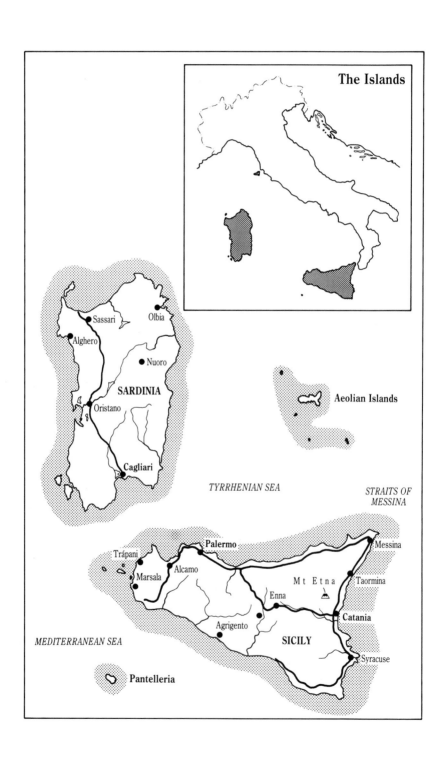

The Islands

Sassari
Olbia
Alghero
Nuoro
SARDINIA
Oristano
Cagliari

Aeolian Islands

TYRRHENIAN SEA

STRAITS OF
MESSINA

Messina
Palermo
Trápani
Alcamo
Marsala
Mt Etna
Taormina
Enna
Catania
Agrigento
SICILY
MEDITERRANEAN SEA
Syracuse
Pantelleria

SICILY

Alcamo wine country.

I Vini: THE WINES OF SICILY	486
La Gastronomia	488
Le Strade dei Vini: THE WINE ROADS OF SICILY	
Ancient Wines in an Ancient Land	489
Le Sagre: WINE AND OTHER RELATED FESTIVALS	503
Additional Information	503

Sicily, like some great slumbering giant, lies stretched out under the broad-shouldered volcano of Etna. In many ways, the island, separated from mainland Italy only by the narrow Straits of Messina, seems much further away from the rest of the country than it really is. Its separate history and domination – by the Phoenicians, Greeks, Romans, Normans, Angevins, Spanish Bourbons – combined with its unique geographical position almost within sight of north Africa, has left behind myriad influences: contrast Palermo's Islamic pleasure palaces and the amazing Norman-Byzantine cathedral of Monreale; the island's baroque and peasant foods; the lush overwhelming scent of orange blossom and the stench of rotting garbage and poverty; the deep-abiding Sicilian tradition of hospitality and the fearful code of *omertà*.

Sicily is one of Italy's great wine regions, in sheer size alone if nothing else. Although she ranks equal first with Apulia in terms of production, like that other great southern vineyard, much wine seems to be produced with little other ambition than to swell the already overflowing EEC 'wine lake'. The percentage of DOC wine remains a mere 4% of the island's total production, though this is explained partly by the fact that many of Sicily's best wines – certainly the most widely available and best known – are not entitled to geographical *denominazioni*.

Sicily is not an island for the single-minded wine tourist, and indeed most who come here do so for other reasons: the exceptionally mild Mediterranean climate, beautiful beaches and rugged natural scenery, archaeology and ancient ruins that rival even those of Greece, and the opportunity to explore one of the few remaining unspoiled outposts of Europe where life really has changed little over the centuries. Yet those who come to this land

THE ISLANDS

of contrasts will find that their cup is never empty, and that in wine terms at least, the sleeping giant may be about to awake.

ORIENTATION

Sicily is Italy's largest single region and the largest island in the Mediterranean. It is an autonomous region made up of 9 provinces: Palermo, Agrigento, Caltanissetta, Catania, Enna, Messina, Ragusa, Syracuse, and Trapani. Both Palermo, the regional capital, and Catania, its second city, have international airports. By train, there are direct services from northern Italy to Sicily via the ferry port of Villa San Giovanni which also serves for car and passenger ferries. There are car ferry and hydrofoil services from Reggio Calabria, while ferries also operate between Palermo and Naples, Livorno, and Genoa.

Map Touring Club Italiano 1: 200 000 Sicilia.

I VINI: GLOSSARY TO THE WINES OF SICILY

Wines of *Denominazione di Origine Controllata (DOC)*

Alcamo; Bianco di Alcamo DOC
One of Sicily's best dry white wines, produced from mainly Catarratto Bianco grapes, together with Damaschino, Grecanico, and Trebbiano, grown in the province of Trapani primarily in the commune of Alcamo and environs. Minimum alcohol 11.5 degrees.

Cerasuolo di Vittoria DOC
Robust red table wine produced mainly from Frappato and Calabrese grapes in the south-east of the island centred on the wine commune of Vittoria. Minimum alcohol 13 degrees.

Etna DOC Delimited vineyard on the eastern flanks of Mt Etna for the production of red, *rosato*, and white wines. Red and *rosato* are produced mainly from Nerello Mascalese grapes and must reach a minimum of 12.5 degrees. White Etna is produced from Carricante and Catarratto (the Superiore version must include at least 80% of the former); minimum alcohol 11.5 degrees and 12 degrees for Superiore.

Faro DOC Minuscule delimited vineyard on the far north-eastern tip of the island above Messina for

GIUSEPPE GARIBALDI AND 'I MILLE'

Though the seeds of national unification had already been sown during the tumultuous years of the early 19th century, the first tangible steps to the creation of the Italian state took place when Giuseppe Garibaldi and a motley band of soldiers and volunteers calling themselves *'I Mille'* – the Thousand – landed in the grubby little wine town of Marsala, in western Sicily, on 11 May 1860.

Garibaldi and his troops, their numbers swelled by local peasants who joined the popular uprising, swiftly defeated the much larger Neapolitan army, seized Palermo, and took control of the island. They then began their famous march on to the mainland, liberating first Calabria, then Naples, and continuing towards Rome, the Papal State, and the eventual liberation and unification of the whole Italian peninsula.

The great soldier visited the Florio winery on a subsequent and less action-packed visit to Marsala, and out of respect the company named a style of wine after him: Garibaldi Dolce (GB), a mark which is still used today.

the production of red wine from varieties of Nerello. Minimum alcohol 12 degrees.

Malvasia delle Lipari DOC Rare dessert wine from the Aeolian islands produced from Malvasia di Lipari grapes in 3 versions: sweet (minimum alcohol 11.5 degrees), *passito dolce naturale* (minimum alcohol 18 degrees), and *liquoroso* (minimum alcohol 20 degrees).

Marsala DOC Famous traditional fortified wine produced in western Sicily from Catarratto, Grillo, and Inzolia grapes made into natural wine then blended with *sifone* (a mixture of sweet grape must and grape brandy) and/or *cotto* (cooked grape must) and aged for varying lengths of time, sometimes by the *solera* system. In the past, Marsala was flavoured with egg or syrups, but this has now been eliminated, and the DOC discipline has been revised and tightened up considerably. A number of traditional styles of Marsala are produced, including: Marsala Fine (common grade, with minimum alcohol of 17 degrees and minimum ageing of 1 year: may also be designated IP for Italia Particolare); Marsala Superiore (minimum ageing 2 years: may also be designated SOM for Superior Old Marsala, GD for Garibaldi

Dolce, LP for London Particular, or Vecchio); Marsala Superiore Riserva (minimum ageing 4 years); Marsala Vergine or Solera (minimum ageing 5 years); Marsala Vergine Stravecchio or Riserva (minimum ageing 10 years).

Moscato di Noto DOC Minuscule historic vineyard in the province of Syracuse for the production of Moscato wines in 3 versions: *naturale* (dessert wine with 11.5 degrees alcohol minimum); *liquoroso* (fortified, with minimum alcohol of 16 degrees); and *spumante* (sweet sparkling; minimum alcohol 13 degrees).

Moscato di Siracusa DOC Virtually non-existent dessert Moscato wine from ancient vineyards of Syracuse. Minimum alcohol 16.5 degrees.

Moscato di Pantelleria DOC One of the great dessert wines of Italy, produced from Moscato grapes (known locally as Zibibbo) grown on the tiny volcanic island of Pantelleria. Produced in a variety of both natural and *passito* versions. Natural wine can be sweet, very sweet, or sparkling; Moscato di Pantelleria *passito*, made from grapes dried in the sun, is always very rich and sweet, produced in both *naturale* and *liquoroso* (fortified) versions.

LA GASTRONOMIA: FOODS OF SICILY

Just as Sicily itself has been formed by its unique history of almost continual occupation by foreign forces and influences, so has this had an inevitable influence on shaping the native cuisine of the island. Rice dishes, *cuscusu* (a version of north African *couscous*), stuffed vegetables, and intricate pastries and sweetmeats, for example, are all legacies of the Arabs. But if the Greeks, Normans, Spanish, even the English (with the creation of Marsala wine), all left their mark on Sicily, perhaps the greatest contrast has been – and remains – that between the simple but delicious and innovative *cucina povera* of the ordinary people, and the overblown, bombastic, baroque cuisine of the aristocracy.

PIATTI TIPICI: REGIONAL SPECIALITIES

Antipasti siciliani Most restaurants serve an outstanding array of *antipasti*, including marinated or stuffed vegetables, fried vegetables and fish, marinated sardines and anchovies, roasted peppers, fresh salads, dressed or mashed beans, *arancini di riso* (savoury rice rissoles) and much else.

Pasta cu li sardi Virtually the staple first course: any variety of pasta (*bucatini* and *linguine* are popular) served with sauce made from fresh sardines and wild fennel.

Pasta alla Norma Spaghetti or *penne* served with tomato and fried aubergine sauce garnished with salted *ricotta* cheese. The recipe was created in homage to the composer Bellini, a native of Catania.

Riso alla pescatora Spanish-style rice, shellfish, and seafood pilaff.

Farsumagru Elaborate stuffed meat roll, filled with any number of ingredients: boiled eggs, *mortadella*, cheese, vegetables, raisins, pine nuts, and spices and seasonings.

Cuscusu Sicilian *couscous*: steamed semolina served with a spicy fish stew.

Pesce spada alla siciliana Swordfish steak seasoned with olive oil, lemon juice, chopped parsley, and garlic.

Cassata Famous *ricotta* cheesecake (sometimes made with ice cream) mixed and decorated with candied fruit, pistachio nuts, chocolate, and much else.

Cannoli No visit to Sicily would be complete without enjoying this famous *ricotta*-filled pastry.

ANCIENT WINES IN AN ANCIENT LAND

One of the best wines we ever enjoyed was in Sicily. It was late November, and we had spent the day exploring the remarkable Valley of the Temples at Agrigento, a rare and awesome collection of some 20 Greek temples that

THE ISLANDS

In Brief: Sicily is not a region for the single-minded wine traveller. However, notwithstanding the fact that Sicily's quality wine industry is dominated by a handful of large and very large concerns, wine lovers will rarely go thirsty, and wherever they find themselves there should be interesting local wines to sample. Opportunities for visiting wineries, though, are limited compared to the rest of the country. We make a brief journey around the island to dip into her major wine zones, but there is still ample scope for further exploration.

remain today in a remarkable state of preservation. That night we found a simple *trattoria* near the site, and were looking forward to the extensive array of Sicilian *antipasti* followed by seafood pasta and grilled fish. I had ordered a bottle of white Settesoli, a local wine from the nearby co-operative winery at Menfi, but the waiter returned with a carafe of *vino sfuso* – anonymous 'open wine'. I questioned him, but he assured me that it was *ottimo*. The wine, a strikingly vivid lemon yellow, was indeed exquisite: from the vintage that had been harvested only weeks earlier, it was exceedingly fresh and intensely fruity, and it went so perfectly with the robustly-flavoured foods that it was all you could ask for in a wine. We drank a litre, and then we ordered another ...

To me, that simple, anonymous table wine, so basic, unselfconscious and totally in harmony in place and time, epitomized what we travel the vineyards of the world to find. Yet how rarely is it encountered. In truth, Sicilian wines today make few claims to greatness, and if they can even begin to satisfy this basic prerequisite then we should probably ask for little more.

Yet if Sicily was once known only as the vast source of high-alcohol cutting wines to send north and to France, the best producers today have demonstrated the island's potential for quality, and good wines are widely available. One of the most striking features of viticulture in Sicily, though, is that there is little history of estate wine making on a small scale (as there is, say, in Tuscany, Piedmont, and most other wine zones). Instead, there is a small handful of relatively large companies whose brand-name wines – Corvo, Rapitalà, Regaleali, Donnafugata – are encountered widely by visitors throughout the island, as well as internationally, and who thus continue to dominate the Sicilian wine scene. In recent years, too, co-operative wineries have made great strides by, for example, replanting vineyards on the hills

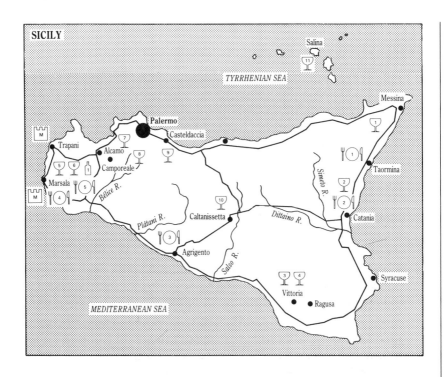

instead of on the sunbaked plains, and investing in modern technology to produce sound, new-style wines that appeal to modern international tastes.

It is none the less worth while making a brief tour of the island to examine it from a vinous point of view. Most visitors will reach Sicily by air, landing at either Palermo or Catania depending on their ultimate destinations. However, the most dramatic entry is by boat from Villa San Giovanni in deepest Calabria, across the Straits of Messina. This narrow body of water was where Homer's wandering hero Odysseus had to endure the twin dangers of the monster Scylla and the whirlpool Charybdis. Take courage, though: the frequent ferries that today ply the straits are reasonably modern and stable, and the crossing takes just 30 minutes.

Messina and its province are the source of two DOC wines. Faro is a traditional red wine produced in the furthest, north-westernmost tip near Cape Peloro in minute quantities almost exclusively by the Bagni winery. Malvasia delle Lipari is even more far-flung, from the off-shore Aeolian archipelago, a classic dessert wine produced in natural sweet versions as well as in the *passito* form from semi-dried grapes. This is as ancient a style of wine as exists, produced by Carlo Hauner on the tiny island of Salina in

THE ISLANDS

minuscule amounts, but it should be sought and tried by all who seek to discover and worship the grape in its myriad manifestations.

Taormina, south of Messina, is one of Sicily's principal tourist destinations. That alone might be reason enough to avoid it, certainly in July and August: but to do so entirely would be to miss one of the great beauty spots of Europe. For the ancient Greeks knew a perfect location when they saw one; it was they who created Taormina's most dramatically-sited amphitheatre, hewn from solid rock on the crest of a steep hill which afforded not only superb acoustics, but also a spectacular and awe-inspiring view across to smouldering Etna and way down below to the pounding, relentless sea. Taormina itself is a charming, mainly medieval town, full of hotels, restaurants, and the usual tourist accoutrements. Indeed, anything that can be passed off on unsuspecting visitors usually will be: the worst, from our wine-biased point of view, are those awful 'lava-encrusted' bottles bearing labels showing the great volcano in full eruption.

The mineral-rich volcanic ash of Etna, of course, has nurtured the vine literally for millennia and the Etna *denominazione* is one of Sicily's more important ones. In fact the wines, both red and white, produced from grapes grown at high altitudes can be quite good – if you are brave enough or silly enough to get past the bizarre packaging. The wine estate of Barone di Villagrande does not resort to such tomfoolery, and its Etna Rosso in particular is a wine worth seeking: produced mainly from an indigenous grape called Nerello Mascalese, it is well rounded and generous with a nice touch of warm peppery spice. Villagrande's Etna Bianco Superiore is also well-made, if less distinctive, produced from 100% Carricante grapes.

In the south-eastern corner of the island lies Syracuse, an ancient Greek city that at its height in the 5th and 4th centuries BC rivalled even Athens in magnificence and influence. Its ruined Greek amphitheatre was the largest in Europe: probably as many as 15,000 people crowded into it over 2000 years ago to watch the first performance of Aeschylus' *Persians*. Other notable remains include the bizarre man-made 'Ear of Dionysus' (probably utilized for its acoustical effects), and the immense Heiron's altar, a sacrificial altar dating from the 3rd century BC. These fragments intimate a past more splendid and golden than we can imagine.

Syracuse once also boasted notable dessert wines produced from the fragrant Moscato grape. But today Moscato di Siracusa DOC is virtually non-existent, while the similar Moscato di Noto, from vineyards around the eponymous baroque 18th-century town to the south, is produced only in the tiniest quantities. Still further south, from the province of Ragusa comes one of Sicily's better delimited table wines, Cerasuolo di Vittorio DOC, a full-bodied, gutsy red wine produced mainly from the local Frappato and Calabrese grapes. Cerasuolo traditionally is a wine capable of lengthy conservation, but today's tastes are for fresher, fruitier, less oxidized styles.

Those who share our passion for ancient ruins will come next to Agrigento, though hardly anywhere else is the dismal contrast between the grubby modern city of today and the splendour of the past more apparent. None the less, a visit to Agrigento's Valley of the Temples should be a must for all who come to Sicily, for it is the sheer scale and immensity of the 20 remaining temples, pocked, time-worn, but still glowing in warm golden sandstone, that is most striking. Here you can well imagine not just important ceremonial sites in isolation but the entire bustle of a great ancient metropolis.

The province of Agrigento produces no wines entitled to DOC status, but the visitor to the great ancient city will not lack for liquid refreshment. We have already noted how superb the simple open carafe wines can be, while the range produced at the Settesoli co-operative winery at nearby Menfi is consistently excellent and has won considerable acclaim. One of the strangest sights, incidentally, in this area and throughout the island is fields of vineyards covered in plastic and bearing plump grapes even until December. No, they are not utilized to produce some strange local late-harvested dessert wine: they are the prized *uva regina* table grapes.

Mazaro del Vallo, located in the far south-western corner of the island, is the home of Sicily's largest fishing fleet, and it is from here that you can catch the ferry to the isolated volcanic island of Pantelleria, a journey that takes 5 hours. From this farthest vinous outpost of Italy, actually closer to sunbaked north Africa than to Sicily, comes one of the nation's greatest dessert wines, Moscato di Pantelleria. The best examples are *passito* wines produced by laying out the fragrant Moscato grapes (locally known as Zibibbo) on straw mats in the blazing sun to dry and shrivel to virtual raisins before pressing and fermentation. The wine that results – two of the best examples are Marco de Bartoli's Bukkurram and the local co-operative's Tanit – is dark amber to walnut, with the complex sticky-rich aromas and flavours of a spicy fruitcake.

Of course, Pantelleria's proximity to north Africa reminds us that Sicily and the western half of the country were under the domination, in ancient times, of the Phoenicians, and in the 9th century of the Saracen Muslims. The town of Marsala was founded by the Phoenicians and later occupied by the Carthaginians, Rome's greatest rival. After the 1st Punic War, when the

Romans defeated the great Hamilcar (father of Hannibal) and succeeded in expelling the Carthaginians from Sicily, Marsala became an important Roman city named Lilybaeum, and the province of Sicily served as '*il granaio*' – the granary – for Imperial Rome. The fascinating remains of a Roman war galley sunk during the 1st Punic War are displayed in Marsala's waterfront archaeological museum.

The name Marsala came many centuries later, from the Arab *Mars-al-Allah*, meaning 'harbour of Allah'. Marsala today is synonymous with the amber-coloured fortified wine to which it gives its name. In truth, though, it is a wine that seems almost entirely at odds and out of harmony with the region of its production. Sitting out in the sun at a waterfront restaurant, eating *spaghetti alle vongole* and grilled swordfish, fortified Marsala hardly seems a wine to contemplate, no more, say, than do Spain's cream sherries when in Sanlucar de Barrameda, or vintage port in sunny Portugal. For, like those other world-famous fortified wines, Marsala developed historically not as a drink of the local people, but as a wine primarily intended for export to London and the British Empire.

An Englishman, John Woodehouse, is credited with its invention, for it was he who first shipped some 70 pipes (a pipe is equivalent to 100 imperial gallons or about 420 litres) back to Britain in 1773. Following the custom of the time, and to make the wine more robust and capable of withstanding

The Florio enoteca, Marsala.

such a voyage, he fortified it with grape brandy. The wine was an immediate success in London, and Admiral Nelson confirmed its popularity by ordering a large consignment for his sailors. After the Battle of Trafalgar, the wine gained the title 'Marsala Victory Wine'. Other Englishmen and Sicilians followed Woodehouse's success, notably Benjamin Ingham and Vicenzo Florio, and Marsala was soon enjoyed not only in Britain, but throughout Europe, and in the United States, South America, Australia, and elsewhere. At the height of the trade, there were some 120 Marsala firms in the town of Marsala itself, though today this number is considerably reduced. Since 1924, Florio, the market leader, has been owned by the vermouth group Cinzano.

Marsala continues to be produced and aged in the vast, whitewashed, low-slung wine warehouses located down by the town's waterfront. Simply follow your nose – the air is heady with evaporating alcohol – to see how this ancient wine is still produced.

The vineyards that produce the base wine for Marsala cover an immense area that extends over much of the western part of the island. The Grillo, Catarratto, and Inzolia vines are planted primarily by the *alberello* or bush system introduced by the Greeks, and the grapes ripen under an intensely hot sun to reach sugar levels with potential alcohol as high as 18 to 20 degrees. Most of the base wine, primarily produced in vast *cantine sociali*, is sold to the Marsala firms and is particularly well-adapted to the production of this unique wine. Indeed, the tendency for these high-alcohol wines to oxidize (or 'marsalize') quickly is one characteristic that distinguishes the finished product.

Marsala warehouses, where this ancient wine ages by the solera *system.*

As in the production of other great fortified wines, the process of fortification with grape brandy, the lengthy ageing in wooden barrels of differing sizes, the addition of cooked grape must (*cotto*) and/or *sifone* (a mixture of sweet grape must and grape brandy) to contribute both sweetness and colour, and many other factors, result in a baffling range of different styles and types of Marsala, ranging from light gold to walnut brown, from virtually bone-dry to very sweet.

Marsala is thus a great historic wine that ought

THE ISLANDS

to proudly take its place in the great vinous tapestry of Italy. However, some time during this century, Marsala's traditional and not inconsiderable pedigree was debased and almost completely lost. In particular, Marsala came to denote not just the classic fortified wine, but any number of bizarre varieties flavoured with egg (Marsala *all'uovo*), and numerous other ingredients, including – believe it or not – bananas and strawberries. Suffice it to say that since 1984 a new and rigorous discipline has been established which should rightly restore Marsala if not to its former glory, then at least to respectability.

Fortified Marsala may be the best-known wine of the Trapani province, but wine co-operatives are investing in modern viticultural equipment and are turning their hands to the production of lighter table wines that can be quite drinkable. Indeed, the potential for quality in this zone and for the capacity to produce distinctive wine of character from the local grape varieties has already been clearly demonstrated in the vineyards that surround the town of Alcamo, located about mid-way betwen Trapani and Palermo.

Alcamo itself is a busy, crazy hill town not far from the famous Doric temple of Segesta. However, the wine country which extends into the hills towards the inland centre of the island is considerably quieter and calmer. Near Camporeale, a French aristocrat from Brittany, Conte Hugues Bernard de la Gatinais, produces one of Sicily's best white wines, Rapitalà Alcamo DOC. Indeed, the wine country between Alcamo and Camporeale is possibly Sicily's most beautiful, the intensive specialized vineyards planted up to 500 metres above sea level on the slopes of rugged, bare mountains interspersed now and then with palm trees, the odd orange orchard, or speckled flocks of sheep. Conte Hugues' father used to produce Muscadet at La Haie-Fouassière near Nantes, and it is hard to imagine a greater contrast than this isolated, dramatic land and the bucolic, charming wine country of the Sèvre-et-Maine.

'Making good white wine in Sicily is really not that different from making good white wine in France,' explained Conte Hugues. 'The modern technology is here today for those who wish to utilize it.' He then proceeded to show us his vast, towering outdoor stainless steel fermentation tanks (what a contrast to the small wooden barrels for the traditional production of Muscadet '*sur lie*'), his refrigeration plant for control of temperature, his modern presses capable of working at the lowest and most delicate levels (only free-run juice, for example, is utilized for Rapitalà), and his computer-controlled bottling lines.

Conte Hugues de la Gatinais.

'Our local Catarratto grape has considerable character and potential in its own right. However, the great problem is that it does have the tendency to oxidize rather quickly. So Rapitalà, like all Sicilian whites, is a wine that must be drunk young. We have now planted both Chardonnay and Sauvignon on the higher slopes and we are quite pleased with the results.' Conte Hugues also produces a warm, well-rounded Rapitalà red as well as an excellent full-bodied *rosato*, though the Alcamo DOC only applies to the white wine. Bouquet di Rapitalà, produced utilizing Chardonnay and Sauvignon, is an extremely light, slightly *frizzante* wine rather in the style of Galestro: on a bakingly hot day it is a refreshingly quenching beverage.

The road from Alcamo leads inevitably to hectic, throbbing Palermo, a city that seems at times more Arab than European. Approaching the city from the hinterland, looking down on Palermo from, say, Monreale, it is hard to imagine a more beautiful setting: the city stretched out languidly along the lovely Bay of Palermo, with the lush Conca d'Oro – the rich, deep green vale of mainly lemon and lime groves – carpeting its surroundings. On closer inspection, the initial impression may be less softly focused, for Palermo must be one of Italy's craziest and most notorious cities, not least because of the Mafia connections that inevitably colour all aspects of life here.

Corvo, Sicily's best-known wine – some might say still its best – comes from an immense winery located to the west of Palermo, at Casteldaccia. Corvo – the crow – more than any other, is the single name that has come to symbolize Sicilian wine, for it is found in any number of restaurants throughout Italy, certainly, as well as in *trattorie* in Manhattan, London, Tokyo, Topsham, anywhere. Though the origins of the winery go back to 1824 when it was the property of the noble Duca di Salaparuta family, today it is owned by a consortium whose largest member is the region of Sicily itself. As such, it functions rather as a co-operative winery might, but instead of restricting its choice to grapes only from its surrounding communities, the Corvo winery selects from growers under contract throughout the island. The winery is thus able to produce a range of extremely well-made

THE ISLANDS

wines – about 10 million bottles a year – which find a ready market throughout the world. The two outstanding whites are the light Corvo Prima Goccia and the more distinctive Corvo Colomba Platino. Corvo Rosso is a typical, generous and rather velvety Sicilian red, but the *cru* Duca Enrico demonstrates that Sicilian wines can reach the very highest level of quality.

Our journey around Sicily has mainly followed the coast, but every visitor should strike out into the interior, too. For the essential contrast between the developed and overdeveloped lush coastal areas and the isolated, parched, but majestically beautiful centre is an enduring feature of Sicily. The interior of the island is furthermore a considerable source of grapes, for each town and community makes wines that serve at least to satisfy its own needs. The town of Caltanissetta, though, located virtually in the middle of the island, has rather higher aspirations. For this is the home of the Regaleali wine estate of the noble Conte Tasca d'Almerita family. The Regaleali wines – white, red, and *rosato* – are among the most widely encountered (alongside Corvo). But widescale availability and popularity should not denote mass-production, for they are undoubtedly among the island's best, combining the twin virtues of consistency with *tipicità* – local character. New top wines of the range include the white Nozze d'Oro and the red Rosso del Conte.

Degustazione: Stop to Taste; Stop to Buy

1

AZIENDA AGRICOLA BAGNI
VIA BELLONE 10
98020 SANTA MARGHERITA DI
   MESSINA ME
TEL: 090/831081

WINE PRODUCED: Faro DOC.
VISITS: by appointment, preferably weekends.
About the only source for this minuscule but historic DOC. English, French spoken.

2

CASA VINICOLA BARONE DI
   VILLAGRANDE
VIA DEL BOSCO 25
95010 MILO CT
OFFICE: VIA TRIESTE 21, CATANIA
TEL: 095/7082175 (*AZIENDA*);
   095/383919 (OFFICE)

WINES PRODUCED: Etna Rosso, Etna Bianco Superiore.
VISITS: by appointment.
This 25-hectare farm located at 650 metres above sea level on the high flanks of Mount Etna has been in the Nicolosi family since 1727, and

wines have been produced and estate bottled since before World War II. Today it is one of the most advanced wineries in the zone, and utilizes modern technology (temperature controlled fermentation, sterile bottling) for the production of high quality red and white wines.
English spoken.

3
AZIENDA AGRICOLA CORIA
VIA CASTELFIDARDO 44-A
97019 VITTORIA RG
TEL: 0932/29229; 985611

WINES PRODUCED: Cerasuolo di Vittoria DOC; Villa Fontane; Moscato di Villa Fontane; Solicchiato di Villa Fontane (*passito*); Perpetuo (aged by the *solera* system); Stravecchio Siciliano.
VISITS: daily, by appointment.

There is an *enoteca* on the premises for direct sales.
Giuseppe Coria is a serious wine maker, noted not only for his traditional Cerasuolo, but also for a range of typical and robust wines that are uniquely Sicilian. He is also a historian of the vine, a gastronome, and the author of books and articles on the subject. Come to the *enoteca* to learn more about the wines of the entire island.

4
AZIENDA AGRICOLA COS
PIAZZA DEL POPOLO 34
97019 VITTORIA RG
TEL: 0932/864042; 994909

WINES PRODUCED: Cerasuolo di Vittoria DOC; Vignalunga Rosso; Terrirussi Bianco.
VISITS: daily, by appointment.
The winery is located in an ancient

typical farmhouse, but it boasts the most modern equipment and technology. The name of the estate is an acronym of the 3 owners and co-partners, Giambattista Cilia, Giusto Occhipinti, and Giuseppina Strano.
French, some English spoken.

5
AZIENDA AGRICOLA VECCHIO
   SAMPERI
CONTRADA FORNARA SAMPERI 292
91025 MARSALA TP
TEL: 0923/962093

WINES PRODUCED: Josephine Doré; Vigna La Miccia; Vecchio Samperi;

Marsala Riserva 20 Y; Moscato di Pantelleria; Bukkuram.
VISITS: daily, preferably afternoons, by appointment.
Marsala as it used to be made: unfortified and aged in the traditional *solera* fashion. Marco de Bartoli's

estate is considered in the first division of Italian wineries and is a member of the select VIDE group. French spoken.

6

CANTINE FLORIO
VIA VINCENZO FLORIO 1
LUNGOMARE
91025 MARSALA TP
TEL: 0923/951122

WINES PRODUCED: Complete range of Marsala wines.

VISITS: Mon–Sat, telephone for an appointment. *Enoteca* open daily 9–12h45; 15–17h30.
Still the market leader and a remarkable and historic winery which should be visited.

7

TENUTA DI RAPITALÀ
CONTRADA RAPITALÀ
90043 CAMPOREALE PA
(OFFICE AND ADMINISTRATION: VIA SEGESTA 9, 90141 PALERMO)
TEL: 091/332088; 322996

WINES PRODUCED: Rapitalà Bianco Alcamo DOC, Rapitalà Rosso,

Rapitalà Rosato, Bouquet di Rapitalà.
VISITS: Mon–Fri, 9–12h.
Appointment advisable.
An immense, modern private winery producing well-made wines of character on a large scale. French spoken.

8

TERRE DI GINESTRA SRL
PIANO PIRAINO
90040 SAN CIPIRELLO PA
TEL: 091/8576767

WINES PRODUCED: Terre di Ginestra Bianco di Sicilia, Terre di Ginestra

Rosso di Sicilia.
VISITS: daily, by appointment.
Well-made red and white Sicilian table wines.
English spoken.

9

CASA VINICOLA DUCA DI SALAPARUTA
VIA NAZIONALE SS113
90014 CASTELDACCIA PA
TEL: 091/953988

WINES PRODUCED: Corvo Rosso e Bianco; Duca Enrico.
VISITS: daily, working hours.
The best-known of all Sicilian table wines.
English, French, German spoken.

10 AZIENDA AGRICOLA REGALEALI
93010 VALLELUNGA DI PRATAMENO
CL
TEL: 0921/52522

WINES PRODUCED: Regaleali Rosso,
Rosato, Bianco; Regaleali Rosso del

Conte; Nozze d'Oro.
VISITS: by appointment.
Aristocratic estate of the Tasca
d'Almerita family located in the
centre of the island.
English spoken.

---

11 AZIENDA AGRICOLA HAUNER
VIA UMBERTO I
98050 LINGUA DI SALINA ME
TEL: 090/9843141

WINES PRODUCED: Malvasia delle
Lipari *naturale* and *passito*; Rosso e
Bianco di Salina.
VISITS: daily, by appointment.

Rare prestigious dessert wines from
this tiny island in the Aeolian
archipelago. There are ferry and
hydrofoil services to the islands
from both Milazzo (north of
Messina) and Naples.
English, French spoken.

Enoteca

1 ENOTECA DI MARSALA
VIA CIRCONVALLAZIONE
91025 MARSALA TP
TEL: 0923/999444

OPEN: daily 9–13h May-Sept. Free
entrance and wine tasting.
Sicily's only regional *enoteca*.

Wine Museums

M ENO AGRI MUSEUM
PROP. SIG. MONTALTO DI MARSALA
SS115 DIRAMAZIONE
   CASTELVETRANO–SELINUNTE
   KM 1040
91025 MARSALA TP

OPEN: daily 9–18h. Free entrance
and wine tasting.

M ENO MUSEUM
CONTRADA BÉRBERO
91100 TRAPANI
TEL: 0923/969697

OPEN: weekdays 9–13h; 15–19h; Sat
9–13h. Free entrance and wine
tasting. In summer open every day.

THE ISLANDS

Ristoranti

1 RISTORANTE GIOVA ROSY SENIOR
CORSO UMBERTO 38
98039 TAORMINA ME
TEL: 0942/24411

Closed Mon.
Our favourite restaurant in
Taormina, located in the medieval
centre: old style in classic
surroundings, serving regional
foods – generous *antipasti, spaghetti
del capitano, linguine del marinaio,
involtini di pesce spada* – and a
good selection of Sicilian wines.
Moderate to Expensive

---

2 HOTEL-RISTORANTE ORIZZONTE
ACIREALE
VIA C. COLOMBO
95024 ACIREALE CT
TEL: 095/886006

Pleasant hotel restaurant with
panoramic views, located just off
SS114.
Moderate

---

3 TRATTORIA 'CAPRICE'
VIA PANORAMICA DEI TEMPLI 51
92100 AGRIGENTO
TEL: 0922/26469

Closed Fri.
Simple *trattoria* located near the
Valley of the Temples serving
*antipasti siciliani, cavatelli con
melanzane, maccheroncini ai pesce
spada*, grilled fish, and good house
wine by the carafe.
Moderate

---

4 HOTEL-RISTORANTE PRESIDENT
VIA NINO BIXIO 1
91025 MARSALA TP
TEL: 0923/999333

Pleasant hotel-*ristorante* in this
important wine town. Restaurant
serves Sicilian foods including
*risotto alla marinara, piccata al
Marsala, involtini siciliani, frittura
del Golfo, triglie dello stagnone.*
Inexpensive to Moderate

---

5 RISTORANTE ZIO CICCIO
LUNGOMARE MEDITERRANEO 211
91025 MARSALA TP
TEL: 0923/981962

Closed Mon except in season.
Popular seafood restaurant not far
from the Florio *cantina* serving
cuscusu, spaghetti Zio Ciccio, and
fresh grilled fish.
Moderate

Wine and Other Related *Sagre* and *Feste*

February	Festival of the Almond Blossom	Agrigento
August	Manifestazioni Folkloristiche e Sagre Gastronomiche	Roccavaldina
early Oct	Salt Festival	Trapani, Marsala
early Oct	Folklore Mediterraneo	Trapani, Marsala, Selinunte

E PER SAPERE DI PIÙ – ADDITIONAL INFORMATION

Azienda Provinciale di Turismo
Piazza Castelnuovo 35
90141 Palermo
tel: 0932/21421

Azienda Provinciale di Turismo
via Calabria-Isolato 301-bis
98100 Messina
tel: 090/775356

Azienda Provinciale di Turismo
Viale Vittoria 255
92100 Agrigento
tel: 0922/26922

Azienda Provinciale di Turismo
via Sorba 15
91100 Trapani
tel: 0923/27273

Associazione Agriturist Regionale
via Alessio di Giovanni 14
90144 Palermo
tel: 091/346046

THE ISLANDS

SARDINIA

I Vini: THE WINES OF SARDINIA   505

La Gastronomia   507

Le Strade dei Vini: THE WINE ROADS OF
    SARDINIA   509

Le Sagre: WINE AND OTHER RELATED FESTIVALS   512

Additional Information   512

Street market.

Sardinia, even more so than Sicily, stands apart from the rest of Italy. The second largest island in the Mediterranean has only in recent decades been opened up to the outside world through the now large-scale development of its tourist industry, notably along the north-eastern Costa Smeralda. The Aga Khan's multi-million-pound investments here may have made this among the most exclusive of holiday destinations in Europe. Yet Sardinia still remains essentially a rugged, remote, and timeless land, its hinterland hardly touched by time.

The Phoenicians, among the first of a long line of foreign invaders and occupiers, probably first brought the vine to the island, though even this is not certain. Perhaps it was always here, as integral a part of the land as the mysterious and ancient *nuraghi* dry-stone dwellings that are still such an enduring feature. But over the centuries, new cuttings were carried here by the Carthaginians, the Greeks, the Romans, and, much later, the Spanish, who introduced a number of grape varieties that remain in production today, including Carignano, Cannonau, Girò. When Sardinia came under the juris-diction of the House of Savoy in the 19th century, Piedmontese grape varieties as well as methods of viticulture were introduced. But whatever their provenance, native or foreign vines, once transplanted to Sardinia, soon sent down deep roots and established an island character of their own.

Thus an often bewildering range of wines of all styles – light white, robust red, amber sherry-like, red fortified, sweet or dry – is produced on Sardinia today. Most are little known outside their locality of production and the vast majority – indeed the best wines – are not even produced under DOC disciplines, adding further to the confusion. Few wines are exported. Yet, in spite of lack of investment and private initiative, Sardinian wines are dis-tinctive, and a huge potential remains to be fulfilled. Thus there will be much to interest and satisfy the adventurous wine lover visiting the island.

Italy today remains a nation of regions, all with their own separate cul-

ORIENTATION

Sardinia, an autonomous region, comprises 4 provinces: Cagliari, Nuoro, Oristano, and Sassari. There are direct international and domestic flights to Cagliari's Elmas airport (for the south coast), Alghero-Sassari's Fertilia (for the north-west), and Olbia's Costa Smeralda (for the north-east). There are frequent ferry crossings from Genoa and Livorno to Olbia and Cagliari. When on the island, the use of a car is recommended for independent exploration.
Map Touring Club Italiano 1: 200 000 Sardegna.

tures, histories, foods, dialects, and wines. Sardinia, even more so than elsewhere, maintains its own separate, isolated identity. We barely scratch the surface of this secret world, which remains still undiscovered and awaiting further exploration.

I VINI: GLOSSARY TO THE WINES OF SARDINIA

Wines of *Denominazione di Origine Controllata (DOC)*

Arborea DOC Delimited wine zone in the province of Oristano for the production of red (from Sangiovese) and white (from Trebbiano).

Campidano di Terralba DOC Dry red wine produced from Bovale, Pascale di Cagliari, and/or Greco Nero grapes grown on the vast Campidano plain south of Oristano. Minimum alcohol 11.5 degrees.

Cannonau di Sardegna DOC Sardinia's most famous delimited wine, produced from black Cannonau grapes grown throughout the region. Produced in a number of different versions: dry red, with minimum alcohol of 13.5 degrees; *superiore*, with minimum alcohol of 15 degrees: this version may itself be either dry, medium dry, or sweet; and *liquoroso secco* or *dolce*, fortified, with minimum alcohol of 18 degrees. The geographical sub-*denominazioni* Cannonau di Oliena, Capo Ferrato, or Alghero may also be utilized for grapes grown within the respective delimited vineyards.

Carignano del Sulcis DOC Red and *rosato* wines from the Spanish Carignano grape (mainly) grown in the south-west corner of the island in the province of Cagliari. Minimum alcohol 11.5 degrees. Wine may be labelled Invecchiato if aged for minimum of 1 year.

Girò di Cagliari DOC Robust red wine from Girò grapes, produced in dry (minimum alcohol 15.5 degrees), *dolce naturale* (minimum alcohol 15.5 degrees with 2 degrees left as residual), and *liquoroso* (fortified, produced in both sweet and dry versions, both with minimum alcohol of 17.5 degrees).

Malvasia di Bosa DOC White dessert wine from Malvasia grapes grown in the wine commune of Bosa, in the province of Nuoro. Made in both dry and sweet versions (minimum alcohol 15 degrees), as well as *liquoroso* (fortified, either sweet or dry, minimum alcohol 17.5 degrees).

Malvasia di Cagliari DOC Malvasia wine produced in various versions as above, but from grapes grown on the plain of Campidano.

Mandrolisai DOC Red and *rosato* wine produced from Bovale, Cannonau, and Monica grapes grown in the provinces of Nuoro and Oristano. Wines labelled Superiore must be aged for minimum of 2 years, 1 in wood.

Monica di Cagliari DOC Sweet and sometimes dry red wine from Monica grapes grown on the plain of Campidano. Minimum alcohol 15.5 degrees. *Liquoroso* version also produced in both dry and sweet versions (minimum alcohol 17.5 degrees). *Liquoroso riserva* must be aged for 2 years minimum, at least 1 in wood barrel.

Monica di Sardegna DOC Relatively light (by Sardinian standards) red wine produced from Monica grapes (mainly, with the addition of Pascale and Carignano) grown throughout the island. Minimum alcohol 12 degrees; 13 degrees and 1 year's ageing for wines labelled Superiore.

Moscato di Cagliari DOC Dessert wine from the Moscato Bianco grape grown mainly on the plain of Campidano: produced in both *dolce naturale* (minimum alcohol 15 degrees), and *liquoroso dolce* (fortified, minimum alcohol 17.5 degrees).

Moscato di Sardegna Spumante DOC Medium sweet to sweet sparkling wine produced from Moscato Bianco grapes grown throughout Sardinia. Minimum alcohol 11.5 degrees.

Moscato di Sorso Sennori DOC
Still and sparkling wines from
Moscato Bianco grapes grown in
delimited vineyard in the province
of Sassari overlooking the Gulf of
Asinara. Minimum alcohol 13
degrees. *Liquoroso dolce* version is
also produced (minimum alcohol
17.5 degrees).

Nasco di Cagliari DOC Old-style
wine produced from Nasco grapes
grown mainly in the province of
Cagliari in dry, *amabile*, and *dolce
naturale* versions (minimum
alcohol 14 degrees), as well as in
fortified sherry-like *liquoroso dolce*
(minimum alcohol 16.5 degrees).

Nuragus di Cagliari DOC
Distinctive light dry white wine
produced mainly from Nuragus
grapes grown on the plain of
Campidano. Minimum alcohol 11
degrees.

Vermentino di Gallura DOC The
Vermentino is Sardinia's most
famous and distinctive white grape
for the production of dry table
wines. Vermentino di Gallura
comes from Vermentino grapes
grown in the provinces of Sassari
and Nuoro in the north of the
island. Minimum alcohol 12
degrees; 14 degrees for wines
labelled Superiore.

Vernaccia di Oristano DOC
Another classic of Sardinia: aged
sherry-type dessert wine produced
from Vernaccia grapes grown near
Oristano. Minimum alcohol 15
degrees; if 15.5 degrees and 3 years'
minimum ageing in wood then it
may be labelled Superiore. Fortified
liquoroso dolce and *liquoroso secco*
versions are also produced
(minimum alcohol 16.5 degrees).
The latter is the favourite *aperitivo*
on the island.

LA GASTRONOMIA:
FOODS OF SARDINIA

Just as the Sardinian spoken tongue is not simply another of Italy's multifarious dialects, but rather a true Romance language in its own right, so is
the Sardinian *cucina* a true national cuisine that differs profoundly from
that found on the mainland. The Sardinian names of the dishes emphasize
their apparent strangeness, but they are none the less delicious for the
various foreign influences that have shaped them over the centuries. The
foods reflect the harsh terrain of the inland hill country and mountains, as
well as the bounty of the sea.

THE ISLANDS

PIATTI TIPICI:
REGIONAL SPECIALITIES

Pane carasau The famous '*carta di musica*' – music paper – bread of the island, wafer thin, sometimes filled with meats, cheese, or seasoned with olive oil.

Prosciutto di cinghiale Wild boar is still prevalent in the uplands and hill country of the island: raw air-cured ham from it is an island delicacy.

Culorzones; culingiones *Ravioli*-type pasta stuffed with fresh sheep's milk cheese, spinach or chard, eggs, and seasonings.

Malloreddus Sardinian *gnocchi*: small dumplings, sometimes made with saffron, and served with simple tomato sauce, and grated *pecorino* cheese.

Lepudrida cagliaritana Thick meat and vegetable soup from Cagliari.

Coccois de gerda Buns filled with savoury pork and aged cheese.

Sa cassòla Luxuriant fish stew, a sort of local *bouillabaisse.*

Aragosta Lobster, a delicacy much enjoyed in resorts.
Aragosta in insalata Boiled and served cold, dressed in olive oil and lemon juice.

Sa fregula Sardinian *couscous*, made with steamed semolina, garnished with fried onions, sausage, and *pecorino sardo.*

Porceddu Sardinia's most famous and characteristic dish: highly seasoned suckling pig roasted on a spit.

Cheeses: *Pecorino sardo* Probably the finest of all *pecorino* cheese, usually salty, aged, and either for eating or grating. *Latticini* Small *mozzarella*-type cheeses made from both cow's or sheep's milk. *Su casizzolu* Small, rather strong cow's milk cheeses. *Fresa* Buttery, creamy rather sweet cheese.

SARDINIA

In Brief: Sardinian wines are nothing if not heavyweights, so it is not surprising that they traditionally served as high-alcohol *vini da taglio* – cutting wines – which were sent in bulk to the mainland and to France. However, as the market for such wines has diminished in recent years, the island's large-scale wineries – private and co-operative cellars alike – have invested in modern equipment and turned to the production of lighter table wines more suited to international tastes. But there are plenty of the old-style wines still available to sample on the island itself.

The private firm of Sella & Mosca is the paragon of the Sardinian wine scene, and one of the most modern and advanced wineries in Europe. There are scores of *cantine cooperativi* throughout the island, but the Dolianova co-operative has served as something of a model, and its wines are furthermore fairly widely available internationally.

Degustazione: Stop to Taste; Stop to Buy

1

TENUTE SELLA & MOSCA
SOCIETÀ PER AZIONI
LOC. I PIANI
07041 ALGHERO SA
TEL: 079/951281

WINES PRODUCED: Vermentino di Sardegna; Cannonau di Alghero; Tanca Farrà (Cannonau/Cabernet Sauvignon); I Piani; Torbato di Alghero Terre Bianche; Nuraghe Majore Bianco di Alghero; Anghelu Ruju (from *passiti* Cannonau grapes left to dry on mats outside for 15–20 days); Rosé di Alghero; Vermentino di Alghero; Brut di Torbato.
VISITS: Mon–Fri 8h30–13h; 15–18h30. Appointment necessary.

Sella & Mosca is a private winery founded in 1899 by Emilio Sella and Edgardo Mosca, who were both originally from Piedmont. Today the firm has some 400 hectares of vineyards under specialized cultivation, and is able to supply all its own grapes for the production of its outstanding range of wines.

There is a small archaeological museum on the estate.

Alghero itself was once an important outpost of the Spanish Aragon empire, and today the largest resort and centre of the Riviera del Corallo.

English spoken.

THE ISLANDS

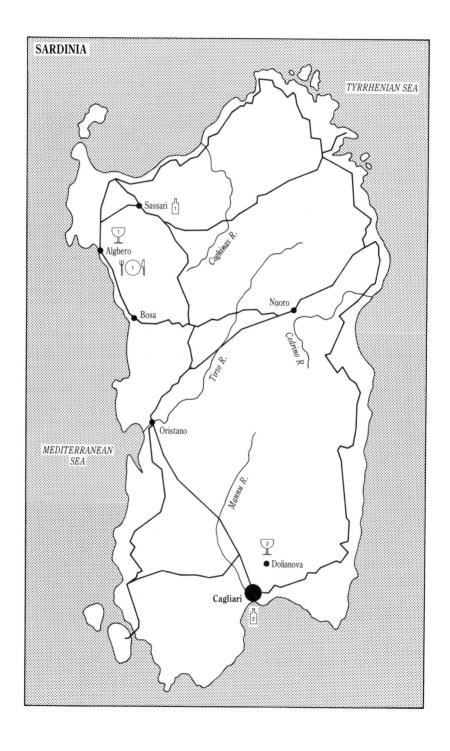

2 CANTINA SOCIALE DI DOLIANOVA
SS387 KM 17
09041 DOLIANOVA CA
TEL: 070/740513

WINES PRODUCED: Cannonau di
Sardegna; Nuragus di Cagliari;
Moscato di Cagliari.
VISITS: daily, by appointment.

Enoteche

1 LA CANTINA DEL BUONGUSTAIO
VIA GIORGIO ASPRONI 24
07100 SASSARI
TEL: 079/274031

OPEN: 8h30–13h; 16–21h.
Extensive collection of Sardinian
wines – Falconara, Doi Cante,

Nuragus, Cannonau, Vermentino,
Capichera, Terre Brune, Vernaccia
di Oristano, Malvasia di Bosa,
and many others – as well as a
selection of wines from throughout
Italy and abroad.
English, Spanish, French spoken.

2 ANTICA ENOTECA CAGLIARITANA
SCALETTE S. CHIARA 21
09100 CAGLIARI
TEL: 070/655611

OPEN: Mon–Fri 8h30–13h; 16–20h;
Sat 8h30–13h.
Long-established *enoteca* near the

Piazza Jenne with a good selection
of Sardinian wines, as well as the
best from throughout the world.
Wines can be both tasted and
purchased.
French spoken.

Ristorante

1 RISTORANTE LA LEPANTO
VIA CARLO ALBERTO 135
07041 ALGHERO SA
TEL: 079/979116

Closed Mon out of season.
Highly-regarded restaurant serving
both Sardinian and Catalan
specialities, reflecting the fact that

Alghero was occupied by the
Catalonians, and the people still
speak the pure Catalan language:
*antipasti di mare, riso ai frutti di
mare, spaghetti al nero di seppia,
aragosta alla catalana.*
Moderate

THE ISLANDS

Wine and Other Related *Sagre* and *Feste*

There are an estimated 1000 festivals that take place throughout Sardinia during the year, most of them of a folkloric and religious nature. While they are not specifically gastronomic, in many there are invariably stalls offering typical foods, specialities, or wines of the zone. It is best to check with local tourist offices for dates on arrival.

E PER SAPERE DI PIÙ – ADDITIONAL INFORMATION

Ente Provinciale per il Turismo
Piazza Deffenu 9
09100 Cagliari
tel: 070/663207

Ente Provinciale per il Turismo
Piazza Italia 19
08100 Nuoro
tel: 0784/32307

Ente Provinciale per il Turismo
via Cagliari 276
09170 Oristano
tel: 0783/74191

Ente Provinciale per il Turismo
Viale Caprera 36
07100 Sassari
tel: 079/233729

Associazione Agriturist Regionale
Viale Trieste 6
09100 Cagliari
tel: 070/668330

Terra Nostra
Associazione Regionale Sarda per
l'Agriturismo
via Sassari 3
09100 Cagliari
tel: 070/668367

SELECT BIBLIOGRAPHY

AA Hachette Guide to Italy (Basingstoke: Automobile Association, 1988)

Anderson, Burton, *Pocket Guide to Italian Wines* (London: Mitchell Beazley, 1987)

Anderson, Burton, *Vino* (London: Macmillan, 1980, 1987)

Belfrage, Nicolas, *Life Beyond Lambrusco* (London: Sidgwick & Jackson, 1985)

Chianti Locations Culture Itineraries Wines (Milan: Edizioni Tecniche Moderne)

Dallas, Philip, *Italian Wines* (London: Faber & Faber, 1989)

Gleave, David, *The Wines of Italy* (London: Salamander Books, 1989)

Guida dell'Ospitalità Rurale (Rome: Agriturist, 1989)

Harris, Valentina, *Edible Italy* (London: Ebury Press, 1988)

Hazan, Victor, *Italian Wine* (New York: Alfred A. Knopf, 1984)

Hobley, Stephen, *Traveller's Wine Guide Italy* (Basingstoke: Waymark, 1990)

Il Mondo del Gallo Nero (Florence: Consorzio del Gallo Nero, 1988)

Lintner, Valerio, *A Traveller's History of Italy* (Gloucestershire: The Windrush Press, 1989)

Michelin Italia (Clermont-Ferrand: Michelin et Cie, 1989)

Millon, Marc and Kim, *The Wine and Food of Europe: An Illustrated Guide* (Exeter: Webb & Bower, 1982)

Millon, Marc and Kim, *The Wine Roads of Europe* (London: Robert Nicholson, 1983)

Paronetto, Lamberto, *Verona Antica Terra di Vini Pregiati* (Verona: Fiorini 1977)

Veronelli, Luigi, *I Ristoranti di Veronelli* (Milan: Giorgio Mondadori, 1989)

Veronelli, Luigi, *Le Cantine di Veronelli* (Milan: Giorgio Mondadori, 1989)

Vini d'Italia (Rome: Gambero Rosso, 1989)

GLOSSARY

Abboccato Slightly sweet; medium dry.
Acciaio inox Stainless steel.
Aceto Vinegar.
Acidità Acidity.
Acido Acid.
Amabile Sweet.
Amaro Bitter.
Ammandorlato Bitter almond.
Annata Year of vintage.
Asciutto Dry.
Attrezzatura Plant; equipment.
Azienda agricola (pl.) *aziende agricole*
   Private wine estate: indicates that
   wines are produced entirely from
   own-grown grapes.
Badia Abbey.
Barrique Small 225-litre wooden barrel,
   usually made from French oak.
Bianco White; white wine.
Botte (pl.) *botti*; *botti di rovere* Cask; oak
   casks (usually large, made from
   Slavonian, not French, oak).
Bricco Hilltop.
Cantina (pl.) *cantine* Cellar.
Cantina sociale (pl.) *cantine sociali*;
   cantina cooperativa Wine
   co-operative.
Carato (pl.) *carati* Wooden barrel.
   Caratello Small wooden barrel,
   usually containing only 50–100 litres;
   utilized for traditional production of
   Vin Santo.
Casa vinicola Winery that buys in all or
   some of its grapes.
Cascina Farm.
Castello Castle.
Classico Wines from the historic
   heartland of the DOC zone.
Coltivatore (pl.) *coltivatori* Grape
   grower.
Corpo Body.
Corposo Full-bodied.
Cru French term widely used in Italy to
   indicate select single vineyard.
Damigiana (pl.) *damigiane* Demi-john:
   usually wicker or plastic covered glass
   container capable of holding 54 or 25
   litres.
Dolce Sweet.
Duro Hard, high in tannin.
Elegante Elegant.

Enologia Oenology.
Etichetta Label.
Ettolitro Hectolitre, or 100 litres. 100
   litres of wine is equivalent to 100
   kilograms (see *quintale*).
Fattoria Farm, wine estate.
Fermentazione naturale Natural
   fermentation.
Fondo Dregs.
Fresco Fresh, with refreshing acidity.
Frizzante Slightly sparkling.
Giovane Young.
Gradevole Pleasant.
Grappa (pl.) *grappe* Distilled spirit made
   from the grape residue (pressed skins,
   pips, stems) left over after the wine
   making process.
Imbottigliato dal produttore all'origine
   Estate bottled: bottled by the
   producer at the source.
Imbottigliato nella zona di produzione
   Bottled in the region or zone, not
   estate-bottled.
Invecchiamento Ageing.
Invecchiato Aged.
Leggero Light.
Legno Wood.
Liquoroso Dessert wine, usually fortified
   with alcohol.
Macerazione carbonica Carbonic
   maceration, utilized for *vino novello*
   wines.
Maturo Mature, bottle aged.
Metodo champenois Classic method for
   the production of sparkling wines by
   secondary fermentation in the bottle.
Metodo Charmat Charmat method
   (known also as the tank method) of
   secondary fermentation in
   hermetically sealed autoclaves: the
   sparkling wine is then transferred
   under pressure to the bottle.
Mosto Unfermented grape juice.
Muffa Mould.
Muffa nobile Noble rot: *Botrytis cinerea*.
Nobile Noble.
Ossidato Oxidized.
Passito (pl.) *passiti* Semi-dried grapes;
   wine made from semi-dried grapes.
Pigiare To press; *pigiatura soffice* light,
   gentle pressure.

Profumo Bouquet that comes from fermentation and ageing.

Pronta beva Wine to drink young.

Quercia Oak.

Quintale (pl.) *quintali* 100 kilograms. Grape yields are usually expressed as *quintali* per hectare (2.47 acres), with the best vineyards usually limiting this yield to as low as possible.

Resa The juice yielded from the grapes, generally expressed as a percentage of their initial weight.

Retrogusto Aftertaste.

Rimontaggio Utilized in the production of red wines whereby the must is sprayed or pumped back periodically to the top of the fermentation tank to extract colour and tannin.

Riserva (pl.) *riserve* Reserve wine.

Riserva speciale Special reserve.

Rosato Rosé wine.

Rosso Red; red wine.

Rovere Oak.

Sapore Flavour, taste.

Spumante Sparkling wine.

Stravecchio Very old wine.

Superiore Wines produced to more stringent set of standards, usually relating to alcohol content and minimum ageing.

Tannino; tannico Tannin; rich in tannin.

Tappo Cork.

Tipicità Typicalness: indicates that a wine demonstrates the character of its grape variety and zone of production.

Uva Grape.

Uvaggio Grape mix or blend.

Vasca (pl.) *vasche* Tank; fermentation vats.

Vecchio Old.

Vellutato Velvety.

Vendemmia Harvest; also indicates year of harvest or vintage.

Vignaiuolo Vine grower.

Vigneto (pl.) *vigneti* Single vineyard.

Vinaccia (pl.) *vinacce* Wine drenched dregs and residue of pressed grapes left over after the wine making process. Used to distil into *grappa*.

Vinificatori-viticoltori Wine estates who vinify only grapes that they have grown on their own vineyards.

Vinificazione Vinification.

Vini tipici New controlled category applying to distinctive table wines with geographical specifications. Equivalent to French *vin de pays*.

Vino da meditazione Term coined to indicate contemplative wine best enjoyed on its own, without food.

Vino da taglio Cutting wine, usually from Mezzogiorno, legally mixed with lighter wines in certain years to boost body, colour and alcohol.

Vino di ripasso Traditional process utilized in the Valpolicella whereby wines are transferred to casks containing the lees remaining after the fermentation of Recioto and Amarone. This induces a secondary fermentation, and contributes body, richness, and character.

Vino novello Wine vinified usually by carbonic maceration to be drunk within weeks or months of the vintage.

Vino sfuso 'Open' wine, that is, not bottled but purchased in bulk, usually by the demi-john.

Vite Vine.

Viticoltura Vine cultivation.

Vitigno Grape variety.

Zucchero residuo Residual sugar.

ACKNOWLEDGEMENTS

This book has been a long time in preparation, and many people have helped us considerably. We would like to thank the Italian State Tourist Office; the Italian Trade Centre; and CIT.

We have furthermore received considerable advice and assistance from members of the British wine trade specializing in Italian wine. We would particularly like to thank Richard Hobson of Italian Wine Agencies; the Istituto Enologico Italiano; Renato Trestini; Winecellars; G. Belloni & Co.; and Enotria Wines Ltd.

In Italy, we owe an enormous debt to the scores of wine producers who received us so kindly, gave us their time, supplied wines for tasting, and generously made this project such an enjoyable one to research. Our friends throughout Italy, furthermore, contributed greatly not only to the content of this book but to making our work so pleasurable. Special thanks are due to Alder Zonari, Elia and Elda Rossetti, Pino Pagano, Conte Giovanni Michon Pecori, Franca Michon Pecori, Fernanda Maurigi, and Giuliano and Agnese Corti. Back home, our dear friends Mariangela and Trevor Williams were a constant source of advice and encouragement. Nello Ghezzo kept us fed and sane in the frantic weeks leading to our copy deadline.

Finally we could not have completed this project without the help and support of both of our families.

INDEX

Note: Entries in bold type refer to maps. Alphabetical arrangement is word-by-word, thus La Versa Brut precedes Lacrima di Morro.

abbeys
Badia a Passignano, 256
Coltibuono, 259, 267, 274
Grottaferrata, 396
Neustift, 204, 205
Sant'Antimo, 294
see also monasteries
Abruzzi and Molise wine region, 405–13
Abruzzi, The, wine zone, 409–11, **410**
DOC wines, 405, 406–7
foods, 407–8
Molise, 411–12, **412**
orientation, 406
aceto (vinegar), 150, 360
Acqui Terme, 60, 61, 66
Aglianico (grape), 3, 422, 461–2, 463, 464
Aglianico del Vulture DOC, 457, 458, 460, 462
Aglianico di Taburno DOC, 417
agriturismo (farmhouse tourism), 9, 34, 75, 108, 226, 233
Abruzzi, the, 410, 411
Avellino Hills, 427
Calabria, 477
Carmignano zone, 284
Chianti zone, 248, 265
in Colli Albani, 398
Falernum, 427, 429
Marches, 383
Montalcino, 287
Montefalco, 353
Murge trulli, 437, 444
Romagna Hills, 367
Salentine Peninsula, 445, 447, 452, 455
Alba, 34–5, 37
Albana di Romagna DOCG, 357
albeisa bottle, 44
Alcamo DOC, 496, 497
Bianco di Alcamo DOC, 486
Aleatico di Gradoli DOC, 388
Alezio DOC, 432, 447
Alicante (grape), 323
Allegrini family, 140
Alto Adige (Südtiroler), DOC, 181

Amarone, 125, 141, 143
Recioto della Valpolicella Amarone DOC, 123
amphora bottle, 377
Ancona, 376–7
Antinori, Marchese Piero, 244, 258
Aprilia DOC, 388
Apulia wine region, 4, 23, 431–56
agriturismo, 9
DOC wines, 432–7
foods, 437
Murge, 437–44, **439**
orientation, 432
regional specialities, 438
sagre, 456
Salentine Peninsula see Salentine Peninsula wine zone
wine roads, 441–2, 447–50
Aquileia DOC, 209, 223–4
Arborea DOC, 505
Arnad Montjovet, 31
Asti (town), 60–1
Asti and the Monferrato, 34–5, 59–75
agriturismo, 71, 75
degustazione, 62, 66–8, 74
enoteche regionali, 69, 73, 74
ristoranti, 69–71
wine roads, 61–71, **62**, 71–8, **72**
Asti Spumante, 17, 19, 58, 59, 63–5
Avellino (town), 419–21
Avellino wine zone, 418–27, **420**
degustazione, 425–6
ristoranti, 426
wines, 422–4
aziende agricole (private wine estates), 6
Blangé Ceretto, 58
Giuseppe Quintarelli, 142
Pojer and Sandri, 187, 190
see also estates

Barbaresco (town), 52
Barbaresco DOCG, 17, 19–20, 51
Barbaresco wine road, 50–5, **51**
botteghe del vino, 54–5
degustazione, 53–4
enoteche regionali, 52–3, 54–5
ristoranti, 55
Barbera (grape), 20, 59, 63, 68
Barbera, 17, 20, 63, 103
d'Alba DOC, 20, 52

Barbera *cont.*
  d'Asti, 59
  del Monferrato DOC, 20, 59
Bardolino DOC, 120, 127, 129
Bardolino wine zone, 126–36
  degustazione, 131–5
  punti di ristoro agrituristico, 135–6
  ristoranti, 134–5
Bari, 437–9
Barolo DOCG, 17, 20
Barolo wine road, 37–50, **39**, 144
  botteghe del vino, 47–9
  degustazione, 44–7
  enoteche regionali, 42, 43, 47–9
  ristoranti, 49–50
  vineyard classification, 40
  wine of, 37–8
barriques, oak, 216, 251, 252, 256, 258, 303,
  310, 379
  in Avellino Hills, 423
  in Falernum, 428
  in the Maremma, 319
Basilicata wine region, 457–67, **461**
  DOC wine, 458
  foods, 458–60
  orientation, 458
  regional specialities, 459
  Vulture vineyards, 460–7
Bassano del Grappa, 163, 166
Bianchello del Metuaro DOC, 373
Bianchi-Bernetti family, 378
Bianco Capena DOC, 388
Bianco d'Arquà, 174
Bianco dei Colli Maceratesi DOC, 373
Bianco di Custoza DOC, 120–1
Bianco di Custoza wine zone, 156–9
  degustazione, 158
  ristoranti, 159
  wine road, 156–8, **157**
Bianco di Pitigliano DOC, 234, 320, 321
Bianco di Scandiano DOC, 357–8
Bianco Pisano San Torpe DOC, 234
Bianco Valdinievole DOC, 234
Bianco Vergine Valdichiana DOC, 234
Biferno DOC, 406, 411
Biondi-Santi, Ferrucio, 286–90
Blauburgunder (Pinot Noir grape), 205, 206
Boca DOC, 20, 80
Bolgheri DOC, 234
Bolla firm, 151–2
Bonarda (grape), 103

Boscaini family, 137–8, 139, 141, 144
Bossi Fedrigotti family, 188–9
Botrytis cinerea: see muffa nobile
Botticino DOC, 97
Bouquet di Rapitalà, 497
Bozen, 194–5
Brachetto d'Acqui DOC, 17, 20, 60, 66
Breganze DOC, 121
Brescia Hills and Lombardy Lakes
  wine road, 111–14, **112**
  degustazione, 111–13
  enoteca, 113
  ristoranti, 113–14
  sagre, 114
Brindisi DOC, 434, 442
Briona DOC, 80
Brunello (grape), 287
Brunello, 291–3, 294
Brunello di Montalcino DOCG, 231, 234,
  286–9
Brusco dei Barbi, 292
Bukkurram, 493
Buschenschank, the, 203
Buttafuoco, 104

'Ca' de Be' drinking houses, 369–70
Cabernet Franc (grape), 211
Cabernet Sauvignon (grape), 211–12, 278–9
Cacc'e Mmitte di Lucera DOC, 434
Cagnina DOC, 358
Calabria wine region, 468–82
  Cirò wine zone *see* separate entry
  DOC wines, 469–71
  foods, 471–2
  Greco di Bianco wine zone, 478–81, **479**
  orientation, 469
  wine roads, 473–7, **474**, 478–81, **479**
Caldaro (Kalterersee) DOC, 181
Caluso Passito DOC, 21
Campania wine region, 3, 414–30
  Avellino Hills, 418–27, **420**
  DOC wines, 415–7
  Falernum, 427–9, **428**
  foods, 418
  orientation, 415
  regional specialities, 419
  wine roads, 418–27, **420**, 427–9, **428**
Campidano di Terralba DOC, 505
Candia Colli Apuani DOC, 234
Canelli, 61, 63, 65
Cannonau di Sardegna DOC, 505

cantine sociali (wine co-operatives), 91–2, 94, 159, 167–8
Càvit, 188
Colognola ai Colli, 152, 153
Cormòns, 215, 218
Custoza, 156–7
Locorotondo, 440–1, 443
Santa Maria della Versa, 103
Soave, 152
Valdobbiàdene, 162–3
Valpolicella, 142, 149
Vini Steverjan, 217, 219
see also co-operatives
'*capitel*' wines, 142
Capri DOC, 415
Capriano del Colle DOC, 97
Carema DOC, 20–1
Carignano del Sulcis DOC, 506
Carmignano DOC, 4, 231–2, 234–5
Carmignano wine road, 276–86, **277**
  degustazione, 282–4
  enoteche, 284
  punto di ristoro agrituristico, 286
  ristoranti, 284–6
  wine road, 279–81
  wines, 277–9, 280–1
Carso DOC, 209, 244
Cartizze zone, 162
Casal de' Ronchi, 147
Casal di Serra vineyard, 378–9
Castel del Monte DOC, 434
Casteller DOC, 181, 188
Castelli di Jesi and Cònero wine road *see*
  Marches, The, wine region
Castelli Romani, 395–6, 398
Castello di Brolio, 259–60
Castello di Vicchiomaggio, 254–6
Castello Guerrieri, 133
castles, 30, 37, 41, 43, 66, 71, 197
  Barolo, 48
  Brolio, 259–60, 268
  Canelli, 65
  Castel del Monte, Bari, 440
  Conegliano, 161
  Costigliole, 62
  Gavi Ligure, 76
  Lagopesole, 465
  Melfi, 460, 462–3, 464
  Mezzolombardo, 187
  Moncalvo, 72
  Montalcino, 293

Montemagno, 73
Roppolo, 81
Rovereto, 188
Schloß Sigmundskron, 197
Soave, 153
Valeggio, 157
Verrazzano, 262
Catarratto (grape), 495, 497
Cavalieri del Tartufo e dei Vini di Alba, Ordine dei, 43
Cellatica DOC, 97
Cerasuolo di Vittoria DOC, 486, 493
Ceretto brothers, 58
Cerveteri DOC, 390
Cesanese
  del Piglio DOC, 390
  di Affile DOC, 390
  di Olevano Romano DOC, 390
Chambave, 30
Charmat tank production method, 64, 162, 358
chestnuts (*castagne*), 346
Chianti Classico wine zone, 231, 242, 247–75
  degustazione, 261–70
  enoteche, 271–2
  family and estate names, 252
  punti di ristoro agrituristico, 275
  ristoranti, 272–5
Chianti DOCG, 3–4, 235, 252–3, 255–6, 301
Chiaretto, 111, 127
Chiavennasca (grape), 108
churches, 57
  Bardolino, 129
  Bari, San Nicola, 440
  Carmignano, 280
  Casarenello, 448
  Cisano, 129–30
  Copertino, 449
  Moncalvo, 72
  Montefalco, 349, 350
  Padua, 172
  Orvieto Cathedral (Duomo), 337
  Riomaggiore, 91
  San Floriano, 141–2
  San Giorgio, 140
  San Pietro di Feletto, 162
  Tramin, 199
Cinque Terre DOC, 86, 89–90
  Sciacchetrà DOC, 86–7, 90, 94
Cinque Terre wine road, 89–95, **90**
  degustazione, 93–4

Cinque Terre wine road *cont.*
  enoteca, 94
  ristoranti, 94–5
  sagre, 95
Cinzano wine firm, 58, 495
Cirò DOC, 469, 475
Cirò wine zone, 473–7, **474**
Cìvita di Bagnoregio, 338, 339
classification, vineyard, 40, 144
Colli Albani DOC, 390
Colli Albani wine zone, 392–402, **394**
  wine roads, 395–8
Colli Altoberini DOC, 330
Colli Berici DOC, 121
Colli Bolognese DOC, 358–9
Colli del Trasimeno DOC, 330
Colli di Bolzano (Bozner Leiten) DOC, 181
Colli di Parma DOC, 359
Colli Euganei DOC, 121–2
Colli Euganei region, 170–8
  wine road, **171**, 172–4
Colli Lanuvini DOC, 390
Colli Morenici Mantovani del Garda DOC,
  97–8
Colli Orientali del Friuli DOC, 209–10, 222
Colli Perugini DOC, 330
Colli Piacentini DOC, 359, 363
Colli Tortonesi DOC, 21
Colline Lucchesi DOC, 235
Collio DOC, 210, 216
Collio, wine road, 209, 213–20
coltura biologica, 32, 104, 105, 133, 148, 262,
  295
  in Calabria, 480
  in Colli Albani, 398
  in Maremma, 325
  in Montefalco, 353
Conegliano, 160–1
Cònero promontory, 380
cookery schools, 274
co-operatives, 30, 52, 197, 338, 354
  Barbaresco, 54
  Colli Albani, 394, 395
  Grevepesa, 269
  Groppo, 90, 91
  Sardinia, 509
  Scansano, 320, 324
  Sicily, 490–1, 493, 496
  see also cantine sociale
Copertino DOC, 434
Cori DOC, 390

Cortese (grape), 75
Cortese dell'Alto Monferrato DOC, 21, 75
Cortese di Gavi DOC, 22
Corvo, 497–8
crete Senese, 260, 290
Crimisa, Greek town of, 473–4
cru wines, 39–40, 144–5
cucina piemontese, 18

Dante Alighieri, 146, 242
degustazione: see individual wine regions
denominazione di origine controllata (DOC),
  4, 12
*denominazione di origine controllata e
  garantita* (DOCG), 12
'designer' wines, 4, 251, 286
distillery, *grappa* (*distilleria artigianale*),
  134, 224
Dolceacqua DOC, 87
Dolcetto (grape), 59–60
Dolcetto, 17, 21, 52
Donne del Vino, Le, 270
Donnici DOC, 469

earthquake, 419–22, 457, 463
Eisacktaler (Valle di Isarco) DOC, 204
Elba DOC, 235
Emilia Romagna wine region, 356–71
  Colli Piacentini, 362–5, **362**
  DOC and DOCG wines, 357–61
  foods, 361–2
  orientation, 357
  Parma–Reggio–Modena–Bologna, 365–6
  Romagna Hills, 367–70
Empoli, 273
en primeur market, 254
Enfer d'Arvier, 29
enoteche (wine libraries), 7, 369–70, 391
  see also individual wine regions
Erbaluce (grape), 82
Erbaluce di Caluso DOC, 21
Est! Est!! Est!!! di Montefiascone DOC, 390,
  402–3
estates, wine, 5–6, 9, 215–16
  Baccheretto, 284
  Ca' del Bosco, 113
  Capezzana, 277–8, 280–1, 283
  Castello di Nipozzano, 308–9
  in Chianti, 259
  Fattoria dei Barbi, 290–1
  Fattoria di Calavria, 282

Fattoria di Selvapiana, 311
Le Velette, 338, 341
Lungarotti, 348
Montagliari, 257
Pagliarese, 259–60, 269
Pomino, 310
Regaleali, 498
Serègo Alighieri, 3, 138, 146–7
Tenuta San Leonardo, 189
Tenuta Trerose, 304
Vicchiomaggio, 274
Vignamaggio, 256, 261
Villa Belvedere, 130
Villa dei Vescovi, 173
see also aziende agricole
Etna DOC, 486, 492
Etruscans, 1, 36, 276, 331, 334
  in Maremma, 318, 321–3
  in Orvieto, 335, 338
  tombs of, 279–80, 302, 338
    Montefortini, 279–80, 282

Falanghina (grape), 427
Falerio dei Colli Ascolani DOC, 374
Falerno DOC, 415, 428–9
Falernum wine zone, 427–9, **428**
Fara DOC, 21, 80
Faro DOC, 486–7, 491
Favorita (grape), 57
Favorita, 17, 21
fermentation control, 336
Ferrari firm, 188
feste: see sagre and *feste*
Fiano (grape), 3, 422–3
Fiano di Avellino DOC, 414, 417, 422–3
fiasco, 248, 273
Fiera del Levante, 440
'Five Roses', 450
floral abortion, 222, 422
Florence and Siena wine road, 242–6
  Enoteca Italica Permanente, 246
Foianeghe, 189, 191
Franciacorta DOC, 98
frascata huts, 396
Frascati DOC, 390, 395
Frederick II of Swabia, 380, 462, 463
Freisa, 17, 21, 60
Frescobaldi family, 244–5, 308–9
Friuli-Venezia, 208–27, **214**
  agriturismo, 226
  Aquileia, 223–4

Carso, 224
Colli Orientali del Friuli, 222
Collio wine road *see* separate entry
DOC wines, 209–10
foods, 212–13
Grave del Friuli, 223
Isonzo wine zone, 220–2
Latisana, 224
orientation, 209
principal grape varieties, 210–12
regional specialities, 213
ristoranti, 225
sagre, 226
fruit, 172, 175, 217
funghi, 26, 287

Gabiano DOC, 22
Gaglioppo (grape), 474, 475
Galestro, 252, 281
Gallipoli, 447
Gambellara DOC, 122
Gancia firm, 68
Garibaldi, Giuseppe, 487
Garibaldi Dolce (GB), 487
Gattinara DOC, 22
Gavi DOC, 22, 75
Gavi Ligure, 75, 76
Gavi wine region, 75–8, **76**
Gewürztraminer (grape), 198–9
Ghemme DOC, 22, 80
Gioia del Colle DOC, 434
Gioia di Riecine, 267
Giradelli family, 132
Girò di Cagliari DOC, 506
governo production method, 263
grape cure (*cura dell'uva*), 129, 206
grape varieties, Friuli, 210–11
grappa, 31, 166
  home distillation, 288
Grave del Friuli DOC, 210, 216, 223
Gravina DOC, 434
Grechetto (grape), 337, 352
Greco (grape), 3, 422, 474, 480
Greco di Bianco DOC, 469, 478–80
Greco di Tufo DOC, 414, 417, 422–3, 424, 425–6
Greeks, 1, 3, 36, 422, 457, 492
Greve, 253–4
Grignolino (grape), 60
Grignolino, 17, 22, 74
Grillo (grape), 495

grolla, la, 31
Guelph–Ghibelline conflict, 146, 242, 256–7, 313
Guerrieri Rizzardi family, 133

Hapsburgs, 179, 183, 204, 208, 215, 216
Horace, 462
House of Savoy, 18, 19

Il Canneto, 465
Institut Agricol Regional, 29
investment, 250, 286, 304, 319, 350
Irpinia tribe, 423
Ischia DOC, 417
Isonzo DOC, 210, 216
Isonzo wine zone, 220–2
Istituto Agrario Provinciale, 186
Istituto Enologico Italiano, 126

Kaltern (Caldaro), 197–8

La Salle vineyards, 27, 29, 31
La Versa Brut, 103
Lacrima di Morro d'Alba DOC, 374
lacrima method, 448
Lacryma Christi del Vesuvio DOC, 424
Lago di Caldaro (Kalterersee) DOC, 181, 198
Lagrein (grape), 197
Lake Nemi, 397
Lambrusco, 98, 356, 358, 359, 365–6
Lamezia DOC, 469–70
Langhe, The, wine region, 37–59
    Barbaresco wine road, 50–5
    Barolo wine road, 37–50
    Roero, the, 56–9
Latisana DOC, 210, 224
Latium wine region, 387–404
    agriturismo, 9
    Colli Albani *see* Colli Albani wine zone
    DOC wines, 388–91
    foods, 391–2
    Montefiascone, 402–4
    orientation, 388
    Rome *enoteca,* 391
Le Busche, 379
Lega del Chianti, 231, 242, 257
Lessini Durello DOC, 122
Lessona DOC, 22
Leverano DOC, 434–5

Liguria, 85–95
    Cinque Terre wine road *see* separate entry
    foods, 87–8
    wines, 86–7
Lison-Pramaggiore DOC, 122
Locorotondo DOC, 435, 440–1
Lombardy, 96–115
    Brescia Hills and Lombardy Lakes *see* Brescia Hills and Lombardy Lakes wine road
    foods, 100
    Oltrepò Pavese *see* Oltrepò Pavese wine road
    Valtellina *see* Valtellina wine road
    wines, 97–100
Lugana DOC, 98, 111
Lungarotti, Giorgio, 345–7
Lungarotti Brut, 347

Magna Grecia, 470, 474
Malvasia, 22, 72, 487, 491–2, 506
Malvasia Istriana (grape), 210
Malvasia Nera (grape), 60
Mandrolisai DOC, 506
Maraschino liqueur, 172, 175
Marca Trevignana *see* Treviso region
Marches, The, wine region, 372–83
    Castelli di Jesi and Cònero wine road, 376–83, **377**
    DOC wines, 373–4
    foods, 375–6
    orientation, 373
Maremma, The, wine road, 318–27, **319**
    degustazione, 323–5
    enoteca, 325
    ristoranti, 326
    sagre, 326–7
    wine road, 318–23
Marino DOC, 390
marogne (dry-stone walls), 140–1
Marsala DOC, 487–8, 495–6
Martina Franca DOC, 435, 440, 441
Marzemino (grape), 188
Masi firm, 3, 143–5
masserie farmhouses, 445–6
Mastroberardino family, 3, 421, 422–3
Matino DOC, 435
Matta, John, 254–6, 261, 274
Mazzano vineyard, 143, 144
Mazzei family, 257

Medici, the, 246, 276, 277–8, 279, 280, 281–4, 314
Melfi, 460, 462–3, 464
Melissa DOC, 470
Meranese di Collina (Meraner Hügel) DOC, 181
Merlot (grape), 212
Messapican civilization, 445, 447, 449, 450
metodo champenois, 64, 99
metodo rustico wines, 163
mezzadria (sharecropping), 138, 146, 233, 248, 307–8, 309
Milan, 96
monasteries, 192, 193
  Badia a Coltibuono, 259, 267
  Convento di San Colombano, 128
  Neustift, 204, 205
  San Colombano, 130
  San Zeno, 143, 157
  see also abbeys
Monferrato *see* Asti and the Monferrato
Monfortino *riserva*, 42–3
Monica DOC, 506
Montalcino wine road, 286–300, **289**
  degustazione, 294–9
  enoteche, 293, 299
  punto di ristoro agrituristico, 300
  ristoranti, 299–300
  town, 287, 293
  vineyards, 290
  wines, 286–93
Montebuono, 105
Montecarlo DOC, 235
Montecompatri Colonna DOC, 391
Montefalco DOC, 330–1
Montefalco wine zone, 349–55, **350**
Montefiascone wine zone, 402–4, **403**
Montello e Colli Asolani DOC, 122
Montepulciano (grape), 409
Montepulciano d'Abruzzo DOC, 406
Montepulciano wine road, 231, 300–7, **301**
  noble wine of, 301–3
Montescudaio DOC, 236
Montuni del Reno DOC, 359
Morellino di Scansano DOC, 236, 318, 319–20
Morgex vineyards, 31
Moscadello di Montalcino DOC, 236
Moscato (grape), 64, 65, 171
Moscato, 170–1
  d'Asti DOC, 58, 65

d'Asti Spumante DOC, 19, 22
di Cagliari DOC, 506
di Pantelleria DOC, 493
di Sardegna Spumante DOC, 506
di Sorso Sennori DOC, 507
di Trani DOC, 435
Fior d'Arancio, 171, 177
mosto, 346
Mostra Mercato del Tartufo, 61
muffa nobile (noble rot or *Botrytis cinerea*), 125, 303, 332, 340, 382
Müller-Thurgau (grape), 187
Murge wine zone, 437–44, **439**
  wine roads, 441–2
museums, 41, 140, 368
  Conegliano, 161
  country-life, 63
  Etruscan, 280, 338
  folk, 199, 202
  Irpino, 423
  Leonardo da Vinci, 281
  Martini, 36
  olive oil, 129, 132
  Sicily, 501
  Storico della Guerra, 188
  Treviso, 160
  Vite e del Vino, 311, 312
  wine, 201–2, 217, 220, 281, 344, 347–8

Nardò DOC, 435, 449
Nasco di Cagliari DOC, 507
Nebbiolo (grape), 79, 108
Nebbiolo d'Alba DOC, 22
Negrar valley, 142–3
Negro Amaro (grape), 449
Nerello Mascalese (grape), 492
Nino Negri wine road, 108–9
norcinerie (pork butchers), 333
nuraghi dwellings, 504
Nuragus di Cagliari DOC, 507
Nus Rouge, 30

Occhio di Pernice (grape), 278
Occhio di Pernice, 304
oenologists, 60, 250, 258, 297, 443, 463–4
olive oil, 129, 132, 282
  in Gallipoli, 433, 447
  in Liguria, 87–8
  olio extra vergine d'oliva, 240–1, 283, 284
Olive Riviera, 129, 132
Oltrepò Pavese DOC, 98

Oltrepò Pavese wine road, 100–8, **102**
  degustazione, 105–6
  enoteca, 106
  regional specialities, 101
  ristoranti, 107
  wines, 102–4
Ortanova DOC, 435
Orvieto DOC, 331, 391
Orvieto wine zone, 334–44, **335**
  degustazione, 340–2
  enoteche, 342–3
  punto di ristoro agrituristico, 344
  ristoranti, 343
  town, 337–8
  vineyard, 332
  wine road, 338
  wines, 329, 336–7
Ostuni DOC, 435–6, 442

Padua, 172
Pagadebit DOC, 359
palazzi, 37, 66, 76, 123, 162
  Antinori, 244
  Callori, 73
  Communale, 293
  Montepulciano, 302
  del Podestà, 257
Parrina DOC, 236, 323
passito dessert wine, 30
Pentro di Isernia DOC, 406–7, 411
pesto, 87
Petrarch, 173–4
Phoenicians, 493–4, 504
phylloxera, 138, 428
Piave DOC, 122
Piave wine road, 167–9, **168**
Piedmont and Valle d'Aosta wine region, 5,
  17–84, 144
  agriturismo, 34
  Asti and the Monferrato *see* separate entry
  botteghe del vino, 35, 47–9
  degustazione, 31–3
  DOC and DOCG wines, 19–24
  enoteche regionali, 18, 33, 35, 41, 42,
    43
  foods, 24–6
  Gavi *see* Gavi wine region
  Langhe wine region *see* separate entry
  Northern Piedmont, 78–84, **79**
  orientation, 18
  regional specialities, 25–6

ristoranti, 24, 33–4
wine roads, 27–31, **28**, 34–5 *see also*
  individual wine zones
pieve: see churches
Picolit (grape), 211
Picolit DOC, 222
Pinot Bianco (grape), 211
Pinot Grigio (grape), 211
Pinot Nero (grape), 212
Plinius, 425
polenta (cornmeal mush), 66, 123, 212,
  295
polipi (octopus), 177
Pollino DOC, 470
Pomino DOC, 4, 236, 310
Pompeii, 416
prices, 8
Primitivo (grape), 436, 450
Primitivo di Manduria DOC, 436, 450
promiscuous cultivation, 331, 345
Prosecco (grape), 162
Prosecco di Conegliano-Valdobbiàdene DOC,
  122, 160

Querciagrande, 252, 265

Rapitalà Alcamo DOC, 496–7
Ratti family, 40, 44–5, 144
Recioto, 125, 136, 141, 142
  di Soave DOC, 123, 125, 152–3, 154
Refosco dal Peduncolo Rosso (grape), 212
refrigeration, 336
Refrontolo, 162
renaissance, wine, 3–4, 186, 232, 242–3,
  250–2, 450
restaurants (*ristoranti*), 7–8
  see also individual wine regions and
    zones
Ribolla Gialla (grape), 211
Ricasoli family, 259–60
rice growing, 80
Riesling Italico (grape), 211
Riesling Renano (grape), 211
Rionero, 460, 463, 464
ripasso method, 139
Risorgimento, 19, 80
Riviera del Garda Bresciano DOC, 98
Riviera di Ponente DOC, 87
Roero, The, 56–9, **56**
Roero Arneis DOC, 22–3
Roero DOC, 23

Romans, 1, 36, 170–1, 223, 449
  aqueduct of, 66
  cities of, 29, 60, 79
  in Sicily, 494
Rosa del Golfo, 446, 447–8
Rossese (grape), 87
Rossese di Dolceacqua DOC, 87
Rosso Barletta DOC, 436
Rosso Canosa DOC, 436
Rosso Cònero DOC, 374, 380
Rosso di Cerignola DOC, 436
Rosso di Montalcino DOC, 237, 287, 292–3
Rosso di Montefalco DOC, 350–2
Rosso di Montepulciano DOC, 236
Rovescala zone, 103
Rubino di Cantavenna DOC, 23
Ruchè di Castagnole del Monferrato DOC, 23, 73
Rufina and Pomino wine road, 232, 307–12, **308**

Sagrantino (grape), 351–2
Sagrantino di Montefalco DOC, 350–2
sagre and *feste* (festivals), 11, 84, 397
  Douja d'Or, 61, 62
  Il Mostro Mercato del Chianti Classico, 254
  Polentone, 66
  Soave grape, 153
Salentine Peninsula wine zone, 445–55, **446**
  agriturismo, 455
  degustazione, 451–4
  enoteca, 454
  ristoranti, 454–5
  wine roads, 447–50
Salice Salentino DOC, 436
Salterio, 306
San Colombano al Lambro DOC, 98
San Floriano, 140, 141–2, 217
San Gimignano wine road, 313–18, **314**
San Giorgio, 347
San Severo DOC, 436
Sangiovese (grape), 251, 319
Sangiovese dei Colli Pesaresi DOC, 374
Sangiovese di Romagna DOC, 359
Sangioveto di Coltibuono, 267
Santa Maddalena (St Magdalener) DOC, 181
Sant'Anna di Isola di Capo Rizzuto DOC, 470
Saracen Muslims, 493
Sardinia, 504–12, **510**
  degustazione, 509, 511
  DOC wine, 504, 505–7

enoteche, 511
  foods, 507–8
  ristorante, 511
Saturnia hot springs, 318, 320–1
Sauvignon (grape), 211
Savuto DOC, 471
Schiava (grape), 187, 206
schools of viticulture, 41, 141–2, 145
  Valpolicella, 139
seafood, 212, 375–6, 471–2, 507–8
Sella and Mosca firm, 509
Serègo Alighieri family, 3, 138, 146–7
Serègo Alighieri Valpolicella Classico, 3
Serprino, 173
Sfursat (or Sforzato), 109
Sicily 485–503, **491**
  degustazione, 498–501
  DOC wine, 485, 486–8
  enoteca, 501
  foods, 488–9
  orientation, 486
  ristoranti, 502
  sagre, 503
  wine museums, 501
  wine tour, 491–8
Siena *see* Florence and Siena wine road
Sizzano DOC, 23, 80
Soave DOC, 122–3, 152
Soave wine zone, 151–5, **152**
  wine road, 153
soils, 43–4, 220, 394
Solativo, 82
Solopaca DOC, 417
Sorni DOC, 181
spa towns, 60, 170, 172, 173, 206, 300, 465
Spanna (grape), 79, 80, 81
Spanna, 24
Spumante delle Marche, 375
Squinzano DOC, 436–7
Südtirol, 9, 179, 193–207
  Eisacktal (Isarco) Valley, 204
  Etsch (Adige) Valley, 205–6
  Südtiroler Weinstraße, 195–204, **196**
    weinkellerei/enoteca, 202
    weinproben/degustazione, 199–201
  wine and folk museums, 201–2
  vineyard, 193–4
Syracuse, 492

Tanit, 493
Taurasi DOC, 414, 417, 422–3

technology, modern, 4, 216, 304, 345, 425, 431
Tedeschi family, 137, 142, 147
Terlano (Terlaner) DOC, 182
Teroldego Rotaliano DOC, 182, 186, 187–8
terrain 174, 260–1, 320, 457
  clay and chalk, 290
  Collio, 216–17
  galestro, 257
  limestone, 277, 440
  volcanic, 403, 424, 492
Tignanello, 251–2, 258
Tocai di San Martino della Battaglia DOC, 98
Tocai Friulano (grape), 211
Torgiano DOCG, 329, 331–2, 346
Torgiano wine zone, 344–9, **345**
tourism, 447, 468, 473, 478, 480
  in Sardinia, 504
  in Sicily, 492
  wine, 4–6, 34–5
Traminer Aromatico (grape), 211
transhumance, 407
Trebbiano d'Abruzzo DOC, 407
Trebbiano di Romagna DOC, 361
Trebbiano Toscano (grape), 314
Trentino-Alto Adige region, 179–207
  DOC wines, 181–2
  foods, 183, 186
  orientation, 180
  Südtirol wine and wine gardens *see* Südtirol
  Trentino wine country *see* Trentino wine region
Trentino DOC, 182, 187
Trentino wine region, 183–93, **185**
  degustazione, 189–92
  enoteca, 192
  regional specialities, 184
  ristoranti, 192–3
Treviso region, 159–69
  Piave wine road, 167–9, **168**
  Vino Bianco wine road, 160–7, **161**
truffles, 24, 26, 72, 332
  auctions, 73
  white, 61, 63, 73, 332
trulli houses, 9, 437, 439–40
tufa, 72–3, 257, 302, 321–2, 440
  carvings, 445
  caves, 73, 129, 336, 340, 459
  cellars, 420, 425, 464
  in Orvieto, 334–6, 339

Tufo (town), 420–1, 424
Tuscany region, 3–4, 5–6, 9, 232–328
  Carmignano *see* Carmignano wine road
  Chianti Classico wine zone *see* separate entry
  DOC and DOCG wines, 234–7
  Florence and Siena wine road, 242–6
  foods, 238–40
  Maremma, The *see* Maremma, The, wine road
  Montalcino *see* Montalcino wine road
  Montepulciano *see* Montepulciano wine road
  orientation, 232
  regional specialities, 239–40
  Rufina and Pomino *see* Rufina and Pomino wine road
  sagre, 326
  San Gimignano *see* San Gimignano wine road

Umbria wine region, 9, 329–55
  DOC wines, 330–2
  foods, 332–4
  Montefalco wine road *see* Montefalco wine zone
  orientation, 330
  Orvieto wine road *see* Orvieto wine zone
  regional specialities, 333–4
  sagre, 355
  Torgiano wine road *see* Torgiano wine zone
uva regina (grape), 493

Vajo Armaron, 147
Val d'Arbia DOC, 237
Valcalepio DOC, 99
Valdadige (Etschtaler) DOC, 182
Valle d'Aosta *see* Piedmont and Valle d'Aosta wine region
Valle d'Aosta DOC, 24
Valle Isarco (Eisacktaler) DOC, 182
Valley of the Temples, 489–90, 493
Valpolicella, La, wine zone, 136–51, **138**
  degustazione, 143–9
  ristoranti, 149–51
  wine road, 140–3
Valpolicella DOC, 3, 123, 139, 146
Valpolicella-Valpantena DOC, 143
Valtellina DOC, 99
Valtellina Superiore, 108
Valtellina wine road, 108–11, **109**